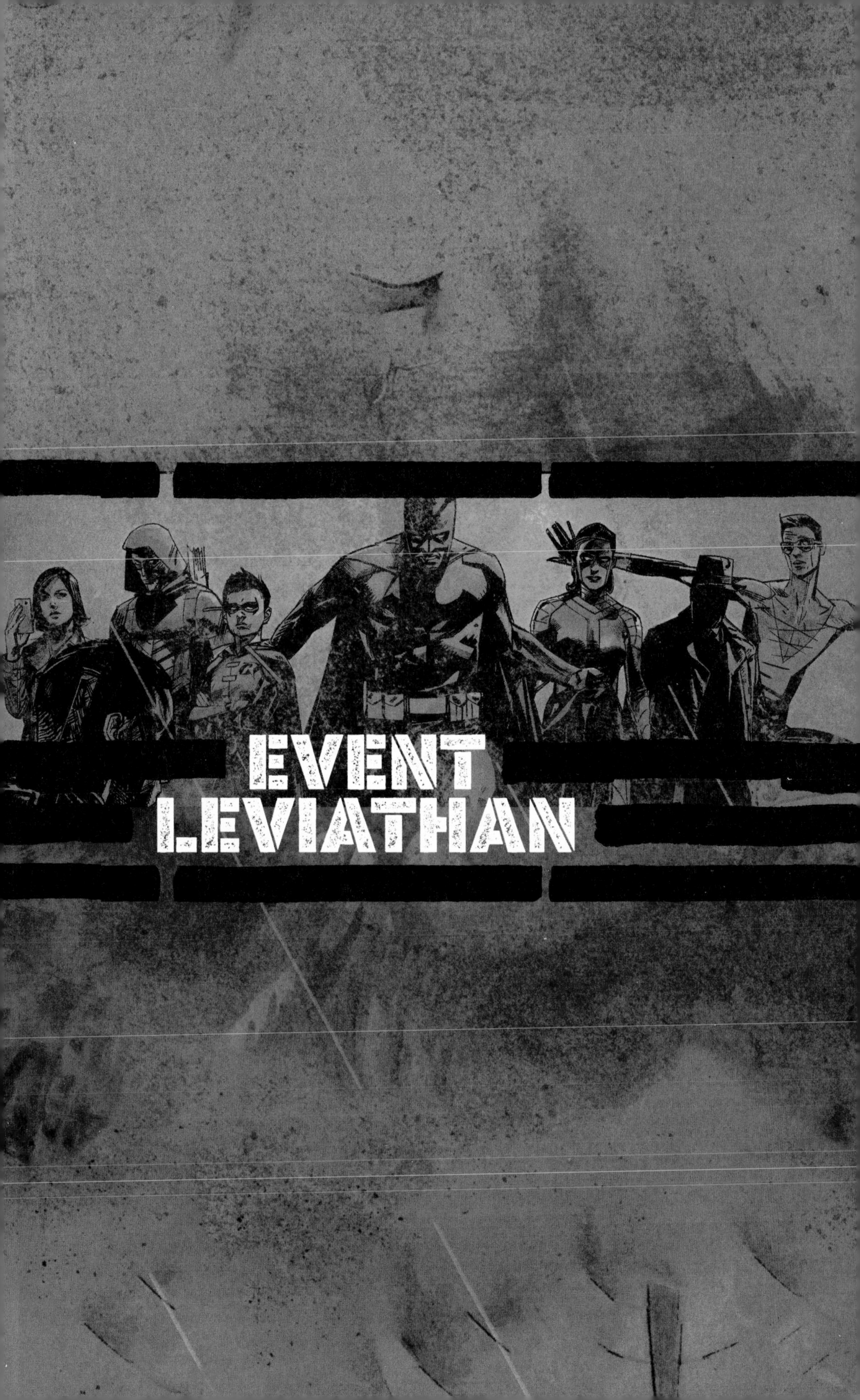
EVENT
LEVIATHAN

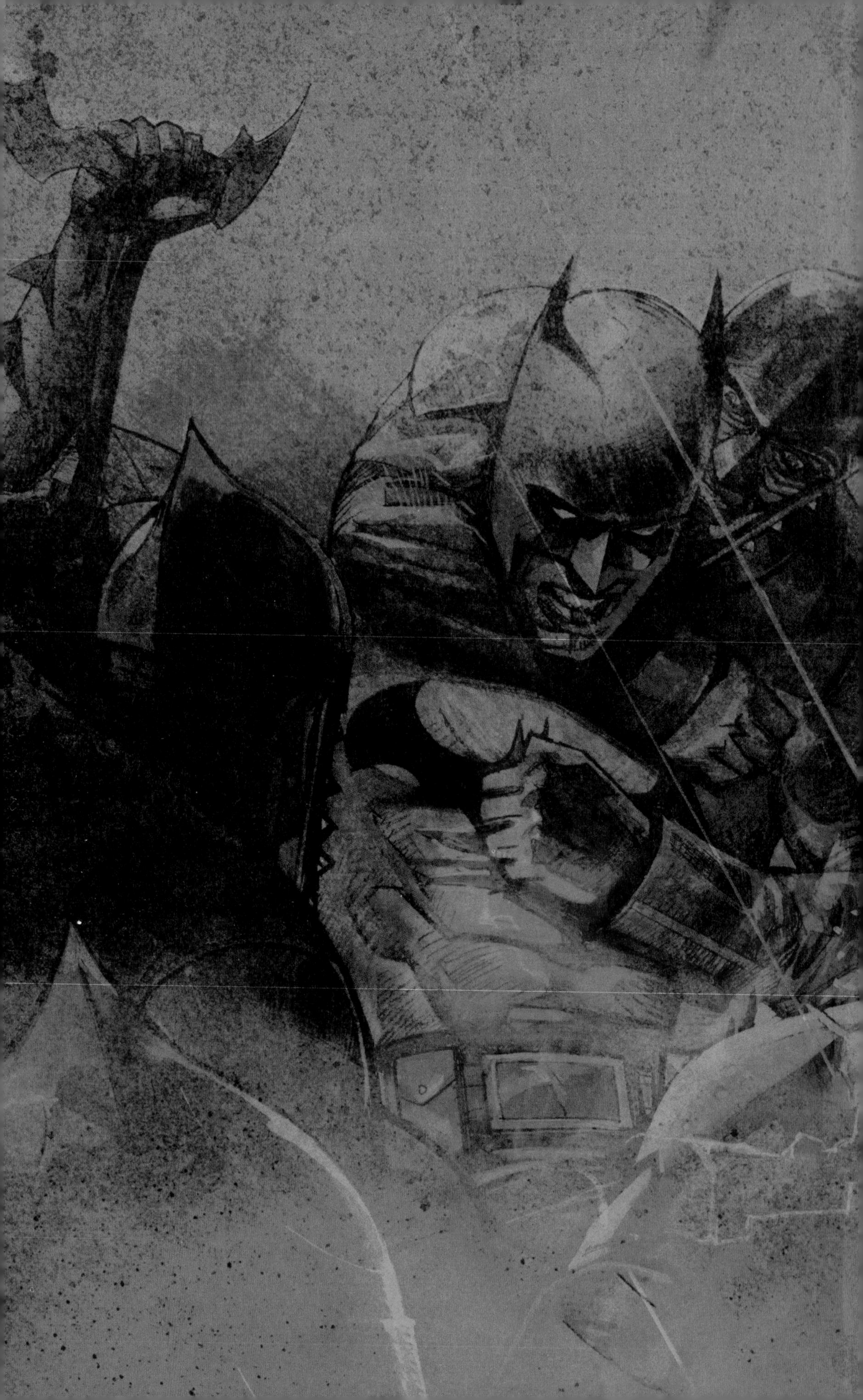

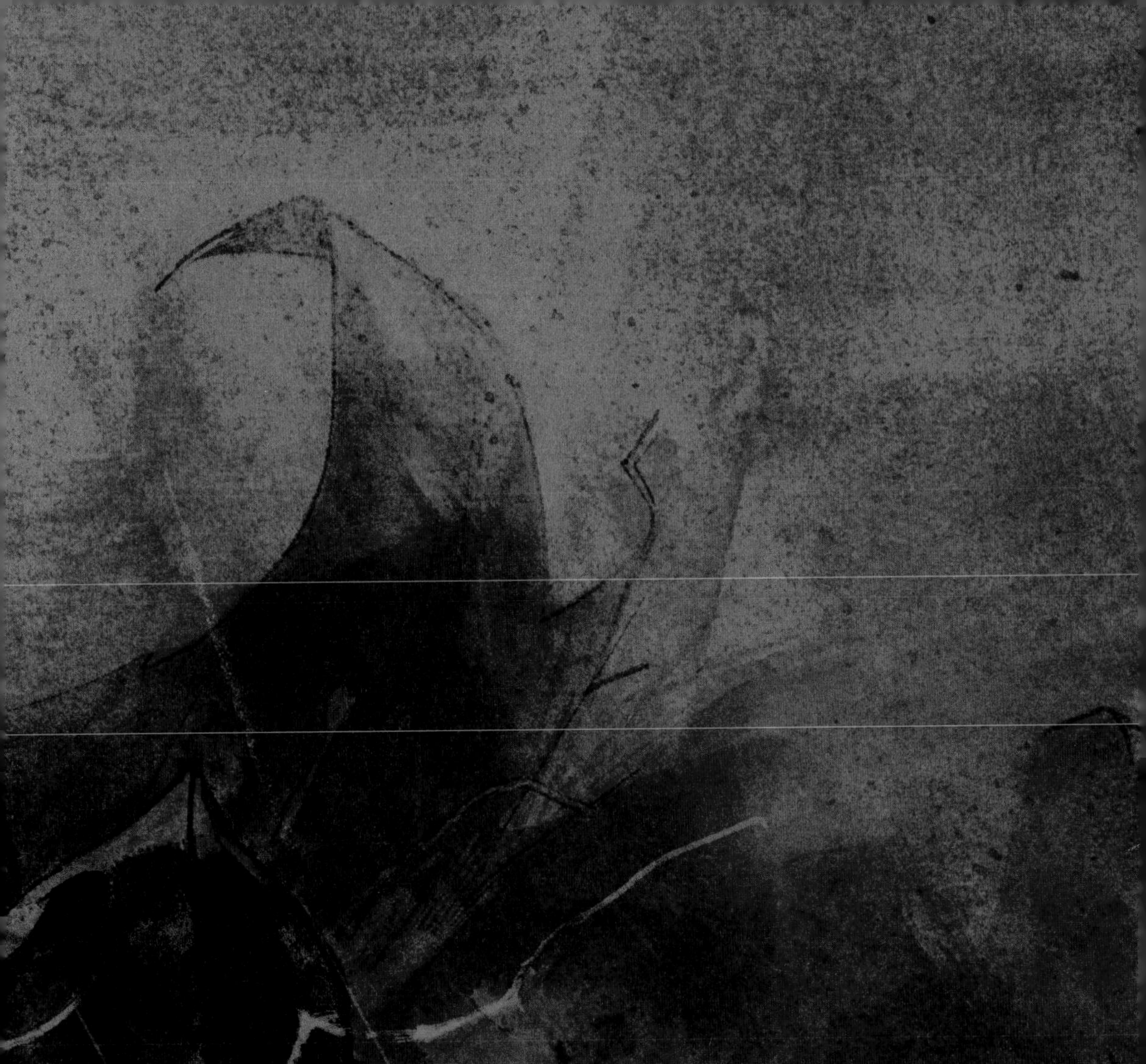

EVENT LEVIATHAN

BRIAN MICHAEL BENDIS GREG RUCKA MATT FRACTION MARC ANDREYKO writers
ALEX MALEEV YANICK PAQUETTE MIKE PERKINS
STEVE LIEBER EDUARDO PANSICA JÚLIO FERREIRA artists
NATHAN FAIRBAIRN PAUL MOUNTS FCO PLASCENCIA colorists
JOSHUA REED DAVE SHARPE SIMON BOWLAND CLAYTON COWLES
TOM NAPOLITANO ALW'S TROY PETERI letterers
ALEX MALEEV collection cover art and original series covers

MIKE COTTON Editor – Original Series
JESSICA CHEN Associate Editor – Original Series
JEB WOODARD Group Editor – Collected Editions
SCOTT NYBAKKEN Editor – Collected Edition
STEVE COOK Design Director – Books
LOUIS PRANDI Publication Design
CHRISTY SAWYER Publication Production

BOB HARRAS Senior VP – Editor-in-Chief, DC Comics
PAT McCALLUM Executive Editor, DC Comics

DAN DiDIO Publisher
JIM LEE Publisher & Chief Creative Officer
BOBBIE CHASE VP – New Publishing Initiatives & Talent Development
DON FALLETTI VP – Manufacturing Operations & Workflow Management
LAWRENCE GANEM VP – Talent Services
ALISON GILL Senior VP – Manufacturing & Operations
HANK KANALZ Senior VP – Publishing Strategy & Support Services
DAN MIRON VP – Publishing Operations
NICK J. NAPOLITANO VP – Manufacturing Administration & Design
NANCY SPEARS VP – Sales
MICHELE R. WELLS VP & Executive Editor, Young Reader

EVENT LEVIATHAN

DC Comics, 2900 West Alameda Ave., Burbank, CA 91505
Printed by Transcontinental Interglobe, Beauceville, QC,
Canada. 2/21/20. First Printing.
ISBN: 978-1-4012-9959-0

Library of Congress Cataloging-in-Publication Data is available.

PEFC Certified

This product is
from sustainably
managed forests and
controlled sources

PEFC/01-31-106   www.pefc.org

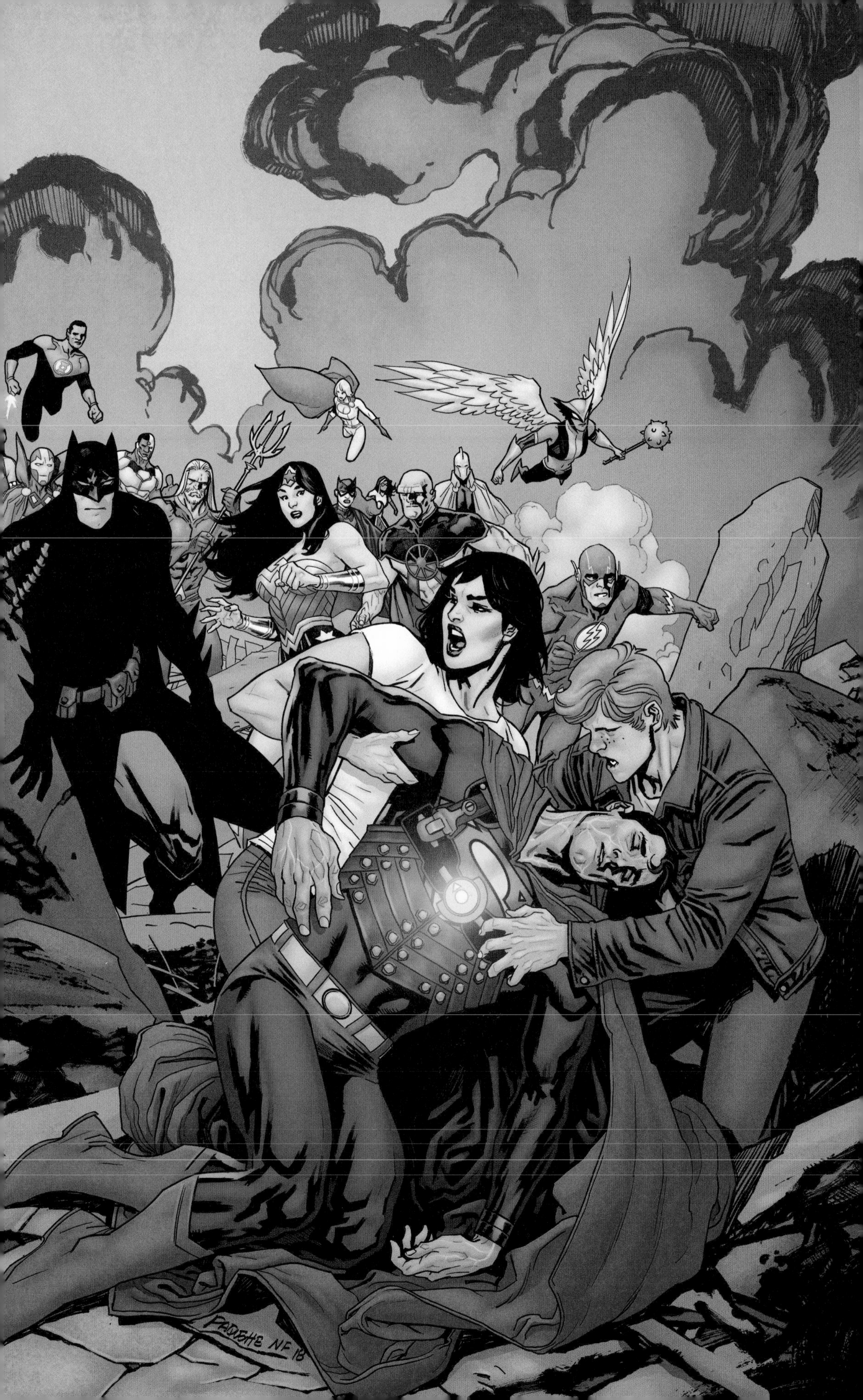
PAQUETTE NF 18

DC COMICS PROUDLY PRESENTS

SUPERMAN LEVIATHAN RISING

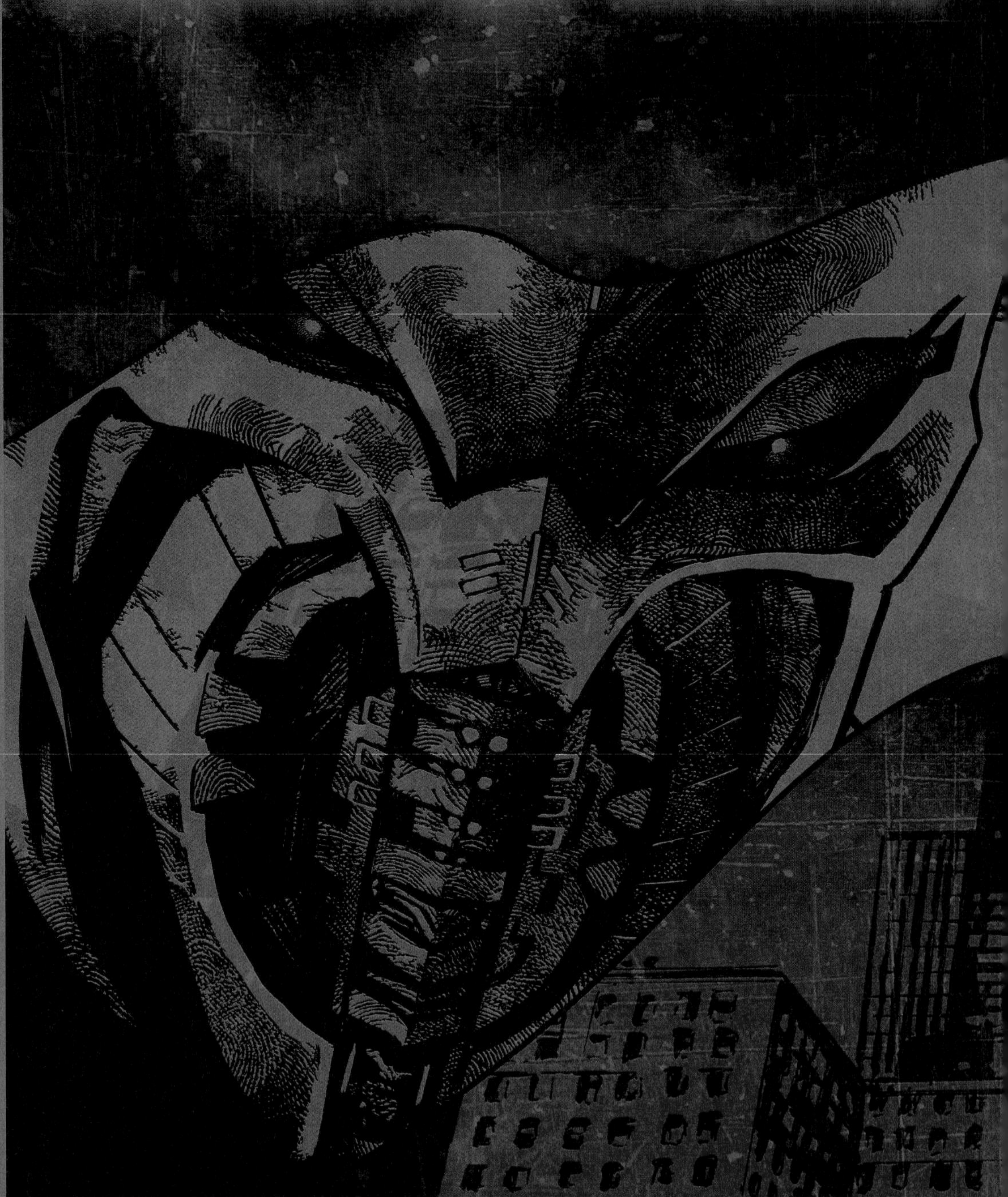

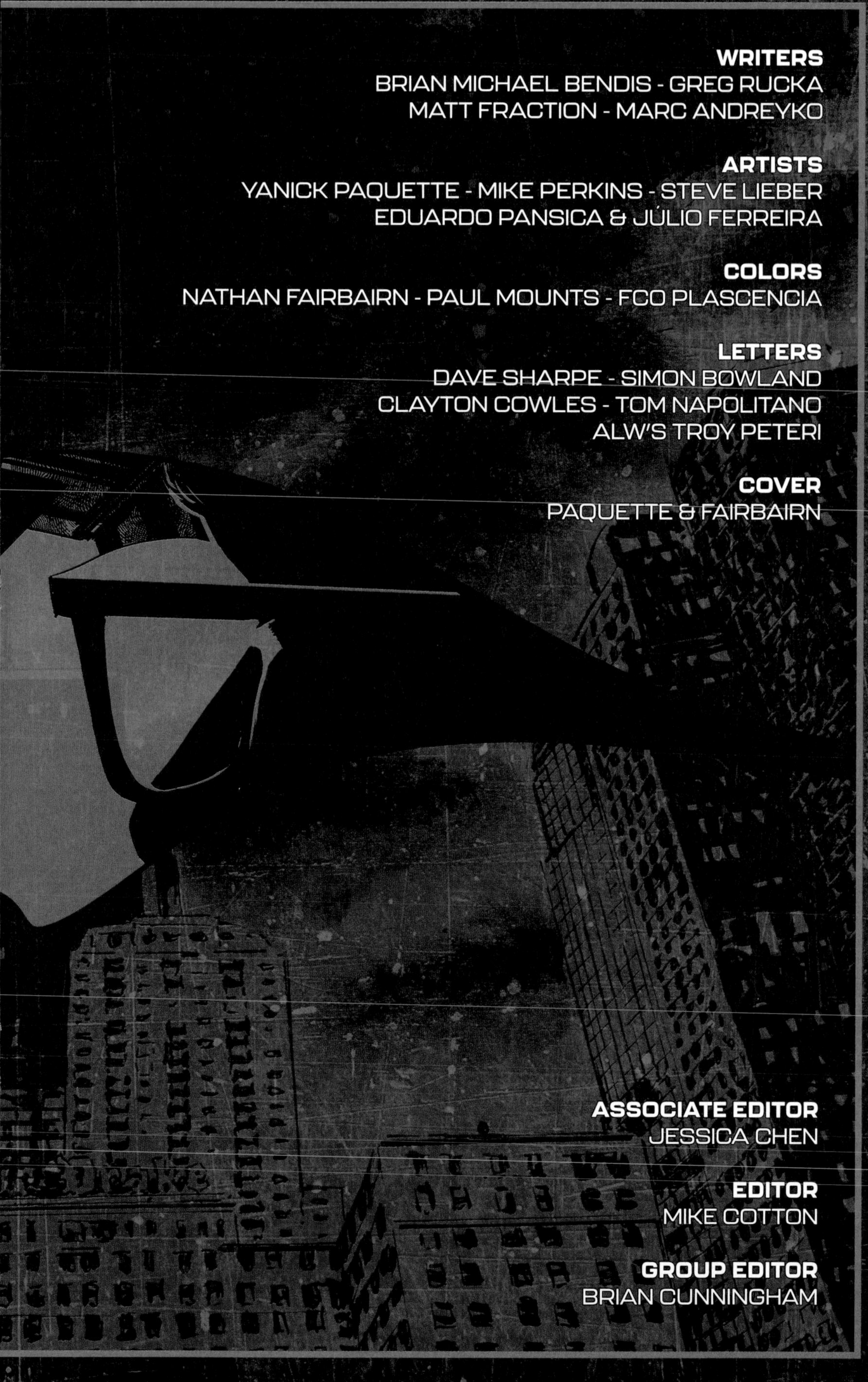

WRITERS
BRIAN MICHAEL BENDIS - GREG RUCKA
MATT FRACTION - MARC ANDREYKO

ARTISTS
YANICK PAQUETTE - MIKE PERKINS - STEVE LIEBER
EDUARDO PANSICA & JÚLIO FERREIRA

COLORS
NATHAN FAIRBAIRN - PAUL MOUNTS - FCO PLASCENCIA

LETTERS
DAVE SHARPE - SIMON BOWLAND
CLAYTON COWLES - TOM NAPOLITANO
ALW'S TROY PETERI

COVER
PAQUETTE & FAIRBAIRN

ASSOCIATE EDITOR
JESSICA CHEN

EDITOR
MIKE COTTON

GROUP EDITOR
BRIAN CUNNINGHAM

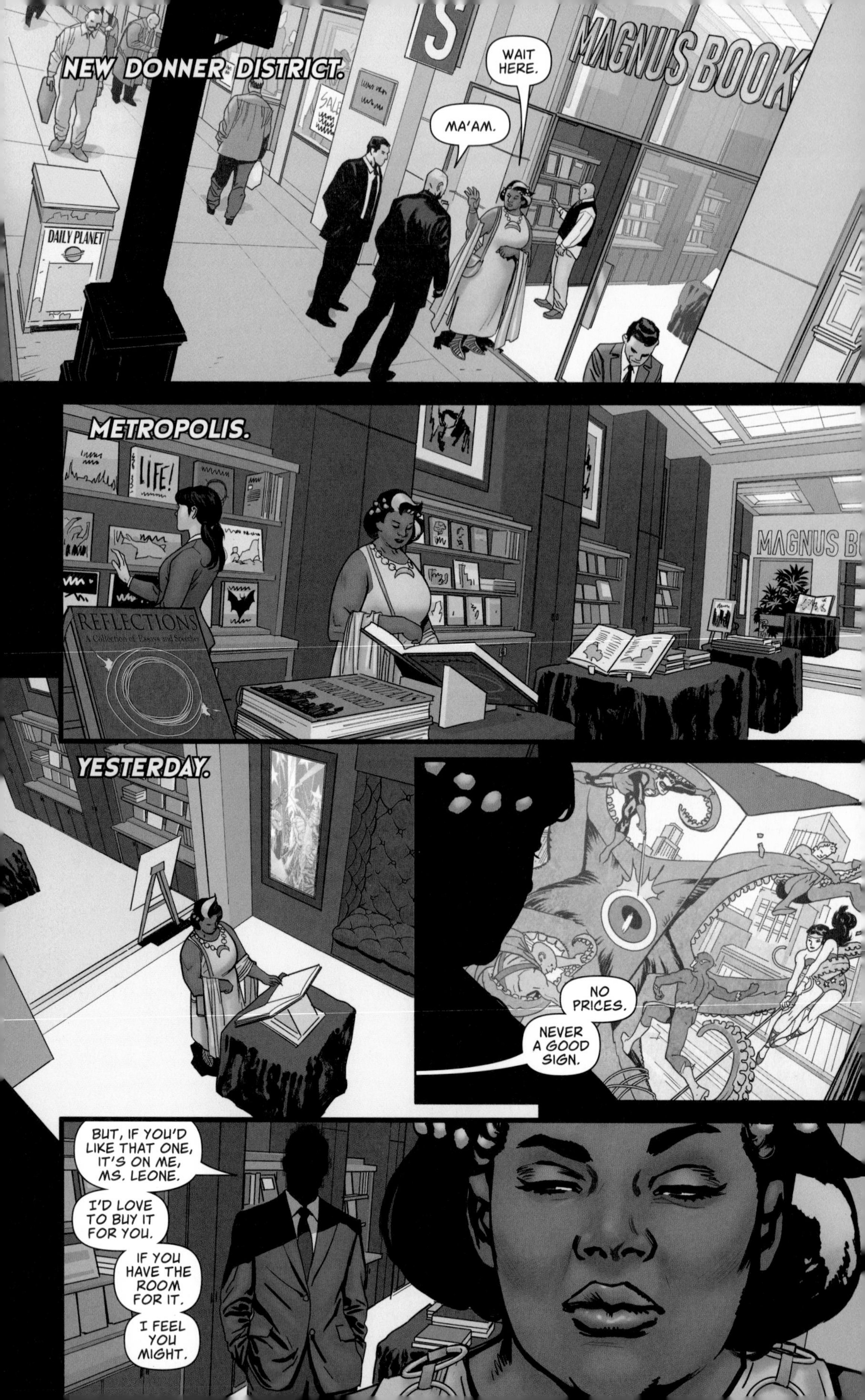

NEW DONNER DISTRICT.
MAGNUS BOOK
DAILY PLANET
SALE
WAIT HERE.
MA'AM.
METROPOLIS.
LIFE!
REFLECTIONS
A Collection of Essays and Speeches
MAGNUS BO
YESTERDAY.
NO PRICES.
NEVER A GOOD SIGN.
BUT, IF YOU'D LIKE THAT ONE, IT'S ON ME, MS. LEONE.
I'D LOVE TO BUY IT FOR YOU.
IF YOU HAVE THE ROOM FOR IT.
I FEEL YOU MIGHT.

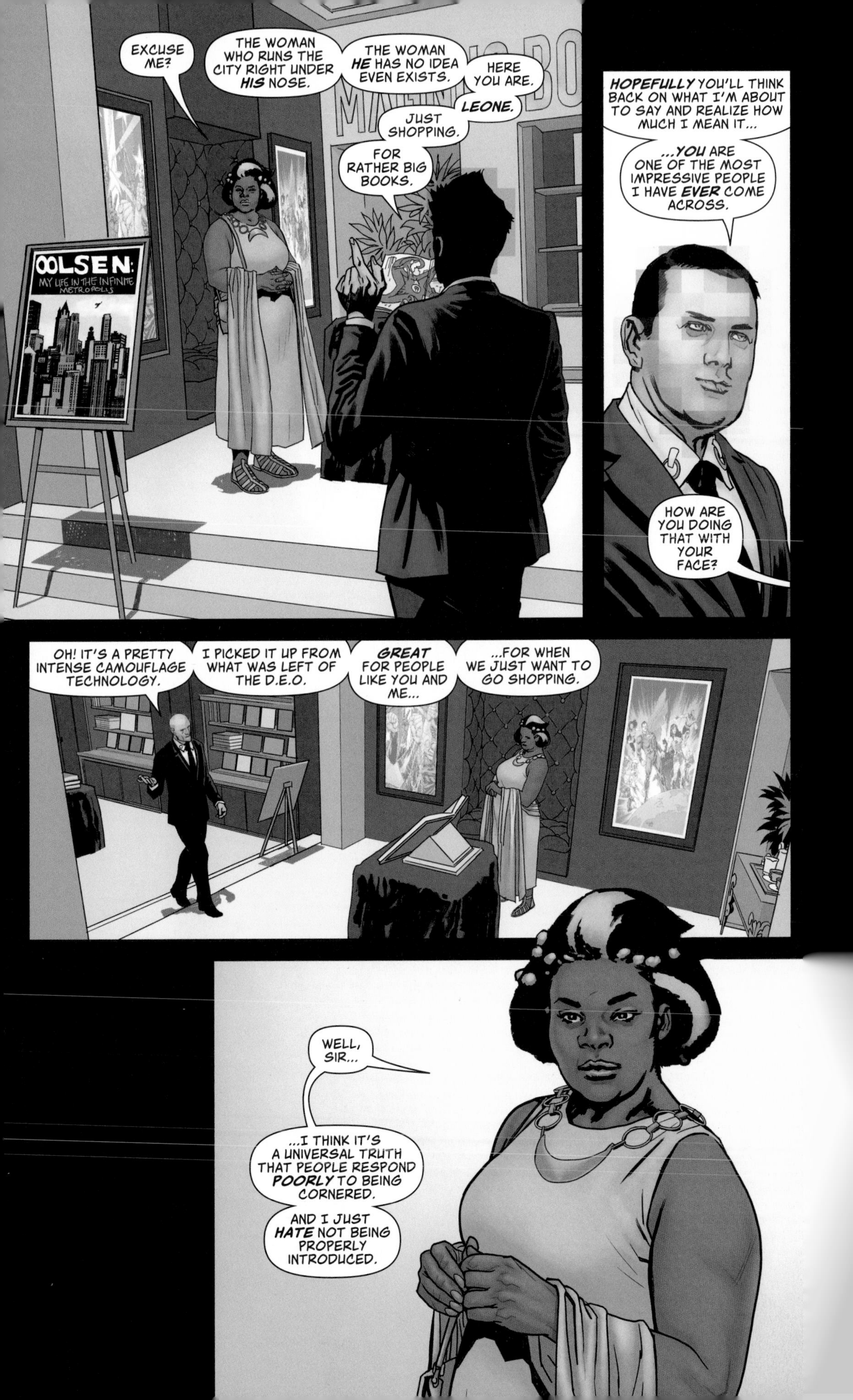
EXCUSE ME?
THE WOMAN WHO RUNS THE CITY RIGHT UNDER HIS NOSE.
THE WOMAN HE HAS NO IDEA EVEN EXISTS.
HERE YOU ARE.
LEONE.
JUST SHOPPING.
FOR RATHER BIG BOOKS.
OLSEN: MY LIFE IN THE INFINITE METROPOLIS
HOPEFULLY YOU'LL THINK BACK ON WHAT I'M ABOUT TO SAY AND REALIZE HOW MUCH I MEAN IT...
...YOU ARE ONE OF THE MOST IMPRESSIVE PEOPLE I HAVE EVER COME ACROSS.
HOW ARE YOU DOING THAT WITH YOUR FACE?
OH! IT'S A PRETTY INTENSE CAMOUFLAGE TECHNOLOGY.
I PICKED IT UP FROM WHAT WAS LEFT OF THE D.E.O.
GREAT FOR PEOPLE LIKE YOU AND ME...
...FOR WHEN WE JUST WANT TO GO SHOPPING.
WELL, SIR...
...I THINK IT'S A UNIVERSAL TRUTH THAT PEOPLE RESPOND POORLY TO BEING CORNERED.
AND I JUST HATE NOT BEING PROPERLY INTRODUCED.

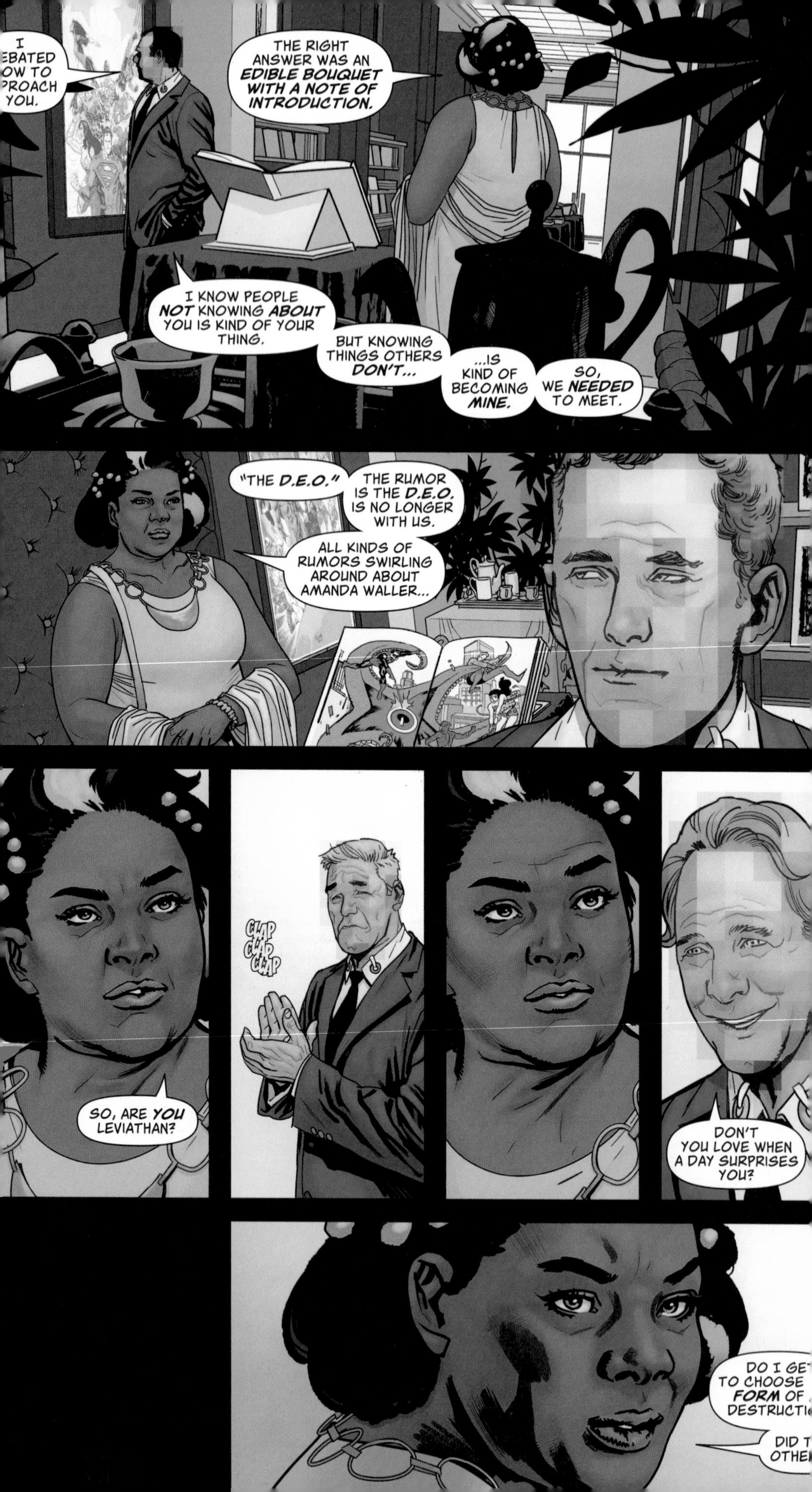
I EBATED OW TO PROACH YOU.
THE RIGHT ANSWER WAS AN EDIBLE BOUQUET WITH A NOTE OF INTRODUCTION.
I KNOW PEOPLE NOT KNOWING ABOUT YOU IS KIND OF YOUR THING.
BUT KNOWING THINGS OTHERS DON'T...
...IS KIND OF BECOMING MINE.
SO, WE NEEDED TO MEET.
"THE D.E.O."
THE RUMOR IS THE D.E.O. IS NO LONGER WITH US.
ALL KINDS OF RUMORS SWIRLING AROUND ABOUT AMANDA WALLER...
SO, ARE YOU LEVIATHAN?
CLAP CLAP CLAP
DON'T YOU LOVE WHEN A DAY SURPRISES YOU?
DO I GE TO CHOOSE FORM OF DESTRUCTI
DID T OTHE

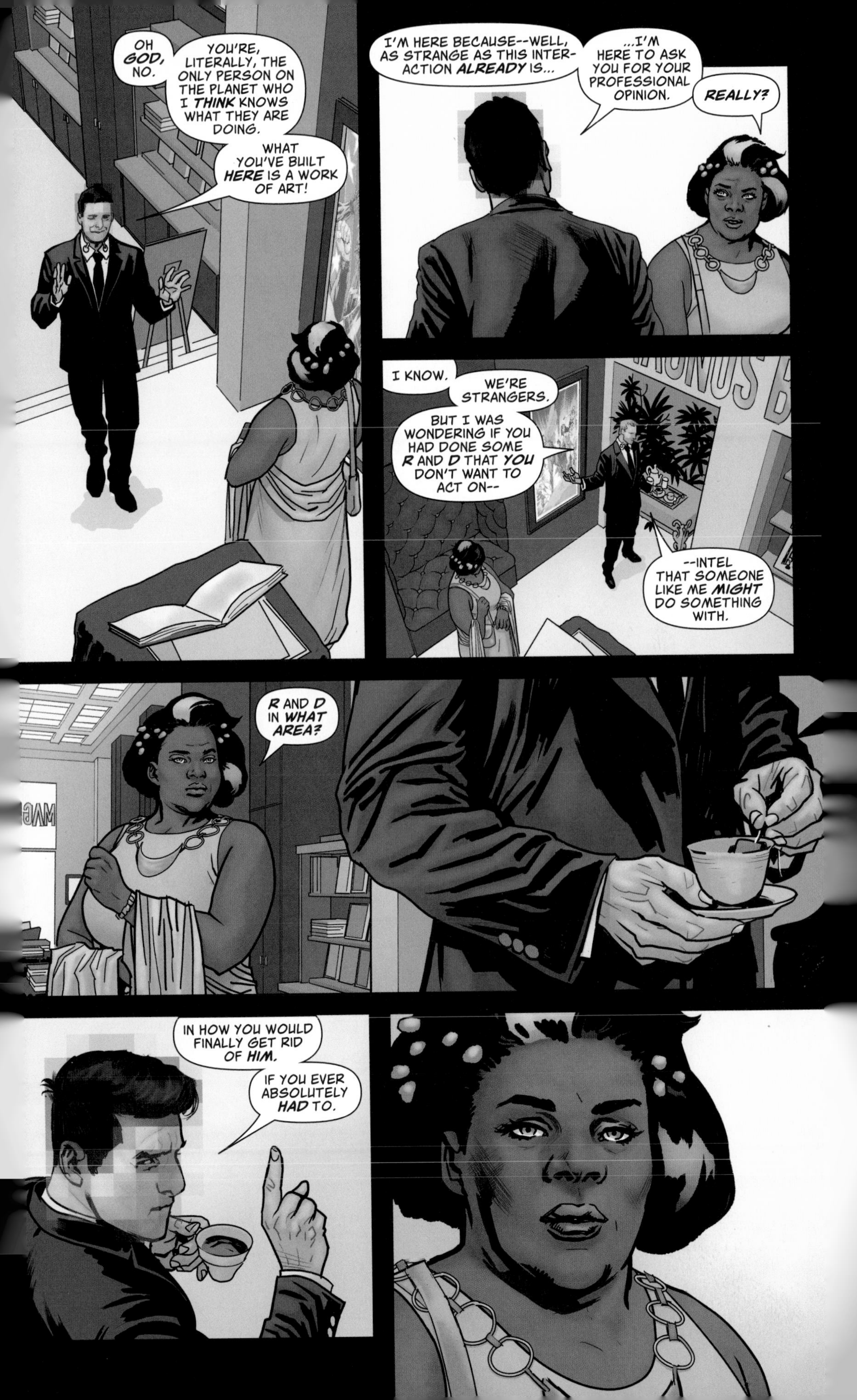
OH GOD, NO.
YOU'RE, LITERALLY, THE ONLY PERSON ON THE PLANET WHO I THINK KNOWS WHAT THEY ARE DOING.
WHAT YOU'VE BUILT HERE IS A WORK OF ART!
I'M HERE BECAUSE--WELL, AS STRANGE AS THIS INTERACTION ALREADY IS...
...I'M HERE TO ASK YOU FOR YOUR PROFESSIONAL OPINION.
REALLY?
I KNOW.
WE'RE STRANGERS.
BUT I WAS WONDERING IF YOU HAD DONE SOME R AND D THAT YOU DON'T WANT TO ACT ON--
--INTEL THAT SOMEONE LIKE ME MIGHT DO SOMETHING WITH.
R AND D IN WHAT AREA?
IN HOW YOU WOULD FINALLY GET RID OF HIM.
IF YOU EVER ABSOLUTELY HAD TO.

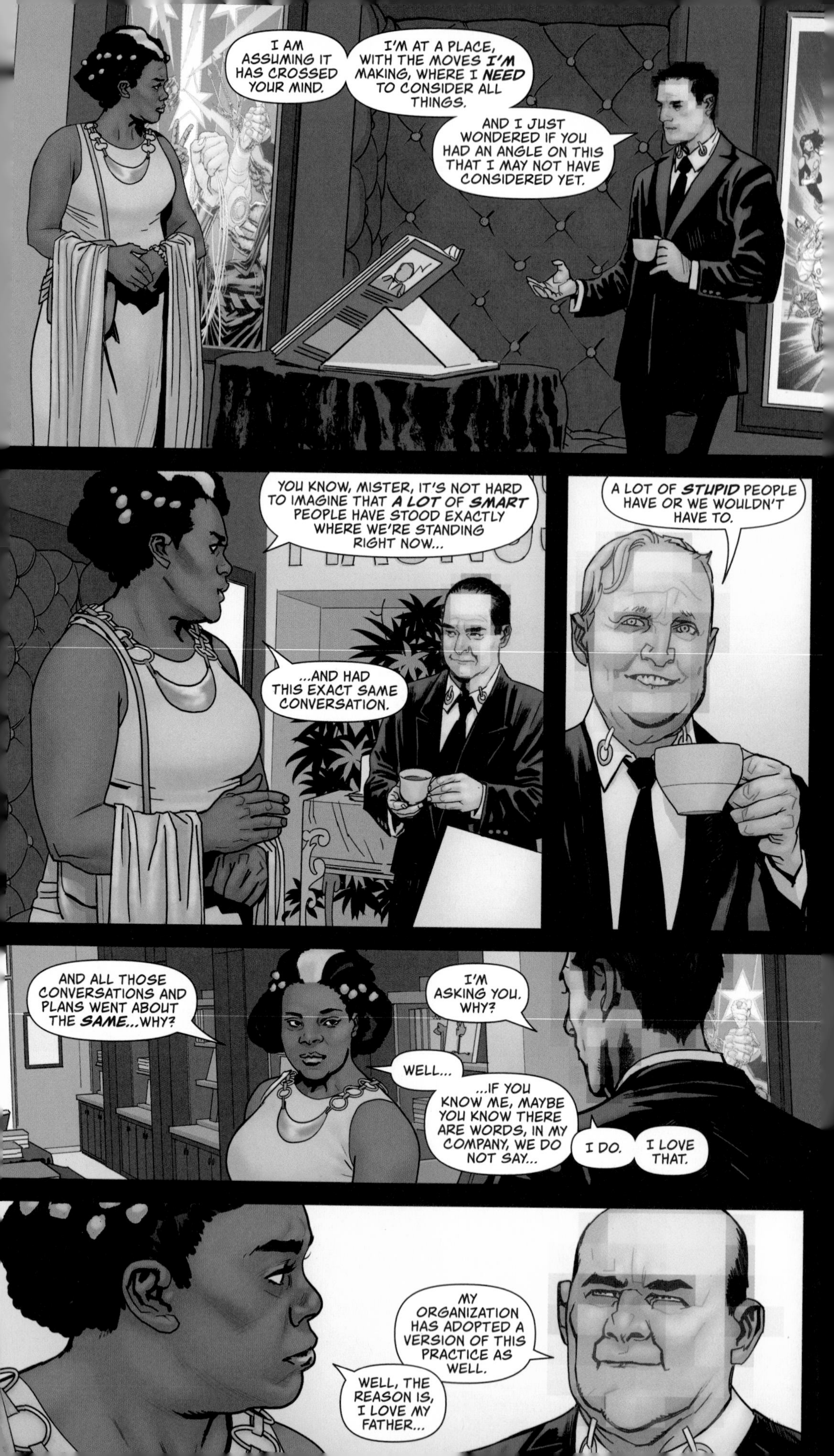
I AM ASSUMING IT HAS CROSSED YOUR MIND.
I'M AT A PLACE, WITH THE MOVES I'M MAKING, WHERE I NEED TO CONSIDER ALL THINGS.
AND I JUST WONDERED IF YOU HAD AN ANGLE ON THIS THAT I MAY NOT HAVE CONSIDERED YET.
YOU KNOW, MISTER, IT'S NOT HARD TO IMAGINE THAT A LOT OF SMART PEOPLE HAVE STOOD EXACTLY WHERE WE'RE STANDING RIGHT NOW...
...AND HAD THIS EXACT SAME CONVERSATION.
A LOT OF STUPID PEOPLE HAVE OR WE WOULDN'T HAVE TO.
AND ALL THOSE CONVERSATIONS AND PLANS WENT ABOUT THE SAME... WHY?
I'M ASKING YOU. WHY?
WELL...
...IF YOU KNOW ME, MAYBE YOU KNOW THERE ARE WORDS, IN MY COMPANY, WE DO NOT SAY...
I DO.
I LOVE THAT.
MY ORGANIZATION HAS ADOPTED A VERSION OF THIS PRACTICE AS WELL.
WELL, THE REASON IS, I LOVE MY FATHER...

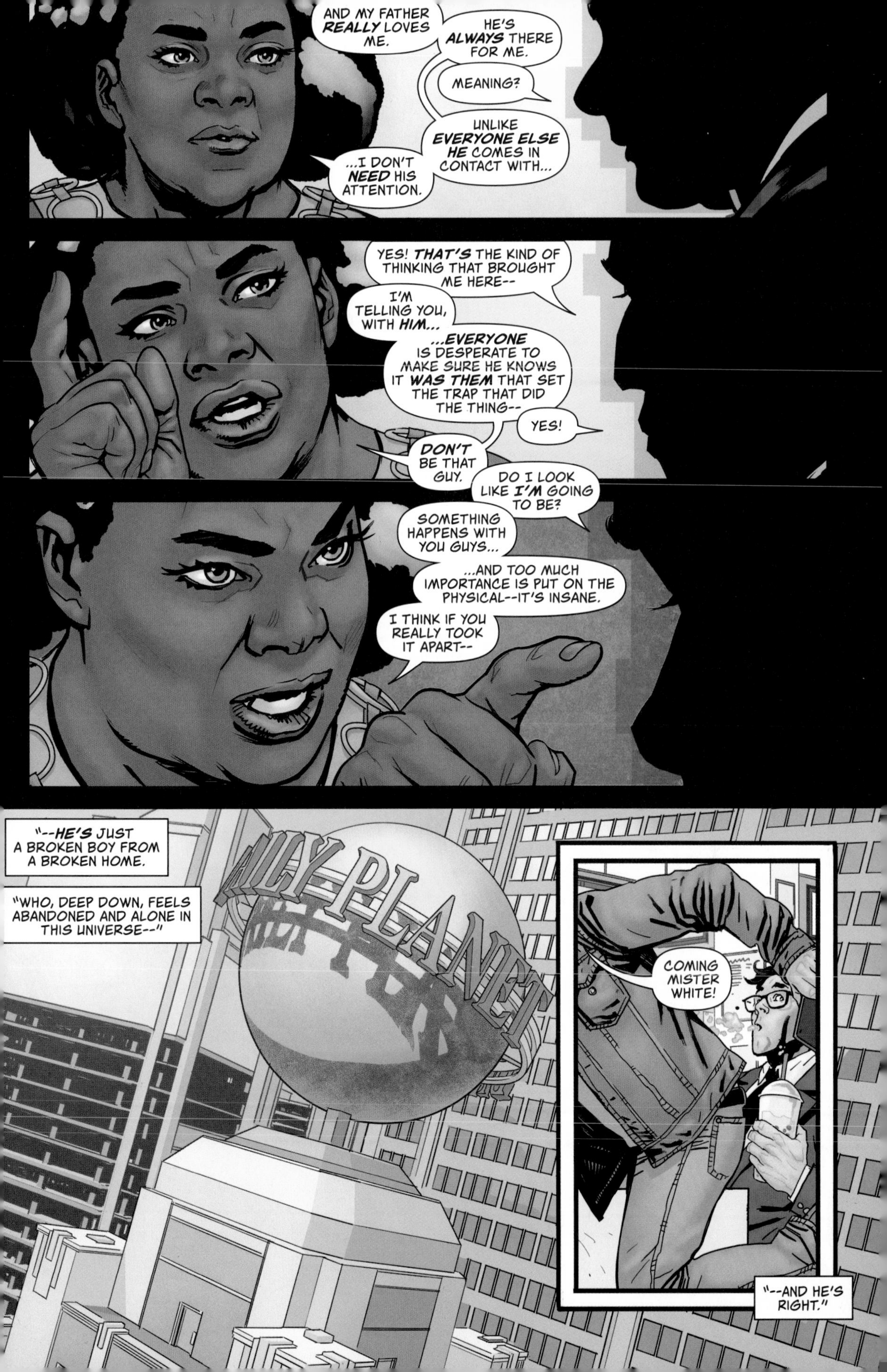

AND MY FATHER REALLY LOVES ME.
HE'S ALWAYS THERE FOR ME.
MEANING?
UNLIKE EVERYONE ELSE HE COMES IN CONTACT WITH...
...I DON'T NEED HIS ATTENTION.
YES! THAT'S THE KIND OF THINKING THAT BROUGHT ME HERE--
I'M TELLING YOU, WITH HIM...
...EVERYONE IS DESPERATE TO MAKE SURE HE KNOWS IT WAS THEM THAT SET THE TRAP THAT DID THE THING--
YES!
DON'T BE THAT GUY.
DO I LOOK LIKE I'M GOING TO BE?
SOMETHING HAPPENS WITH YOU GUYS...
...AND TOO MUCH IMPORTANCE IS PUT ON THE PHYSICAL--IT'S INSANE.
I THINK IF YOU REALLY TOOK IT APART--
"--HE'S JUST A BROKEN BOY FROM A BROKEN HOME.
"WHO, DEEP DOWN, FEELS ABANDONED AND ALONE IN THIS UNIVERSE--"
COMING MISTER WHITE!
"--AND HE'S RIGHT."

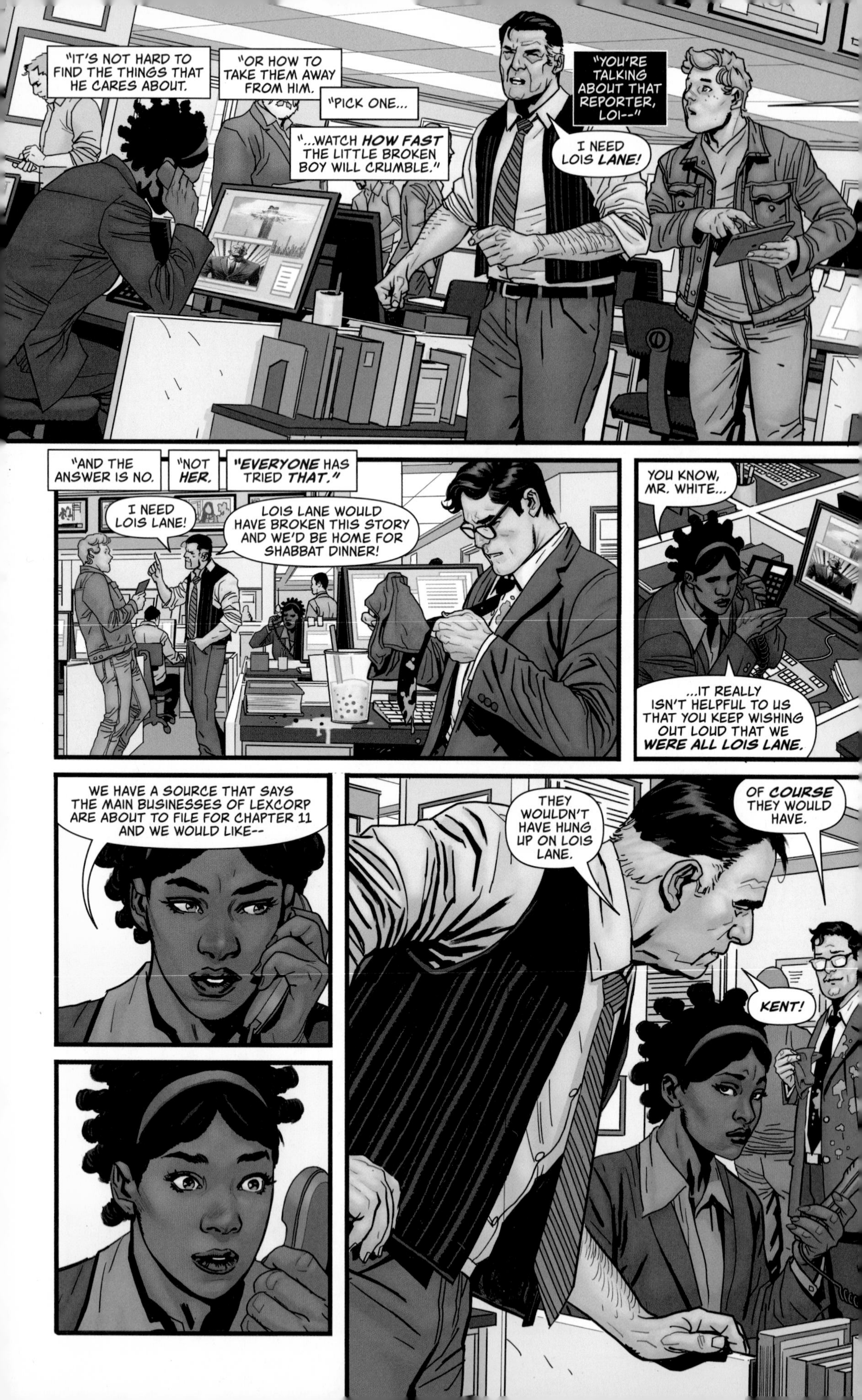
"IT'S NOT HARD TO FIND THE THINGS THAT HE CARES ABOUT.
"OR HOW TO TAKE THEM AWAY FROM HIM.
"PICK ONE...
"...WATCH **HOW FAST** THE LITTLE BROKEN BOY WILL CRUMBLE."
"YOU'RE TALKING ABOUT THAT REPORTER, LOI--"
I NEED LOIS **LANE!**
"AND THE ANSWER IS NO.
"NOT **HER.**
"EVERYONE HAS TRIED **THAT."**
I NEED LOIS LANE!
LOIS LANE WOULD HAVE BROKEN THIS STORY AND WE'D BE HOME FOR SHABBAT DINNER!
YOU KNOW, MR. WHITE...
...IT REALLY ISN'T HELPFUL TO US THAT YOU KEEP WISHING OUT LOUD THAT WE **WERE ALL LOIS LANE.**
WE HAVE A SOURCE THAT SAYS THE MAIN BUSINESSES OF LEXCORP ARE ABOUT TO FILE FOR CHAPTER 11 AND WE WOULD LIKE--
THEY WOULDN'T HAVE HUNG UP ON LOIS LANE.
OF **COURSE** THEY WOULD HAVE.
KENT!

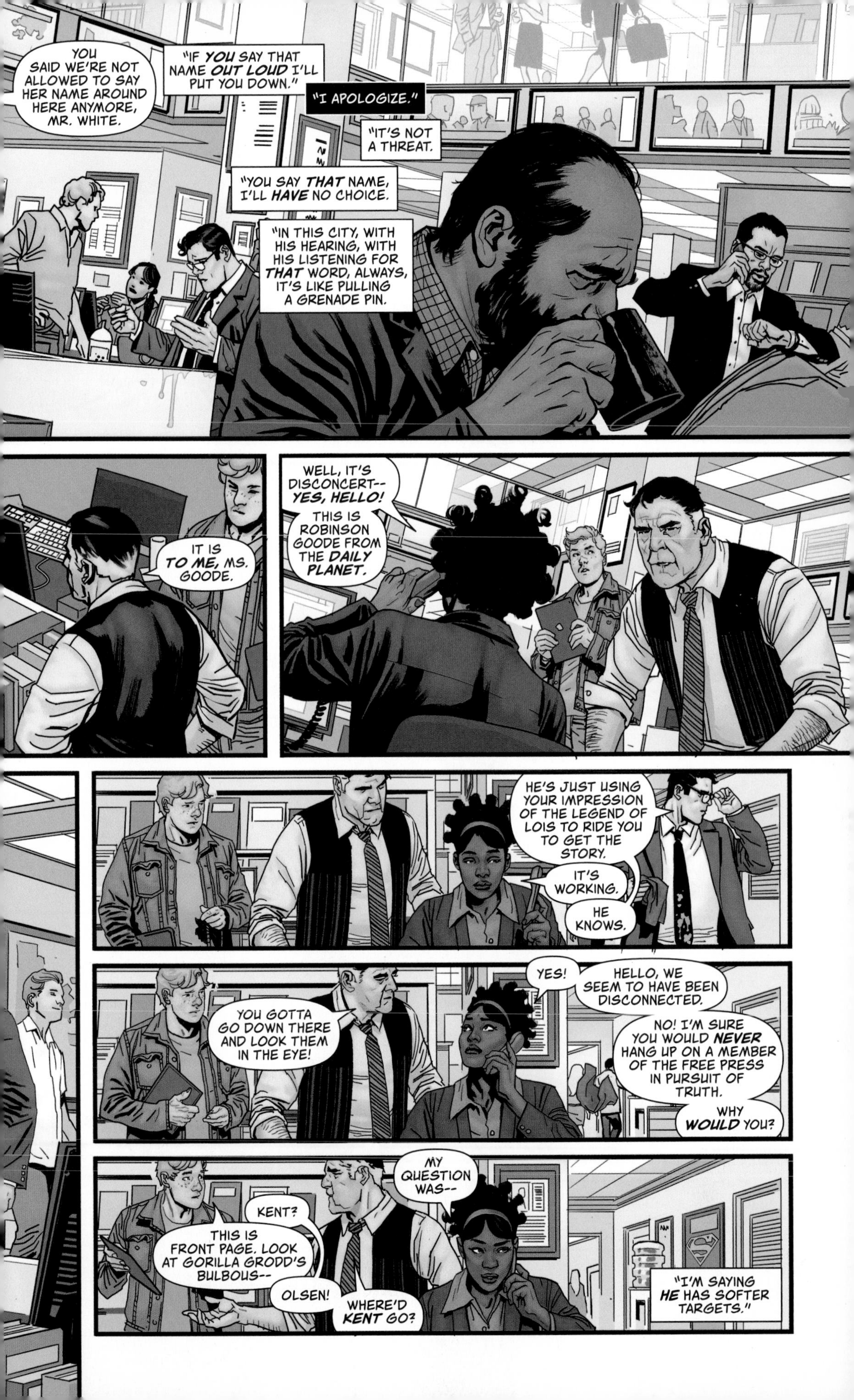

YOU SAID WE'RE NOT ALLOWED TO SAY HER NAME AROUND HERE ANYMORE, MR. WHITE.
"IF YOU SAY THAT NAME OUT LOUD I'LL PUT YOU DOWN."
"I APOLOGIZE."
"IT'S NOT A THREAT.
"YOU SAY THAT NAME, I'LL HAVE NO CHOICE.
"IN THIS CITY, WITH HIS HEARING, WITH HIS LISTENING FOR THAT WORD, ALWAYS, IT'S LIKE PULLING A GRENADE PIN.
IT IS TO ME, MS. GOODE.
WELL, IT'S DISCONCERT-- YES, HELLO! THIS IS ROBINSON GOODE FROM THE DAILY PLANET.
HE'S JUST USING YOUR IMPRESSION OF THE LEGEND OF LOIS TO RIDE YOU TO GET THE STORY.
IT'S WORKING.
HE KNOWS.
YOU GOTTA GO DOWN THERE AND LOOK THEM IN THE EYE!
YES!
HELLO, WE SEEM TO HAVE BEEN DISCONNECTED.
NO! I'M SURE YOU WOULD NEVER HANG UP ON A MEMBER OF THE FREE PRESS IN PURSUIT OF TRUTH.
WHY WOULD YOU?
MY QUESTION WAS--
KENT?
THIS IS FRONT PAGE. LOOK AT GORILLA GRODD'S BULBOUS--
OLSEN!
WHERE'D KENT GO?
"I'M SAYING HE HAS SOFTER TARGETS."

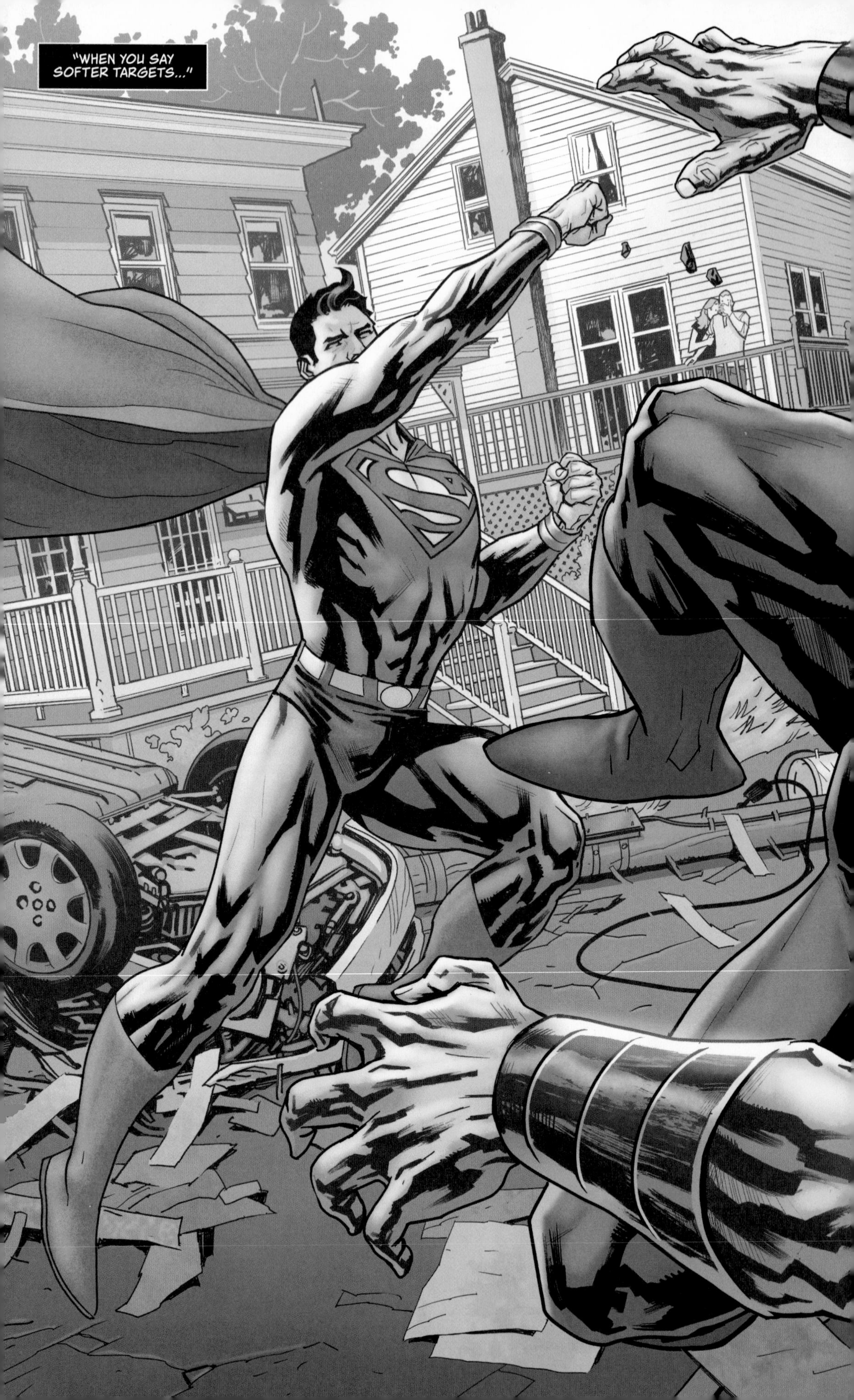
"WHEN YOU SAY SOFTER TARGETS..."

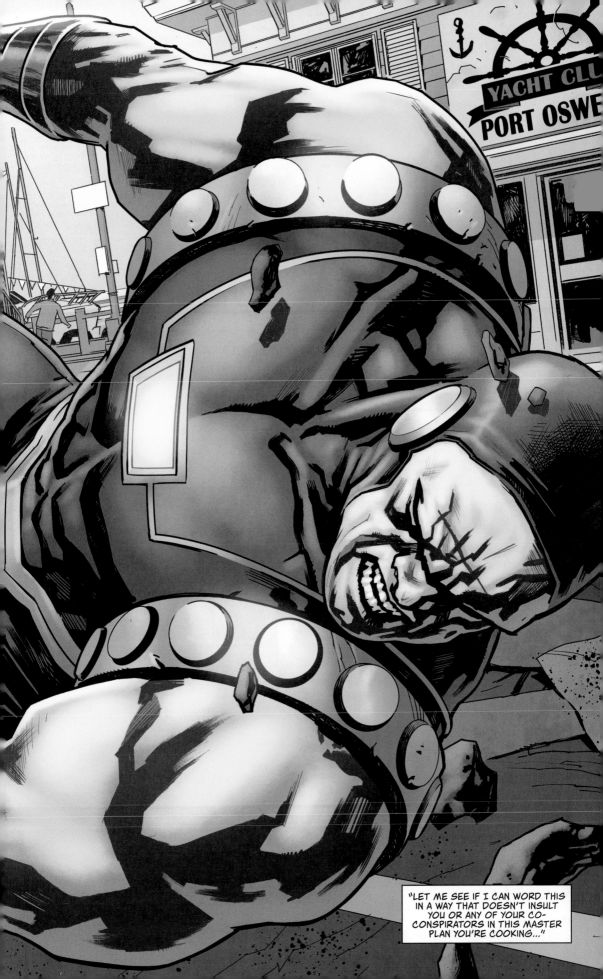

"LET ME SEE IF I CAN WORD THIS IN A WAY THAT DOESN'T INSULT YOU OR ANY OF YOUR CO-CONSPIRATORS IN THIS MASTER PLAN YOU'RE COOKING..."

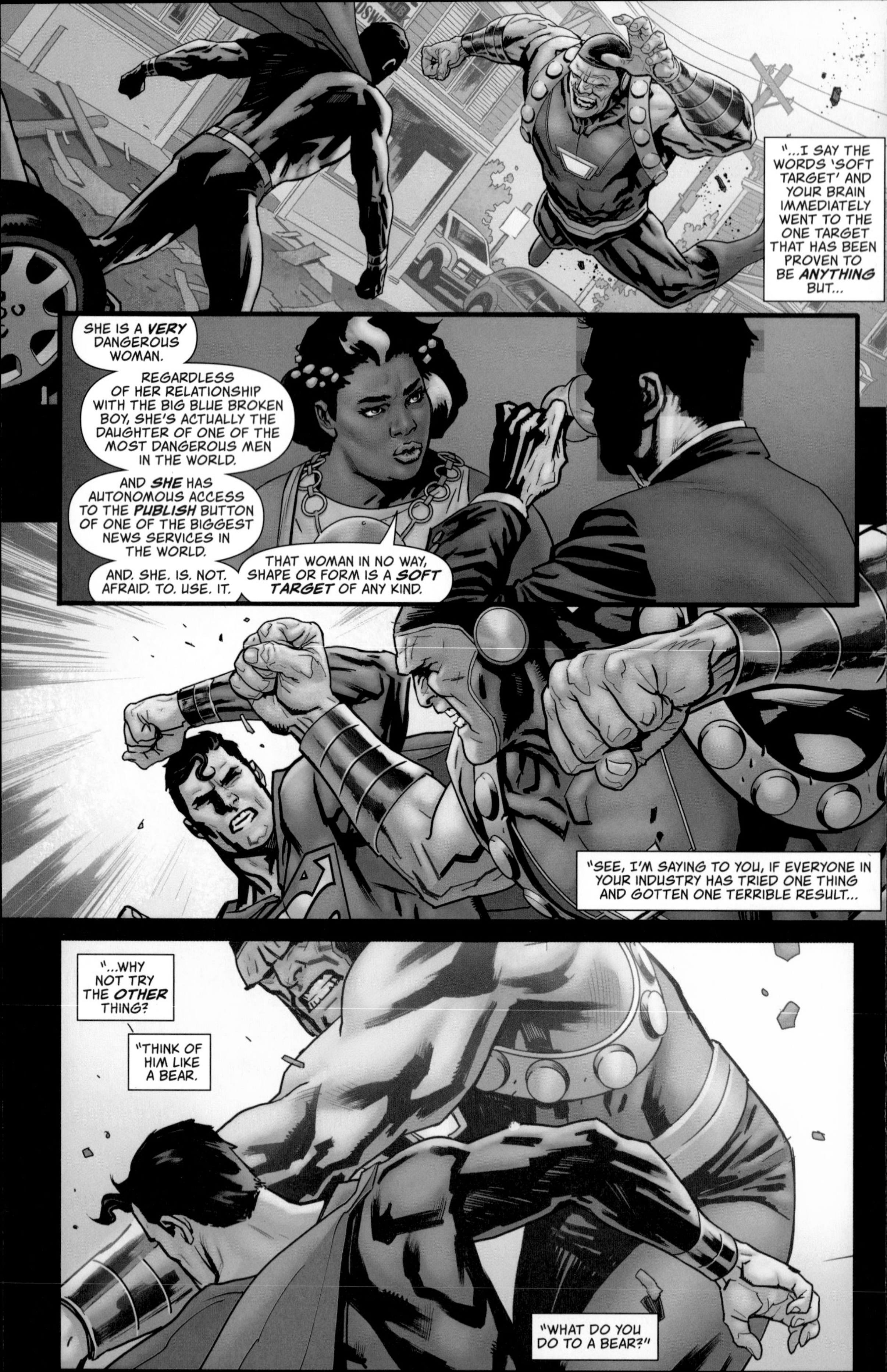
"...I SAY THE WORDS 'SOFT TARGET' AND YOUR BRAIN IMMEDIATELY WENT TO THE ONE TARGET THAT HAS BEEN PROVEN TO BE ANYTHING BUT...
SHE IS A VERY DANGEROUS WOMAN.
REGARDLESS OF HER RELATIONSHIP WITH THE BIG BLUE BROKEN BOY, SHE'S ACTUALLY THE DAUGHTER OF ONE OF THE MOST DANGEROUS MEN IN THE WORLD.
AND SHE HAS AUTONOMOUS ACCESS TO THE PUBLISH BUTTON OF ONE OF THE BIGGEST NEWS SERVICES IN THE WORLD.
AND. SHE. IS. NOT. AFRAID. TO. USE. IT.
THAT WOMAN IN NO WAY, SHAPE OR FORM IS A SOFT TARGET OF ANY KIND.
"SEE, I'M SAYING TO YOU, IF EVERYONE IN YOUR INDUSTRY HAS TRIED ONE THING AND GOTTEN ONE TERRIBLE RESULT...
"...WHY NOT TRY THE OTHER THING?
"THINK OF HIM LIKE A BEAR.
"WHAT DO YOU DO TO A BEAR?"

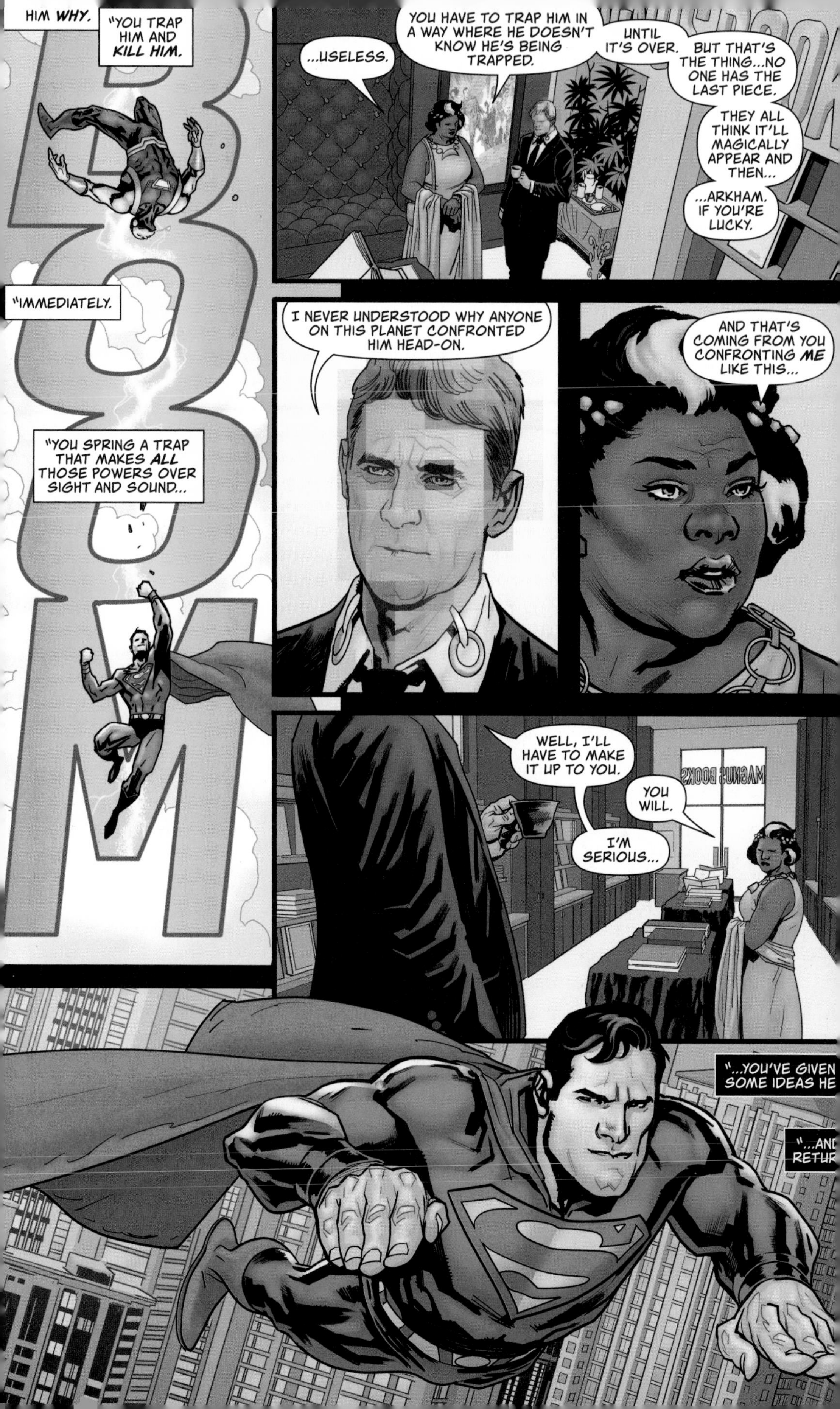
HIM WHY.
"YOU TRAP HIM AND KILL HIM.
...USELESS.
YOU HAVE TO TRAP HIM IN A WAY WHERE HE DOESN'T KNOW HE'S BEING TRAPPED.
UNTIL IT'S OVER.
BUT THAT'S THE THING...NO ONE HAS THE LAST PIECE.
THEY ALL THINK IT'LL MAGICALLY APPEAR AND THEN...
...ARKHAM. IF YOU'RE LUCKY.
"IMMEDIATELY.
I NEVER UNDERSTOOD WHY ANYONE ON THIS PLANET CONFRONTED HIM HEAD-ON.
AND THAT'S COMING FROM YOU CONFRONTING ME LIKE THIS...
"YOU SPRING A TRAP THAT MAKES ALL THOSE POWERS OVER SIGHT AND SOUND...
BOOM
WELL, I'LL HAVE TO MAKE IT UP TO YOU.
YOU WILL.
I'M SERIOUS...
MAGNUS BOOKS
"...YOU'VE GIVEN SOME IDEAS HE
"...AND RETUR

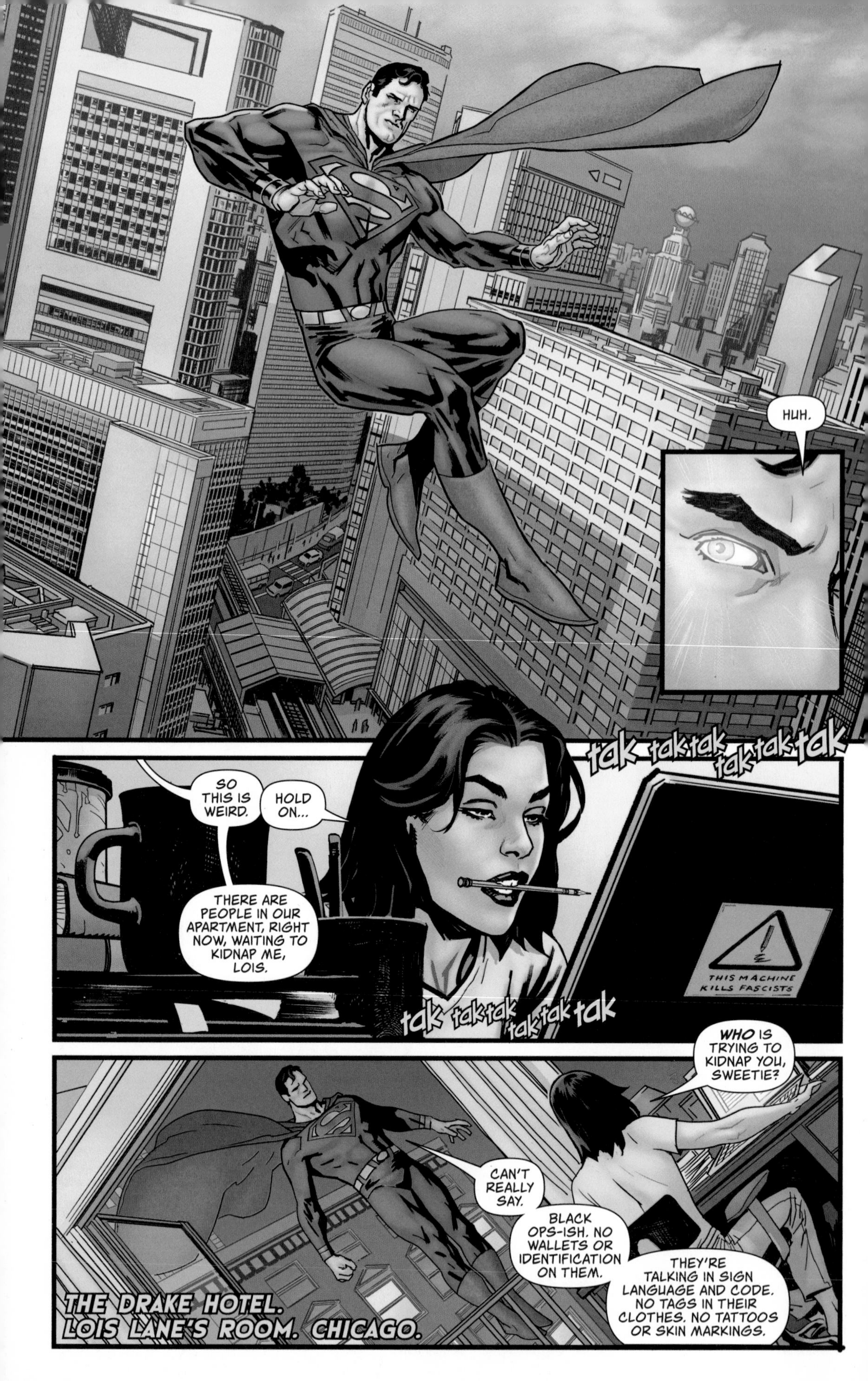
HUH.
tak tak tak tak tak tak
SO THIS IS WEIRD.
HOLD ON...
THERE ARE PEOPLE IN OUR APARTMENT, RIGHT NOW, WAITING TO KIDNAP ME, LOIS.
THIS MACHINE KILLS FASCISTS
tak tak tak tak tak tak
THE DRAKE HOTEL. LOIS LANE'S ROOM. CHICAGO.
WHO IS TRYING TO KIDNAP YOU, SWEETIE?
CAN'T REALLY SAY.
BLACK OPS-ISH. NO WALLETS OR IDENTIFICATION ON THEM.
THEY'RE TALKING IN SIGN LANGUAGE AND CODE. NO TAGS IN THEIR CLOTHES. NO TATTOOS OR SKIN MARKINGS.

AND THEY'RE JUST HIDING IN OUR APARTMENT?

BACK IN METROPOLIS.

RIGHT NOW.

LOOKING TO KIDNAP *YOU?*

"THAT PART WAS CLEAR."

NOT *ME?*

HUH.

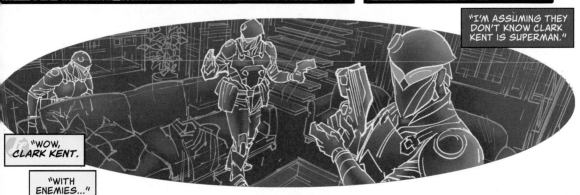

"I'M ASSUMING THEY DON'T KNOW CLARK KENT IS SUPERMAN."

"WOW, CLARK KENT.

"WITH ENEMIES..."

CLARK KENT IS A LAW-ABIDING CITIZEN, WHO--

S.T.A.R. LABS EXPOSÉ.

OH, YES.

THEY *MIGHT* HAVE A BEEF WITH ME.

THAT HATCHET PIECE ON *YOUNG JUSTICE.*

HATCHET PIECE? THOSE KIDS NEED A LESSON IN CLEANING UP AFTER--

LET'S CALL THE POLICE.

LET'S CALL METROPOLIS SPECIAL FORCES--GIVE MAGGIE SAWYER A THRILL.

ACTUALLY, I'M THINKING ABOUT GOING ALONG WITH IT.

WHAT?

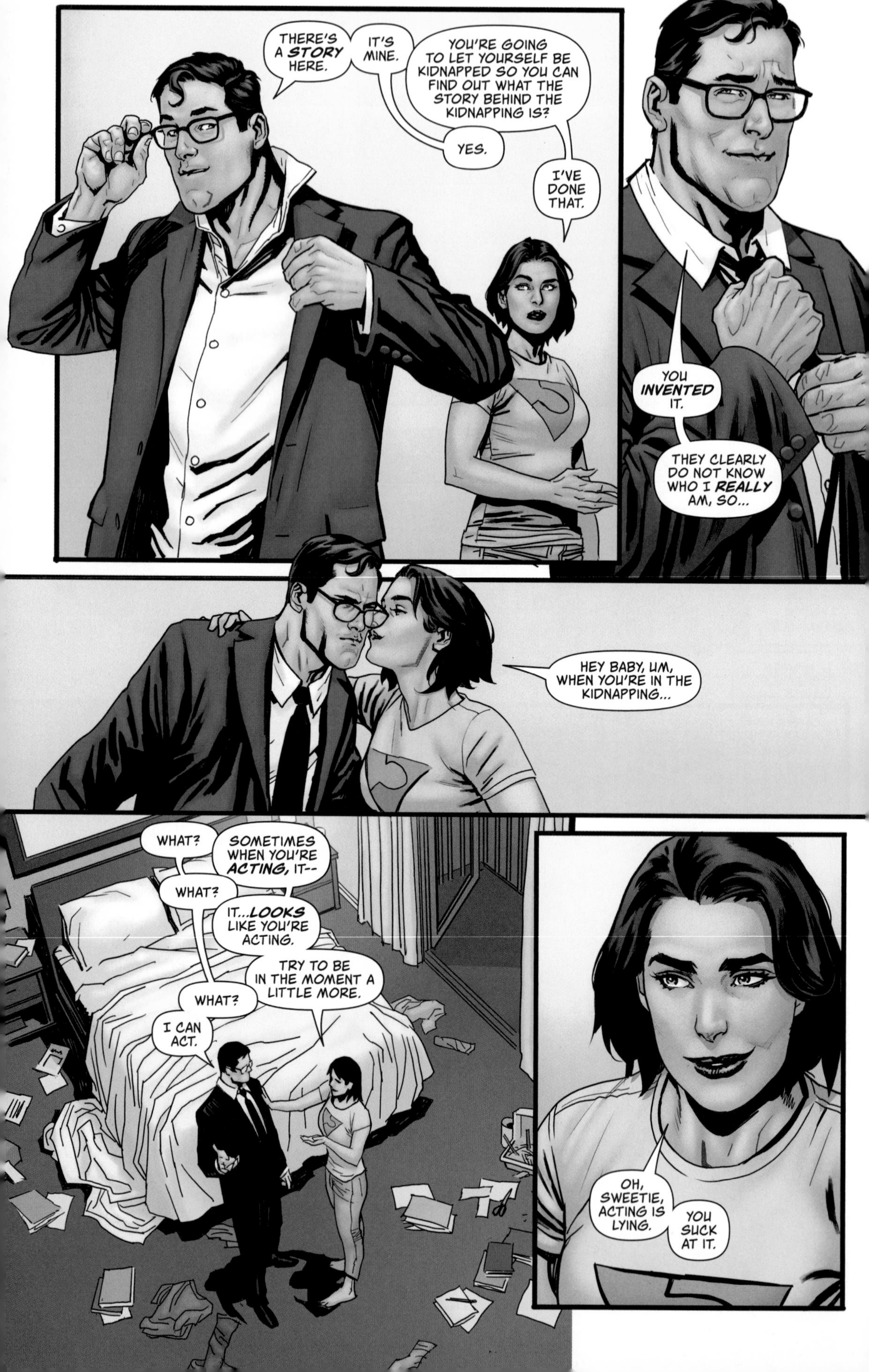
THERE'S A STORY HERE.
IT'S MINE.
YOU'RE GOING TO LET YOURSELF BE KIDNAPPED SO YOU CAN FIND OUT WHAT THE STORY BEHIND THE KIDNAPPING IS?
YES.
I'VE DONE THAT.
YOU INVENTED IT.
THEY CLEARLY DO NOT KNOW WHO I REALLY AM, SO...
HEY BABY, UM, WHEN YOU'RE IN THE KIDNAPPING...
WHAT?
SOMETIMES WHEN YOU'RE ACTING, IT--
WHAT?
IT...LOOKS LIKE YOU'RE ACTING.
TRY TO BE IN THE MOMENT A LITTLE MORE.
WHAT?
I CAN ACT.
OH, SWEETIE, ACTING IS LYING.
YOU SUCK AT IT.

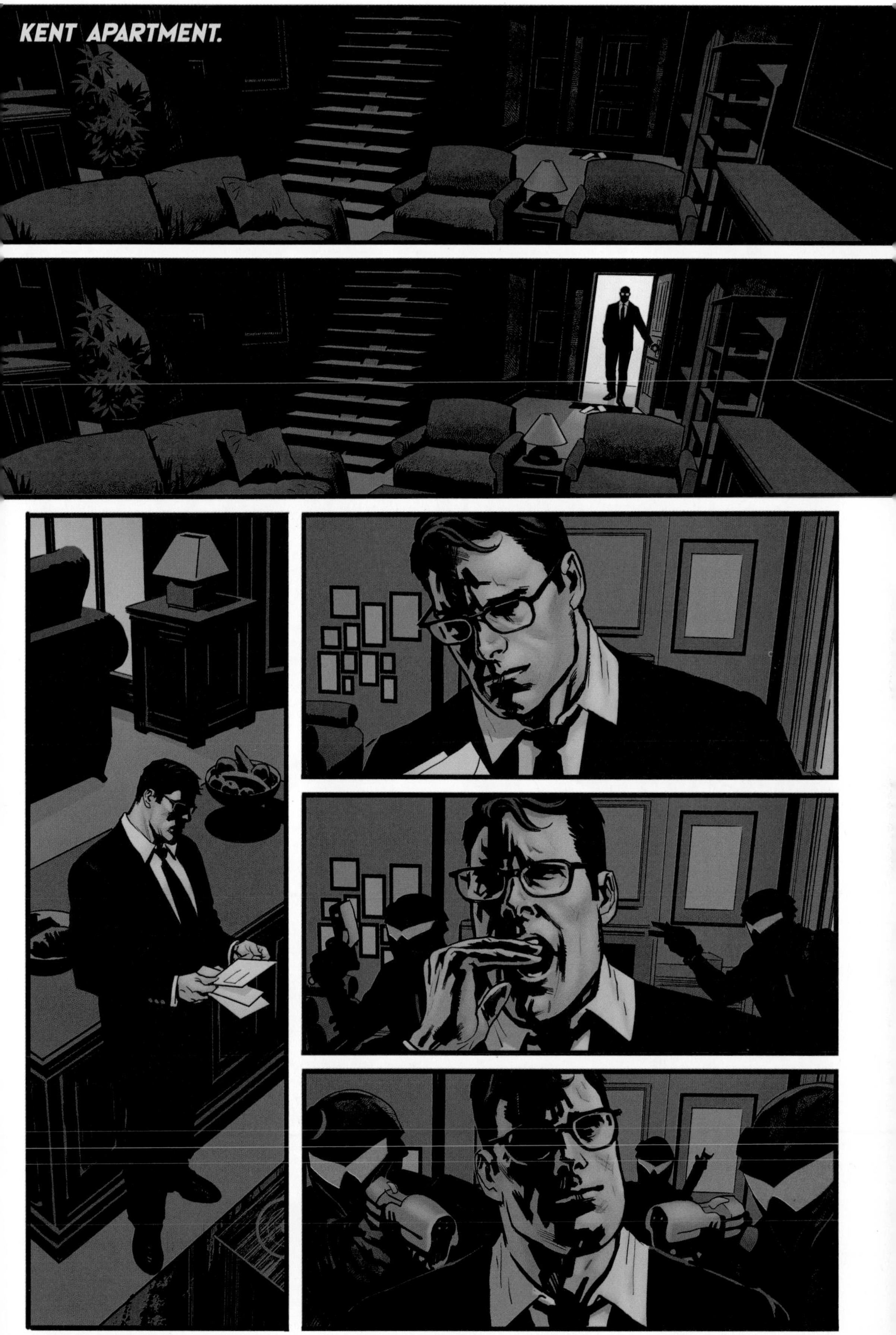
KENT APARTMENT.

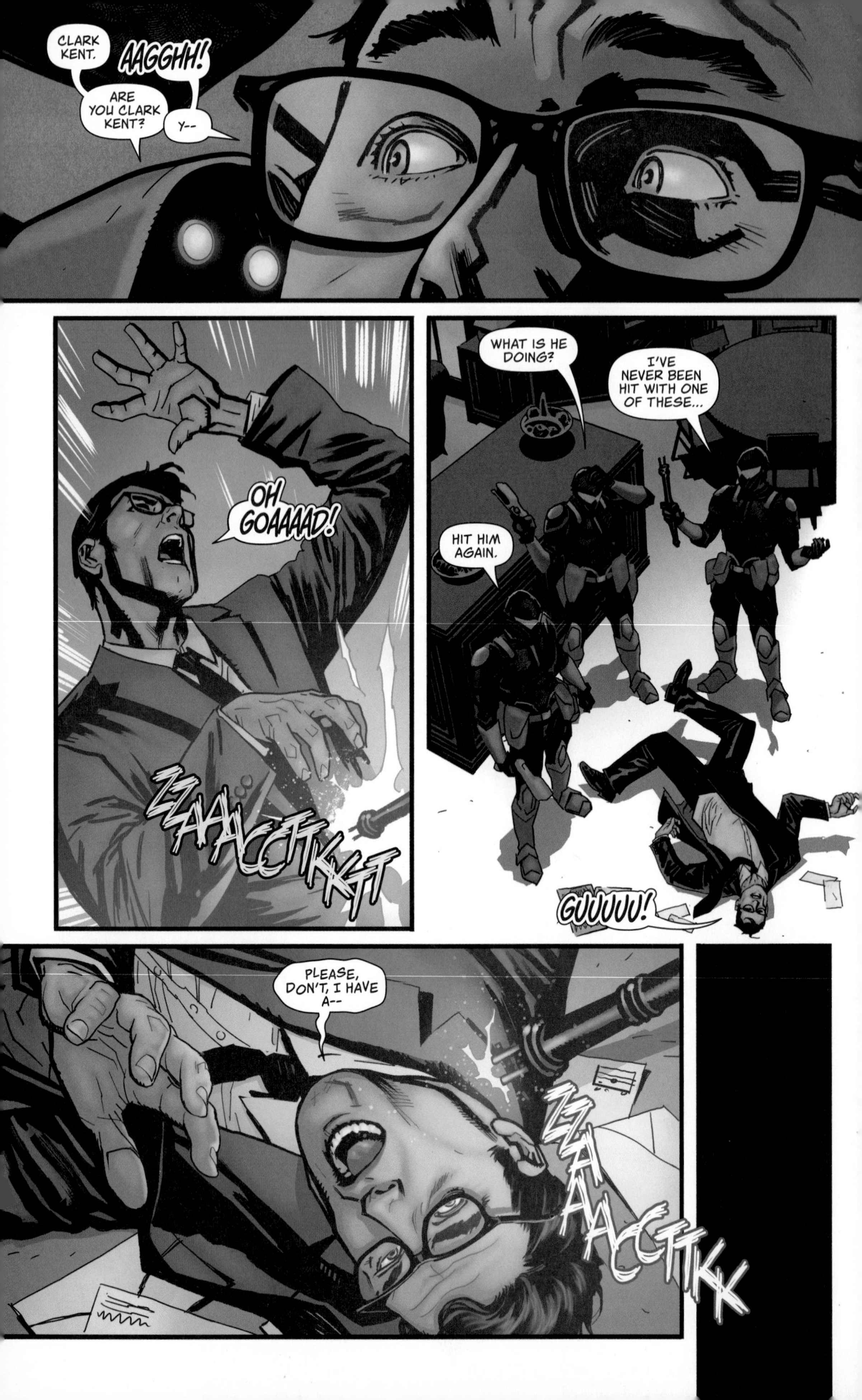
CLARK KENT.
ARE YOU CLARK KENT?
AAGGHH!
Y--
OH GOAAAAD!
ZZAAACCTTKKTT
WHAT IS HE DOING?
I'VE NEVER BEEN HIT WITH ONE OF THESE...
HIT HIM AGAIN.
GUUUUU!
PLEASE, DON'T, I HAVE A--
ZZAAACCTTKK

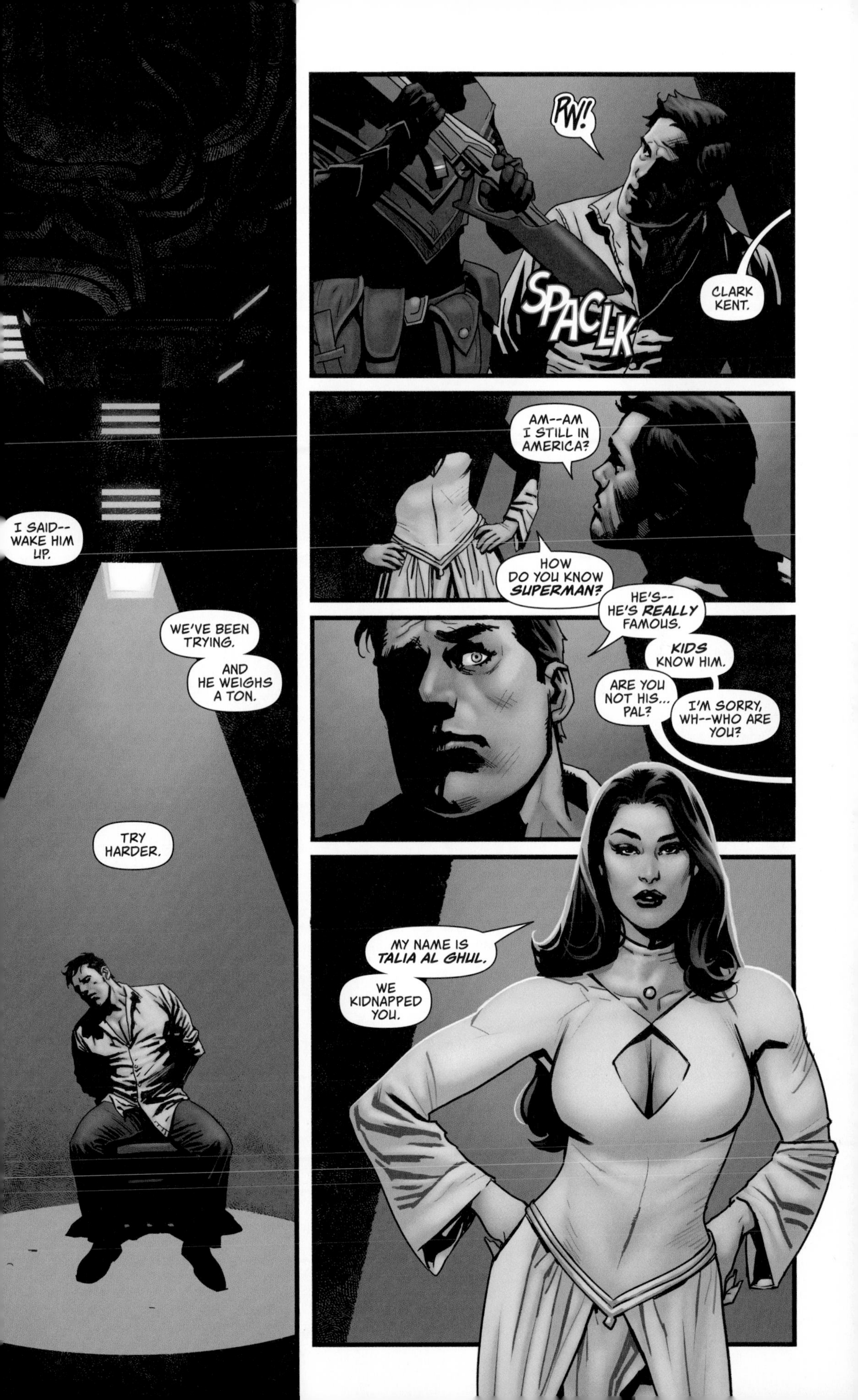
I SAID-- WAKE HIM UP.
WE'VE BEEN TRYING.
AND HE WEIGHS A TON.
TRY HARDER.
PW!
SPACLK
CLARK KENT.
AM--AM I STILL IN AMERICA?
HOW DO YOU KNOW SUPERMAN?
HE'S-- HE'S REALLY FAMOUS.
KIDS KNOW HIM.
ARE YOU NOT HIS... PAL?
I'M SORRY, WH--WHO ARE YOU?
MY NAME IS TALIA AL GHUL.
WE KIDNAPPED YOU.

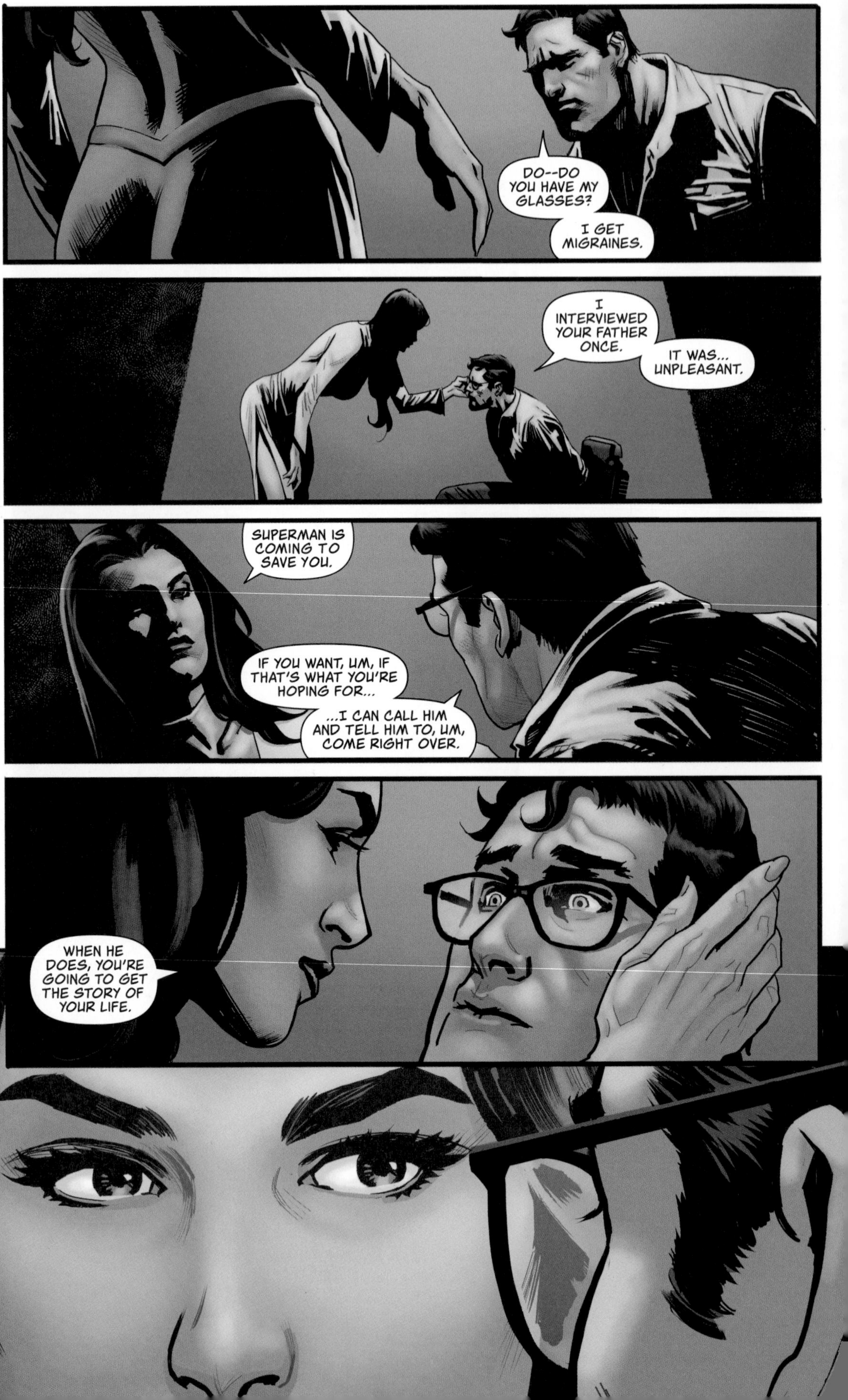
DO--DO YOU HAVE MY GLASSES?
I GET MIGRAINES.
I INTERVIEWED YOUR FATHER ONCE.
IT WAS... UNPLEASANT.
SUPERMAN IS COMING TO SAVE YOU.
IF YOU WANT, UM, IF THAT'S WHAT YOU'RE HOPING FOR...
...I CAN CALL HIM AND TELL HIM TO, UM, COME RIGHT OVER.
WHEN HE DOES, YOU'RE GOING TO GET THE STORY OF YOUR LIFE.

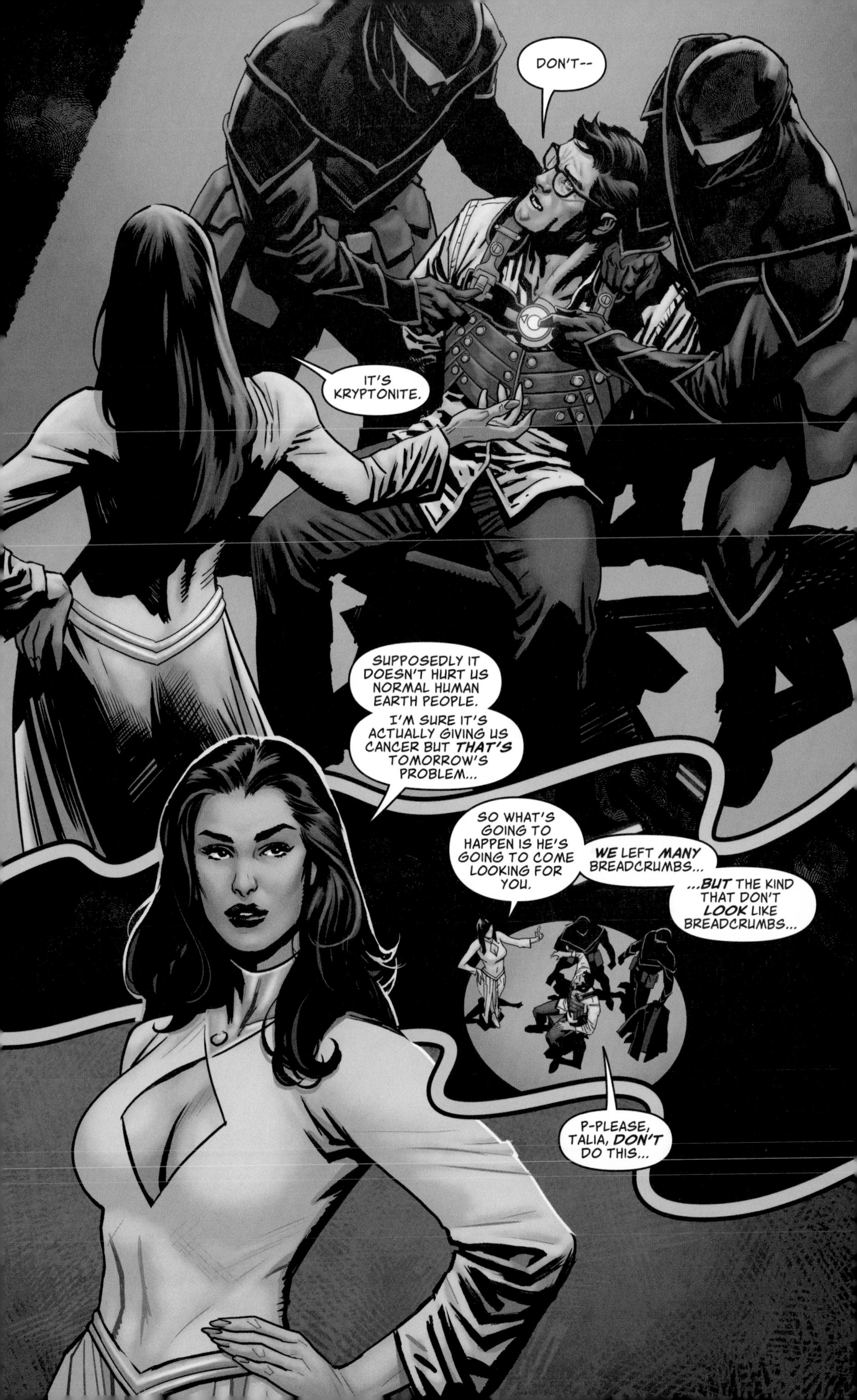
DON'T--
IT'S KRYPTONITE.
SUPPOSEDLY IT DOESN'T HURT US NORMAL HUMAN EARTH PEOPLE.
I'M SURE IT'S ACTUALLY GIVING US CANCER BUT THAT'S TOMORROW'S PROBLEM...
SO WHAT'S GOING TO HAPPEN IS HE'S GOING TO COME LOOKING FOR YOU.
WE LEFT MANY BREADCRUMBS...
...BUT THE KIND THAT DON'T LOOK LIKE BREADCRUMBS...
P-PLEASE, TALIA, DON'T DO THIS...

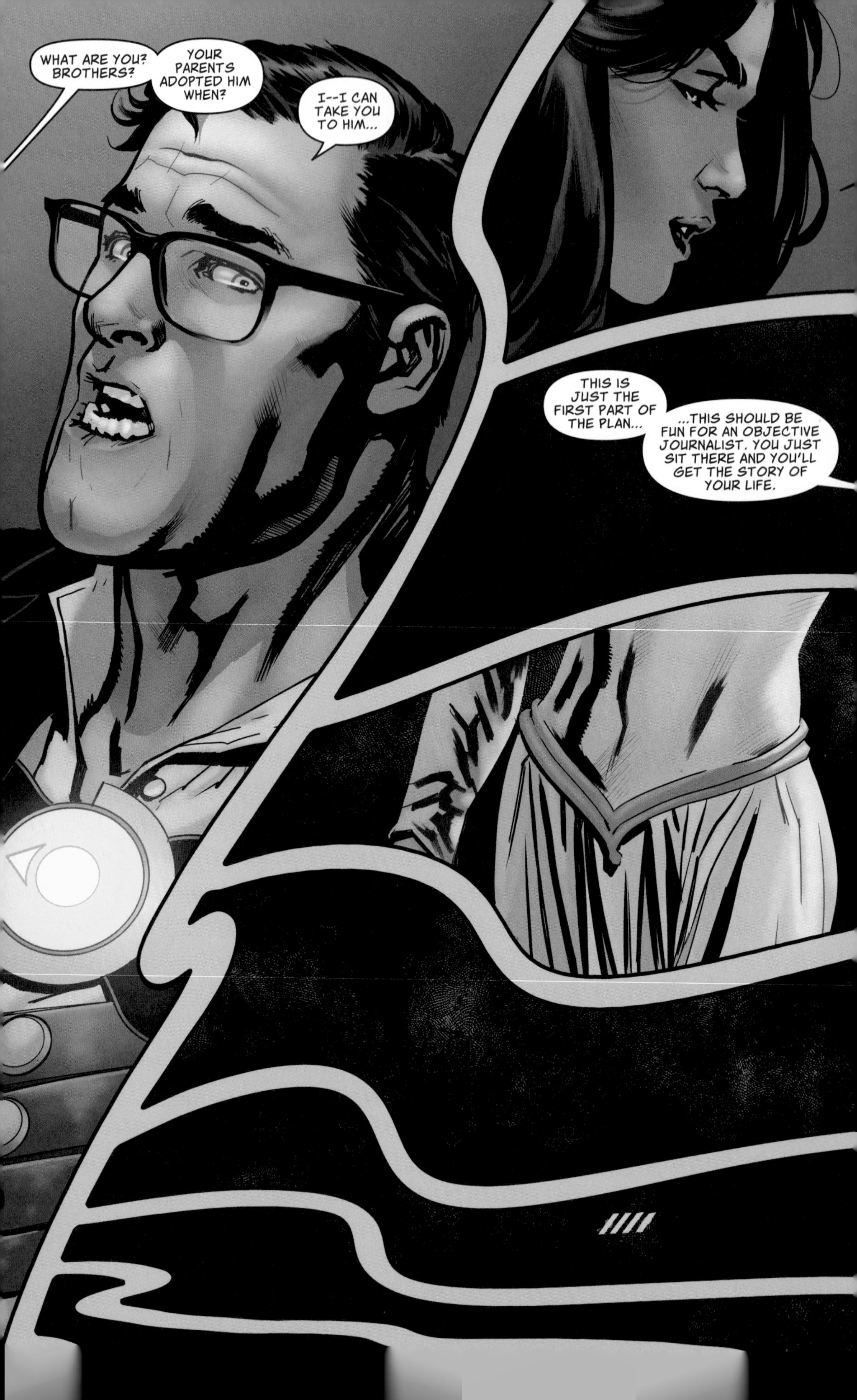
WHAT ARE YOU? BROTHERS?
YOUR PARENTS ADOPTED HIM WHEN?
I--I CAN TAKE YOU TO HIM...
THIS IS JUST THE FIRST PART OF THE PLAN...
...THIS SHOULD BE FUN FOR AN OBJECTIVE JOURNALIST. YOU JUST SIT THERE AND YOU'LL GET THE STORY OF YOUR LIFE.

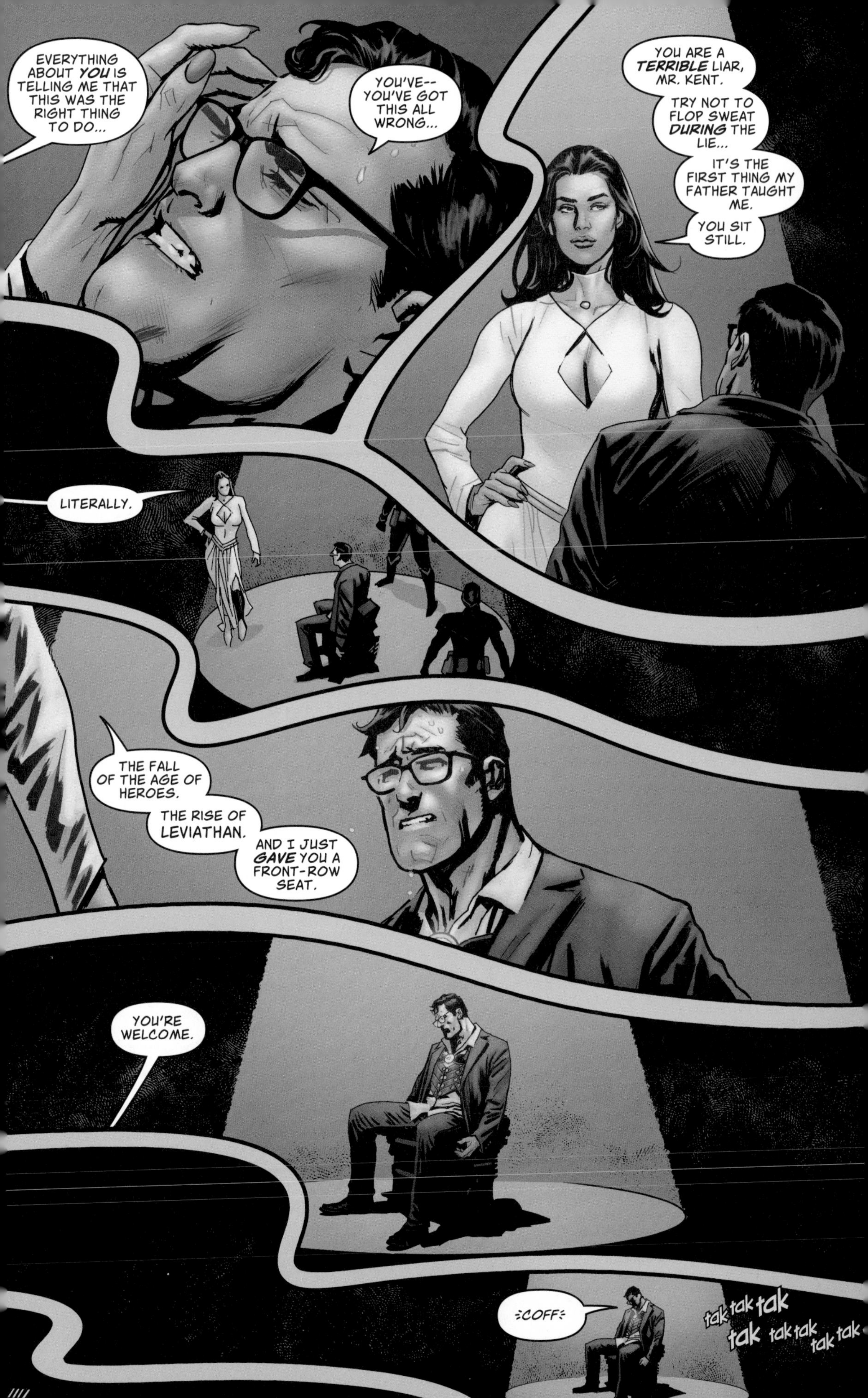
EVERYTHING ABOUT YOU IS TELLING ME THAT THIS WAS THE RIGHT THING TO DO...
YOU'VE-- YOU'VE GOT THIS ALL WRONG...
YOU ARE A TERRIBLE LIAR, MR. KENT.
TRY NOT TO FLOP SWEAT DURING THE LIE...
IT'S THE FIRST THING MY FATHER TAUGHT ME.
YOU SIT STILL.
LITERALLY.
THE FALL OF THE AGE OF HEROES.
THE RISE OF LEVIATHAN.
AND I JUST GAVE YOU A FRONT-ROW SEAT.
YOU'RE WELCOME.
=COFF=
tak tak tak
tak tak tak tak tak

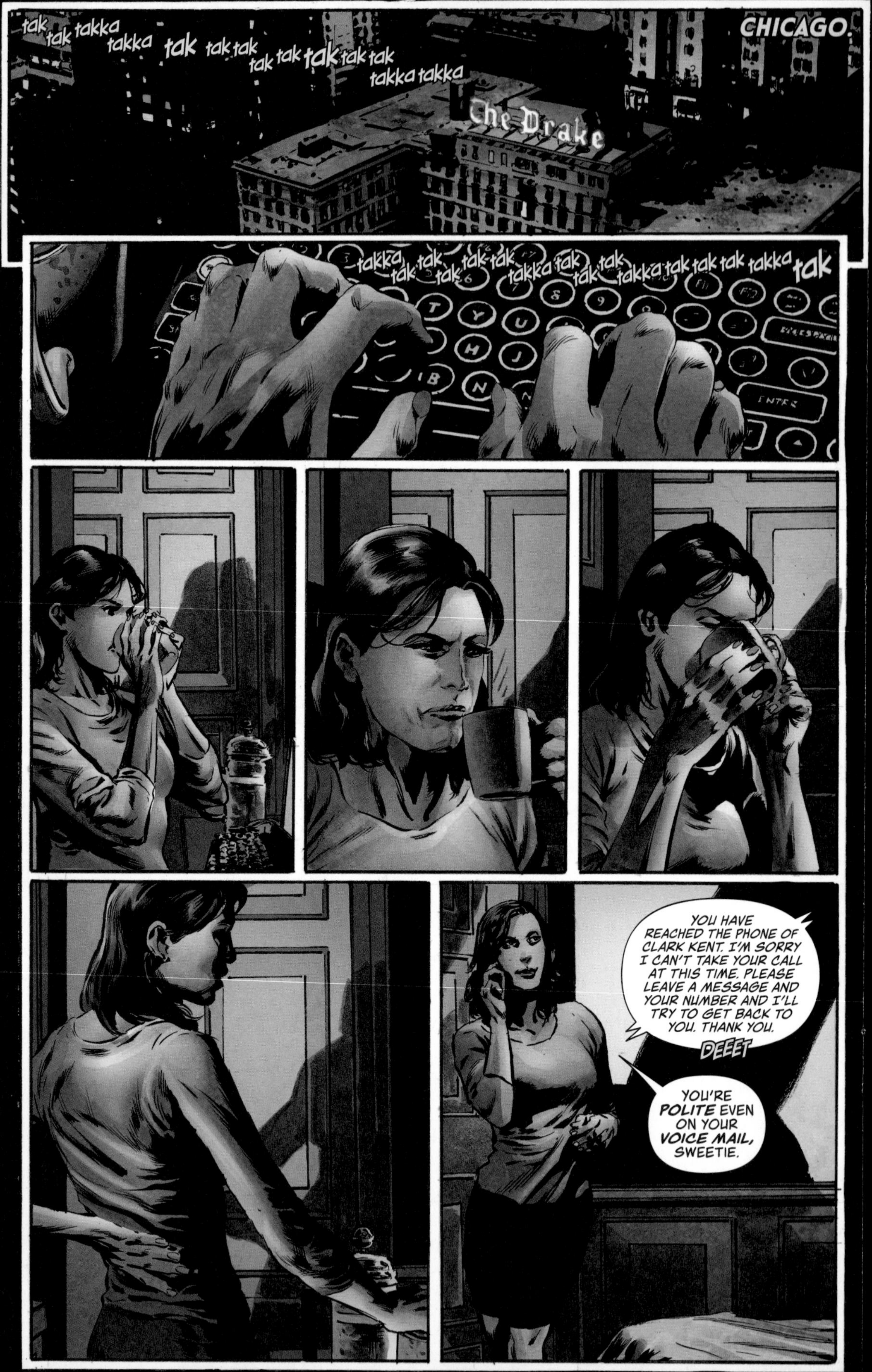
tak tak takka takka tak tak tak tak tak tak tak tak takka takka
CHICAGO.
The Drake
takka tak tak tak tak tak tak takka tak tak tak takka tak tak tak takka tak
YOU HAVE REACHED THE PHONE OF CLARK KENT. I'M SORRY I CAN'T TAKE YOUR CALL AT THIS TIME. PLEASE LEAVE A MESSAGE AND YOUR NUMBER AND I'LL TRY TO GET BACK TO YOU. THANK YOU.
DEEET
YOU'RE POLITE EVEN ON YOUR VOICE MAIL, SWEETIE.

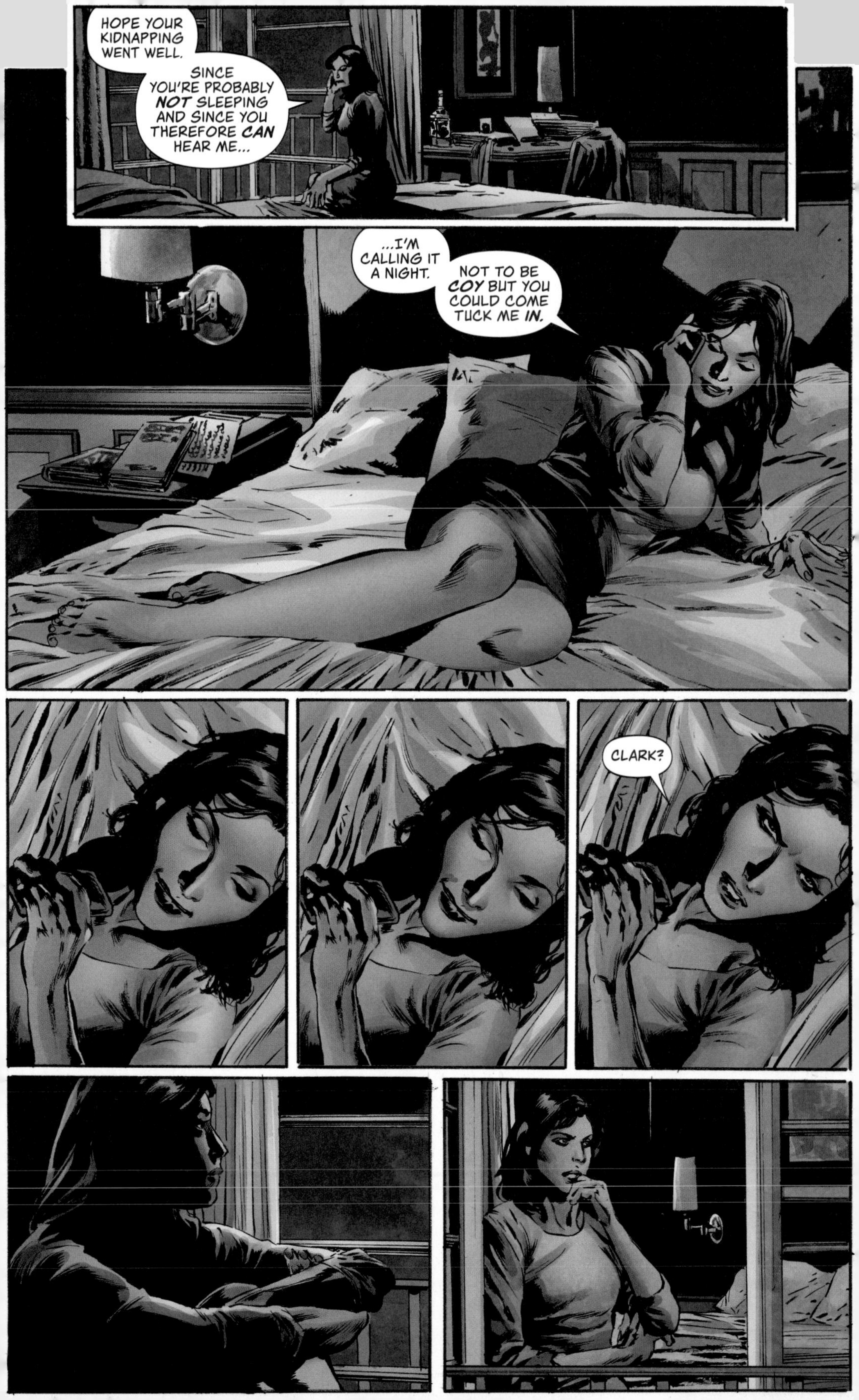
HOPE YOUR KIDNAPPING WENT WELL.
SINCE YOU'RE PROBABLY **NOT** SLEEPING AND SINCE YOU THEREFORE **CAN** HEAR ME...
...I'M CALLING IT A NIGHT.
NOT TO BE **COY** BUT YOU COULD COME TUCK ME **IN.**
CLARK?

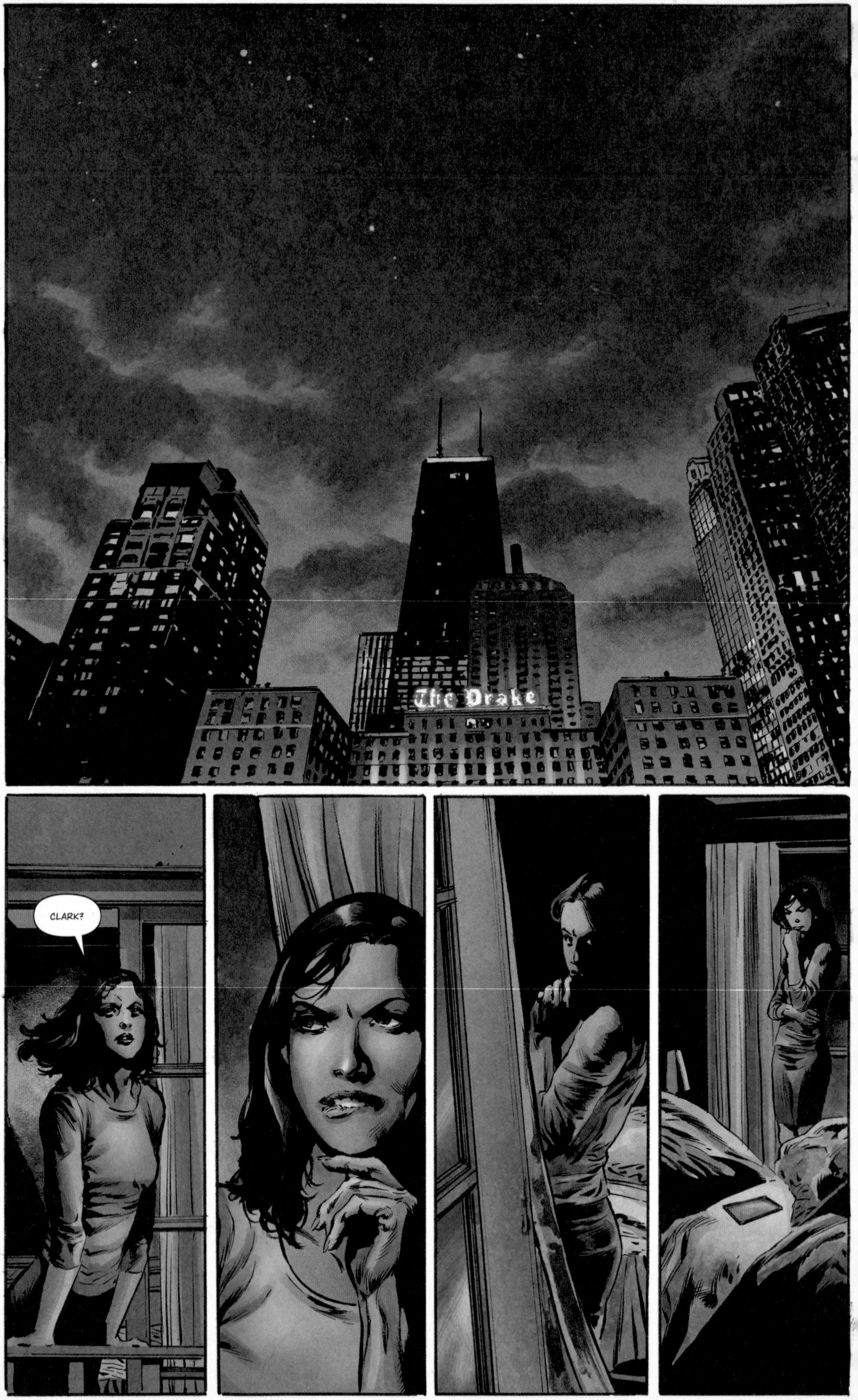
The Drake
CLARK?

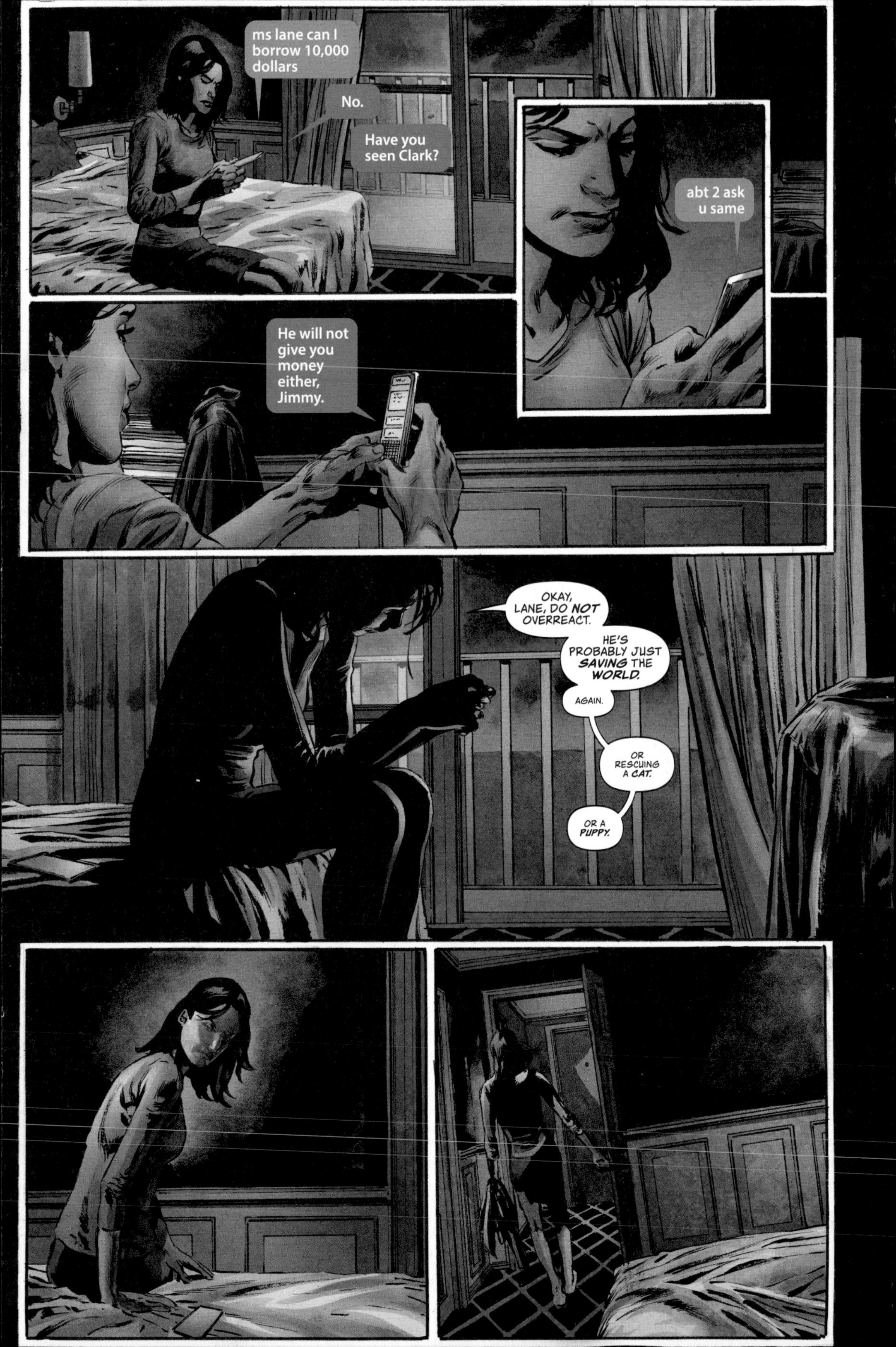
ms lane can I borrow 10,000 dollars
No.
Have you seen Clark?
abt 2 ask u same
He will not give you money either, Jimmy.
OKAY, LANE, DO *NOT* OVERREACT.
HE'S PROBABLY JUST *SAVING* THE *WORLD.*
AGAIN.
OR RESCUING A *CAT.*
OR A *PUPPY.*

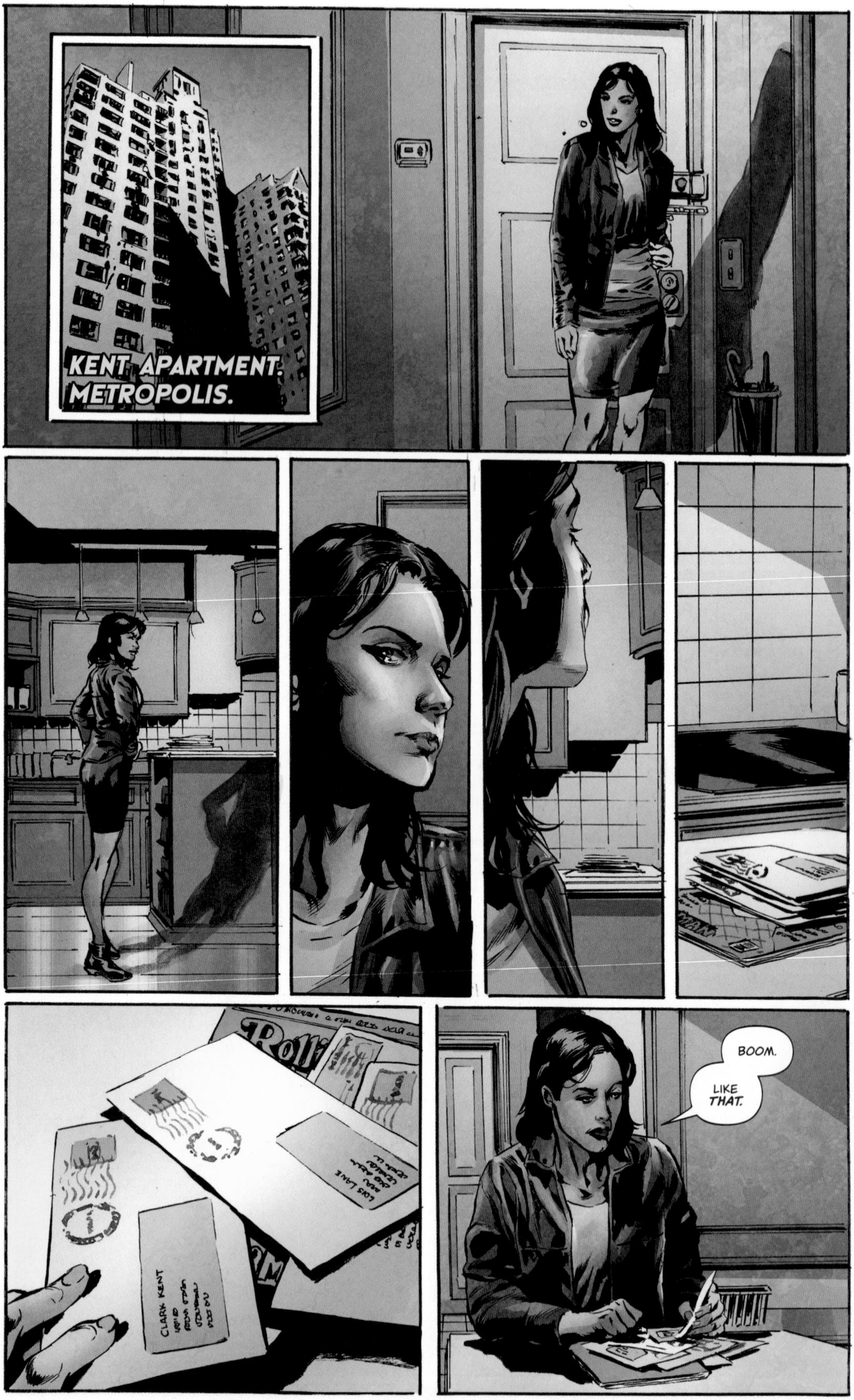
KENT APARTMENT.
METROPOLIS.
LOIS LANE
CLARK KENT
BOOM.
LIKE *THAT.*

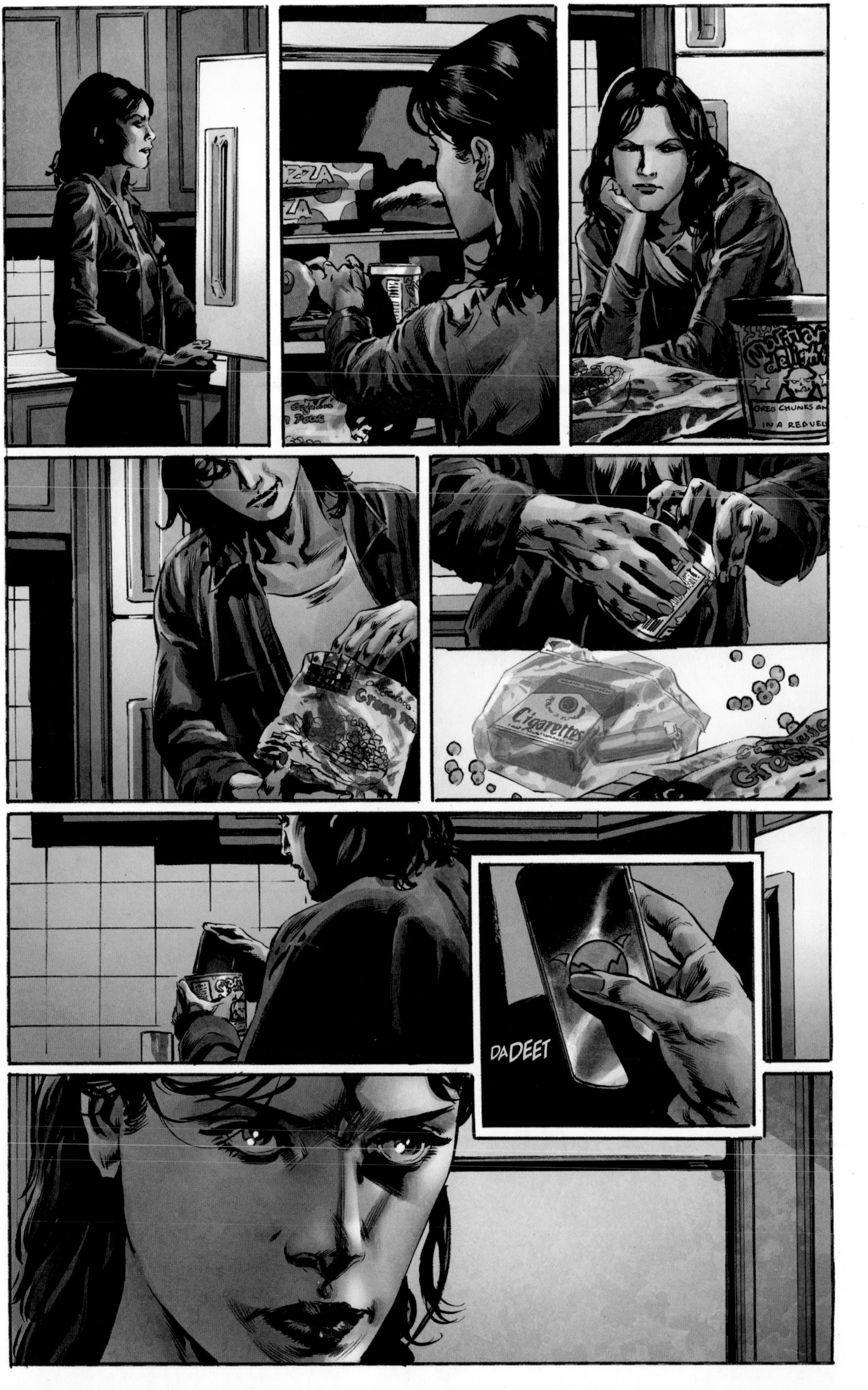
Cigarettes
DADEET

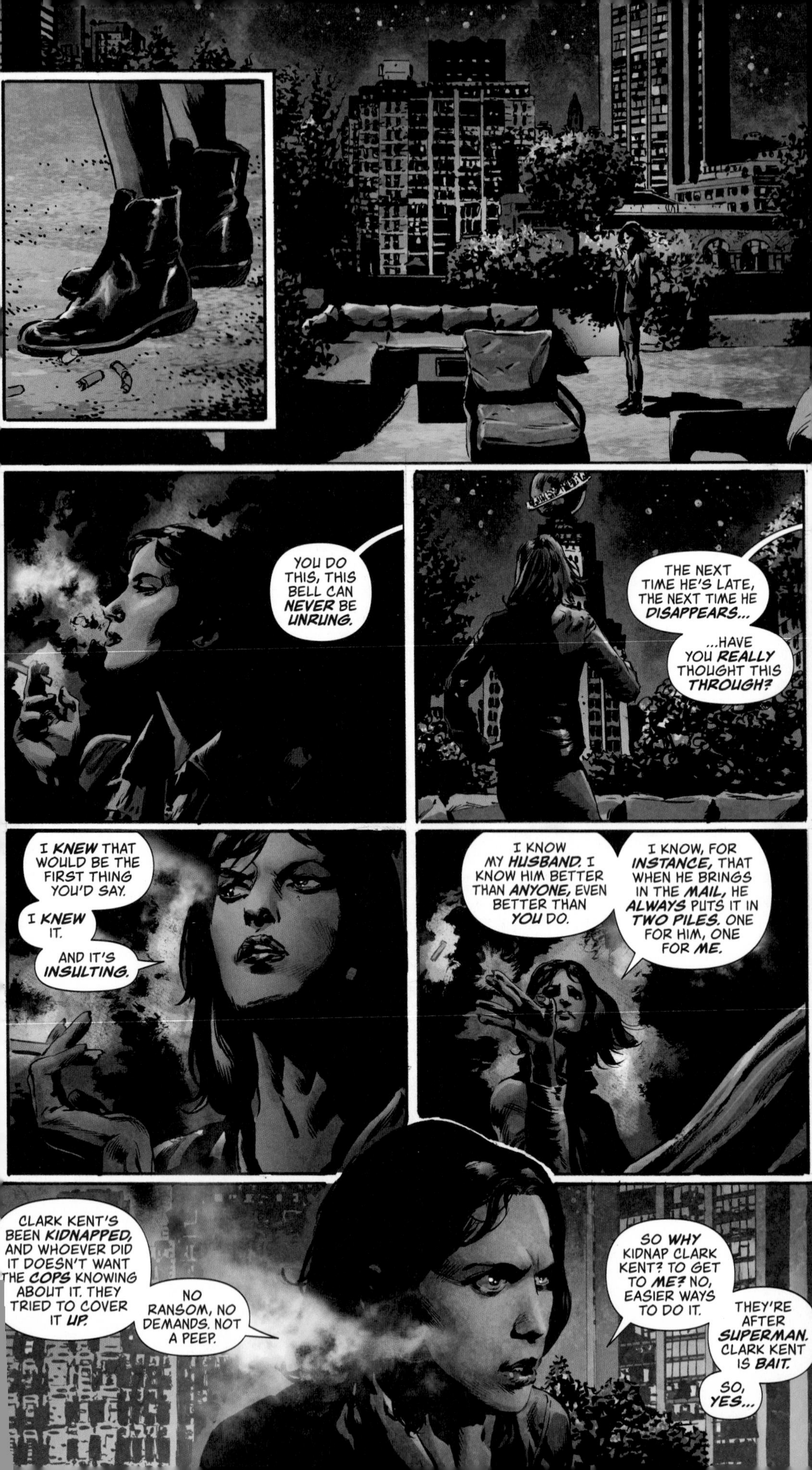
YOU DO THIS, THIS BELL CAN NEVER BE UNRUNG.
THE NEXT TIME HE'S LATE, THE NEXT TIME HE DISAPPEARS...
...HAVE YOU REALLY THOUGHT THIS THROUGH?
I KNEW THAT WOULD BE THE FIRST THING YOU'D SAY.
I KNEW IT.
AND IT'S INSULTING.
I KNOW MY HUSBAND. I KNOW HIM BETTER THAN ANYONE, EVEN BETTER THAN YOU DO.
I KNOW, FOR INSTANCE, THAT WHEN HE BRINGS IN THE MAIL, HE ALWAYS PUTS IT IN TWO PILES. ONE FOR HIM, ONE FOR ME.
CLARK KENT'S BEEN KIDNAPPED, AND WHOEVER DID IT DOESN'T WANT THE COPS KNOWING ABOUT IT. THEY TRIED TO COVER IT UP.
NO RANSOM, NO DEMANDS. NOT A PEEP.
SO WHY KIDNAP CLARK KENT? TO GET TO ME? NO, EASIER WAYS TO DO IT.
THEY'RE AFTER SUPERMAN. CLARK KENT IS BAIT.
SO, YES...

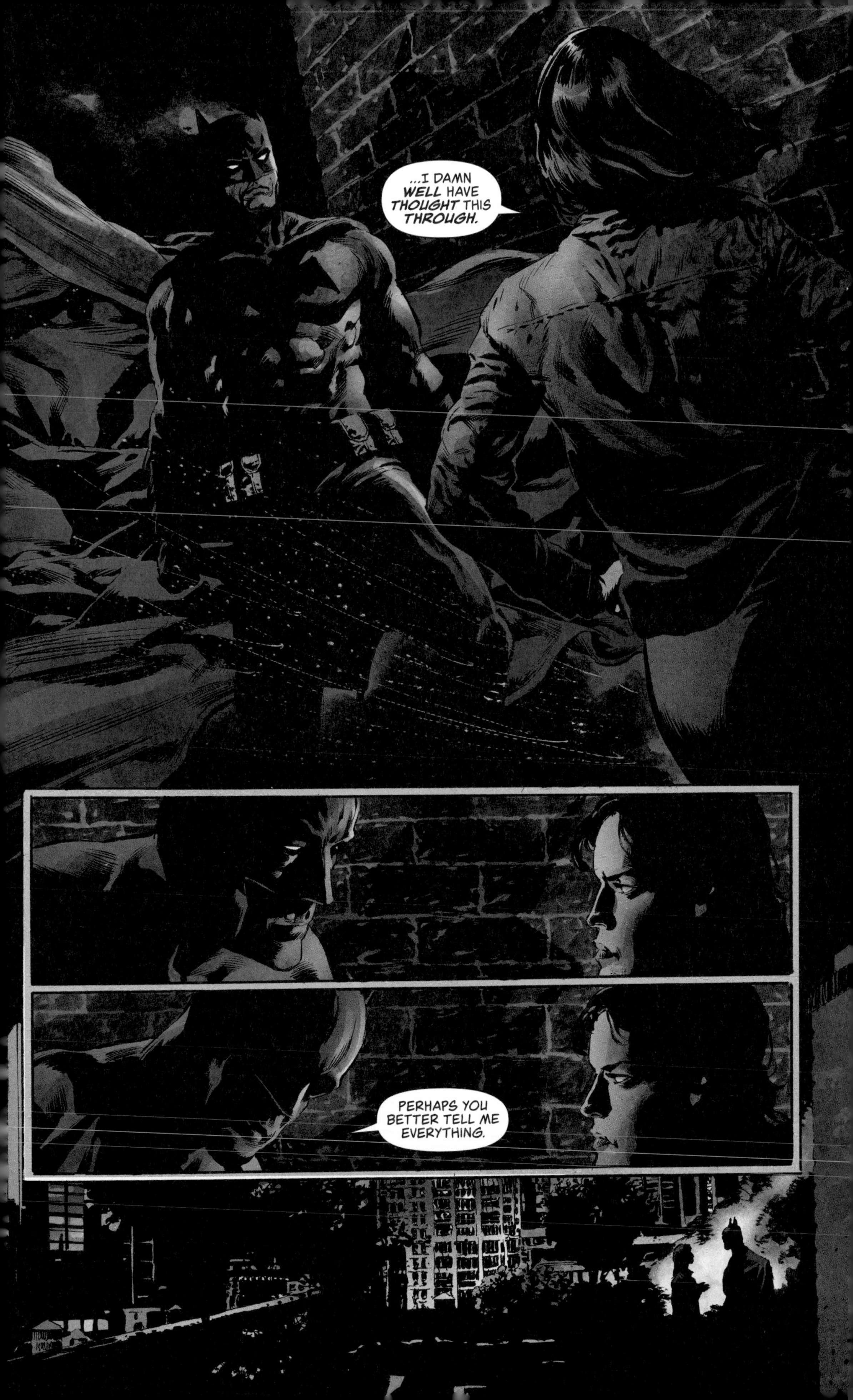
...I DAMN WELL HAVE THOUGHT THIS THROUGH.
PERHAPS YOU BETTER TELL ME EVERYTHING.

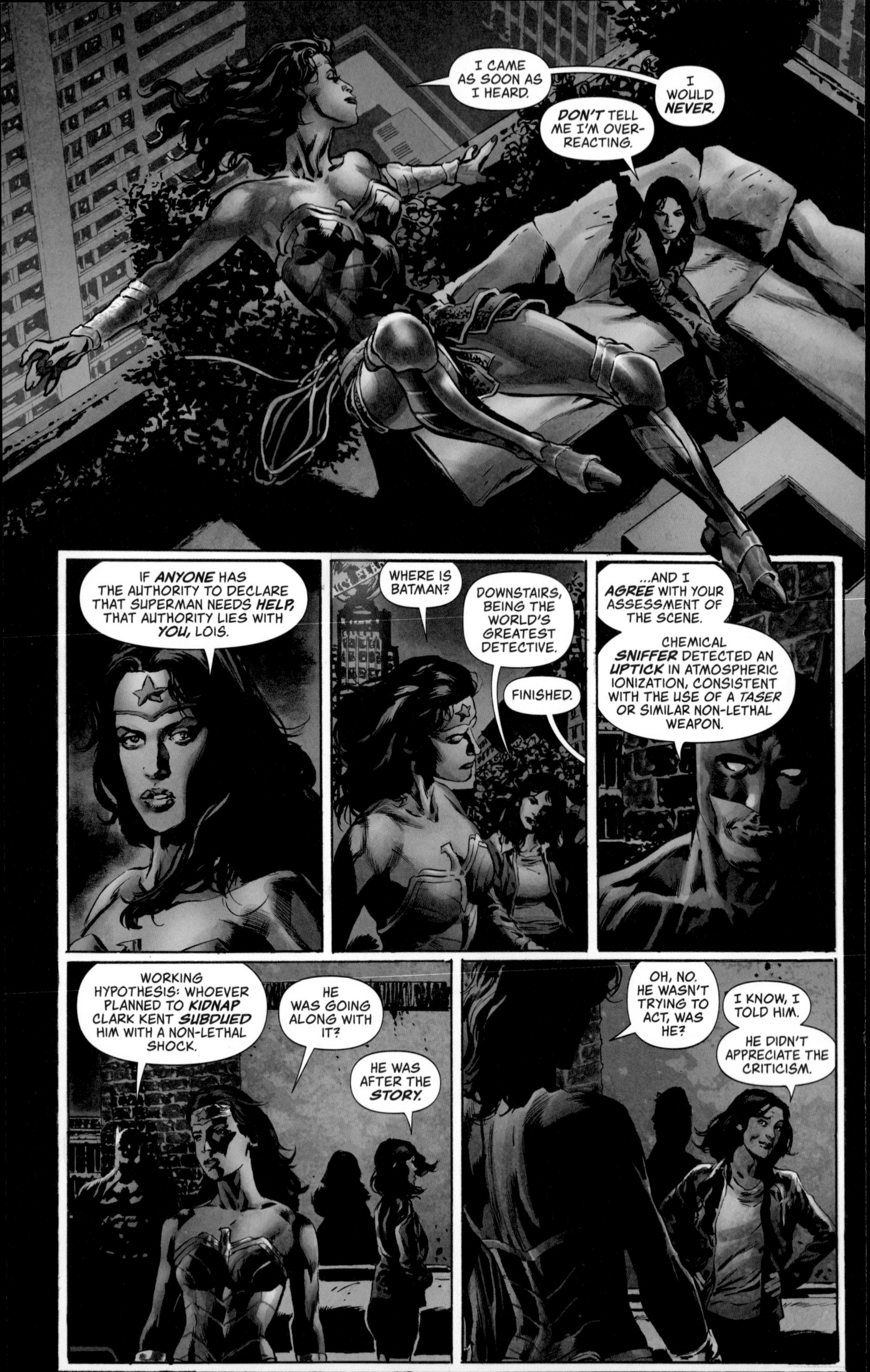

I CAME AS SOON AS I HEARD.
DON'T TELL ME I'M OVER-REACTING.
I WOULD NEVER.
IF ANYONE HAS THE AUTHORITY TO DECLARE THAT SUPERMAN NEEDS HELP, THAT AUTHORITY LIES WITH YOU, LOIS.
WHERE IS BATMAN?
DOWNSTAIRS, BEING THE WORLD'S GREATEST DETECTIVE.
FINISHED.
...AND I AGREE WITH YOUR ASSESSMENT OF THE SCENE.
CHEMICAL SNIFFER DETECTED AN UPTICK IN ATMOSPHERIC IONIZATION, CONSISTENT WITH THE USE OF A TASER OR SIMILAR NON-LETHAL WEAPON.
WORKING HYPOTHESIS: WHOEVER PLANNED TO KIDNAP CLARK KENT SUBDUED HIM WITH A NON-LETHAL SHOCK.
HE WAS GOING ALONG WITH IT?
HE WAS AFTER THE STORY.
OH, NO. HE WASN'T TRYING TO ACT, WAS HE?
I KNOW, I TOLD HIM.
HE DIDN'T APPRECIATE THE CRITICISM.

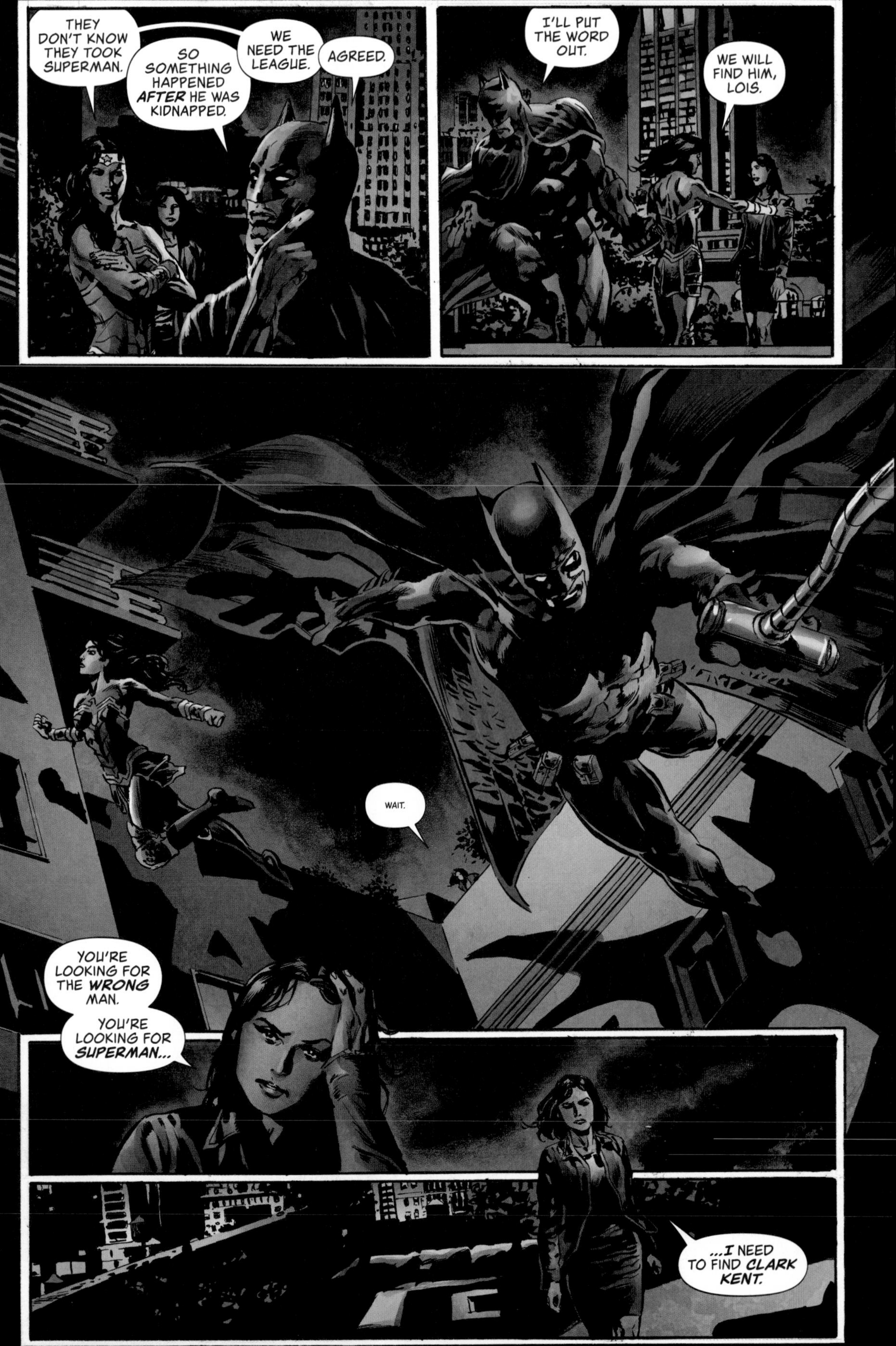
THEY DON'T KNOW THEY TOOK SUPERMAN.
SO SOMETHING HAPPENED AFTER HE WAS KIDNAPPED.
WE NEED THE LEAGUE.
AGREED.
I'LL PUT THE WORD OUT.
WE WILL FIND HIM, LOIS.
WAIT.
YOU'RE LOOKING FOR THE WRONG MAN.
YOU'RE LOOKING FOR SUPERMAN...
...I NEED TO FIND CLARK KENT.

WHAT'S THIS? WHILE ON A WILDLY SUCCESSFUL WORLDWIDE BOOK TOUR FOR HIS WILDLY SUCCESSFUL (WORLDWIDE) BOOK OF PHOTOGRAPHY, OUR PAL JIMMY AWAKENS WITH THE FAINT TASTE OF GORILLA CHAMPAGNE ON HIS BREATH, WEARING ONLY BOW TIE AND BIRTHDAY SUIT, IN A HONEYMOON SUITE SOMEWHERE IN GORILLA CITY--SHOCKED TO DISCOVER HE'S NOT ALONE!

THE LADY IN QUESTION APPEARS TO HAVE JUST AS MANY QUESTIONS ABOUT WHAT HAPPENED LAST NIGHT FOR...

SUPERMAN'S MARRIED FRIEND

JIMMY OLSEN

ESPECIALLY BECAUSE THE LADY IN QUESTION IS NO ORDINARY LADY IN QUESTION! DEAR READER, IT TURNS OUT THAT ANYTHING IS POSSIBLE IN THE COLD LIGHT OF DAY AFTER JUST

ONE WILD NIGHT IN GORILLA CITY!

AAAAAAA!

AAAAAAAA!

OLSEN
MY LIFE IN THE INFINITE METROPOLIS

YOU! YOU.

WHO ARE YOU? HOW DID--

AAA!

GETITOFFGETIT**OFF**--

I, UHH... IS IT--

--JESSSSZZZZAMINNNTH?

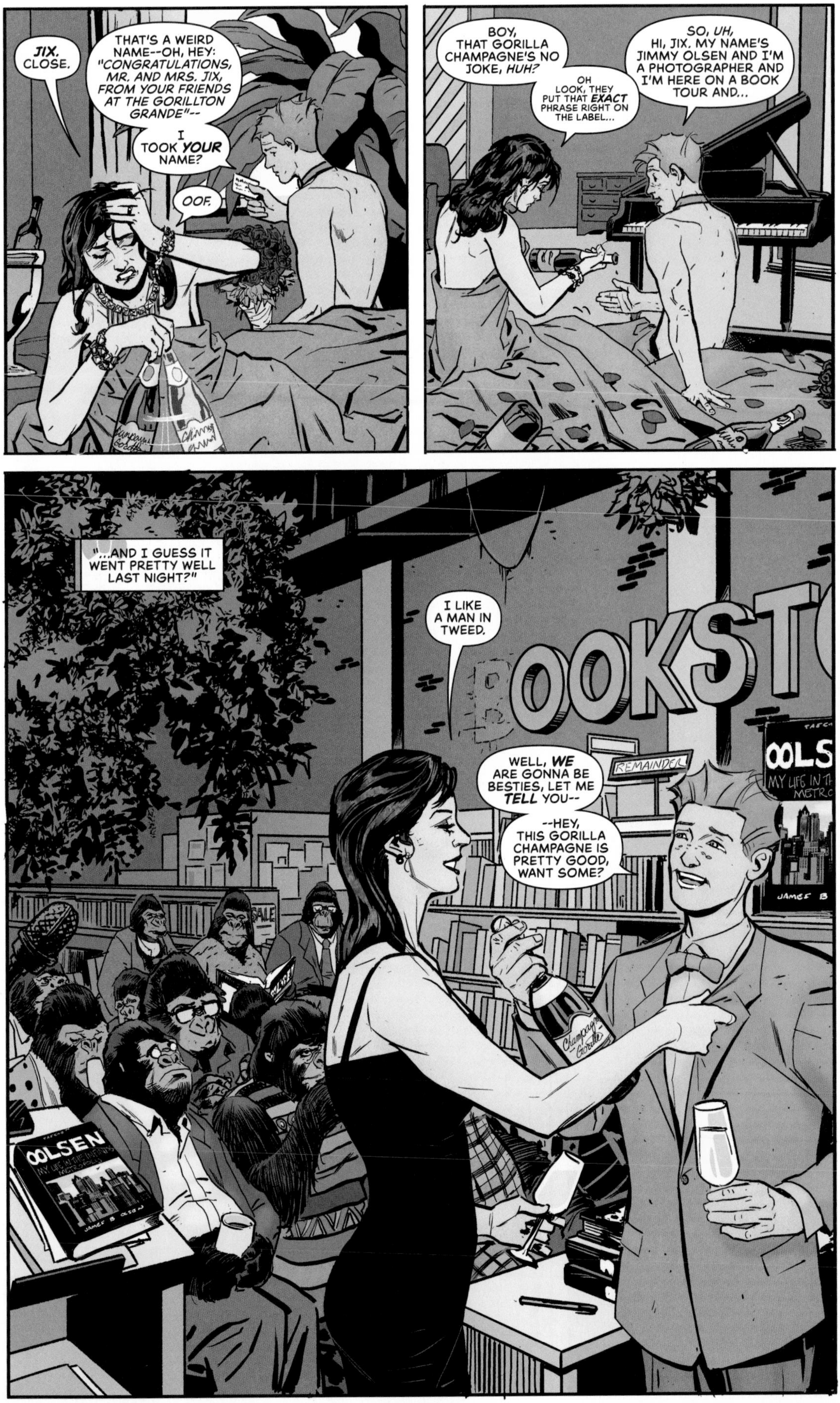
JIX. CLOSE.
THAT'S A WEIRD NAME--OH, HEY: "CONGRATULATIONS, MR. AND MRS. JIX, FROM YOUR FRIENDS AT THE GORILLTON GRANDE"--
I TOOK YOUR NAME?
OOF.
BOY, THAT GORILLA CHAMPAGNE'S NO JOKE, HUH?
OH LOOK, THEY PUT THAT EXACT PHRASE RIGHT ON THE LABEL...
SO, UH, HI, JIX. MY NAME'S JIMMY OLSEN AND I'M A PHOTOGRAPHER AND I'M HERE ON A BOOK TOUR AND...
"...AND I GUESS IT WENT PRETTY WELL LAST NIGHT?"
I LIKE A MAN IN TWEED.
WELL, WE ARE GONNA BE BESTIES, LET ME TELL YOU--
--HEY, THIS GORILLA CHAMPAGNE IS PRETTY GOOD, WANT SOME?
REMAINDER
OLSEN

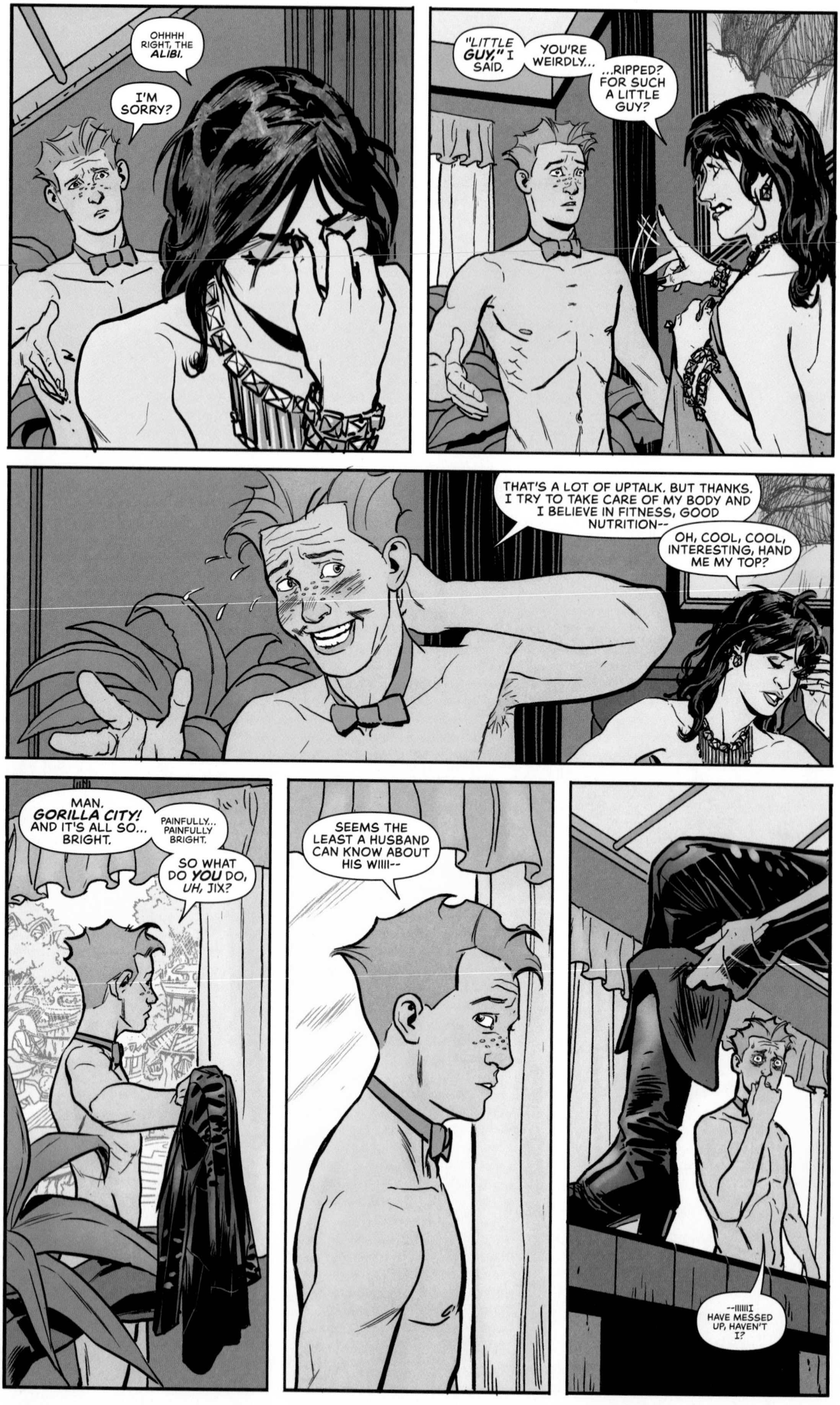
OHHHH RIGHT, THE ALIBI.
I'M SORRY?
"LITTLE GUY," I SAID.
YOU'RE WEIRDLY...
...RIPPED? FOR SUCH A LITTLE GUY?
THAT'S A LOT OF UPTALK. BUT THANKS. I TRY TO TAKE CARE OF MY BODY AND I BELIEVE IN FITNESS, GOOD NUTRITION--
OH, COOL, COOL, INTERESTING, HAND ME MY TOP?
MAN. GORILLA CITY! AND IT'S ALL SO... BRIGHT.
PAINFULLY... PAINFULLY BRIGHT.
SO WHAT DO YOU DO, UH, JIX?
SEEMS THE LEAST A HUSBAND CAN KNOW ABOUT HIS WIIII--
--IIIIII HAVE MESSED UP, HAVEN'T I?

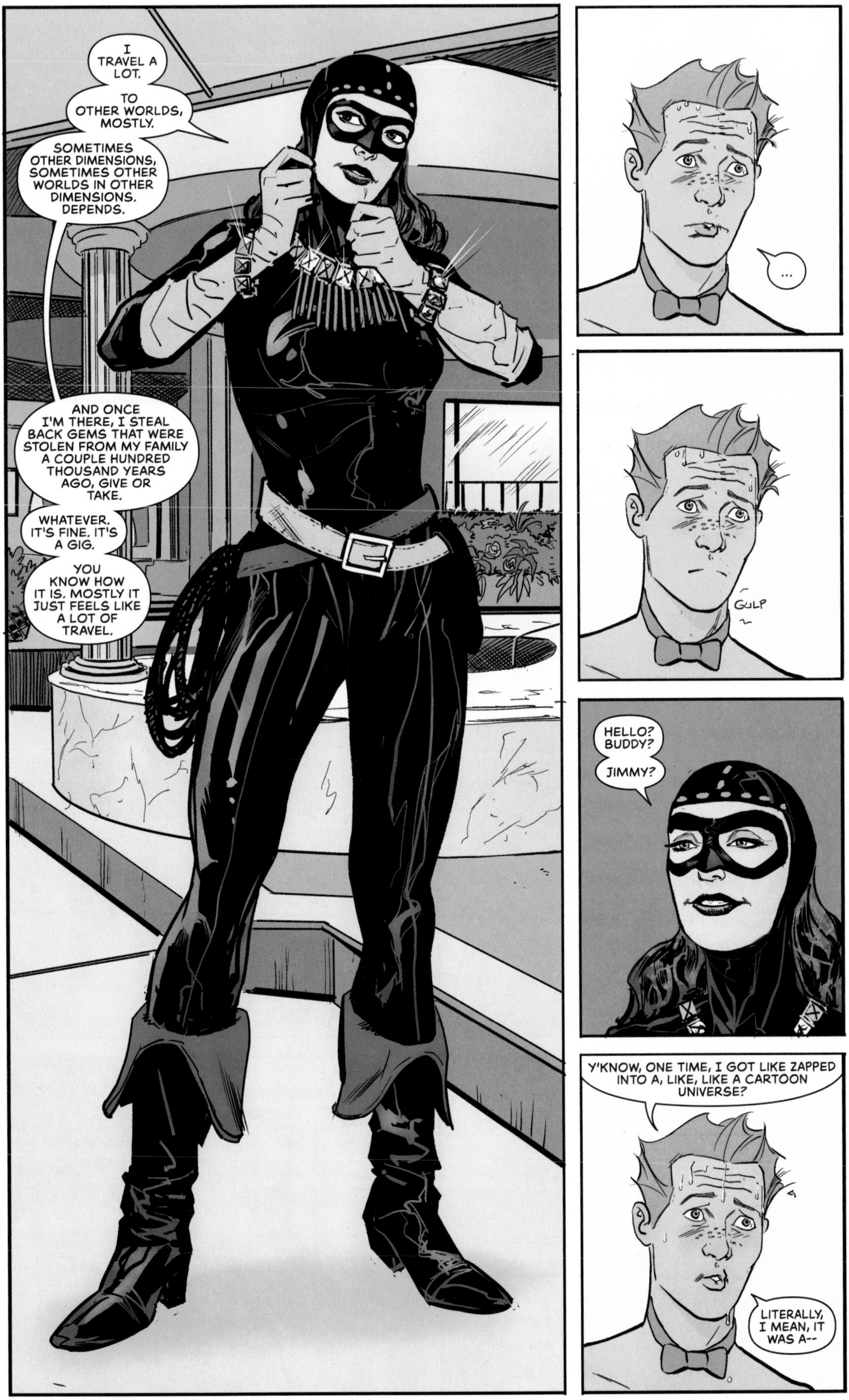

I TRAVEL A LOT.
TO OTHER WORLDS, MOSTLY.
SOMETIMES OTHER DIMENSIONS, SOMETIMES OTHER WORLDS IN OTHER DIMENSIONS. DEPENDS.
AND ONCE I'M THERE, I STEAL BACK GEMS THAT WERE STOLEN FROM MY FAMILY A COUPLE HUNDRED THOUSAND YEARS AGO, GIVE OR TAKE.
WHATEVER. IT'S FINE. IT'S A GIG.
YOU KNOW HOW IT IS. MOSTLY IT JUST FEELS LIKE A LOT OF TRAVEL.
...
GULP
HELLO? BUDDY?
JIMMY?
Y'KNOW, ONE TIME, I GOT LIKE ZAPPED INTO A, LIKE, LIKE A CARTOON UNIVERSE?
LITERALLY, I MEAN, IT WAS A--

THE **MAN OF STEEL** AND THE PAL OF A **PRETTY-STRONG-METAL-NOT-STEEL-STRONG-BUT-NOT-LIKE-TIN-OR-SOMETHING** WOKE UP ON THE WRONG SIDE OF **REALITY** THIS MORNING!

THAT 5-D IMP-ERNEL MR. MXYZPTLK AND MR. MXYZPTLK'S PAL, 4·QQ&BE4J*O(@NXX HAVE YOUR FAVORITE **GOOD TIME PARTY BOYS** ON THE RUN IN A **CRAZY CARTOON DIMENSION** WHERE PHYSICS ITSELF SEEMS TO HAVE GOTTEN A PUNCH-UP IN REWRITE!

HOW CAN THEY ESCAPE, LET ALONE TRICK THESE DASTARDLY LITTLE WEIRDOS INTO SAYING THEIR OWN NAMES BACKWARD? WHAT HAPPENS IF THEY GET CHASED INTO AN ANVIL FACTORY? ARE THERE COMMERCIAL BREAKS? AND SOMEHOW WE **ALL** KNOW THIS IS JIMMY'S FAULT, RIGHT?

READ ON TO FIND OUT HOW

SUPERMAN'S TOYETIC SIDEKICK

JIMMY OLSEN

ALMOST GOT HIMSELF AMUSED TO DEATH IN...

THE FIFTH-DIMENSION FUNNIES

JIMMY? JIMMY, WHY ARE YOU TELLING ME THIS?

I JUST...

I WAS REALLY GLAD NOT TO BE THERE ANYMORE JUST THEN.

BECAUSE MY EYES WOULD'VE POPPED OUT OF MY HEAD AND MY JAW WOULD BE ON THE FLOOR AND THERE'D BE A BIG **AROOGA AROOGA** NOISE.

EMBARRASSING.

HEY, WAIT.

WHERE ARE **MY** CLOTHES?

UH, I DUNNO, CLOSET MAYBE?

DIDN'T REALLY LOOK LIKE WE WERE IN THE TAKE-THE-TIME-TO-HANG-OUR-CLOTHES-UP SORTA PLACE LAST NIGHT...

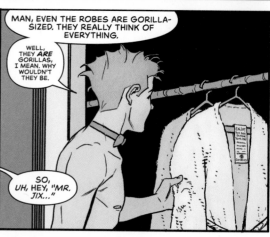

MAN, EVEN THE ROBES ARE GORILLA-SIZED, THEY REALLY THINK OF EVERYTHING.

WELL, THEY **ARE** GORILLAS, I MEAN. WHY WOULDN'T THEY BE.

SO, UH, HEY, "MR. JIX..."

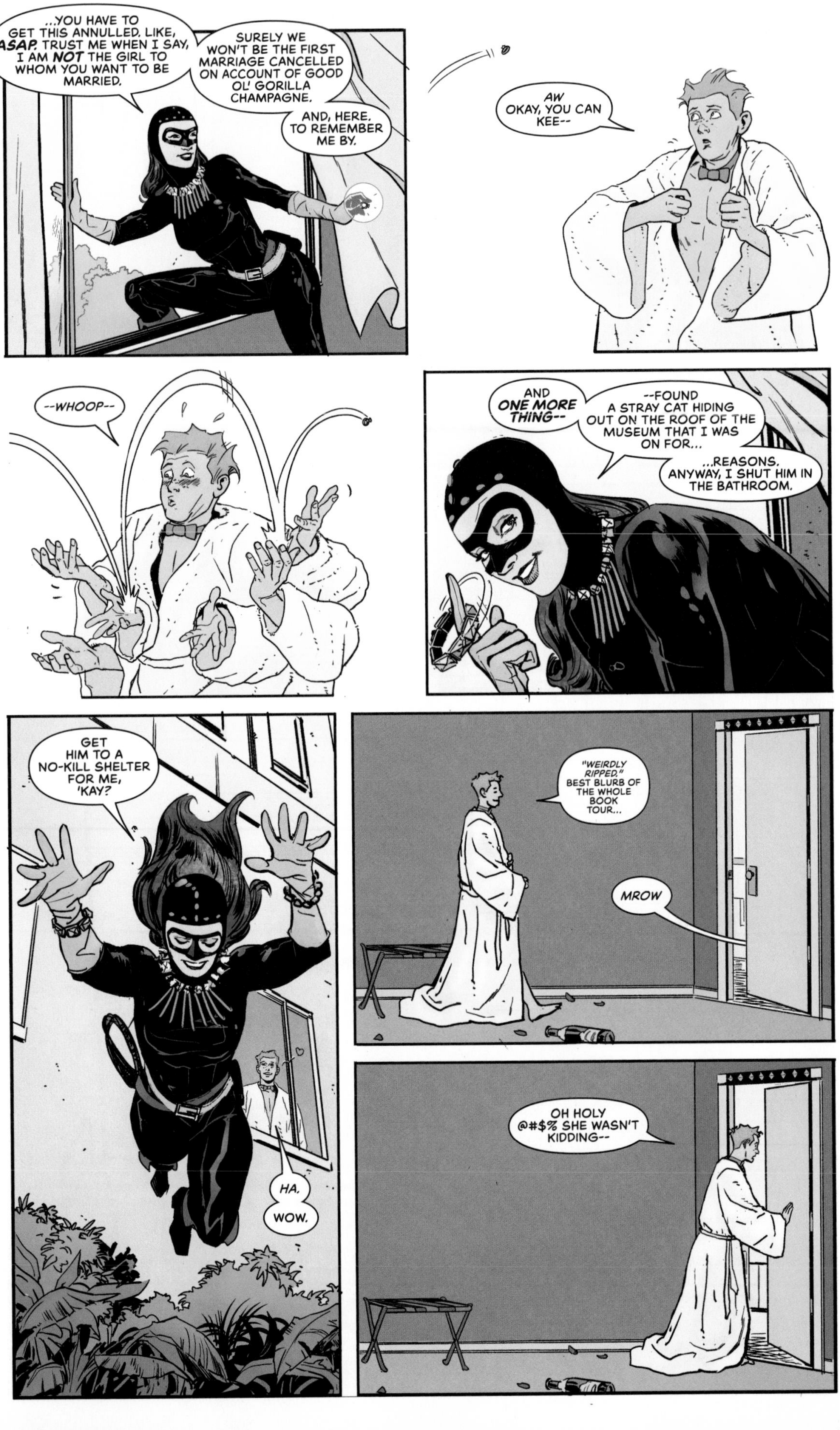
...YOU HAVE TO GET THIS ANNULLED. LIKE, ASAP. TRUST ME WHEN I SAY, I AM NOT THE GIRL TO WHOM YOU WANT TO BE MARRIED.
SURELY WE WON'T BE THE FIRST MARRIAGE CANCELLED ON ACCOUNT OF GOOD OL' GORILLA CHAMPAGNE.
AND, HERE. TO REMEMBER ME BY.
AW OKAY, YOU CAN KEE--
--WHOOP--
AND ONE MORE THING--
--FOUND A STRAY CAT HIDING OUT ON THE ROOF OF THE MUSEUM THAT I WAS ON FOR...
...REASONS. ANYWAY, I SHUT HIM IN THE BATHROOM.
GET HIM TO A NO-KILL SHELTER FOR ME, 'KAY?
HA.
WOW.
"WEIRDLY RIPPED." BEST BLURB OF THE WHOLE BOOK TOUR...
MROW
OH HOLY @#$% SHE WASN'T KIDDING--

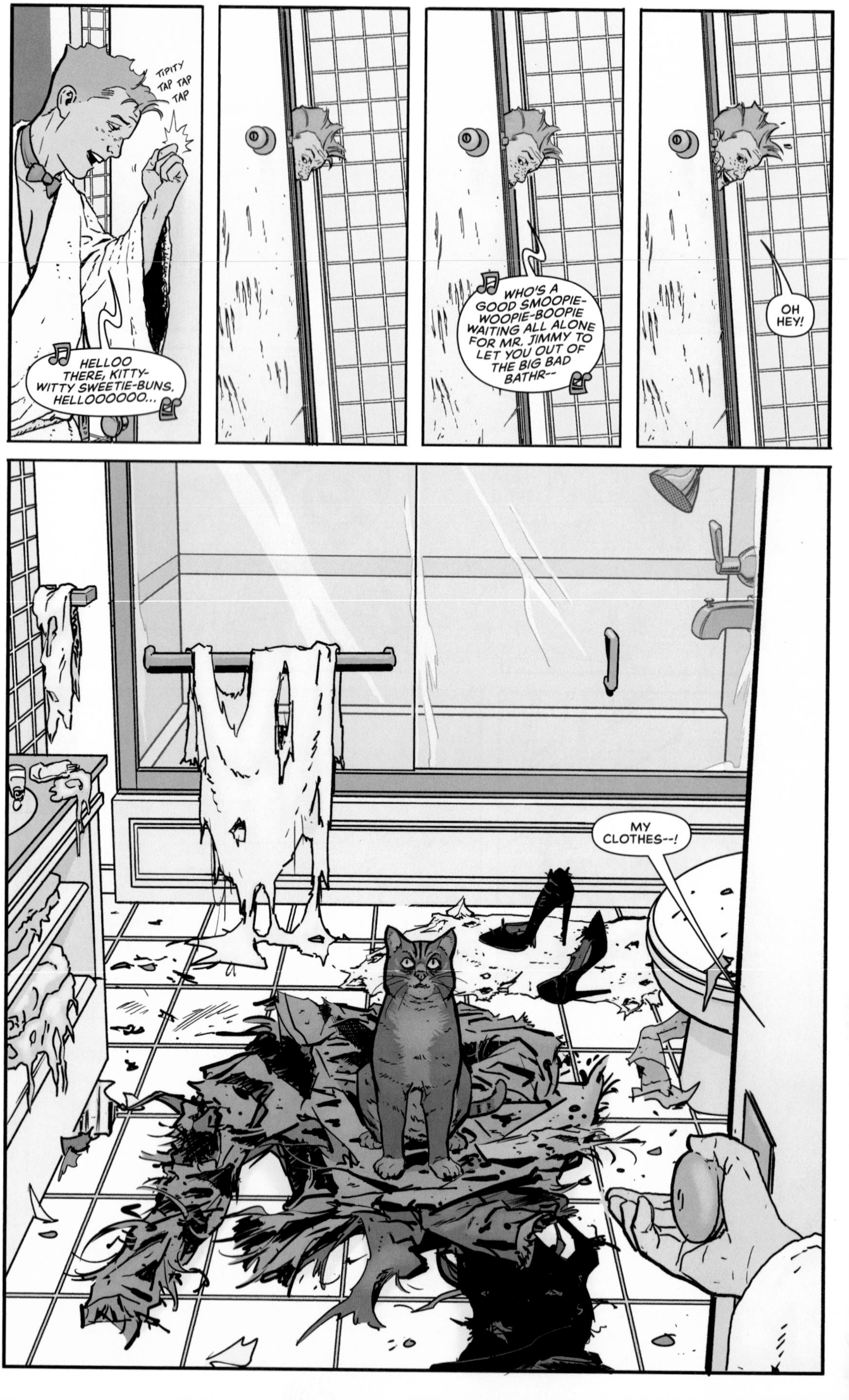
TIPITY TAP TAP TAP
HELLOO THERE, KITTY-WITTY SWEETIE-BUNS. HELLOOOOOO...
WHO'S A GOOD SMOOPIE-WOOPIE-BOOPIE WAITING ALL ALONE FOR MR. JIMMY TO LET YOU OUT OF THE BIG BAD BATHR--
OH HEY!
MY CLOTHES--!

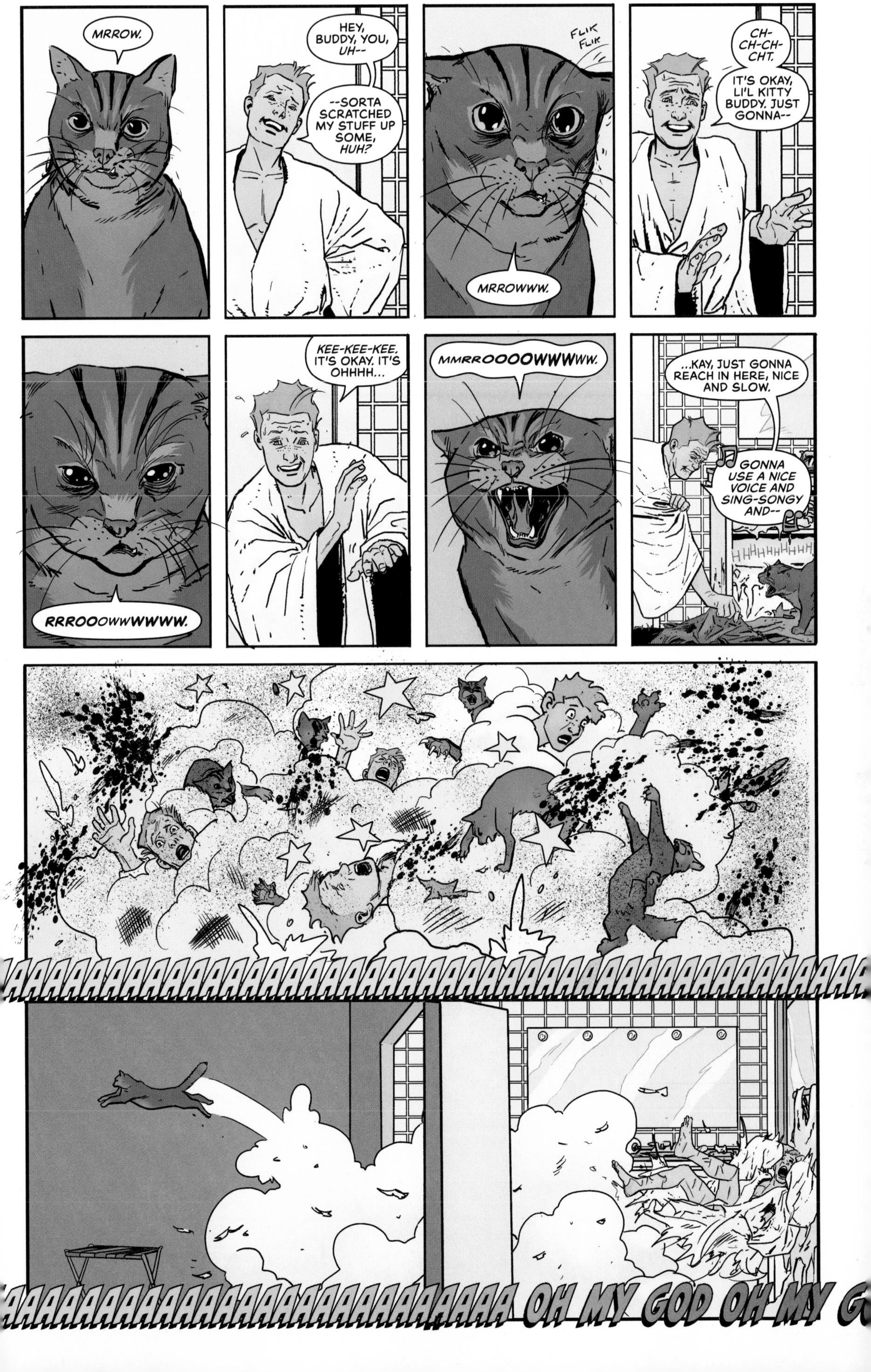
MRROW.
HEY, BUDDY, YOU, UH--
--SORTA SCRATCHED MY STUFF UP SOME, HUH?
FLIK FLIK
MRROWWW.
CH-CH-CH-CHT.
IT'S OKAY, LI'L KITTY BUDDY. JUST GONNA--
RRROOOWWWWWW.
KEE-KEE-KEE. IT'S OKAY. IT'S OHHHH...
MMRROOOOWWWWW.
...KAY, JUST GONNA REACH IN HERE, NICE AND SLOW.
GONNA USE A NICE VOICE AND SING-SONGY AND--
HHHHHHHHHH
AAAAAAAAAAAAAAAAAAAAAAAAAAAAAAAAAAAAAAAAAAAAAA
AAAAAAAAAAAAAAAAAAAAAAAAAAAA OH MY GOD OH MY G

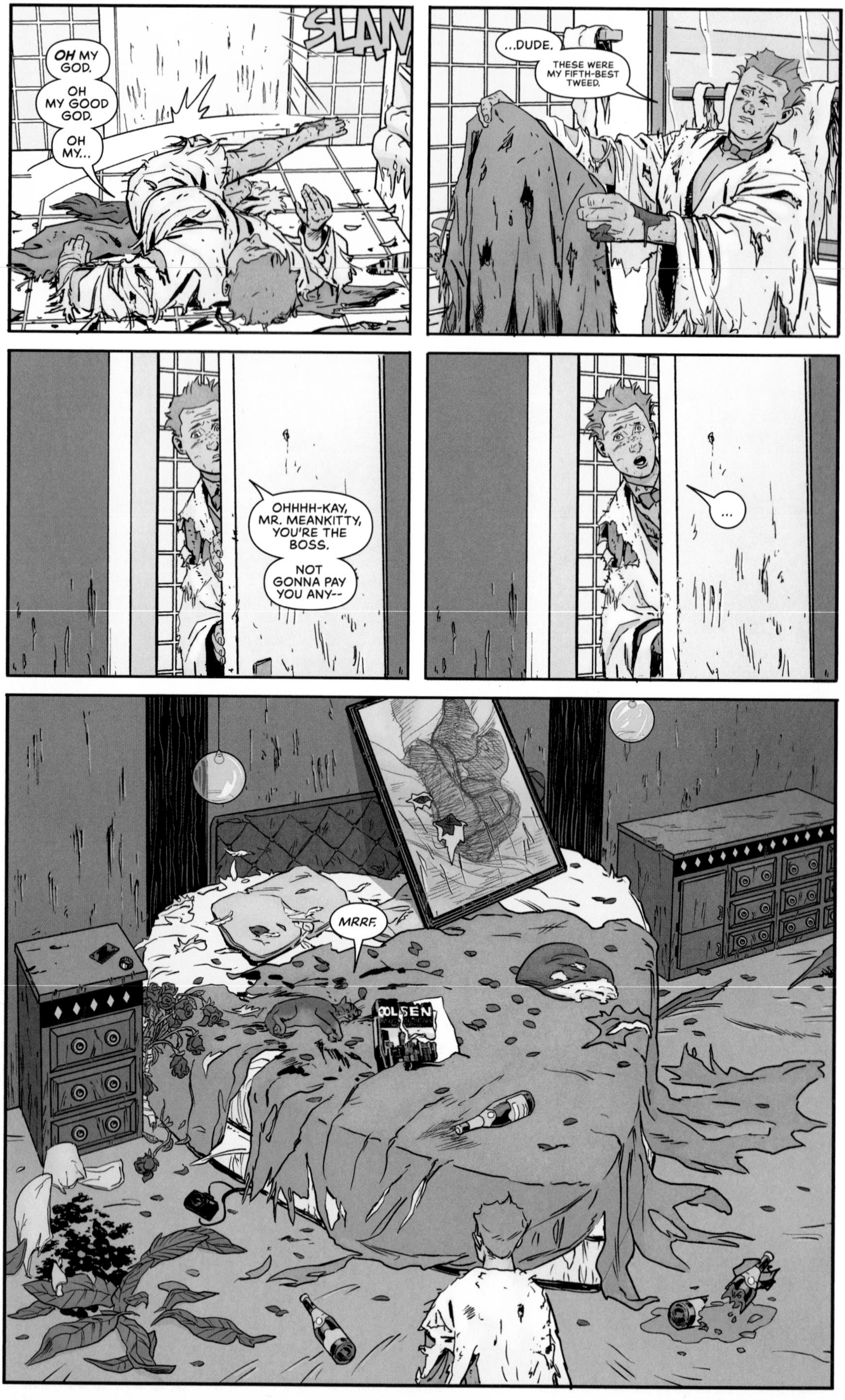
OH MY GOD.
OH MY GOOD GOD.
OH MY...
...DUDE.
THESE WERE MY FIFTH-BEST TWEED.
OHHHH-KAY, MR. MEANKITTY, YOU'RE THE BOSS.
NOT GONNA PAY YOU ANY--
...
MRRF.

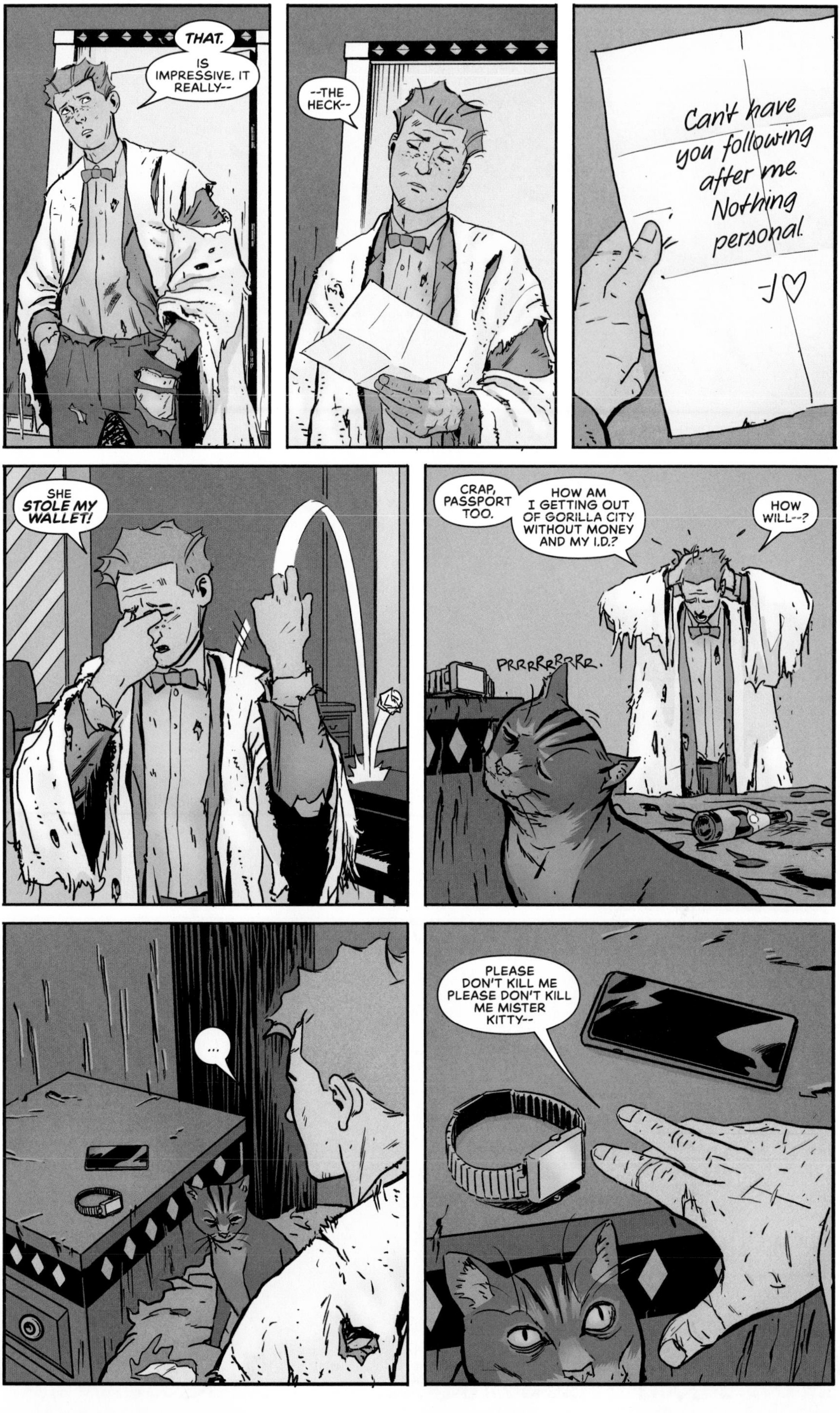
THAT.
IS IMPRESSIVE. IT REALLY--
--THE HECK--
Can't have you following after me. Nothing personal.
-J ♡
SHE STOLE MY WALLET!
CRAP, PASSPORT TOO.
HOW AM I GETTING OUT OF GORILLA CITY WITHOUT MONEY AND MY I.D.?
HOW WILL--?
PRRRRRRRRR.
...
PLEASE DON'T KILL ME PLEASE DON'T KILL ME MISTER KITTY--

YOINK!

THIS DOESN'T EVEN RATE IN MY, LIKE, TOP *TWENTY* CALLS OF SHAME, MR. SHREDDIE VEDDER.

SO DON'T YOU JUDGE ME.

WORRF.

ZEEZEEZEEZEEZEEZEEZEEZE

OH NO! HANG ON HANG ON--

HRRK   HRRK

HHHRRRPH.

RRPPH.

KK   KK

--NONONONONONO DON'T BARF ON THE--

EEZEEZEEZEEZEEZEEZEEZEEZE ZEEZEEZEE--

BLLLLLOOORGG

*JIMMY OLSEN'S SUPERMAN SIGNAL WATCH WAS PATCHED WITH A KRYPTONITE-PROXIMITY FIRMWARE UPGRADE, ALERTING THE MAN OF STEEL'S BEST PAL WHENEVER SOMEONE IS CAUSING HIM TROUBLE WITH A CAPITAL K! --Editor

RRT.RRT.RRTRRT.RRTRRT.RRTRRTRR

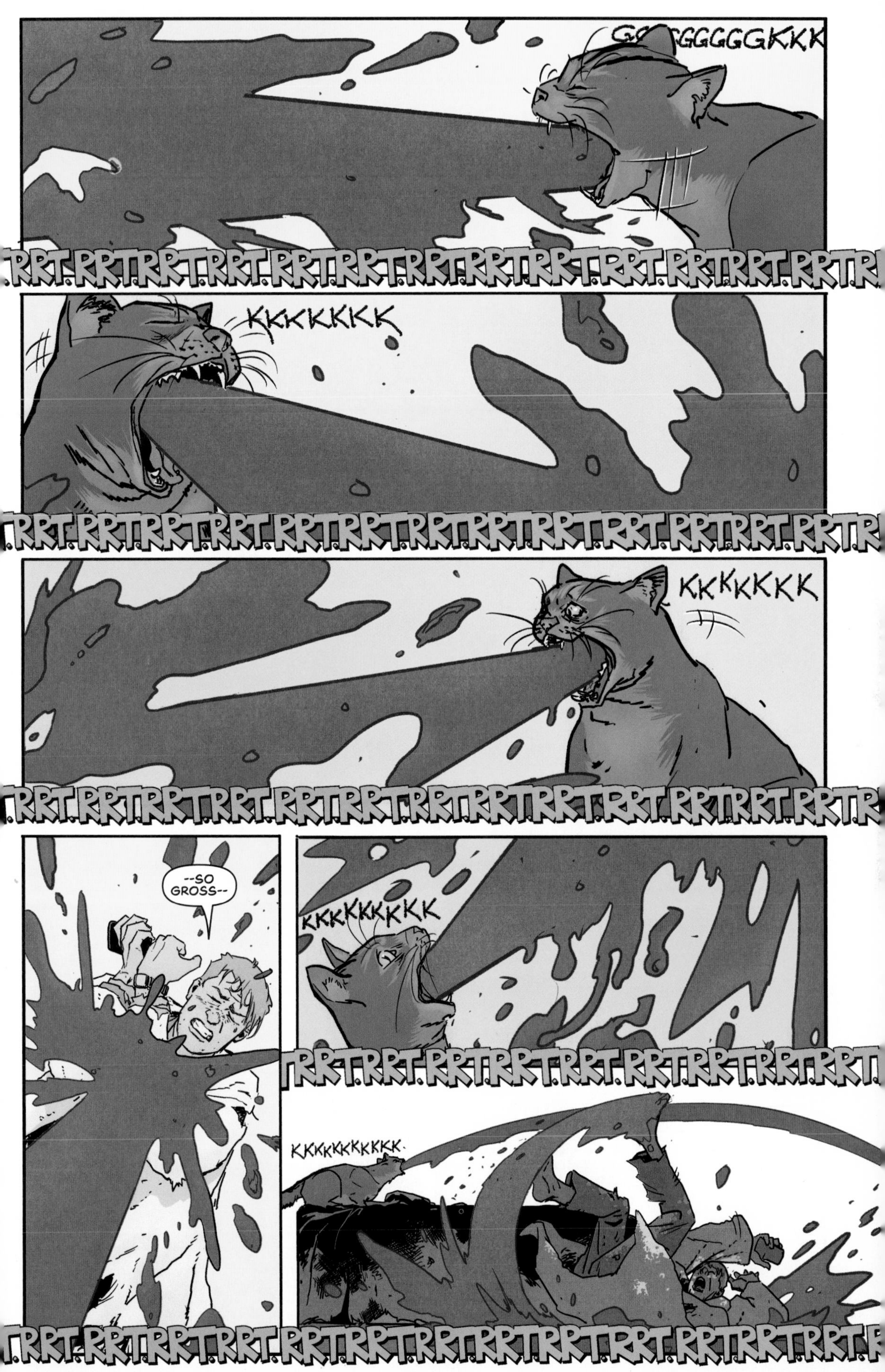
GGGGGGGGKKK
T.RRT.RRT.RRT.RRT.RRT.RRT.RRT.RRT.RRT.RRT.RRT.RRT.RRT.RRT.RRT.R
KKKKKKK
T.RRT.RRT.RRT.RRT.RRT.RRT.RRT.RRT.RRT.RRT.RRT.RRT.RRT.RRT.RRT.R
KKKKKKK
T.RRT.RRT.RRT.RRT.RRT.RRT.RRT.RRT.RRT.RRT.RRT.RRT.RRT.RRT.RRT.R
--SO GROSS--
KKKKKKKKKK
T.RRT.RRT.RRT.RRT.RRT.RRT.RRT.RRT.RRT.RRT.R
KKKKKKKKKKK
T.RRT.RRT.RRT.RRT.RRT.RRT.RRT.RRT.RRT.RRT.RRT.RRT.RRT.RRT.RRT.R

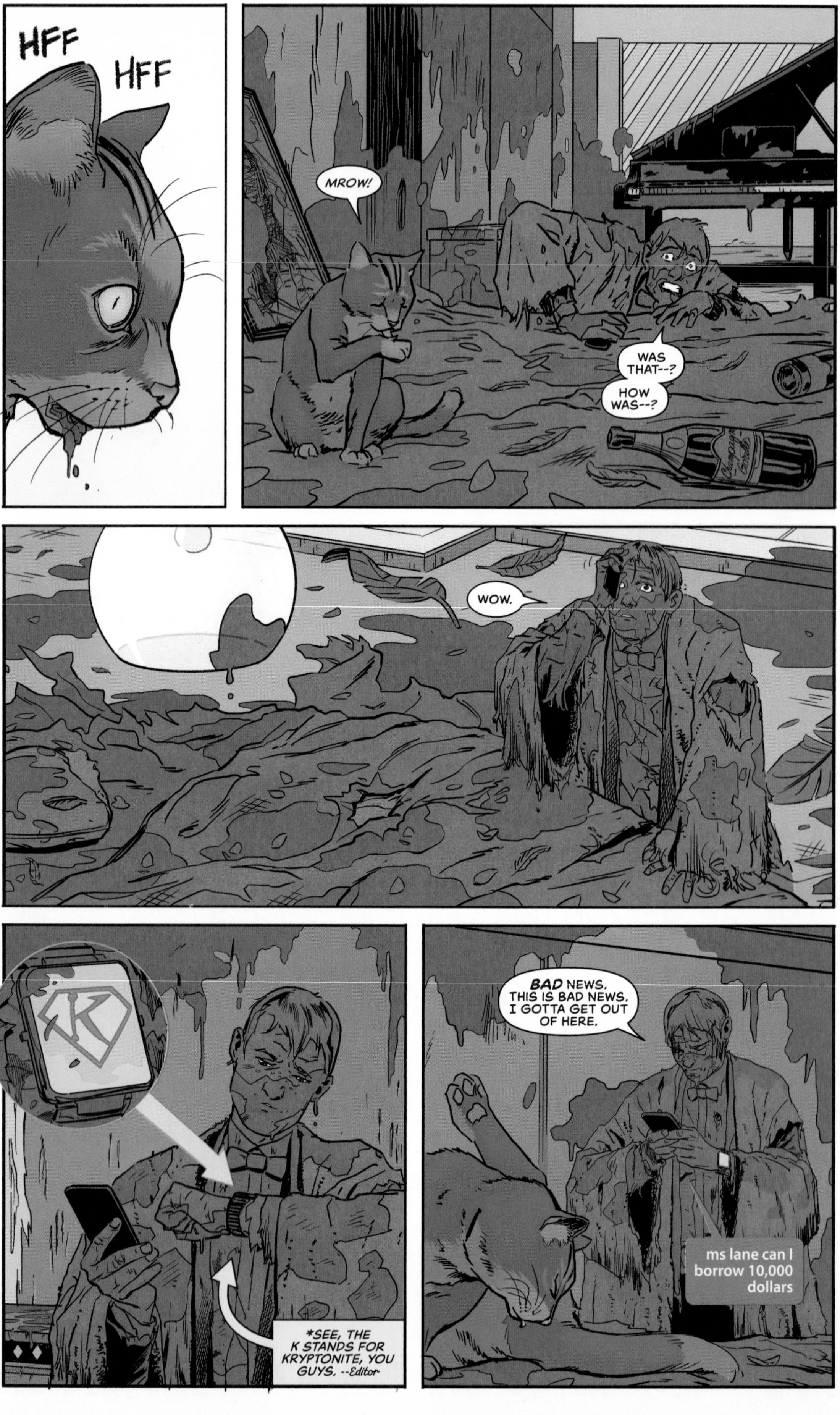
HFF
HFF
MROW!
WAS THAT--?
HOW WAS--?
WOW.
*SEE, THE K STANDS FOR KRYPTONITE, YOU GUYS. --Editor
BAD NEWS. THIS IS BAD NEWS. I GOTTA GET OUT OF HERE.
ms lane can I borrow 10,000 dollars

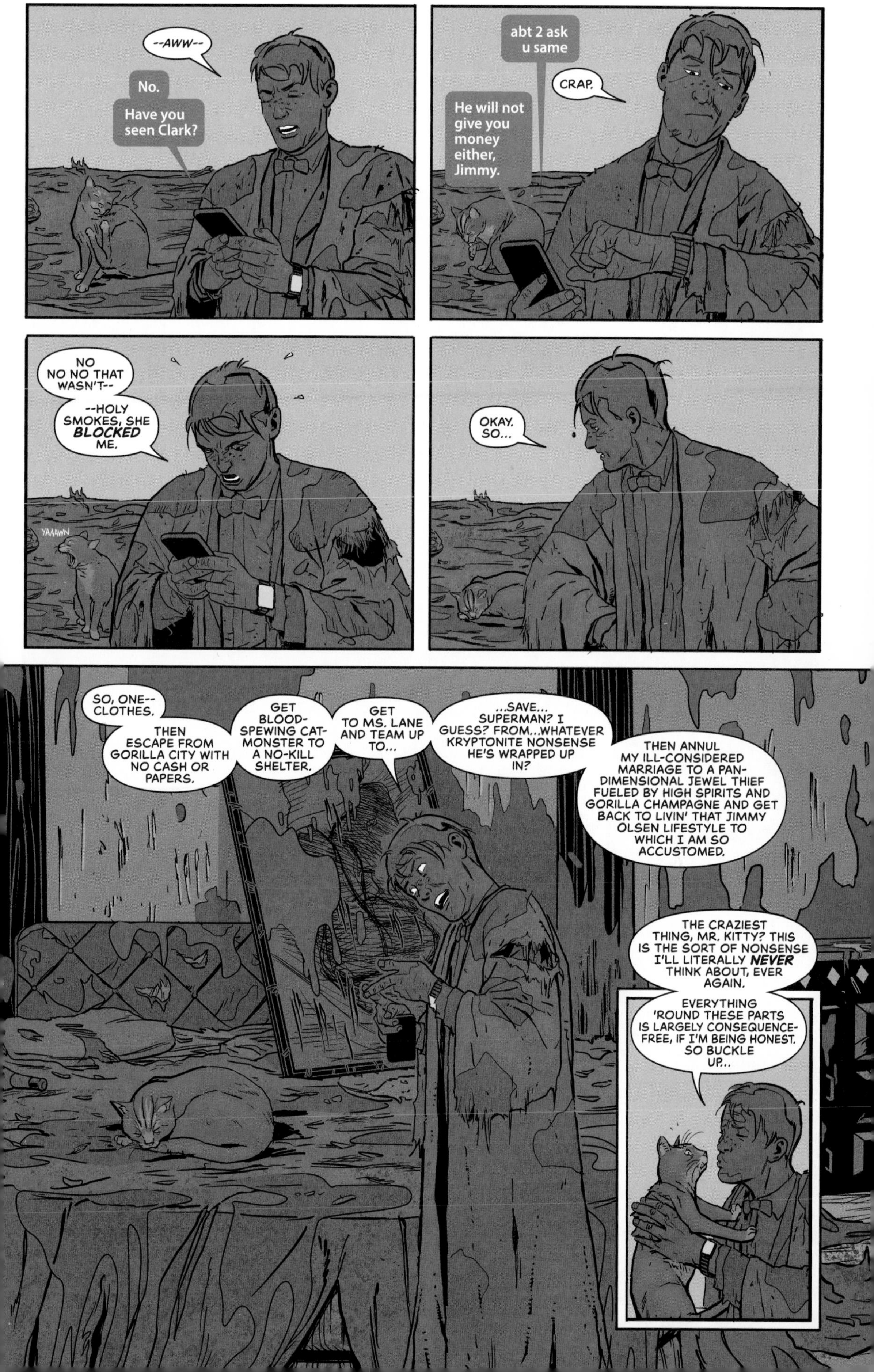
--AWW--
No.
Have you seen Clark?
abt 2 ask u same
CRAP.
He will not give you money either, Jimmy.
NO NO NO THAT WASN'T--
--HOLY SMOKES, SHE BLOCKED ME.
YAAAWN
OKAY. SO...
SO, ONE-- CLOTHES.
THEN ESCAPE FROM GORILLA CITY WITH NO CASH OR PAPERS.
GET BLOOD-SPEWING CAT-MONSTER TO A NO-KILL SHELTER.
GET TO MS. LANE AND TEAM UP TO...
...SAVE... SUPERMAN? I GUESS? FROM...WHATEVER KRYPTONITE NONSENSE HE'S WRAPPED UP IN?
THEN ANNUL MY ILL-CONSIDERED MARRIAGE TO A PAN-DIMENSIONAL JEWEL THIEF FUELED BY HIGH SPIRITS AND GORILLA CHAMPAGNE AND GET BACK TO LIVIN' THAT JIMMY OLSEN LIFESTYLE TO WHICH I AM SO ACCUSTOMED.
THE CRAZIEST THING, MR. KITTY? THIS IS THE SORT OF NONSENSE I'LL LITERALLY NEVER THINK ABOUT, EVER AGAIN.
EVERYTHING 'ROUND THESE PARTS IS LARGELY CONSEQUENCE-FREE, IF I'M BEING HONEST. SO BUCKLE UP...

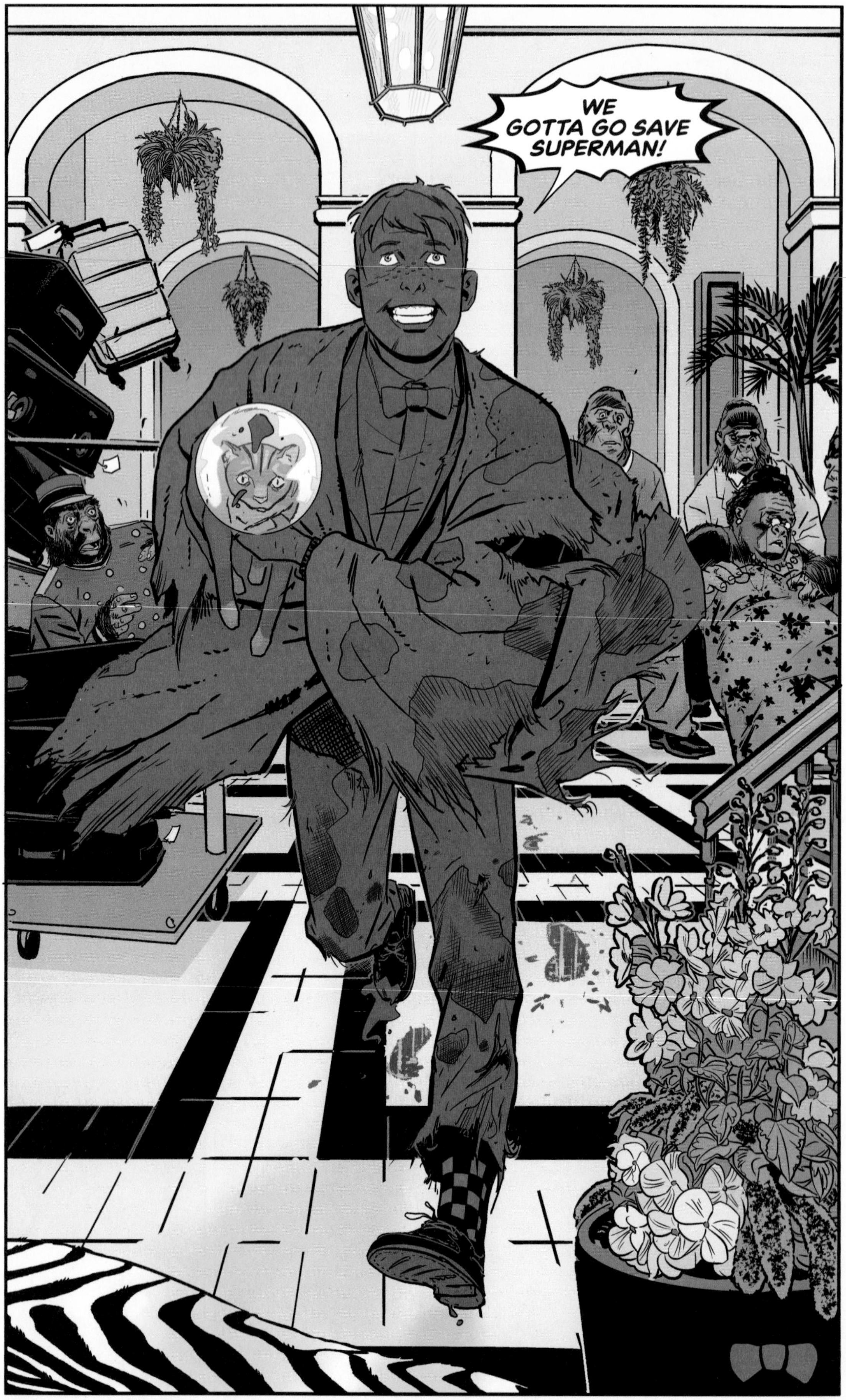
WE GOTTA GO SAVE SUPERMAN!

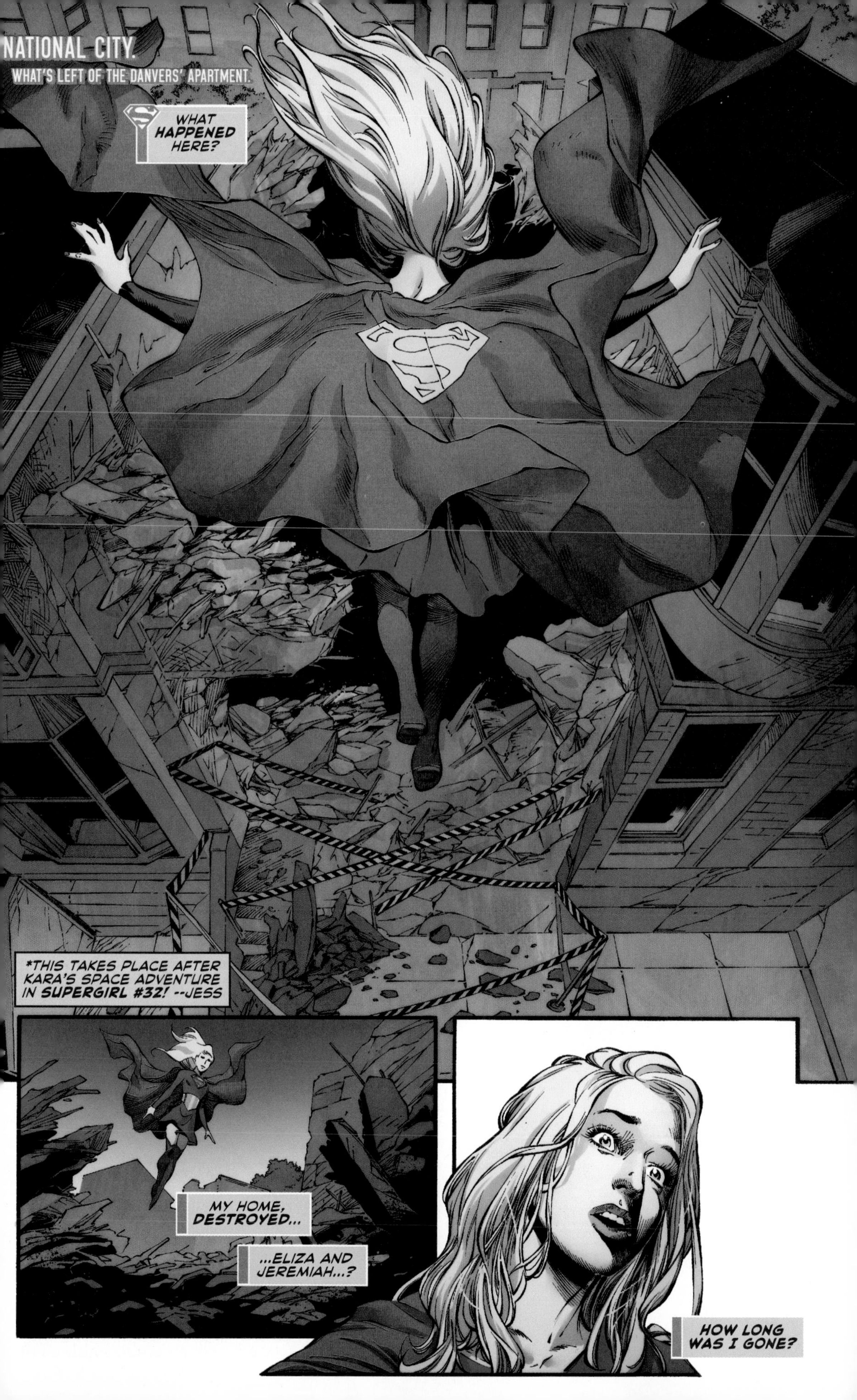
NATIONAL CITY.
WHAT'S LEFT OF THE DANVERS' APARTMENT.
WHAT HAPPENED HERE?
*THIS TAKES PLACE AFTER KARA'S SPACE ADVENTURE IN SUPERGIRL #32! --JESS
MY HOME, DESTROYED...
...ELIZA AND JEREMIAH...?
HOW LONG WAS I GONE?

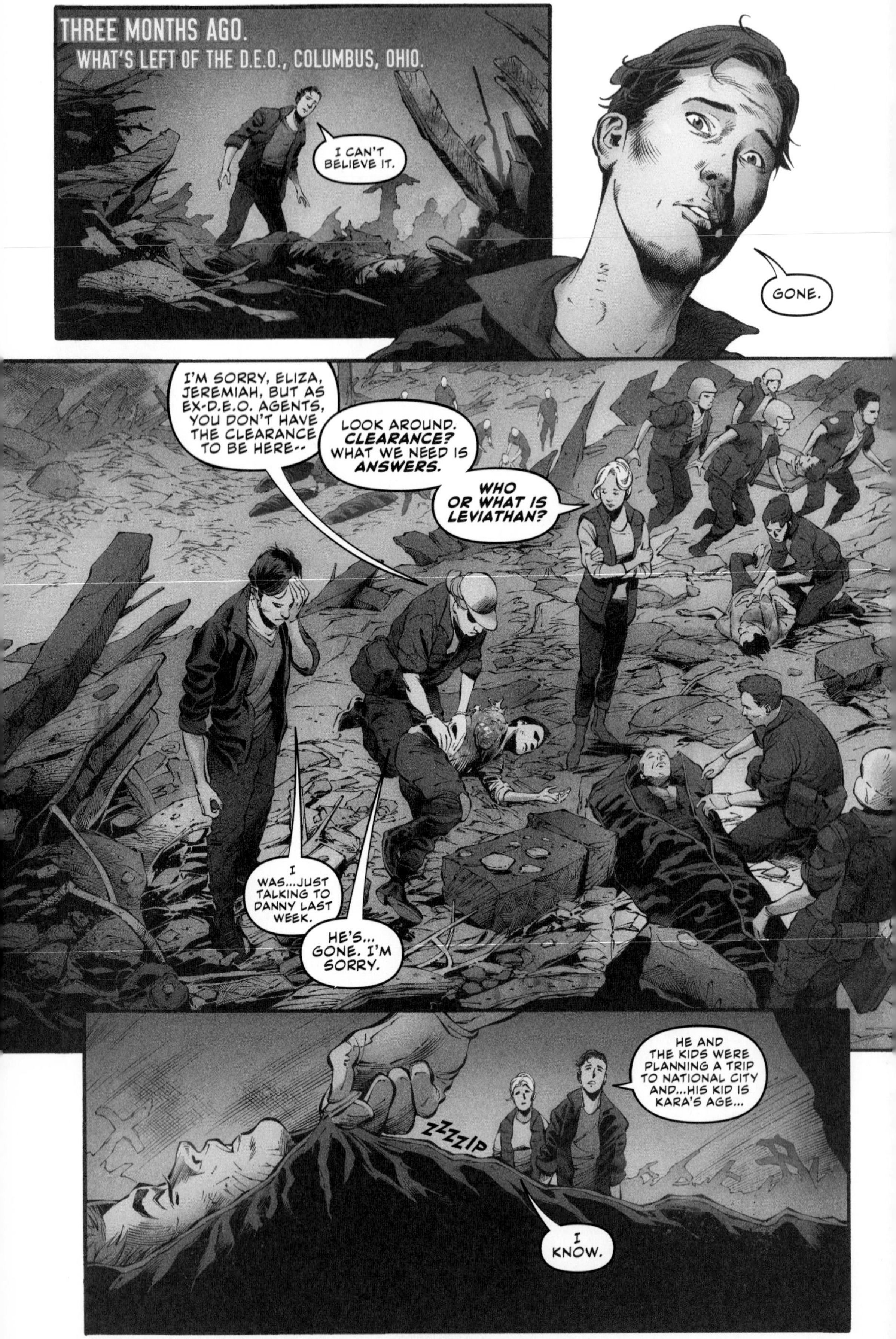
THREE MONTHS AGO.
WHAT'S LEFT OF THE D.E.O., COLUMBUS, OHIO.
I CAN'T BELIEVE IT.
GONE.
I'M SORRY, ELIZA, JEREMIAH, BUT AS EX-D.E.O. AGENTS, YOU DON'T HAVE THE CLEARANCE TO BE HERE--
LOOK AROUND. CLEARANCE? WHAT WE NEED IS ANSWERS.
WHO OR WHAT IS LEVIATHAN?
I WAS...JUST TALKING TO DANNY LAST WEEK.
HE'S... GONE. I'M SORRY.
HE AND THE KIDS WERE PLANNING A TRIP TO NATIONAL CITY AND...HIS KID IS KARA'S AGE...
ZZZZIP
I KNOW.

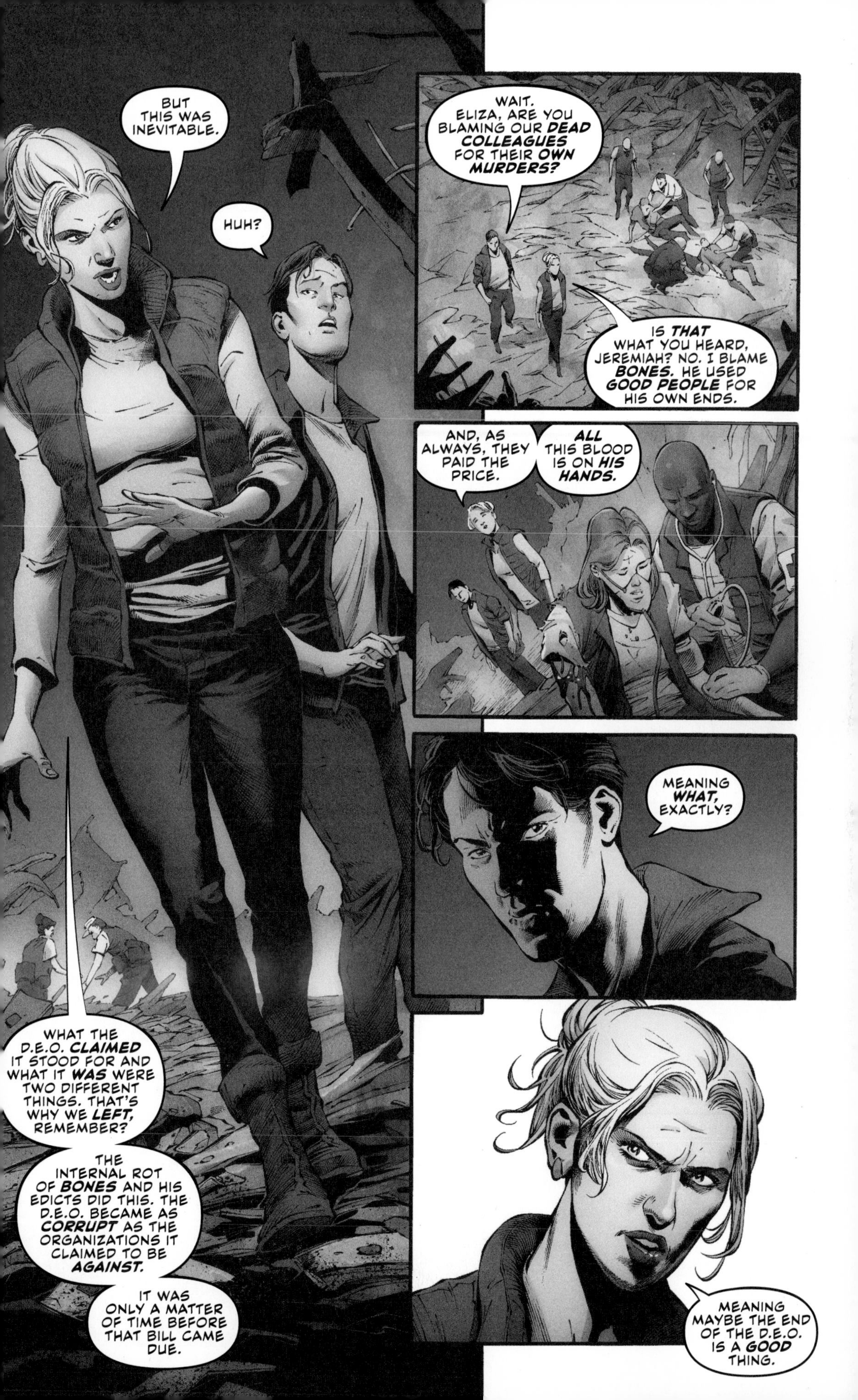
BUT THIS WAS INEVITABLE.
HUH?
WHAT THE D.E.O. CLAIMED IT STOOD FOR AND WHAT IT WAS WERE TWO DIFFERENT THINGS. THAT'S WHY WE LEFT, REMEMBER?
THE INTERNAL ROT OF BONES AND HIS EDICTS DID THIS. THE D.E.O. BECAME AS CORRUPT AS THE ORGANIZATIONS IT CLAIMED TO BE AGAINST.
IT WAS ONLY A MATTER OF TIME BEFORE THAT BILL CAME DUE.
WAIT. ELIZA, ARE YOU BLAMING OUR DEAD COLLEAGUES FOR THEIR OWN MURDERS?
IS THAT WHAT YOU HEARD, JEREMIAH? NO. I BLAME BONES. HE USED GOOD PEOPLE FOR HIS OWN ENDS.
AND, AS ALWAYS, THEY PAID THE PRICE.
ALL THIS BLOOD IS ON HIS HANDS.
MEANING WHAT, EXACTLY?
MEANING MAYBE THE END OF THE D.E.O. IS A GOOD THING.

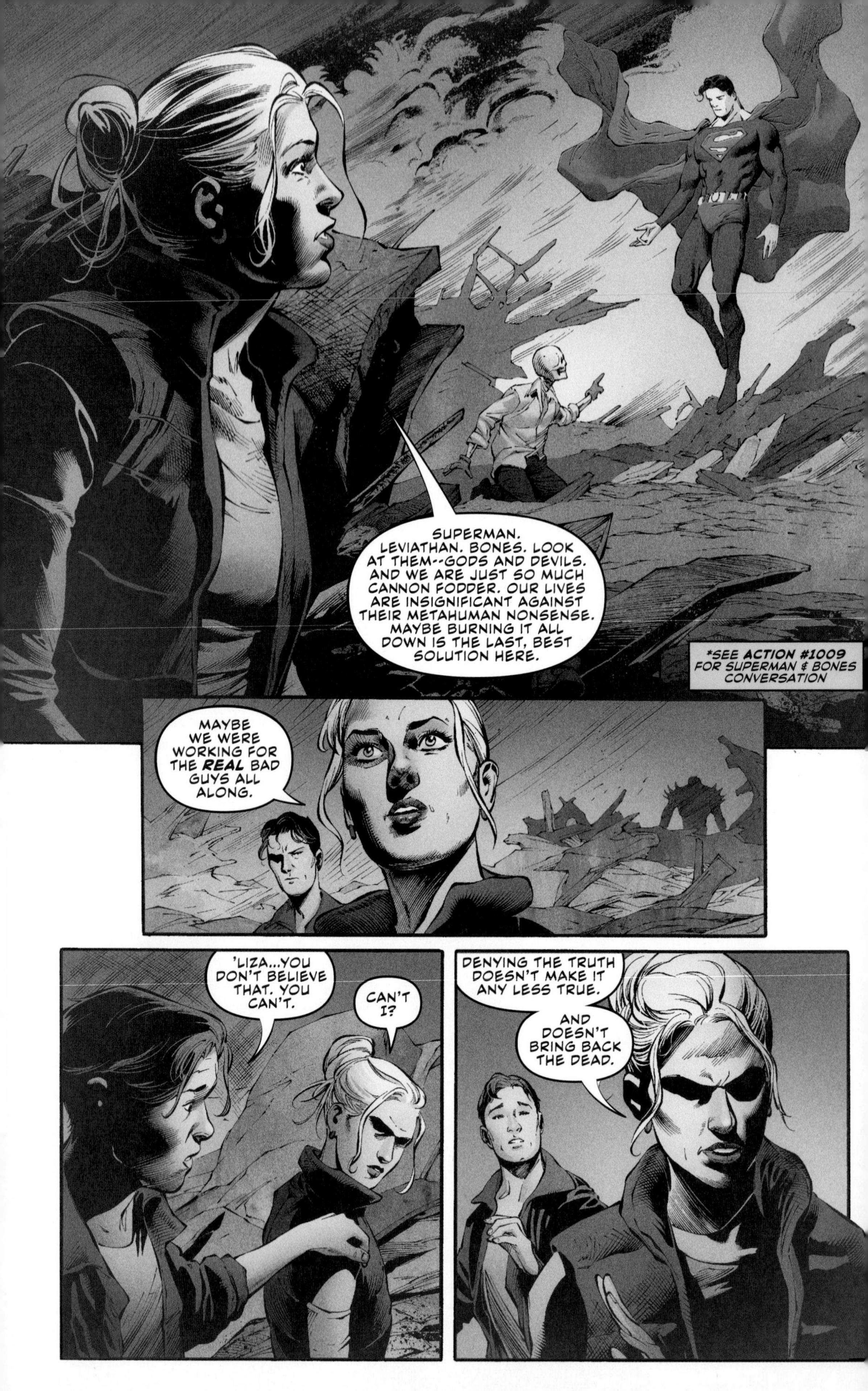
SUPERMAN. LEVIATHAN. BONES. LOOK AT THEM--GODS AND DEVILS. AND WE ARE JUST SO MUCH CANNON FODDER. OUR LIVES ARE INSIGNIFICANT AGAINST THEIR METAHUMAN NONSENSE. MAYBE BURNING IT ALL DOWN IS THE LAST, BEST SOLUTION HERE.
*SEE ACTION #1009 FOR SUPERMAN & BONES CONVERSATION
MAYBE WE WERE WORKING FOR THE REAL BAD GUYS ALL ALONG.
'LIZA...YOU DON'T BELIEVE THAT. YOU CAN'T.
CAN'T I?
DENYING THE TRUTH DOESN'T MAKE IT ANY LESS TRUE.
AND DOESN'T BRING BACK THE DEAD.

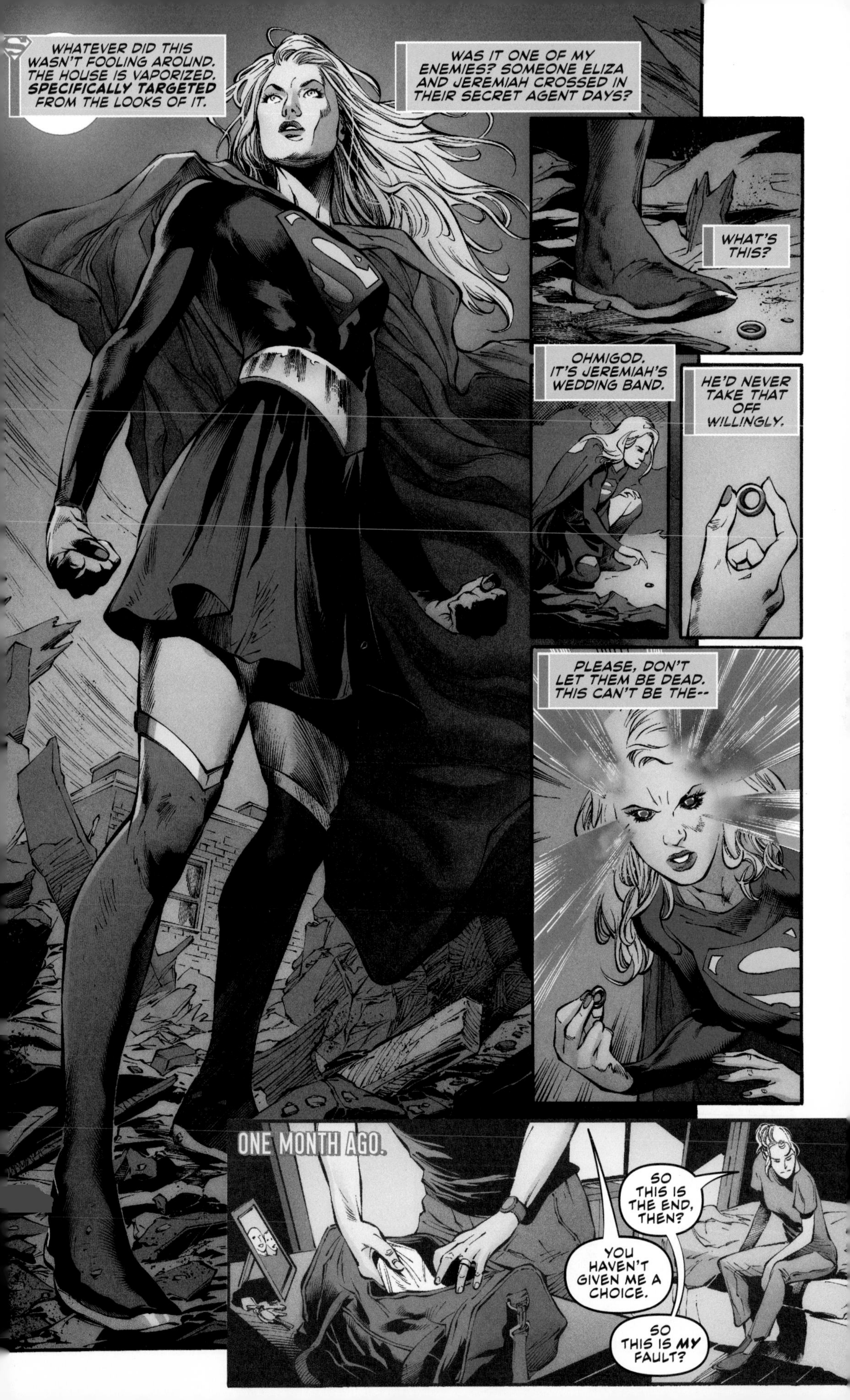
WHATEVER DID THIS WASN'T FOOLING AROUND. THE HOUSE IS VAPORIZED. **SPECIFICALLY TARGETED** FROM THE LOOKS OF IT.
WAS IT ONE OF MY ENEMIES? SOMEONE ELIZA AND JEREMIAH CROSSED IN THEIR SECRET AGENT DAYS?
WHAT'S THIS?
OHMIGOD. IT'S JEREMIAH'S WEDDING BAND.
HE'D NEVER TAKE THAT OFF WILLINGLY.
PLEASE, DON'T LET THEM BE DEAD. THIS CAN'T BE THE--
ONE MONTH AGO.
SO THIS IS THE END, THEN?
YOU HAVEN'T GIVEN ME A CHOICE.
SO THIS IS **MY** FAULT?

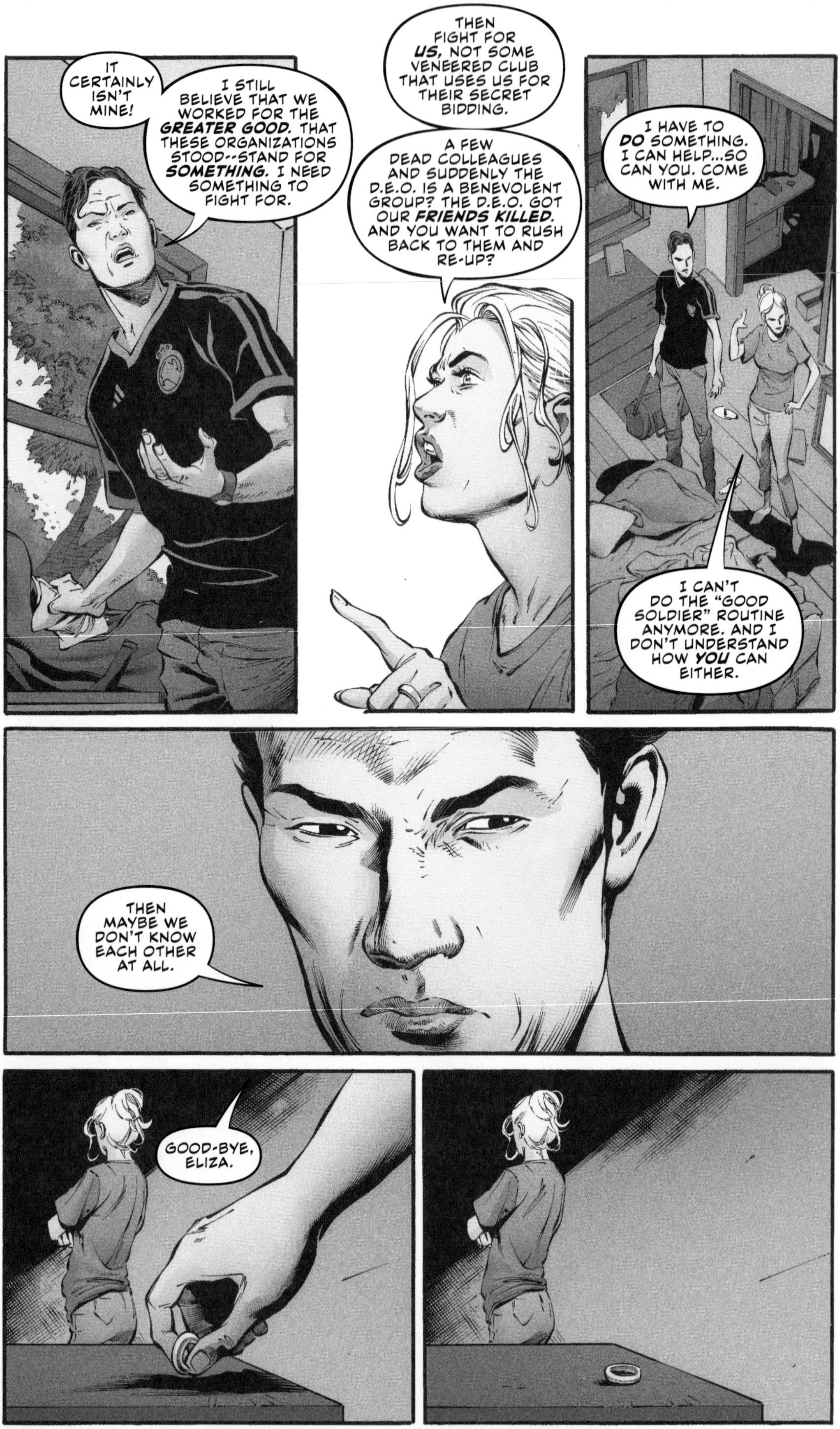
IT CERTAINLY ISN'T MINE!
I STILL BELIEVE THAT WE WORKED FOR THE GREATER GOOD. THAT THESE ORGANIZATIONS STOOD--STAND FOR SOMETHING. I NEED SOMETHING TO FIGHT FOR.
THEN FIGHT FOR US, NOT SOME VENEERED CLUB THAT USES US FOR THEIR SECRET BIDDING.
A FEW DEAD COLLEAGUES AND SUDDENLY THE D.E.O. IS A BENEVOLENT GROUP? THE D.E.O. GOT OUR FRIENDS KILLED. AND YOU WANT TO RUSH BACK TO THEM AND RE-UP?
I HAVE TO DO SOMETHING. I CAN HELP...SO CAN YOU. COME WITH ME.
I CAN'T DO THE "GOOD SOLDIER" ROUTINE ANYMORE. AND I DON'T UNDERSTAND HOW YOU CAN EITHER.
THEN MAYBE WE DON'T KNOW EACH OTHER AT ALL.
GOOD-BYE, ELIZA.

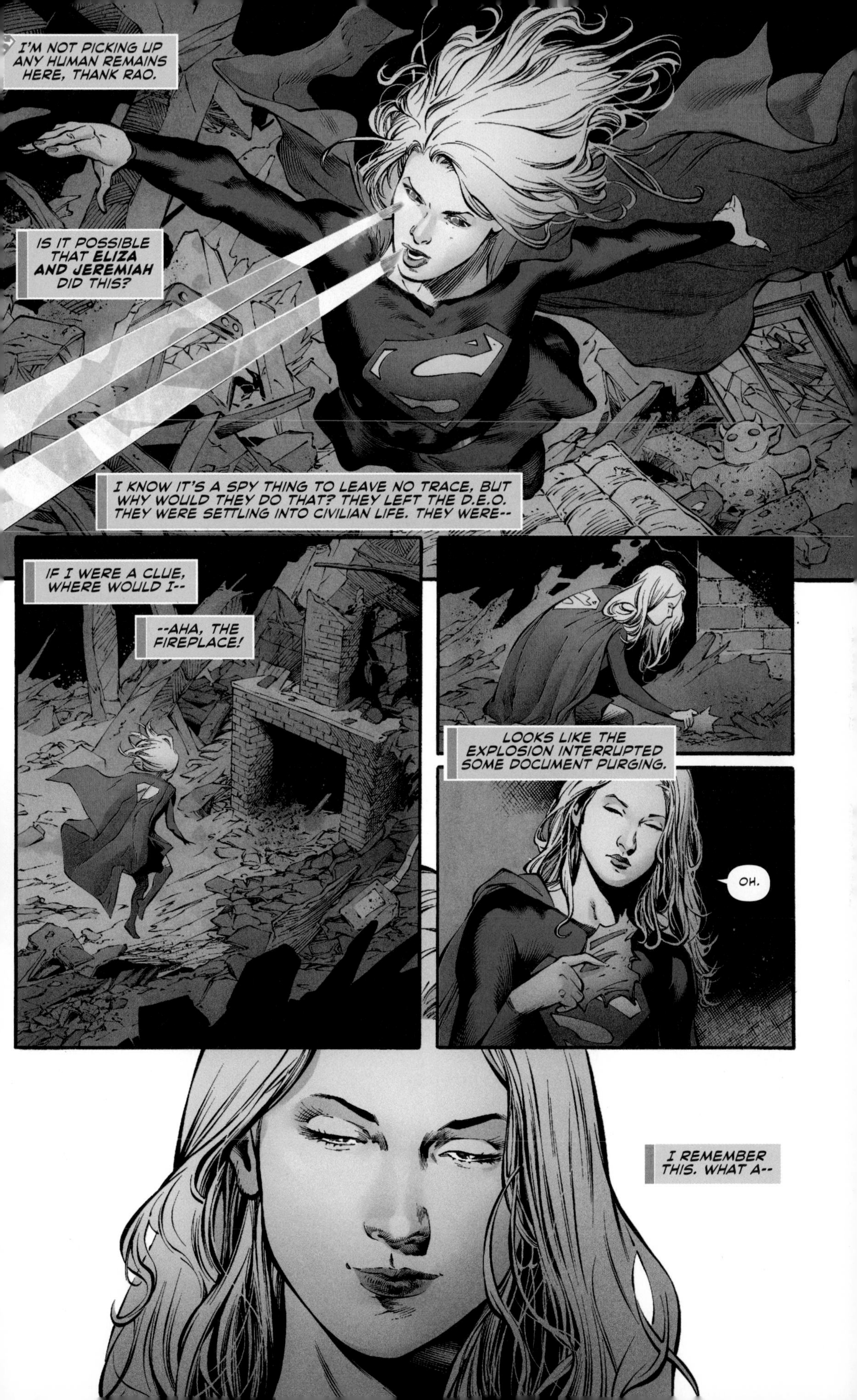
I'M NOT PICKING UP ANY HUMAN REMAINS HERE, THANK RAO.
IS IT POSSIBLE THAT ELIZA AND JEREMIAH DID THIS?
I KNOW IT'S A SPY THING TO LEAVE NO TRACE, BUT WHY WOULD THEY DO THAT? THEY LEFT THE D.E.O. THEY WERE SETTLING INTO CIVILIAN LIFE. THEY WERE--
IF I WERE A CLUE, WHERE WOULD I--
--AHA, THE FIREPLACE!
LOOKS LIKE THE EXPLOSION INTERRUPTED SOME DOCUMENT PURGING.
OH.
I REMEMBER THIS. WHAT A--

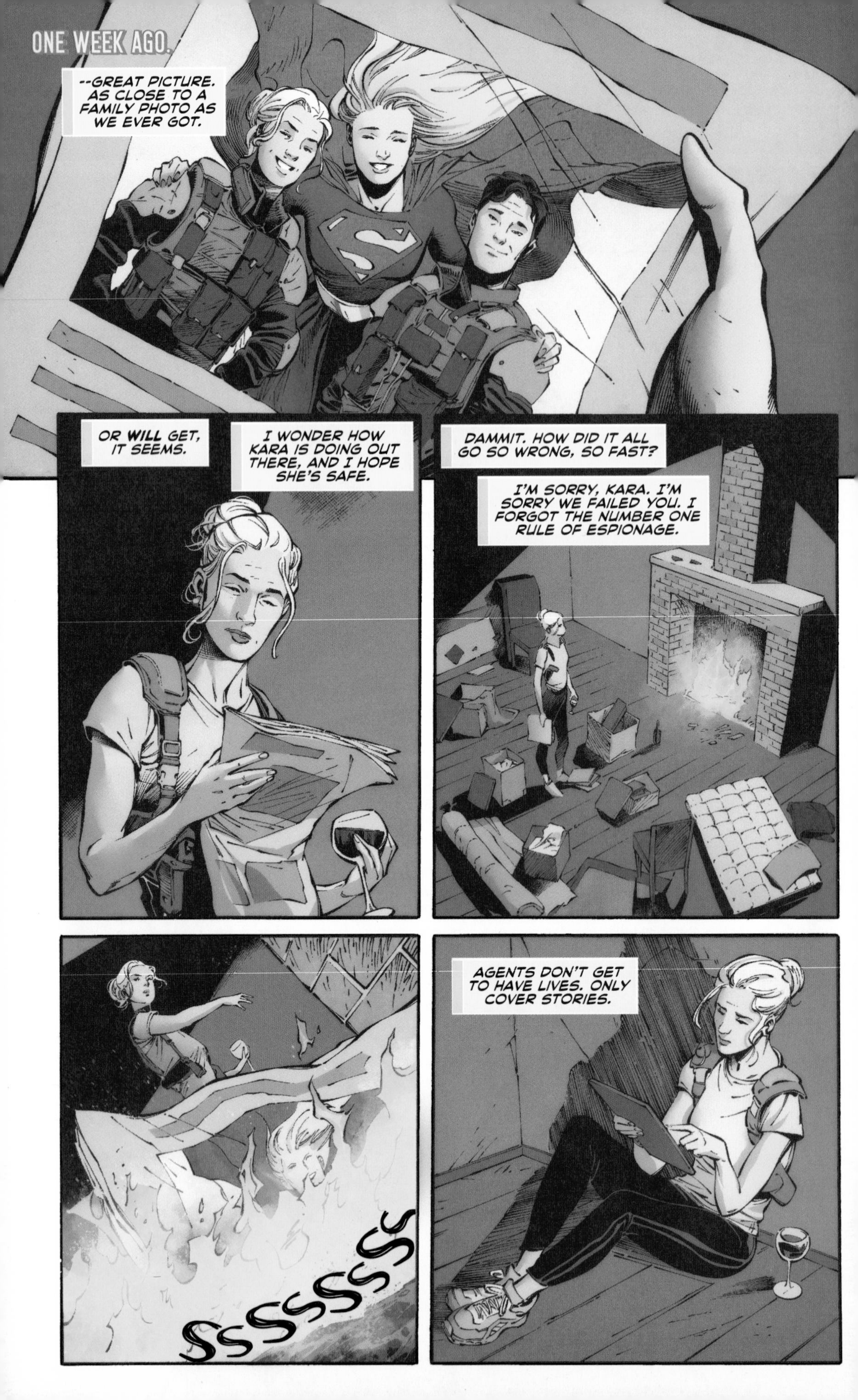
ONE WEEK AGO.
--GREAT PICTURE. AS CLOSE TO A FAMILY PHOTO AS WE EVER GOT.
OR WILL GET, IT SEEMS.
I WONDER HOW KARA IS DOING OUT THERE, AND I HOPE SHE'S SAFE.
DAMMIT. HOW DID IT ALL GO SO WRONG, SO FAST?
I'M SORRY, KARA. I'M SORRY WE FAILED YOU. I FORGOT THE NUMBER ONE RULE OF ESPIONAGE.
SSSSSSSS
AGENTS DON'T GET TO HAVE LIVES. ONLY COVER STORIES.

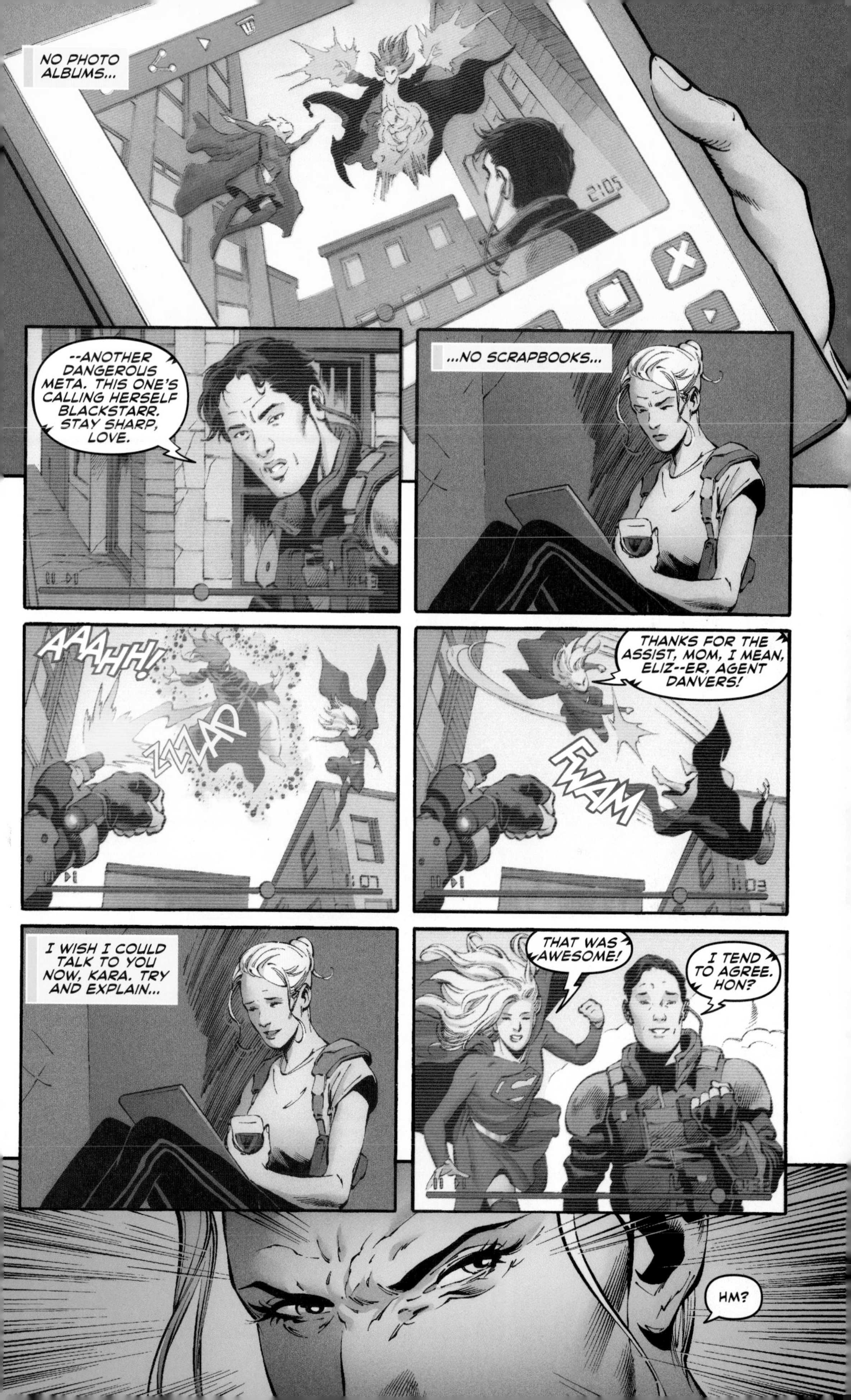
NO PHOTO ALBUMS...
2:05
--ANOTHER DANGEROUS META. THIS ONE'S CALLING HERSELF BLACKSTARR. STAY SHARP, LOVE.
...NO SCRAPBOOKS...
AAAHH!
ZZZAP
THANKS FOR THE ASSIST, MOM, I MEAN, ELIZ--ER, AGENT DANVERS!
FWAM
I WISH I COULD TALK TO YOU NOW, KARA. TRY AND EXPLAIN...
THAT WAS AWESOME!
I TEND TO AGREE. HON?
HM?

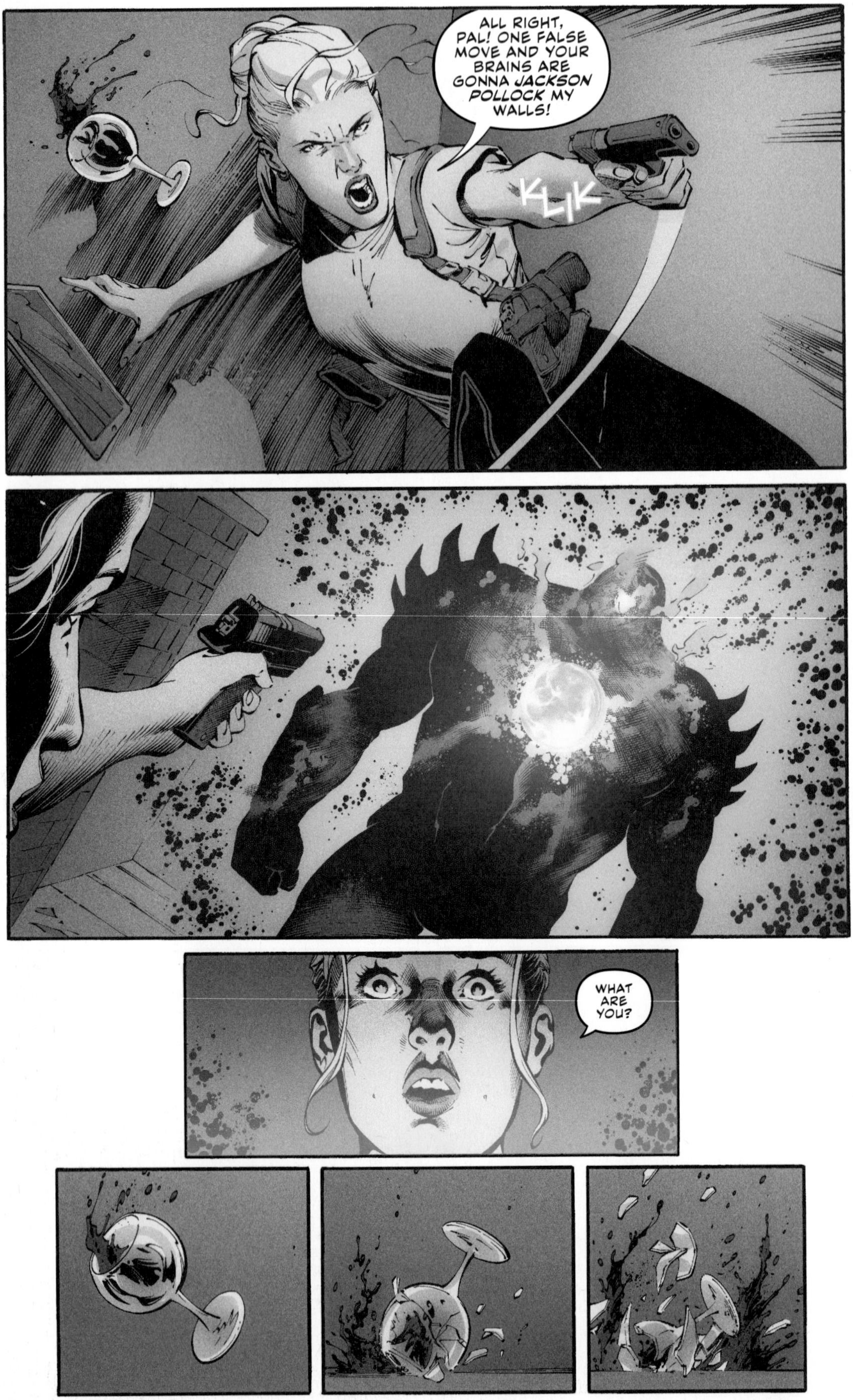
ALL RIGHT, PAL! ONE FALSE MOVE AND YOUR BRAINS ARE GONNA *JACKSON POLLOCK* MY WALLS!
KLIK
WHAT ARE YOU?

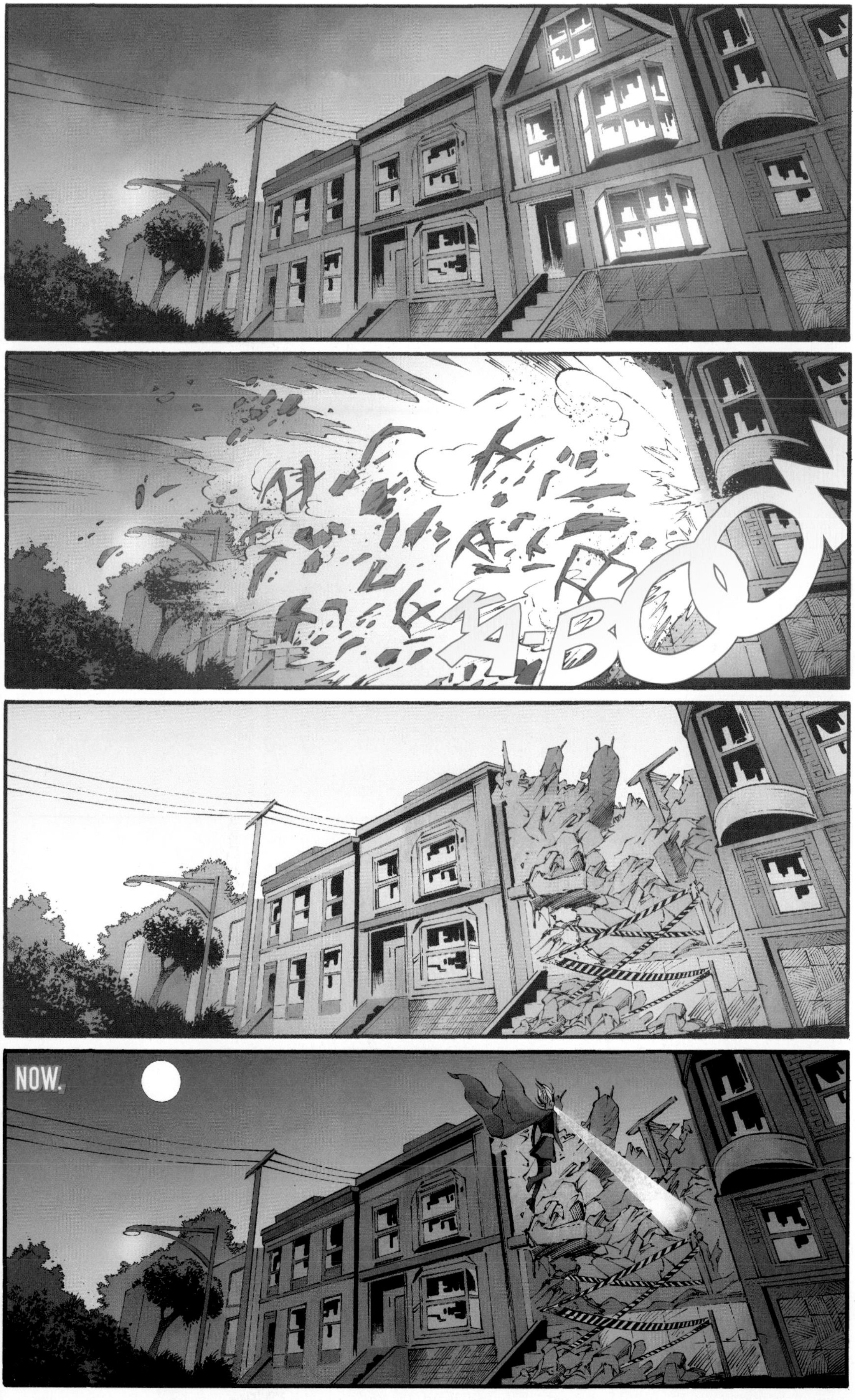
KA-BOOOM
NOW.

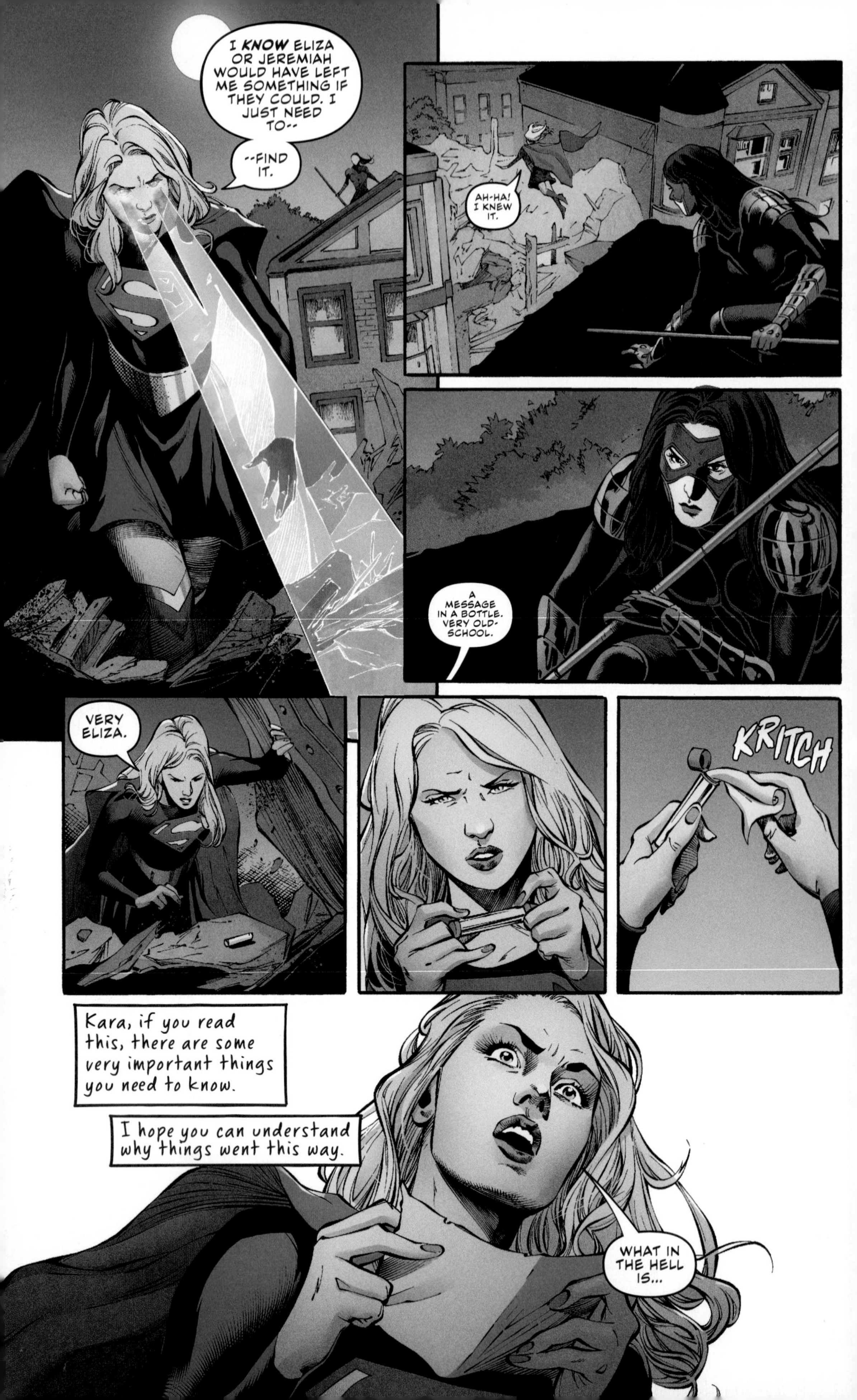
I KNOW ELIZA OR JEREMIAH WOULD HAVE LEFT ME SOMETHING IF THEY COULD. I JUST NEED TO--
--FIND IT.
AH-HA! I KNEW IT.
A MESSAGE IN A BOTTLE. VERY OLD-SCHOOL.
VERY ELIZA.
KRITCH
Kara, if you read this, there are some very important things you need to know.
I hope you can understand why things went this way.
WHAT IN THE HELL IS...

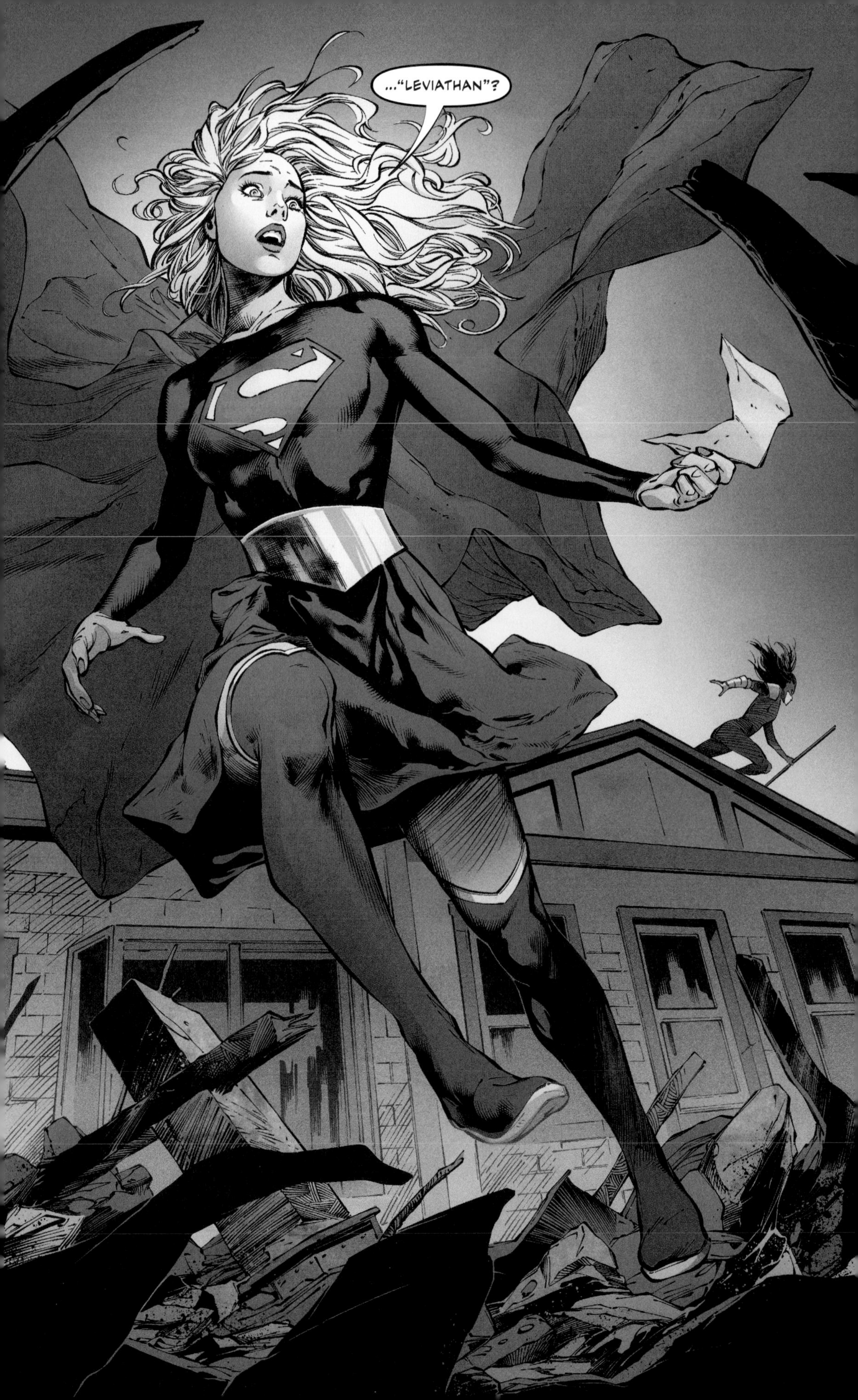
..."LEVIATHAN"?

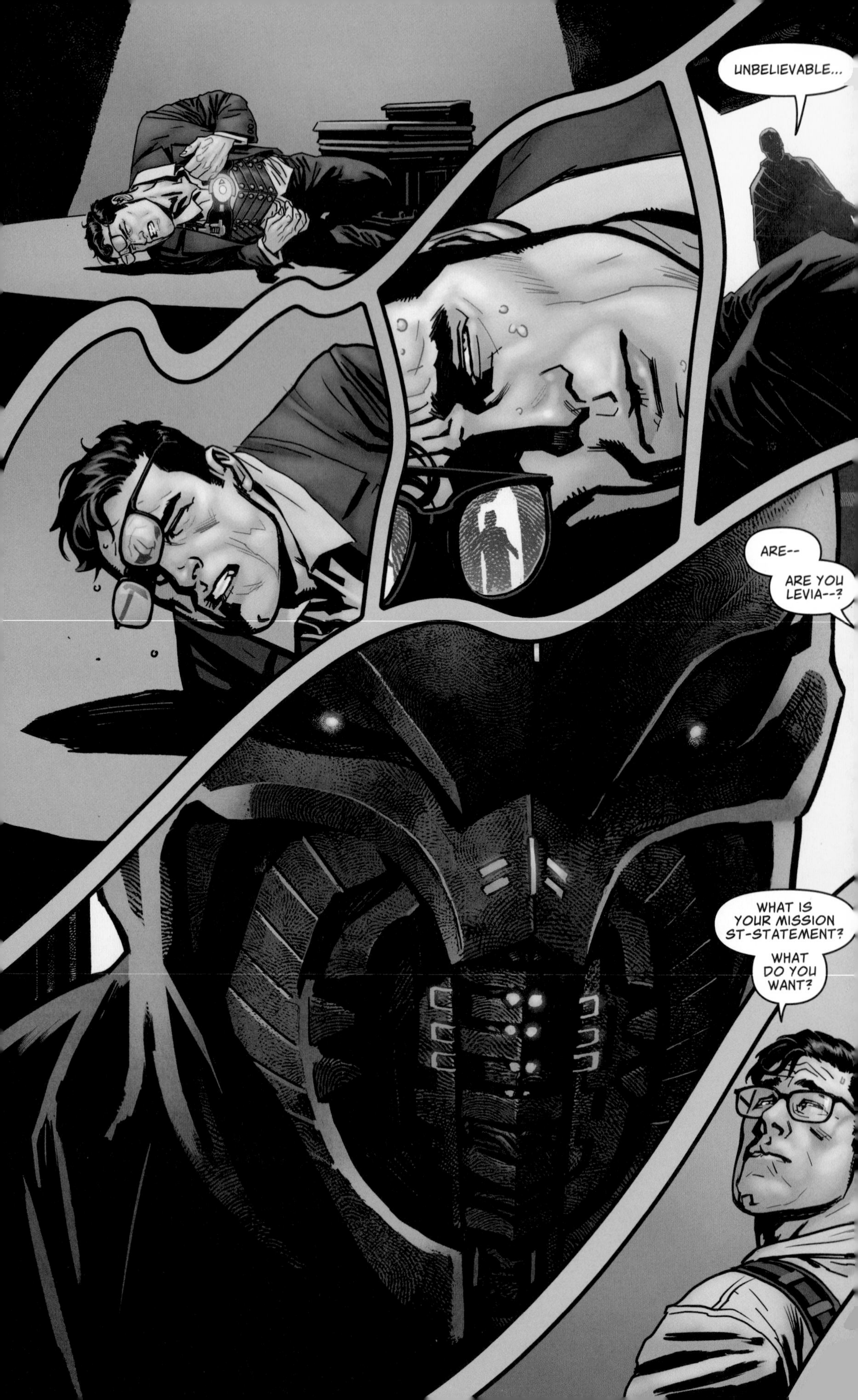
UNBELIEVABLE...
ARE--
ARE YOU LEVIA--?
WHAT IS YOUR MISSION ST-STATEMENT?
WHAT DO YOU WANT?

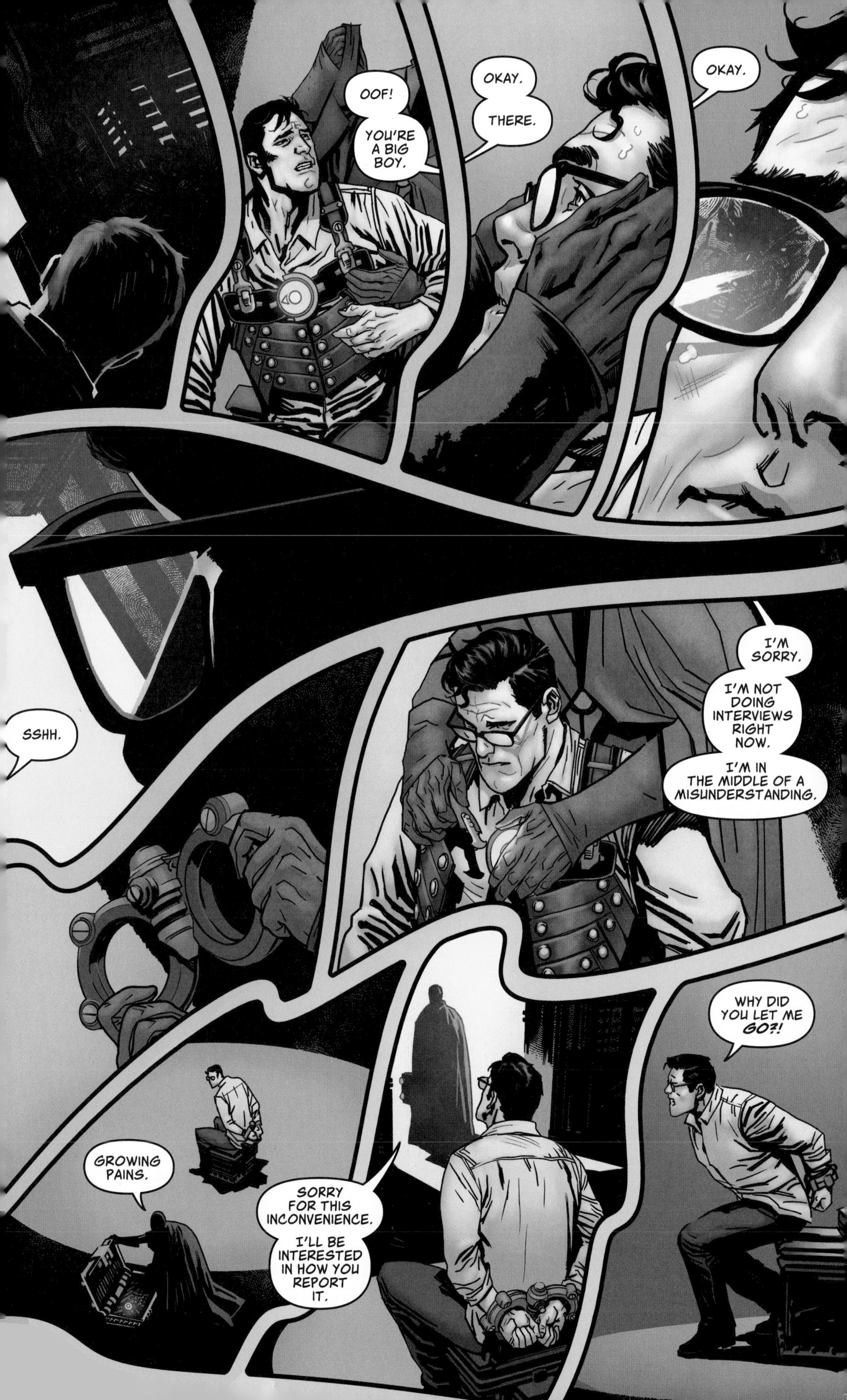
OOF!
YOU'RE A BIG BOY.
OKAY.
THERE.
OKAY.
SSHH.
I'M SORRY.
I'M NOT DOING INTERVIEWS RIGHT NOW.
I'M IN THE MIDDLE OF A MISUNDERSTANDING.
GROWING PAINS.
SORRY FOR THIS INCONVENIENCE.
I'LL BE INTERESTED IN HOW YOU REPORT IT.
WHY DID YOU LET ME GO?!

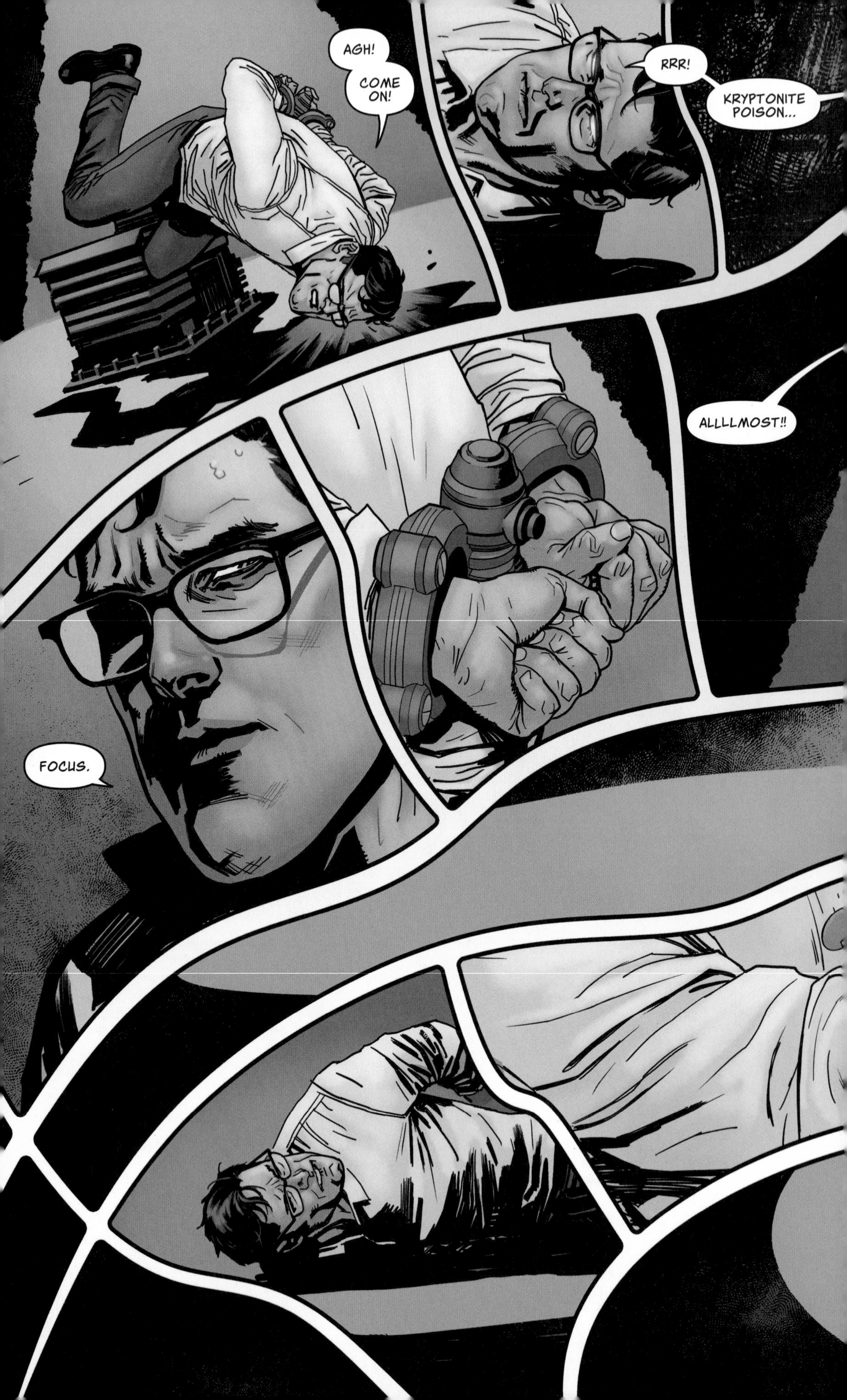
AGH!
COME ON!
RRR!
KRYPTONITE POISON...
ALLLLMOST!!
FOCUS.

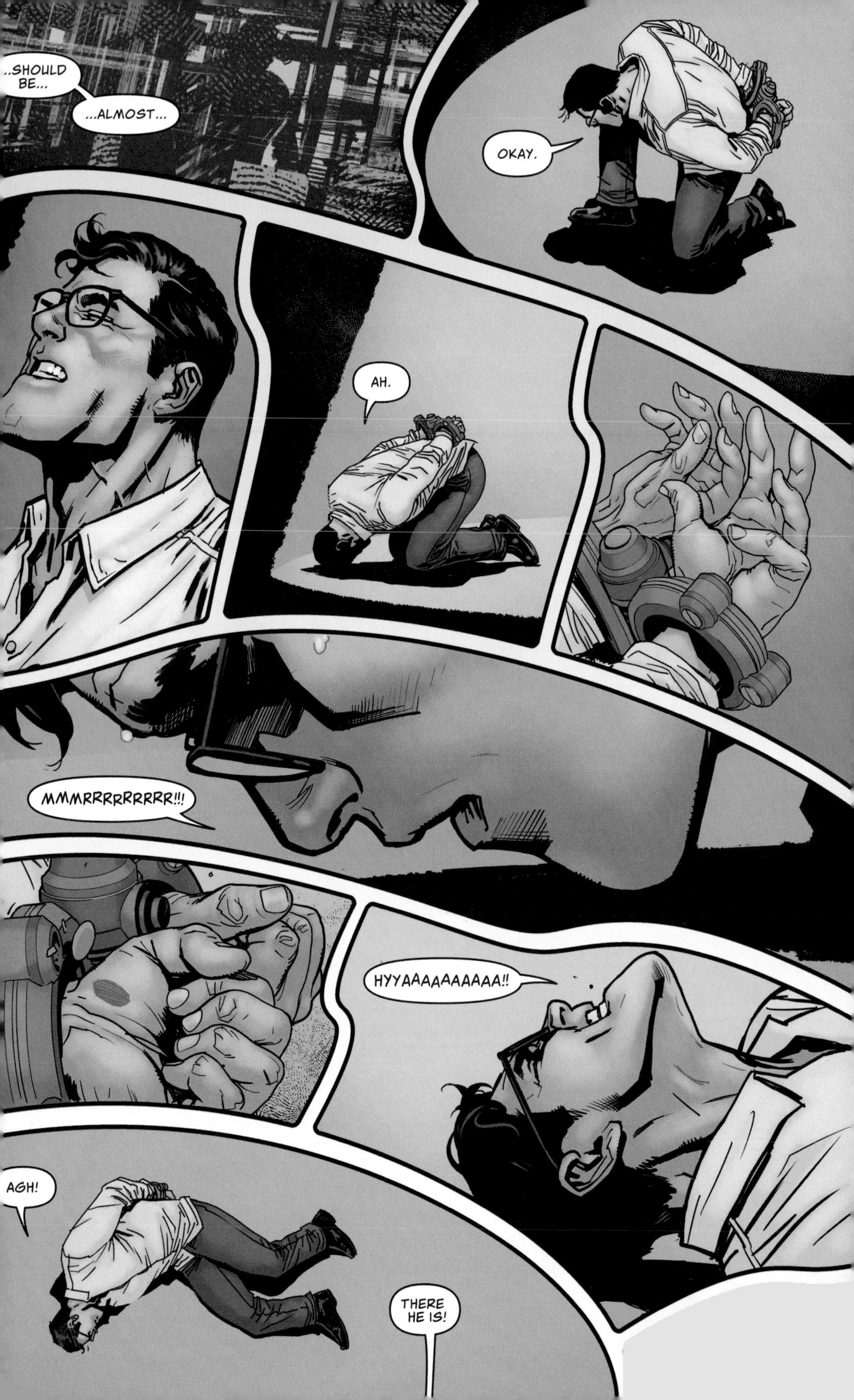
..SHOULD BE...
...ALMOST...
OKAY.
AH.
MMMRRRRRRRR!!!
HYYAAAAAAAAA!!
AGH!
THERE HE IS!

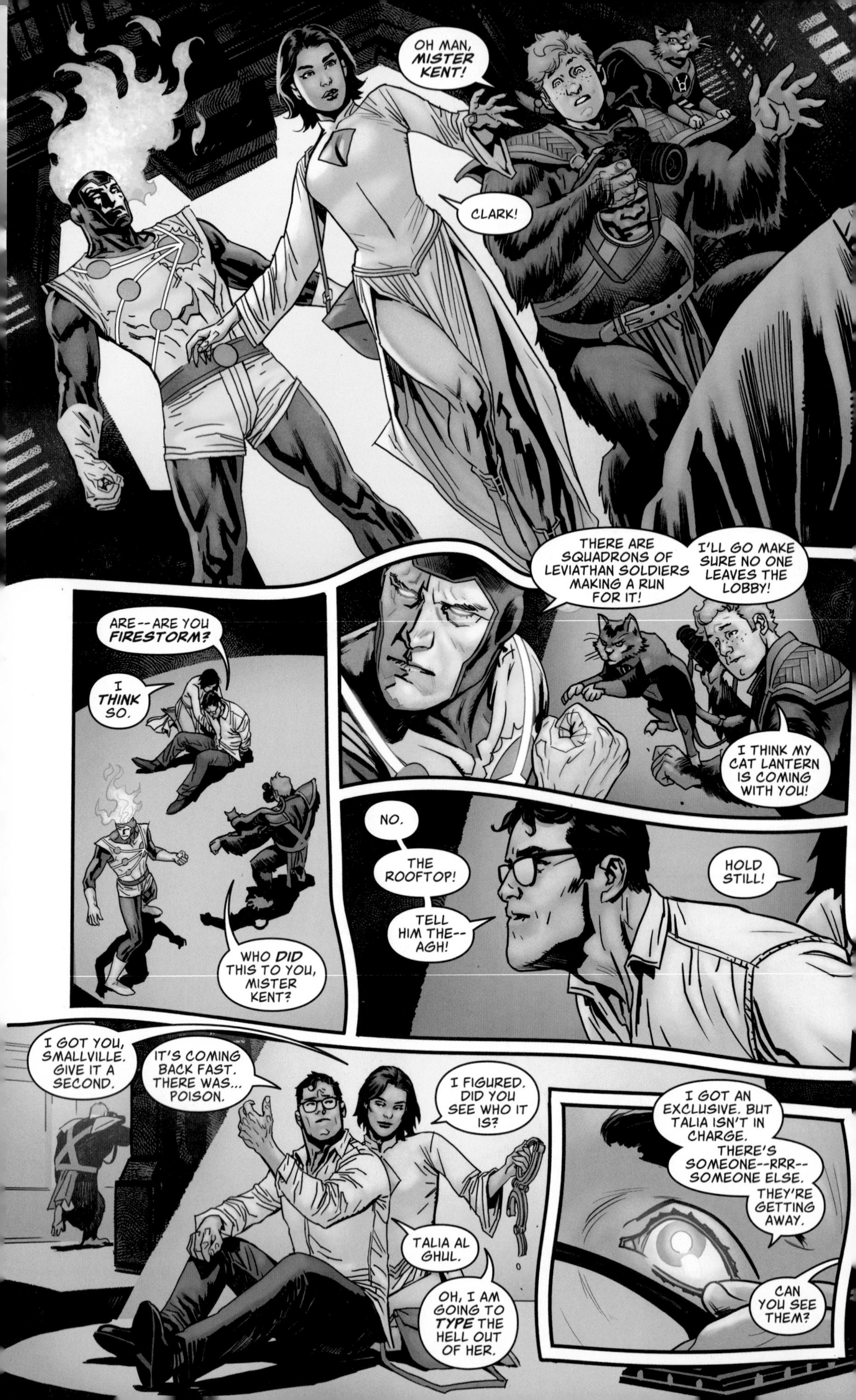
OH MAN, MISTER KENT!
CLARK!
THERE ARE SQUADRONS OF LEVIATHAN SOLDIERS MAKING A RUN FOR IT!
I'LL GO MAKE SURE NO ONE LEAVES THE LOBBY!
ARE--ARE YOU FIRESTORM?
I THINK SO.
I THINK MY CAT LANTERN IS COMING WITH YOU!
NO.
THE ROOFTOP!
TELL HIM THE--AGH!
HOLD STILL!
WHO DID THIS TO YOU, MISTER KENT?
I GOT YOU, SMALLVILLE. GIVE IT A SECOND.
IT'S COMING BACK FAST. THERE WAS... POISON.
I FIGURED. DID YOU SEE WHO IT IS?
TALIA AL GHUL.
OH, I AM GOING TO TYPE THE HELL OUT OF HER.
I GOT AN EXCLUSIVE. BUT TALIA ISN'T IN CHARGE.
THERE'S SOMEONE--RRR--SOMEONE ELSE.
THEY'RE GETTING AWAY.
CAN YOU SEE THEM?

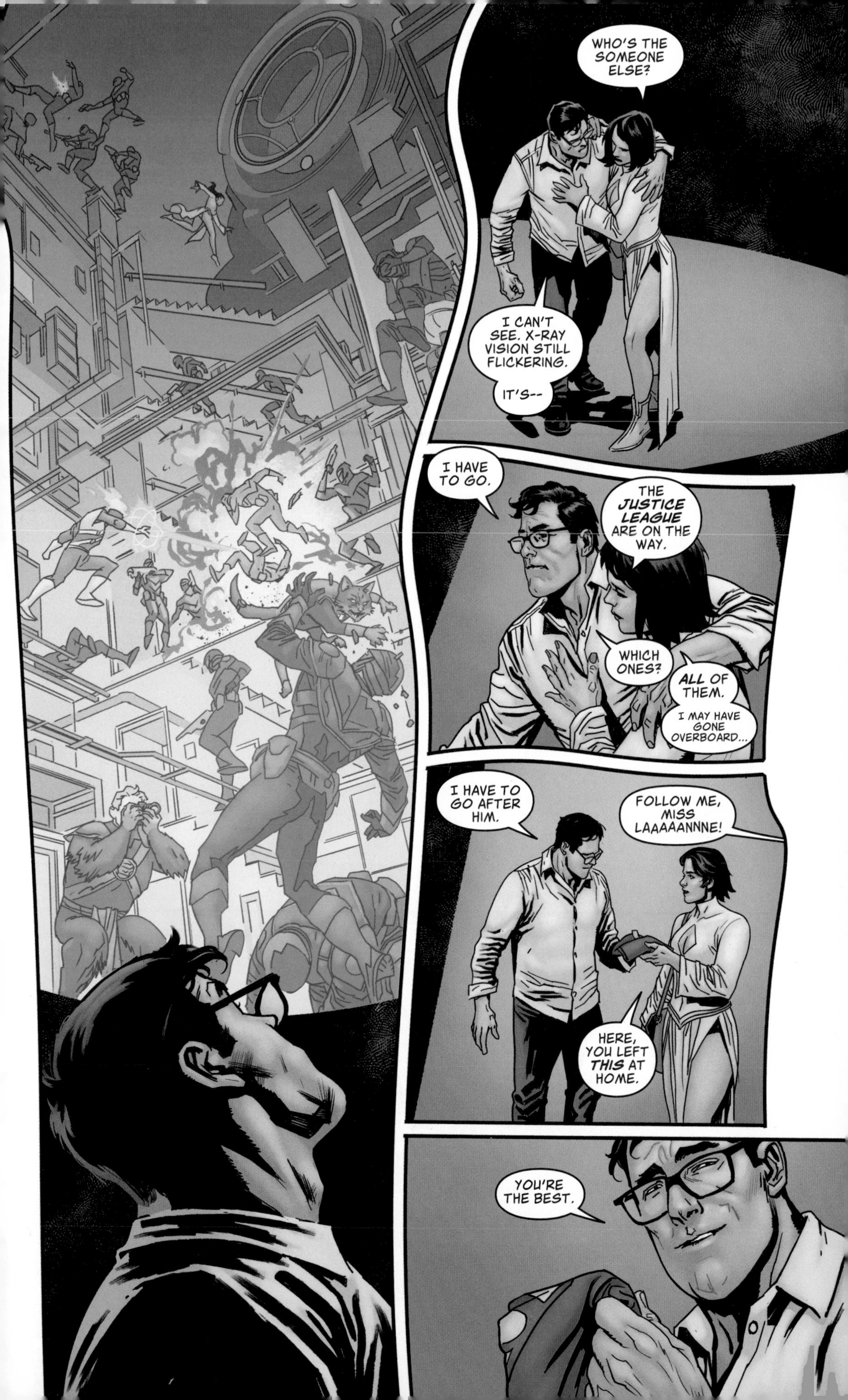
WHO'S THE SOMEONE ELSE?
I CAN'T SEE. X-RAY VISION STILL FLICKERING.
IT'S--
I HAVE TO GO.
THE JUSTICE LEAGUE ARE ON THE WAY.
WHICH ONES?
ALL OF THEM.
I MAY HAVE GONE OVERBOARD...
I HAVE TO GO AFTER HIM.
FOLLOW ME, MISS LAAAAANNNE!
HERE, YOU LEFT THIS AT HOME.
YOU'RE THE BEST.

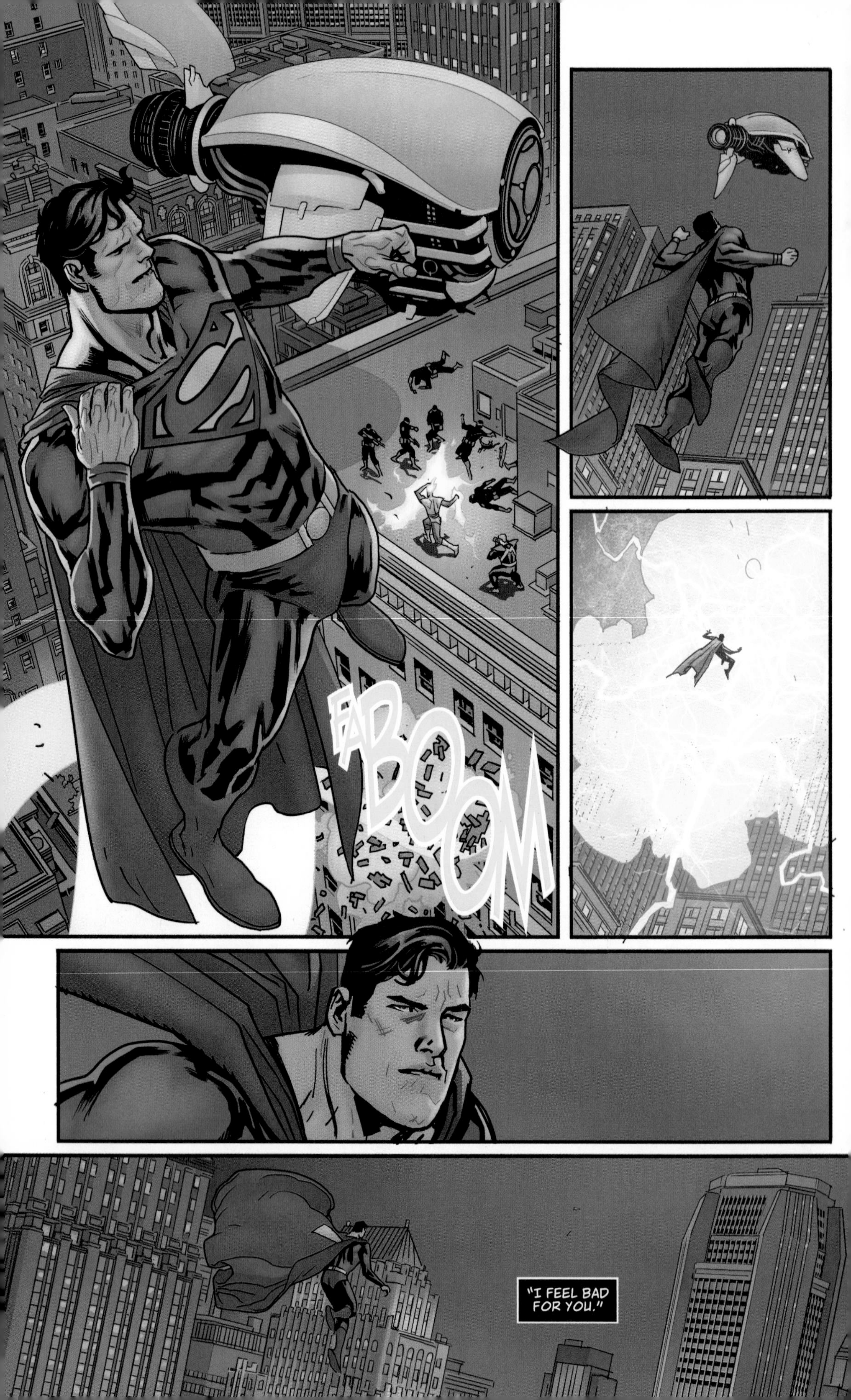
FADBOOM
"I FEEL BAD FOR YOU."

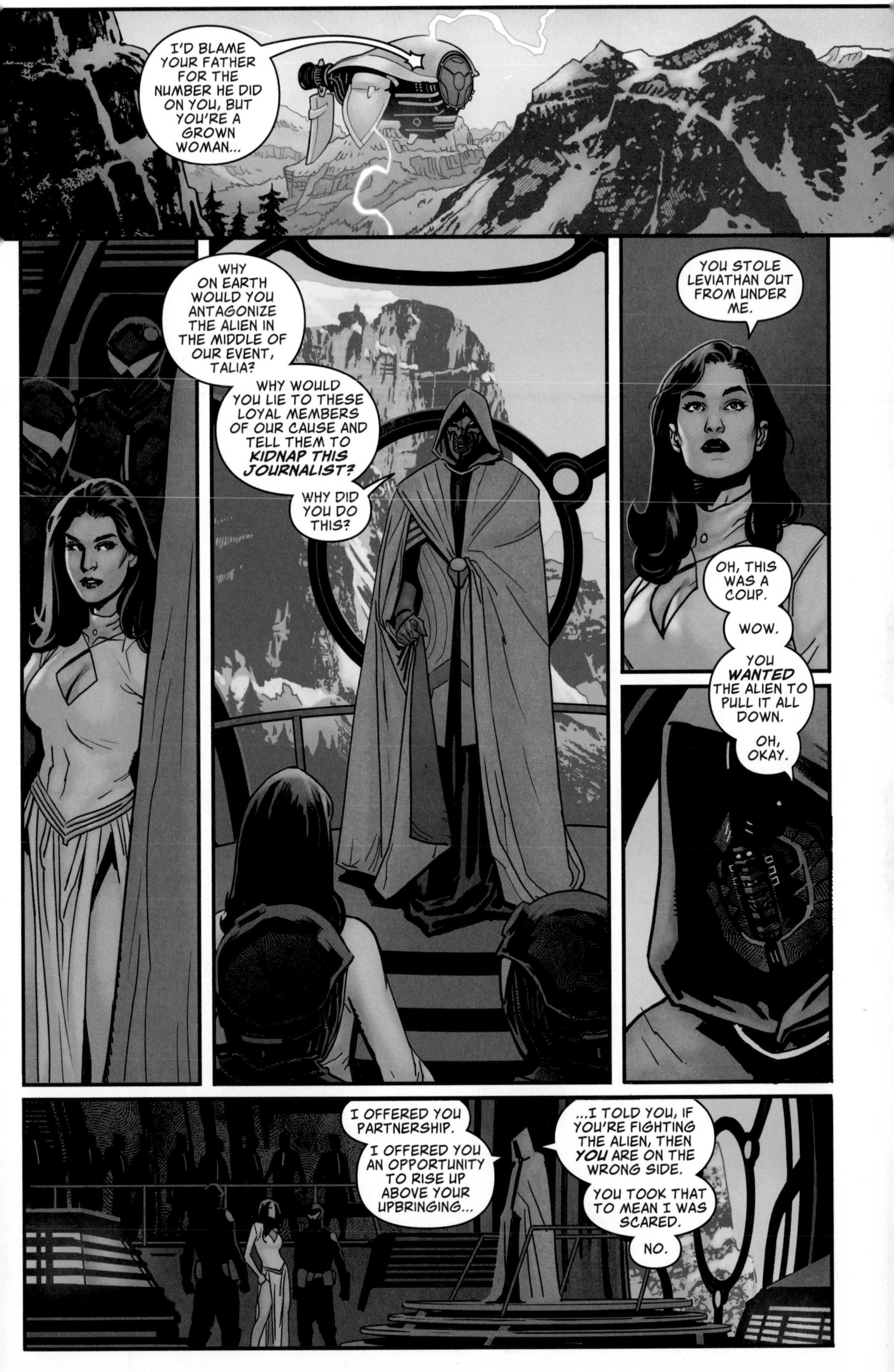

I'D BLAME YOUR FATHER FOR THE NUMBER HE DID ON YOU, BUT YOU'RE A GROWN WOMAN...
WHY ON EARTH WOULD YOU ANTAGONIZE THE ALIEN IN THE MIDDLE OF OUR EVENT, TALIA?
WHY WOULD YOU LIE TO THESE LOYAL MEMBERS OF OUR CAUSE AND TELL THEM TO KIDNAP THIS JOURNALIST?
WHY DID YOU DO THIS?
YOU STOLE LEVIATHAN OUT FROM UNDER ME.
OH, THIS WAS A COUP.
WOW.
YOU WANTED THE ALIEN TO PULL IT ALL DOWN.
OH, OKAY.
I OFFERED YOU PARTNERSHIP.
I OFFERED YOU AN OPPORTUNITY TO RISE UP ABOVE YOUR UPBRINGING...
...I TOLD YOU, IF YOU'RE FIGHTING THE ALIEN, THEN YOU ARE ON THE WRONG SIDE.
YOU TOOK THAT TO MEAN I WAS SCARED.
NO.

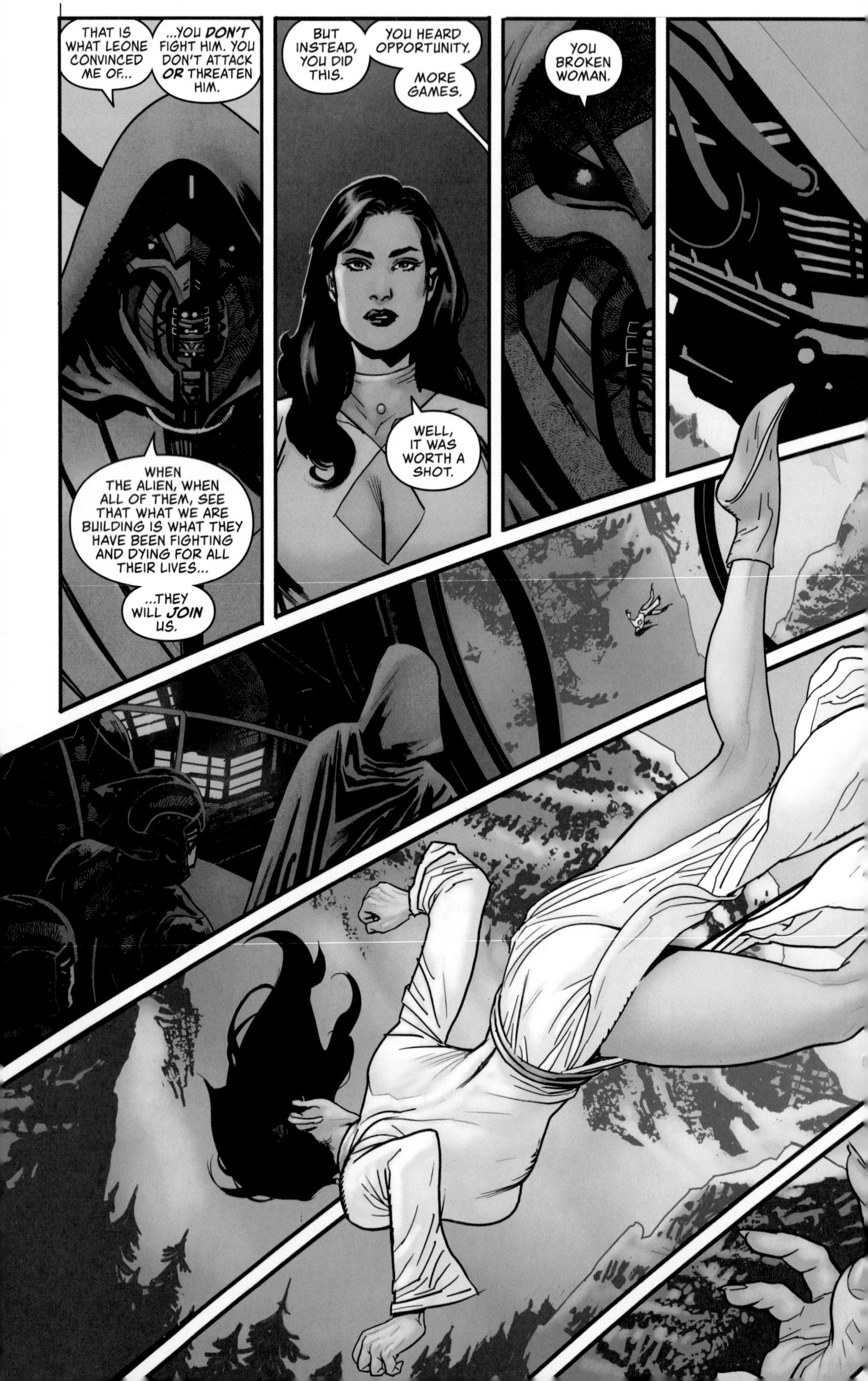
THAT IS WHAT LEONE CONVINCED ME OF...
...YOU DON'T FIGHT HIM. YOU DON'T ATTACK OR THREATEN HIM.
WHEN THE ALIEN, WHEN ALL OF THEM, SEE THAT WHAT WE ARE BUILDING IS WHAT THEY HAVE BEEN FIGHTING AND DYING FOR ALL THEIR LIVES...
...THEY WILL JOIN US.
BUT INSTEAD, YOU DID THIS.
YOU HEARD OPPORTUNITY.
MORE GAMES.
WELL, IT WAS WORTH A SHOT.
YOU BROKEN WOMAN.

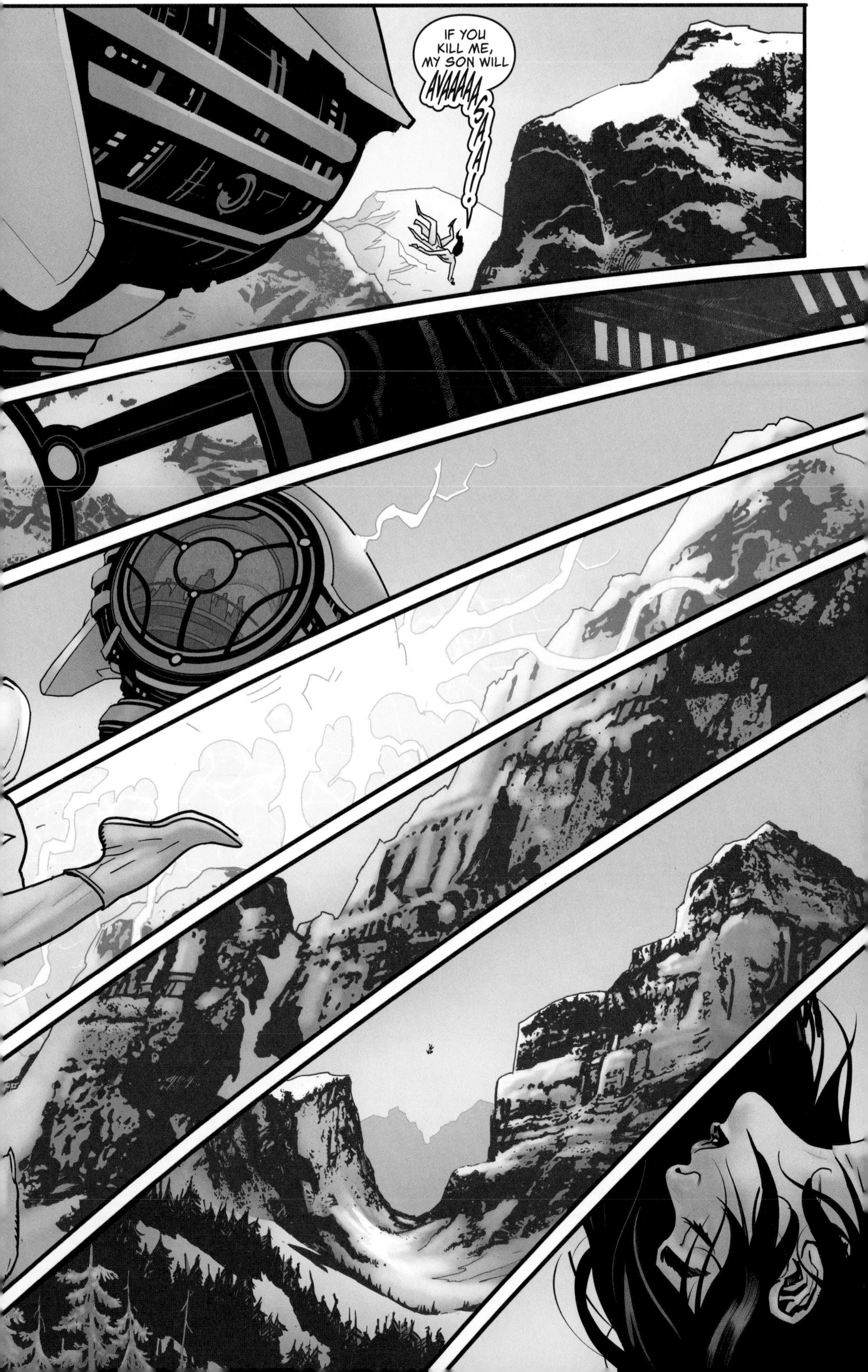
IF YOU KILL ME, MY SON WILL
AVAAAAASAA!

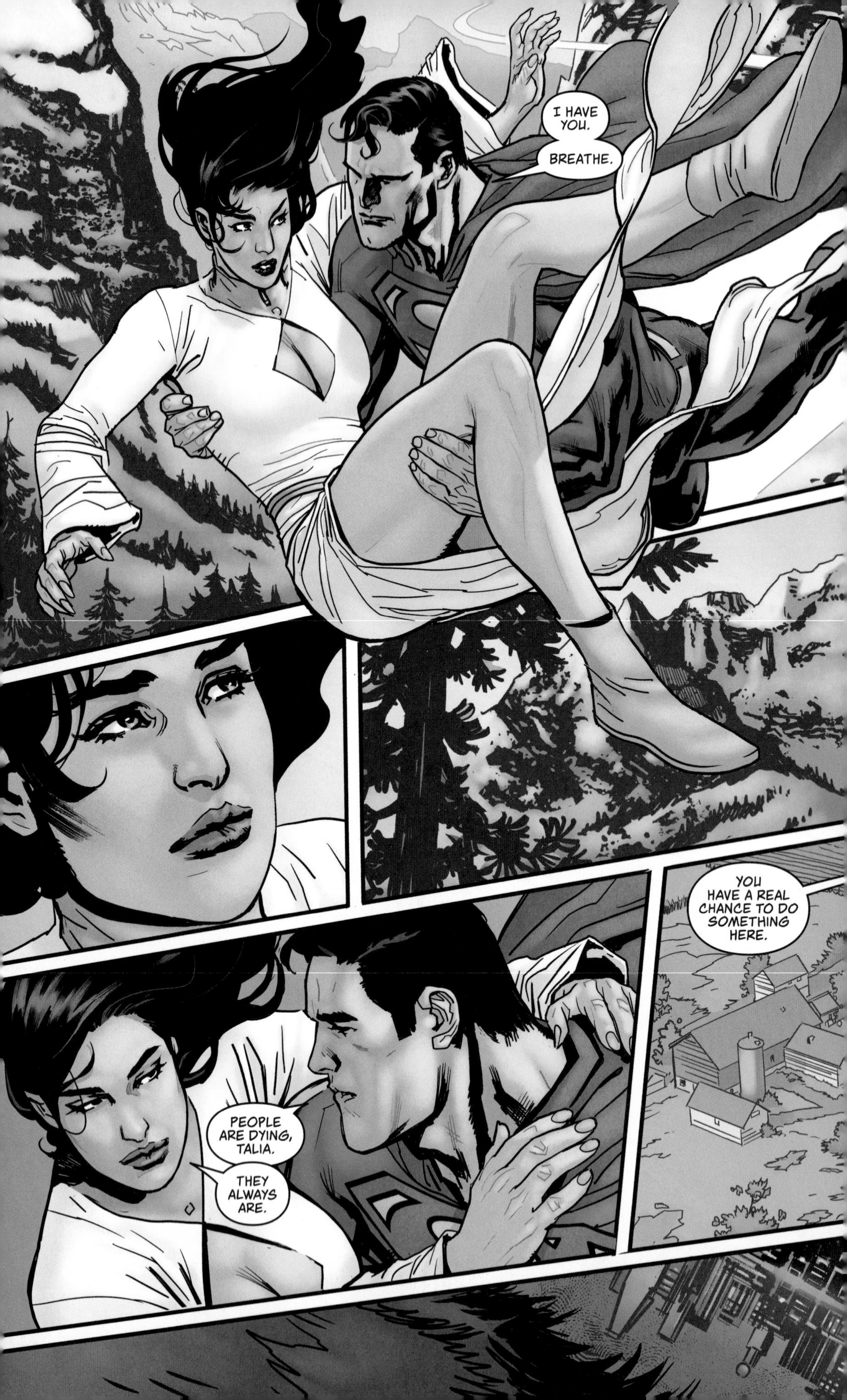
I HAVE YOU.
BREATHE.
YOU HAVE A REAL CHANCE TO DO SOMETHING HERE.
PEOPLE ARE DYING, TALIA.
THEY ALWAYS ARE.

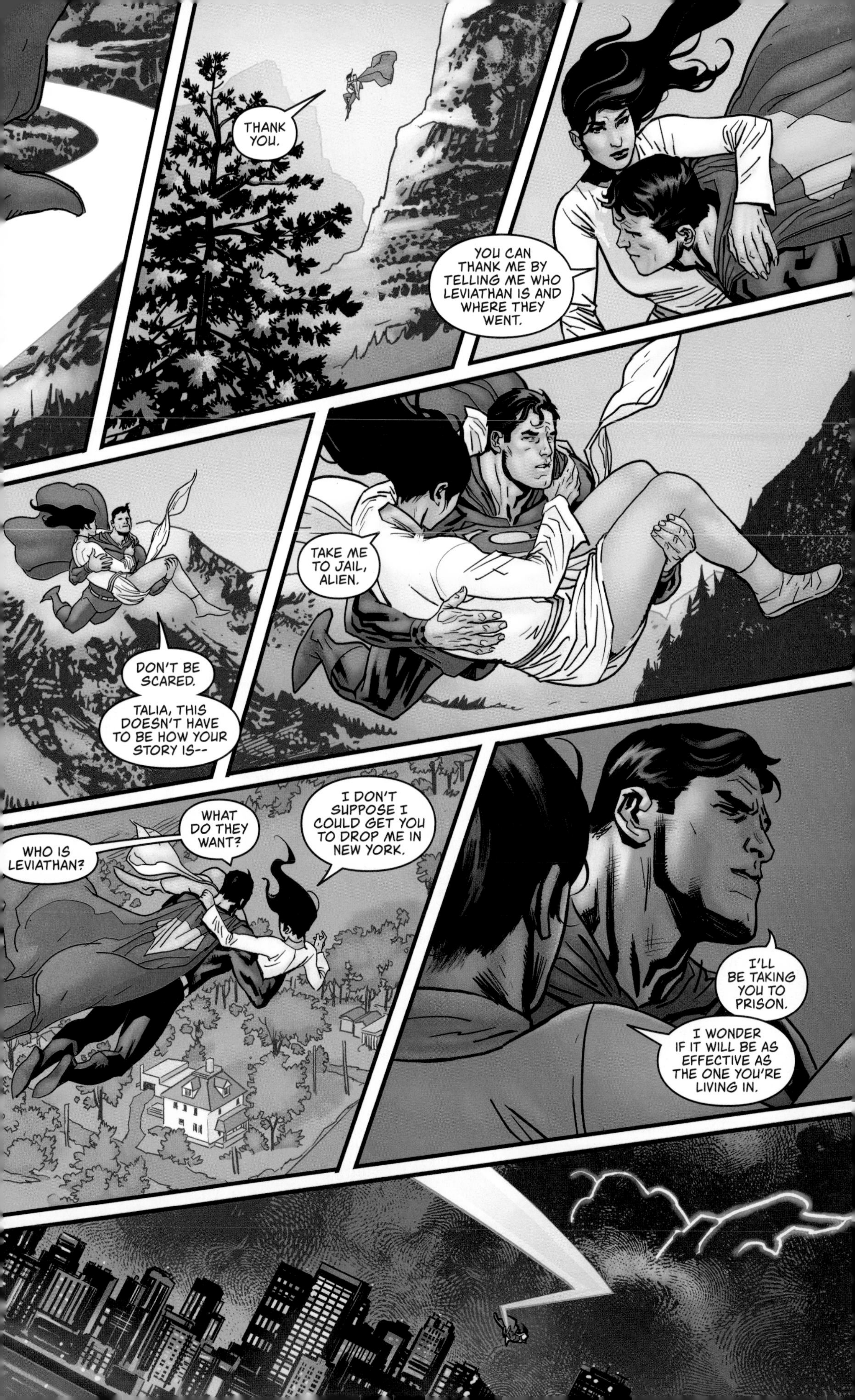
THANK YOU.
YOU CAN THANK ME BY TELLING ME WHO LEVIATHAN IS AND WHERE THEY WENT.
DON'T BE SCARED.
TALIA, THIS DOESN'T HAVE TO BE HOW YOUR STORY IS--
TAKE ME TO JAIL, ALIEN.
WHO IS LEVIATHAN?
WHAT DO THEY WANT?
I DON'T SUPPOSE I COULD GET YOU TO DROP ME IN NEW YORK.
I'LL BE TAKING YOU TO PRISON.
I WONDER IF IT WILL BE AS EFFECTIVE AS THE ONE YOU'RE LIVING IN.

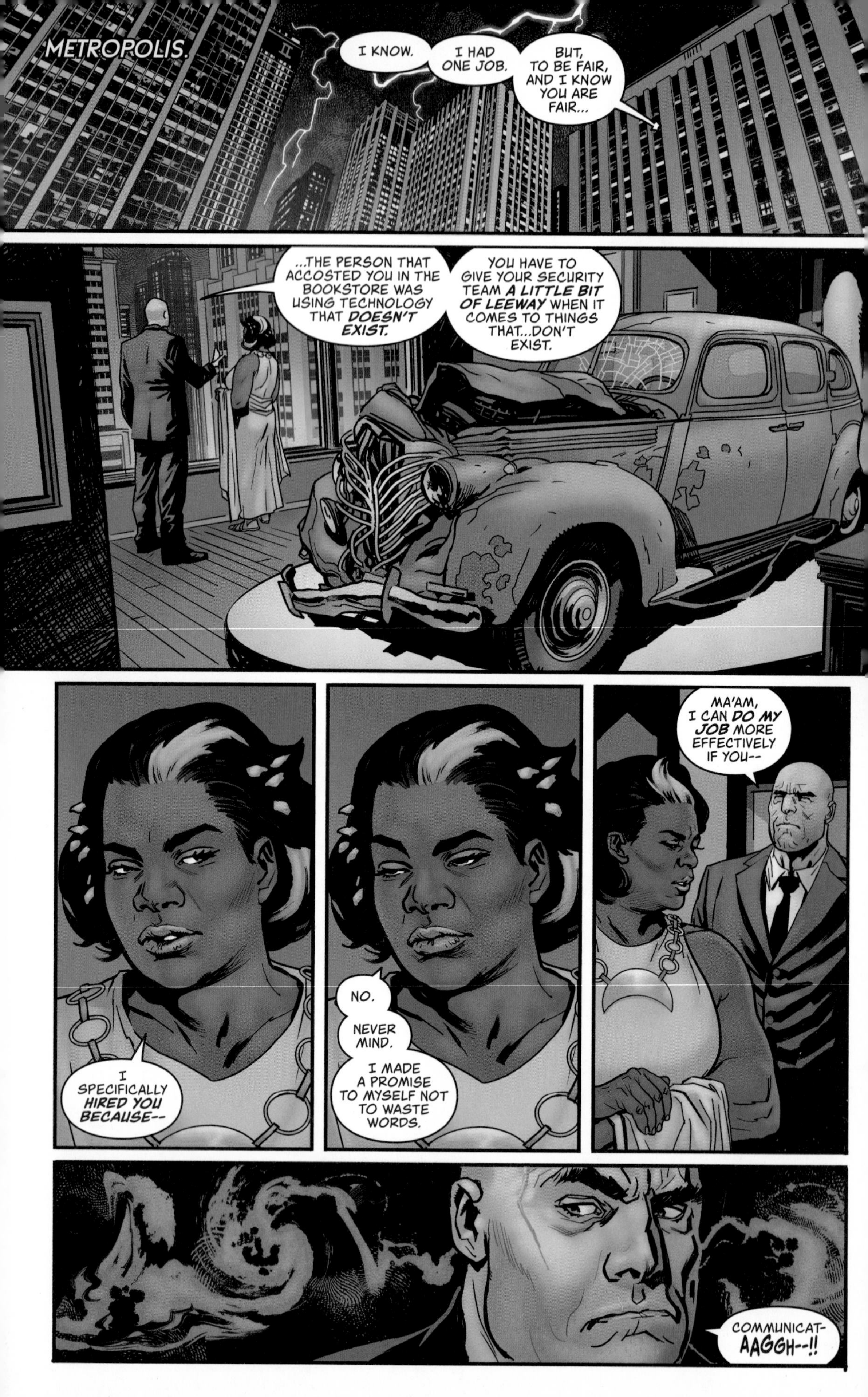
METROPOLIS.
I KNOW.
I HAD ONE JOB.
BUT, TO BE FAIR, AND I KNOW YOU ARE FAIR...
...THE PERSON THAT ACCOSTED YOU IN THE BOOKSTORE WAS USING TECHNOLOGY THAT DOESN'T EXIST.
YOU HAVE TO GIVE YOUR SECURITY TEAM A LITTLE BIT OF LEEWAY WHEN IT COMES TO THINGS THAT...DON'T EXIST.
I SPECIFICALLY HIRED YOU BECAUSE--
NO.
NEVER MIND.
I MADE A PROMISE TO MYSELF NOT TO WASTE WORDS.
MA'AM, I CAN DO MY JOB MORE EFFECTIVELY IF YOU--
COMMUNICAT-AAGGH--!!

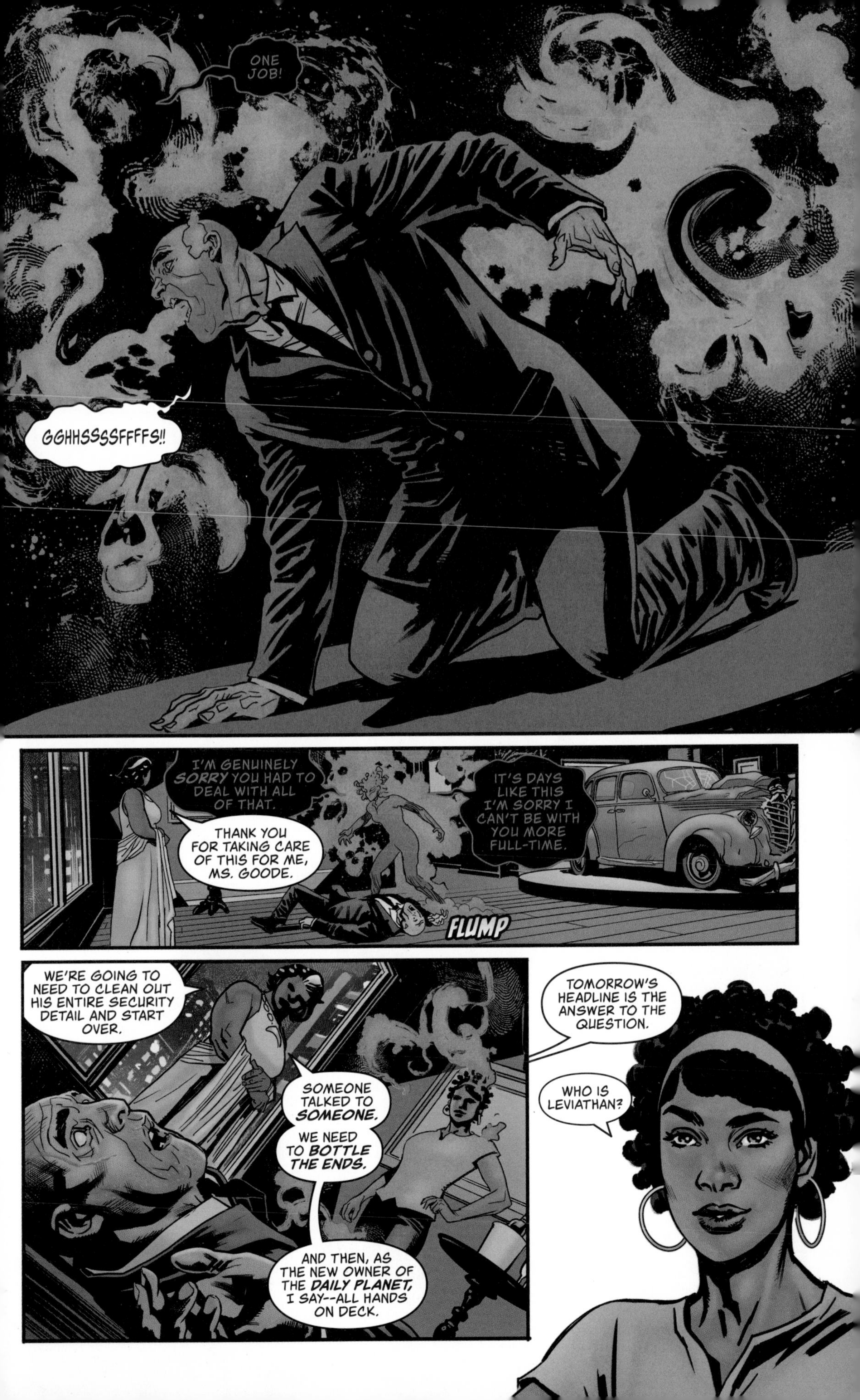
ONE JOB!
GGHHSSSSFFFFS!!
I'M GENUINELY SORRY YOU HAD TO DEAL WITH ALL OF THAT.
THANK YOU FOR TAKING CARE OF THIS FOR ME, MS. GOODE.
IT'S DAYS LIKE THIS I'M SORRY I CAN'T BE WITH YOU MORE FULL-TIME.
FLUMP
WE'RE GOING TO NEED TO CLEAN OUT HIS ENTIRE SECURITY DETAIL AND START OVER.
SOMEONE TALKED TO SOMEONE.
WE NEED TO BOTTLE THE ENDS.
AND THEN, AS THE NEW OWNER OF THE DAILY PLANET, I SAY--ALL HANDS ON DECK.
TOMORROW'S HEADLINE IS THE ANSWER TO THE QUESTION.
WHO IS LEVIATHAN?

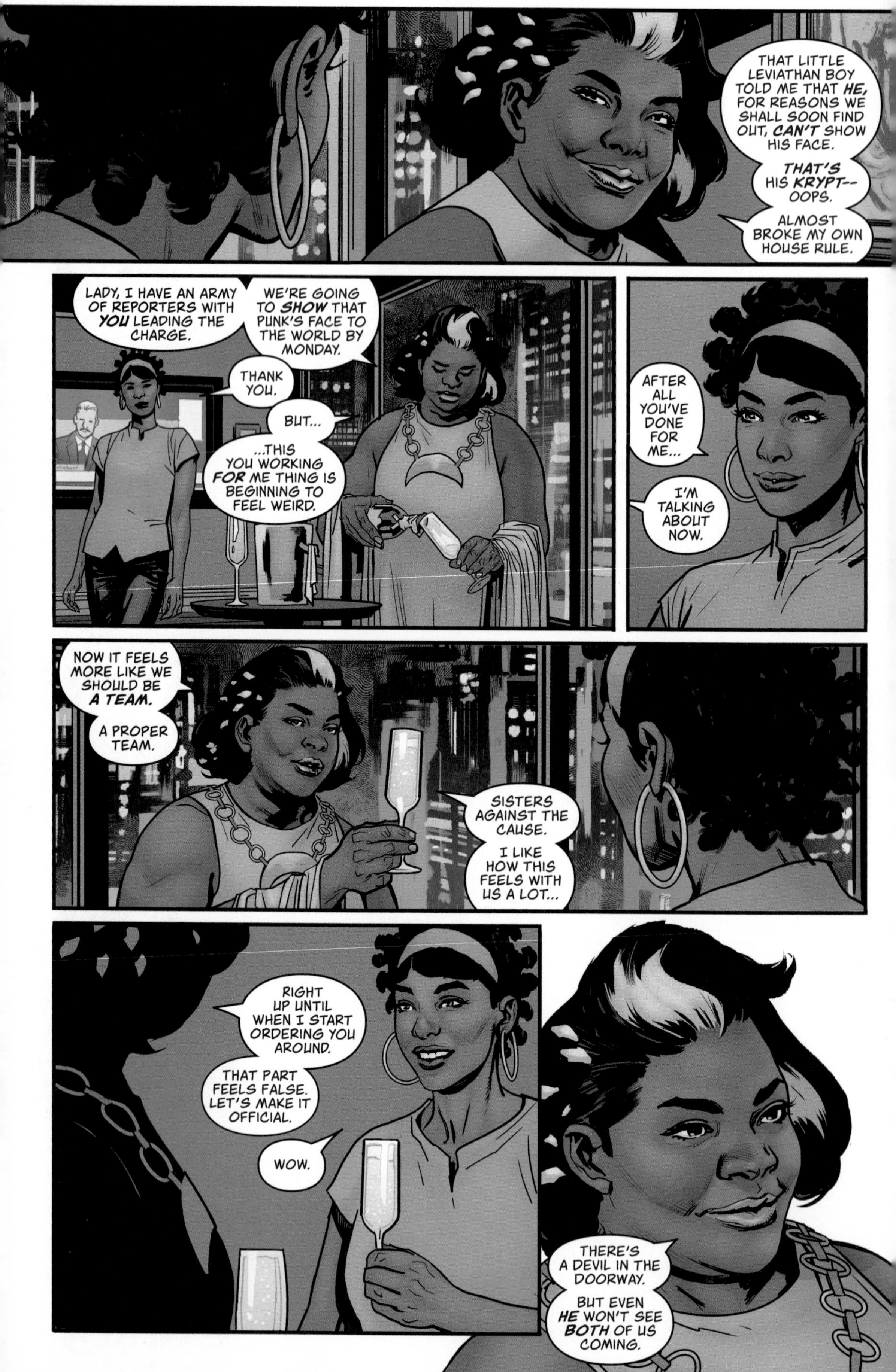
THAT LITTLE LEVIATHAN BOY TOLD ME THAT *HE,* FOR REASONS WE SHALL SOON FIND OUT, *CAN'T* SHOW HIS FACE.
THAT'S HIS *KRYPT*-- OOPS.
ALMOST BROKE MY OWN HOUSE RULE.
LADY, I HAVE AN ARMY OF REPORTERS WITH *YOU* LEADING THE CHARGE.
WE'RE GOING TO *SHOW* THAT PUNK'S FACE TO THE WORLD BY MONDAY.
THANK YOU.
BUT...
...THIS YOU WORKING *FOR* ME THING IS BEGINNING TO FEEL WEIRD.
AFTER ALL YOU'VE DONE FOR ME...
I'M TALKING ABOUT NOW.
NOW IT FEELS MORE LIKE WE SHOULD BE *A TEAM.*
A PROPER TEAM.
SISTERS AGAINST THE CAUSE.
I LIKE HOW THIS FEELS WITH US A LOT...
RIGHT UP UNTIL WHEN I START ORDERING YOU AROUND.
THAT PART FEELS FALSE. LET'S MAKE IT OFFICIAL.
WOW.
THERE'S A DEVIL IN THE DOORWAY.
BUT EVEN *HE* WON'T SEE *BOTH* OF US COMING.

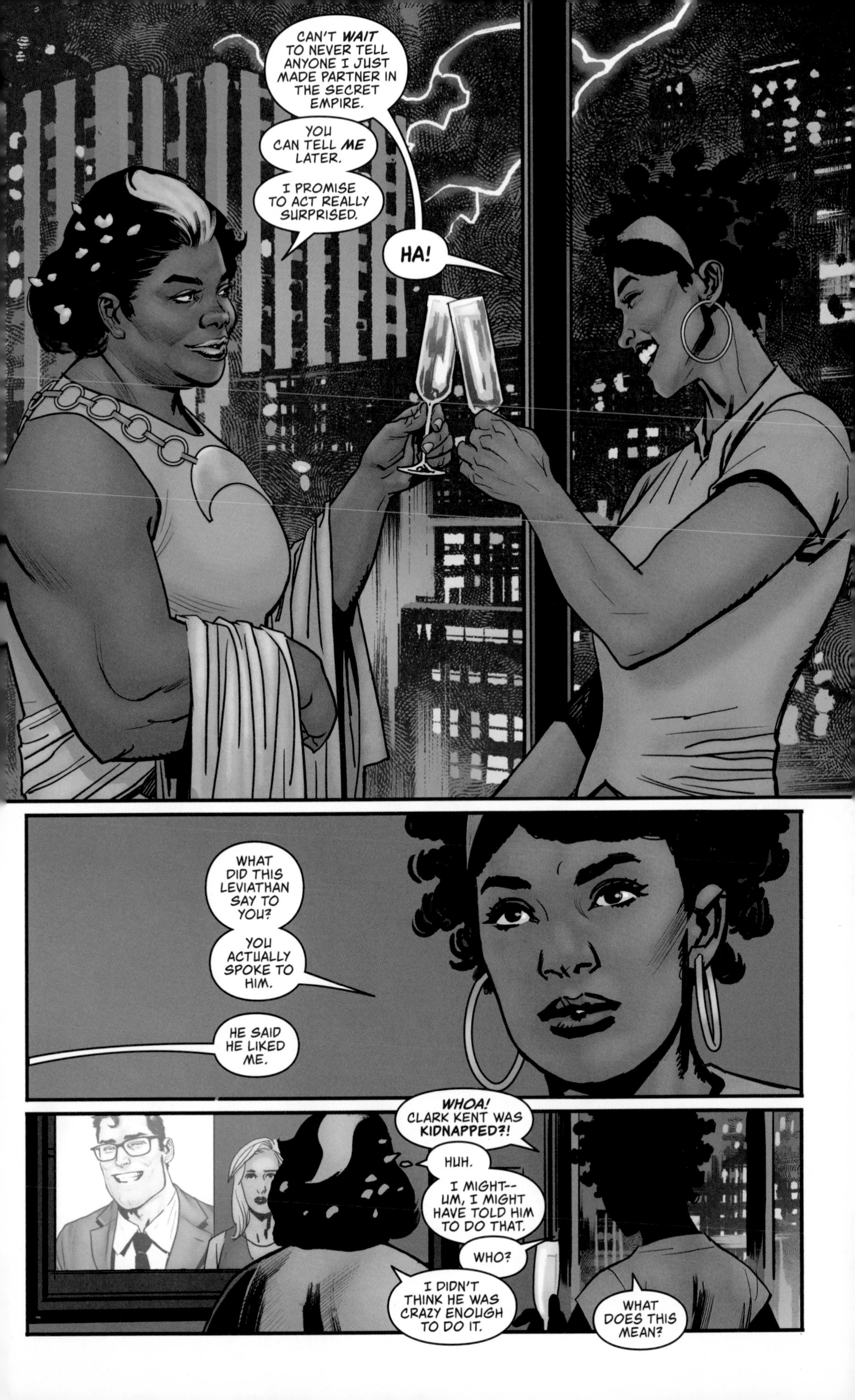
CAN'T WAIT TO NEVER TELL ANYONE I JUST MADE PARTNER IN THE SECRET EMPIRE.
YOU CAN TELL ME LATER.
I PROMISE TO ACT REALLY SURPRISED.
HA!
WHAT DID THIS LEVIATHAN SAY TO YOU?
YOU ACTUALLY SPOKE TO HIM.
HE SAID HE LIKED ME.
WHOA! CLARK KENT WAS KIDNAPPED?!
HUH.
I MIGHT-- UM, I MIGHT HAVE TOLD HIM TO DO THAT.
WHO?
I DIDN'T THINK HE WAS CRAZY ENOUGH TO DO IT.
WHAT DOES THIS MEAN?

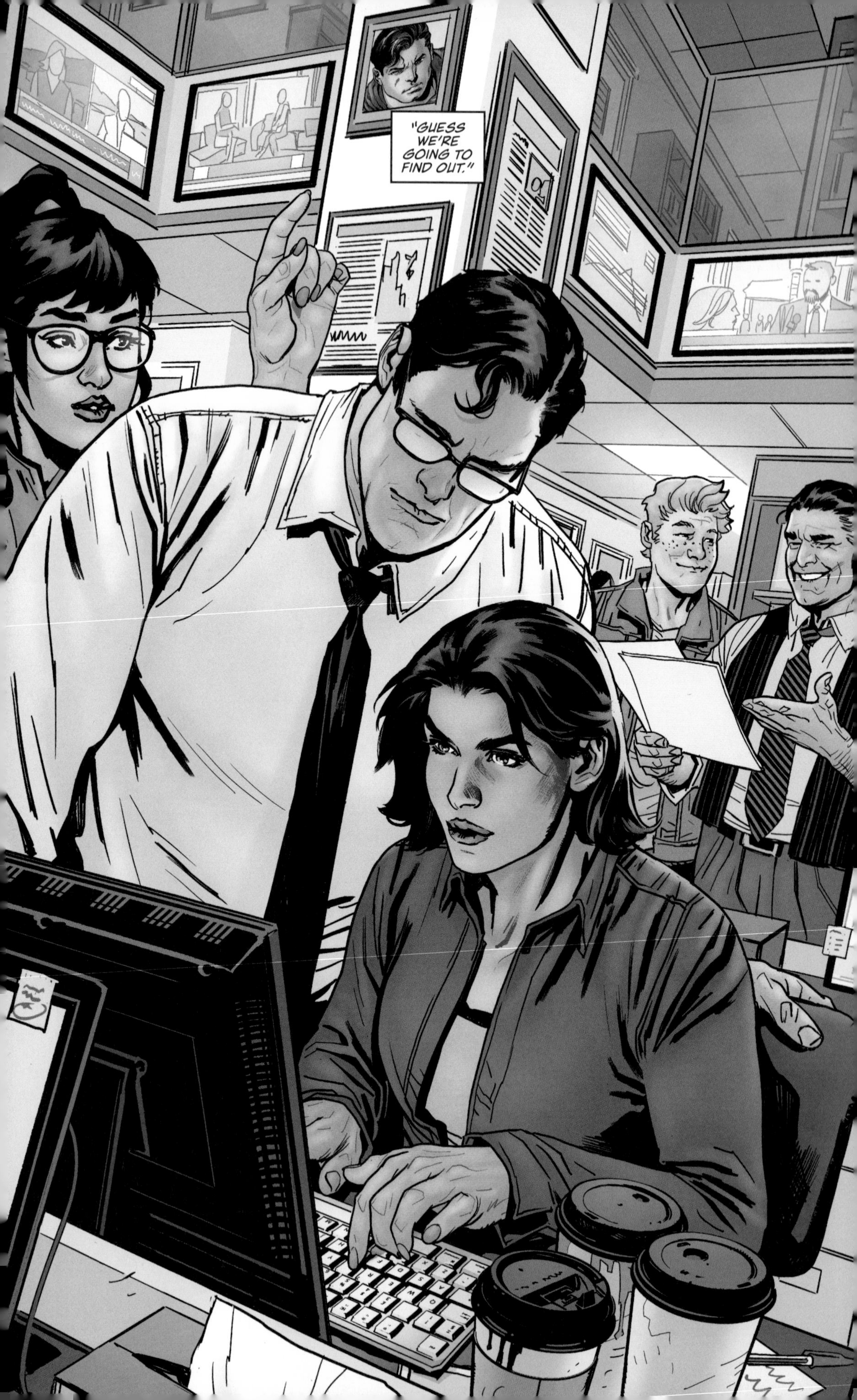
"GUESS WE'RE GOING TO FIND OUT."

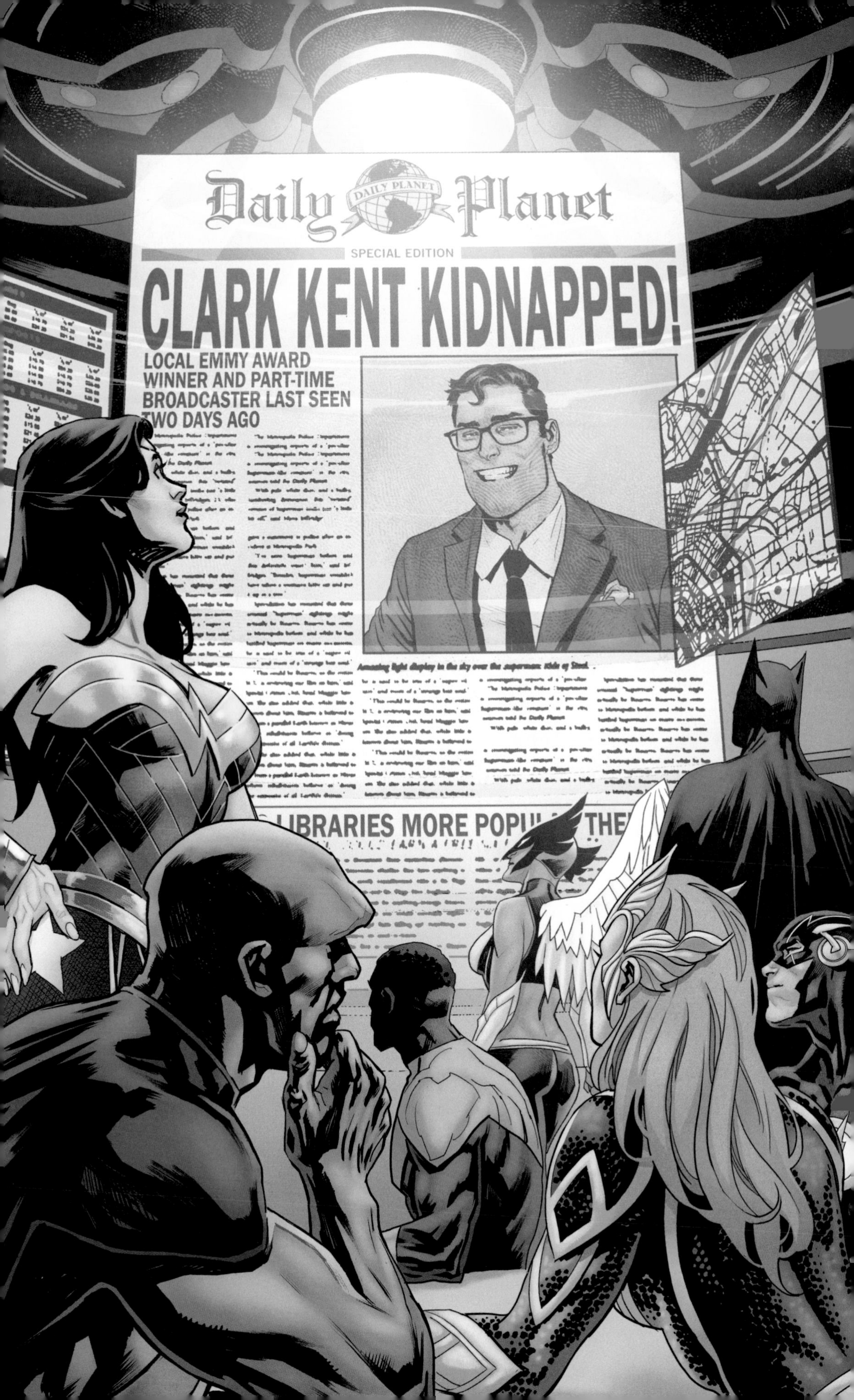
Daily Planet
DAILY PLANET
SPECIAL EDITION
CLARK KENT KIDNAPPED!
LOCAL EMMY AWARD WINNER AND PART-TIME BROADCASTER LAST SEEN TWO DAYS AGO
LIBRARIES MORE POPUL THE

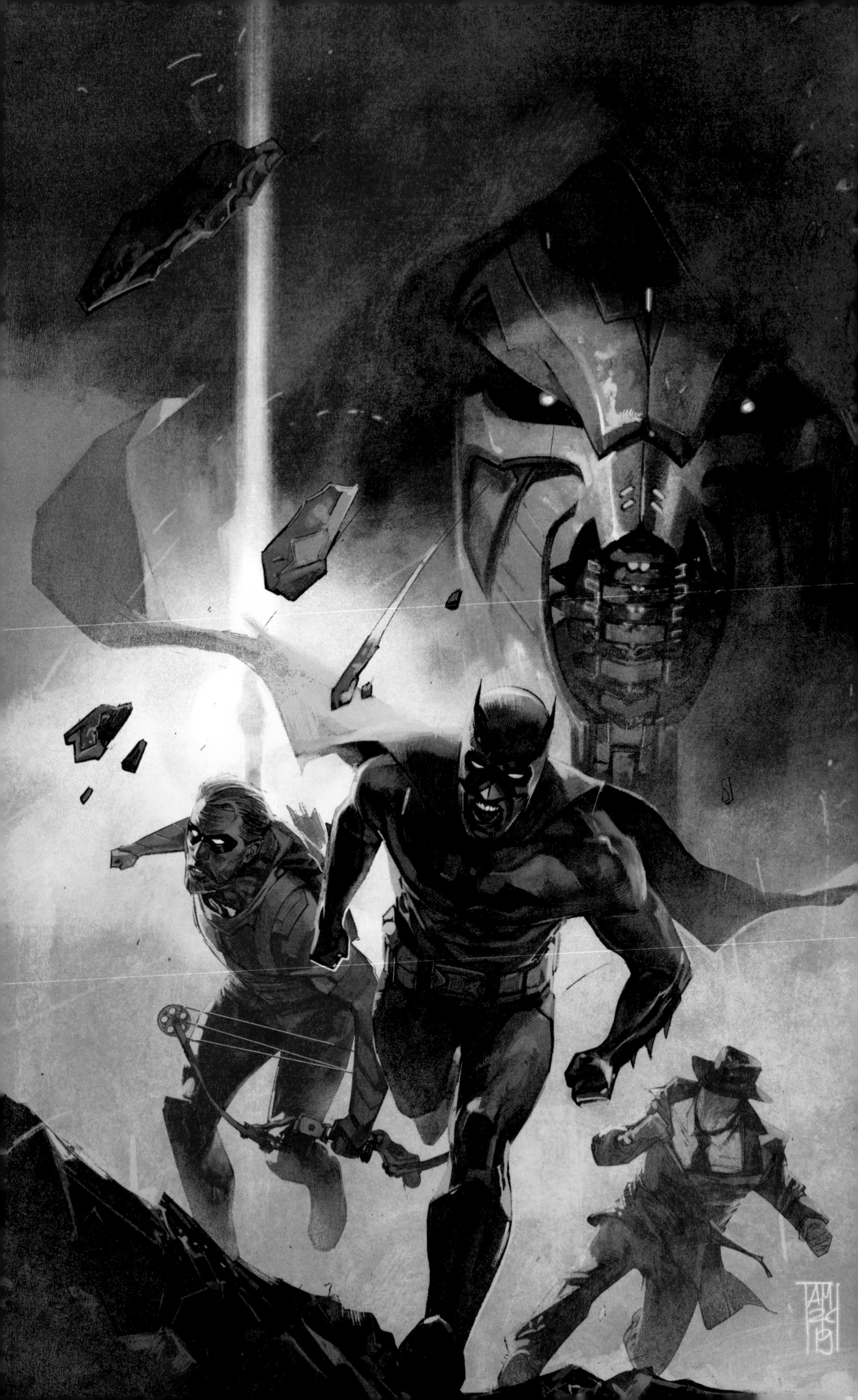

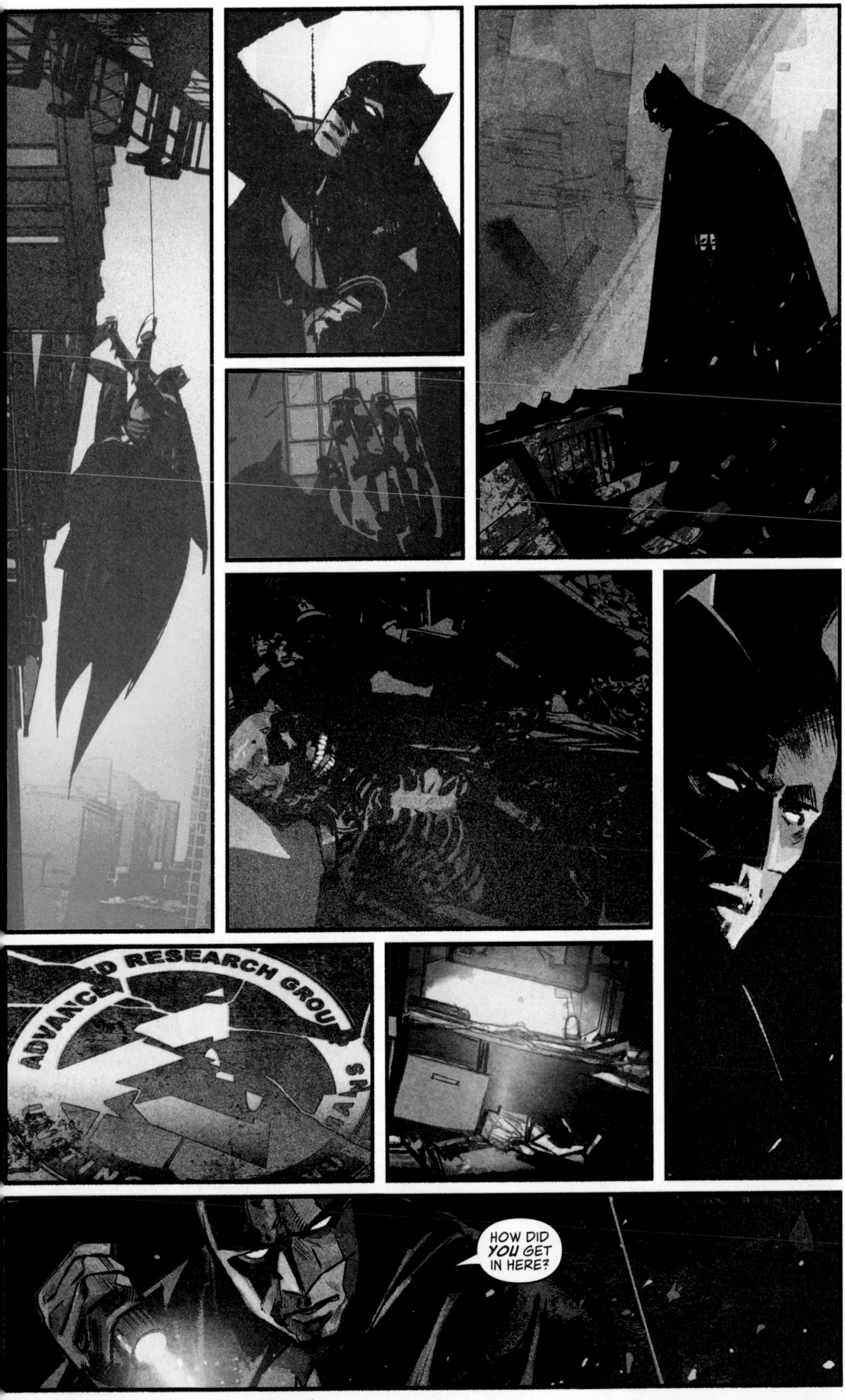
ADVANCED RESEARCH GROUP
HOW DID YOU GET IN HERE?

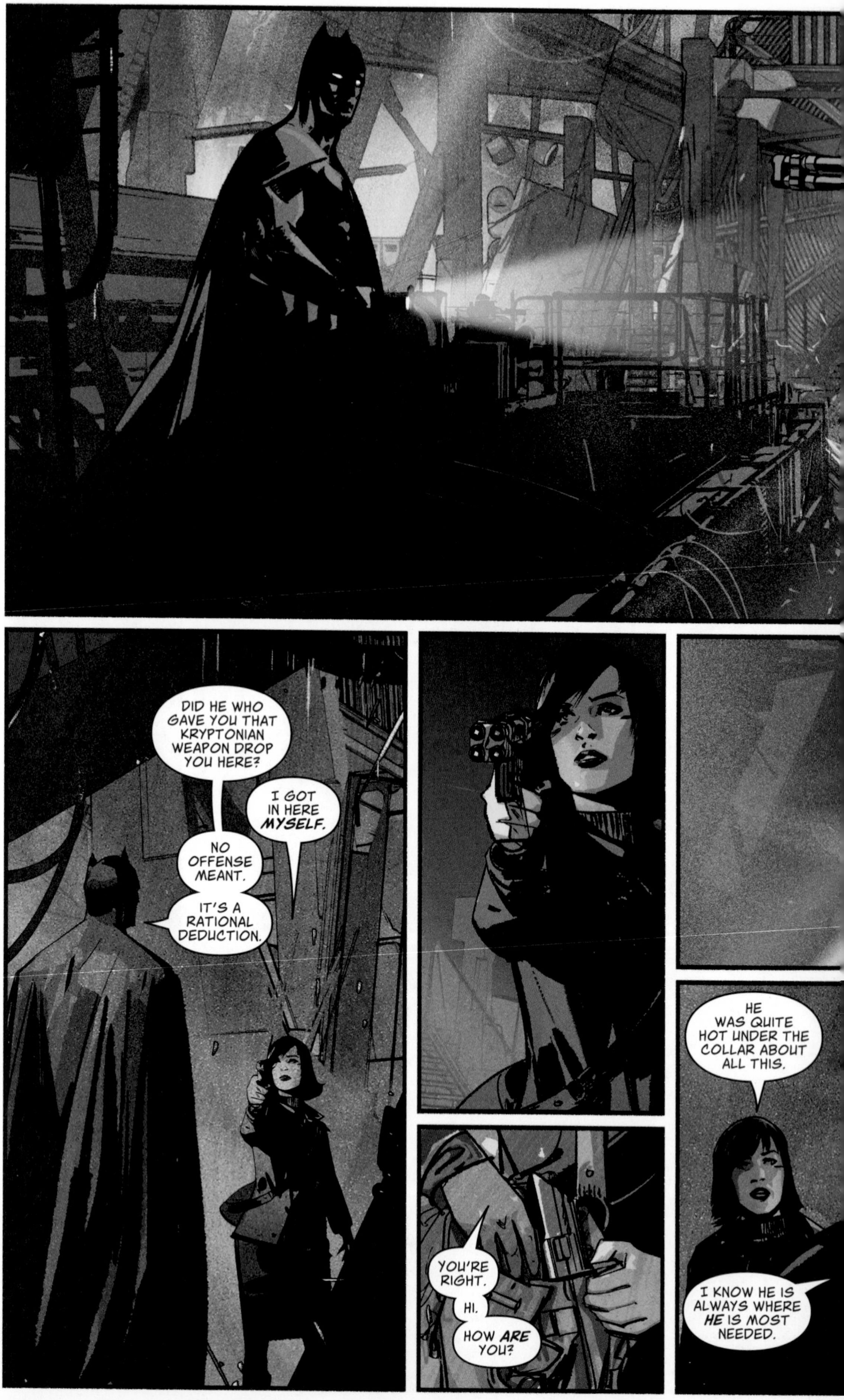
DID HE WHO GAVE YOU THAT KRYPTONIAN WEAPON DROP YOU HERE?
NO OFFENSE MEANT.
IT'S A RATIONAL DEDUCTION.
I GOT IN HERE MYSELF.
HE WAS QUITE HOT UNDER THE COLLAR ABOUT ALL THIS.
I KNOW HE IS ALWAYS WHERE HE IS MOST NEEDED.
YOU'RE RIGHT.
HI.
HOW ARE YOU?

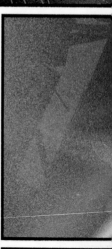

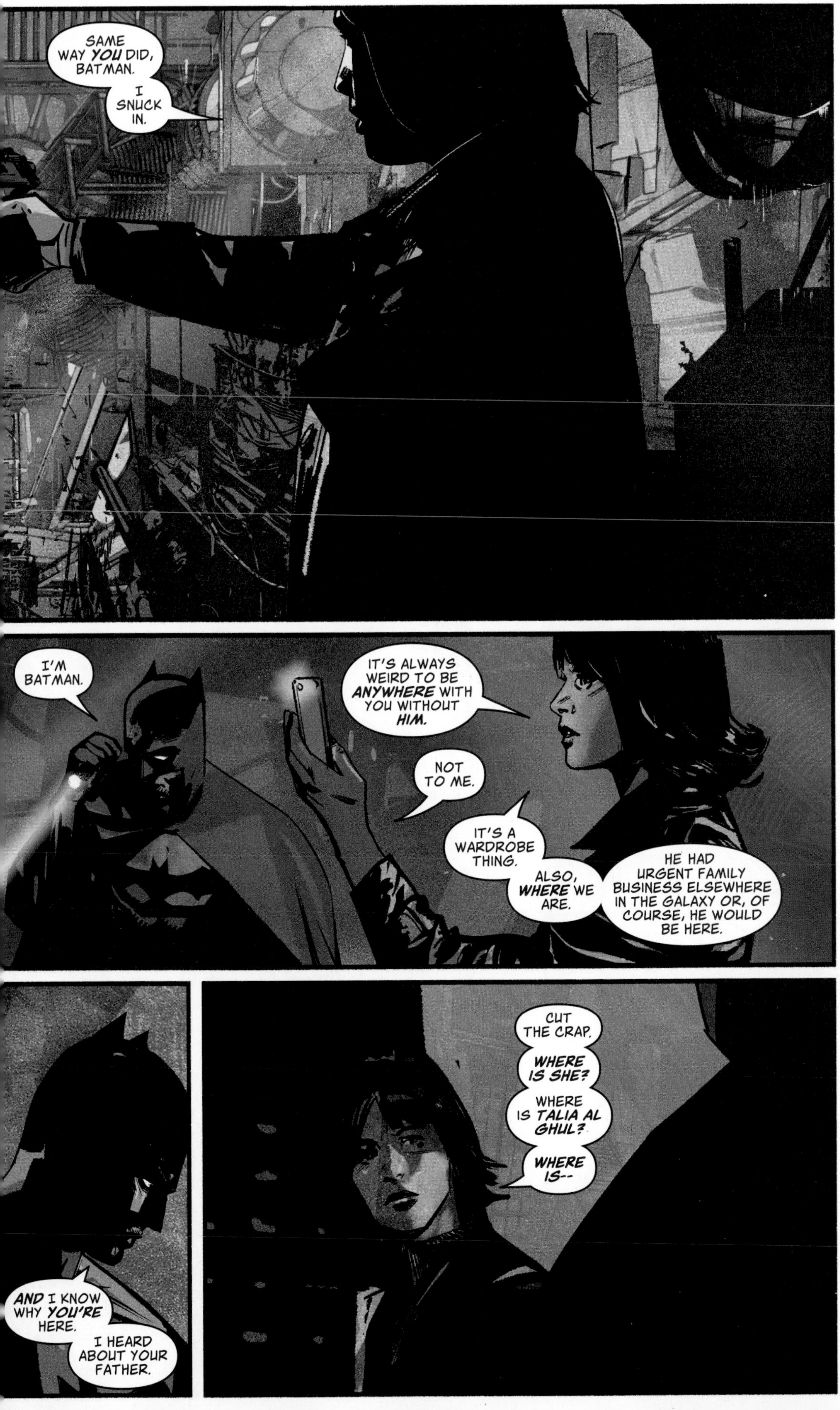
SAME WAY YOU DID, BATMAN.
I SNUCK IN.
I'M BATMAN.
IT'S ALWAYS WEIRD TO BE ANYWHERE WITH YOU WITHOUT HIM.
NOT TO ME.
IT'S A WARDROBE THING.
ALSO, WHERE WE ARE.
HE HAD URGENT FAMILY BUSINESS ELSEWHERE IN THE GALAXY OR, OF COURSE, HE WOULD BE HERE.
CUT THE CRAP.
WHERE IS SHE?
WHERE IS TALIA AL GHUL?
WHERE IS--
AND I KNOW WHY YOU'RE HERE.
I HEARD ABOUT YOUR FATHER.

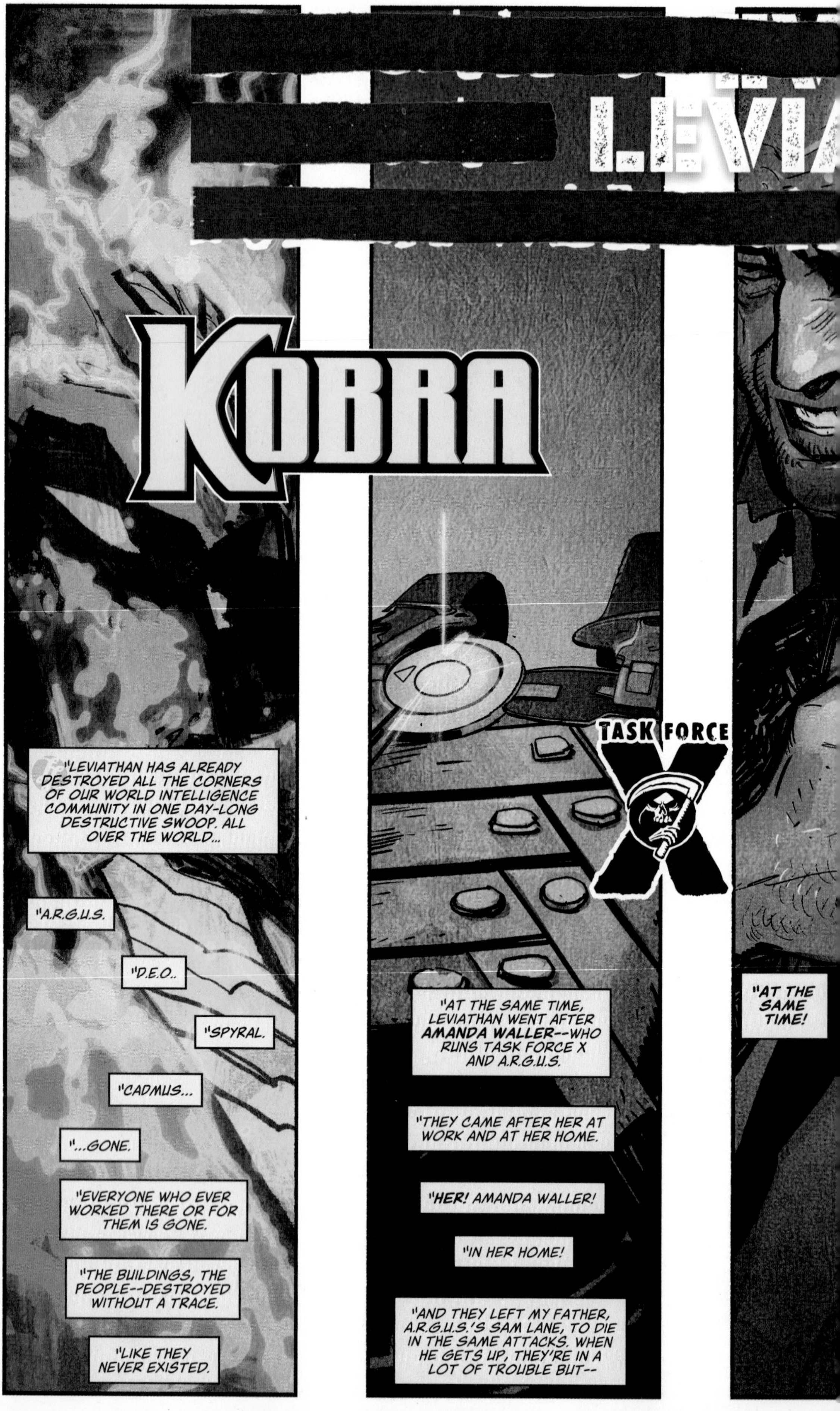
[redacted]
KOBRA
"LEVIATHAN HAS ALREADY DESTROYED ALL THE CORNERS OF OUR WORLD INTELLIGENCE COMMUNITY IN ONE DAY-LONG DESTRUCTIVE SWOOP. ALL OVER THE WORLD...
"A.R.G.U.S.
"D.E.O..
"SPYRAL.
"CADMUS...
"...GONE.
"EVERYONE WHO EVER WORKED THERE OR FOR THEM IS GONE.
"THE BUILDINGS, THE PEOPLE--DESTROYED WITHOUT A TRACE.
"LIKE THEY NEVER EXISTED.
TASK FORCE X
"AT THE SAME TIME, LEVIATHAN WENT AFTER AMANDA WALLER--WHO RUNS TASK FORCE X AND A.R.G.U.S.
"THEY CAME AFTER HER AT WORK AND AT HER HOME.
"HER! AMANDA WALLER!
"IN HER HOME!
"AND THEY LEFT MY FATHER, A.R.G.U.S.'S SAM LANE, TO DIE IN THE SAME ATTACKS. WHEN HE GETS UP, THEY'RE IN A LOT OF TROUBLE BUT--
"AT THE SAME TIME!

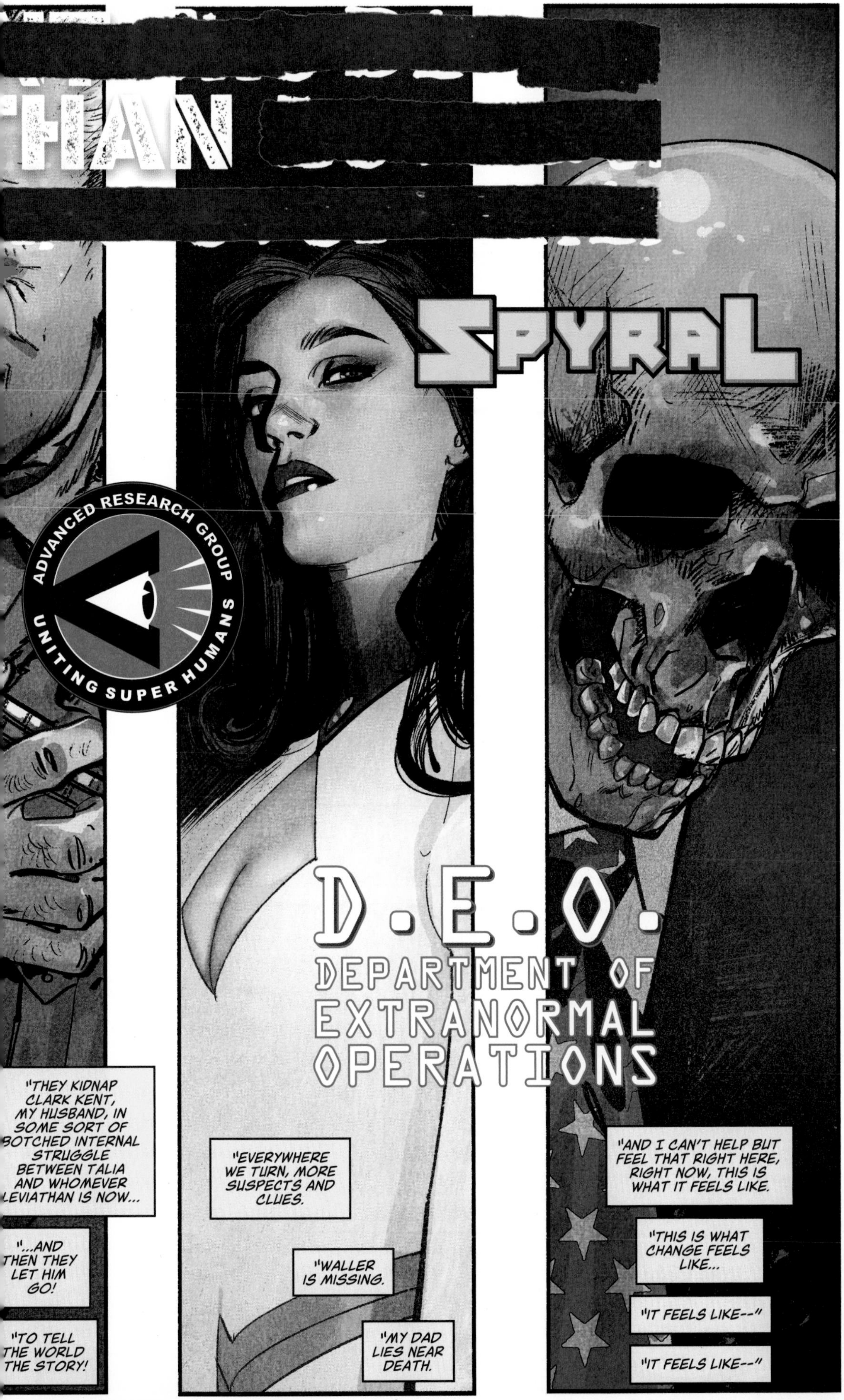

[redacted]
HAN [redacted]
SPYRAL
ADVANCED RESEARCH GROUP
UNITING SUPER HUMANS
D.E.O.
DEPARTMENT OF EXTRANORMAL OPERATIONS
"THEY KIDNAP CLARK KENT, MY HUSBAND, IN SOME SORT OF BOTCHED INTERNAL STRUGGLE BETWEEN TALIA AND WHOMEVER LEVIATHAN IS NOW...
"...AND THEN THEY LET HIM GO!
"TO TELL THE WORLD THE STORY!
"EVERYWHERE WE TURN, MORE SUSPECTS AND CLUES.
"WALLER IS MISSING.
"MY DAD LIES NEAR DEATH.
"AND I CAN'T HELP BUT FEEL THAT RIGHT HERE, RIGHT NOW, THIS IS WHAT IT FEELS LIKE.
"THIS IS WHAT CHANGE FEELS LIKE...
"IT FEELS LIKE--"
"IT FEELS LIKE--"

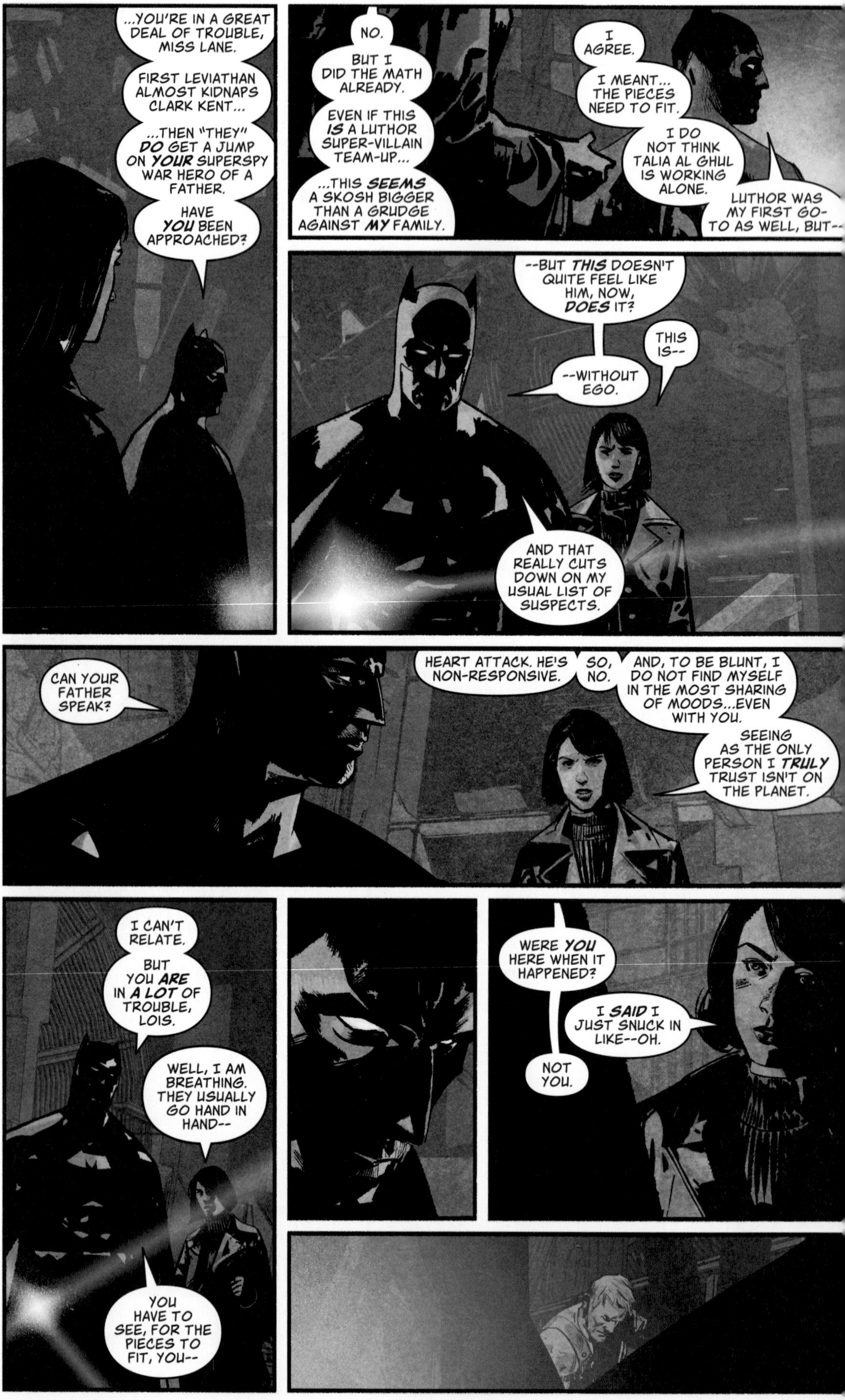
...YOU'RE IN A GREAT DEAL OF TROUBLE, MISS LANE.
FIRST LEVIATHAN ALMOST KIDNAPS CLARK KENT...
...THEN "THEY" DO GET A JUMP ON YOUR SUPERSPY WAR HERO OF A FATHER.
HAVE YOU BEEN APPROACHED?
NO.
BUT I DID THE MATH ALREADY.
EVEN IF THIS IS A LUTHOR SUPER-VILLAIN TEAM-UP...
...THIS SEEMS A SKOSH BIGGER THAN A GRUDGE AGAINST MY FAMILY.
I AGREE.
I MEANT... THE PIECES NEED TO FIT.
I DO NOT THINK TALIA AL GHUL IS WORKING ALONE.
LUTHOR WAS MY FIRST GO-TO AS WELL, BUT--
--BUT THIS DOESN'T QUITE FEEL LIKE HIM, NOW, DOES IT?
THIS IS--
--WITHOUT EGO.
AND THAT REALLY CUTS DOWN ON MY USUAL LIST OF SUSPECTS.
CAN YOUR FATHER SPEAK?
HEART ATTACK. HE'S NON-RESPONSIVE.
SO, NO.
AND, TO BE BLUNT, I DO NOT FIND MYSELF IN THE MOST SHARING OF MOODS...EVEN WITH YOU.
SEEING AS THE ONLY PERSON I TRULY TRUST ISN'T ON THE PLANET.
I CAN'T RELATE.
BUT YOU ARE IN A LOT OF TROUBLE, LOIS.
WELL, I AM BREATHING. THEY USUALLY GO HAND IN HAND--
YOU HAVE TO SEE, FOR THE PIECES TO FIT, YOU--
WERE YOU HERE WHEN IT HAPPENED?
I SAID I JUST SNUCK IN LIKE--OH.
NOT YOU.

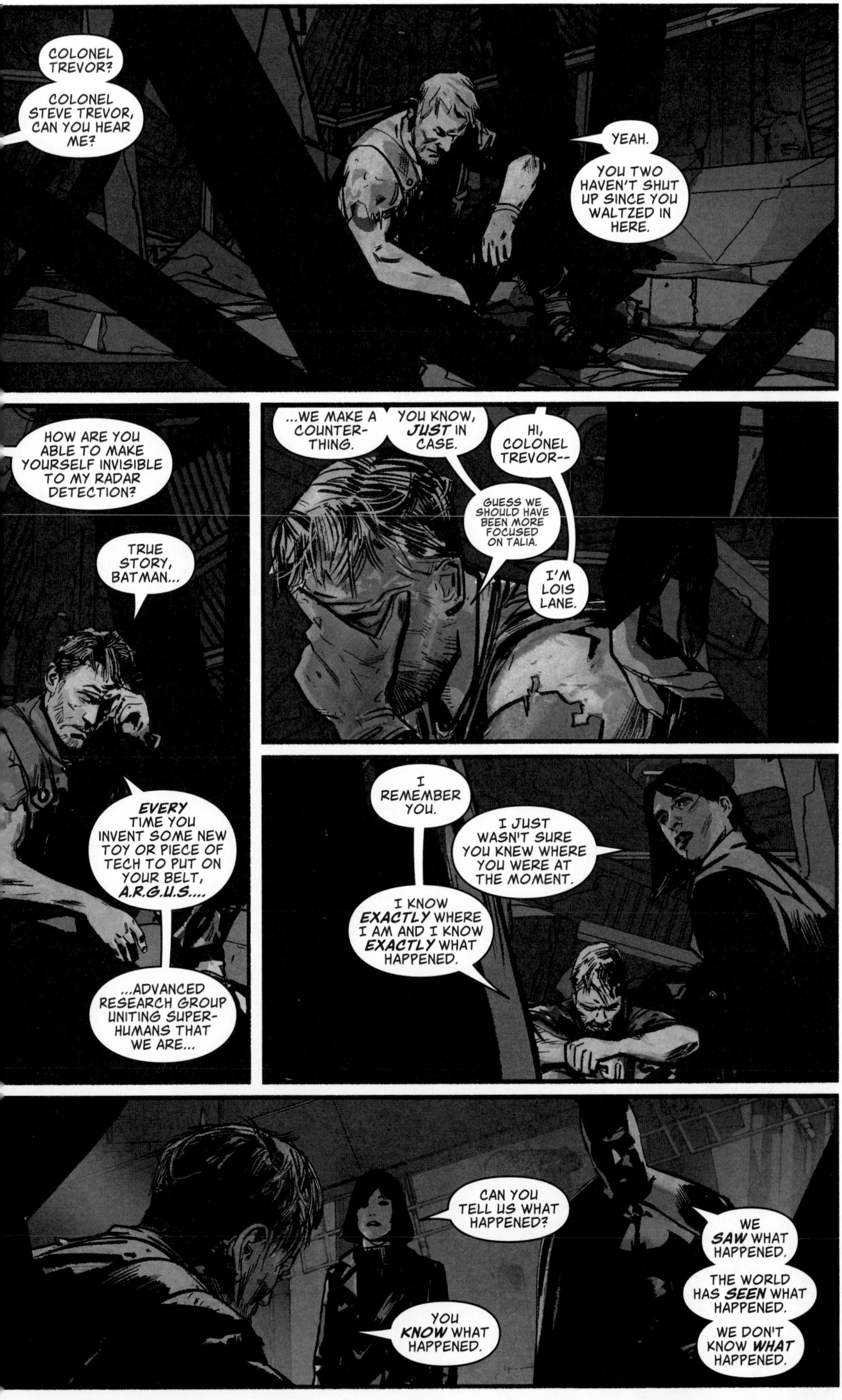

COLONEL TREVOR?
COLONEL STEVE TREVOR, CAN YOU HEAR ME?
YEAH.
YOU TWO HAVEN'T SHUT UP SINCE YOU WALTZED IN HERE.
HOW ARE YOU ABLE TO MAKE YOURSELF INVISIBLE TO MY RADAR DETECTION?
TRUE STORY, BATMAN...
EVERY TIME YOU INVENT SOME NEW TOY OR PIECE OF TECH TO PUT ON YOUR BELT, A.R.G.U.S....
...ADVANCED RESEARCH GROUP UNITING SUPER-HUMANS THAT WE ARE...
...WE MAKE A COUNTER-THING.
YOU KNOW, JUST IN CASE.
GUESS WE SHOULD HAVE BEEN MORE FOCUSED ON TALIA.
HI, COLONEL TREVOR--
I'M LOIS LANE.
I REMEMBER YOU.
I JUST WASN'T SURE YOU KNEW WHERE YOU WERE AT THE MOMENT.
I KNOW EXACTLY WHERE I AM AND I KNOW EXACTLY WHAT HAPPENED.
CAN YOU TELL US WHAT HAPPENED?
YOU KNOW WHAT HAPPENED.
WE SAW WHAT HAPPENED.
THE WORLD HAS SEEN WHAT HAPPENED.
WE DON'T KNOW WHAT HAPPENED.

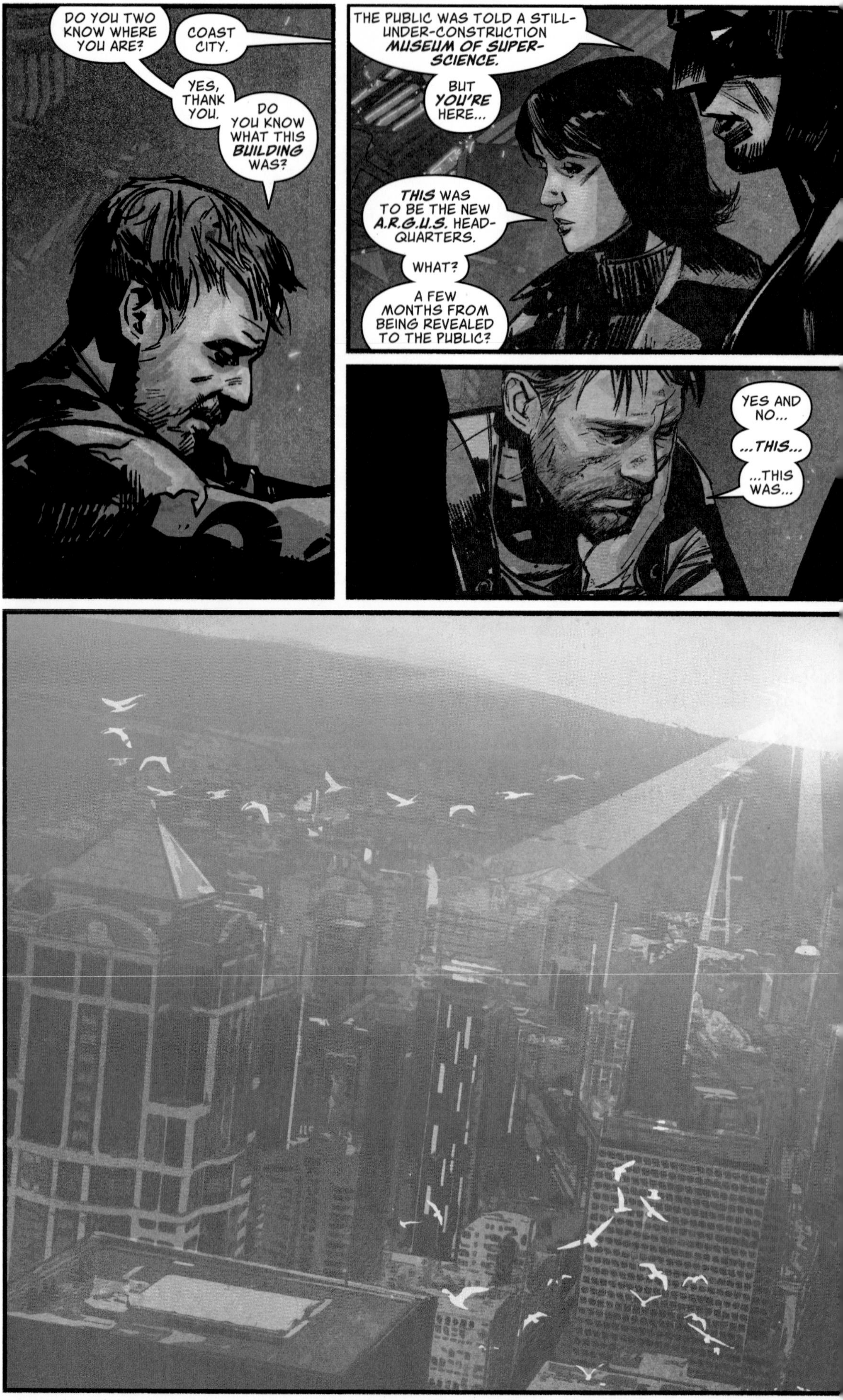
DO YOU TWO KNOW WHERE YOU ARE?
COAST CITY.
YES, THANK YOU.
DO YOU KNOW WHAT THIS BUILDING WAS?
THE PUBLIC WAS TOLD A STILL-UNDER-CONSTRUCTION MUSEUM OF SUPER-SCIENCE.
BUT YOU'RE HERE...
THIS WAS TO BE THE NEW A.R.G.U.S. HEAD-QUARTERS.
WHAT?
A FEW MONTHS FROM BEING REVEALED TO THE PUBLIC?
YES AND NO...
...THIS...
...THIS WAS...

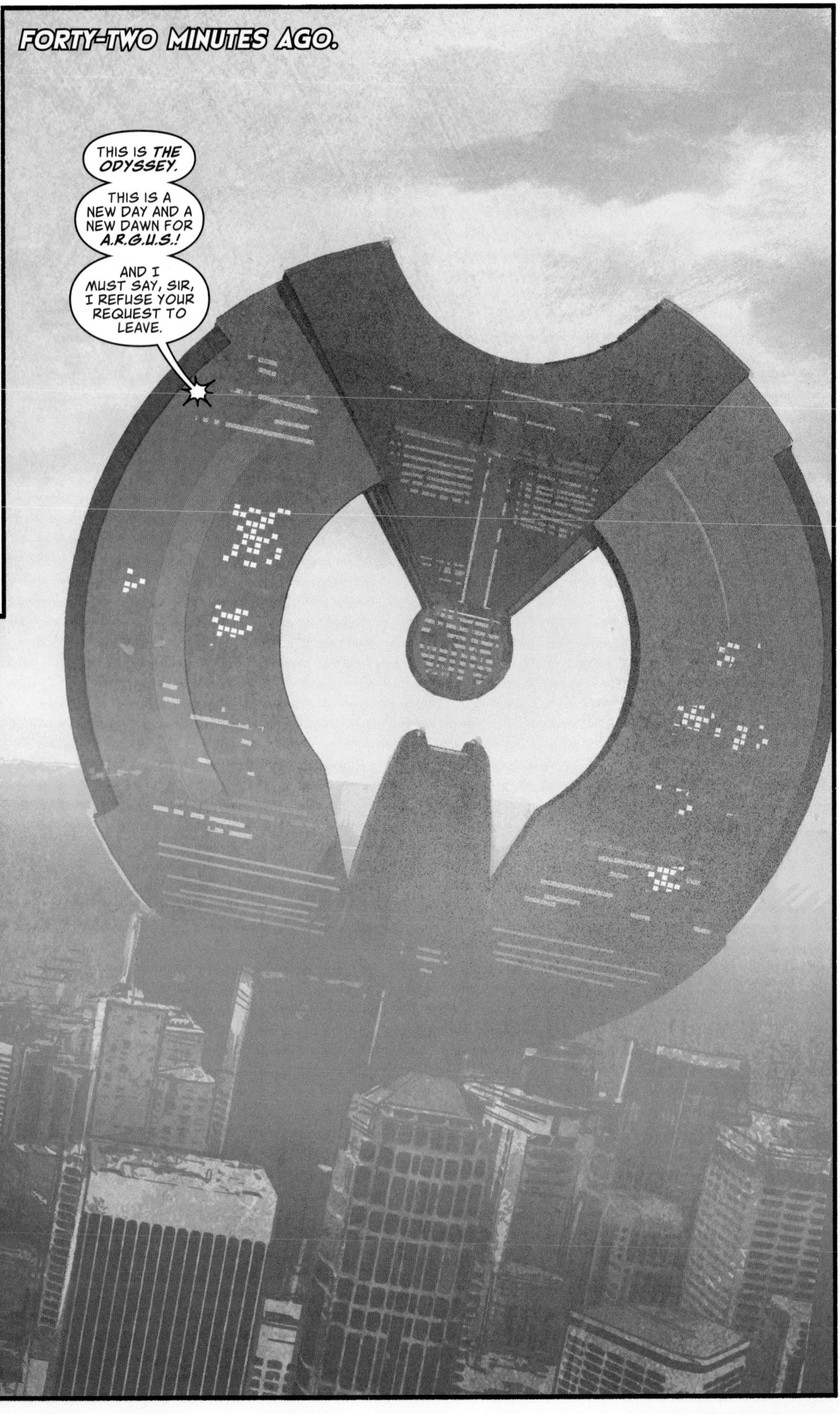
FORTY-TWO MINUTES AGO.
THIS IS *THE ODYSSEY.*
THIS IS A NEW DAY AND A NEW DAWN FOR *A.R.G.U.S.!*
AND I MUST SAY, SIR, I REFUSE YOUR REQUEST TO LEAVE.

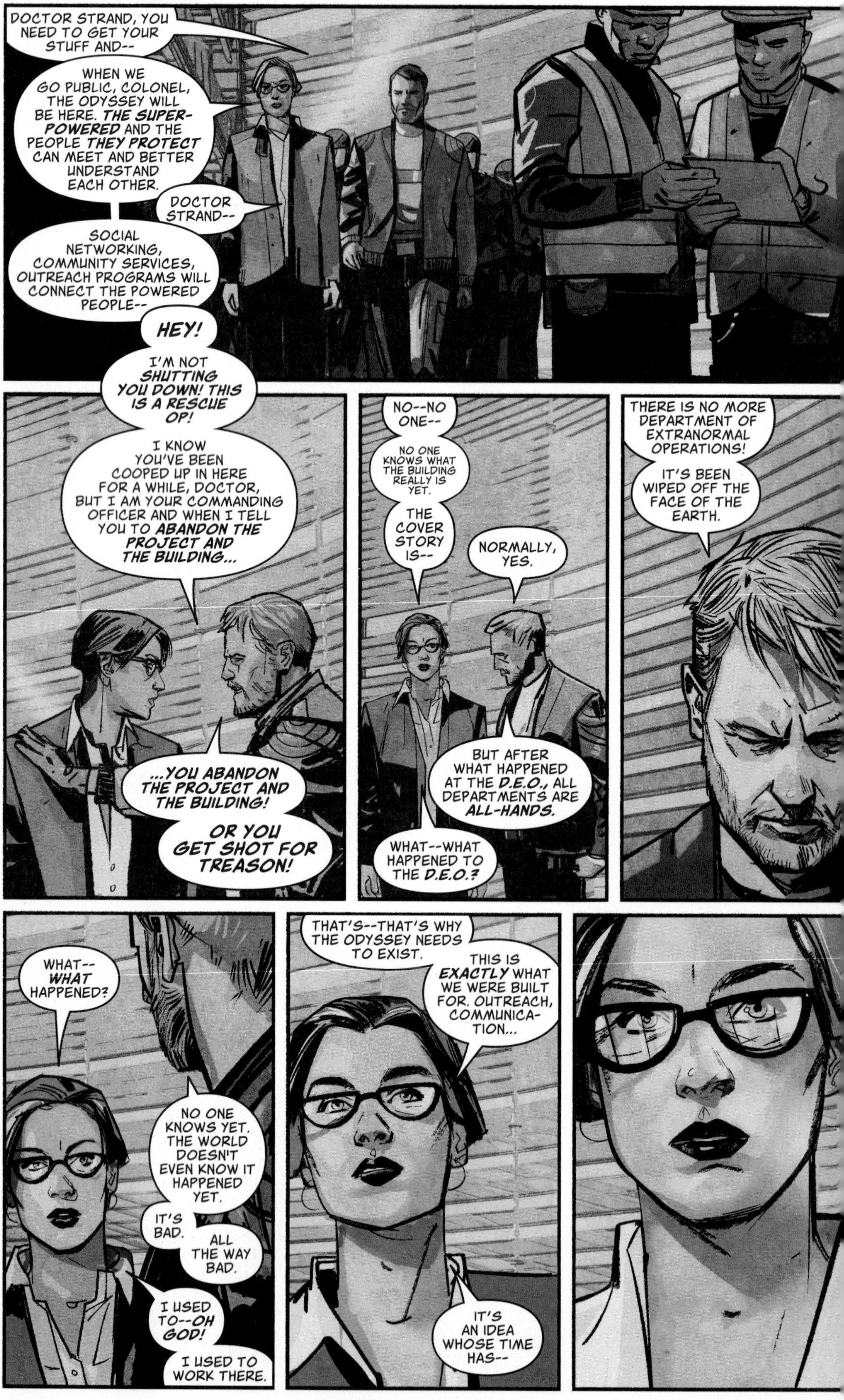

DOCTOR STRAND, YOU NEED TO GET YOUR STUFF AND--
WHEN WE GO PUBLIC, COLONEL, THE ODYSSEY WILL BE HERE. THE SUPER-POWERED AND THE PEOPLE THEY PROTECT CAN MEET AND BETTER UNDERSTAND EACH OTHER.
DOCTOR STRAND--
SOCIAL NETWORKING, COMMUNITY SERVICES, OUTREACH PROGRAMS WILL CONNECT THE POWERED PEOPLE--
HEY!
I'M NOT SHUTTING YOU DOWN! THIS IS A RESCUE OP!
I KNOW YOU'VE BEEN COOPED UP IN HERE FOR A WHILE, DOCTOR, BUT I AM YOUR COMMANDING OFFICER AND WHEN I TELL YOU TO ABANDON THE PROJECT AND THE BUILDING...
...YOU ABANDON THE PROJECT AND THE BUILDING!
OR YOU GET SHOT FOR TREASON!
NO--NO ONE--
NO ONE KNOWS WHAT THE BUILDING REALLY IS YET.
THE COVER STORY IS--
NORMALLY, YES.
BUT AFTER WHAT HAPPENED AT THE D.E.O., ALL DEPARTMENTS ARE ALL-HANDS.
WHAT--WHAT HAPPENED TO THE D.E.O.?
THERE IS NO MORE DEPARTMENT OF EXTRANORMAL OPERATIONS!
IT'S BEEN WIPED OFF THE FACE OF THE EARTH.
WHAT-- WHAT HAPPENED?
NO ONE KNOWS YET. THE WORLD DOESN'T EVEN KNOW IT HAPPENED YET.
IT'S BAD.
ALL THE WAY BAD.
I USED TO--OH GOD!
I USED TO WORK THERE.
THAT'S--THAT'S WHY THE ODYSSEY NEEDS TO EXIST.
THIS IS EXACTLY WHAT WE WERE BUILT FOR. OUTREACH, COMMUNICA-TION...
IT'S AN IDEA WHOSE TIME HAS--

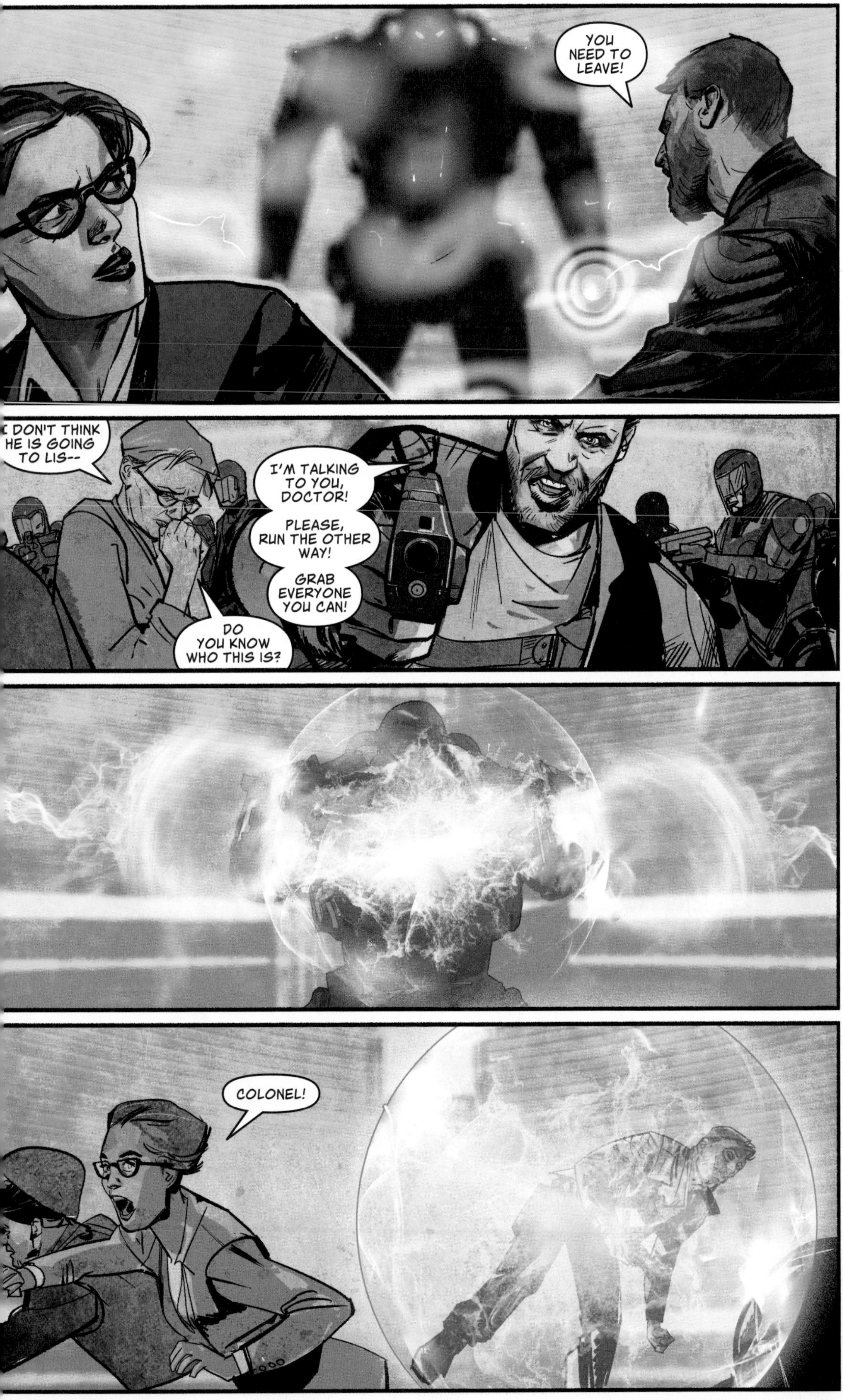
YOU NEED TO LEAVE!
I DON'T THINK HE IS GOING TO LIS--
I'M TALKING TO YOU, DOCTOR!
PLEASE, RUN THE OTHER WAY!
GRAB EVERYONE YOU CAN!
DO YOU KNOW WHO THIS IS?
COLONEL!

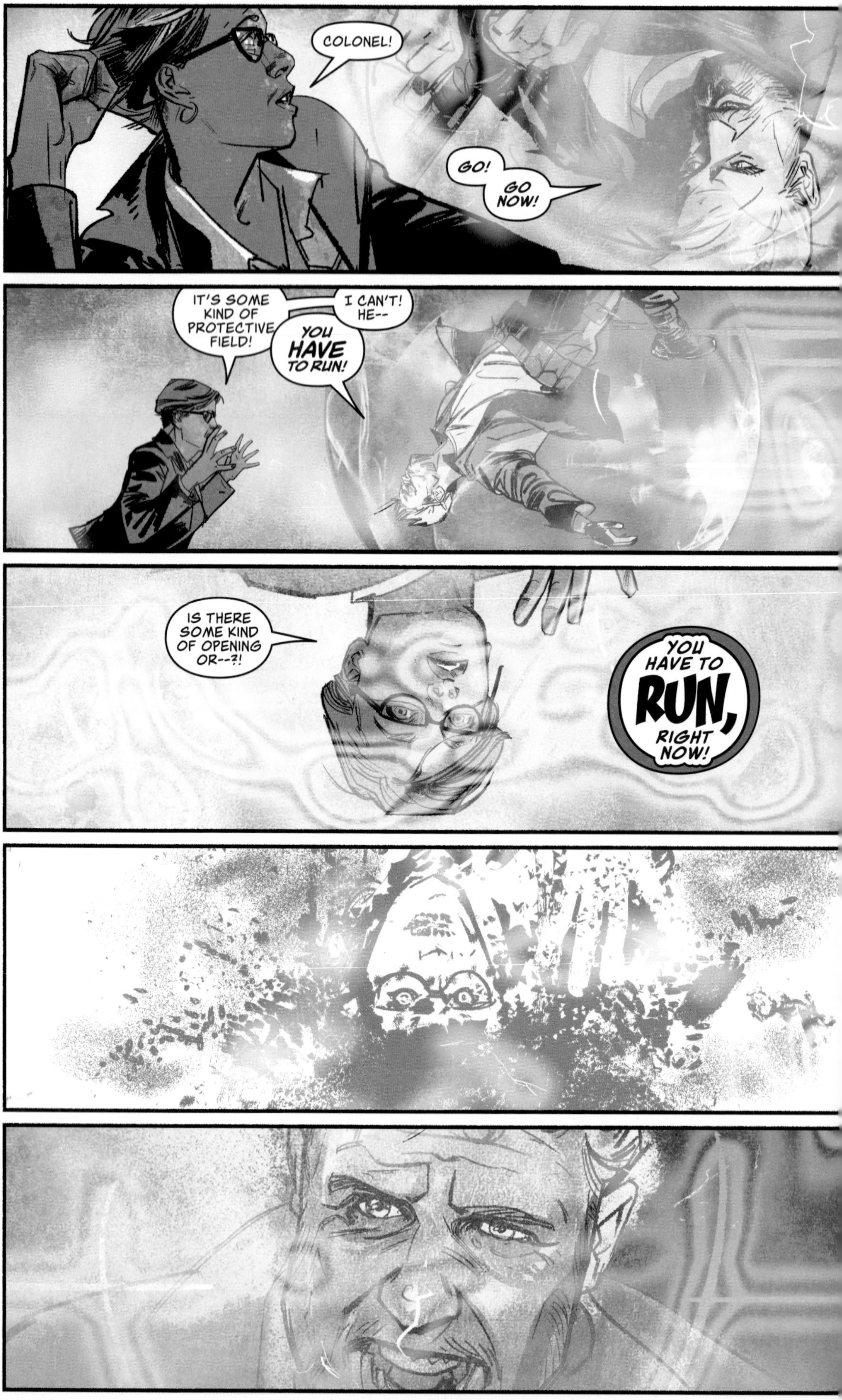
COLONEL!
GO! GO NOW!
IT'S SOME KIND OF PROTECTIVE FIELD!
I CAN'T! HE--
YOU HAVE TO RUN!
IS THERE SOME KIND OF OPENING OR--?!
YOU HAVE TO RUN, RIGHT NOW!

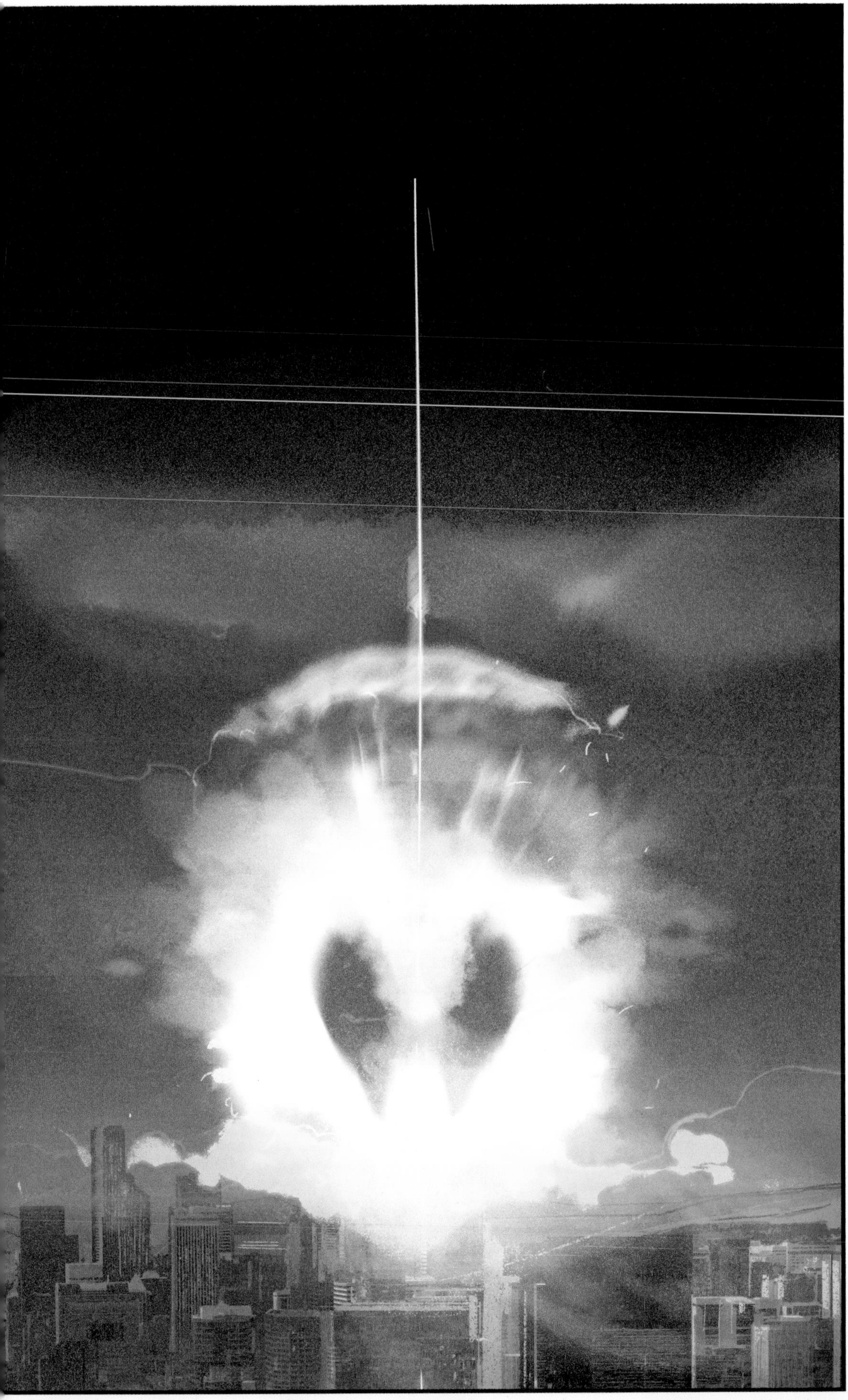

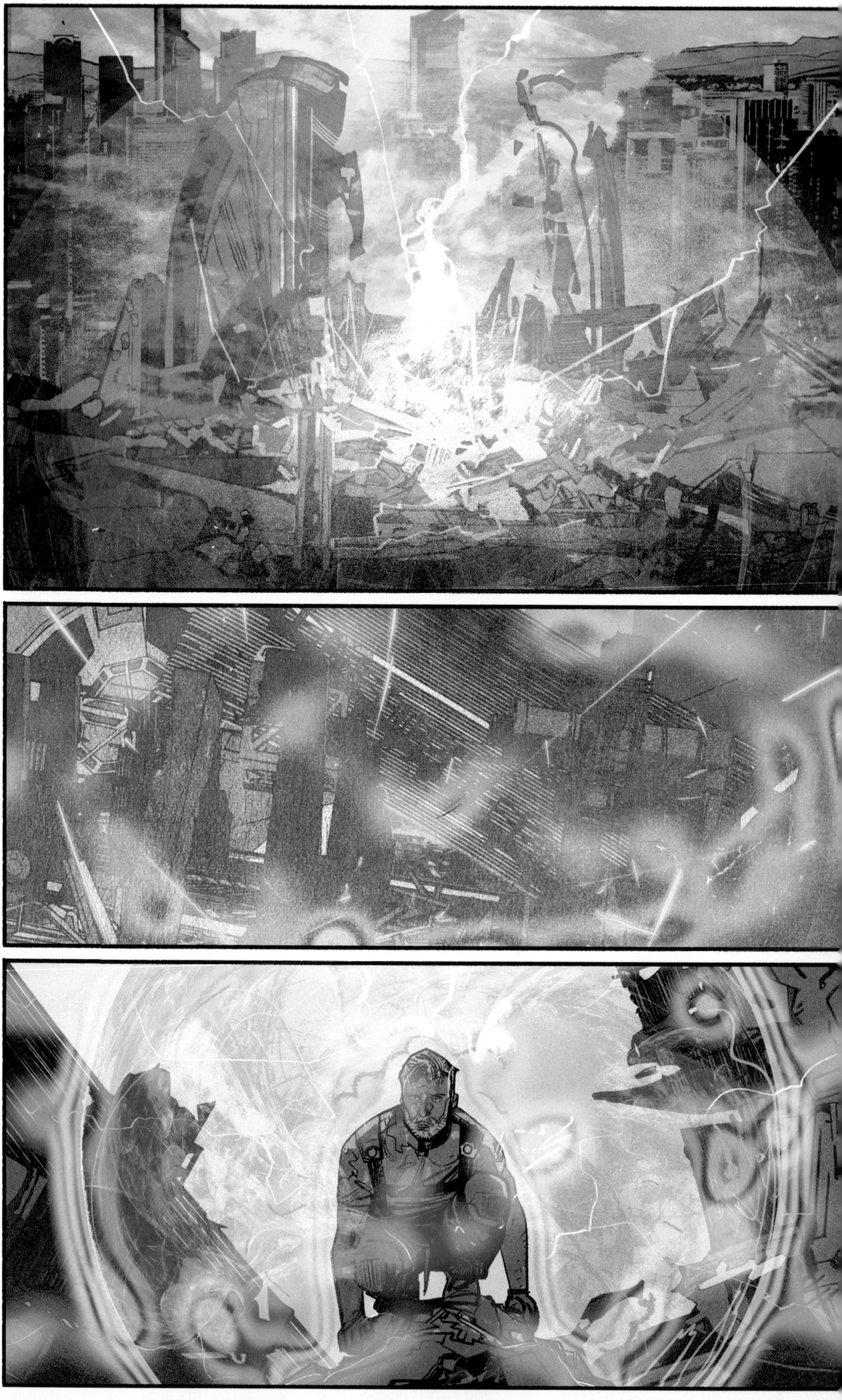

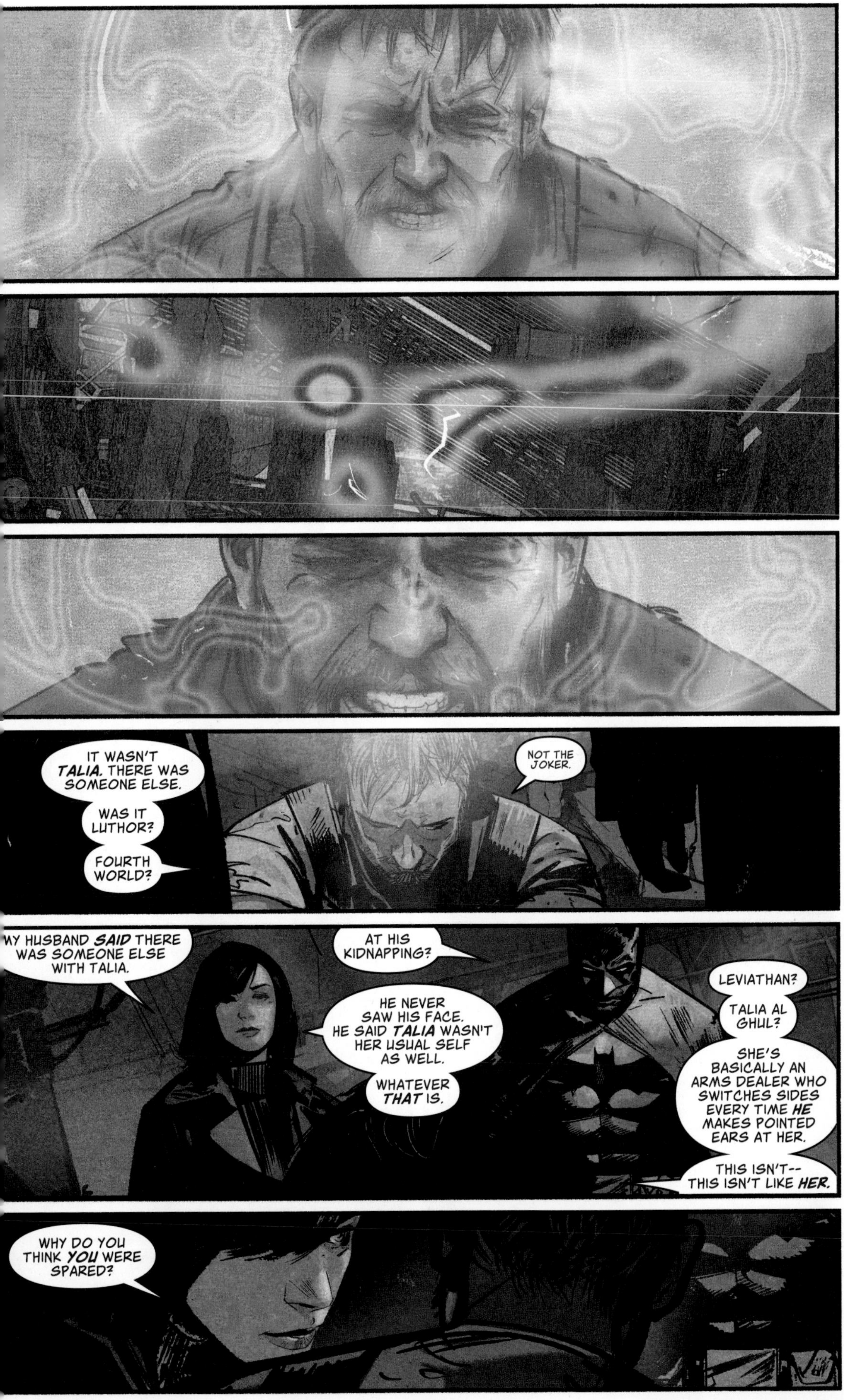
IT WASN'T TALIA. THERE WAS SOMEONE ELSE.
WAS IT LUTHOR?
FOURTH WORLD?
NOT THE JOKER.
MY HUSBAND SAID THERE WAS SOMEONE ELSE WITH TALIA.
AT HIS KIDNAPPING?
HE NEVER SAW HIS FACE. HE SAID TALIA WASN'T HER USUAL SELF AS WELL.
WHATEVER THAT IS.
LEVIATHAN?
TALIA AL GHUL?
SHE'S BASICALLY AN ARMS DEALER WHO SWITCHES SIDES EVERY TIME HE MAKES POINTED EARS AT HER.
THIS ISN'T-- THIS ISN'T LIKE HER.
WHY DO YOU THINK YOU WERE SPARED?

RIGHT *THIS* SECOND...

...DOESN'T FEEL LIKE I WAS.

YOU WERE LEFT TO BEAR WITNESS.

TO TELL THE STORY...

MY PUNISHMENT FOR "PAST SINS"?

WHAT SINS?

ASK TALIA AND ASK HER LEVIA--

NO.

NO.

DON'T YOU SEE?

I SURVIVED. *I AM LEVIATHAN.*

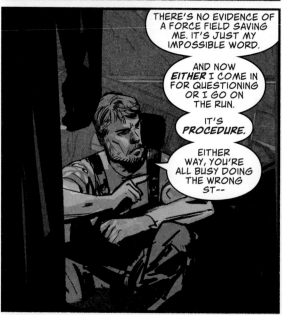

THERE'S NO EVIDENCE OF A FORCE FIELD SAVING ME. IT'S JUST MY IMPOSSIBLE WORD.

AND NOW *EITHER* I COME IN FOR QUESTIONING OR I GO ON THE RUN.

IT'S *PROCEDURE.*

EITHER WAY, YOU'RE ALL BUSY DOING THE WRONG ST--

--*OH!* BUT IT *CAN'T* BE ME.

IT'S *YOU*--

--YOU'RE LEVIATHAN, LOIS LANE.

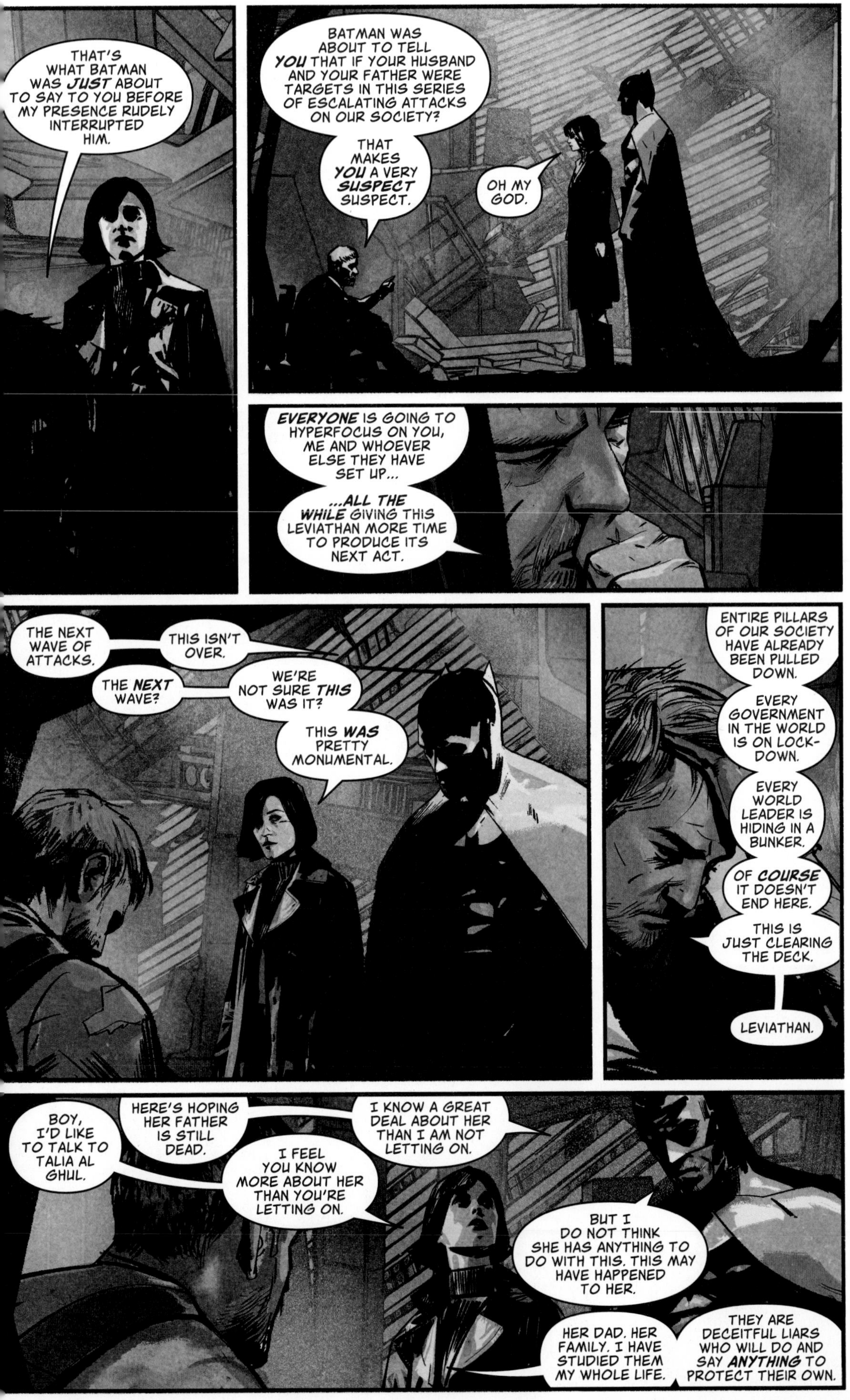
THAT'S WHAT BATMAN WAS JUST ABOUT TO SAY TO YOU BEFORE MY PRESENCE RUDELY INTERRUPTED HIM.
BATMAN WAS ABOUT TO TELL YOU THAT IF YOUR HUSBAND AND YOUR FATHER WERE TARGETS IN THIS SERIES OF ESCALATING ATTACKS ON OUR SOCIETY?
THAT MAKES YOU A VERY SUSPECT SUSPECT.
OH MY GOD.
EVERYONE IS GOING TO HYPERFOCUS ON YOU, ME AND WHOEVER ELSE THEY HAVE SET UP...
...ALL THE WHILE GIVING THIS LEVIATHAN MORE TIME TO PRODUCE ITS NEXT ACT.
THE NEXT WAVE OF ATTACKS.
THIS ISN'T OVER.
THE NEXT WAVE?
WE'RE NOT SURE THIS WAS IT?
THIS WAS PRETTY MONUMENTAL.
ENTIRE PILLARS OF OUR SOCIETY HAVE ALREADY BEEN PULLED DOWN.
EVERY GOVERNMENT IN THE WORLD IS ON LOCK-DOWN.
EVERY WORLD LEADER IS HIDING IN A BUNKER.
OF COURSE IT DOESN'T END HERE.
THIS IS JUST CLEARING THE DECK.
LEVIATHAN.
BOY, I'D LIKE TO TALK TO TALIA AL GHUL.
HERE'S HOPING HER FATHER IS STILL DEAD.
I FEEL YOU KNOW MORE ABOUT HER THAN YOU'RE LETTING ON.
I KNOW A GREAT DEAL ABOUT HER THAN I AM NOT LETTING ON.
BUT I DO NOT THINK SHE HAS ANYTHING TO DO WITH THIS. THIS MAY HAVE HAPPENED TO HER.
HER DAD. HER FAMILY. I HAVE STUDIED THEM MY WHOLE LIFE.
THEY ARE DECEITFUL LIARS WHO WILL DO AND SAY ANYTHING TO PROTECT THEIR OWN.

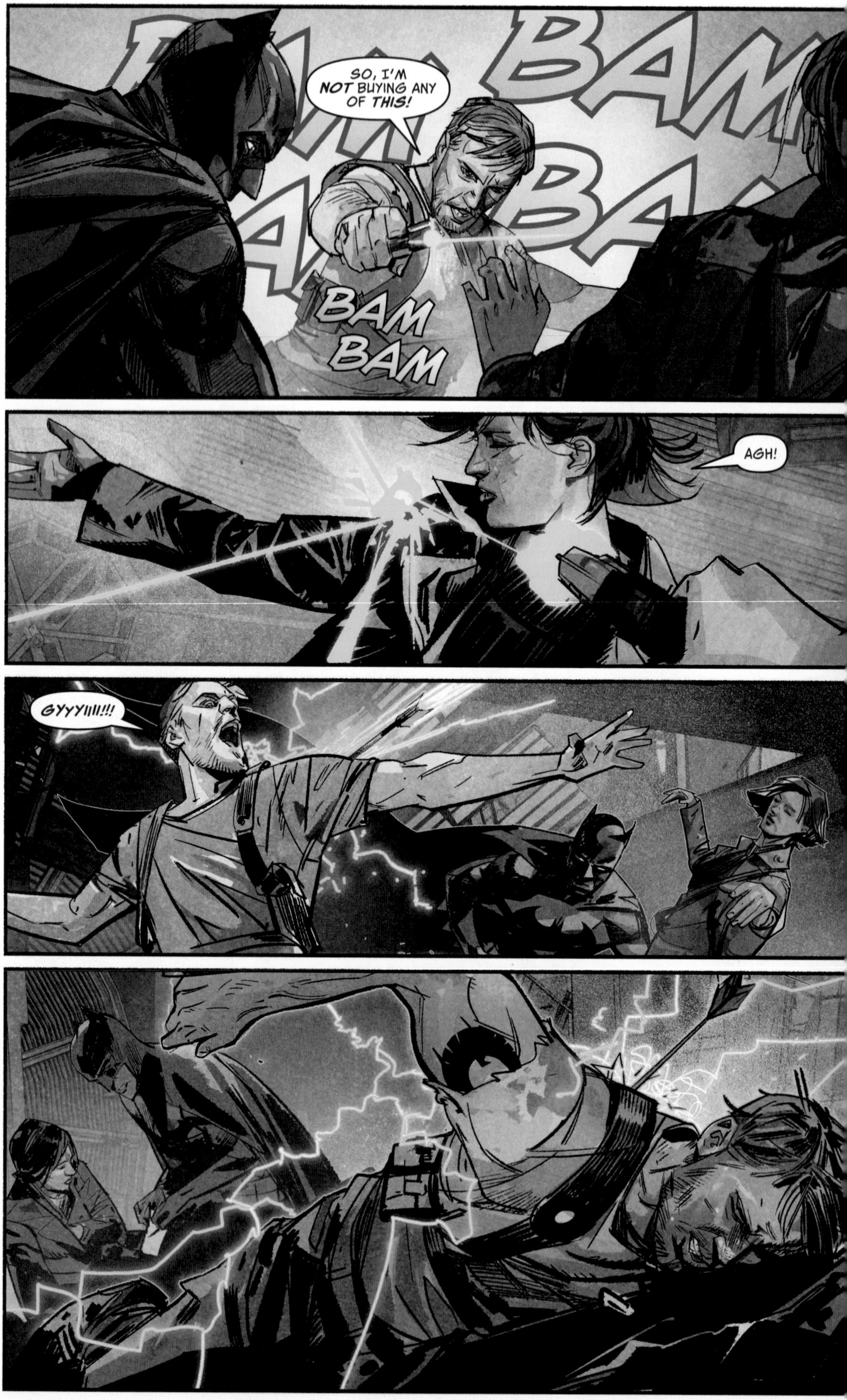
BAM
SO, I'M NOT BUYING ANY OF THIS!
BAM BAM
AGH!
GYYIIII!!!

TASER ARROW. STAY DOWN, STEVE.

OH, AND, UH, DON'T TOUCH HIM FOR THREE MINUTES.

HIT HIM *AGAIN!*

NO, GREEN ARROW. HE'S NOT A SUSPECT.

I DON'T THINK HE'S THE GUY EITHER, BUT HE JUST ACTED *REALLY GUILTY* AND EITHER WAY--

THIS HAPPENED ON YOUR WATCH, TREVOR!

STEVE TREVOR WAS RIGHT.

DAMN IT!

THIS CRIME SCENE...THE ENTIRE THING...IS IMMACULATE.

THE DESTRUCTION CLEANED ITSELF OF ANY AND ALL SIGNATURE, CLUE OR DETAIL AS IT WENT.

SO YOU DON'T *KNOW* ANYTHING.

I KNOW THIS *MASSIVE* CRIME SCENE IS IMMACULATE...

THAT IN ITSELF... IS A CLUE.

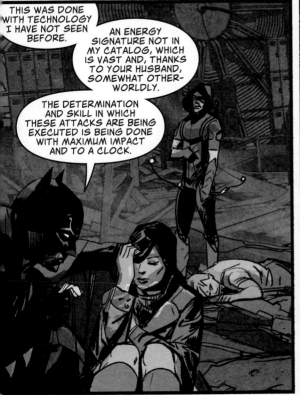

THIS WAS DONE WITH TECHNOLOGY I HAVE NOT SEEN BEFORE.

AN ENERGY SIGNATURE NOT IN MY CATALOG, WHICH IS VAST AND, THANKS TO YOUR HUSBAND, SOMEWHAT OTHER-WORLDLY.

THE DETERMINATION AND SKILL IN WHICH THESE ATTACKS ARE BEING EXECUTED IS BEING DONE WITH MAXIMUM IMPACT AND TO A CLOCK.

AND ON *OUR* COLLECTIVE WATCH.

OUR WATCH.

ATTACKS PLANNED TO TRIGGER THOSE LEFT BEHIND TO *TURN* ON EACH OTHER.

TO ACCUSE.

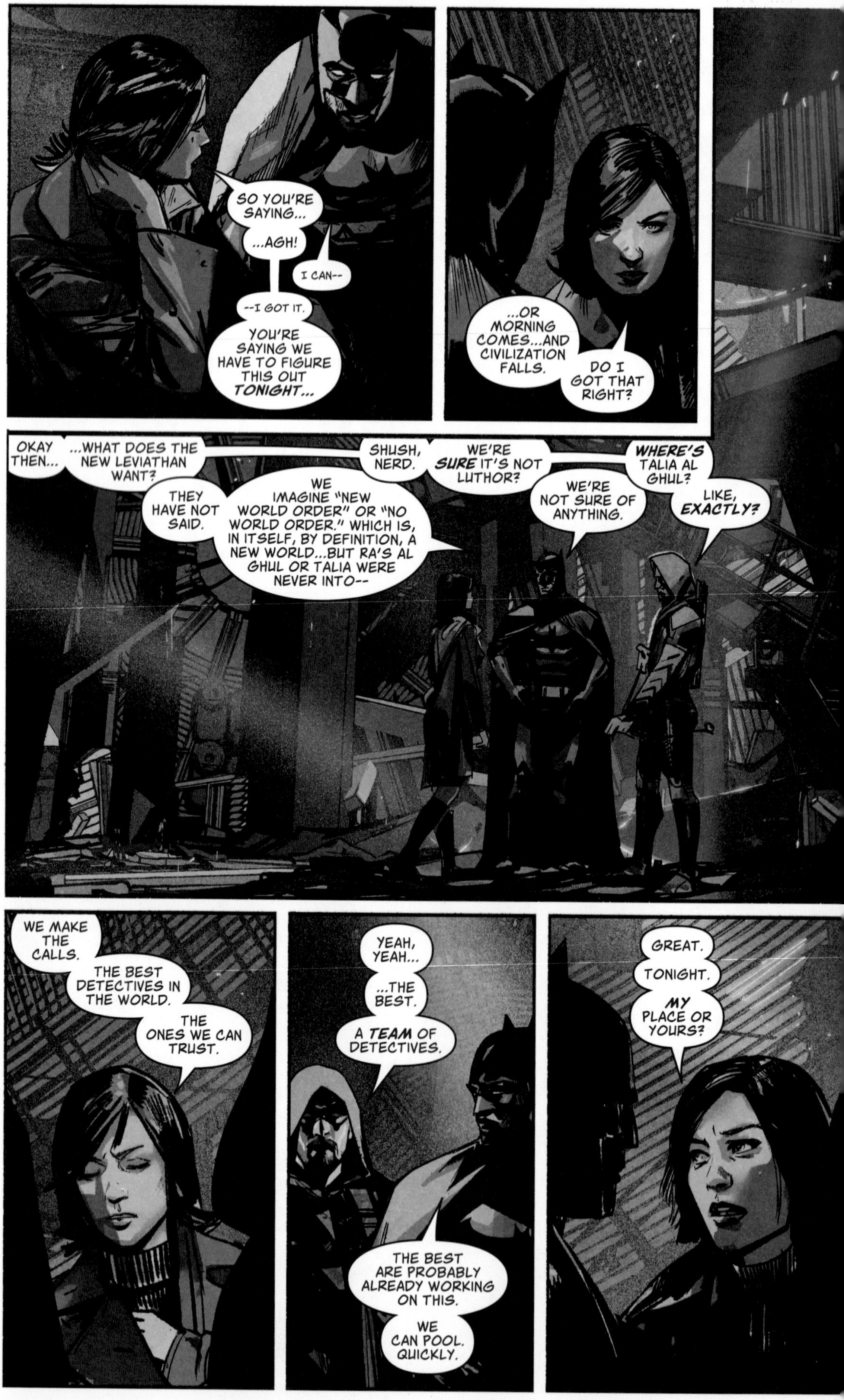
SO YOU'RE SAYING...
...AGH!
I CAN--
--I GOT IT.
YOU'RE SAYING WE HAVE TO FIGURE THIS OUT TONIGHT...
...OR MORNING COMES...AND CIVILIZATION FALLS.
DO I GOT THAT RIGHT?
OKAY THEN...
...WHAT DOES THE NEW LEVIATHAN WANT?
THEY HAVE NOT SAID.
WE IMAGINE "NEW WORLD ORDER" OR "NO WORLD ORDER." WHICH IS, IN ITSELF, BY DEFINITION, A NEW WORLD...BUT RA'S AL GHUL OR TALIA WERE NEVER INTO--
SHUSH, NERD.
WE'RE SURE IT'S NOT LUTHOR?
WE'RE NOT SURE OF ANYTHING.
WHERE'S TALIA AL GHUL?
LIKE, EXACTLY?
WE MAKE THE CALLS.
THE BEST DETECTIVES IN THE WORLD.
THE ONES WE CAN TRUST.
YEAH, YEAH...
...THE BEST.
A TEAM OF DETECTIVES.
THE BEST ARE PROBABLY ALREADY WORKING ON THIS.
WE CAN POOL. QUICKLY.
GREAT.
TONIGHT.
MY PLACE OR YOURS?

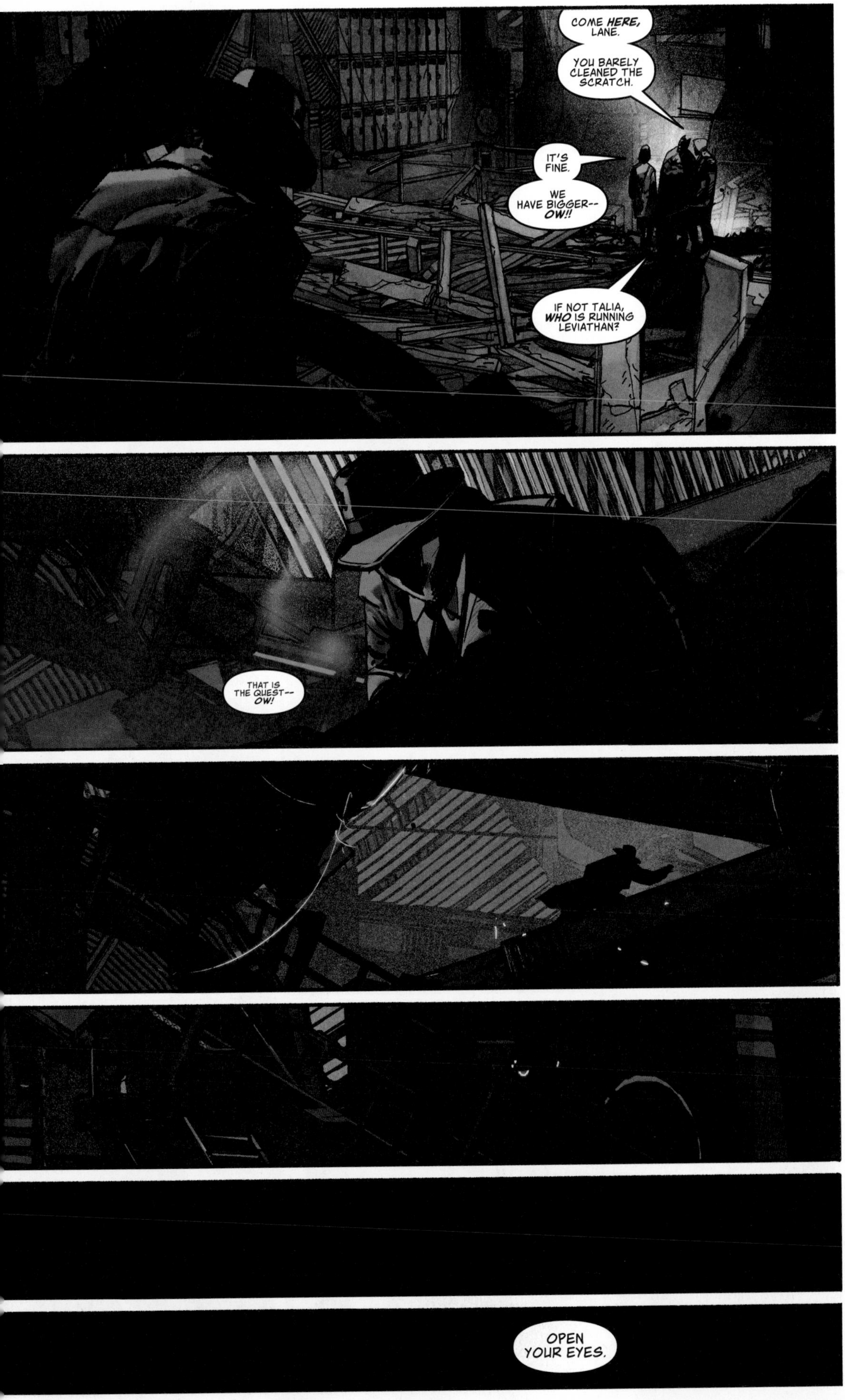
COME HERE, LANE.
YOU BARELY CLEANED THE SCRATCH.
IT'S FINE.
WE HAVE BIGGER-- OW!!
IF NOT TALIA, WHO IS RUNNING LEVIATHAN?
THAT IS THE QUEST-- OW!
OPEN YOUR EYES.

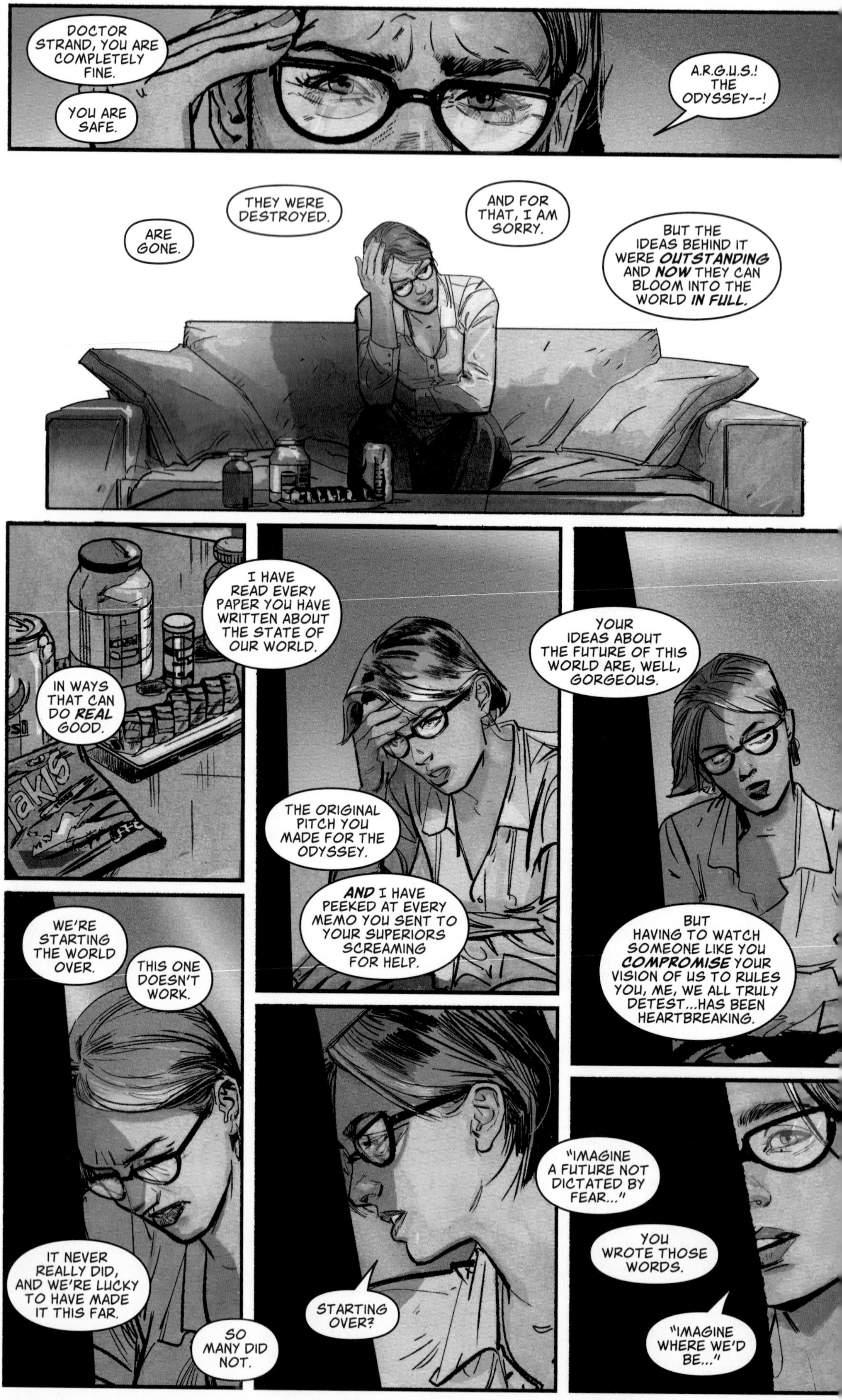

DOCTOR STRAND, YOU ARE COMPLETELY FINE.
YOU ARE SAFE.
A.R.G.U.S.! THE ODYSSEY--!
ARE GONE.
THEY WERE DESTROYED.
AND FOR THAT, I AM SORRY.
BUT THE IDEAS BEHIND IT WERE **OUTSTANDING** AND **NOW** THEY CAN BLOOM INTO THE WORLD **IN FULL.**
IN WAYS THAT CAN DO **REAL** GOOD.
I HAVE READ EVERY PAPER YOU HAVE WRITTEN ABOUT THE STATE OF OUR WORLD.
THE ORIGINAL PITCH YOU MADE FOR THE ODYSSEY.
AND I HAVE PEEKED AT EVERY MEMO YOU SENT TO YOUR SUPERIORS SCREAMING FOR HELP.
YOUR IDEAS ABOUT THE FUTURE OF THIS WORLD ARE, WELL, GORGEOUS.
BUT HAVING TO WATCH SOMEONE LIKE YOU **COMPROMISE** YOUR VISION OF US TO RULES YOU, ME, WE ALL TRULY DETEST...HAS BEEN HEARTBREAKING.
WE'RE STARTING THE WORLD OVER.
THIS ONE DOESN'T WORK.
IT NEVER REALLY DID, AND WE'RE LUCKY TO HAVE MADE IT THIS FAR.
SO MANY DID NOT.
STARTING OVER?
"IMAGINE A FUTURE NOT DICTATED BY FEAR..."
YOU WROTE THOSE WORDS.
"IMAGINE WHERE WE'D BE..."

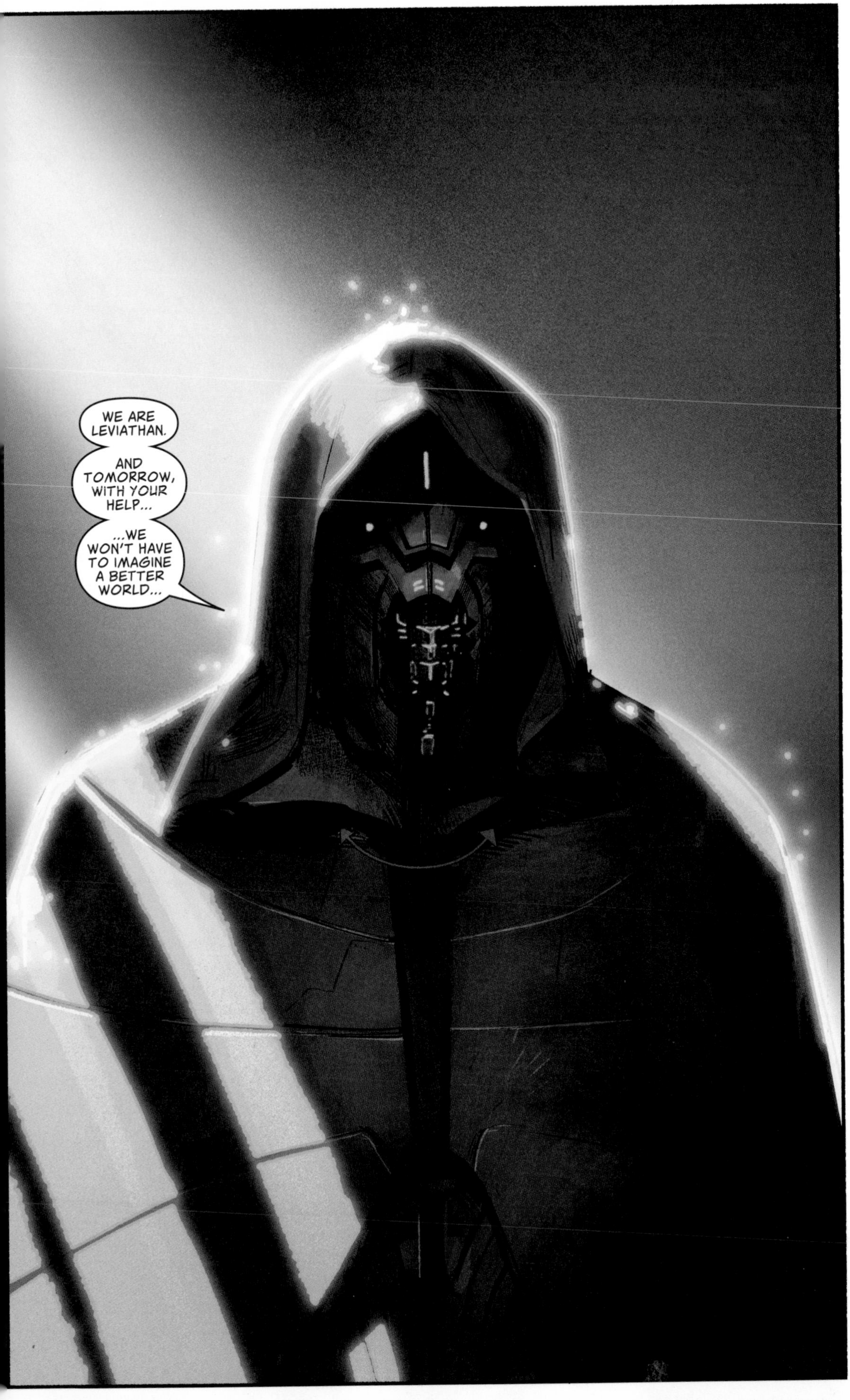
WE ARE LEVIATHAN.
AND TOMORROW, WITH YOUR HELP...
...WE WON'T HAVE TO IMAGINE A BETTER WORLD...

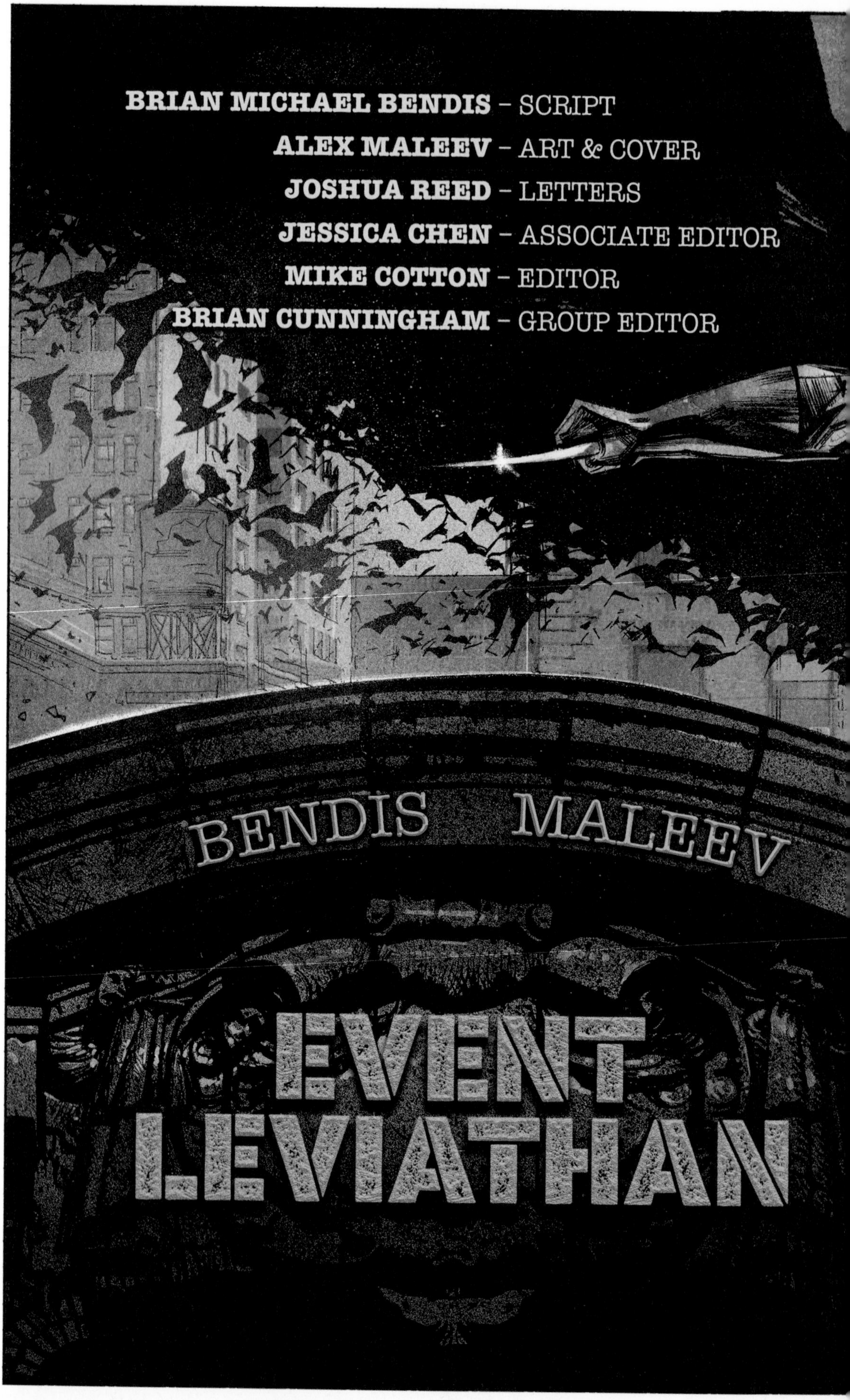
BRIAN MICHAEL BENDIS - SCRIPT
ALEX MALEEV - ART & COVER
JOSHUA REED - LETTERS
JESSICA CHEN - ASSOCIATE EDITOR
MIKE COTTON - EDITOR
BRIAN CUNNINGHAM - GROUP EDITOR
BENDIS MALEEV
EVENT LEVIATHAN

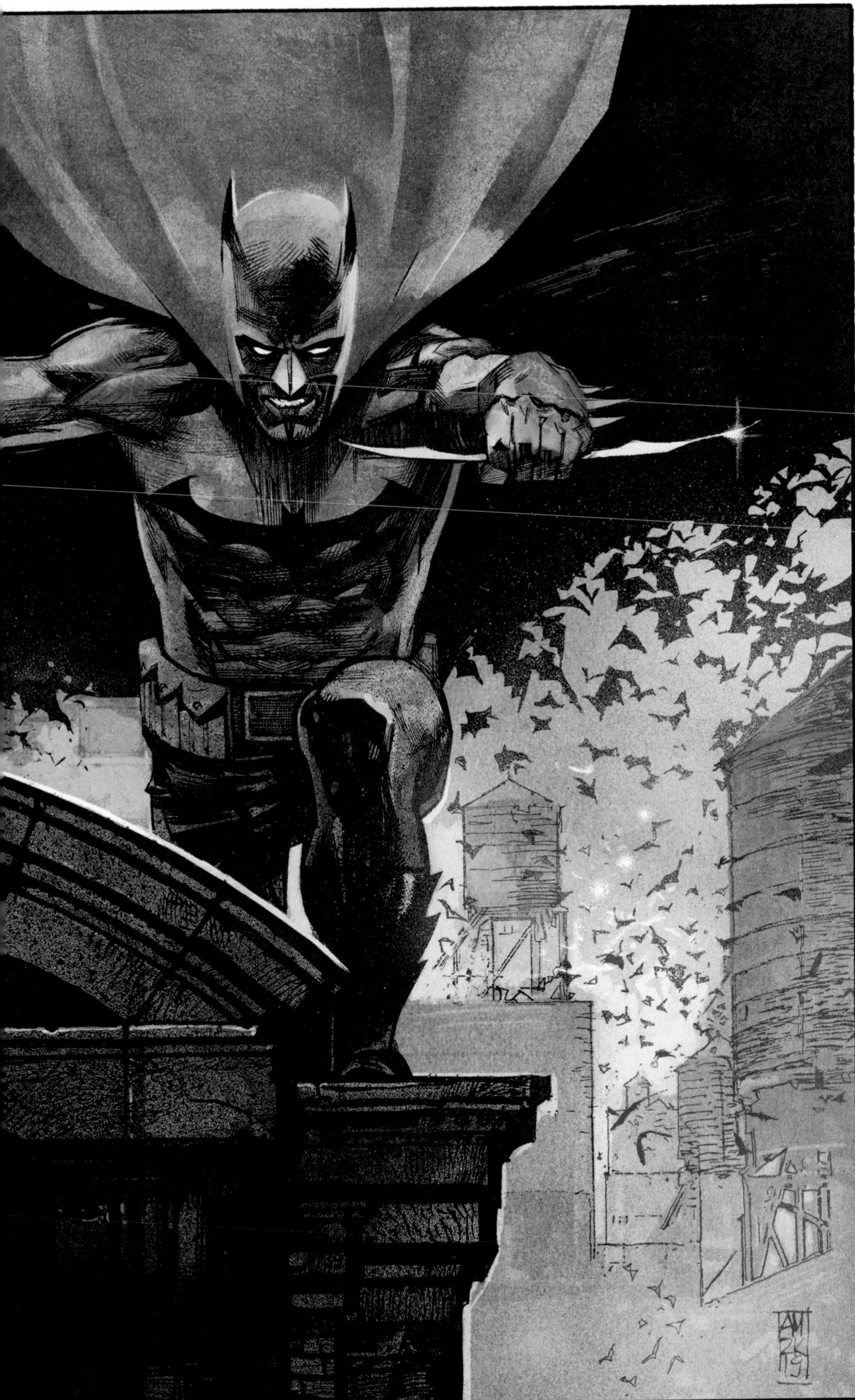

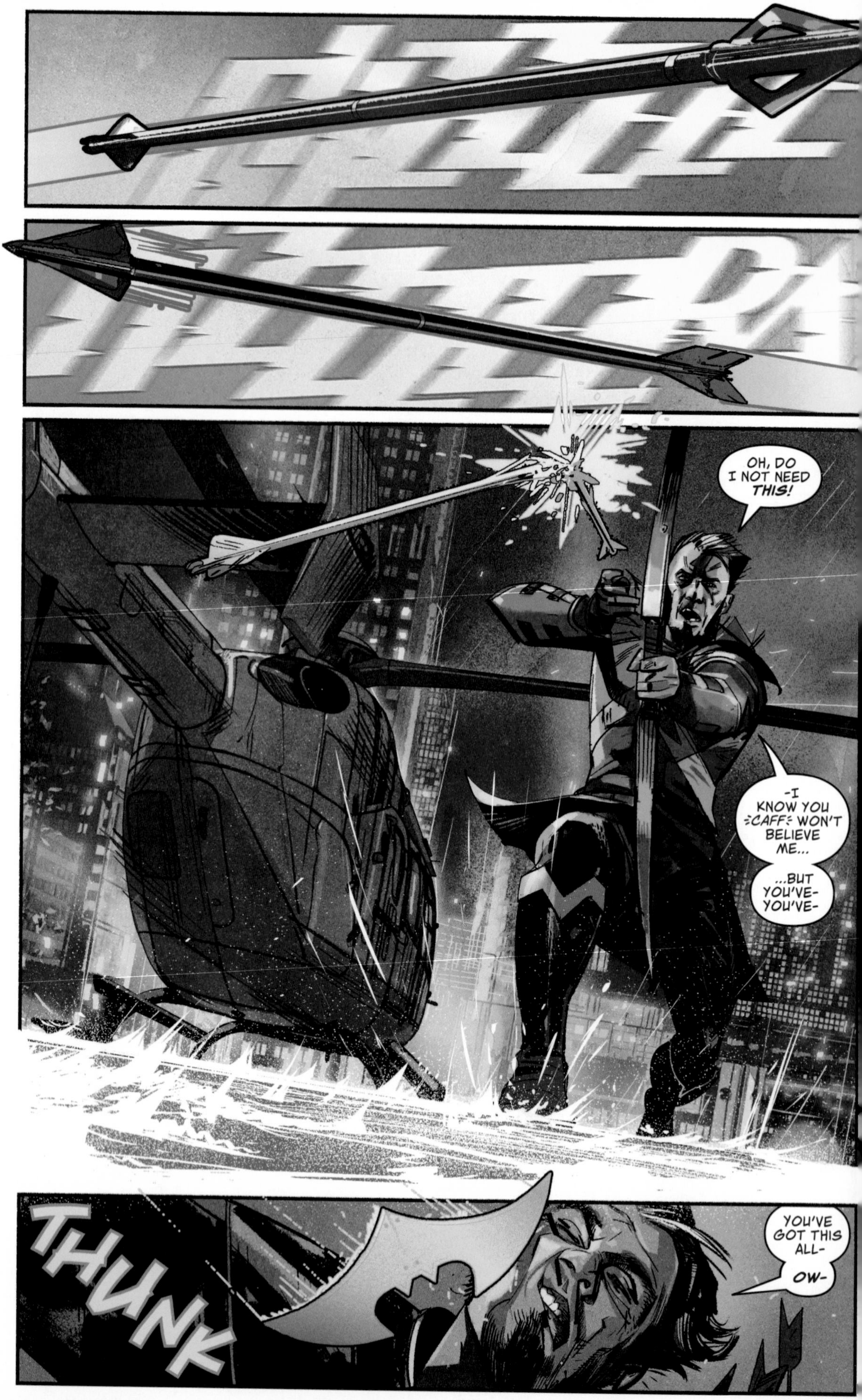
OH, DO I NOT NEED *THIS!*
-I KNOW YOU =CAFF= WON'T BELIEVE ME...
...BUT YOU'VE- YOU'VE-
THUNK
YOU'VE GOT THIS ALL-
OW-

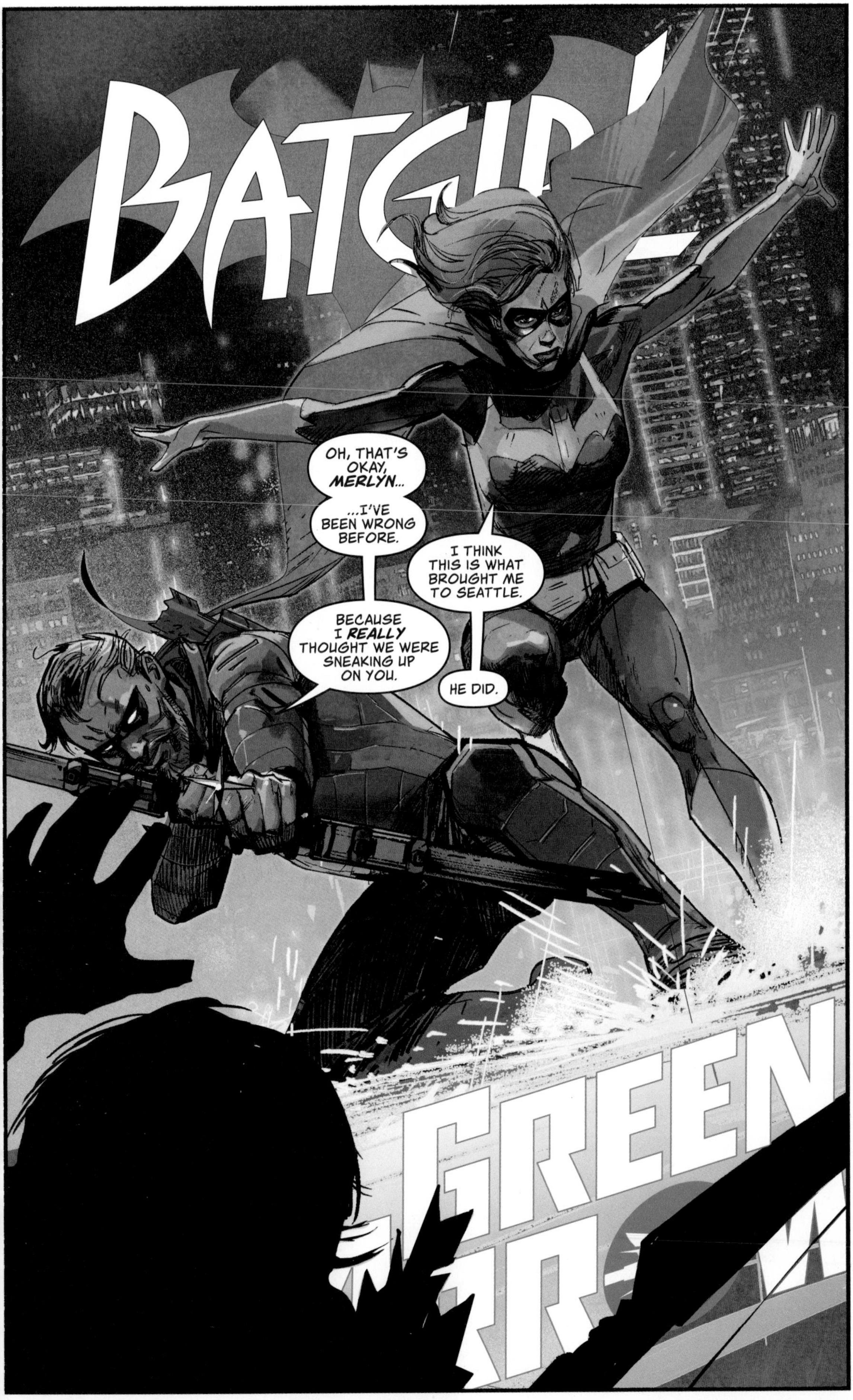

BATGIRL
OH, THAT'S OKAY, MERLYN...
...I'VE BEEN WRONG BEFORE.
BECAUSE I REALLY THOUGHT WE WERE SNEAKING UP ON YOU.
I THINK THIS IS WHAT BROUGHT ME TO SEATTLE.
HE DID.
GREEN

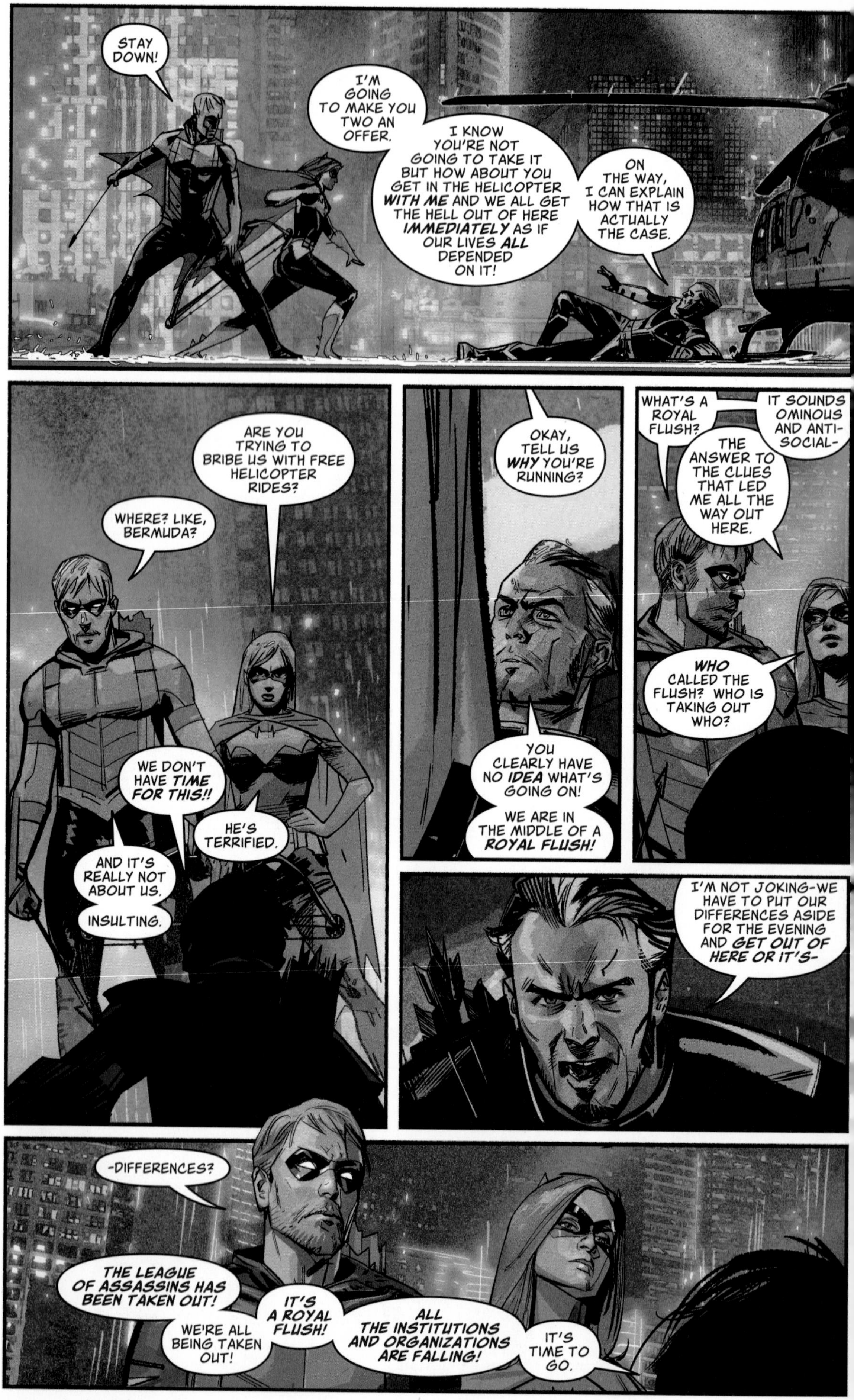
STAY DOWN!
I'M GOING TO MAKE YOU TWO AN OFFER.
I KNOW YOU'RE NOT GOING TO TAKE IT BUT HOW ABOUT YOU GET IN THE HELICOPTER WITH ME AND WE ALL GET THE HELL OUT OF HERE IMMEDIATELY AS IF OUR LIVES ALL DEPENDED ON IT!
ON THE WAY, I CAN EXPLAIN HOW THAT IS ACTUALLY THE CASE.
ARE YOU TRYING TO BRIBE US WITH FREE HELICOPTER RIDES?
WHERE? LIKE, BERMUDA?
WE DON'T HAVE TIME FOR THIS!!
HE'S TERRIFIED.
AND IT'S REALLY NOT ABOUT US.
INSULTING.
OKAY, TELL US WHY YOU'RE RUNNING?
YOU CLEARLY HAVE NO IDEA WHAT'S GOING ON!
WE ARE IN THE MIDDLE OF A ROYAL FLUSH!
WHAT'S A ROYAL FLUSH?
IT SOUNDS OMINOUS AND ANTI-SOCIAL-
THE ANSWER TO THE CLUES THAT LED ME ALL THE WAY OUT HERE.
WHO CALLED THE FLUSH? WHO IS TAKING OUT WHO?
I'M NOT JOKING-WE HAVE TO PUT OUR DIFFERENCES ASIDE FOR THE EVENING AND GET OUT OF HERE OR IT'S-
-DIFFERENCES?
THE LEAGUE OF ASSASSINS HAS BEEN TAKEN OUT!
WE'RE ALL BEING TAKEN OUT!
IT'S A ROYAL FLUSH!
ALL THE INSTITUTIONS AND ORGANIZATIONS ARE FALLING!
IT'S TIME TO GO.

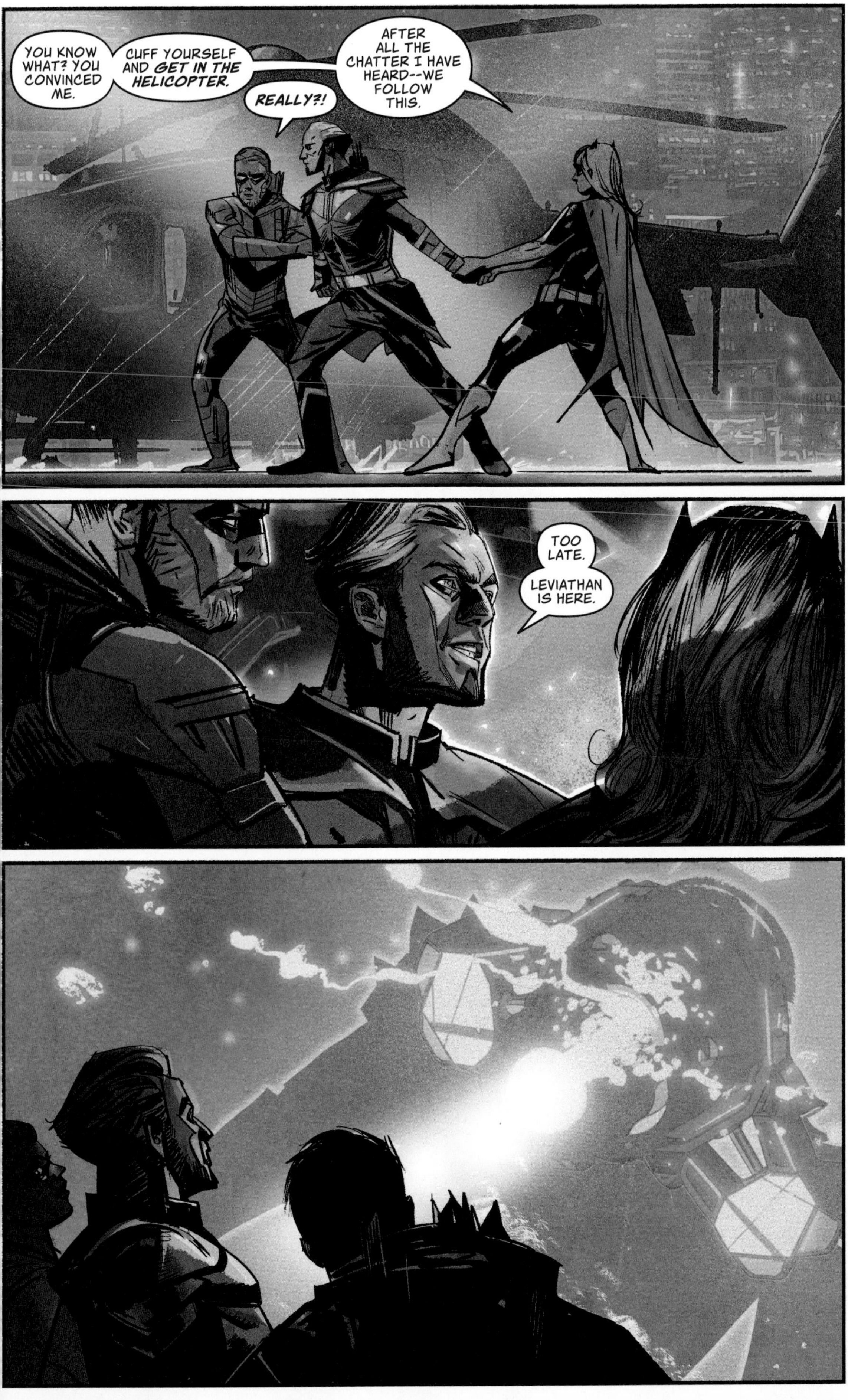
YOU KNOW WHAT? YOU CONVINCED ME.
CUFF YOURSELF AND GET IN THE HELICOPTER.
REALLY?!
AFTER ALL THE CHATTER I HAVE HEARD--WE FOLLOW THIS.
TOO LATE.
LEVIATHAN IS HERE.

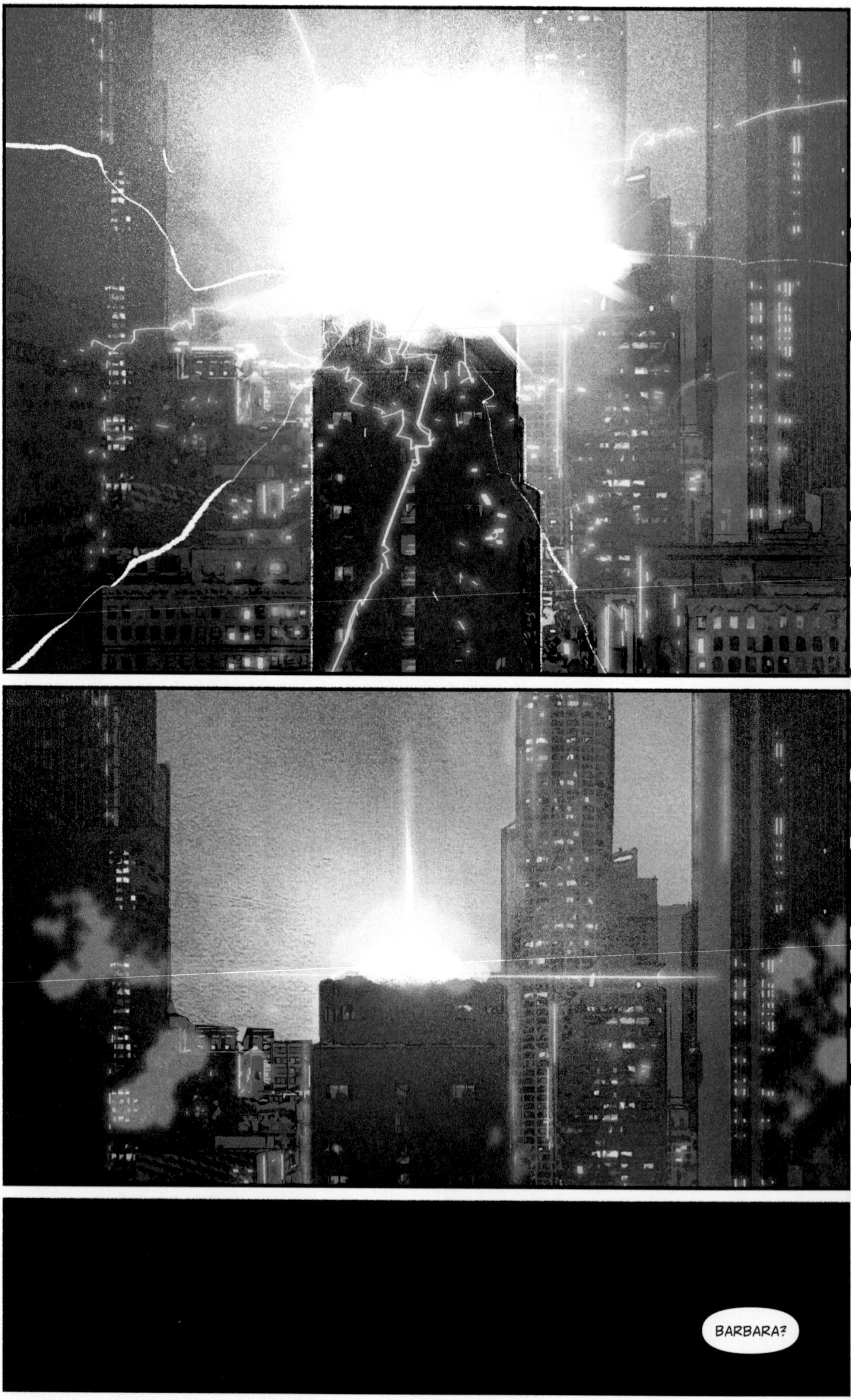
BARBARA?

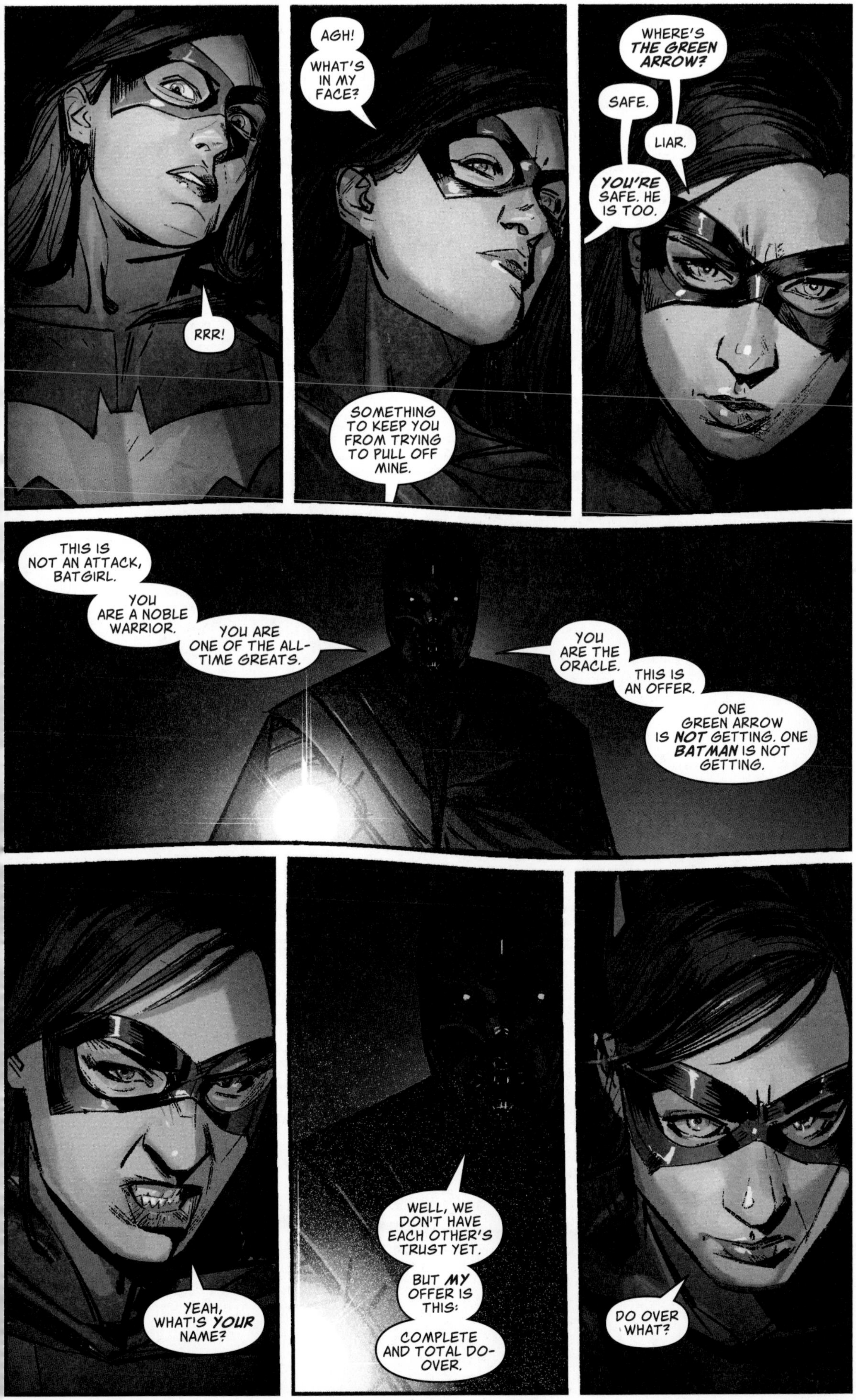
RRR!
AGH!
WHAT'S IN MY FACE?
SOMETHING TO KEEP YOU FROM TRYING TO PULL OFF MINE.
WHERE'S THE GREEN ARROW?
SAFE.
LIAR.
YOU'RE SAFE. HE IS TOO.
THIS IS NOT AN ATTACK, BATGIRL.
YOU ARE A NOBLE WARRIOR.
YOU ARE ONE OF THE ALL-TIME GREATS.
YOU ARE THE ORACLE.
THIS IS AN OFFER.
ONE GREEN ARROW IS NOT GETTING. ONE BATMAN IS NOT GETTING.
YEAH, WHAT'S YOUR NAME?
WELL, WE DON'T HAVE EACH OTHER'S TRUST YET.
BUT MY OFFER IS THIS:
COMPLETE AND TOTAL DO-OVER.
DO OVER WHAT?

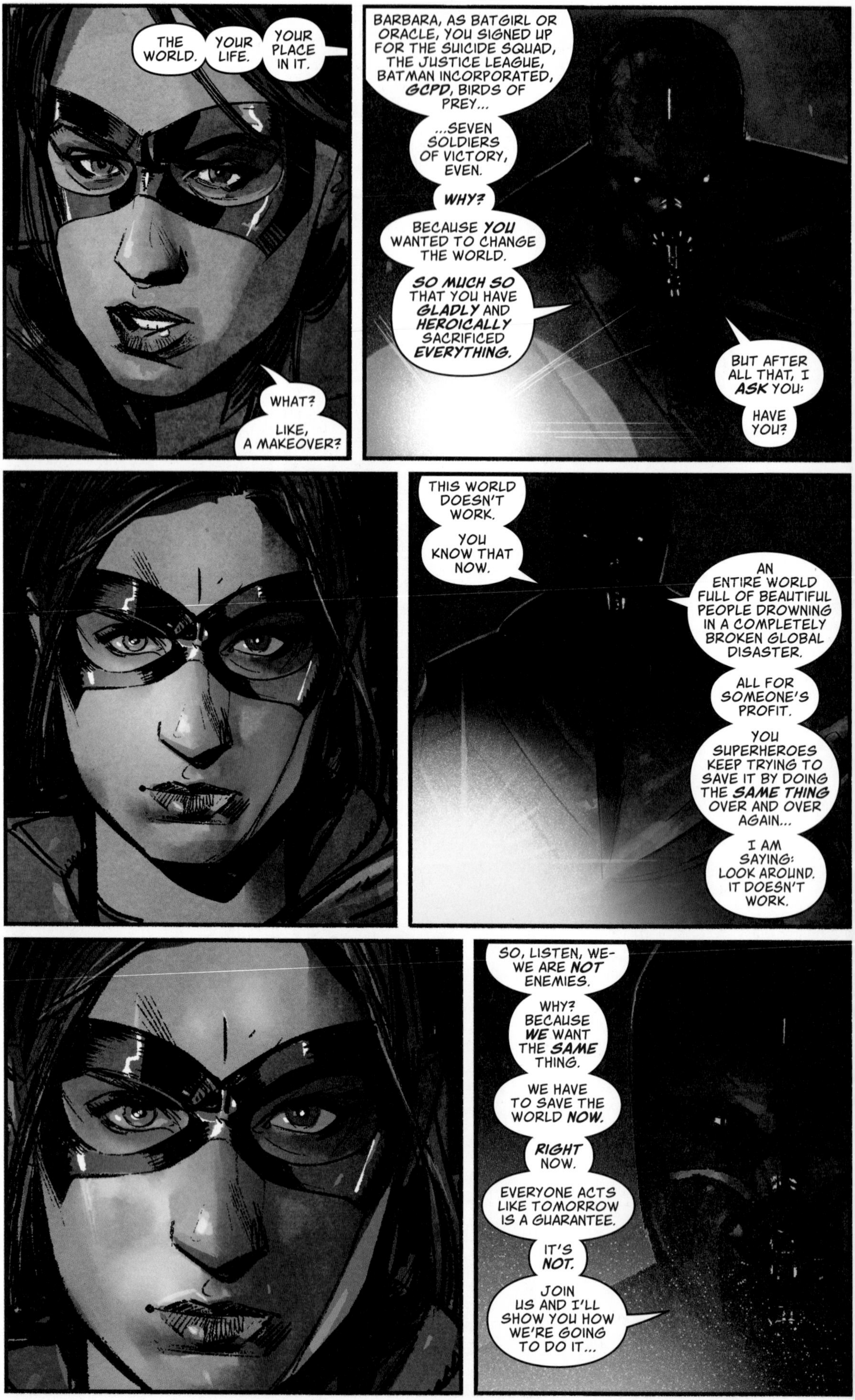

THE WORLD.
YOUR LIFE.
YOUR PLACE IN IT.
BARBARA, AS BATGIRL OR ORACLE, YOU SIGNED UP FOR THE SUICIDE SQUAD, THE JUSTICE LEAGUE, BATMAN INCORPORATED, GCPD, BIRDS OF PREY...
...SEVEN SOLDIERS OF VICTORY, EVEN.
WHY?
BECAUSE YOU WANTED TO CHANGE THE WORLD.
SO MUCH SO THAT YOU HAVE GLADLY AND HEROICALLY SACRIFICED EVERYTHING.
WHAT?
LIKE, A MAKEOVER?
BUT AFTER ALL THAT, I ASK YOU:
HAVE YOU?
THIS WORLD DOESN'T WORK.
YOU KNOW THAT NOW.
AN ENTIRE WORLD FULL OF BEAUTIFUL PEOPLE DROWNING IN A COMPLETELY BROKEN GLOBAL DISASTER.
ALL FOR SOMEONE'S PROFIT.
YOU SUPERHEROES KEEP TRYING TO SAVE IT BY DOING THE SAME THING OVER AND OVER AGAIN...
I AM SAYING: LOOK AROUND. IT DOESN'T WORK.
SO, LISTEN, WE- WE ARE NOT ENEMIES.
WHY? BECAUSE WE WANT THE SAME THING.
WE HAVE TO SAVE THE WORLD NOW.
RIGHT NOW.
EVERYONE ACTS LIKE TOMORROW IS A GUARANTEE.
IT'S NOT.
JOIN US AND I'LL SHOW YOU HOW WE'RE GOING TO DO IT...

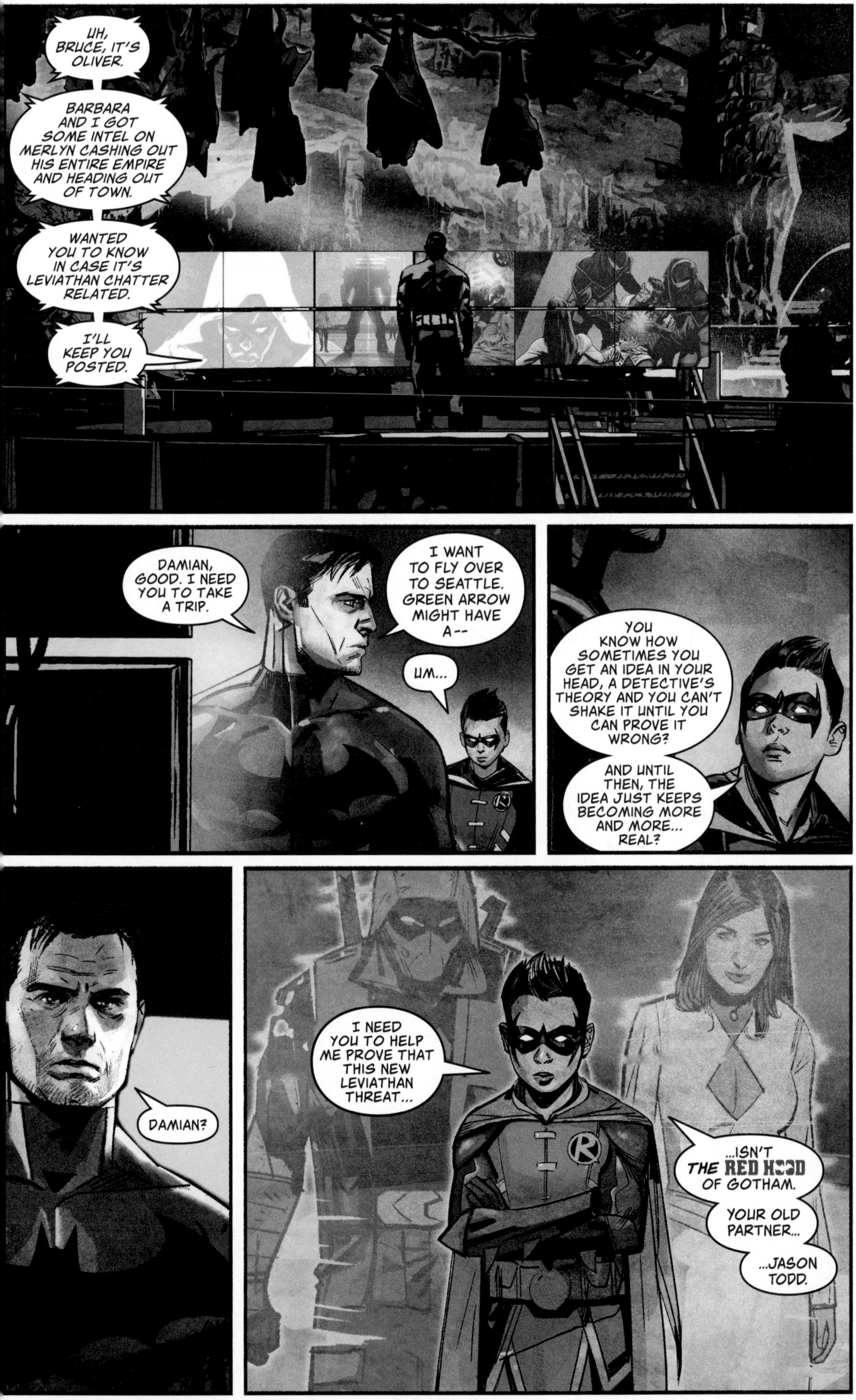
UH, BRUCE, IT'S OLIVER.
BARBARA AND I GOT SOME INTEL ON MERLYN CASHING OUT HIS ENTIRE EMPIRE AND HEADING OUT OF TOWN.
WANTED YOU TO KNOW IN CASE IT'S LEVIATHAN CHATTER RELATED.
I'LL KEEP YOU POSTED.
DAMIAN, GOOD. I NEED YOU TO TAKE A TRIP.
I WANT TO FLY OVER TO SEATTLE. GREEN ARROW MIGHT HAVE A--
UM...
YOU KNOW HOW SOMETIMES YOU GET AN IDEA IN YOUR HEAD, A DETECTIVE'S THEORY AND YOU CAN'T SHAKE IT UNTIL YOU CAN PROVE IT WRONG?
AND UNTIL THEN, THE IDEA JUST KEEPS BECOMING MORE AND MORE... REAL?
DAMIAN?
I NEED YOU TO HELP ME PROVE THAT THIS NEW LEVIATHAN THREAT...
...ISN'T THE RED HOOD OF GOTHAM.
YOUR OLD PARTNER...
...JASON TODD.

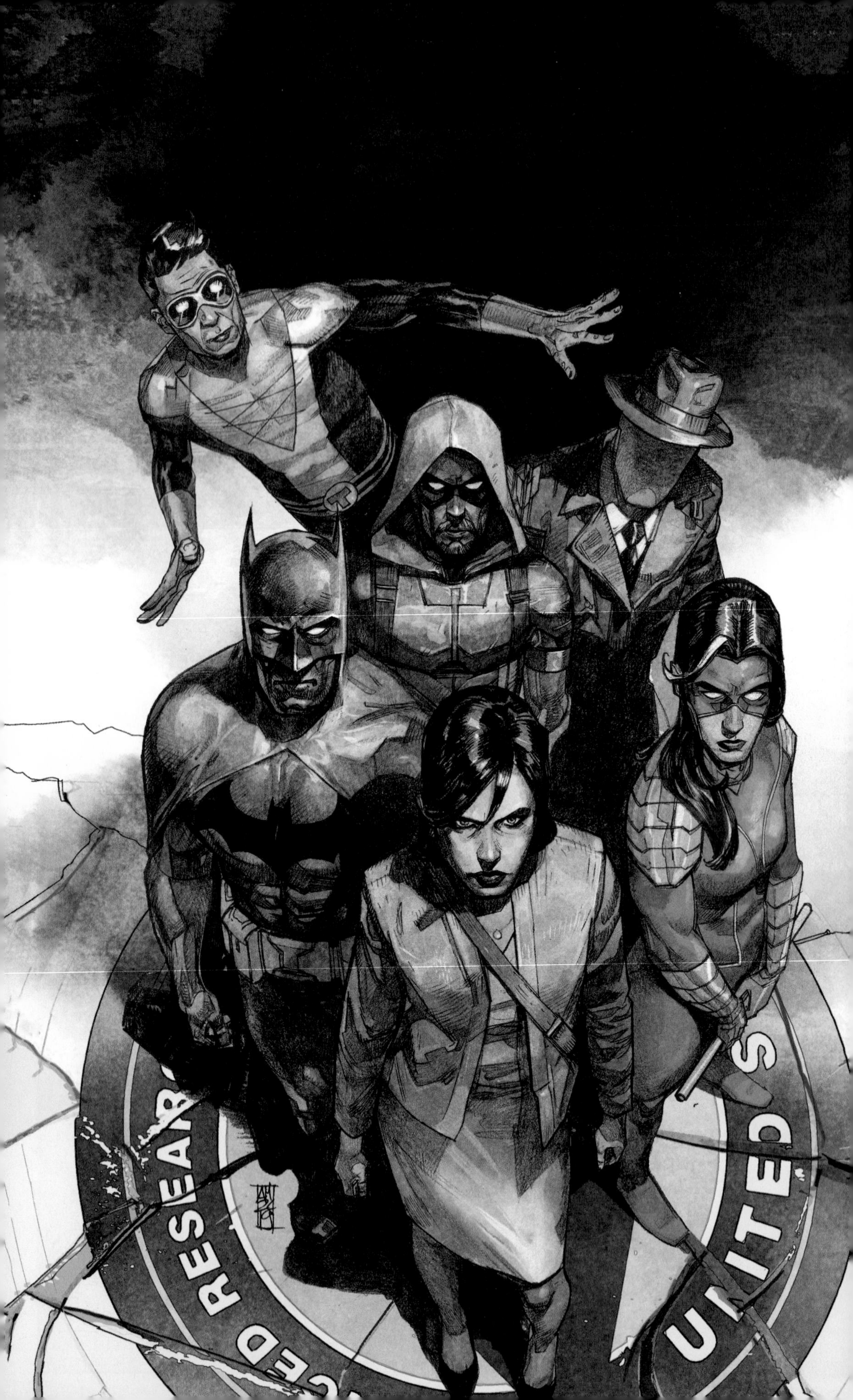
UNITED

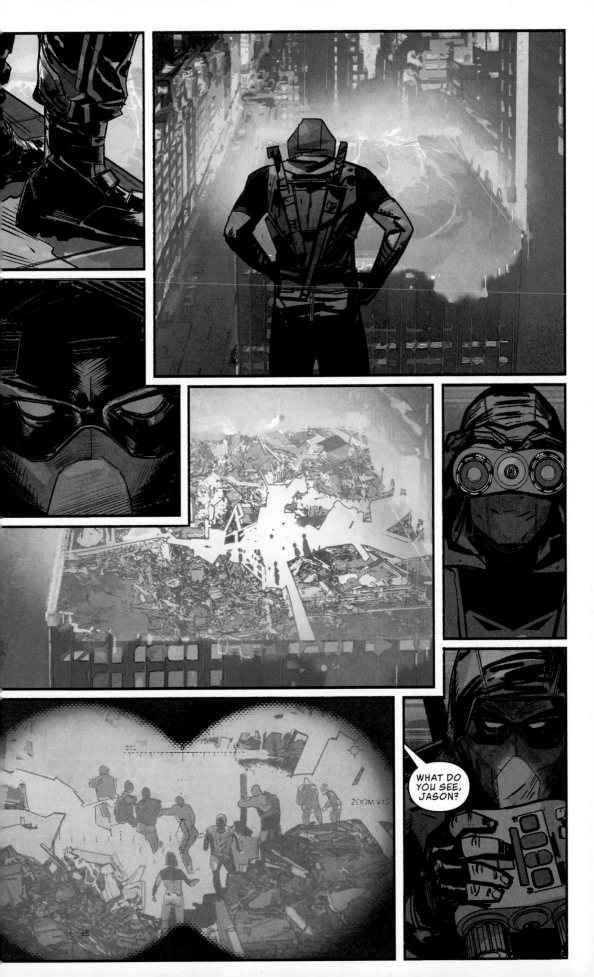

WHAT DO YOU SEE, JASON?

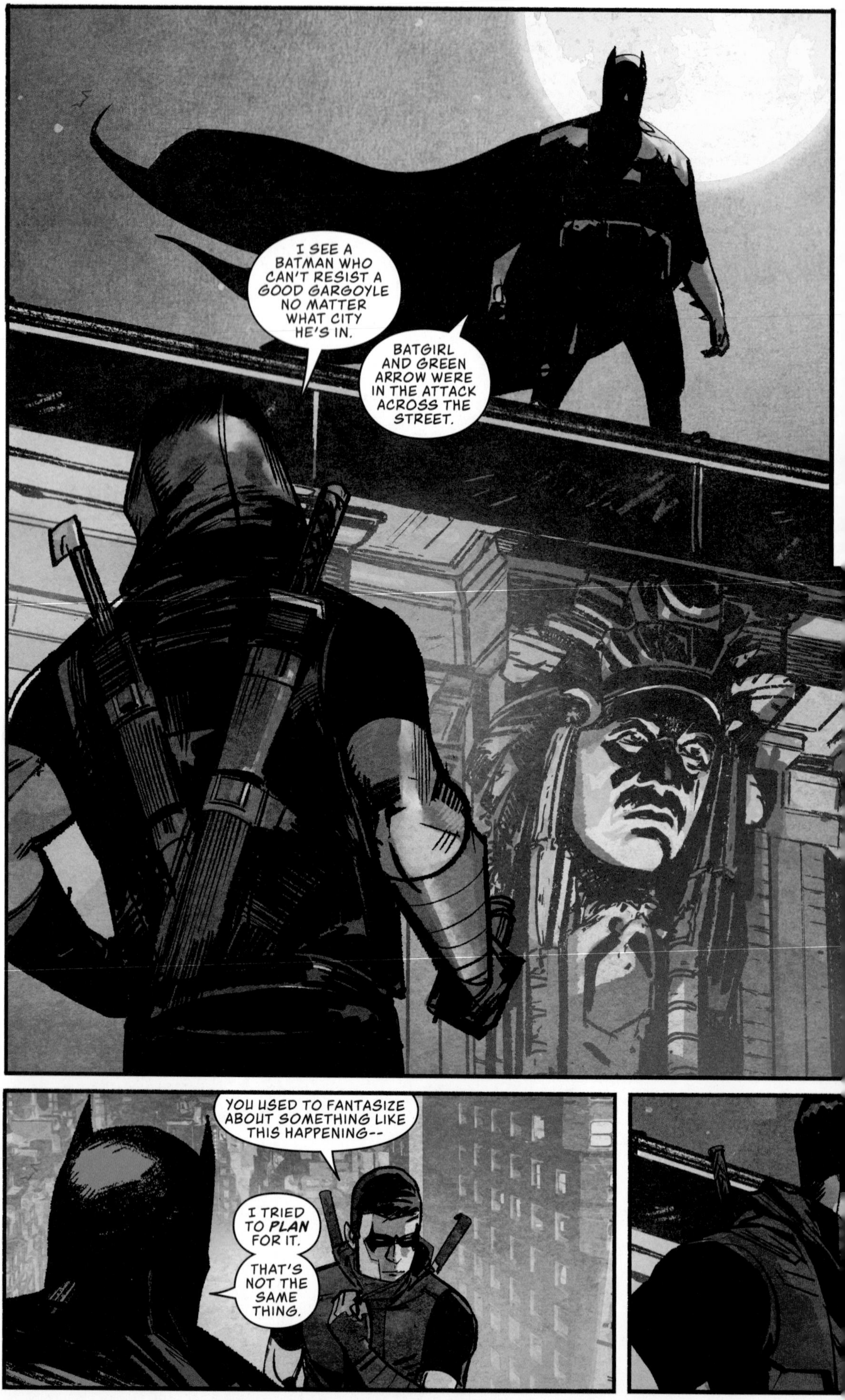
I SEE A BATMAN WHO CAN'T RESIST A GOOD GARGOYLE NO MATTER WHAT CITY HE'S IN.
BATGIRL AND GREEN ARROW WERE IN THE ATTACK ACROSS THE STREET.
YOU USED TO FANTASIZE ABOUT SOMETHING LIKE THIS HAPPENING--
I TRIED TO *PLAN* FOR IT.
THAT'S NOT THE SAME THING.

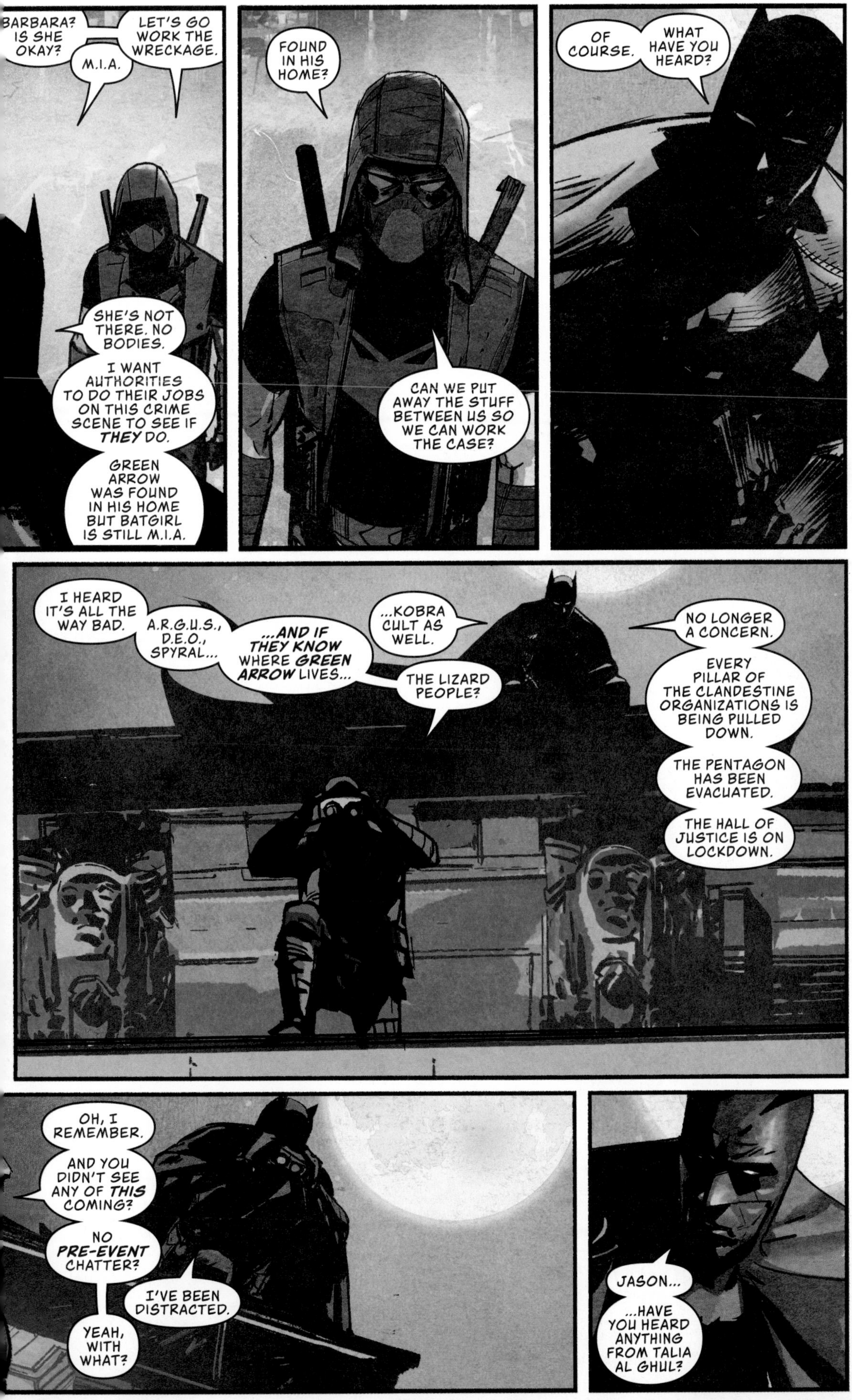
BARBARA? IS SHE OKAY?
M.I.A.
LET'S GO WORK THE WRECKAGE.
SHE'S NOT THERE. NO BODIES.
I WANT AUTHORITIES TO DO THEIR JOBS ON THIS CRIME SCENE TO SEE IF THEY DO.
GREEN ARROW WAS FOUND IN HIS HOME BUT BATGIRL IS STILL M.I.A.
FOUND IN HIS HOME?
CAN WE PUT AWAY THE STUFF BETWEEN US SO WE CAN WORK THE CASE?
OF COURSE.
WHAT HAVE YOU HEARD?
I HEARD IT'S ALL THE WAY BAD.
A.R.G.U.S., D.E.O., SPYRAL...
...AND IF THEY KNOW WHERE GREEN ARROW LIVES...
...KOBRA CULT AS WELL.
THE LIZARD PEOPLE?
NO LONGER A CONCERN.
EVERY PILLAR OF THE CLANDESTINE ORGANIZATIONS IS BEING PULLED DOWN.
THE PENTAGON HAS BEEN EVACUATED.
THE HALL OF JUSTICE IS ON LOCKDOWN.
OH, I REMEMBER.
AND YOU DIDN'T SEE ANY OF THIS COMING?
NO PRE-EVENT CHATTER?
I'VE BEEN DISTRACTED.
YEAH, WITH WHAT?
JASON...
...HAVE YOU HEARD ANYTHING FROM TALIA AL GHUL?

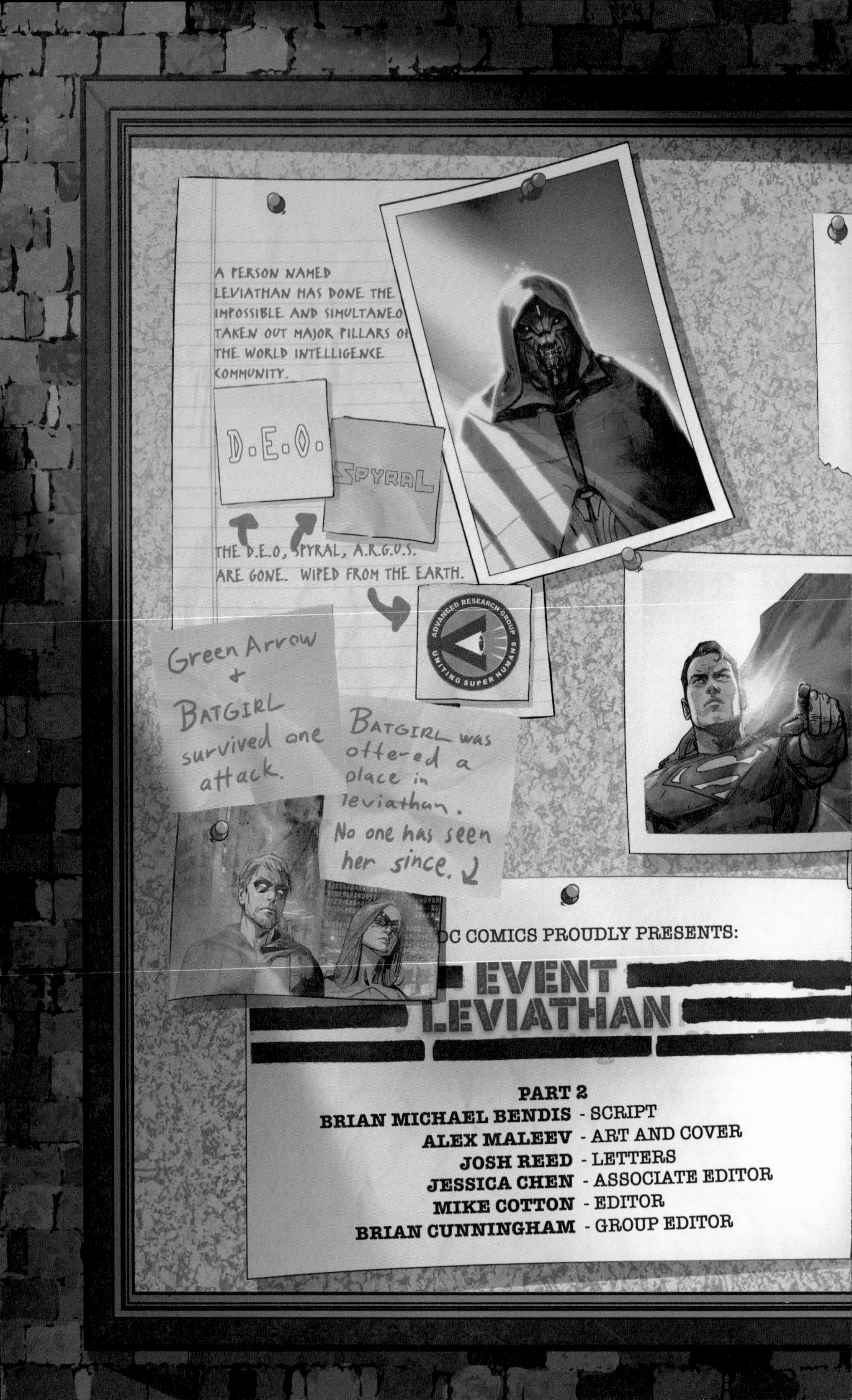

A PERSON NAMED LEVIATHAN HAS DONE THE IMPOSSIBLE AND SIMULTANEO TAKEN OUT MAJOR PILLARS OF THE WORLD INTELLIGENCE COMMUNITY.
D.E.O.
SPYRAL
THE D.E.O, SPYRAL, A.R.G.U.S. ARE GONE. WIPED FROM THE EARTH.
ADVANCED RESEARCH GROUP
UNITING SUPER HUMANS
Green Arrow & Batgirl survived one attack.
Batgirl was offered a place in Leviathan. No one has seen her since.
DC COMICS PROUDLY PRESENTS:
[redacted] EVENT [redacted]
[redacted] LEVIATHAN [redacted]
PART 2
BRIAN MICHAEL BENDIS - SCRIPT
ALEX MALEEV - ART AND COVER
JOSH REED - LETTERS
JESSICA CHEN - ASSOCIATE EDITOR
MIKE COTTON - EDITOR
BRIAN CUNNINGHAM - GROUP EDITOR

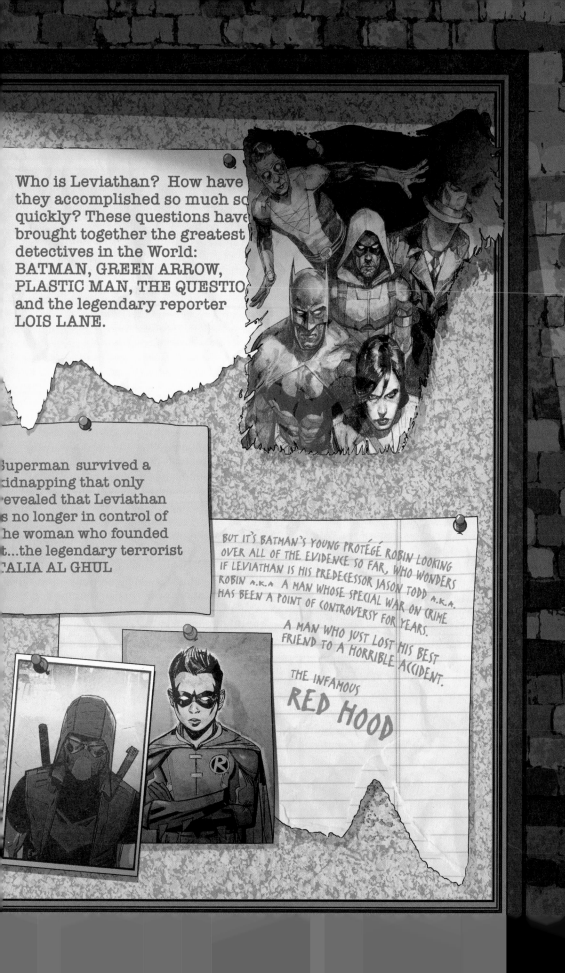

Who is Leviathan? How have they accomplished so much so quickly? These questions have brought together the greatest detectives in the World: BATMAN, GREEN ARROW, PLASTIC MAN, THE QUESTIO and the legendary reporter LOIS LANE.

Superman survived a kidnapping that only revealed that Leviathan s no longer in control of he woman who founded t...the legendary terrorist TALIA AL GHUL

BUT IT'S BATMAN'S YOUNG PROTÉGÉ ROBIN LOOKING OVER ALL OF THE EVIDENCE SO FAR, WHO WONDERS IF LEVIATHAN IS HIS PREDECESSOR JASON TODD a.k.a ROBIN a.k.a A MAN WHOSE SPECIAL WAR ON CRIME HAS BEEN A POINT OF CONTROVERSY FOR YEARS.

A MAN WHO JUST LOST HIS BEST FRIEND TO A HORRIBLE ACCIDENT.

THE INFAMOUS
RED HOOD

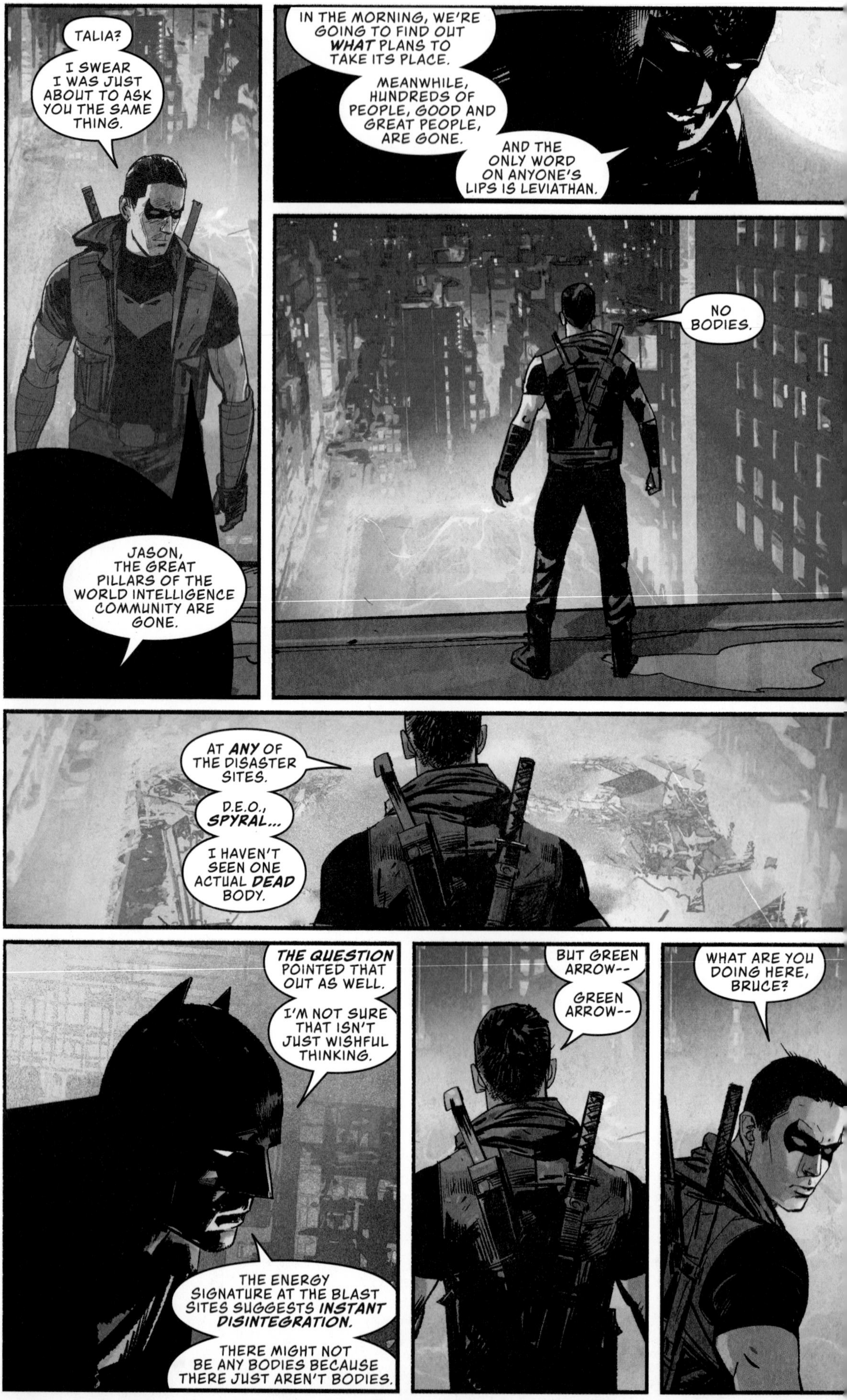

TALIA?
I SWEAR I WAS JUST ABOUT TO ASK YOU THE SAME THING.
JASON, THE GREAT PILLARS OF THE WORLD INTELLIGENCE COMMUNITY ARE GONE.
IN THE MORNING, WE'RE GOING TO FIND OUT WHAT PLANS TO TAKE ITS PLACE.
MEANWHILE, HUNDREDS OF PEOPLE, GOOD AND GREAT PEOPLE, ARE GONE.
AND THE ONLY WORD ON ANYONE'S LIPS IS LEVIATHAN.
NO BODIES.
AT ANY OF THE DISASTER SITES.
D.E.O., SPYRAL...
I HAVEN'T SEEN ONE ACTUAL DEAD BODY.
THE QUESTION POINTED THAT OUT AS WELL.
I'M NOT SURE THAT ISN'T JUST WISHFUL THINKING.
THE ENERGY SIGNATURE AT THE BLAST SITES SUGGESTS INSTANT DISINTEGRATION.
THERE MIGHT NOT BE ANY BODIES BECAUSE THERE JUST AREN'T BODIES.
BUT GREEN ARROW--
GREEN ARROW--
WHAT ARE YOU DOING HERE, BRUCE?

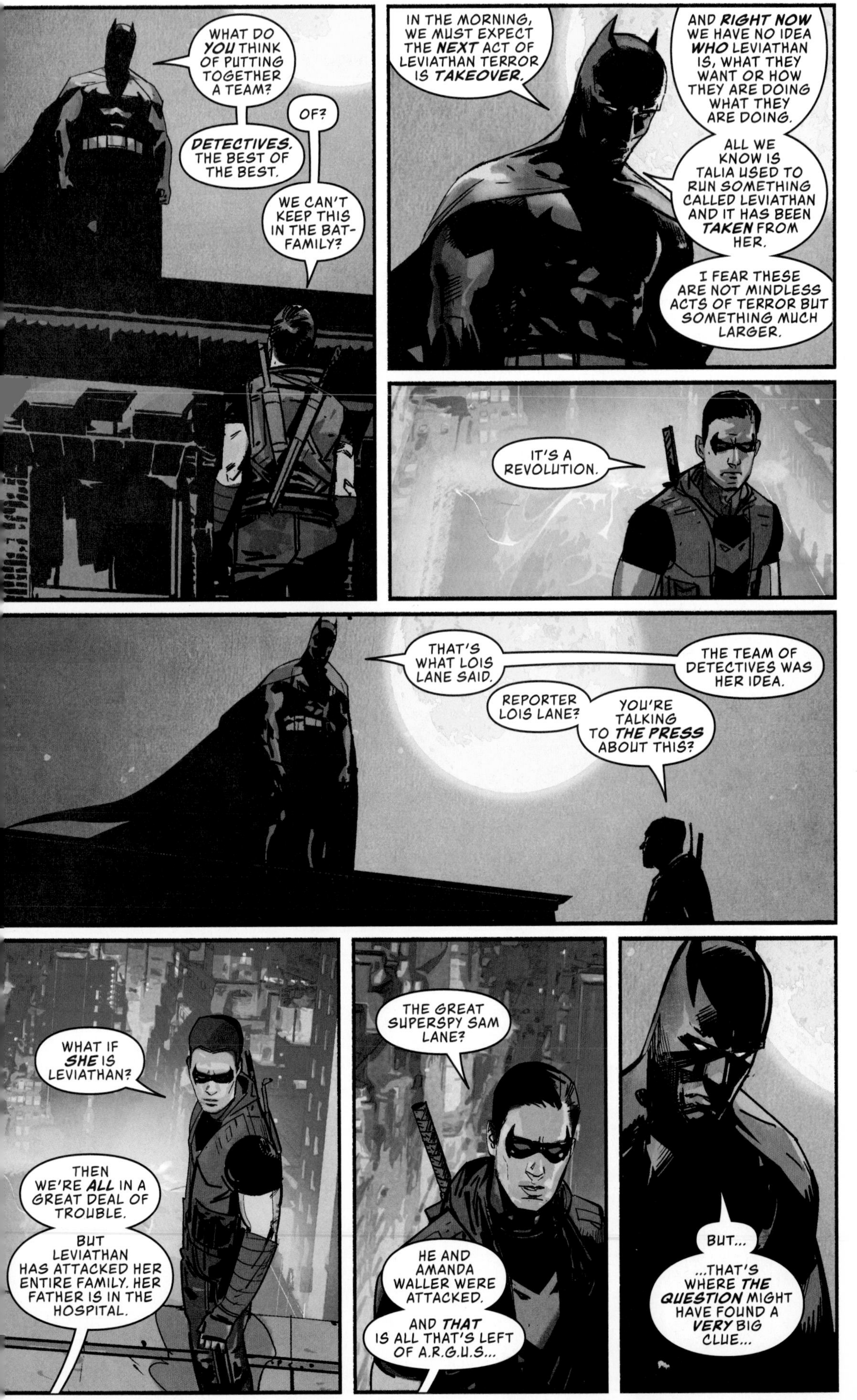
WHAT DO YOU THINK OF PUTTING TOGETHER A TEAM?
OF?
DETECTIVES. THE BEST OF THE BEST.
WE CAN'T KEEP THIS IN THE BAT-FAMILY?
IN THE MORNING, WE MUST EXPECT THE NEXT ACT OF LEVIATHAN TERROR IS TAKEOVER.
AND RIGHT NOW WE HAVE NO IDEA WHO LEVIATHAN IS, WHAT THEY WANT OR HOW THEY ARE DOING WHAT THEY ARE DOING.
ALL WE KNOW IS TALIA USED TO RUN SOMETHING CALLED LEVIATHAN AND IT HAS BEEN TAKEN FROM HER.
I FEAR THESE ARE NOT MINDLESS ACTS OF TERROR BUT SOMETHING MUCH LARGER.
IT'S A REVOLUTION.
THAT'S WHAT LOIS LANE SAID.
THE TEAM OF DETECTIVES WAS HER IDEA.
REPORTER LOIS LANE?
YOU'RE TALKING TO THE PRESS ABOUT THIS?
WHAT IF SHE IS LEVIATHAN?
THEN WE'RE ALL IN A GREAT DEAL OF TROUBLE.
BUT LEVIATHAN HAS ATTACKED HER ENTIRE FAMILY. HER FATHER IS IN THE HOSPITAL.
THE GREAT SUPERSPY SAM LANE?
HE AND AMANDA WALLER WERE ATTACKED.
AND THAT IS ALL THAT'S LEFT OF A.R.G.U.S...
BUT...
...THAT'S WHERE THE QUESTION MIGHT HAVE FOUND A VERY BIG CLUE...

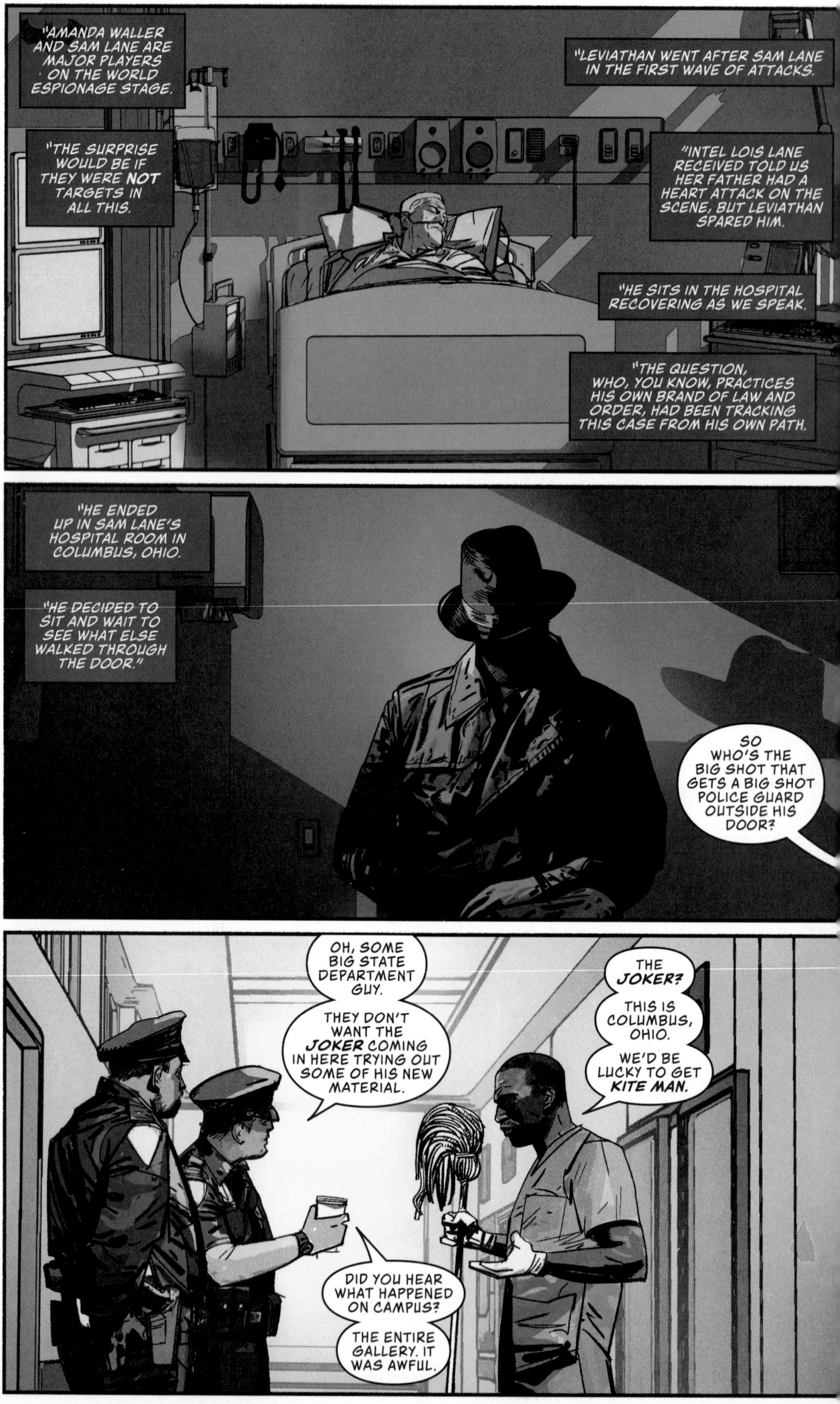
"AMANDA WALLER AND SAM LANE ARE MAJOR PLAYERS ON THE WORLD ESPIONAGE STAGE.
"THE SURPRISE WOULD BE IF THEY WERE NOT TARGETS IN ALL THIS.
"LEVIATHAN WENT AFTER SAM LANE IN THE FIRST WAVE OF ATTACKS.
"INTEL LOIS LANE RECEIVED TOLD US HER FATHER HAD A HEART ATTACK ON THE SCENE, BUT LEVIATHAN SPARED HIM.
"HE SITS IN THE HOSPITAL RECOVERING AS WE SPEAK.
"THE QUESTION, WHO, YOU KNOW, PRACTICES HIS OWN BRAND OF LAW AND ORDER, HAD BEEN TRACKING THIS CASE FROM HIS OWN PATH.
"HE ENDED UP IN SAM LANE'S HOSPITAL ROOM IN COLUMBUS, OHIO.
"HE DECIDED TO SIT AND WAIT TO SEE WHAT ELSE WALKED THROUGH THE DOOR."
SO WHO'S THE BIG SHOT THAT GETS A BIG SHOT POLICE GUARD OUTSIDE HIS DOOR?
OH, SOME BIG STATE DEPARTMENT GUY.
THEY DON'T WANT THE JOKER COMING IN HERE TRYING OUT SOME OF HIS NEW MATERIAL.
THE JOKER?
THIS IS COLUMBUS, OHIO.
WE'D BE LUCKY TO GET KITE MAN.
DID YOU HEAR WHAT HAPPENED ON CAMPUS?
THE ENTIRE GALLERY. IT WAS AWFUL.

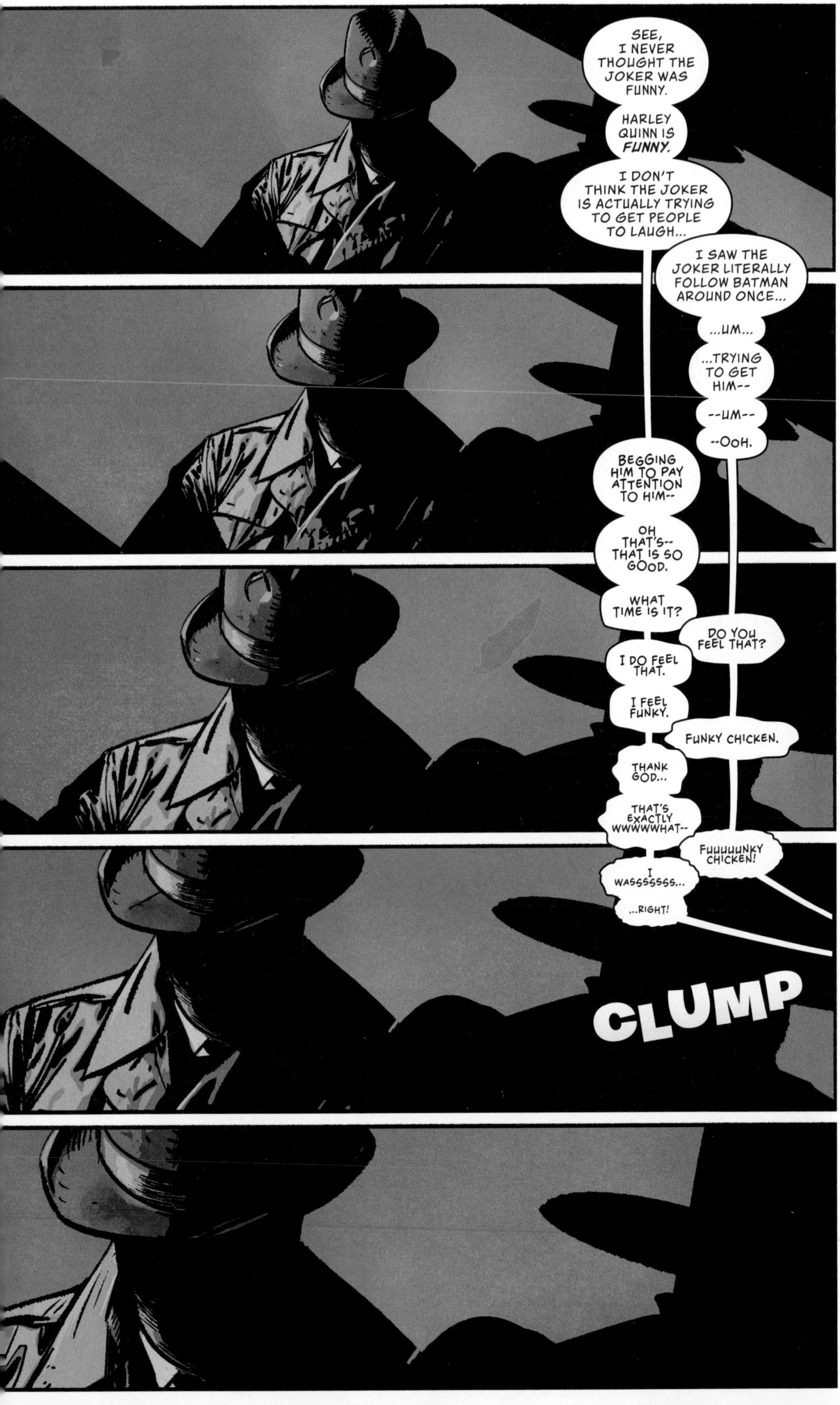
SEE, I NEVER THOUGHT THE JOKER WAS FUNNY.
HARLEY QUINN IS FUNNY.
I DON'T THINK THE JOKER IS ACTUALLY TRYING TO GET PEOPLE TO LAUGH...
I SAW THE JOKER LITERALLY FOLLOW BATMAN AROUND ONCE...
...UM...
...TRYING TO GET HIM--
--UM--
--OOH.
BEGGING HIM TO PAY ATTENTION TO HIM--
OH THAT'S-- THAT IS SO GOOD.
WHAT TIME IS IT?
DO YOU FEEL THAT?
I DO FEEL THAT.
I FEEL FUNKY.
FUNKY CHICKEN.
THANK GOD...
THAT'S EXACTLY WWWWWHAT--
FUUUUUNKY CHICKEN!
I WASSSSSSS...
...RIGHT!
CLUMP

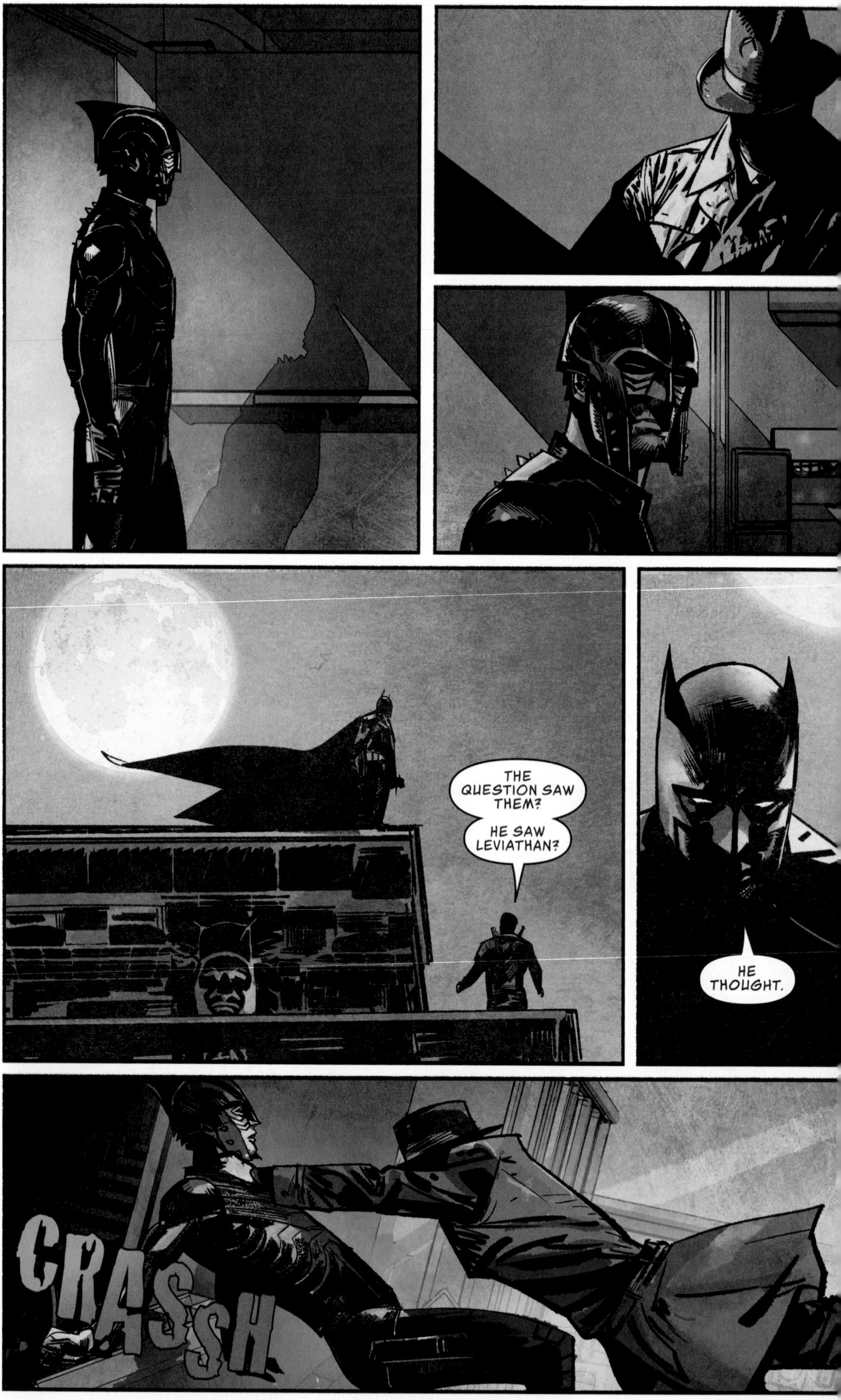
THE QUESTION SAW THEM?
HE SAW LEVIATHAN?
HE THOUGHT.
CRASSH

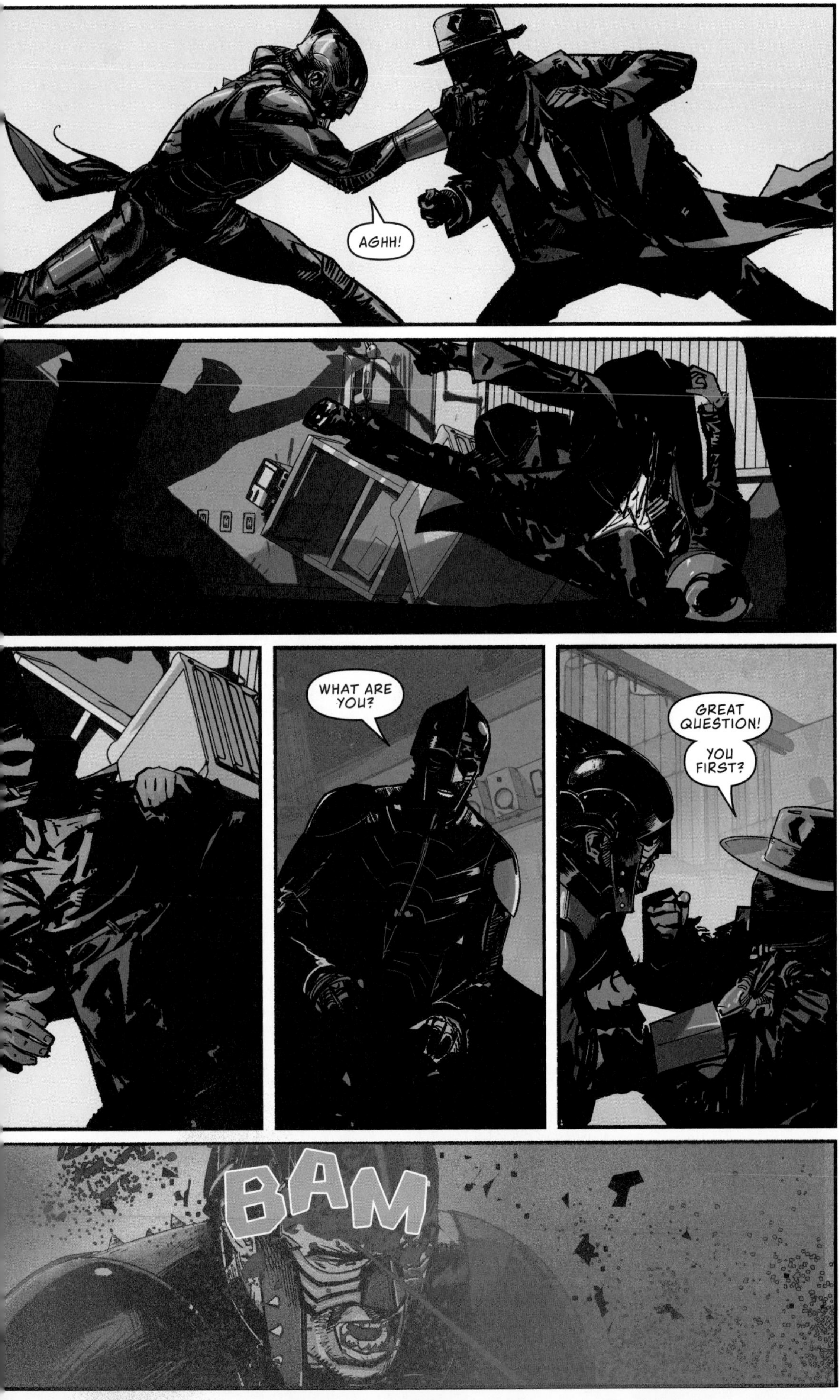
AGHH!
WHAT ARE YOU?
GREAT QUESTION!
YOU FIRST?
BAM

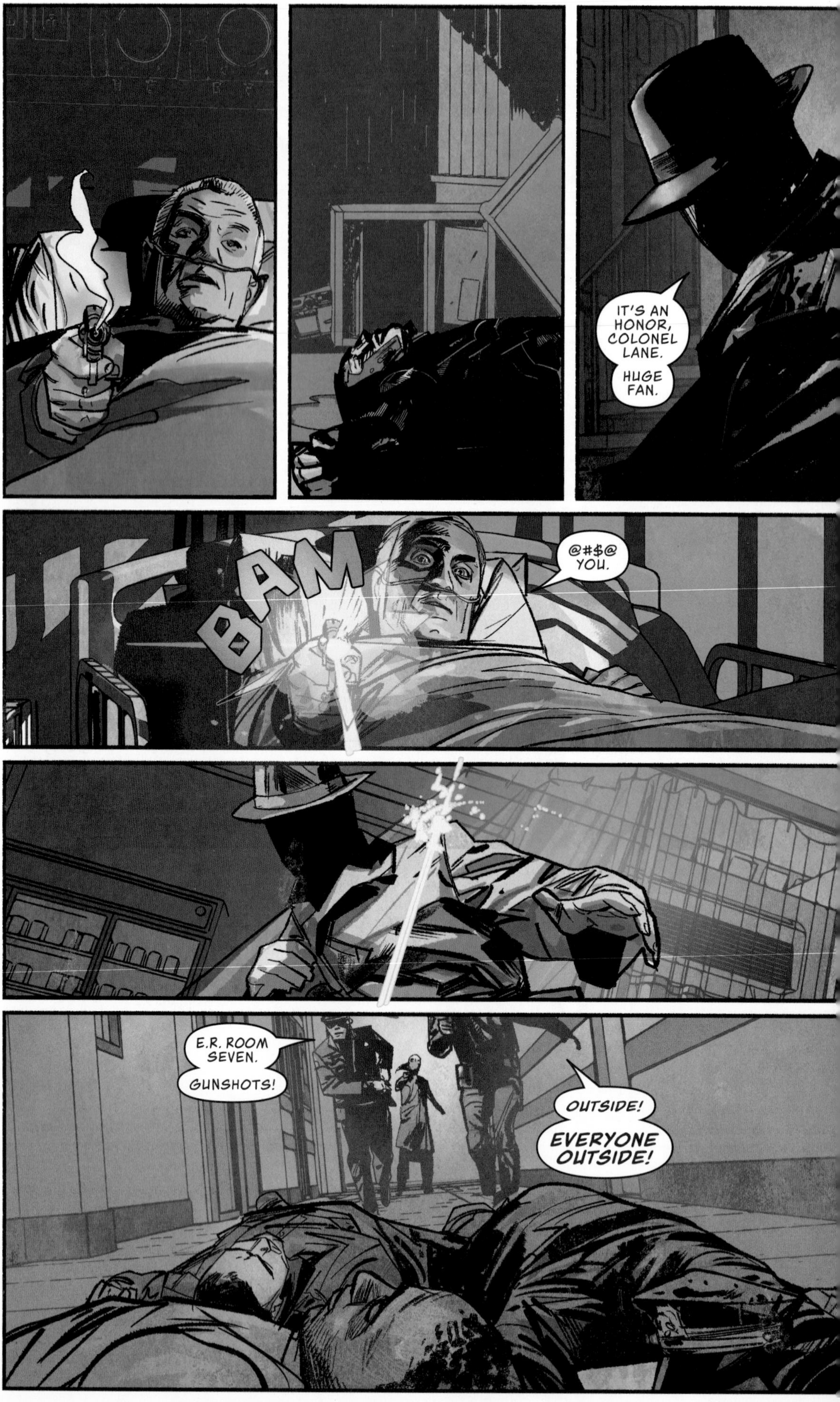
IT'S AN HONOR, COLONEL LANE.
HUGE FAN.
BAM
@#$@ YOU.
E.R. ROOM SEVEN.
GUNSHOTS!
OUTSIDE!
EVERYONE OUTSIDE!

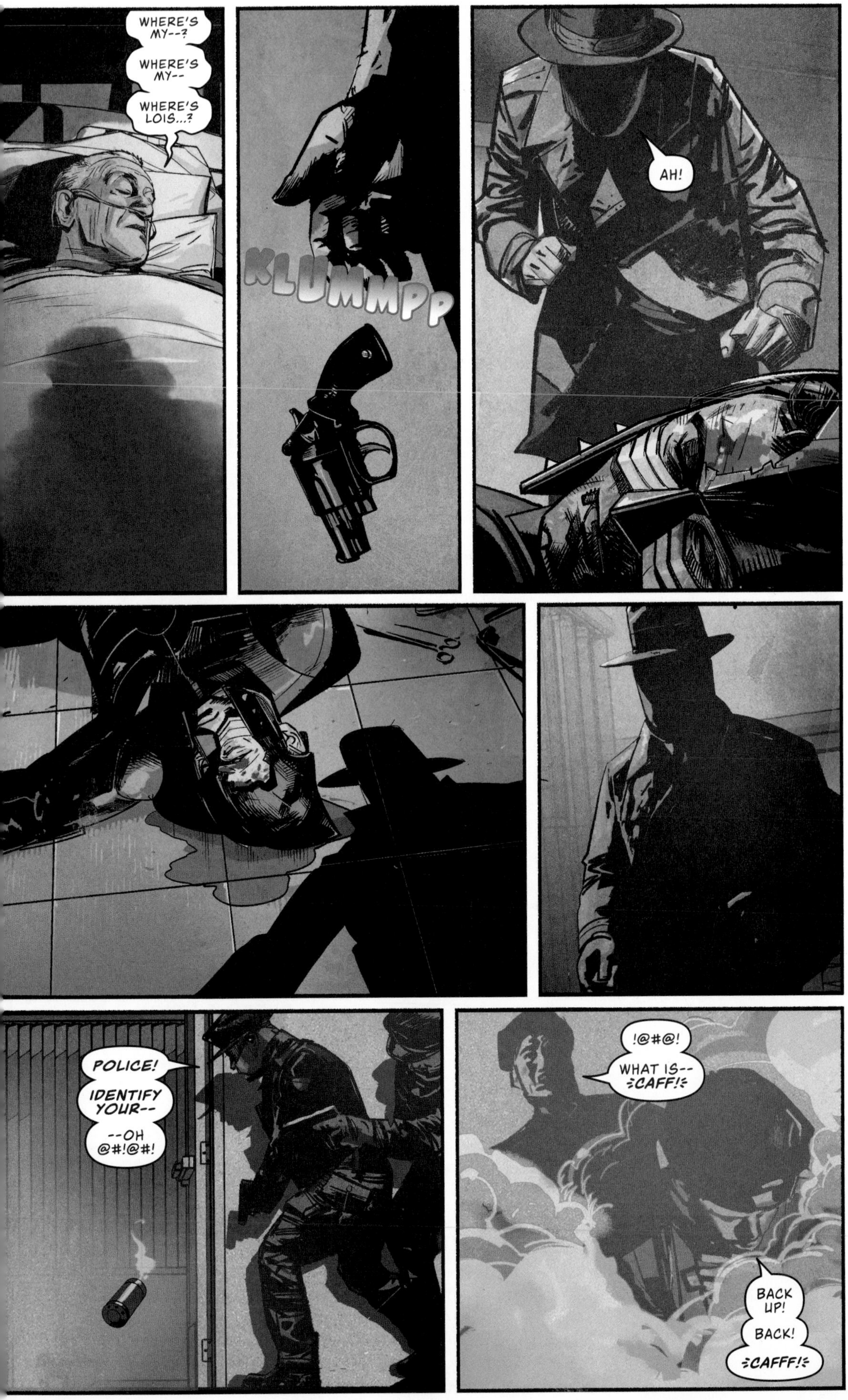
WHERE'S MY--?
WHERE'S MY--
WHERE'S LOIS...?
KLUMMPP
AH!
POLICE!
IDENTIFY YOUR--
--OH @#!@#!
!@#@!
WHAT IS-- *CAFF!*
BACK UP!
BACK!
CAFFF!

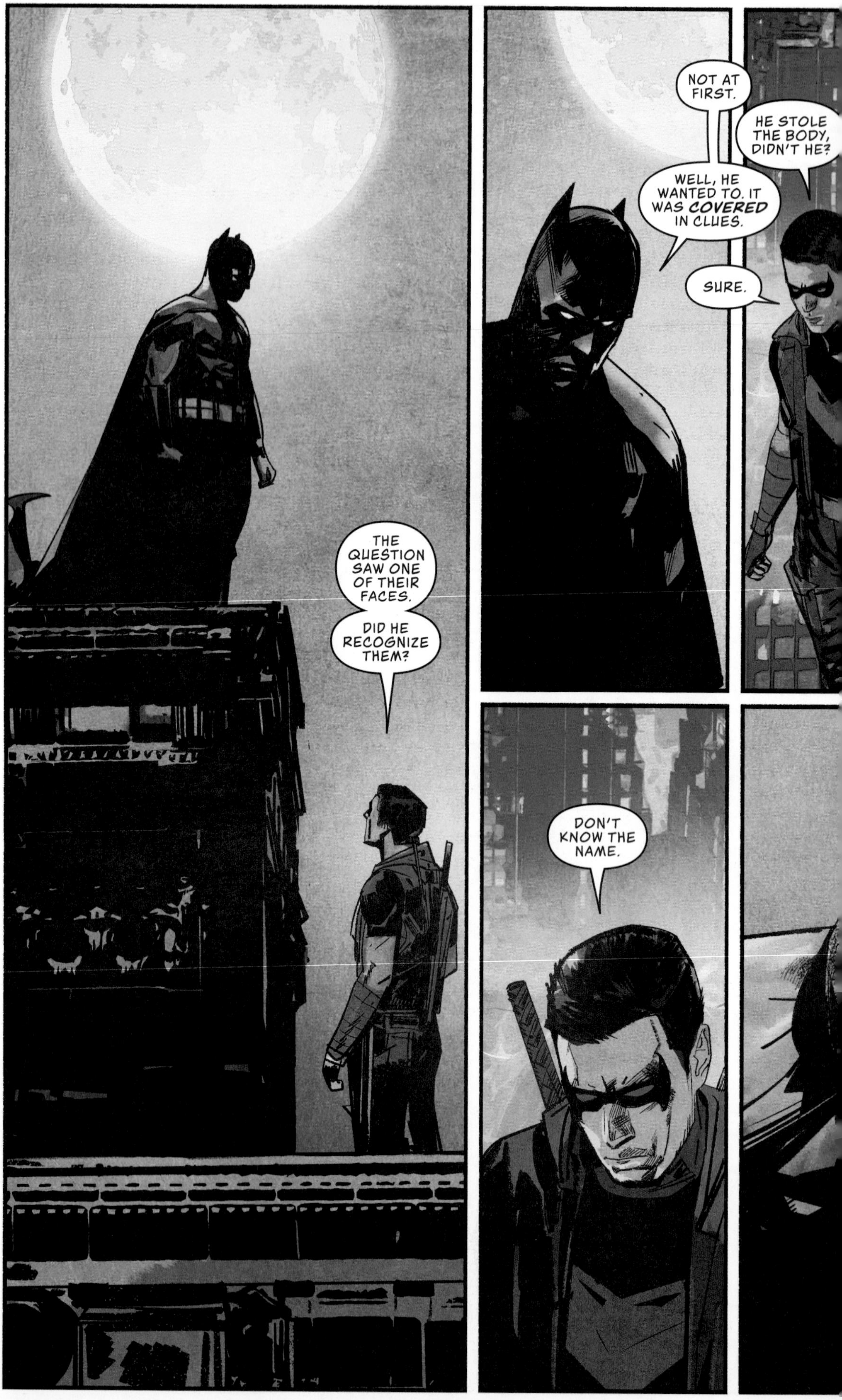
THE QUESTION SAW ONE OF THEIR FACES.
DID HE RECOGNIZE THEM?
NOT AT FIRST.
WELL, HE WANTED TO. IT WAS COVERED IN CLUES.
HE STOLE THE BODY, DIDN'T HE?
SURE.
DON'T KNOW THE NAME.

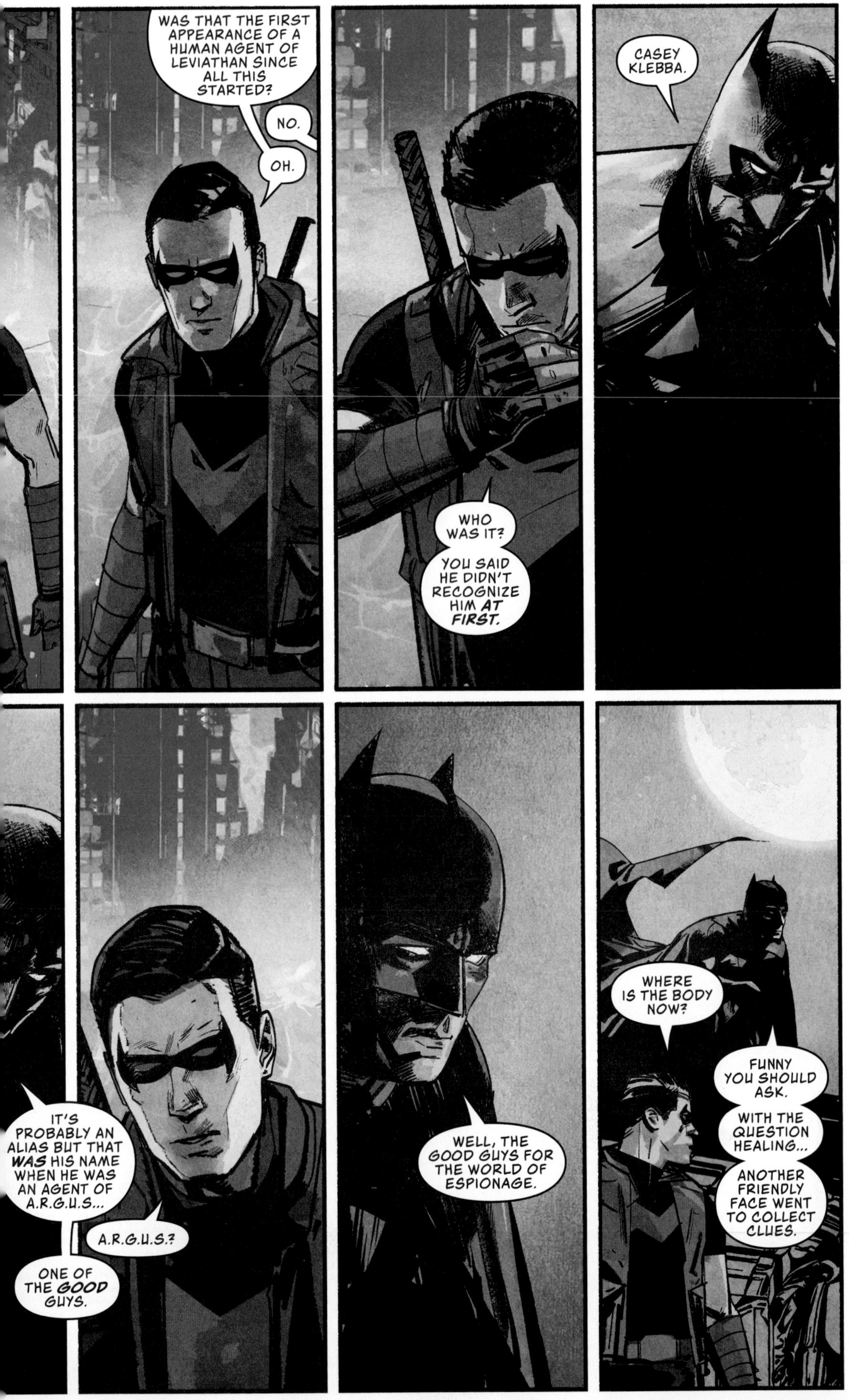
WAS THAT THE FIRST APPEARANCE OF A HUMAN AGENT OF LEVIATHAN SINCE ALL THIS STARTED?
NO.
OH.
WHO WAS IT?
YOU SAID HE DIDN'T RECOGNIZE HIM AT FIRST.
CASEY KLEBBA.
IT'S PROBABLY AN ALIAS BUT THAT WAS HIS NAME WHEN HE WAS AN AGENT OF A.R.G.U.S...
A.R.G.U.S.?
ONE OF THE GOOD GUYS.
WELL, THE GOOD GUYS FOR THE WORLD OF ESPIONAGE.
WHERE IS THE BODY NOW?
FUNNY YOU SHOULD ASK.
WITH THE QUESTION HEALING...
ANOTHER FRIENDLY FACE WENT TO COLLECT CLUES.

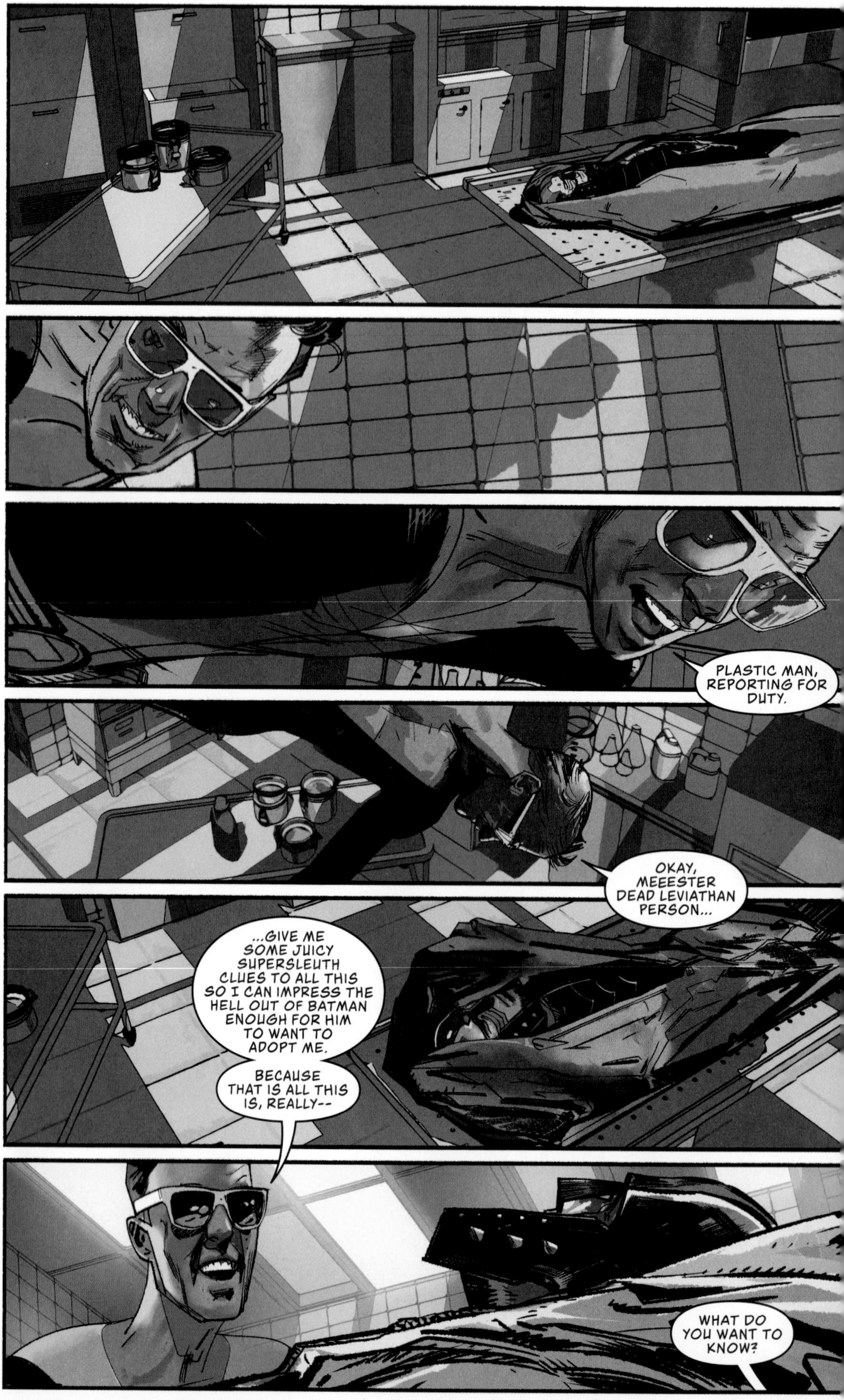
PLASTIC MAN, REPORTING FOR DUTY.
OKAY, MEEESTER DEAD LEVIATHAN PERSON...
...GIVE ME SOME JUICY SUPERSLEUTH CLUES TO ALL THIS SO I CAN IMPRESS THE HELL OUT OF BATMAN ENOUGH FOR HIM TO WANT TO ADOPT ME.
BECAUSE THAT IS ALL THIS IS, REALLY--
WHAT DO YOU WANT TO KNOW?

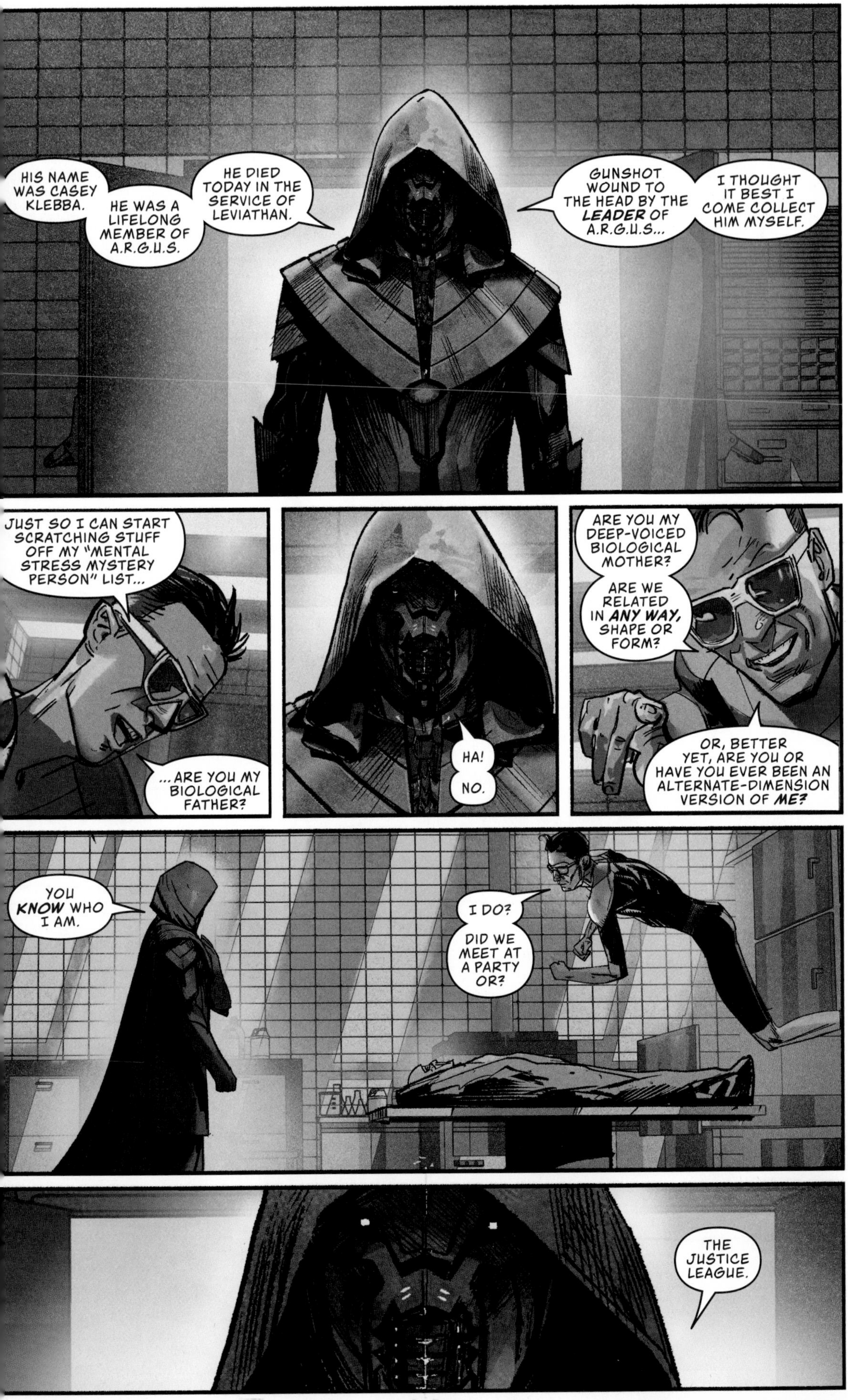
HIS NAME WAS CASEY KLEBBA.
HE WAS A LIFELONG MEMBER OF A.R.G.U.S.
HE DIED TODAY IN THE SERVICE OF LEVIATHAN.
GUNSHOT WOUND TO THE HEAD BY THE **LEADER** OF A.R.G.U.S...
I THOUGHT IT BEST I COME COLLECT HIM MYSELF.
JUST SO I CAN START SCRATCHING STUFF OFF MY "MENTAL STRESS MYSTERY PERSON" LIST...
...ARE YOU MY BIOLOGICAL FATHER?
HA!
NO.
ARE YOU MY DEEP-VOICED BIOLOGICAL MOTHER?
ARE WE RELATED IN **ANY WAY,** SHAPE OR FORM?
OR, BETTER YET, ARE YOU OR HAVE YOU EVER BEEN AN ALTERNATE-DIMENSION VERSION OF **ME?**
YOU **KNOW** WHO I AM.
I DO?
DID WE MEET AT A PARTY OR?
THE JUSTICE LEAGUE.

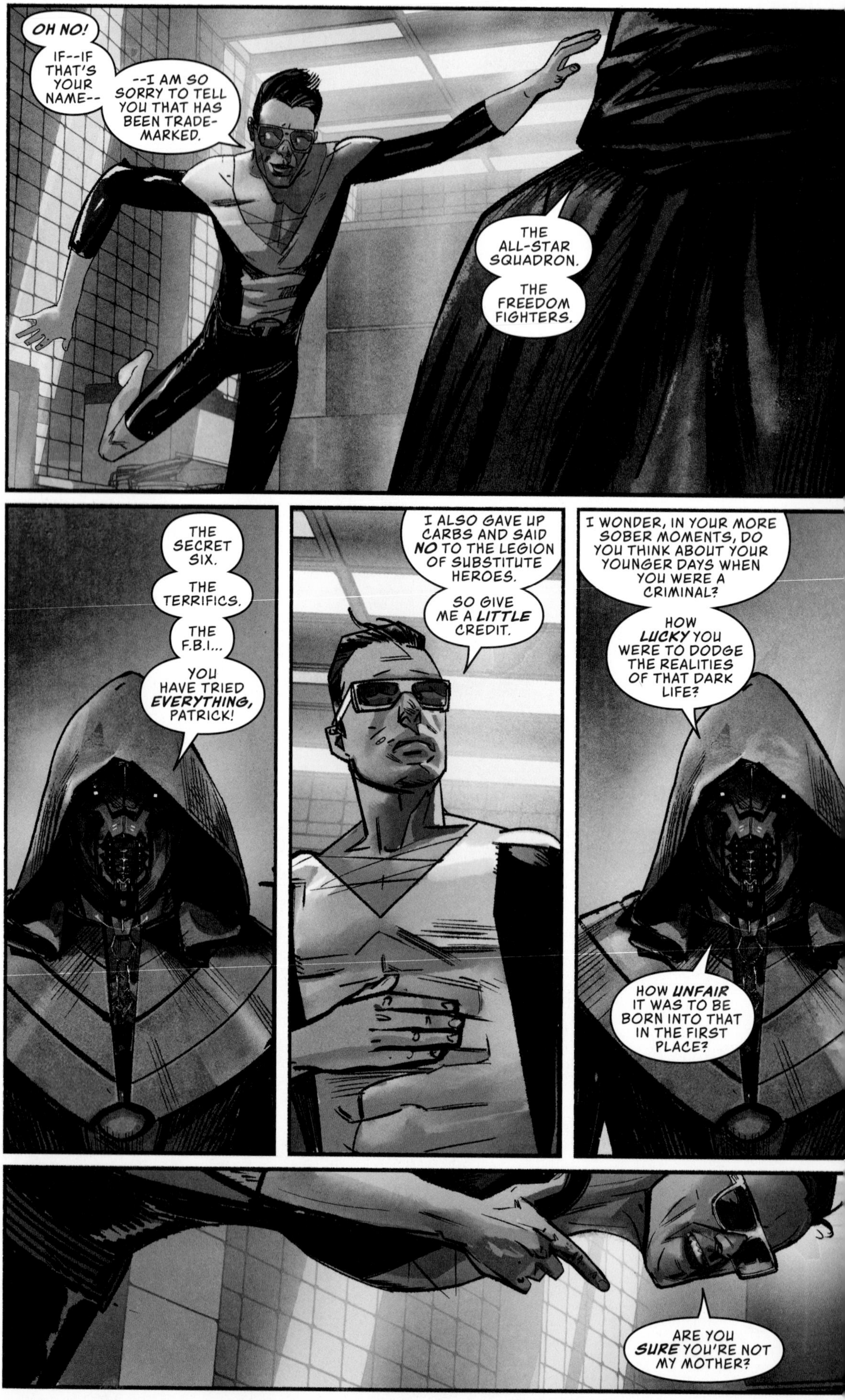
OH NO!
IF--IF THAT'S YOUR NAME--
--I AM SO SORRY TO TELL YOU THAT HAS BEEN TRADE-MARKED.
THE ALL-STAR SQUADRON.
THE FREEDOM FIGHTERS.
THE SECRET SIX.
THE TERRIFICS.
THE F.B.I...
YOU HAVE TRIED EVERYTHING, PATRICK!
I ALSO GAVE UP CARBS AND SAID NO TO THE LEGION OF SUBSTITUTE HEROES.
SO GIVE ME A LITTLE CREDIT.
I WONDER, IN YOUR MORE SOBER MOMENTS, DO YOU THINK ABOUT YOUR YOUNGER DAYS WHEN YOU WERE A CRIMINAL?
HOW LUCKY YOU WERE TO DODGE THE REALITIES OF THAT DARK LIFE?
HOW UNFAIR IT WAS TO BE BORN INTO THAT IN THE FIRST PLACE?
ARE YOU SURE YOU'RE NOT MY MOTHER?

YOU AND I WERE BORN INTO A BROKEN WORLD AND IT ALMOST KILLED US.

WHAT YOU AND I HAVE IN COMMON IS THAT WE TOOK A STEP BACK, ASSESSED OUR SITUATION OURSELVES, AND FIGURED OUT WE NEEDED TO START AGAIN *BEFORE* THIS WORLD ROLLED US OVER LIKE IT DOES SO MANY OTHERS.

I AM SO HONORED THAT YOU TOOK THE TIME TO READ MY UNAUTHORIZED BIOGRAPHY THAT I WROTE MYSELF UNDER A PEN NAME.

I MAKE YOU NERVOUS. I GET IT. THESE ARE HARD WORDS TO HEAR.

THE WORLD *HAS* TO BE CHANGED.

YOU HAVE COME *SO FAR* FROM *SO* LITTLE.

AND YOU HAVE FOUGHT SO HARD SINCE...

I MAKE YOU NERVOUS. I GET IT. THESE ARE HARD WORDS TO HEAR.

I KNOW YOU AND OTHERS ARE WORKING WITH BATMAN TO FIGURE THIS OUT.

PLEASE GIVE HIM AND EVERYONE MY REGARDS.

AND I HOPE THAT EVERY STEP YOU TAKE TOWARD ME, YOU DO WITH AN OPEN MIND...

...BY THE TIME YOU *DO* GET TO ME...

...I HOPE YOU CAN SEE THE TRUTH IN WHAT WE'RE DOING...

...I KNOW YOU LIKE TO JOKE AND YOU'RE GOING TO MAKE A JOKE NOW--

TUSHY BURP!

BUT IN YOUR QUIETER MOMENTS, I WANT YOU TO *REALLY* THINK ABOUT WHAT I'M SAYING.

THE WORLD NEEDS US TO DO BETTER.

RIGHT.

NOW.

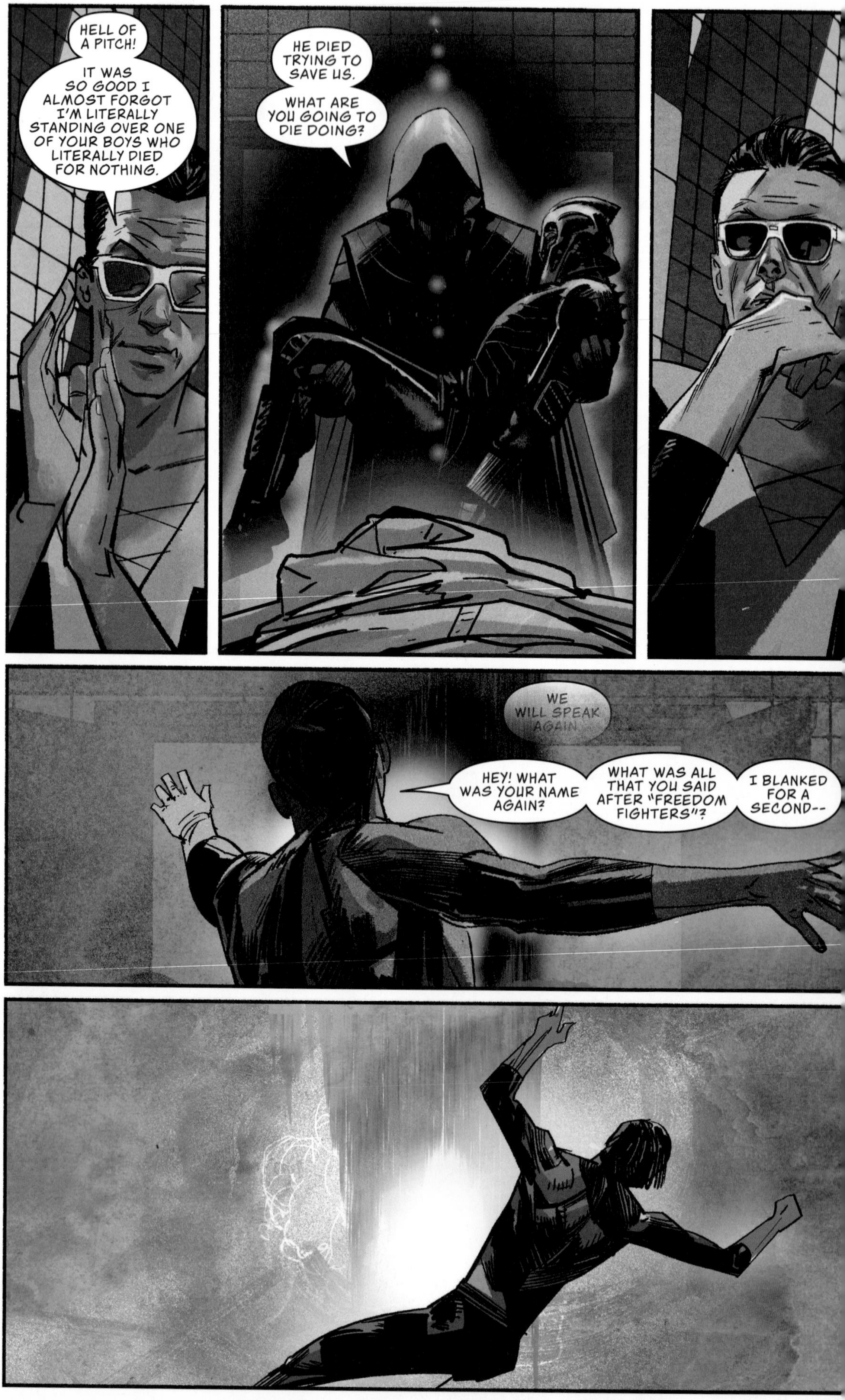
HELL OF A PITCH!
IT WAS SO GOOD I ALMOST FORGOT I'M LITERALLY STANDING OVER ONE OF YOUR BOYS WHO LITERALLY DIED FOR NOTHING.
HE DIED TRYING TO SAVE US.
WHAT ARE YOU GOING TO DIE DOING?
WE WILL SPEAK AGAIN
HEY! WHAT WAS YOUR NAME AGAIN?
WHAT WAS ALL THAT YOU SAID AFTER "FREEDOM FIGHTERS"?
I BLANKED FOR A SECOND--

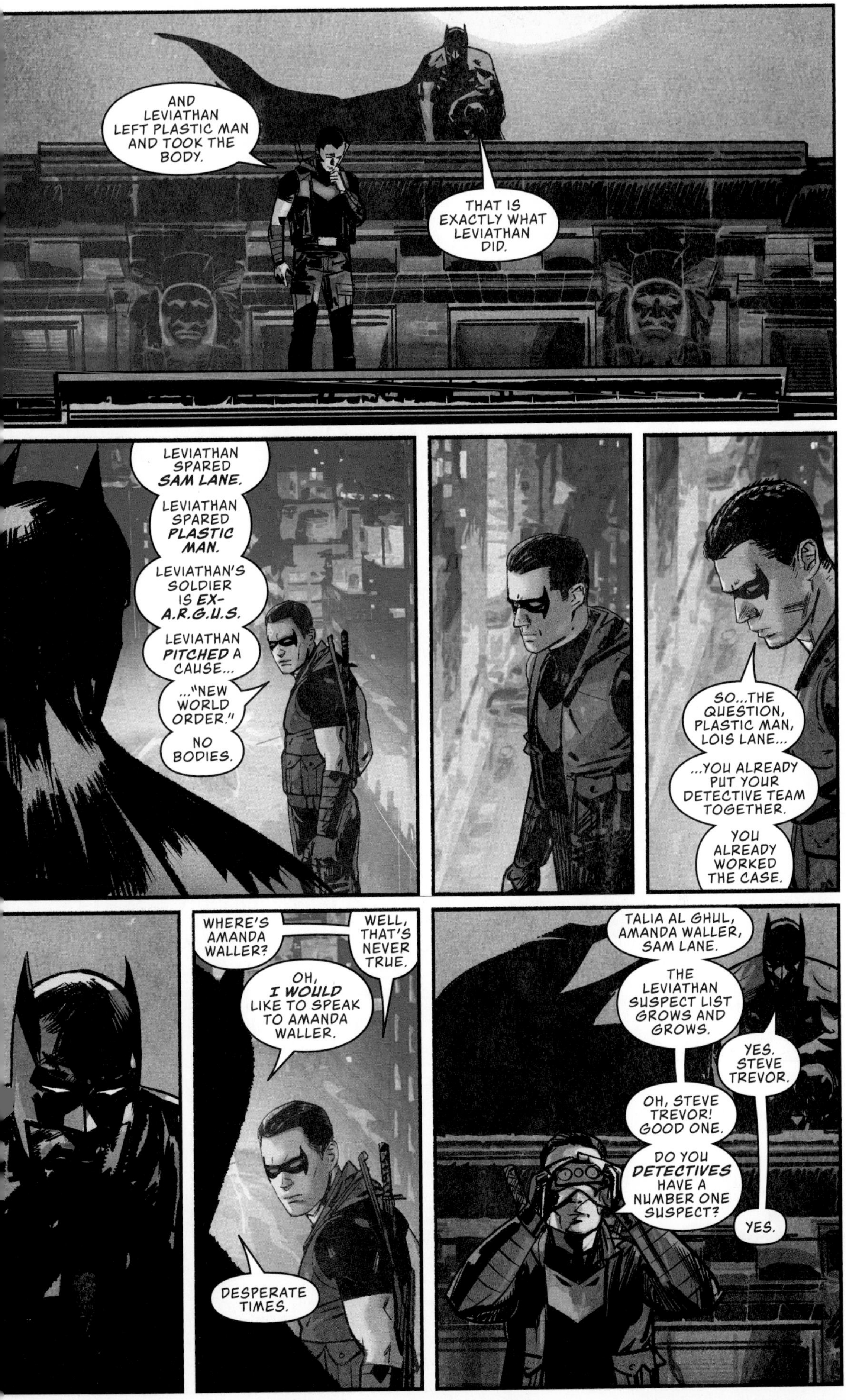
AND LEVIATHAN LEFT PLASTIC MAN AND TOOK THE BODY.
THAT IS EXACTLY WHAT LEVIATHAN DID.
LEVIATHAN SPARED **SAM LANE.**
LEVIATHAN SPARED **PLASTIC MAN.**
LEVIATHAN'S SOLDIER IS **EX-A.R.G.U.S.**
LEVIATHAN **PITCHED** A CAUSE...
..."NEW WORLD ORDER."
NO BODIES.
SO...THE QUESTION, PLASTIC MAN, LOIS LANE...
...YOU ALREADY PUT YOUR DETECTIVE TEAM TOGETHER.
YOU ALREADY WORKED THE CASE.
WHERE'S AMANDA WALLER?
WELL, THAT'S NEVER TRUE.
OH, ***I WOULD*** LIKE TO SPEAK TO AMANDA WALLER.
DESPERATE TIMES.
TALIA AL GHUL, AMANDA WALLER, SAM LANE.
THE LEVIATHAN SUSPECT LIST GROWS AND GROWS.
YES. STEVE TREVOR.
OH, STEVE TREVOR! GOOD ONE.
DO YOU ***DETECTIVES*** HAVE A NUMBER ONE SUSPECT?
YES.

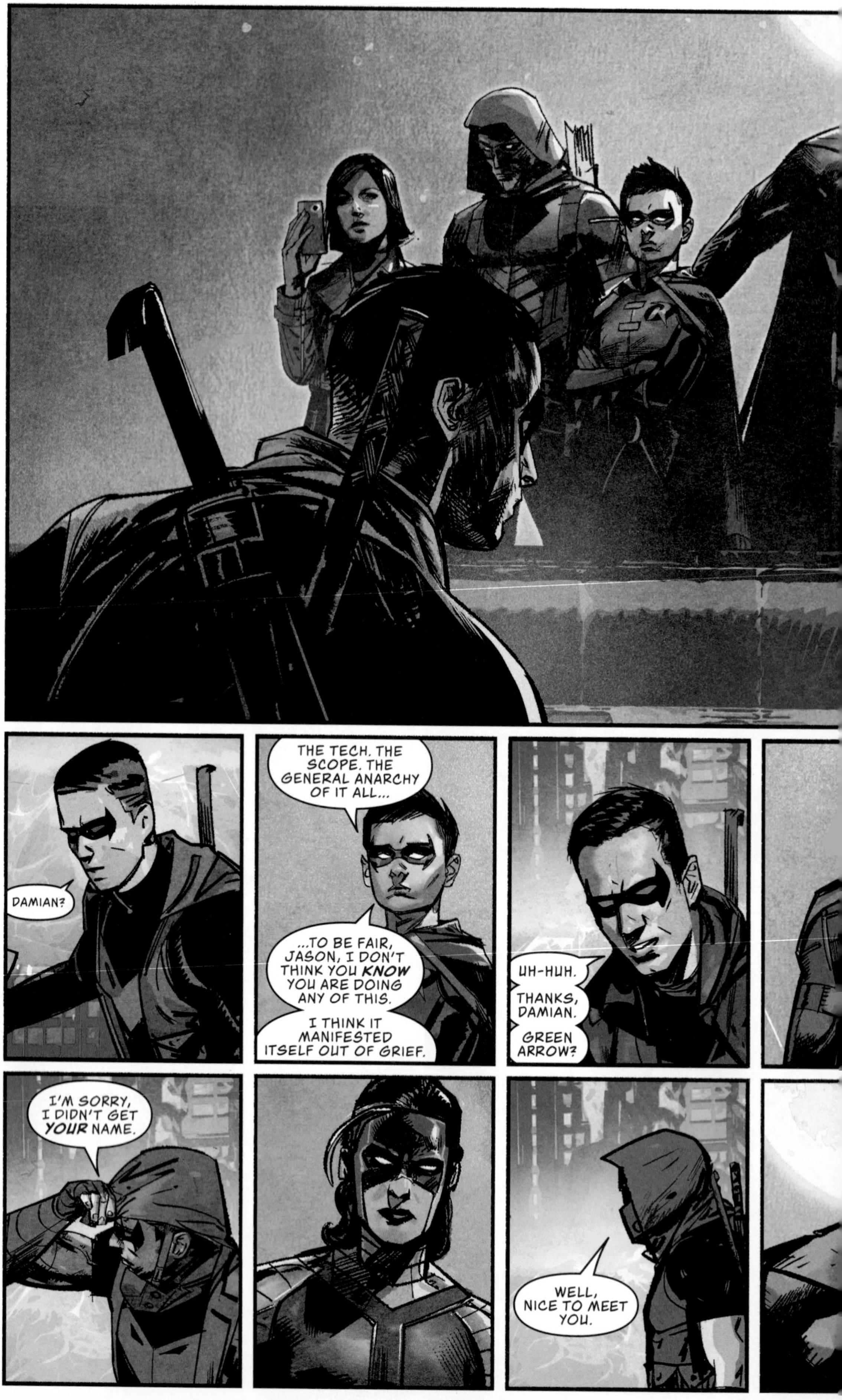
DAMIAN?
THE TECH. THE SCOPE. THE GENERAL ANARCHY OF IT ALL...
...TO BE FAIR, JASON, I DON'T THINK YOU **KNOW** YOU ARE DOING ANY OF THIS.
I THINK IT MANIFESTED ITSELF OUT OF GRIEF.
UH-HUH.
THANKS, DAMIAN.
GREEN ARROW?
I'M SORRY, I DIDN'T GET **YOUR** NAME.
WELL, NICE TO MEET YOU.

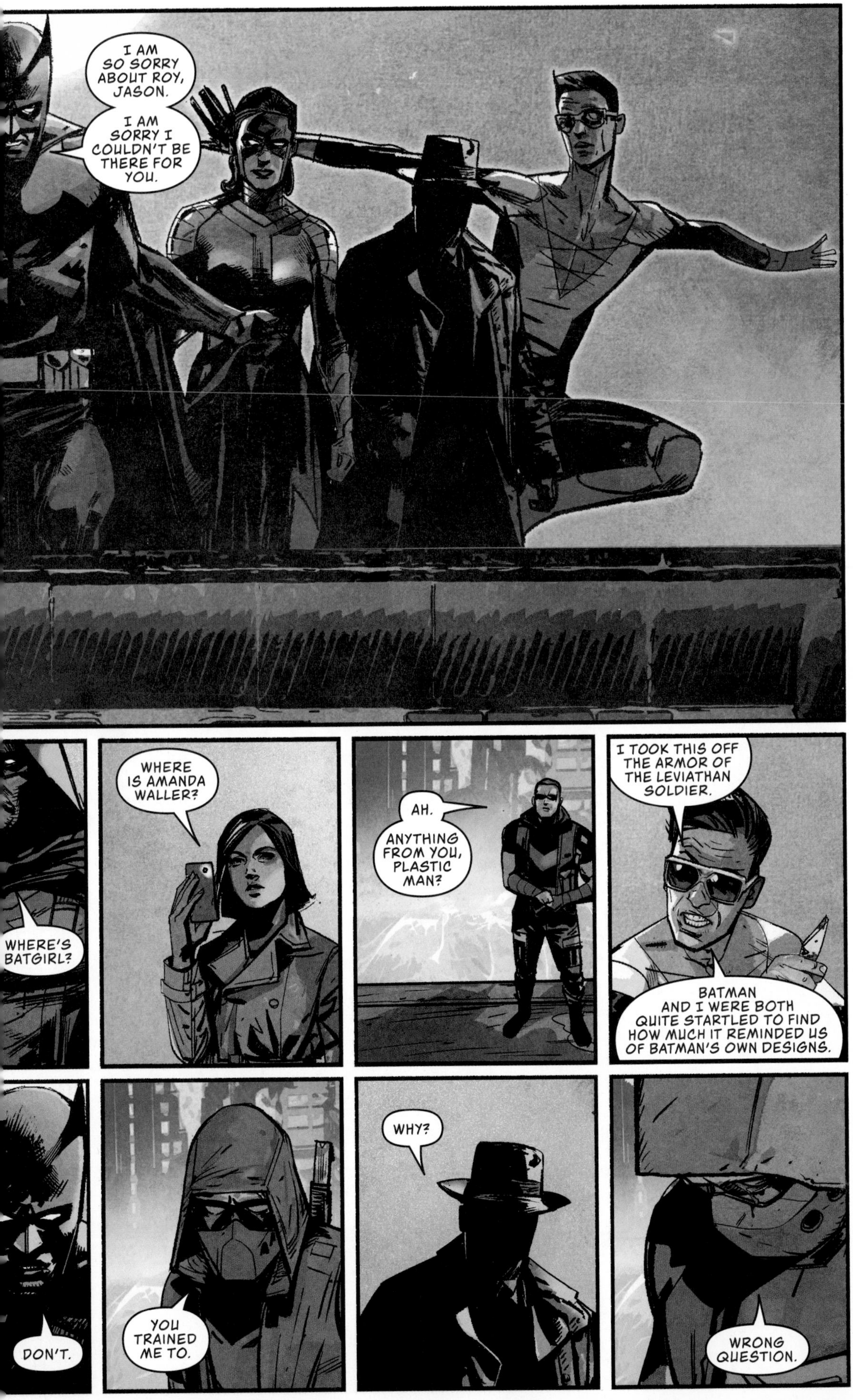
I AM SO SORRY ABOUT ROY, JASON.
I AM SORRY I COULDN'T BE THERE FOR YOU.
WHERE'S BATGIRL?
WHERE IS AMANDA WALLER?
AH.
ANYTHING FROM YOU, PLASTIC MAN?
I TOOK THIS OFF THE ARMOR OF THE LEVIATHAN SOLDIER.
BATMAN AND I WERE BOTH QUITE STARTLED TO FIND HOW MUCH IT REMINDED US OF BATMAN'S OWN DESIGNS.
DON'T.
YOU TRAINED ME TO.
WHY?
WRONG QUESTION.

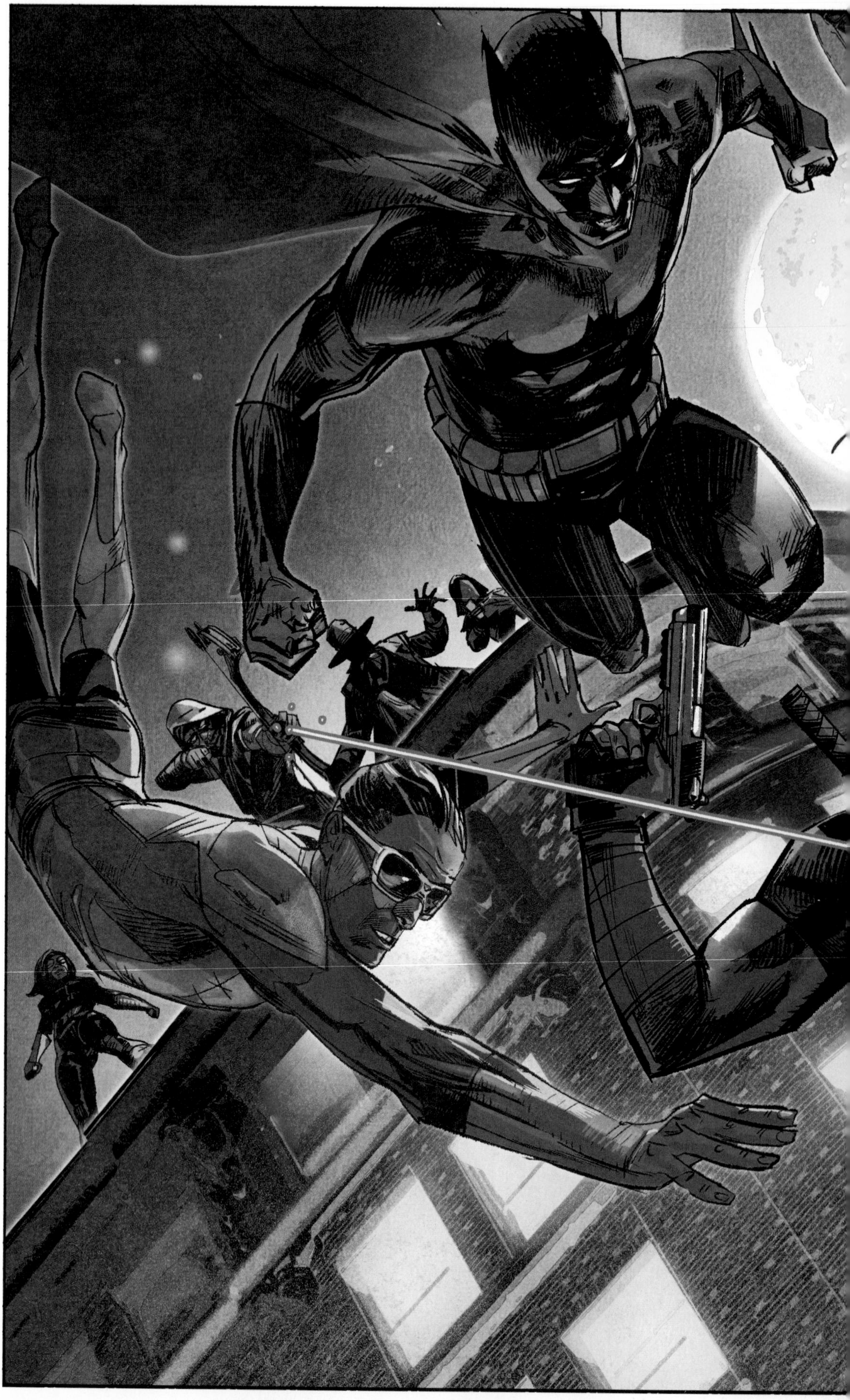

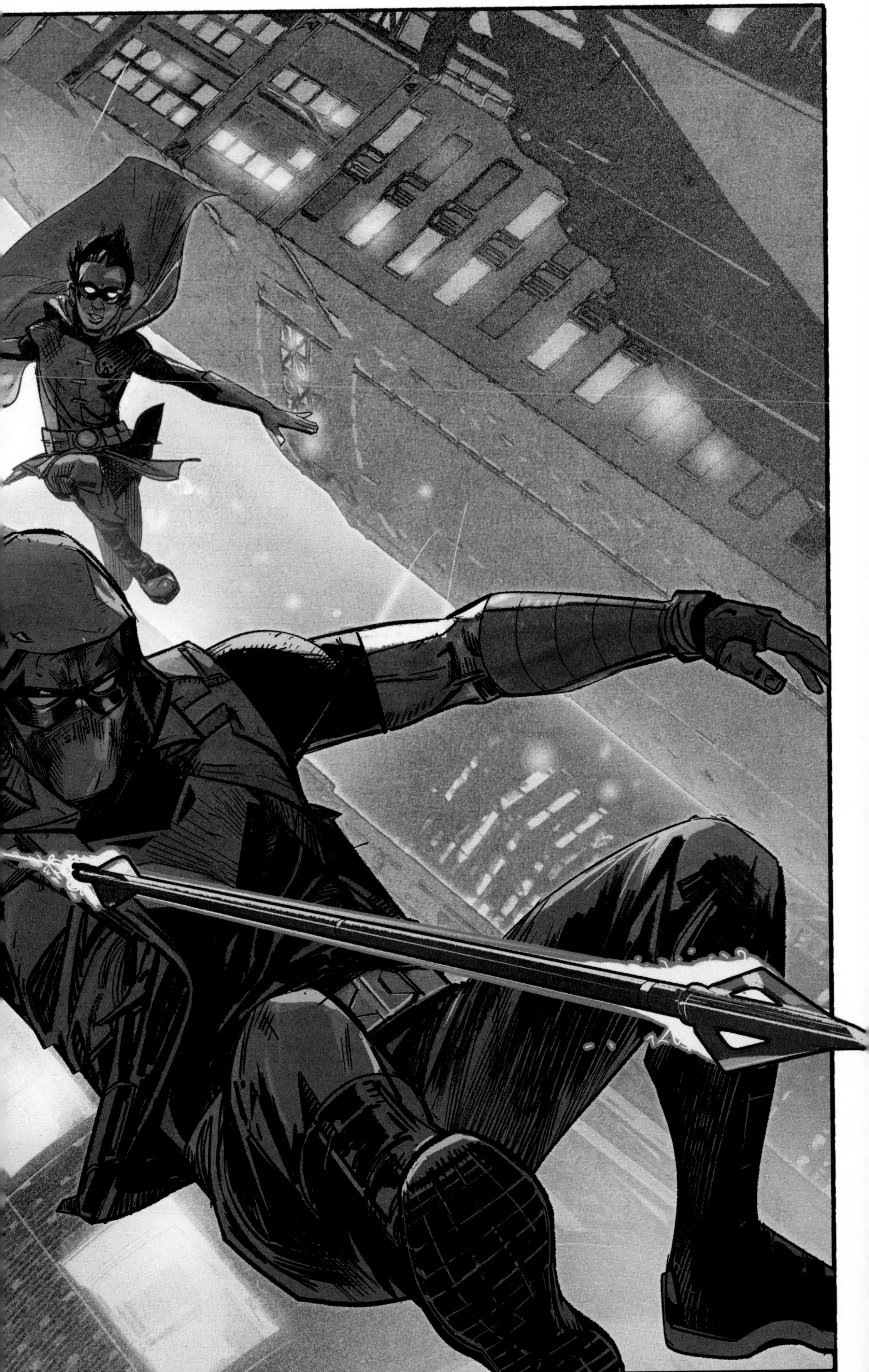

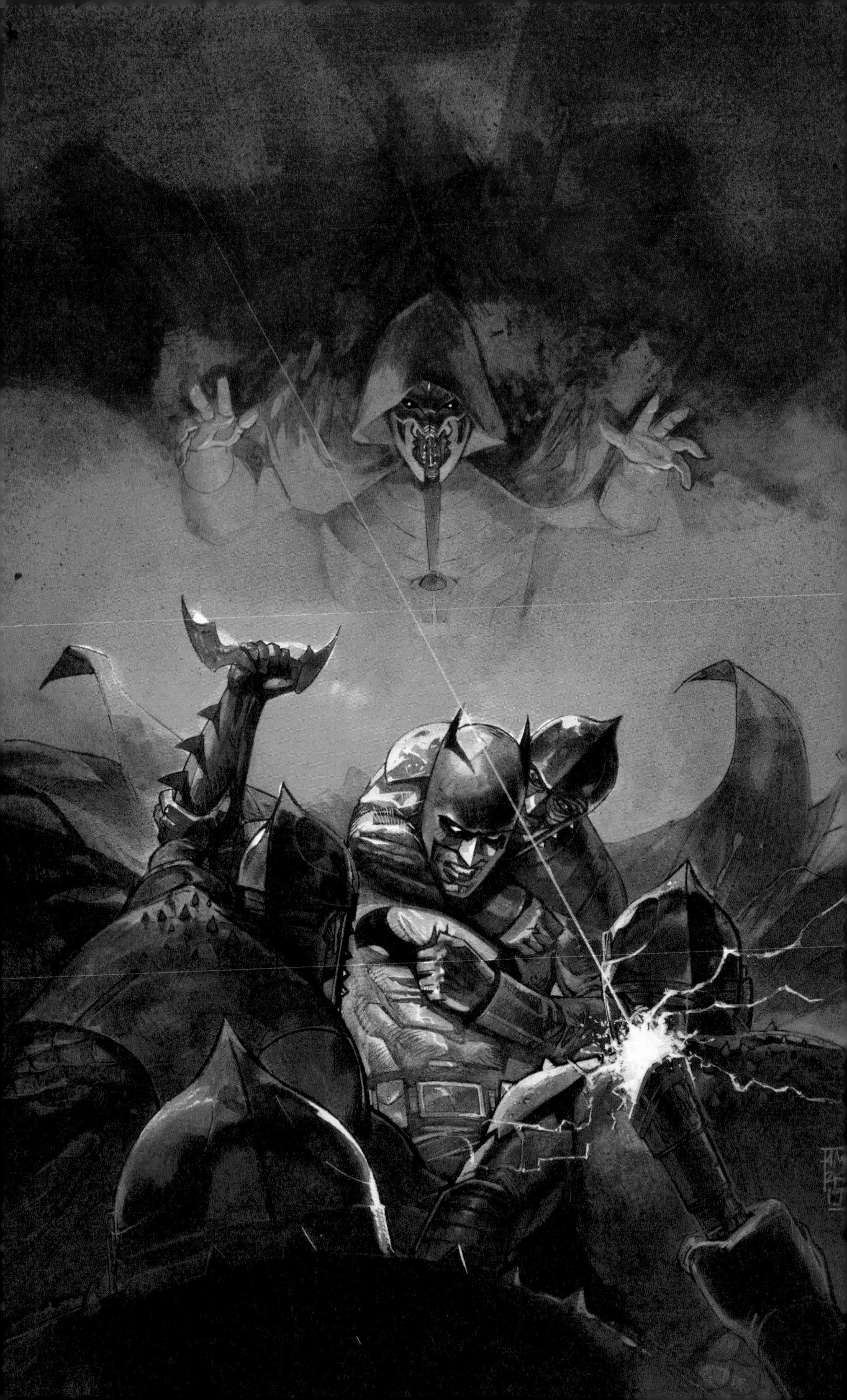

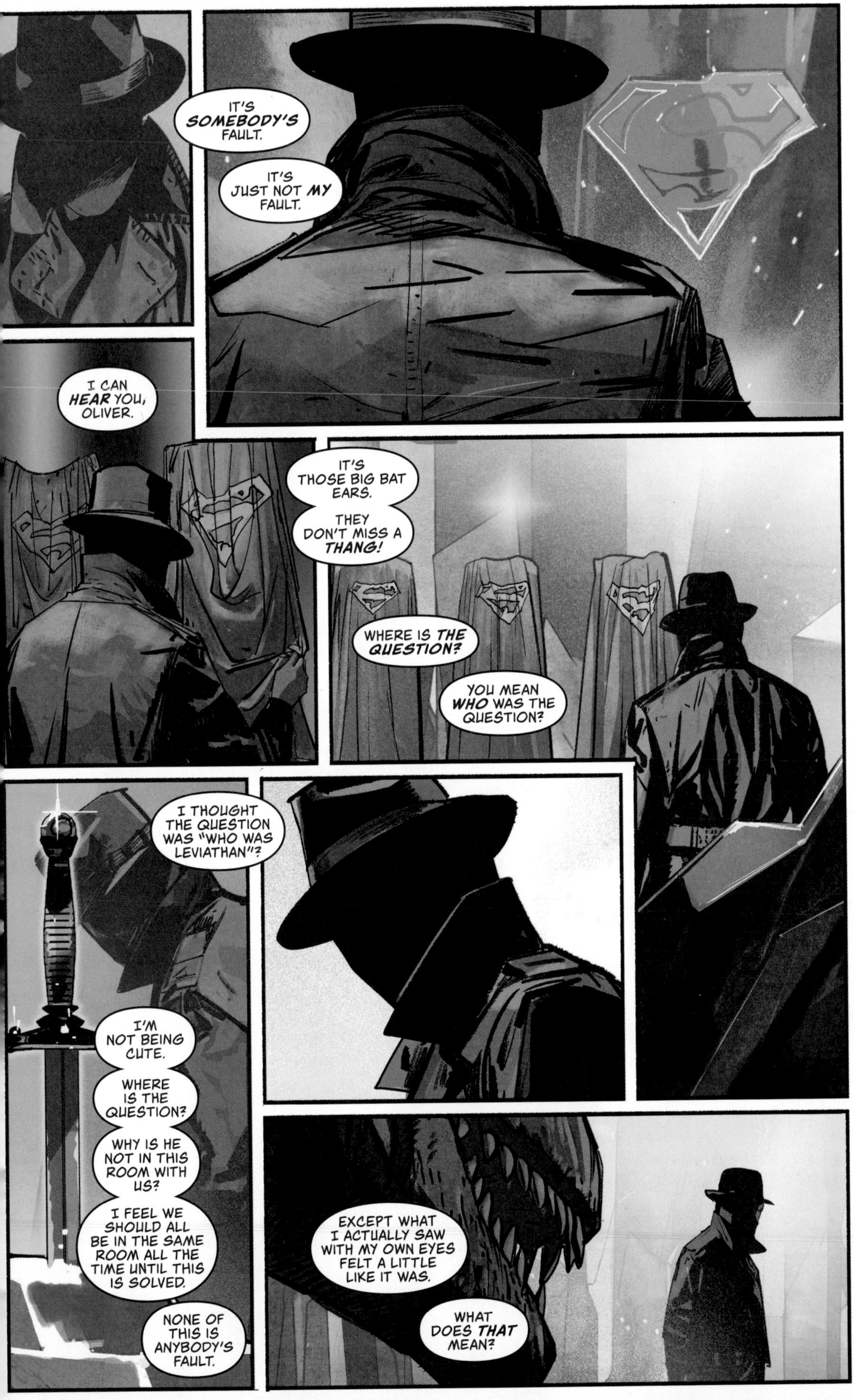

IT'S SOMEBODY'S FAULT.
IT'S JUST NOT MY FAULT.
I CAN HEAR YOU, OLIVER.
IT'S THOSE BIG BAT EARS.
THEY DON'T MISS A THANG!
WHERE IS THE QUESTION?
YOU MEAN WHO WAS THE QUESTION?
I THOUGHT THE QUESTION WAS "WHO WAS LEVIATHAN"?
I'M NOT BEING CUTE.
WHERE IS THE QUESTION?
WHY IS HE NOT IN THIS ROOM WITH US?
I FEEL WE SHOULD ALL BE IN THE SAME ROOM ALL THE TIME UNTIL THIS IS SOLVED.
NONE OF THIS IS ANYBODY'S FAULT.
EXCEPT WHAT I ACTUALLY SAW WITH MY OWN EYES FELT A LITTLE LIKE IT WAS.
WHAT DOES THAT MEAN?

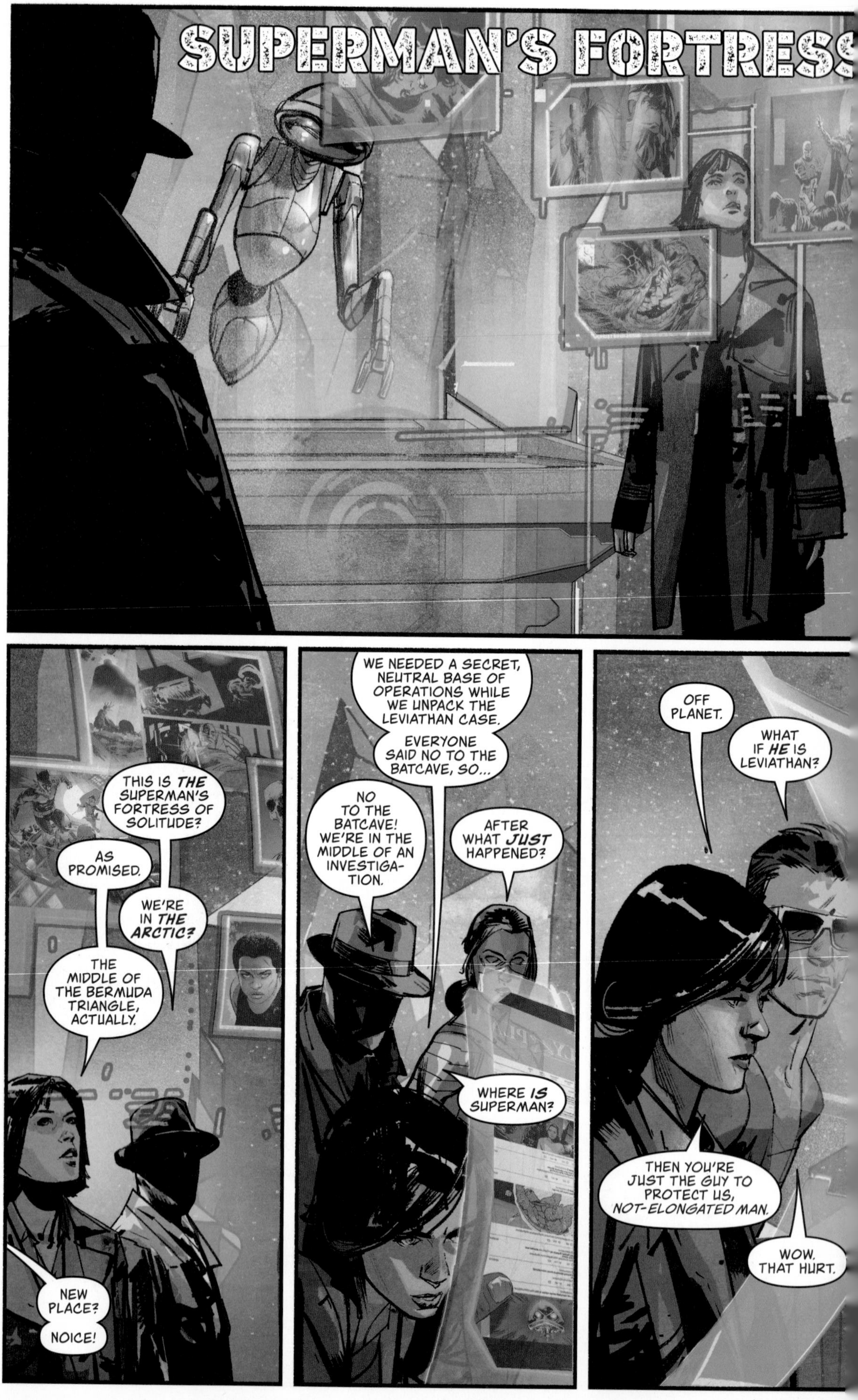
SUPERMAN'S FORTRESS
THIS IS THE SUPERMAN'S FORTRESS OF SOLITUDE?
AS PROMISED.
WE'RE IN THE ARCTIC?
THE MIDDLE OF THE BERMUDA TRIANGLE, ACTUALLY.
NEW PLACE?
NOICE!
WE NEEDED A SECRET, NEUTRAL BASE OF OPERATIONS WHILE WE UNPACK THE LEVIATHAN CASE.
EVERYONE SAID NO TO THE BATCAVE, SO...
NO TO THE BATCAVE! WE'RE IN THE MIDDLE OF AN INVESTIGA- TION.
AFTER WHAT JUST HAPPENED?
WHERE IS SUPERMAN?
OFF PLANET.
WHAT IF HE IS LEVIATHAN?
THEN YOU'RE JUST THE GUY TO PROTECT US, NOT-ELONGATED MAN.
WOW. THAT HURT.

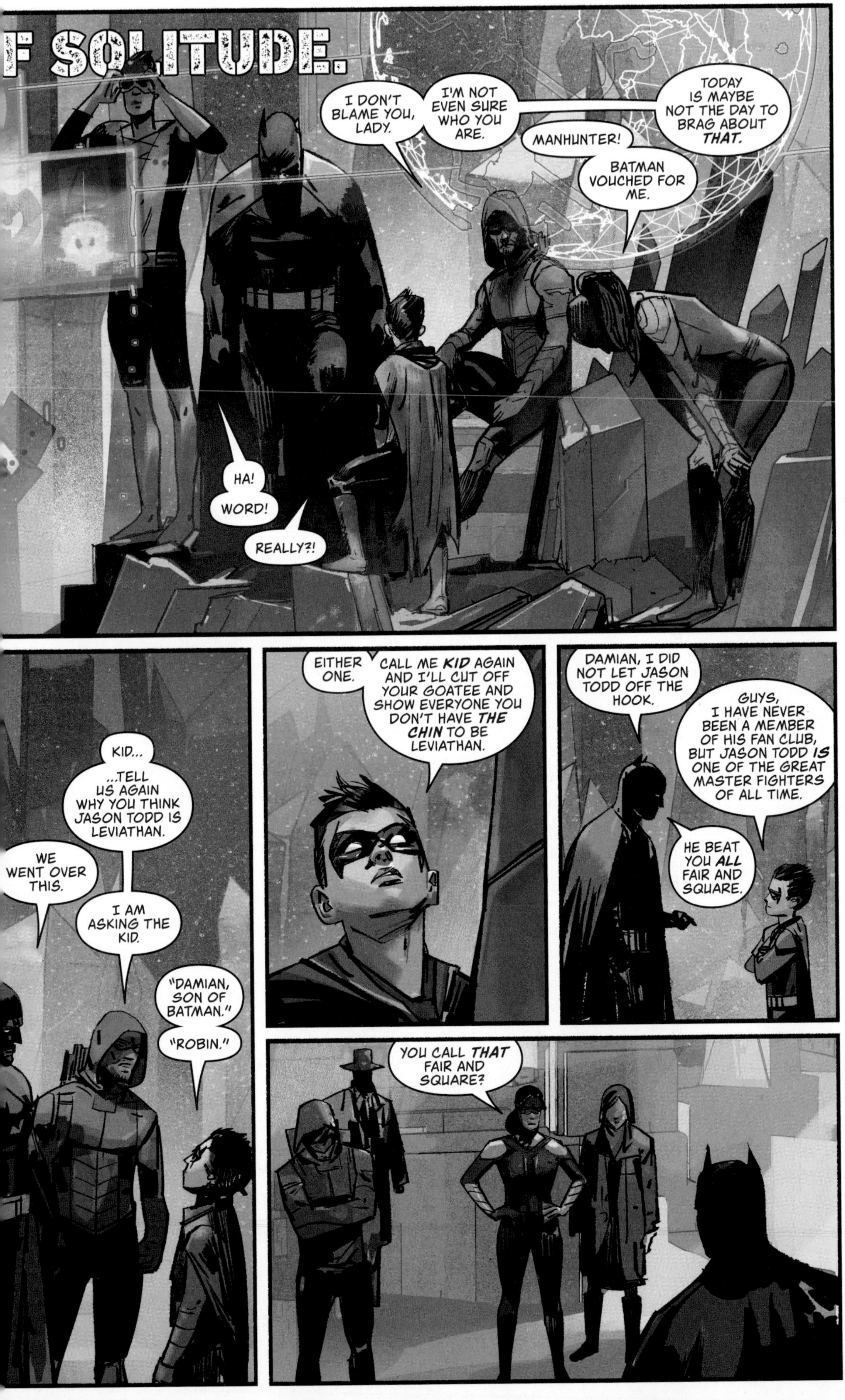
F SOLITUDE.
I DON'T BLAME YOU, LADY.
I'M NOT EVEN SURE WHO YOU ARE.
TODAY IS MAYBE NOT THE DAY TO BRAG ABOUT THAT.
MANHUNTER!
BATMAN VOUCHED FOR ME.
HA!
WORD!
REALLY?!
KID...
...TELL US AGAIN WHY YOU THINK JASON TODD IS LEVIATHAN.
WE WENT OVER THIS.
I AM ASKING THE KID.
"DAMIAN, SON OF BATMAN."
"ROBIN."
EITHER ONE.
CALL ME KID AGAIN AND I'LL CUT OFF YOUR GOATEE AND SHOW EVERYONE YOU DON'T HAVE THE CHIN TO BE LEVIATHAN.
DAMIAN, I DID NOT LET JASON TODD OFF THE HOOK.
GUYS, I HAVE NEVER BEEN A MEMBER OF HIS FAN CLUB, BUT JASON TODD IS ONE OF THE GREAT MASTER FIGHTERS OF ALL TIME.
HE BEAT YOU ALL FAIR AND SQUARE.
YOU CALL THAT FAIR AND SQUARE?

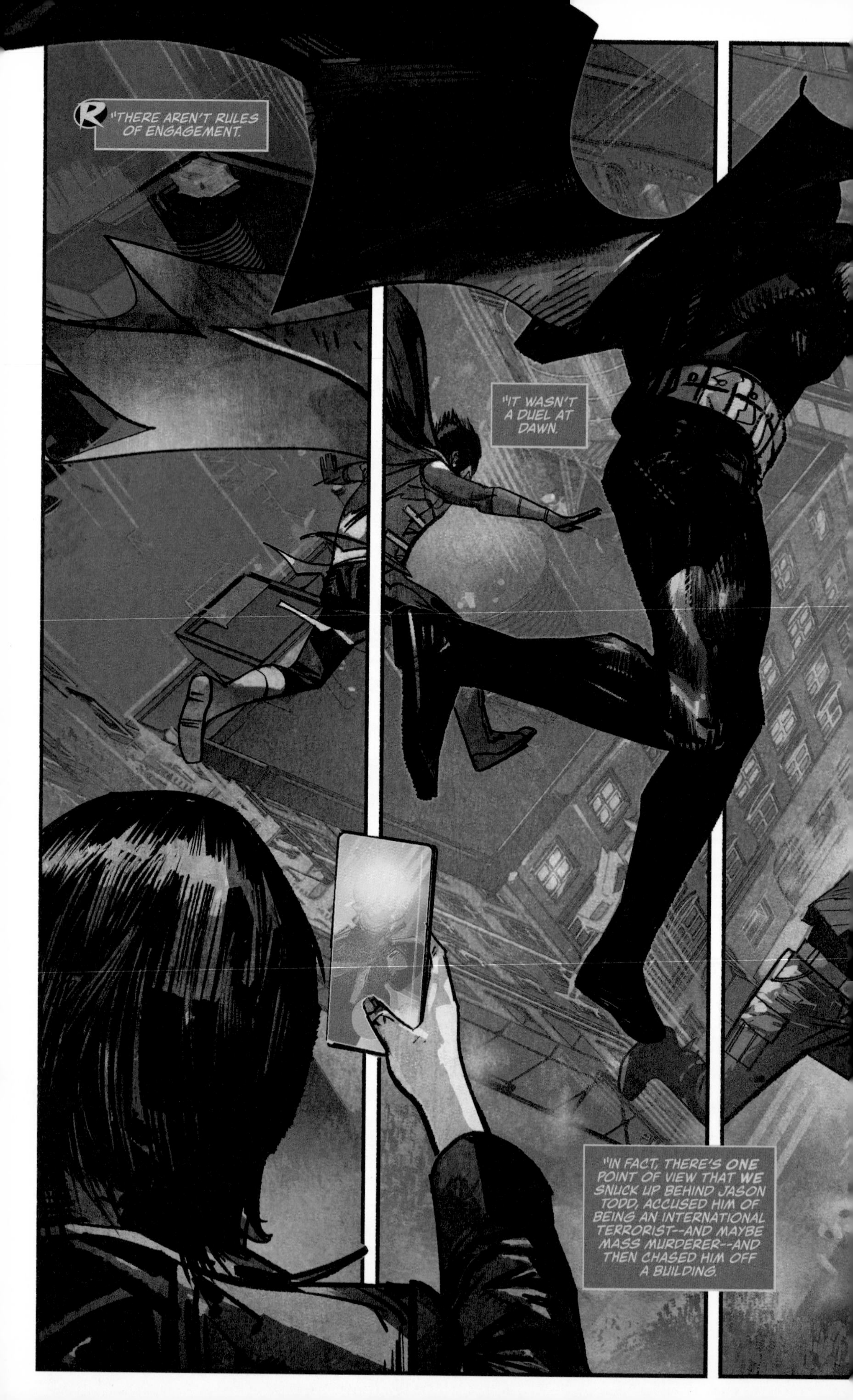
"THERE AREN'T RULES OF ENGAGEMENT.
"IT WASN'T A DUEL AT DAWN.
"IN FACT, THERE'S ONE POINT OF VIEW THAT WE SNUCK UP BEHIND JASON TODD, ACCUSED HIM OF BEING AN INTERNATIONAL TERRORIST--AND MAYBE MASS MURDERER--AND THEN CHASED HIM OFF A BUILDING.

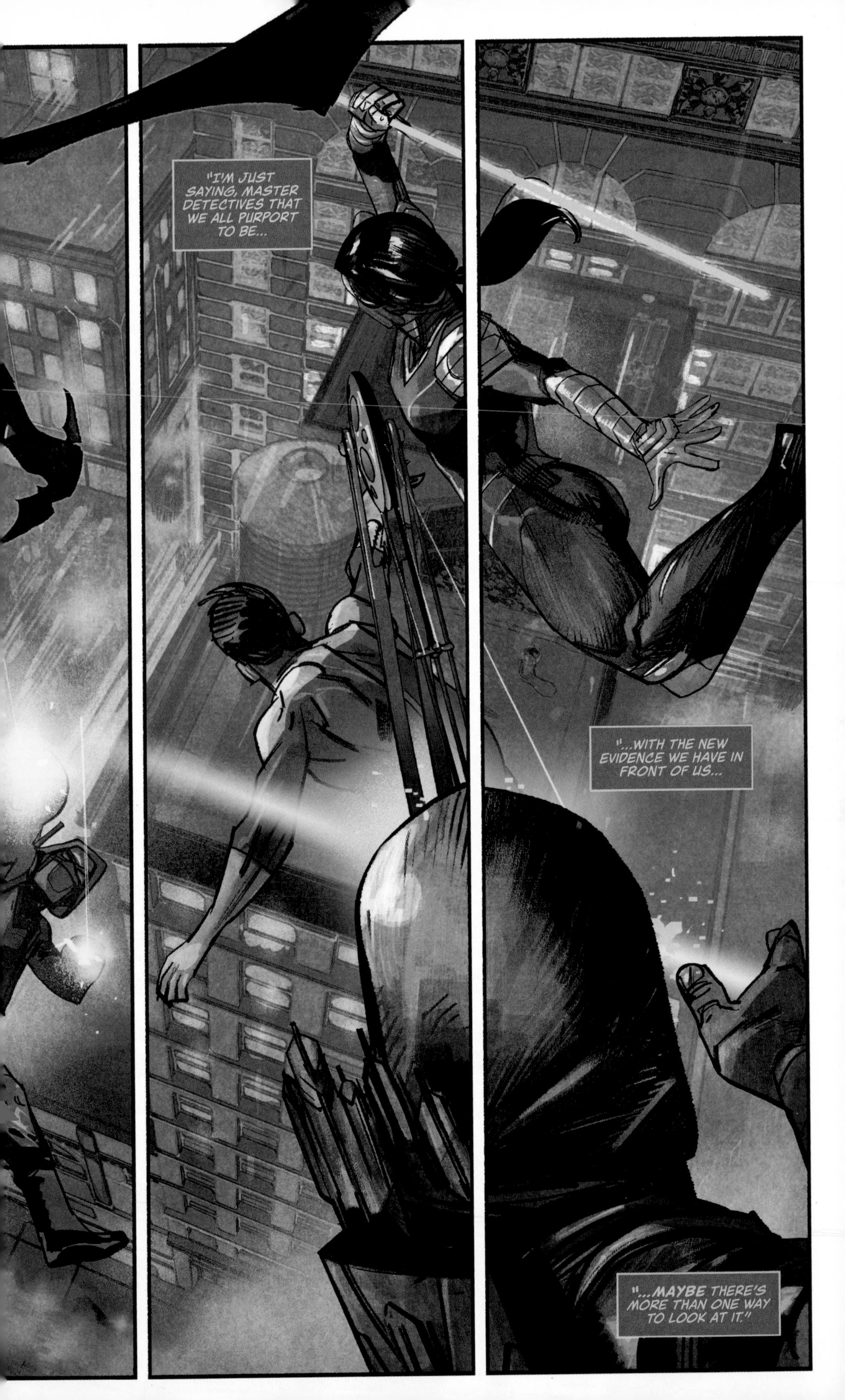
"I'M JUST SAYING, MASTER DETECTIVES THAT WE ALL PURPORT TO BE...
"...WITH THE NEW EVIDENCE WE HAVE IN FRONT OF US...
"...MAYBE THERE'S MORE THAN ONE WAY TO LOOK AT IT."

Files   Editing   Images   Selection   View   Windows   T

TEXT
DOCU
PLAC
HOMI
NEW
OLD
KNOV

Increasingly unknown. A person and organization named LEVIA-THAN has done the impossible and simultaneously taken out major pillars of the world intelligence community.

The D.E.O., Spyral, A.R.G.U.S., and many others are gone. Wiped from the earth.

X ERR

X ERRO

SPYRAL

D.E.O.

RROR

Green Arrow and Batgirl survived one attack. Batgirl was offered a place in Leviathan. No one has seen her since

STATU
UNDE
FONT
GENE

EVENT LEVIATHAN

Part 3
BRIAN MICHAEL BENDIS story
ALEX MALEEV art & cover
JOSH REED letters **JESSICA CHEN** associate editor
MIKE COTTON editor **BRIAN CUNNINGHAM** group editor

TRASH

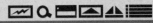

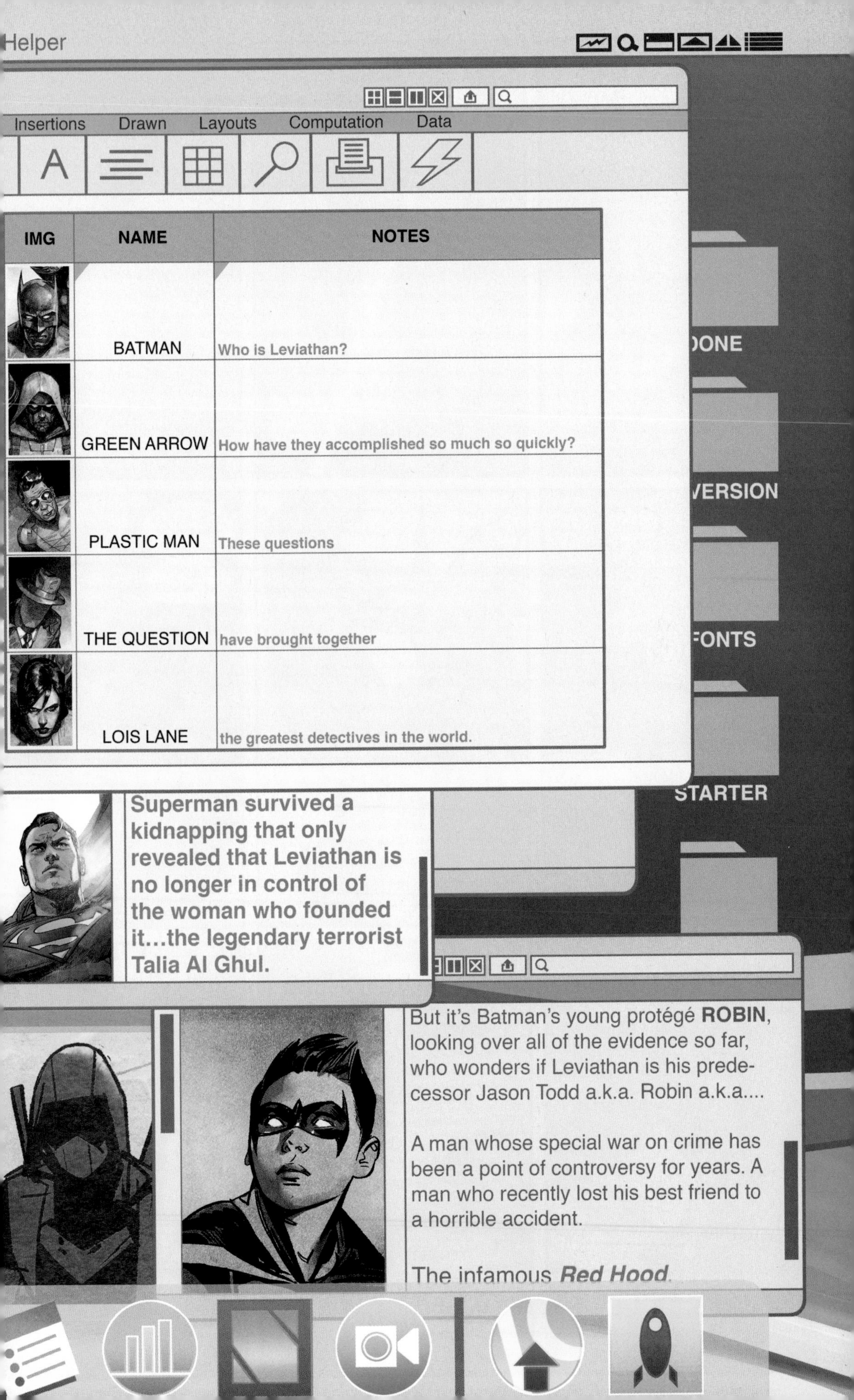

Insertions   Drawn   Layouts   Computation   Data

IMG	NAME	NOTES
	BATMAN	Who is Leviathan?
	GREEN ARROW	How have they accomplished so much so quickly?
	PLASTIC MAN	These questions
	THE QUESTION	have brought together
	LOIS LANE	the greatest detectives in the world.

DONE

VERSION

FONTS

STARTER

 Superman survived a kidnapping that only revealed that Leviathan is no longer in control of the woman who founded it...the legendary terrorist Talia Al Ghul.

 But it's Batman's young protégé **ROBIN**, looking over all of the evidence so far, who wonders if Leviathan is his predecessor Jason Todd a.k.a. Robin a.k.a....

A man whose special war on crime has been a point of controversy for years. A man who recently lost his best friend to a horrible accident.

The infamous *Red Hood*.

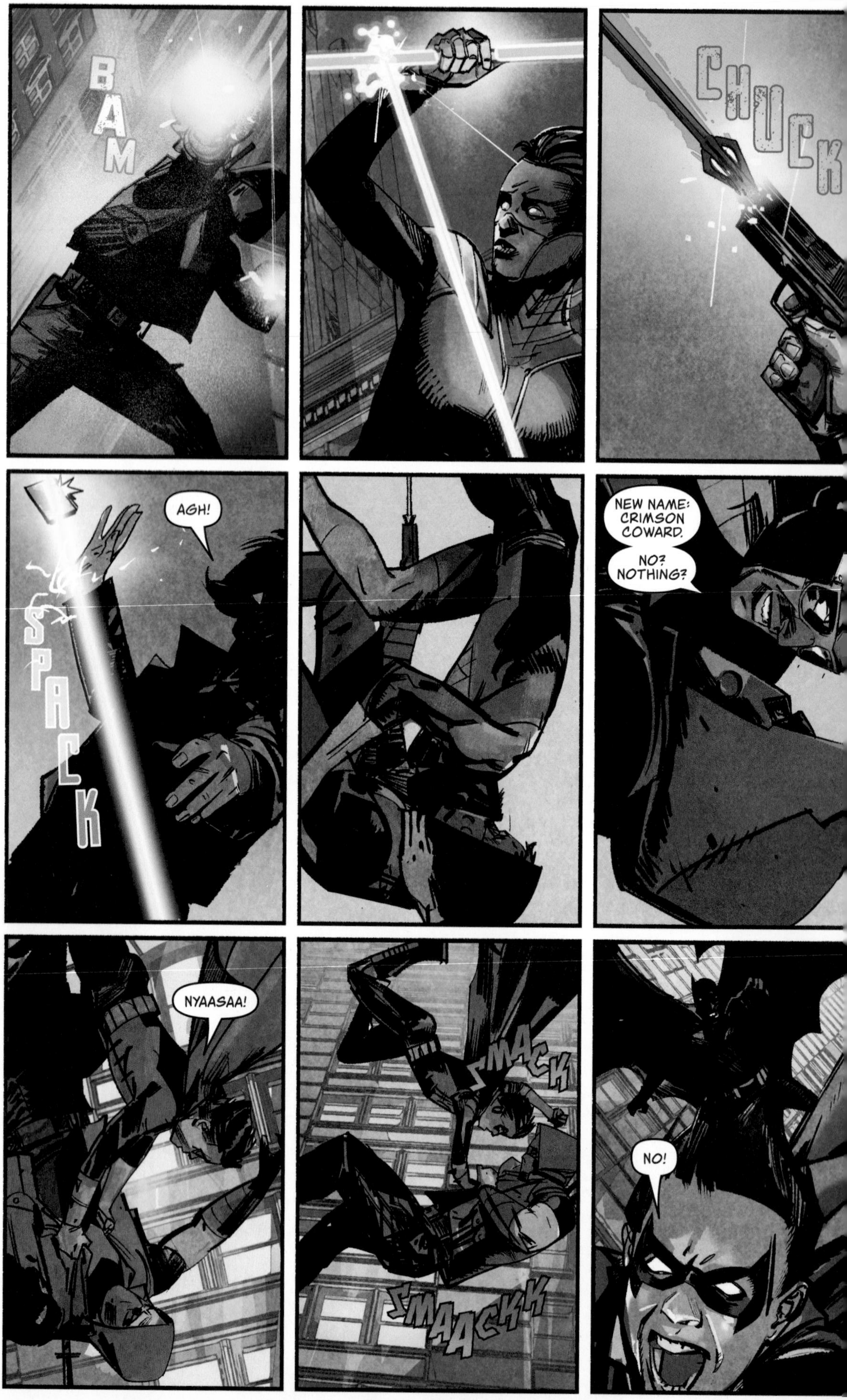
BAM
CHUCK
AGH!
SPACK
NEW NAME: CRIMSON COWARD.
NO? NOTHING?
NYAASAA!
SMACK
SMAACKK
NO!

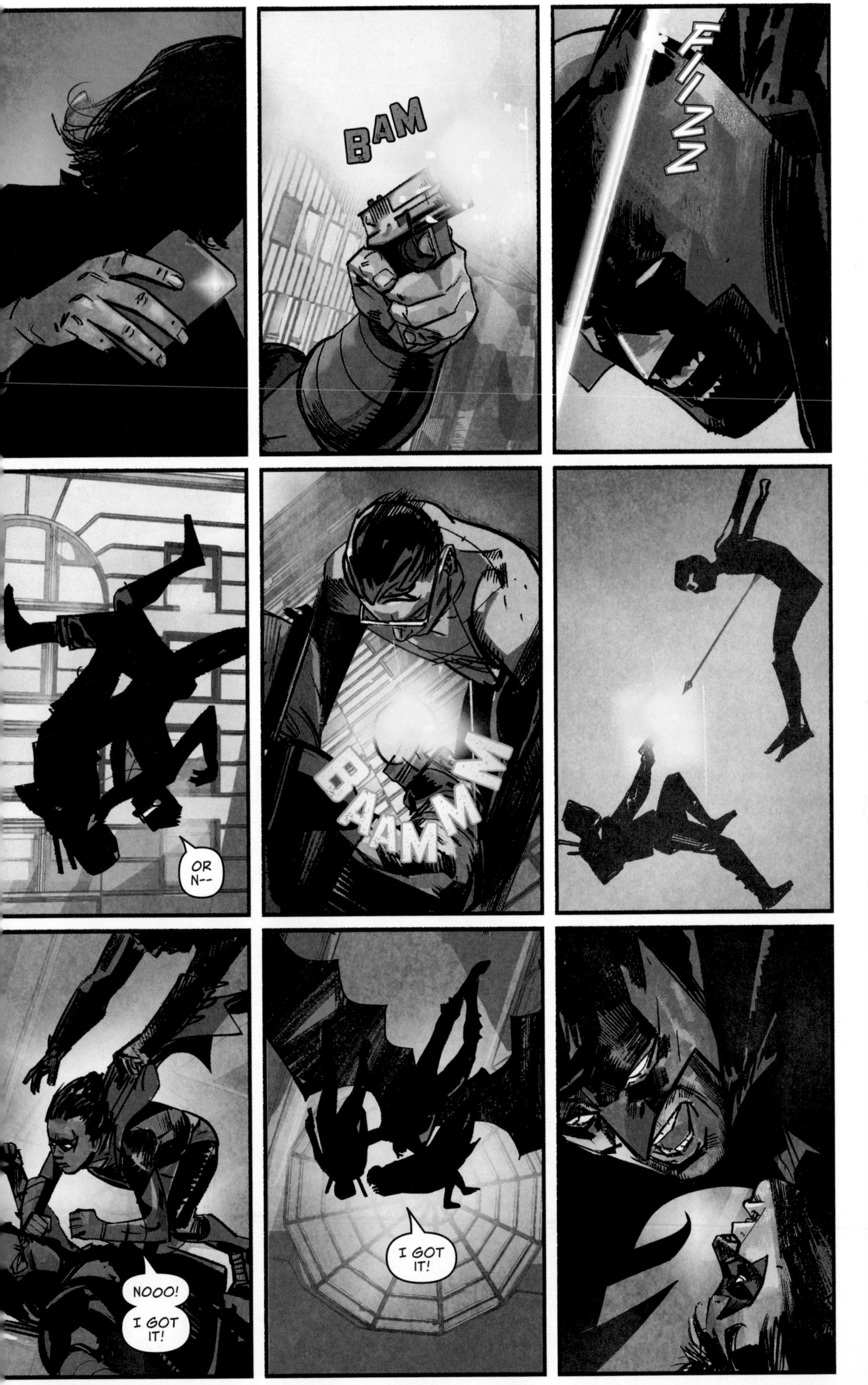
BAM
FIZZ
OR N--
BAAMMM
NOOO!
I GOT IT!
I GOT IT!

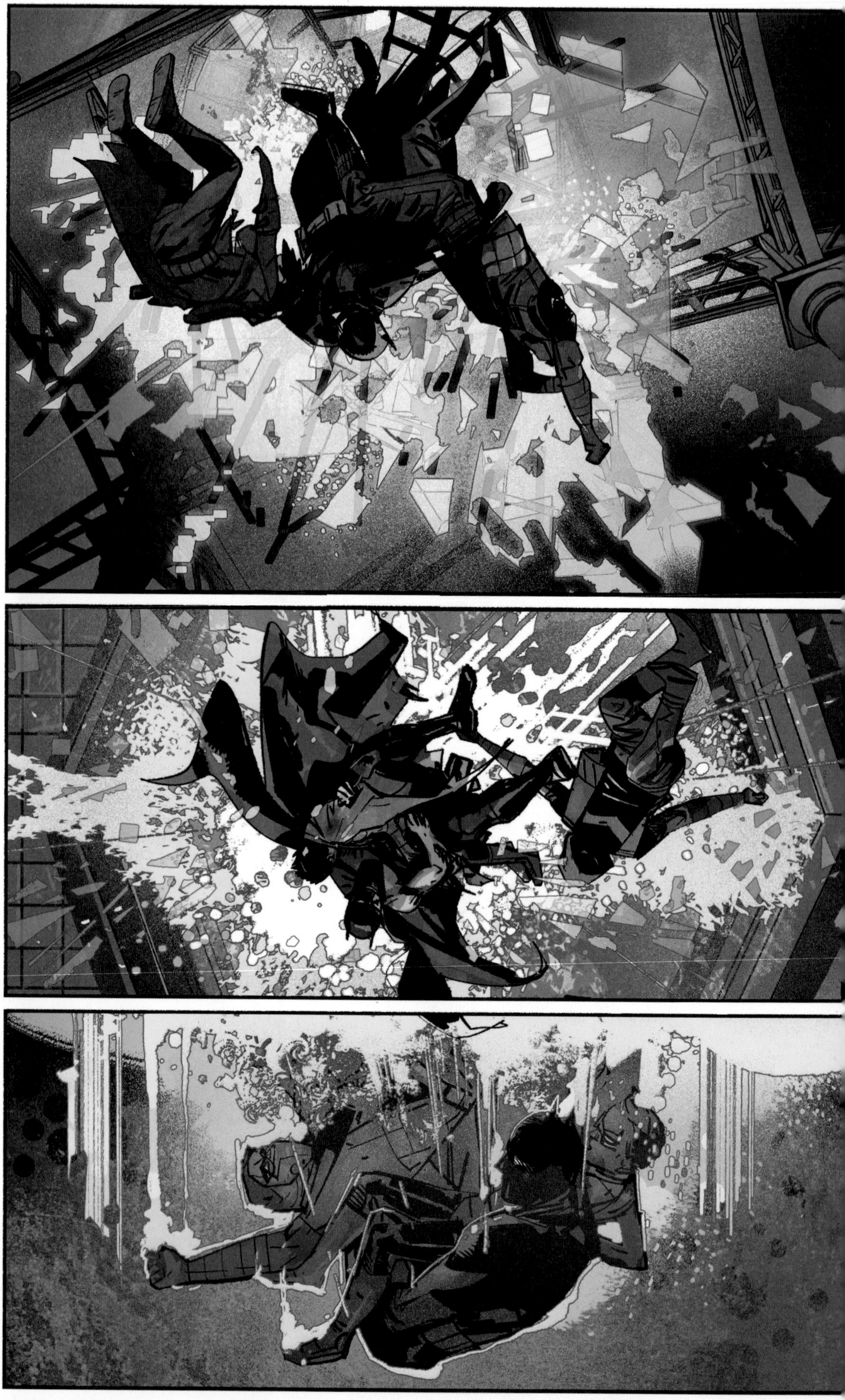

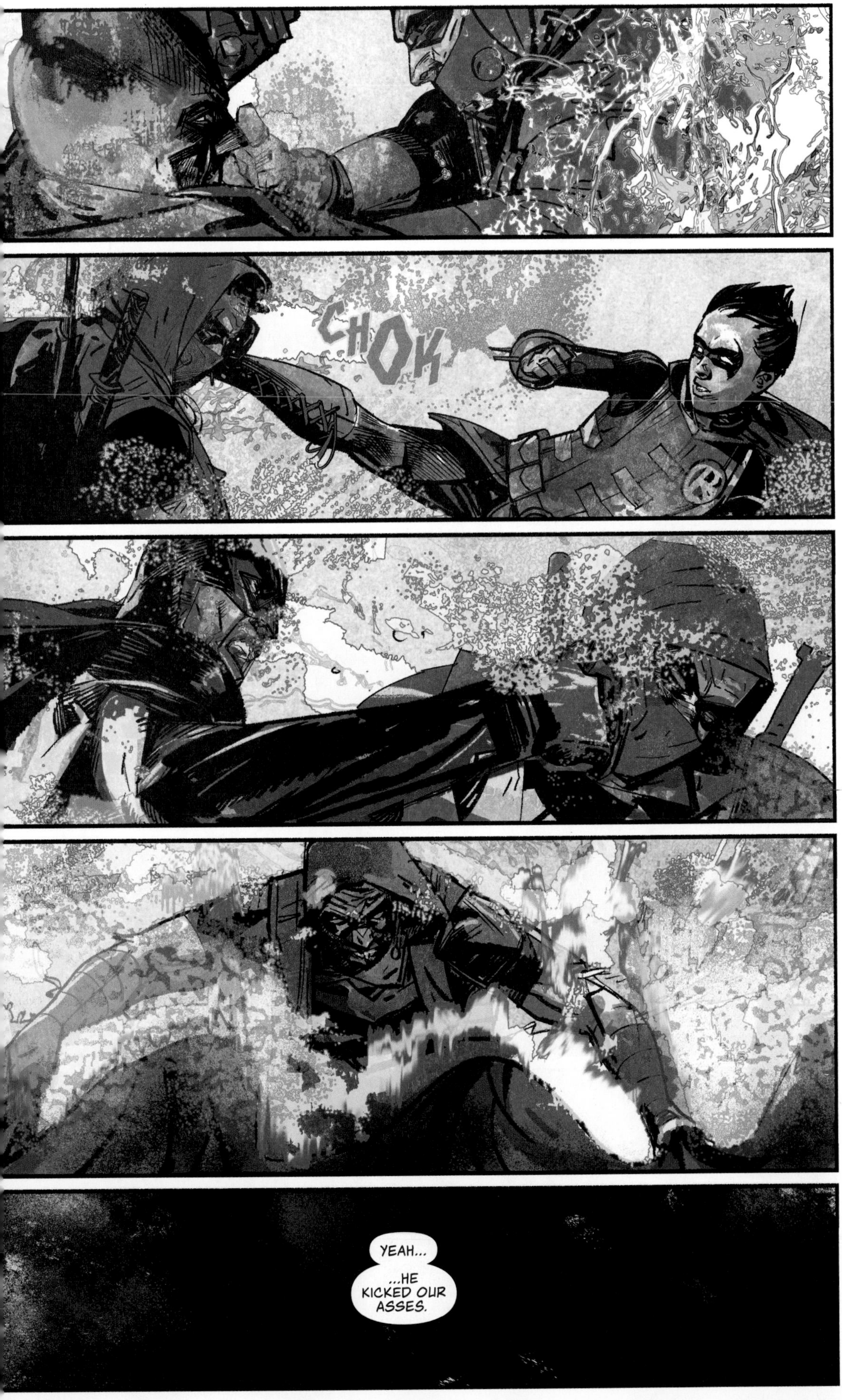
CHOK
YEAH...
...HE KICKED OUR ASSES.

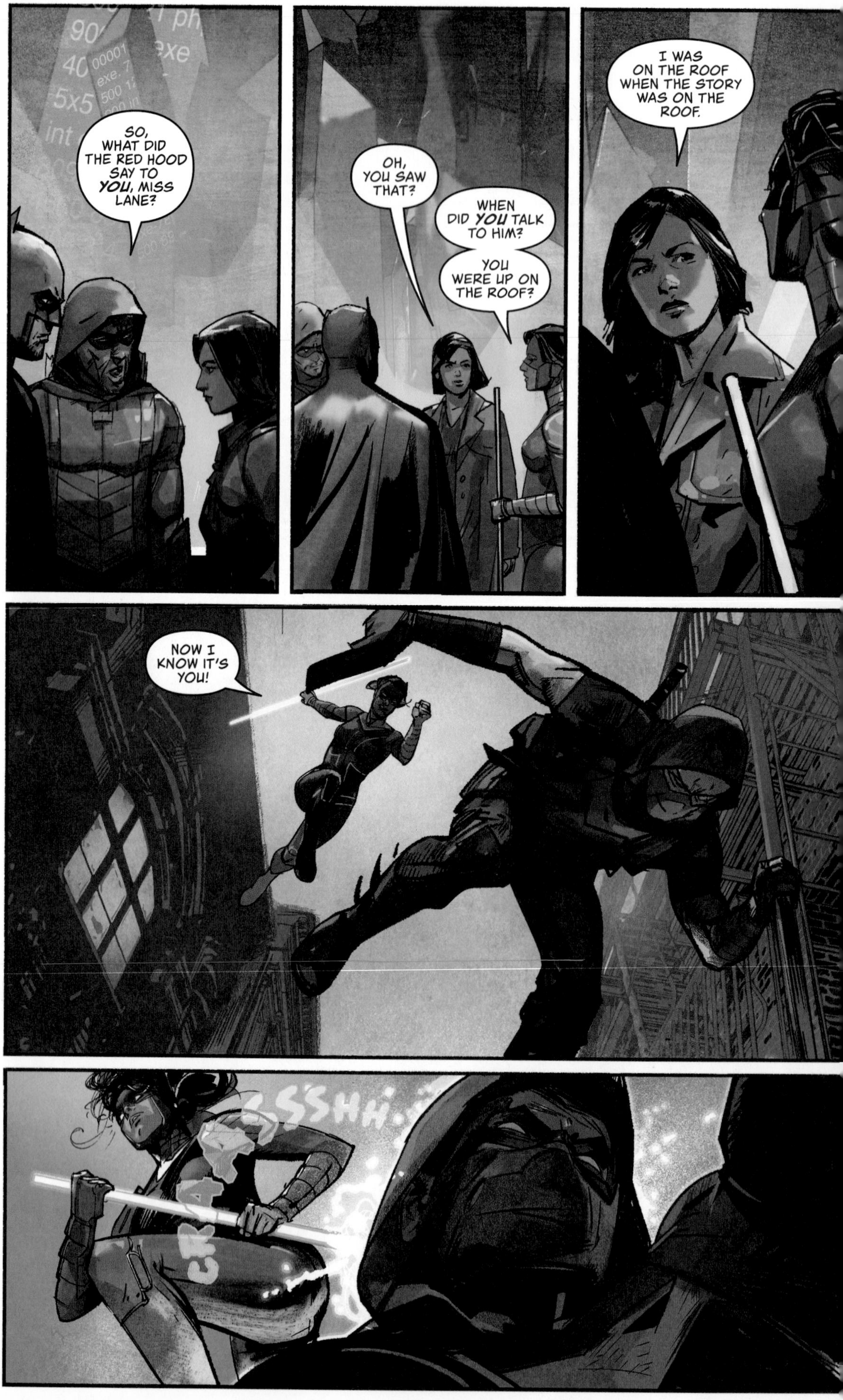
SO, WHAT DID THE RED HOOD SAY TO YOU, MISS LANE?
OH, YOU SAW THAT?
WHEN DID YOU TALK TO HIM?
YOU WERE UP ON THE ROOF?
I WAS ON THE ROOF WHEN THE STORY WAS ON THE ROOF.
NOW I KNOW IT'S YOU!
SSHH

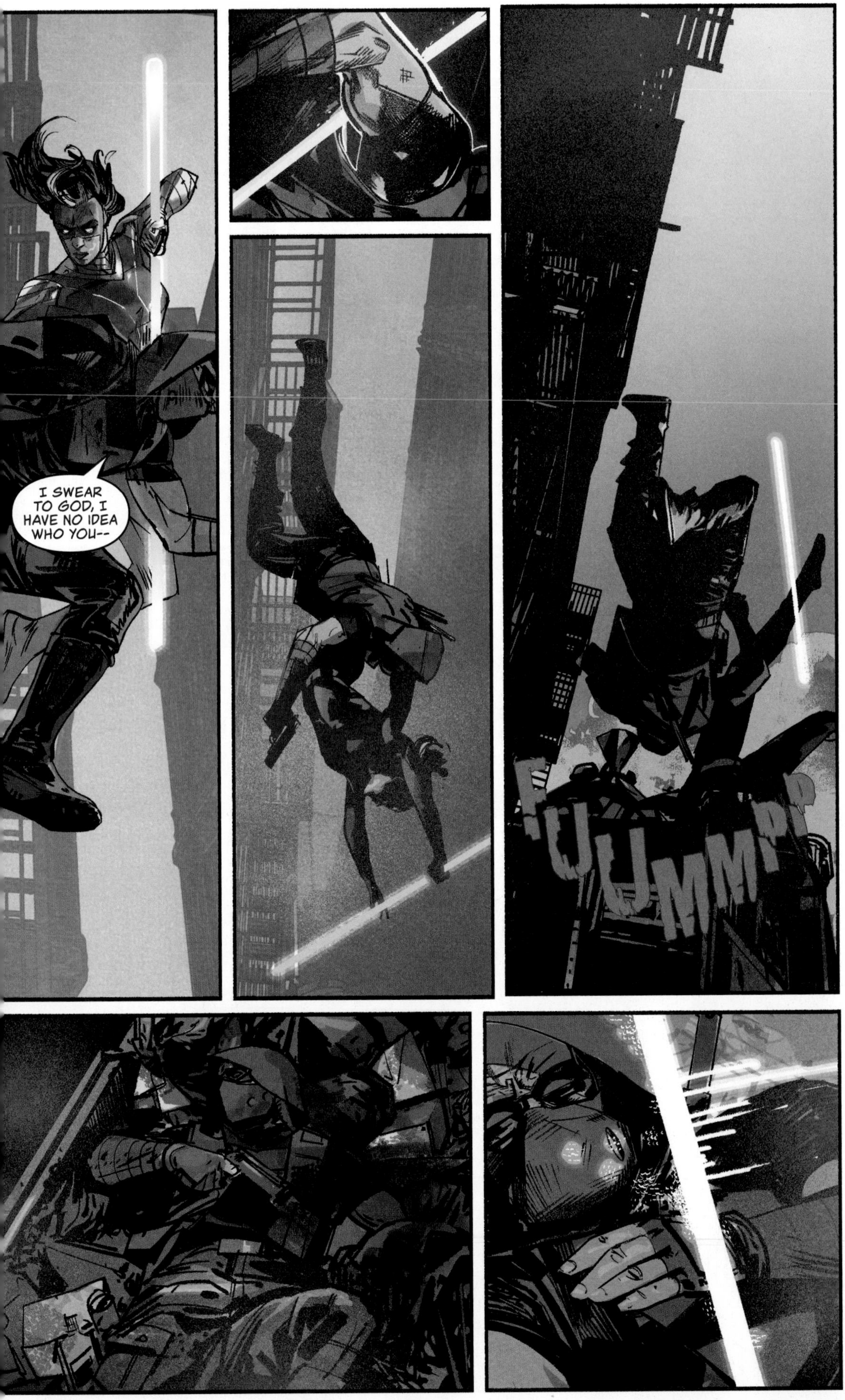
I SWEAR TO GOD, I HAVE NO IDEA WHO YOU--
FUUMMP

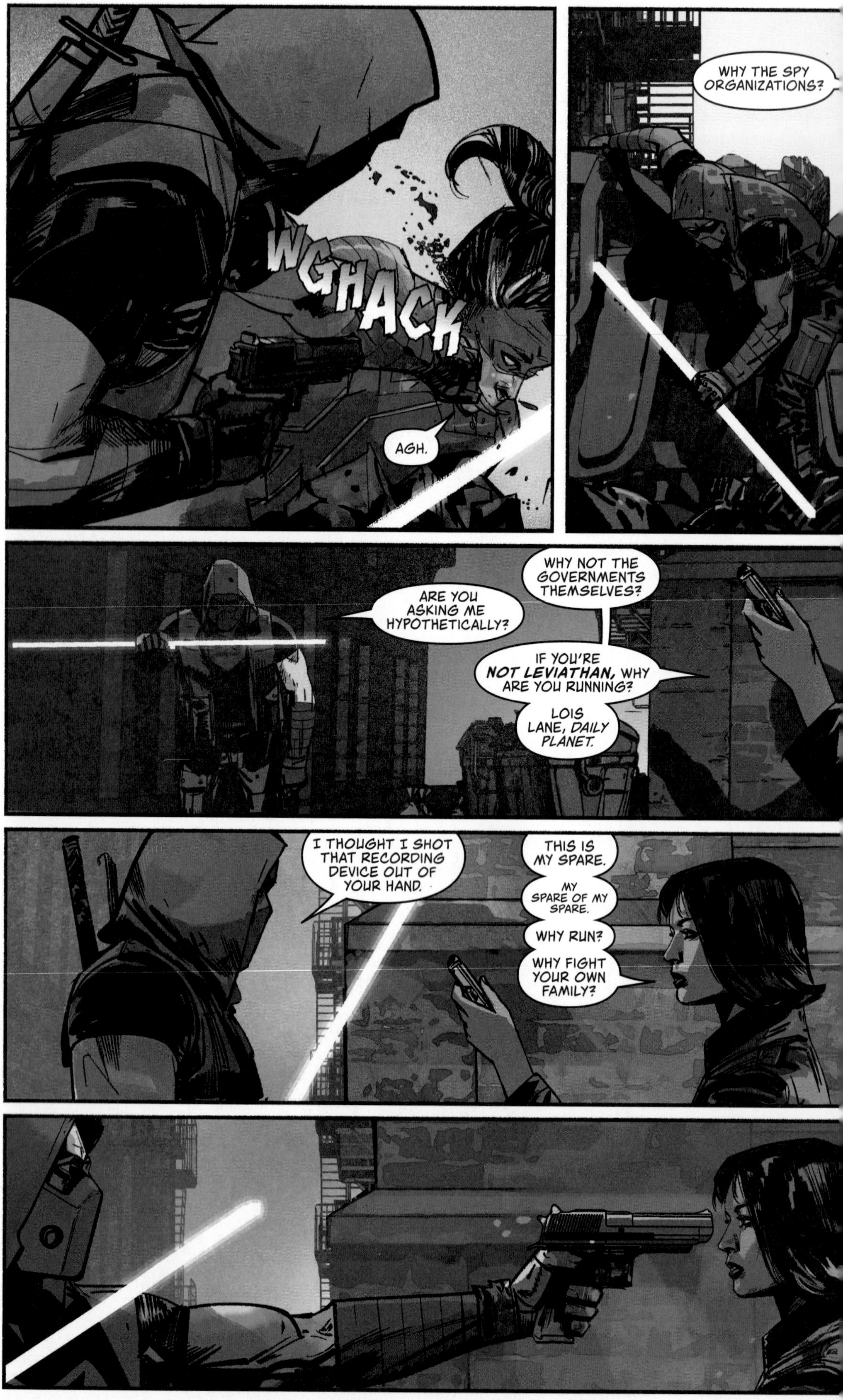
WGHACK
AGH.
WHY THE SPY ORGANIZATIONS?
ARE YOU ASKING ME HYPOTHETICALLY?
WHY NOT THE GOVERNMENTS THEMSELVES?
IF YOU'RE *NOT LEVIATHAN,* WHY ARE YOU RUNNING?
LOIS LANE, *DAILY PLANET.*
I THOUGHT I SHOT THAT RECORDING DEVICE OUT OF YOUR HAND.
THIS IS MY SPARE.
MY SPARE OF MY SPARE.
WHY RUN?
WHY FIGHT YOUR OWN FAMILY?

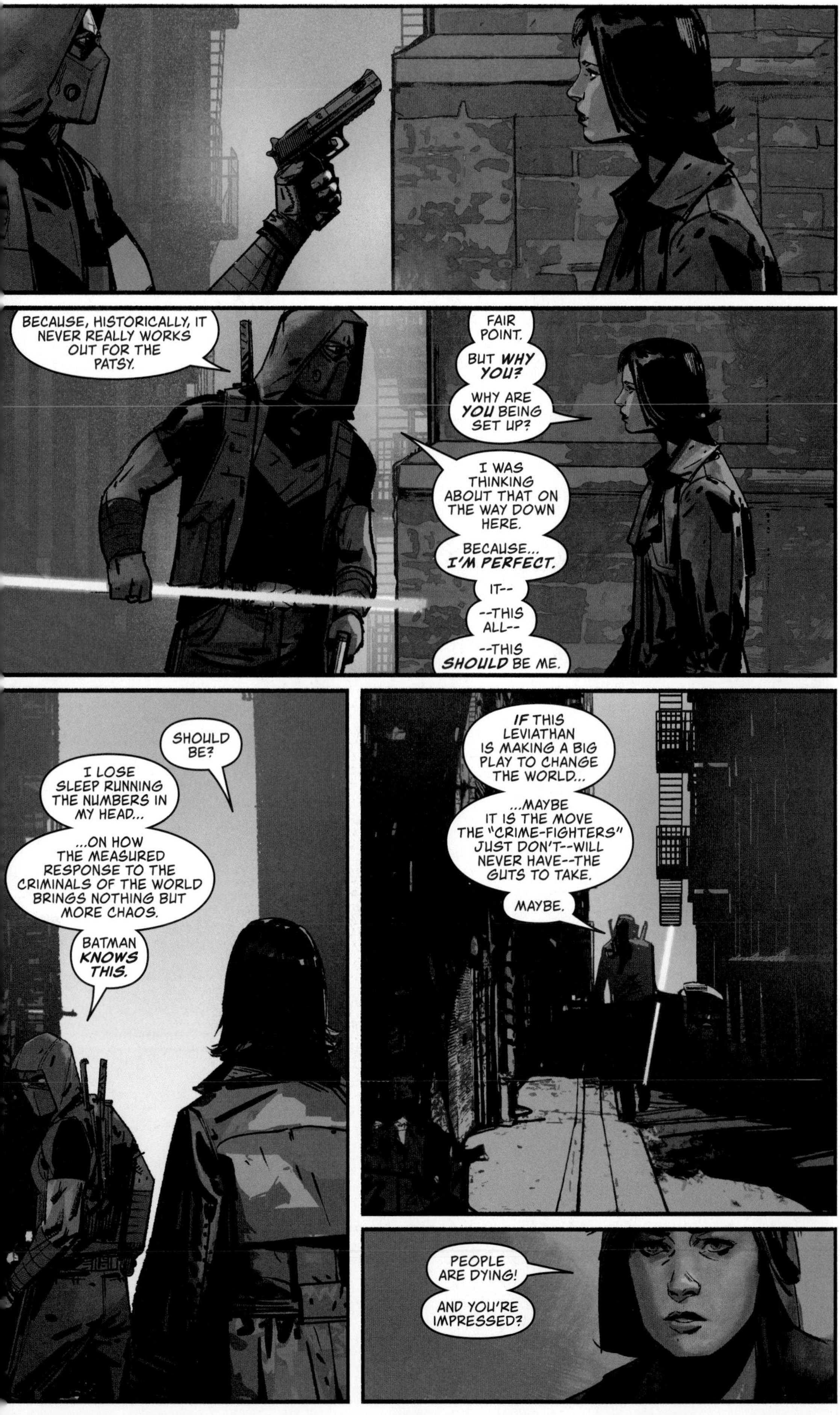
BECAUSE, HISTORICALLY, IT NEVER REALLY WORKS OUT FOR THE PATSY.
FAIR POINT.
BUT *WHY YOU?*
WHY ARE *YOU* BEING SET UP?
I WAS THINKING ABOUT THAT ON THE WAY DOWN HERE.
BECAUSE... *I'M PERFECT.*
IT--
--THIS ALL--
--THIS *SHOULD* BE ME.
SHOULD BE?
I LOSE SLEEP RUNNING THE NUMBERS IN MY HEAD...
...ON HOW THE MEASURED RESPONSE TO THE CRIMINALS OF THE WORLD BRINGS NOTHING BUT MORE CHAOS.
BATMAN *KNOWS THIS.*
IF THIS LEVIATHAN IS MAKING A BIG PLAY TO CHANGE THE WORLD...
...MAYBE IT IS THE MOVE THE "CRIME-FIGHTERS" JUST DON'T--WILL NEVER HAVE--THE GUTS TO TAKE.
MAYBE.
PEOPLE ARE DYING!
AND YOU'RE IMPRESSED?

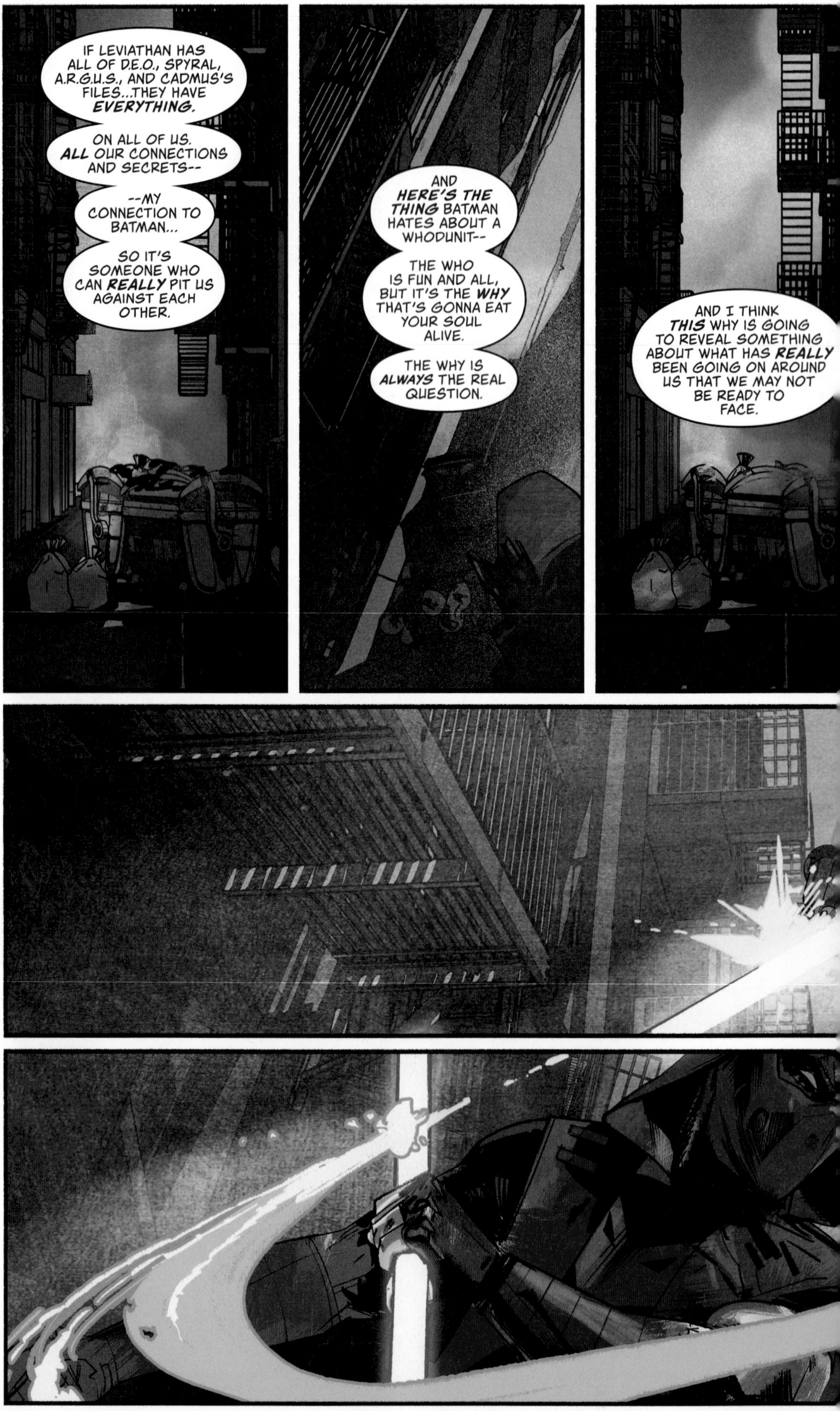
IF LEVIATHAN HAS ALL OF D.E.O., SPYRAL, A.R.G.U.S., AND CADMUS'S FILES...THEY HAVE EVERYTHING.
ON ALL OF US. ALL OUR CONNECTIONS AND SECRETS--
--MY CONNECTION TO BATMAN...
SO IT'S SOMEONE WHO CAN REALLY PIT US AGAINST EACH OTHER.
AND HERE'S THE THING BATMAN HATES ABOUT A WHODUNIT--
THE WHO IS FUN AND ALL, BUT IT'S THE WHY THAT'S GONNA EAT YOUR SOUL ALIVE.
THE WHY IS ALWAYS THE REAL QUESTION.
AND I THINK THIS WHY IS GOING TO REVEAL SOMETHING ABOUT WHAT HAS REALLY BEEN GOING ON AROUND US THAT WE MAY NOT BE READY TO FACE.

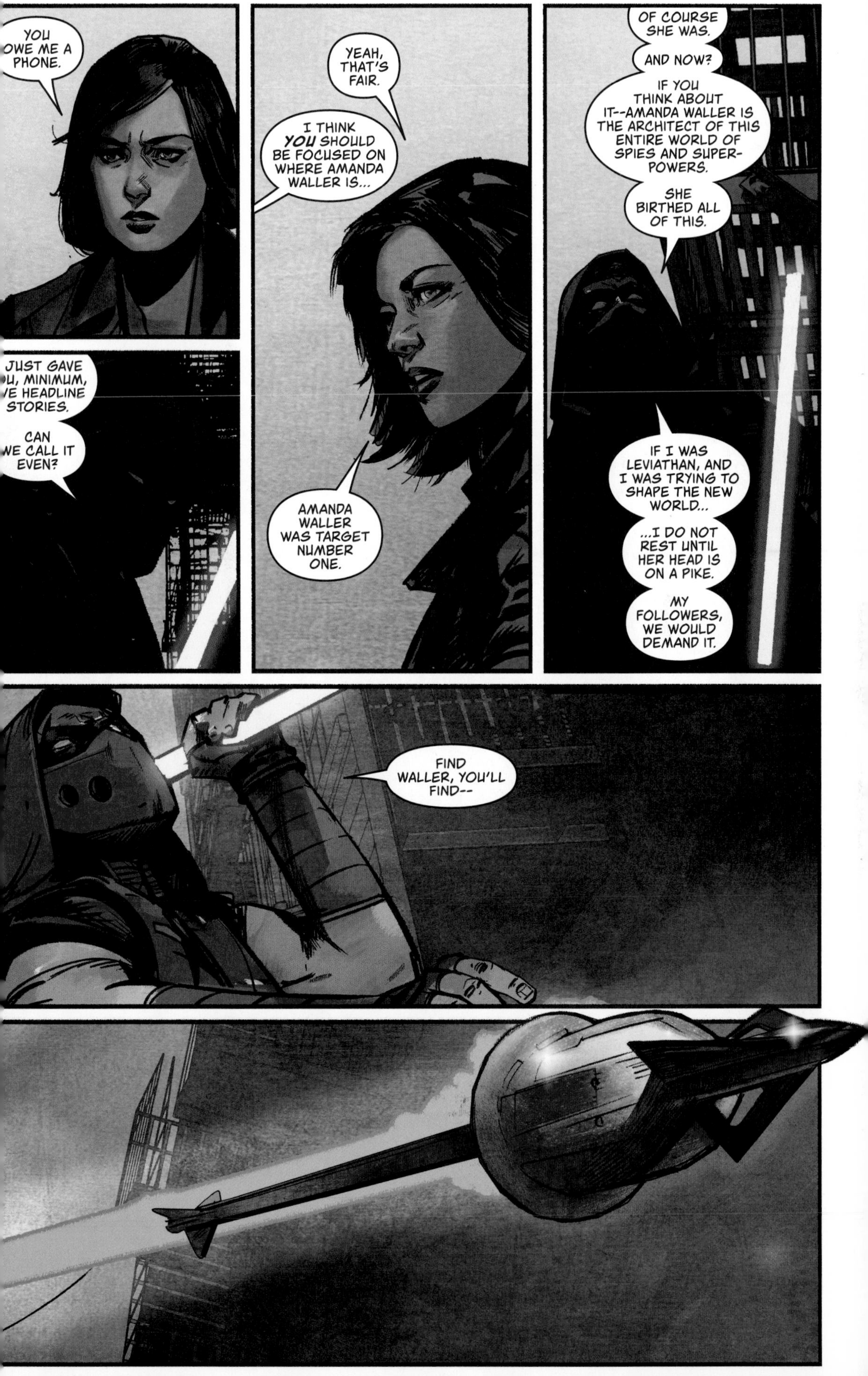
YOU OWE ME A PHONE.
JUST GAVE U, MINIMUM, E HEADLINE STORIES.
CAN WE CALL IT EVEN?
YEAH, THAT'S FAIR.
I THINK *YOU* SHOULD BE FOCUSED ON WHERE AMANDA WALLER IS...
AMANDA WALLER WAS TARGET NUMBER ONE.
OF COURSE SHE WAS.
AND NOW?
IF YOU THINK ABOUT IT--AMANDA WALLER IS THE ARCHITECT OF THIS ENTIRE WORLD OF SPIES AND SUPER-POWERS.
SHE BIRTHED ALL OF THIS.
IF I WAS LEVIATHAN, AND I WAS TRYING TO SHAPE THE NEW WORLD...
...I DO NOT REST UNTIL HER HEAD IS ON A PIKE.
MY FOLLOWERS, WE WOULD DEMAND IT.
FIND WALLER, YOU'LL FIND--

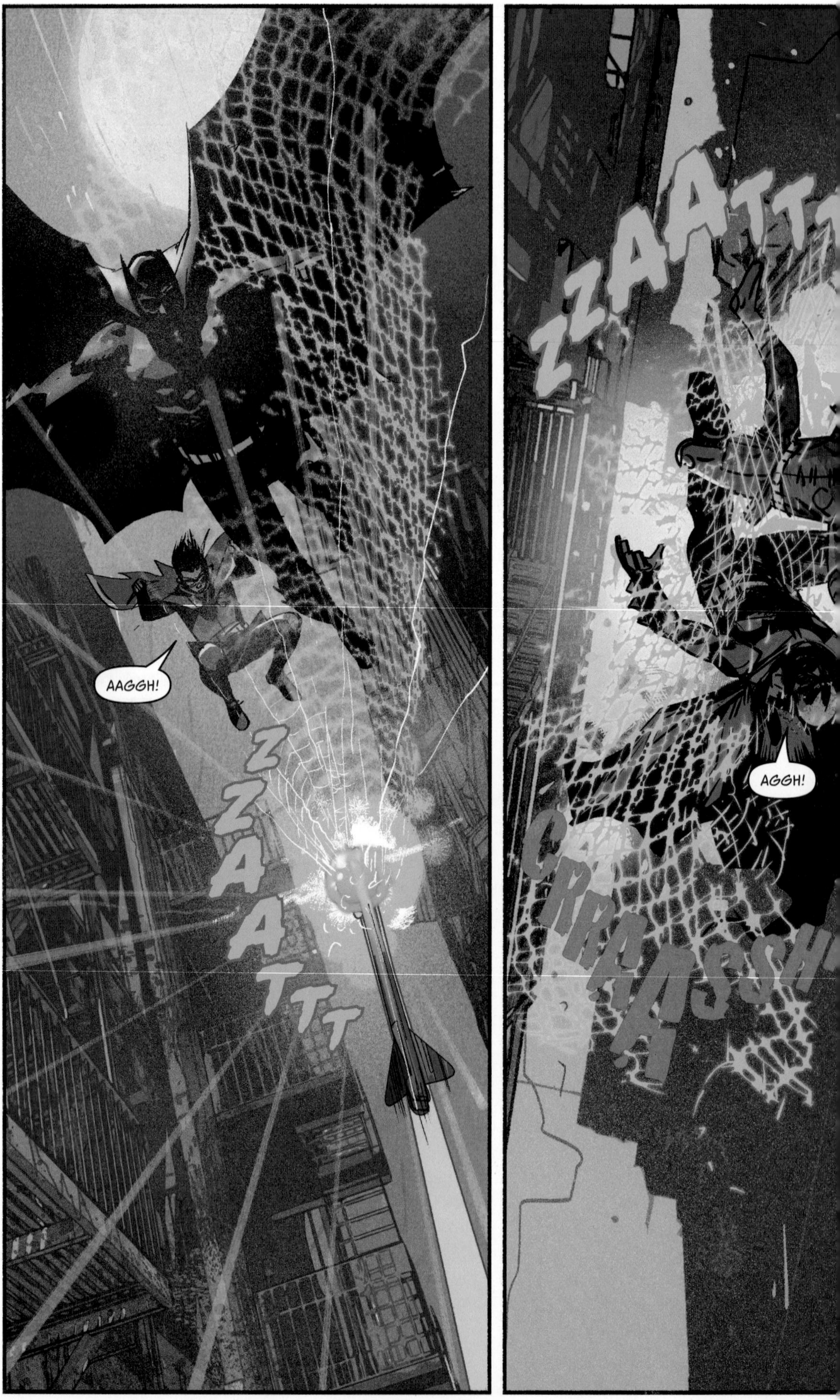
AAGGH!
ZZAATTT
ZZAATT
AGGH!
CRRAASSH

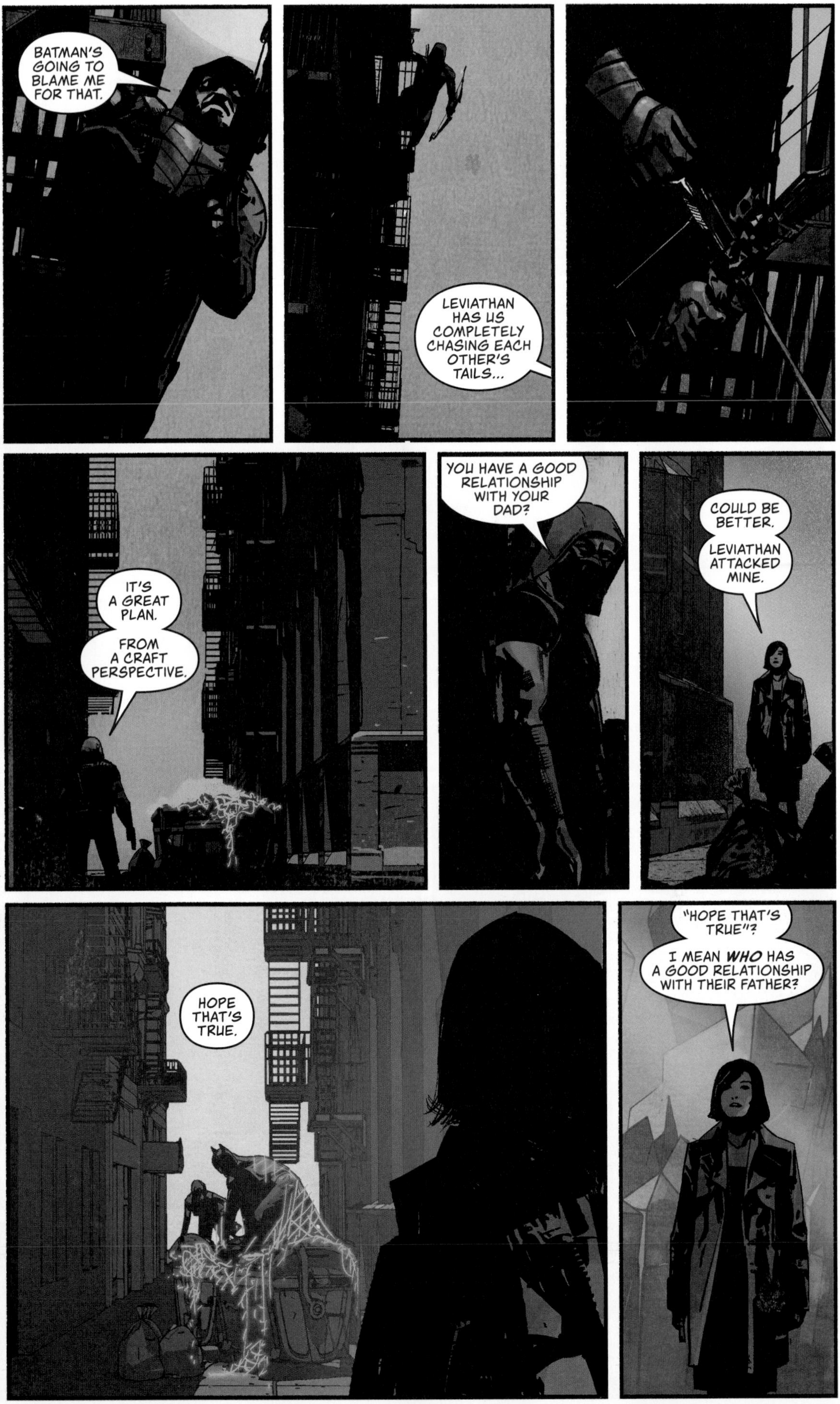
BATMAN'S GOING TO BLAME ME FOR THAT.
LEVIATHAN HAS US COMPLETELY CHASING EACH OTHER'S TAILS...
IT'S A GREAT PLAN.
FROM A CRAFT PERSPECTIVE.
YOU HAVE A GOOD RELATIONSHIP WITH YOUR DAD?
COULD BE BETTER.
LEVIATHAN ATTACKED MINE.
HOPE THAT'S TRUE.
"HOPE THAT'S TRUE"?
I MEAN WHO HAS A GOOD RELATIONSHIP WITH THEIR FATHER?

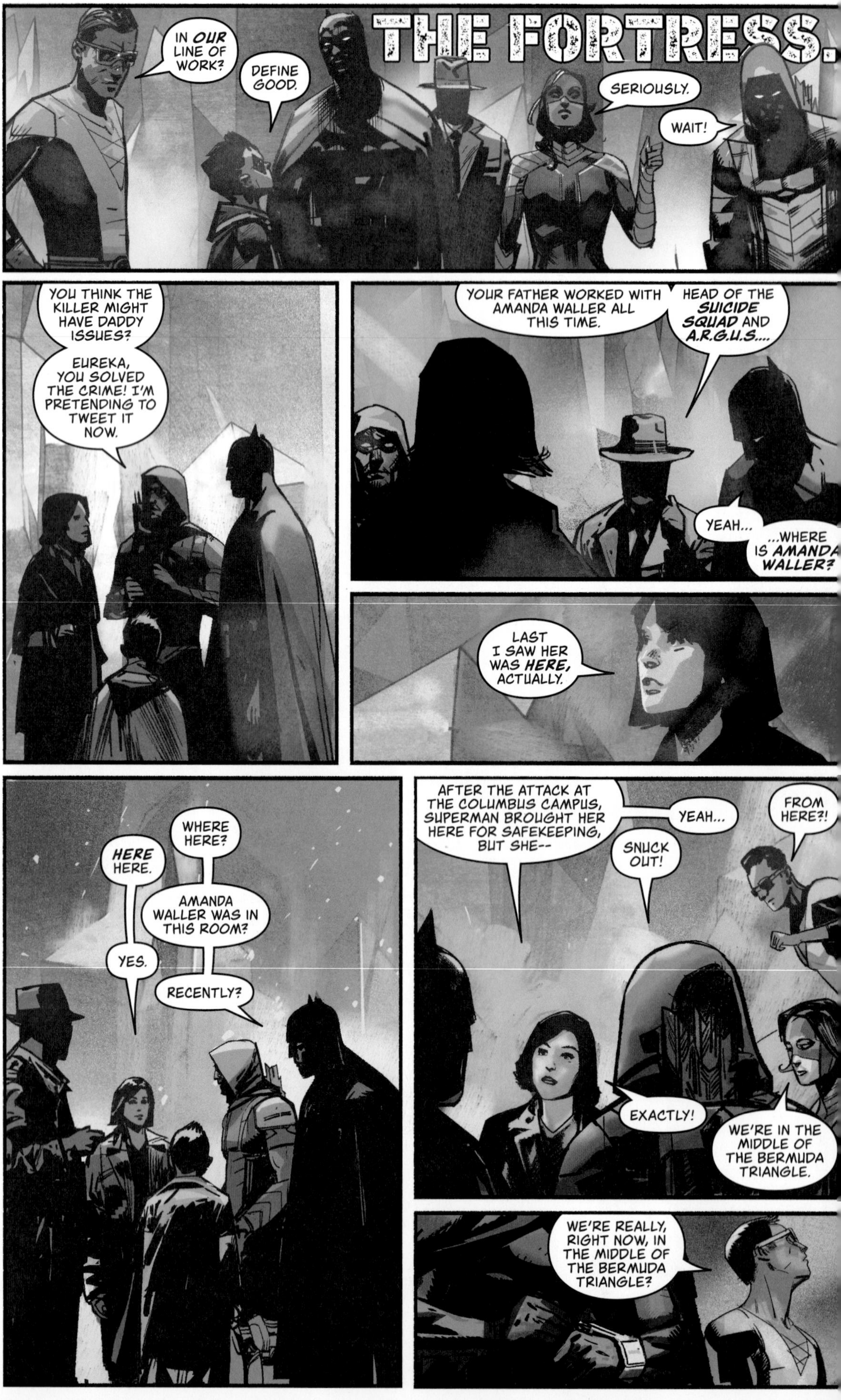
THE FORTRESS.
IN OUR LINE OF WORK?
DEFINE GOOD.
SERIOUSLY.
WAIT!
YOU THINK THE KILLER MIGHT HAVE DADDY ISSUES?
EUREKA, YOU SOLVED THE CRIME! I'M PRETENDING TO TWEET IT NOW.
YOUR FATHER WORKED WITH AMANDA WALLER ALL THIS TIME.
HEAD OF THE SUICIDE SQUAD AND A.R.G.U.S....
YEAH...
...WHERE IS AMANDA WALLER?
LAST I SAW HER WAS HERE, ACTUALLY.
WHERE HERE?
HERE HERE.
AMANDA WALLER WAS IN THIS ROOM?
YES.
RECENTLY?
AFTER THE ATTACK AT THE COLUMBUS CAMPUS, SUPERMAN BROUGHT HER HERE FOR SAFEKEEPING, BUT SHE--
YEAH...
FROM HERE?!
SNUCK OUT!
EXACTLY!
WE'RE IN THE MIDDLE OF THE BERMUDA TRIANGLE.
WE'RE REALLY, RIGHT NOW, IN THE MIDDLE OF THE BERMUDA TRIANGLE?

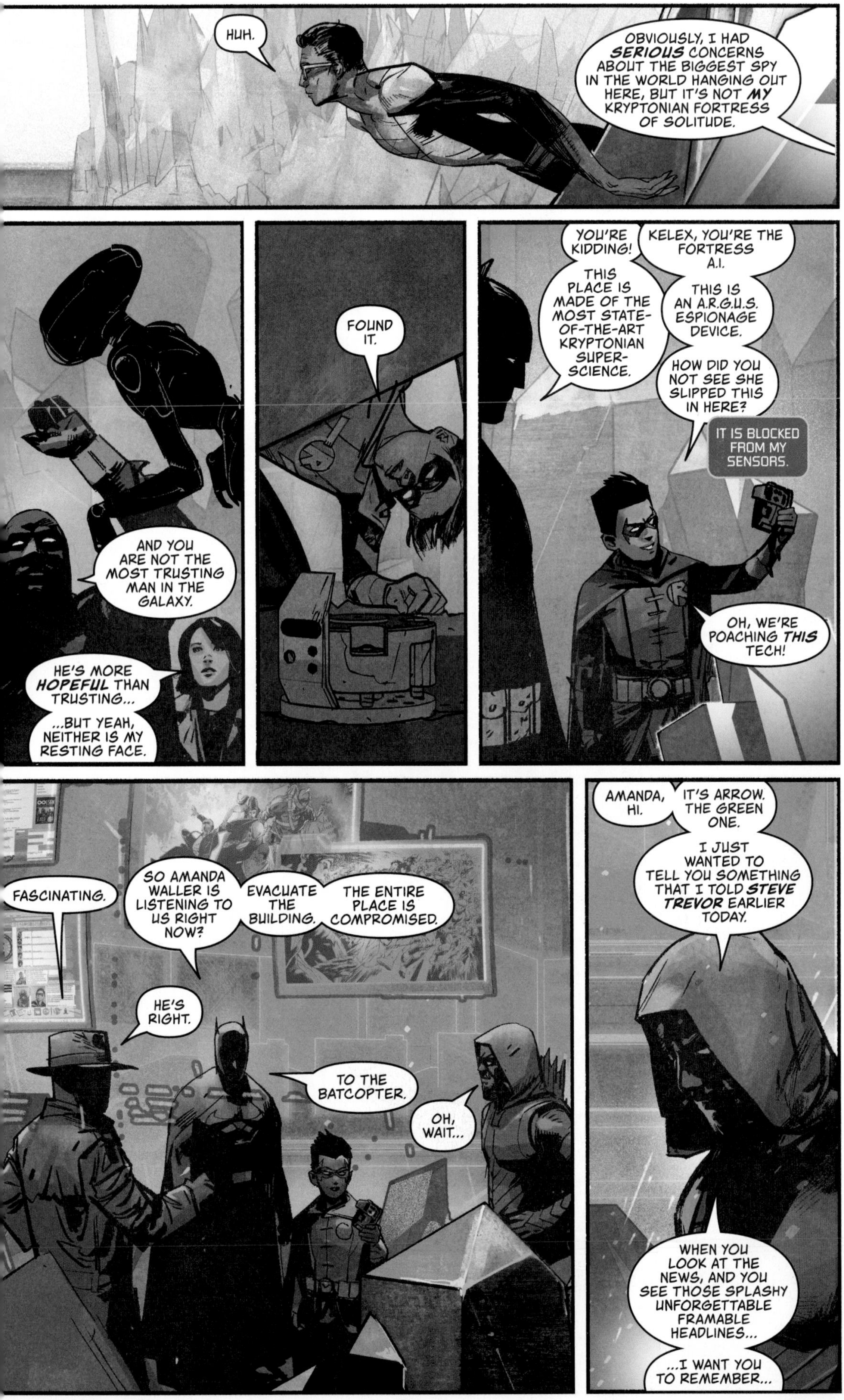
HUH.
OBVIOUSLY, I HAD SERIOUS CONCERNS ABOUT THE BIGGEST SPY IN THE WORLD HANGING OUT HERE, BUT IT'S NOT MY KRYPTONIAN FORTRESS OF SOLITUDE.
AND YOU ARE NOT THE MOST TRUSTING MAN IN THE GALAXY.
HE'S MORE HOPEFUL THAN TRUSTING...
...BUT YEAH, NEITHER IS MY RESTING FACE.
FOUND IT.
YOU'RE KIDDING!
THIS PLACE IS MADE OF THE MOST STATE-OF-THE-ART KRYPTONIAN SUPER-SCIENCE.
KELEX, YOU'RE THE FORTRESS A.I.
THIS IS AN A.R.G.U.S. ESPIONAGE DEVICE.
HOW DID YOU NOT SEE SHE SLIPPED THIS IN HERE?
IT IS BLOCKED FROM MY SENSORS.
OH, WE'RE POACHING THIS TECH!
FASCINATING.
SO AMANDA WALLER IS LISTENING TO US RIGHT NOW?
EVACUATE THE BUILDING.
THE ENTIRE PLACE IS COMPROMISED.
HE'S RIGHT.
TO THE BATCOPTER.
OH, WAIT...
AMANDA, HI.
IT'S ARROW. THE GREEN ONE.
I JUST WANTED TO TELL YOU SOMETHING THAT I TOLD STEVE TREVOR EARLIER TODAY.
WHEN YOU LOOK AT THE NEWS, AND YOU SEE THOSE SPLASHY UNFORGETTABLE FRAMABLE HEADLINES...
...I WANT YOU TO REMEMBER...

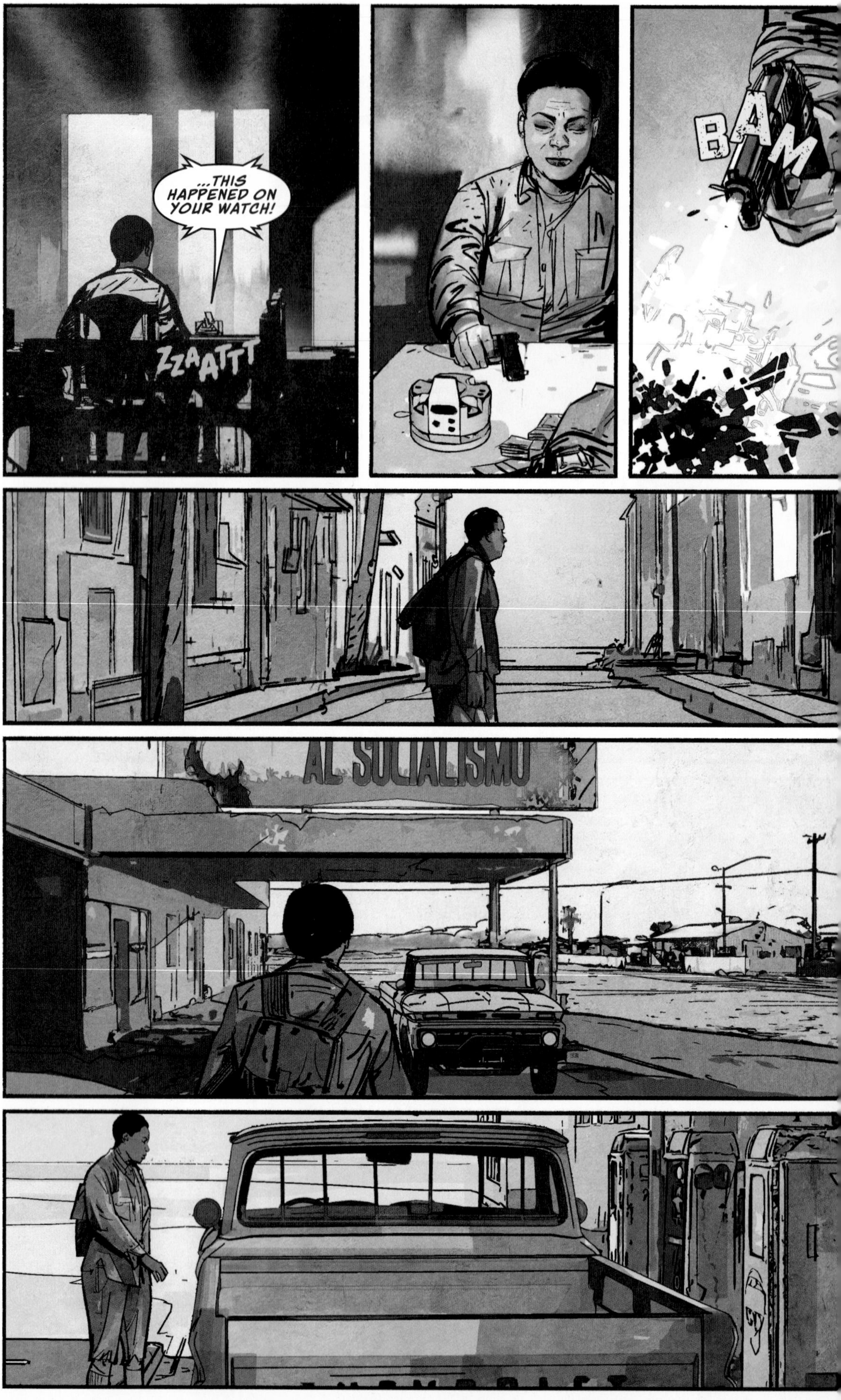
...THIS HAPPENED ON YOUR WATCH!
ZZAATTT
BAM
AL SOCIALISMO

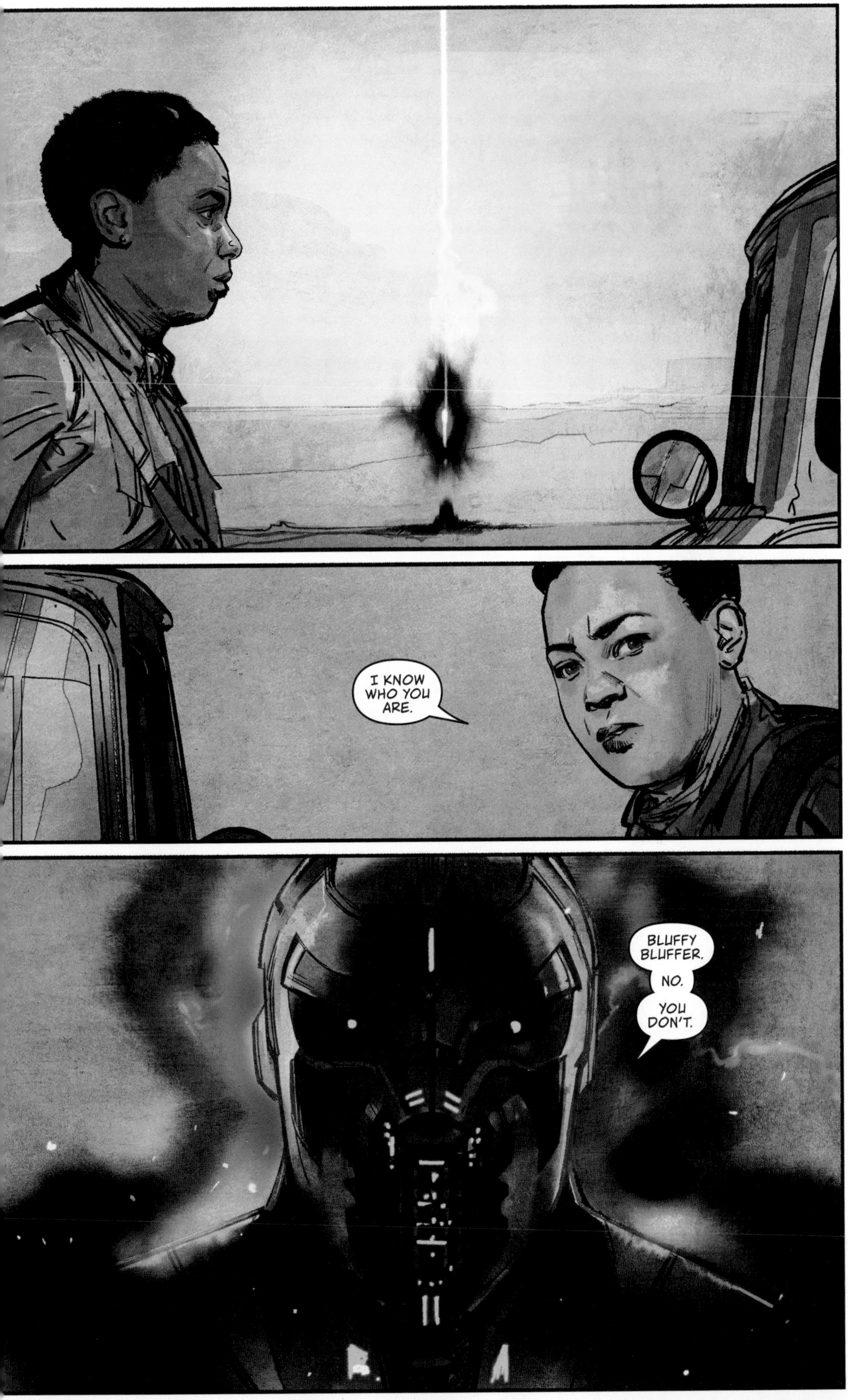
I KNOW WHO YOU ARE.
BLUFFY BLUFFER.
NO.
YOU DON'T.

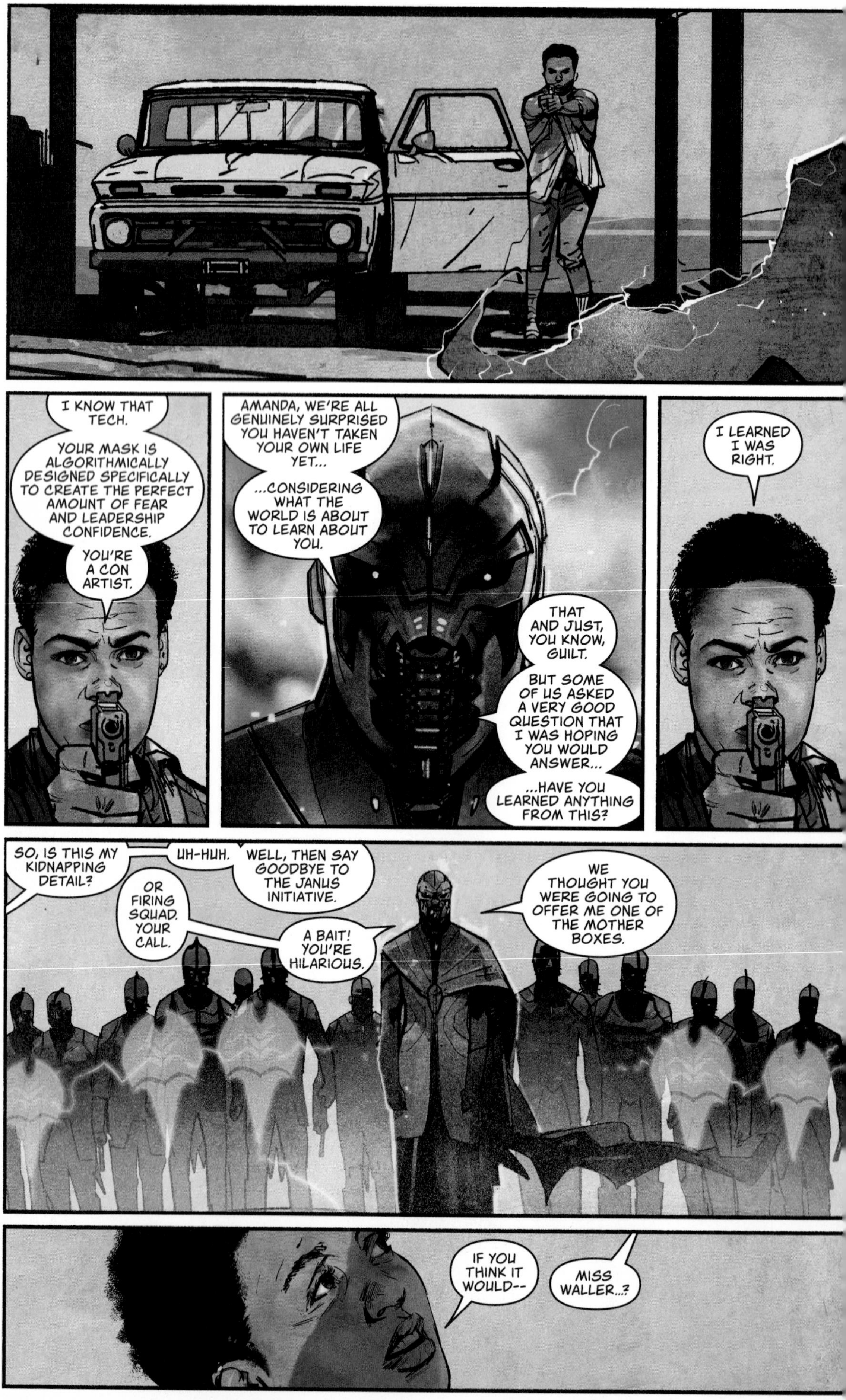
I KNOW THAT TECH.
YOUR MASK IS ALGORITHMICALLY DESIGNED SPECIFICALLY TO CREATE THE PERFECT AMOUNT OF FEAR AND LEADERSHIP CONFIDENCE.
YOU'RE A CON ARTIST.
AMANDA, WE'RE ALL GENUINELY SURPRISED YOU HAVEN'T TAKEN YOUR OWN LIFE YET...
...CONSIDERING WHAT THE WORLD IS ABOUT TO LEARN ABOUT YOU.
THAT AND JUST, YOU KNOW, GUILT.
BUT SOME OF US ASKED A VERY GOOD QUESTION THAT I WAS HOPING YOU WOULD ANSWER...
...HAVE YOU LEARNED ANYTHING FROM THIS?
I LEARNED I WAS RIGHT.
SO, IS THIS MY KIDNAPPING DETAIL?
OR FIRING SQUAD. YOUR CALL.
UH-HUH.
WELL, THEN SAY GOODBYE TO THE JANUS INITIATIVE.
A BAIT! YOU'RE HILARIOUS.
WE THOUGHT YOU WERE GOING TO OFFER ME ONE OF THE MOTHER BOXES.
IF YOU THINK IT WOULD--
MISS WALLER...?

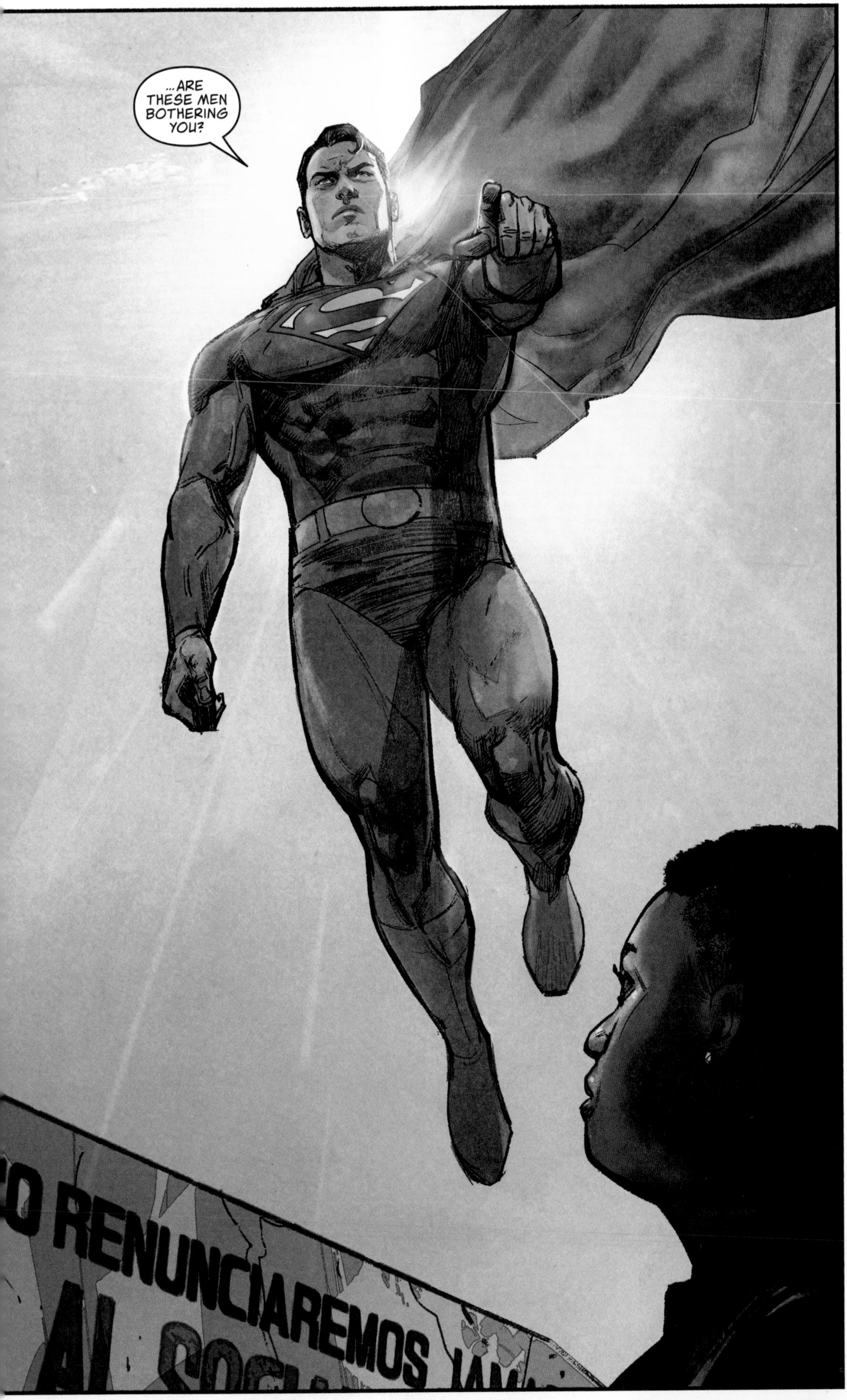
...ARE THESE MEN BOTHERING YOU?
RENUNCIAREMOS

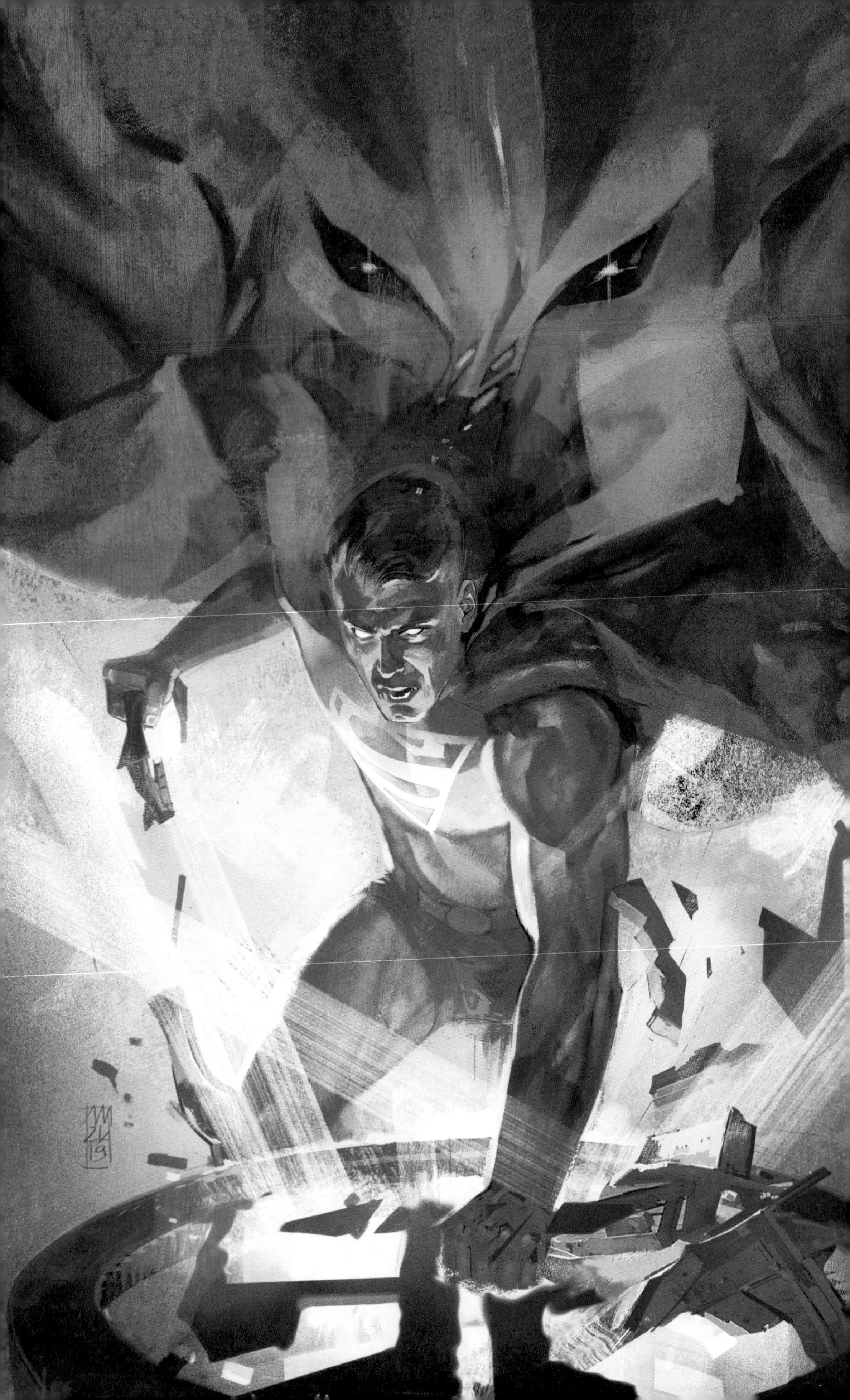

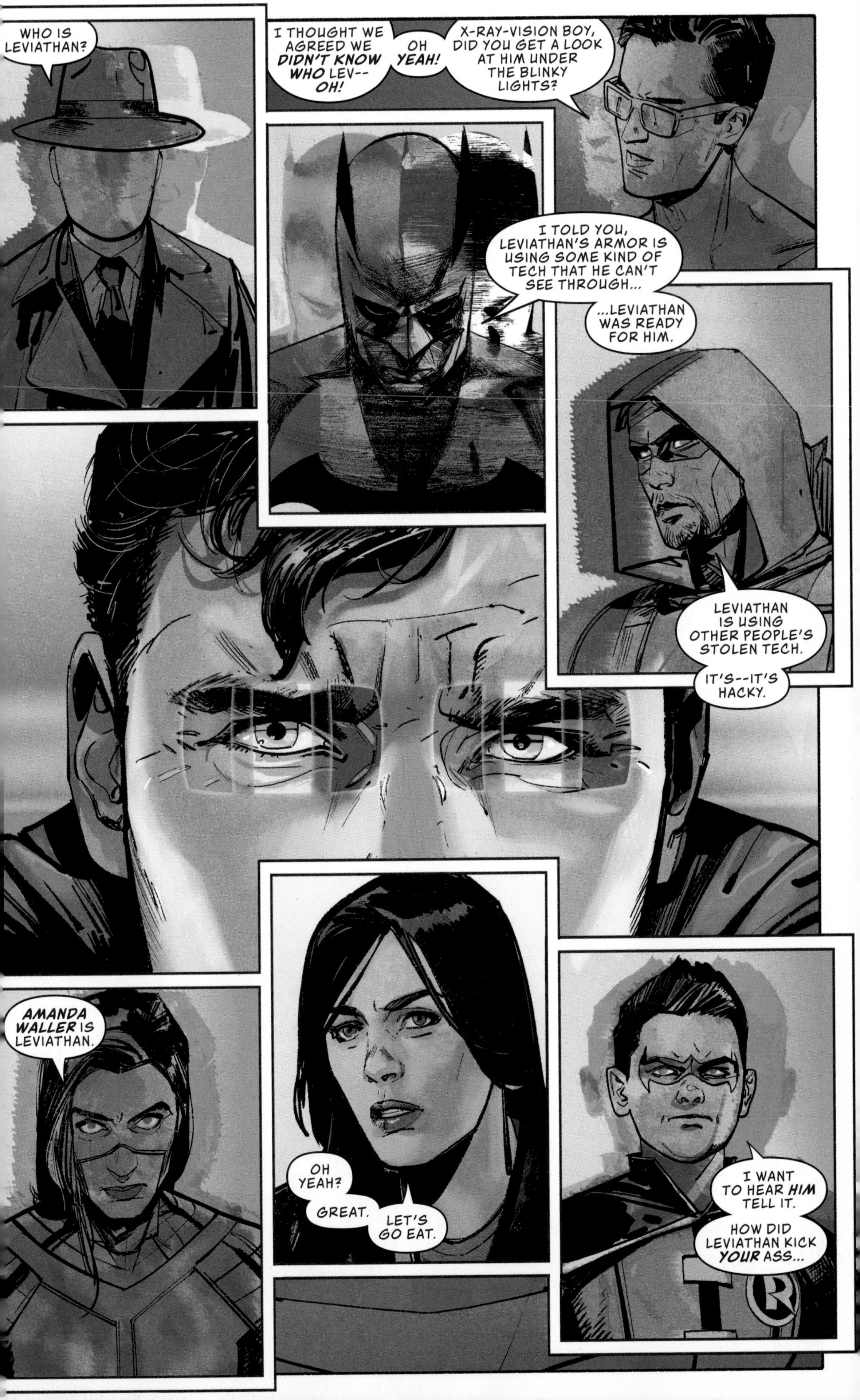

WHO IS LEVIATHAN?
I THOUGHT WE AGREED WE DIDN'T KNOW WHO LEV-- OH!
OH YEAH!
X-RAY-VISION BOY, DID YOU GET A LOOK AT HIM UNDER THE BLINKY LIGHTS?
I TOLD YOU, LEVIATHAN'S ARMOR IS USING SOME KIND OF TECH THAT HE CAN'T SEE THROUGH...
...LEVIATHAN WAS READY FOR HIM.
LEVIATHAN IS USING OTHER PEOPLE'S STOLEN TECH.
IT'S--IT'S HACKY.
AMANDA WALLER IS LEVIATHAN.
OH YEAH?
GREAT.
LET'S GO EAT.
I WANT TO HEAR HIM TELL IT.
HOW DID LEVIATHAN KICK YOUR ASS...

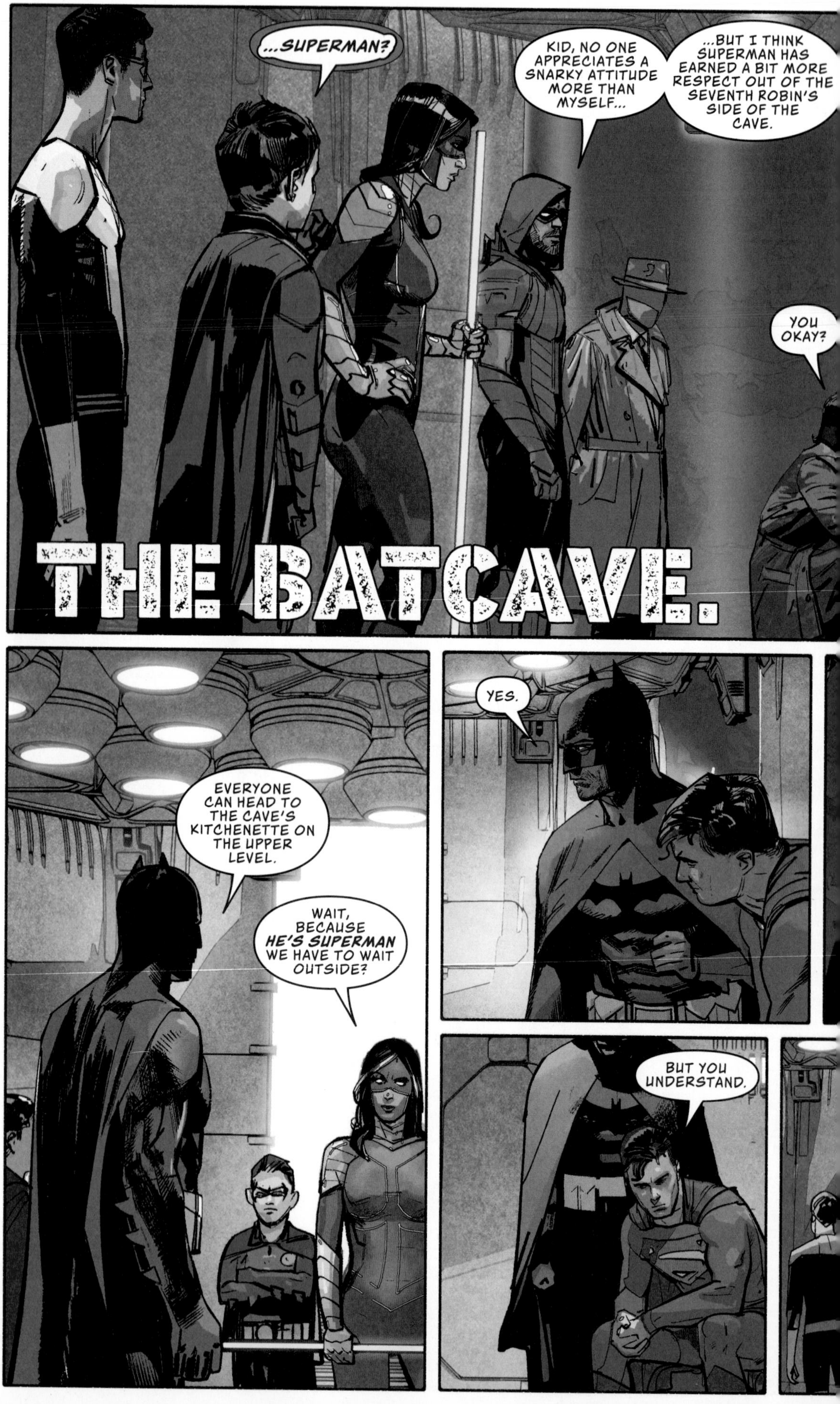
...SUPERMAN?
KID, NO ONE APPRECIATES A SNARKY ATTITUDE MORE THAN MYSELF...
...BUT I THINK SUPERMAN HAS EARNED A BIT MORE RESPECT OUT OF THE SEVENTH ROBIN'S SIDE OF THE CAVE.
YOU OKAY?
THE BATCAVE.
EVERYONE CAN HEAD TO THE CAVE'S KITCHENETTE ON THE UPPER LEVEL.
WAIT, BECAUSE *HE'S SUPERMAN* WE HAVE TO WAIT OUTSIDE?
YES.
BUT YOU UNDERSTAND.

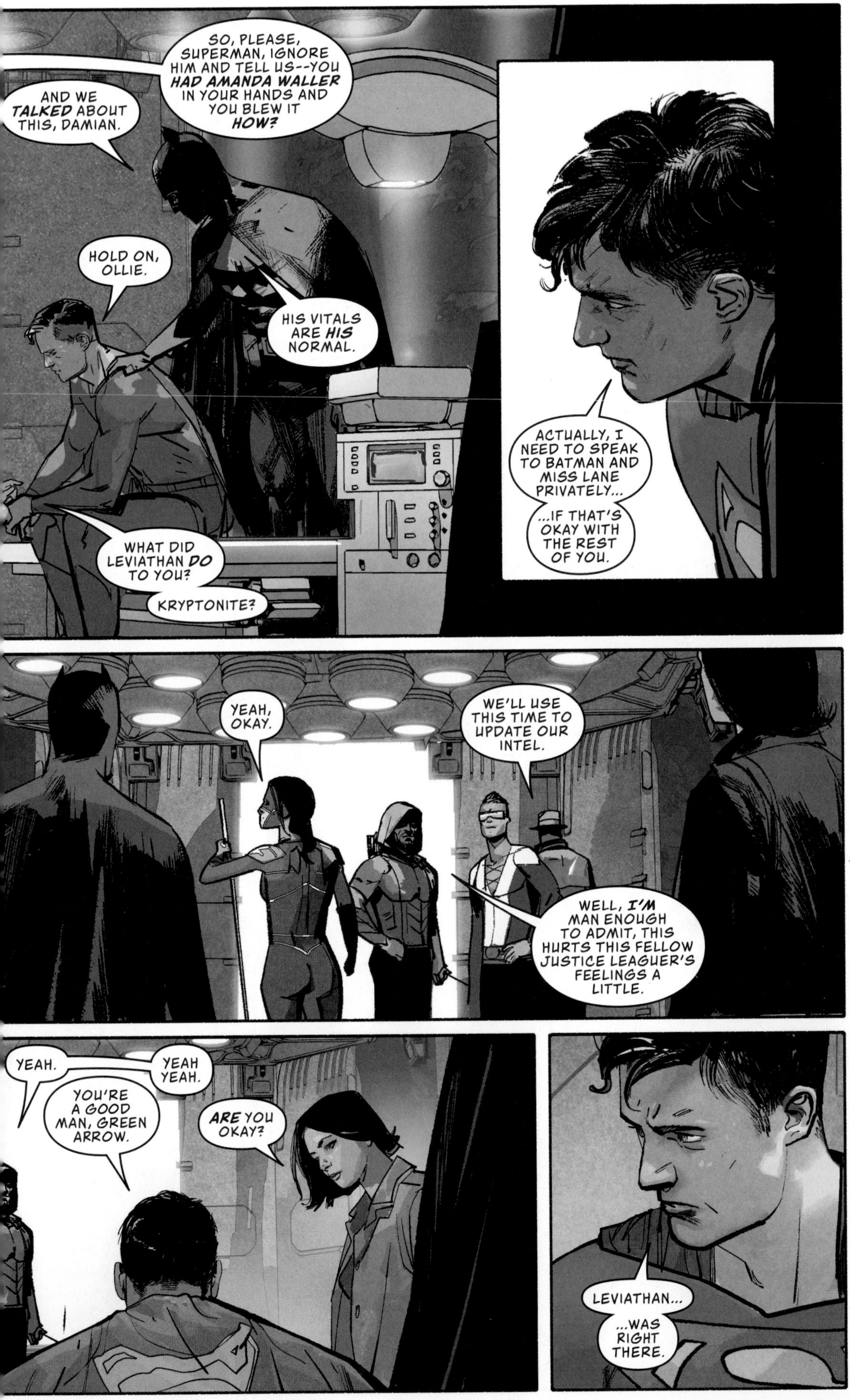
SO, PLEASE, SUPERMAN, IGNORE HIM AND TELL US--YOU HAD AMANDA WALLER IN YOUR HANDS AND YOU BLEW IT HOW?
AND WE TALKED ABOUT THIS, DAMIAN.
HOLD ON, OLLIE.
HIS VITALS ARE HIS NORMAL.
WHAT DID LEVIATHAN DO TO YOU?
KRYPTONITE?
ACTUALLY, I NEED TO SPEAK TO BATMAN AND MISS LANE PRIVATELY...
...IF THAT'S OKAY WITH THE REST OF YOU.
YEAH, OKAY.
WE'LL USE THIS TIME TO UPDATE OUR INTEL.
WELL, I'M MAN ENOUGH TO ADMIT, THIS HURTS THIS FELLOW JUSTICE LEAGUER'S FEELINGS A LITTLE.
YEAH.
YEAH YEAH.
YOU'RE A GOOD MAN, GREEN ARROW.
ARE YOU OKAY?
LEVIATHAN...
...WAS RIGHT THERE.

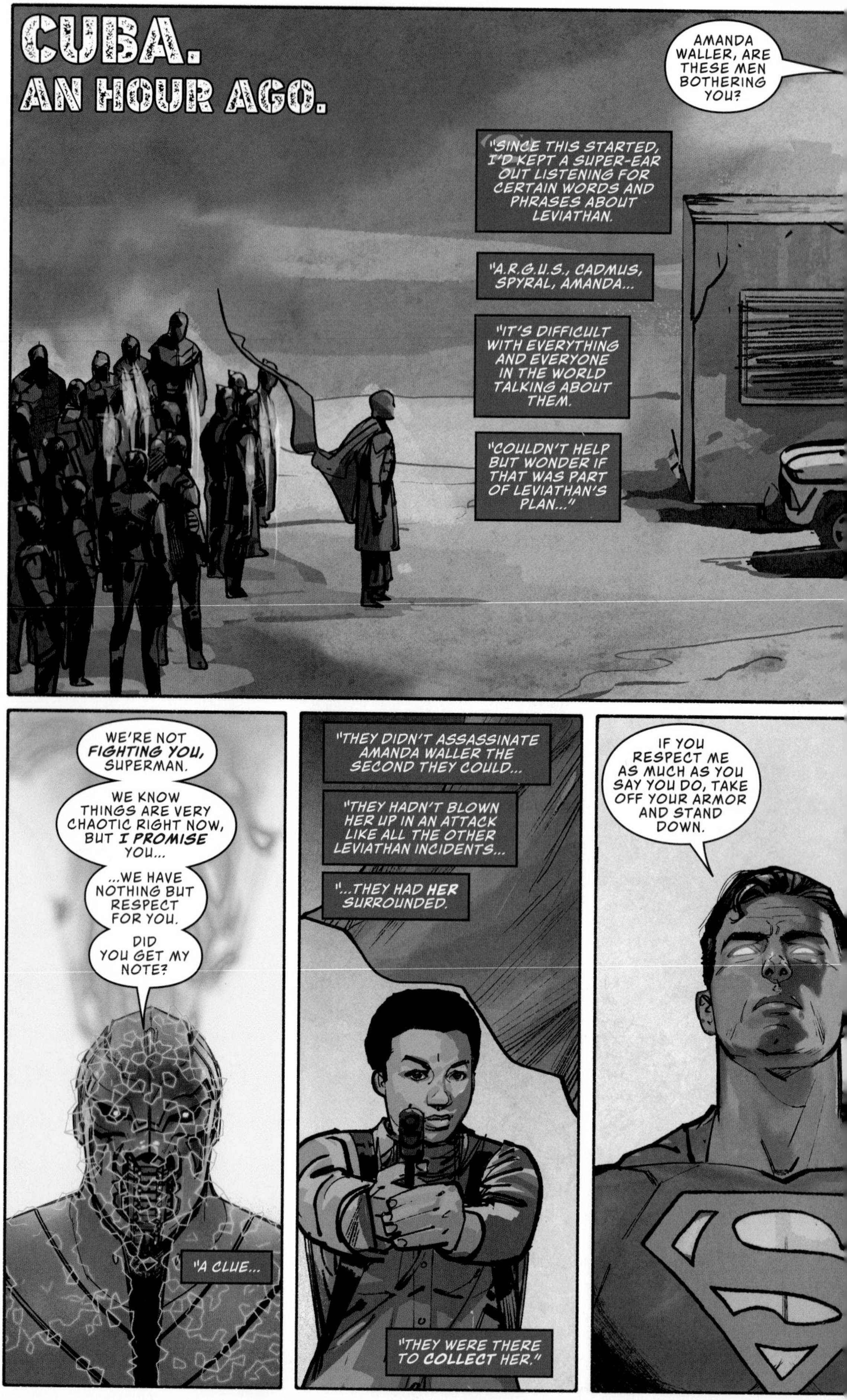
CUBA. AN HOUR AGO.
AMANDA WALLER, ARE THESE MEN BOTHERING YOU?
"SINCE THIS STARTED, I'D KEPT A SUPER-EAR OUT LISTENING FOR CERTAIN WORDS AND PHRASES ABOUT LEVIATHAN.
"A.R.G.U.S., CADMUS, SPYRAL, AMANDA...
"IT'S DIFFICULT WITH EVERYTHING AND EVERYONE IN THE WORLD TALKING ABOUT THEM.
"COULDN'T HELP BUT WONDER IF THAT WAS PART OF LEVIATHAN'S PLAN..."
WE'RE NOT FIGHTING YOU, SUPERMAN.
WE KNOW THINGS ARE VERY CHAOTIC RIGHT NOW, BUT I PROMISE YOU...
...WE HAVE NOTHING BUT RESPECT FOR YOU.
DID YOU GET MY NOTE?
"A CLUE...
"THEY DIDN'T ASSASSINATE AMANDA WALLER THE SECOND THEY COULD...
"THEY HADN'T BLOWN HER UP IN AN ATTACK LIKE ALL THE OTHER LEVIATHAN INCIDENTS...
"...THEY HAD HER SURROUNDED.
"THEY WERE THERE TO COLLECT HER."
IF YOU RESPECT ME AS MUCH AS YOU SAY YOU DO, TAKE OFF YOUR ARMOR AND STAND DOWN.

"THERE'S NO 'CHATTER' BECAUSE IT'S *ALL CHATTER*."

"BUT EVER SINCE AMANDA WALLER ESCAPED OUR *SAFEKEEPING* IN THE FORTRESS OF SOLITUDE, I HAVE KEPT A *SPECIAL EAR* OUT FOR HER."

"AND I *FOUND HER*."

"IN CUBA.

"BUT...LEVIATHAN GOT TO HER FIRST.

"JUST."

AMANDA, GET BEHIND ME.

I WOULD, BUT AFTER WHAT I HAVE SEEN... I DON'T THINK IT'S GOING TO MAKE A DAMN BIT OF DIFFERENCE.

HUMOR ME.

GENTLEMEN, WHATEVER LEVIATHAN HERE HAS BEEN PROMISING...

THINK... ARE THEY *REALLY* GOING TO BE ABLE TO DELIVER?

"I WAS SUPER-SPEED READY FOR WHATEVER HAPPENED NEXT.

"I THOUGHT IF I COULD FOCUS MY X-RAY VISION AND/OR MY TELESCOPIC VISION INTO SOMETHING THAT WOULD HELP ME *SEE THROUGH* THE LEVIATHAN TECHNOLOGY--

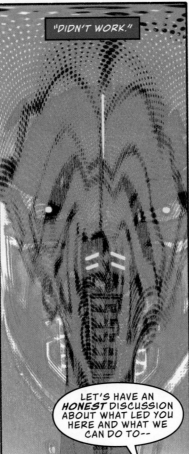

"DIDN'T WORK."

LET'S HAVE AN *HONEST* DISCUSSION ABOUT WHAT LED YOU HERE AND WHAT WE CAN DO TO--

"AN HONEST DISCUSSION"? YOU'RE ADORABLE.

LIVES WERE AT STAKE. I WAS READY.

I HEARD IT.

THE TRIGGER.

A person and organization named LEVIATHAN has done the impossible and simultaneously taken out major pillars of the world intelligence community.

GREEN ARROW and BATGIRL survived one attack. Batgirl was offered a place in Leviathan--no one has seen her since.

ADVANCED RESEARCH GROUP UNITING SUPER HUMANS

D.E.O.
DEPARTMENT OF EXTRANORMAL OPERATIONS

SPYRAL

The DEO, SPYRAL, A.R.G.U.S., and many others are gone.

Who is Leviathan? How have they accomplished so much so quickly? These questions have brought together the greatest detectives in the world: BATMAN, GREEN ARROW, PLASTIC MAN, THE QUESTION, and legendary reporter LOIS LANE.

[redacted] EVENT [redacted]
[redacted] LEVIATHAN [redacted]

Part 4

BRIAN MICHAEL BENDIS
story

ALEX MALEEV
art & cover

JOSH REED
letters

JESSICA CHEN
associate editor

MIKE COTTON
editor

BRIAN CUNNINGHAM
group editor

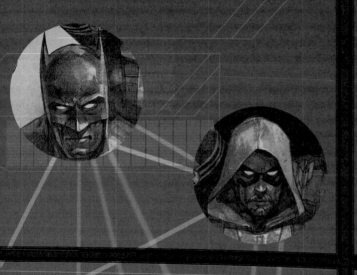

SUPERMAN survived a kidnapping that only revealed that Leviathan is no longer in control of the woman who founded it...the legendary terrorist **TALIA AL GHUL.**

Batman's young protégé **ROBIN,** looking over all of the evidence so far, wonders if Leviathan is his predecessor, **JASON TODD,** but that proved a false lead.

Computer v.9876.0000

System Status: open

Activised location: 192

Login: Admin Verify

Identification open gate ACTIVE

End Line. Version 875629

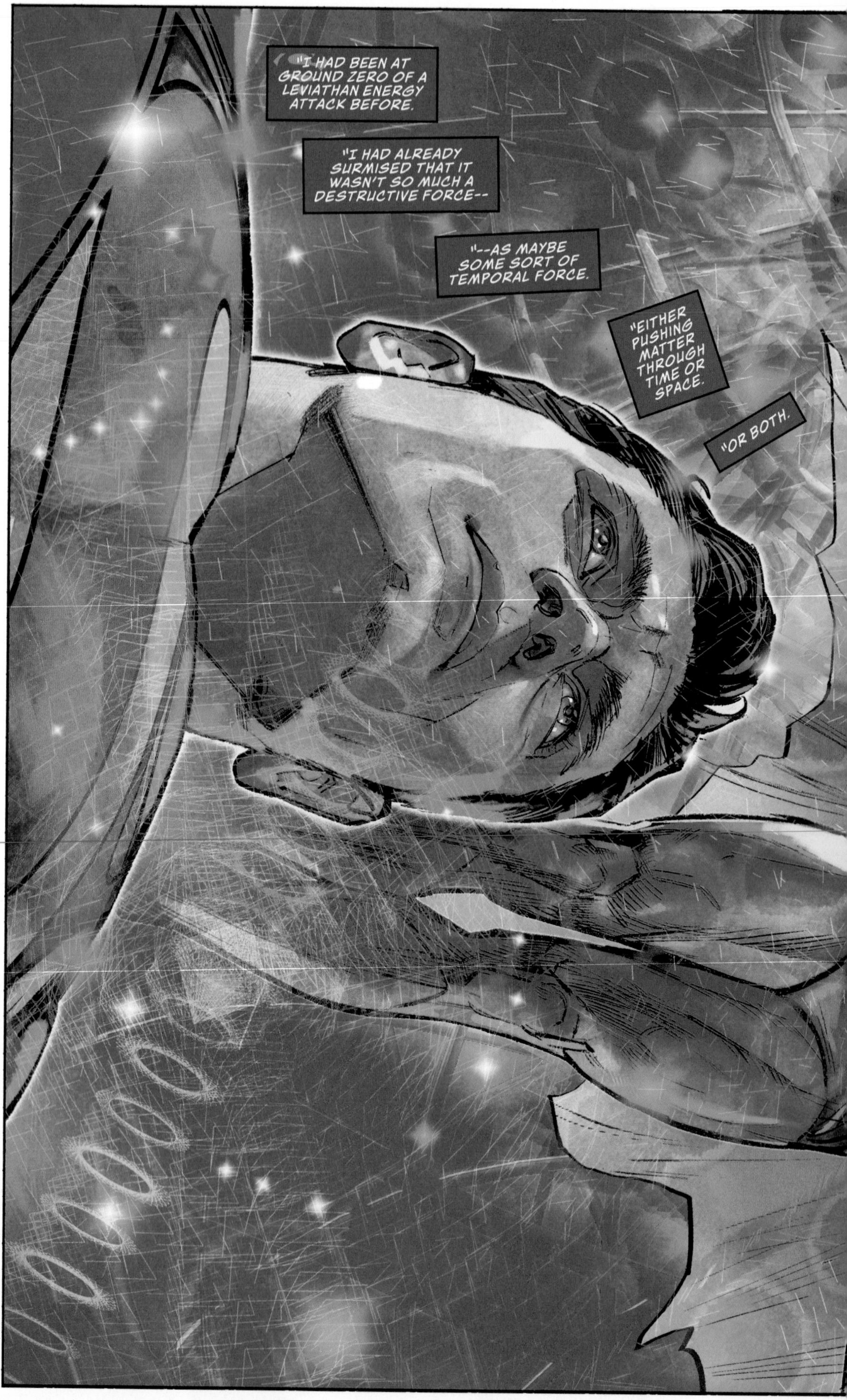
"I HAD BEEN AT GROUND ZERO OF A LEVIATHAN ENERGY ATTACK BEFORE.
"I HAD ALREADY SURMISED THAT IT WASN'T SO MUCH A DESTRUCTIVE FORCE--
"--AS MAYBE SOME SORT OF TEMPORAL FORCE.
"EITHER PUSHING MATTER THROUGH TIME OR SPACE.
"OR BOTH.

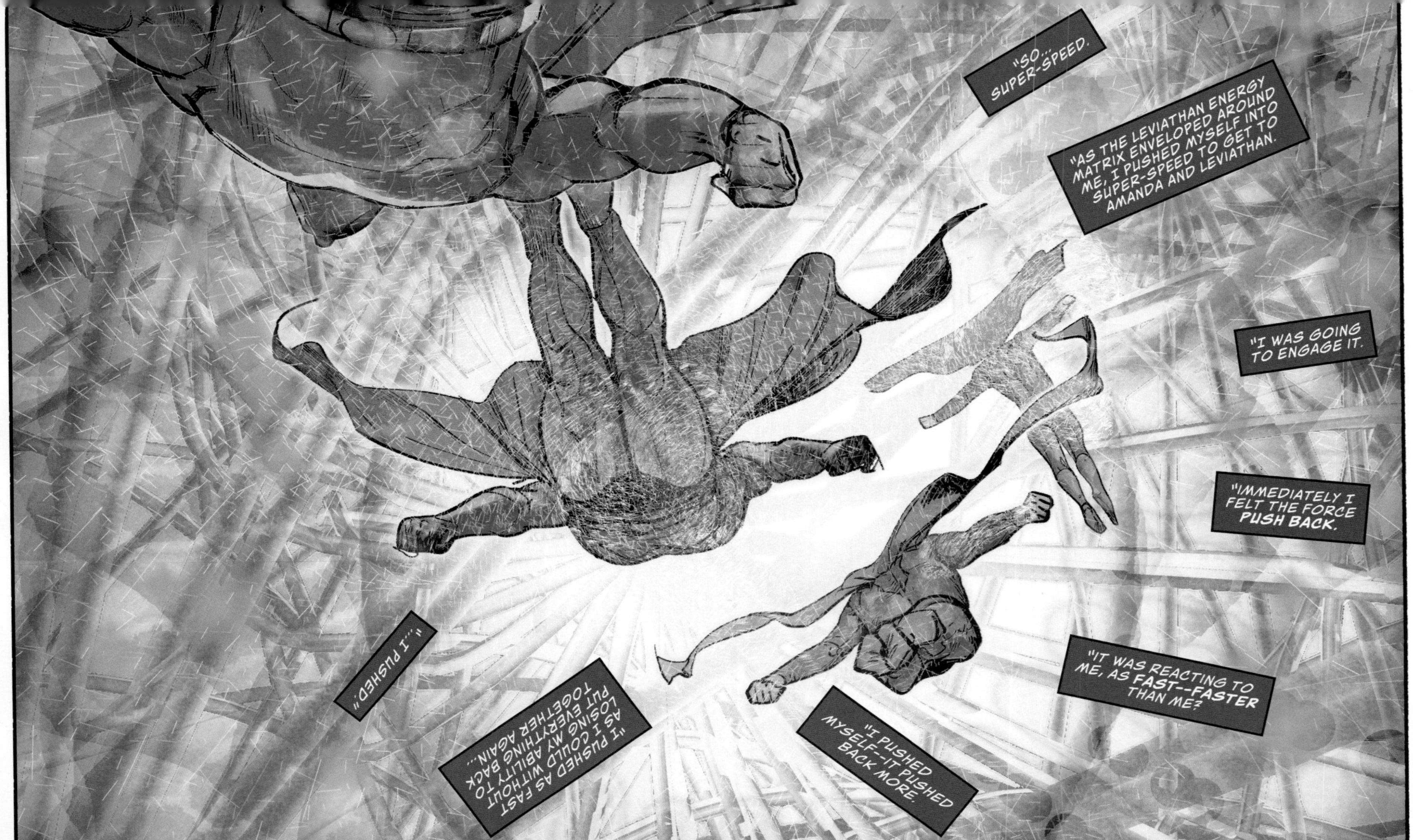
"SO... SUPER-SPEED.
"AS THE LEVIATHAN ENERGY MATRIX ENVELOPED AROUND ME, I PUSHED MYSELF INTO SUPER-SPEED TO GET TO AMANDA AND LEVIATHAN.
"I WAS GOING TO ENGAGE IT.
"IMMEDIATELY I FELT THE FORCE PUSH BACK.
"IT WAS REACTING TO ME, AS FAST--FASTER THAN ME?
"I PUSHED MYSELF--IT PUSHED BACK MORE.
"I PUSHED AS FAST AS I COULD WITHOUT LOSING MY ABILITY TO PUT EVERYTHING BACK TOGETHER AGAIN...
"...I PUSHED."

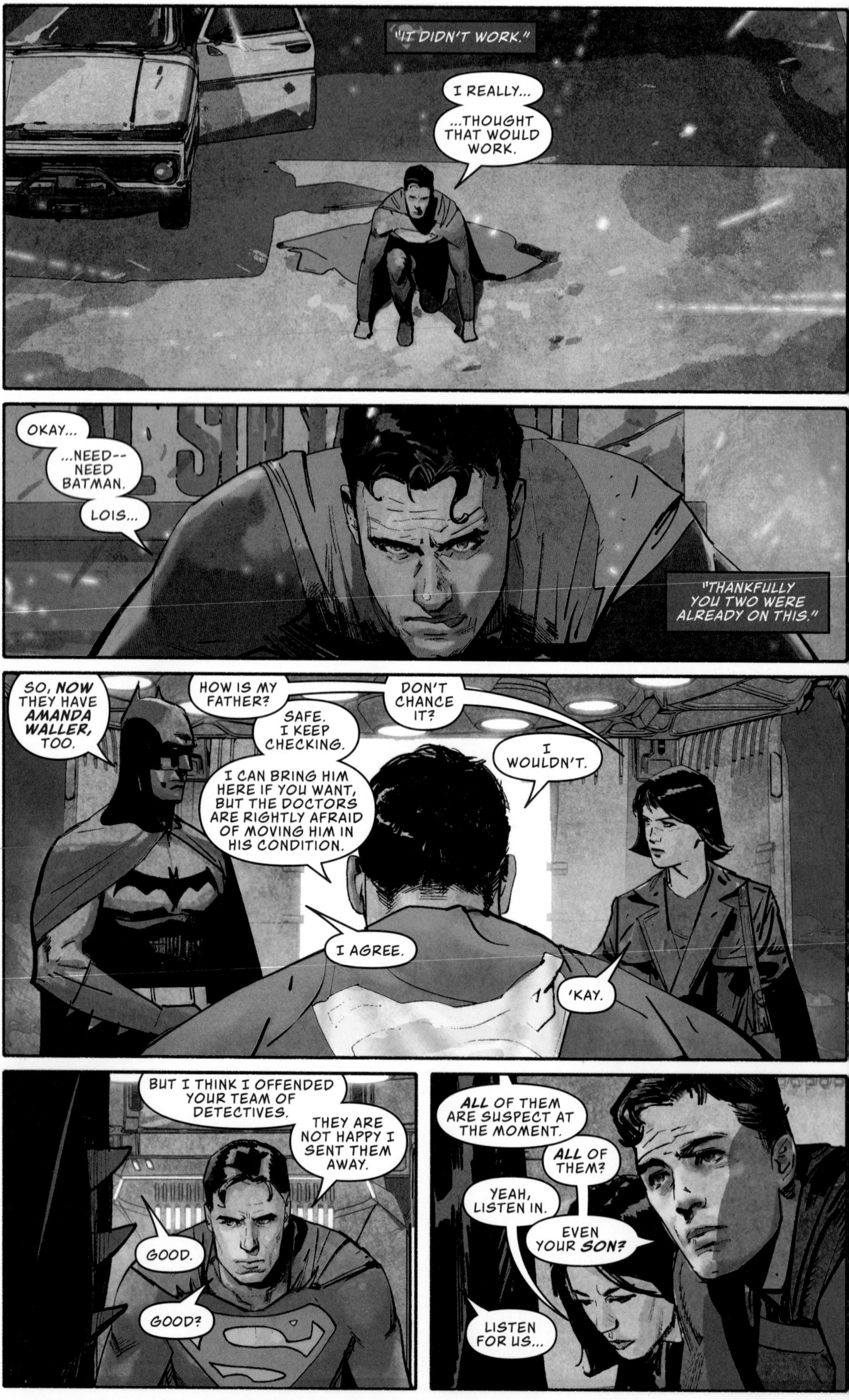
"IT DIDN'T WORK."
I REALLY...
...THOUGHT THAT WOULD WORK.
OKAY...
...NEED-- NEED BATMAN.
LOIS...
"THANKFULLY YOU TWO WERE ALREADY ON THIS."
SO, NOW THEY HAVE AMANDA WALLER, TOO.
HOW IS MY FATHER?
SAFE. I KEEP CHECKING.
DON'T CHANCE IT?
I WOULDN'T.
I CAN BRING HIM HERE IF YOU WANT, BUT THE DOCTORS ARE RIGHTLY AFRAID OF MOVING HIM IN HIS CONDITION.
I AGREE.
'KAY.
BUT I THINK I OFFENDED YOUR TEAM OF DETECTIVES.
THEY ARE NOT HAPPY I SENT THEM AWAY.
GOOD.
GOOD?
ALL OF THEM ARE SUSPECT AT THE MOMENT.
ALL OF THEM?
YEAH, LISTEN IN.
EVEN YOUR SON?
LISTEN FOR US...

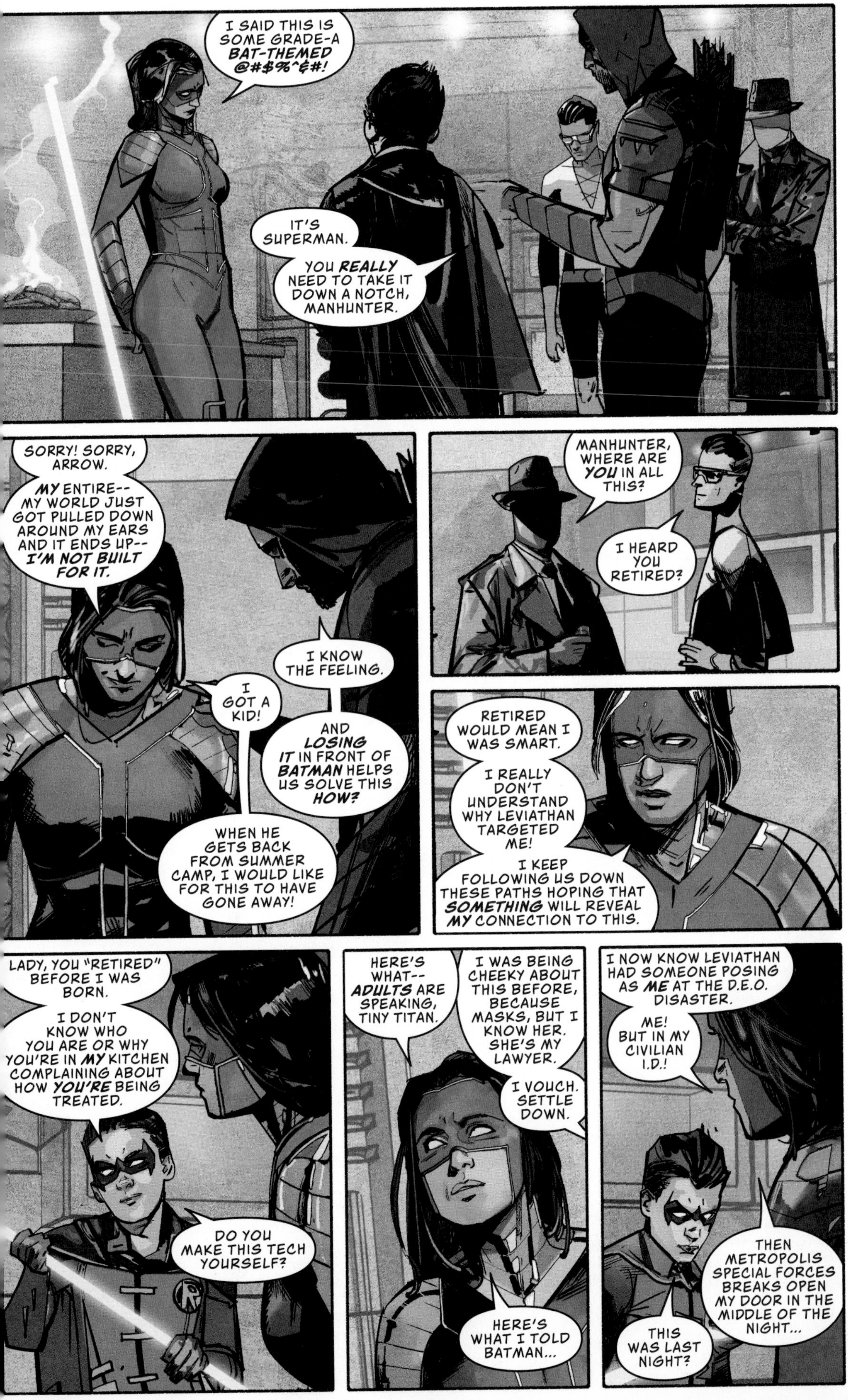
I SAID THIS IS SOME GRADE-A BAT-THEMED @#$%^&#!
IT'S SUPERMAN.
YOU REALLY NEED TO TAKE IT DOWN A NOTCH, MANHUNTER.
SORRY! SORRY, ARROW.
MY ENTIRE-- MY WORLD JUST GOT PULLED DOWN AROUND MY EARS AND IT ENDS UP-- I'M NOT BUILT FOR IT.
I KNOW THE FEELING.
I GOT A KID!
AND LOSING IT IN FRONT OF BATMAN HELPS US SOLVE THIS HOW?
WHEN HE GETS BACK FROM SUMMER CAMP, I WOULD LIKE FOR THIS TO HAVE GONE AWAY!
MANHUNTER, WHERE ARE YOU IN ALL THIS?
I HEARD YOU RETIRED?
RETIRED WOULD MEAN I WAS SMART.
I REALLY DON'T UNDERSTAND WHY LEVIATHAN TARGETED ME!
I KEEP FOLLOWING US DOWN THESE PATHS HOPING THAT SOMETHING WILL REVEAL MY CONNECTION TO THIS.
LADY, YOU "RETIRED" BEFORE I WAS BORN.
I DON'T KNOW WHO YOU ARE OR WHY YOU'RE IN MY KITCHEN COMPLAINING ABOUT HOW YOU'RE BEING TREATED.
DO YOU MAKE THIS TECH YOURSELF?
HERE'S WHAT-- ADULTS ARE SPEAKING, TINY TITAN.
I WAS BEING CHEEKY ABOUT THIS BEFORE, BECAUSE MASKS, BUT I KNOW HER. SHE'S MY LAWYER.
I VOUCH. SETTLE DOWN.
HERE'S WHAT I TOLD BATMAN...
I NOW KNOW LEVIATHAN HAD SOMEONE POSING AS ME AT THE D.E.O. DISASTER.
ME! BUT IN MY CIVILIAN I.D.!
THEN METROPOLIS SPECIAL FORCES BREAKS OPEN MY DOOR IN THE MIDDLE OF THE NIGHT...
THIS WAS LAST NIGHT?

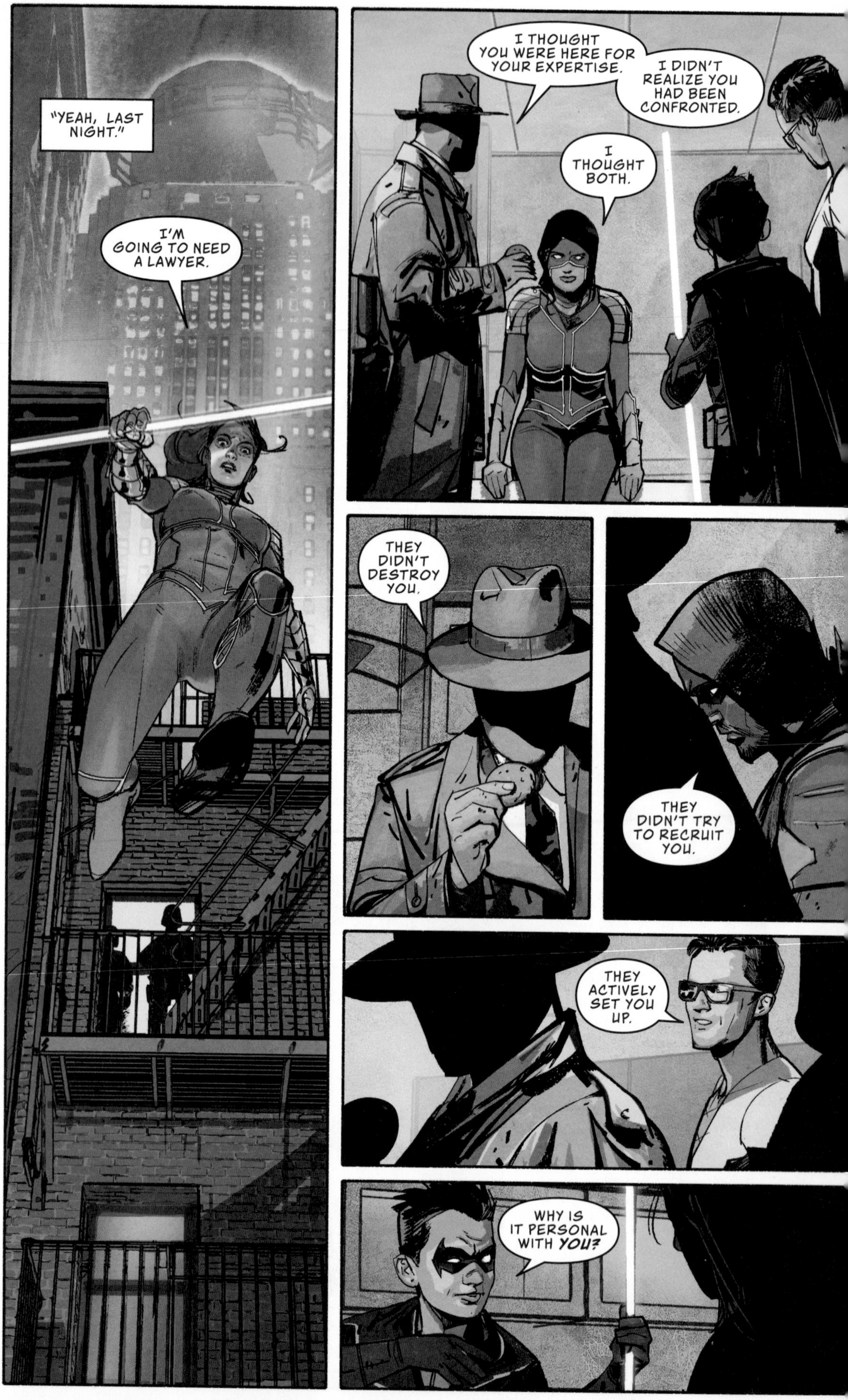
"YEAH, LAST NIGHT."
I'M GOING TO NEED A LAWYER.
I THOUGHT YOU WERE HERE FOR YOUR EXPERTISE.
I DIDN'T REALIZE YOU HAD BEEN CONFRONTED.
I THOUGHT BOTH.
THEY DIDN'T DESTROY YOU.
THEY DIDN'T TRY TO RECRUIT YOU.
THEY ACTIVELY SET YOU UP.
WHY IS IT PERSONAL WITH *YOU?*

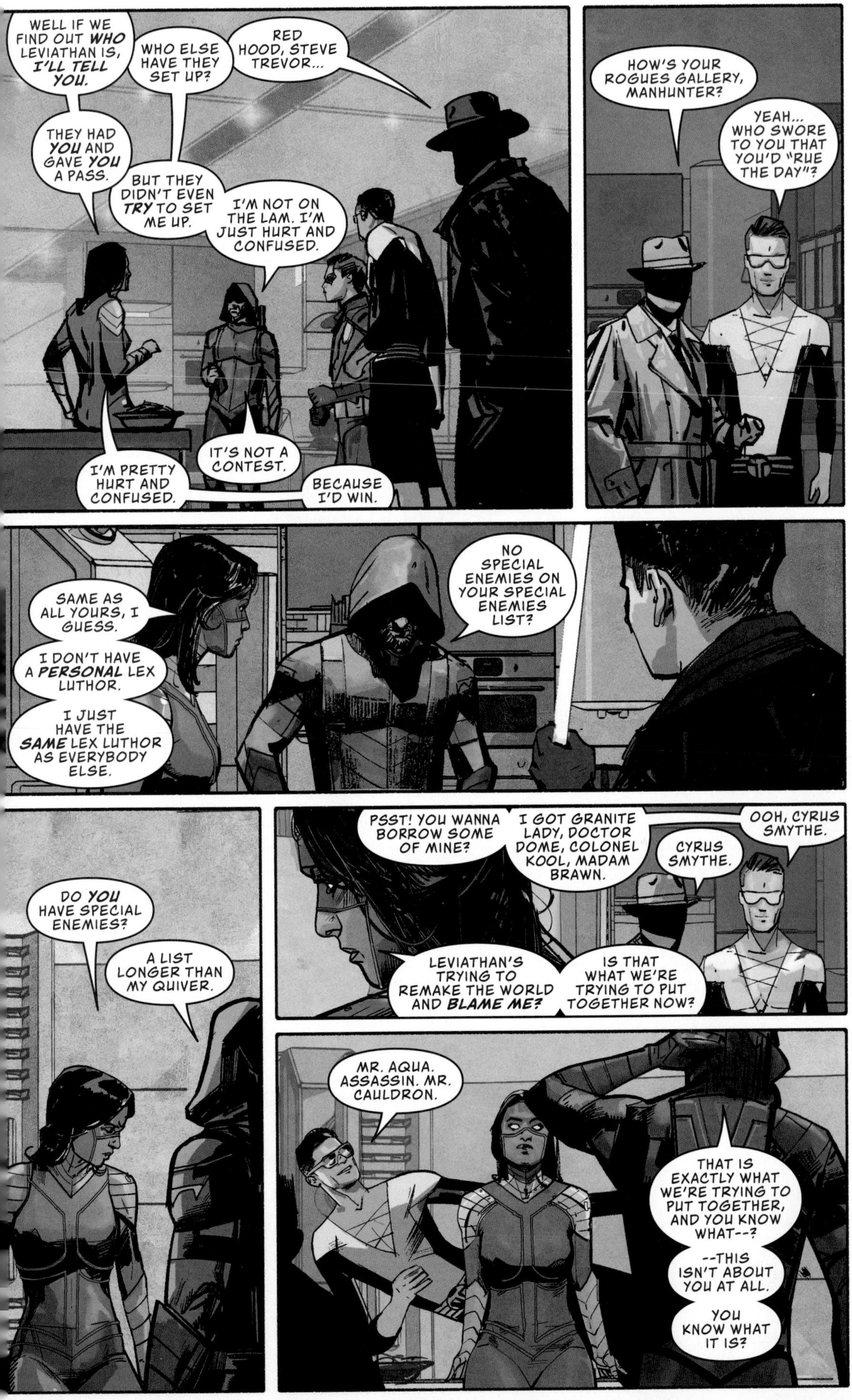
WELL IF WE FIND OUT WHO LEVIATHAN IS, I'LL TELL YOU.
THEY HAD YOU AND GAVE YOU A PASS.
WHO ELSE HAVE THEY SET UP?
RED HOOD, STEVE TREVOR...
BUT THEY DIDN'T EVEN TRY TO SET ME UP.
I'M NOT ON THE LAM. I'M JUST HURT AND CONFUSED.
I'M PRETTY HURT AND CONFUSED.
IT'S NOT A CONTEST.
BECAUSE I'D WIN.
HOW'S YOUR ROGUES GALLERY, MANHUNTER?
YEAH... WHO SWORE TO YOU THAT YOU'D "RUE THE DAY"?
SAME AS ALL YOURS, I GUESS.
I DON'T HAVE A PERSONAL LEX LUTHOR.
I JUST HAVE THE SAME LEX LUTHOR AS EVERYBODY ELSE.
NO SPECIAL ENEMIES ON YOUR SPECIAL ENEMIES LIST?
DO YOU HAVE SPECIAL ENEMIES?
A LIST LONGER THAN MY QUIVER.
PSST! YOU WANNA BORROW SOME OF MINE?
I GOT GRANITE LADY, DOCTOR DOME, COLONEL KOOL, MADAM BRAWN.
CYRUS SMYTHE.
OOH, CYRUS SMYTHE.
LEVIATHAN'S TRYING TO REMAKE THE WORLD AND BLAME ME?
IS THAT WHAT WE'RE TRYING TO PUT TOGETHER NOW?
MR. AQUA. ASSASSIN. MR. CAULDRON.
THAT IS EXACTLY WHAT WE'RE TRYING TO PUT TOGETHER, AND YOU KNOW WHAT--?
--THIS ISN'T ABOUT YOU AT ALL.
YOU KNOW WHAT IT IS?

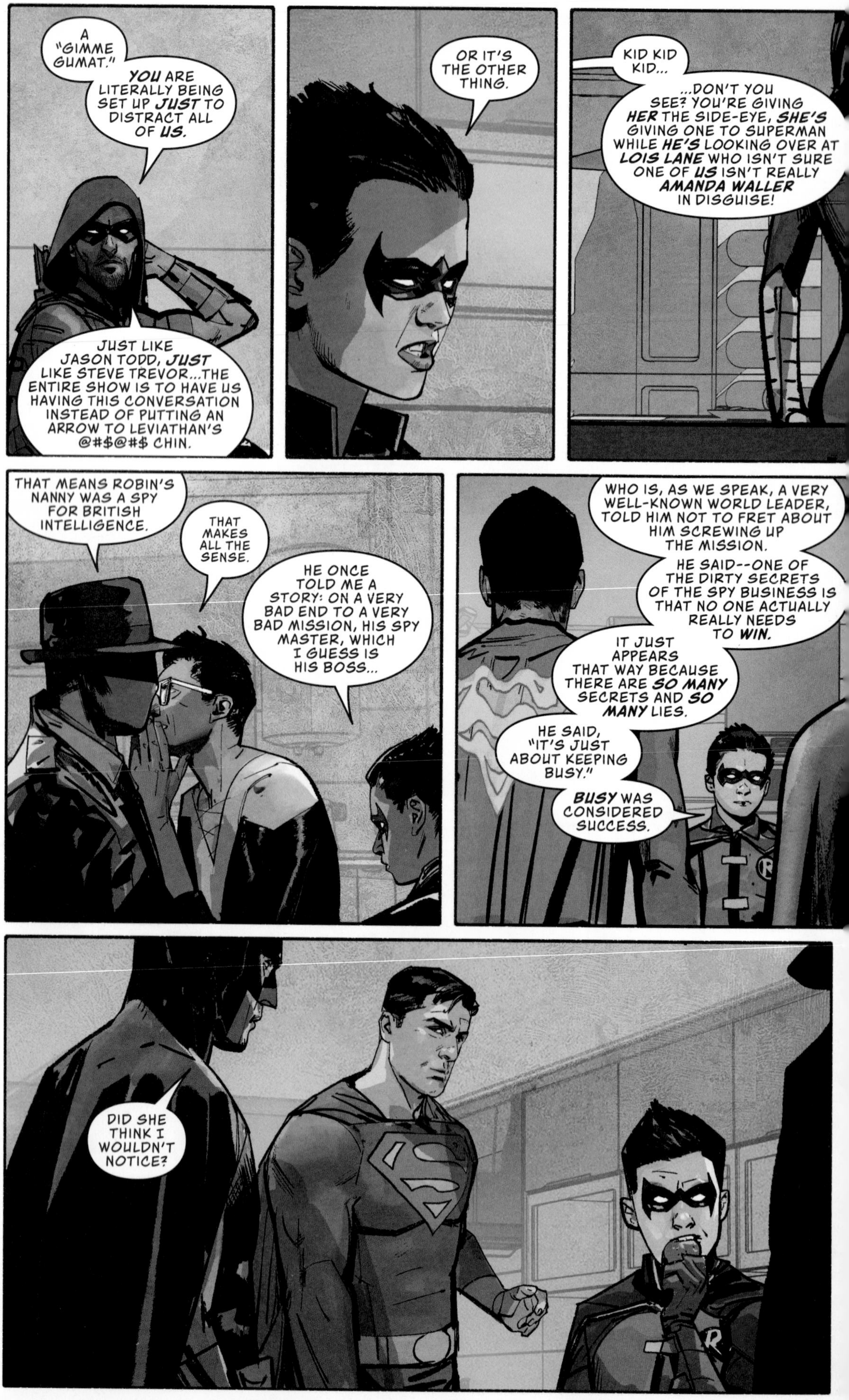
A "GIMME GUMAT." YOU ARE LITERALLY BEING SET UP JUST TO DISTRACT ALL OF US.
JUST LIKE JASON TODD, JUST LIKE STEVE TREVOR...THE ENTIRE SHOW IS TO HAVE US HAVING THIS CONVERSATION INSTEAD OF PUTTING AN ARROW TO LEVIATHAN'S @#$@#$ CHIN.
OR IT'S THE OTHER THING.
KID KID KID...
...DON'T YOU SEE? YOU'RE GIVING HER THE SIDE-EYE, SHE'S GIVING ONE TO SUPERMAN WHILE HE'S LOOKING OVER AT LOIS LANE WHO ISN'T SURE ONE OF US ISN'T REALLY AMANDA WALLER IN DISGUISE!
THAT MEANS ROBIN'S NANNY WAS A SPY FOR BRITISH INTELLIGENCE.
THAT MAKES ALL THE SENSE.
HE ONCE TOLD ME A STORY: ON A VERY BAD END TO A VERY BAD MISSION, HIS SPY MASTER, WHICH I GUESS IS HIS BOSS...
WHO IS, AS WE SPEAK, A VERY WELL-KNOWN WORLD LEADER, TOLD HIM NOT TO FRET ABOUT HIM SCREWING UP THE MISSION.
HE SAID--ONE OF THE DIRTY SECRETS OF THE SPY BUSINESS IS THAT NO ONE ACTUALLY REALLY NEEDS TO WIN.
IT JUST APPEARS THAT WAY BECAUSE THERE ARE SO MANY SECRETS AND SO MANY LIES.
HE SAID, "IT'S JUST ABOUT KEEPING BUSY."
BUSY WAS CONSIDERED SUCCESS.
DID SHE THINK I WOULDN'T NOTICE?

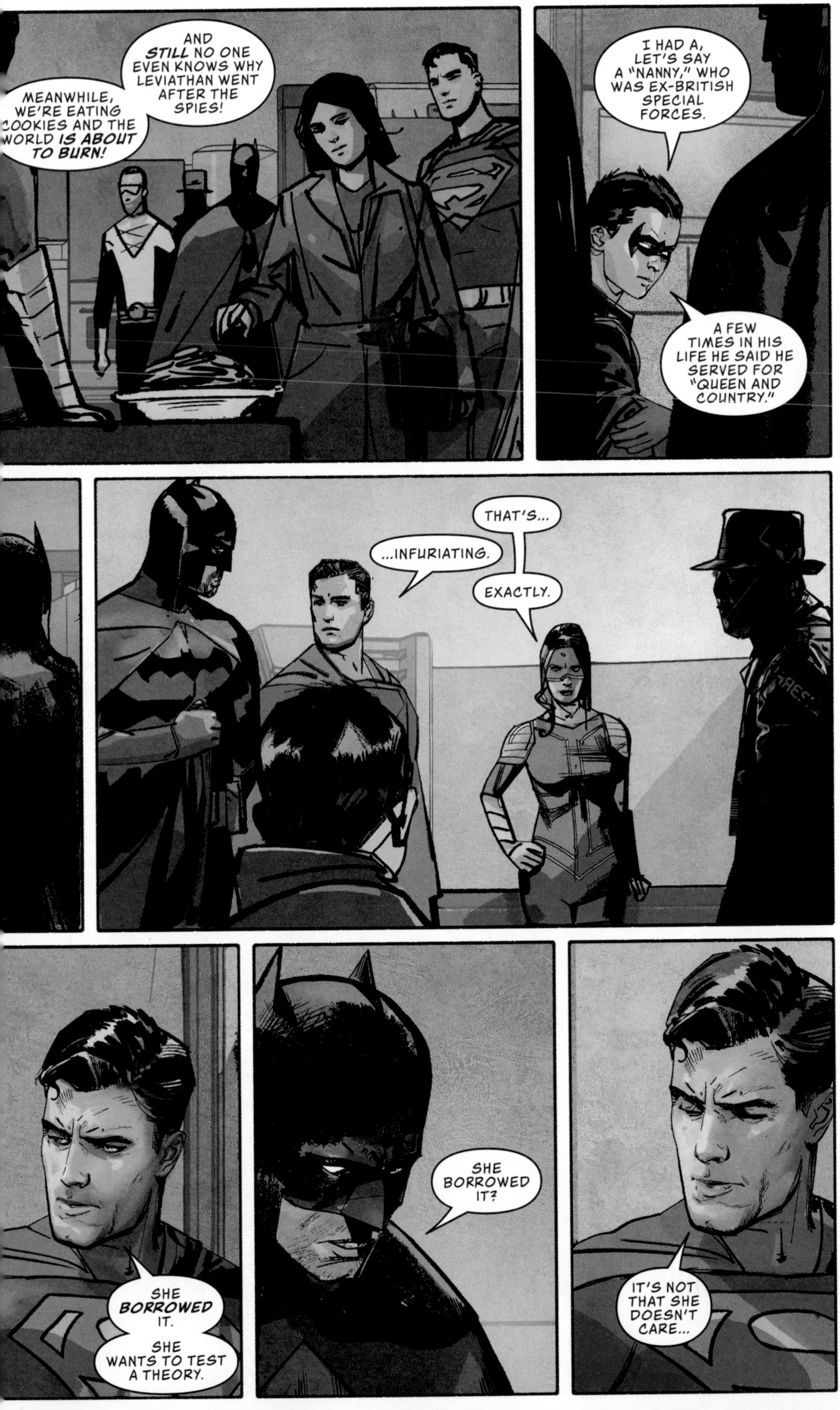

MEANWHILE, WE'RE EATING COOKIES AND THE WORLD **IS ABOUT TO BURN!**
AND **STILL** NO ONE EVEN KNOWS WHY LEVIATHAN WENT AFTER THE SPIES!
I HAD A, LET'S SAY A "NANNY," WHO WAS EX-BRITISH SPECIAL FORCES.
A FEW TIMES IN HIS LIFE HE SAID HE SERVED FOR "QUEEN AND COUNTRY."
THAT'S...
...INFURIATING.
EXACTLY.
SHE **BORROWED** IT.
SHE WANTS TO TEST A THEORY.
SHE BORROWED IT?
IT'S NOT THAT SHE DOESN'T CARE...

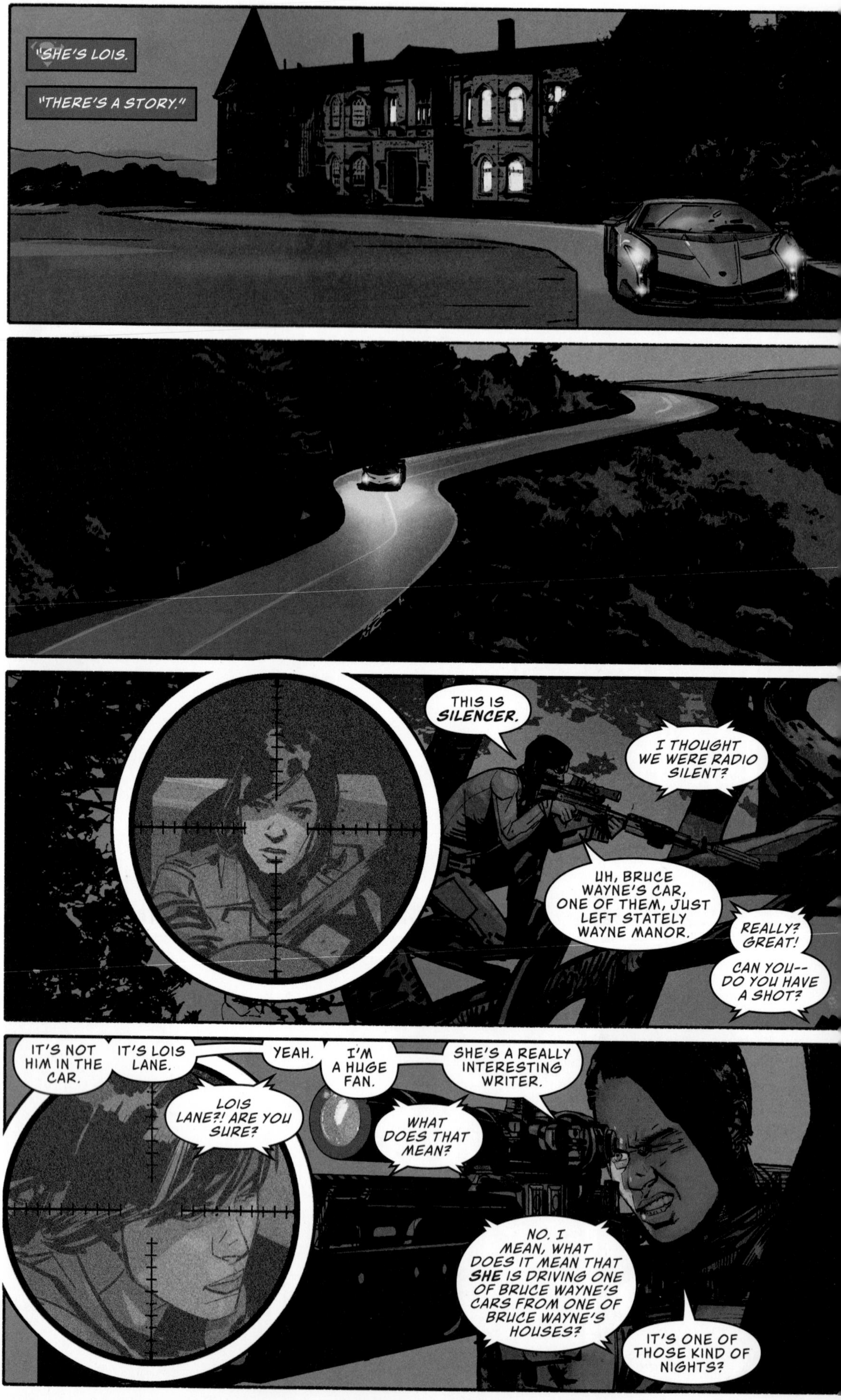
"SHE'S LOIS.
"THERE'S A STORY."
THIS IS SILENCER.
I THOUGHT WE WERE RADIO SILENT?
UH, BRUCE WAYNE'S CAR, ONE OF THEM, JUST LEFT STATELY WAYNE MANOR.
REALLY? GREAT!
CAN YOU-- DO YOU HAVE A SHOT?
IT'S NOT HIM IN THE CAR.
IT'S LOIS LANE.
LOIS LANE?! ARE YOU SURE?
YEAH.
I'M A HUGE FAN.
SHE'S A REALLY INTERESTING WRITER.
WHAT DOES THAT MEAN?
NO. I MEAN, WHAT DOES IT MEAN THAT SHE IS DRIVING ONE OF BRUCE WAYNE'S CARS FROM ONE OF BRUCE WAYNE'S HOUSES?
IT'S ONE OF THOSE KIND OF NIGHTS?

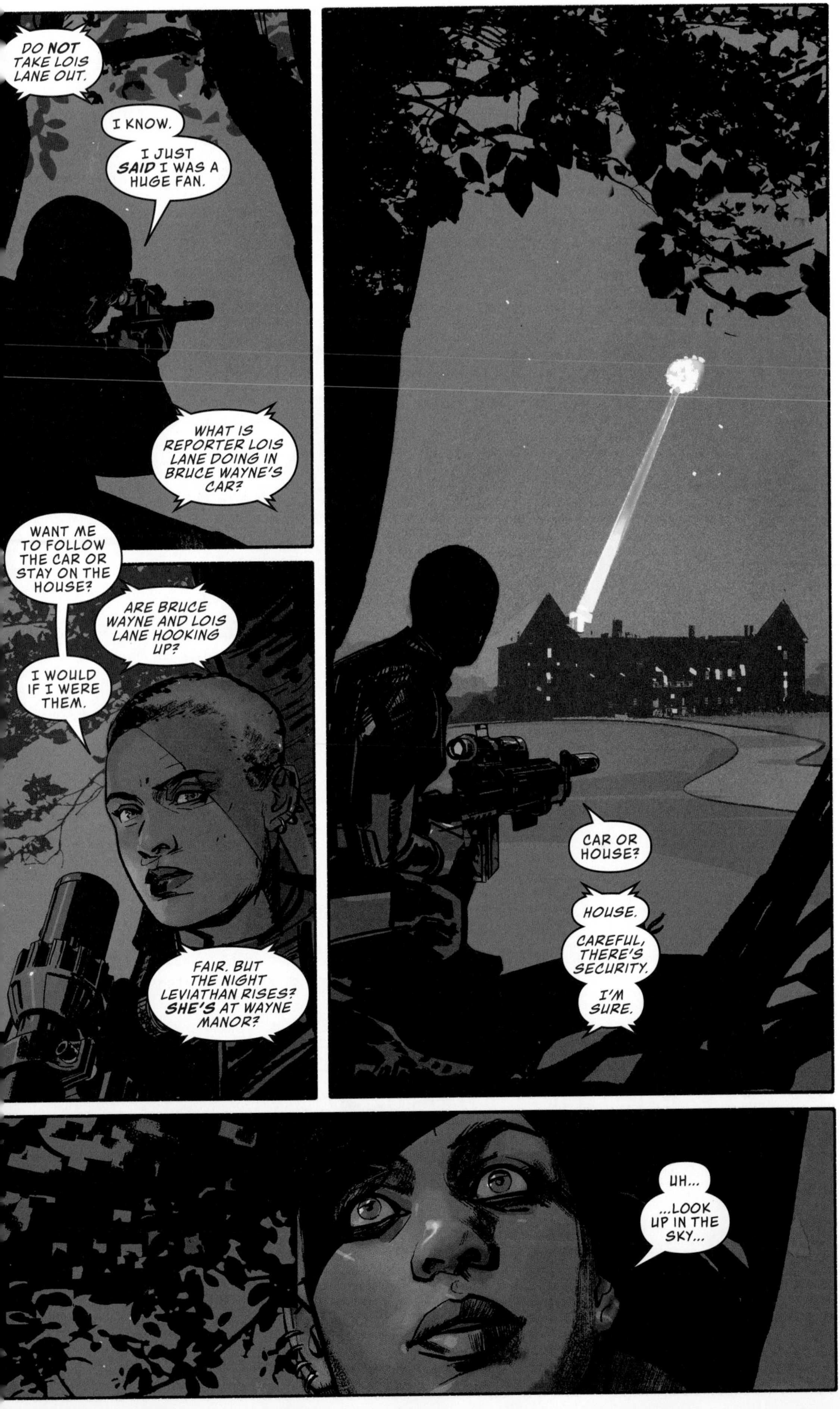
DO NOT TAKE LOIS LANE OUT.
I KNOW.
I JUST SAID I WAS A HUGE FAN.
WHAT IS REPORTER LOIS LANE DOING IN BRUCE WAYNE'S CAR?
WANT ME TO FOLLOW THE CAR OR STAY ON THE HOUSE?
ARE BRUCE WAYNE AND LOIS LANE HOOKING UP?
I WOULD IF I WERE THEM.
FAIR. BUT THE NIGHT LEVIATHAN RISES? SHE'S AT WAYNE MANOR?
CAR OR HOUSE?
HOUSE.
CAREFUL, THERE'S SECURITY.
I'M SURE.
UH...
...LOOK UP IN THE SKY...

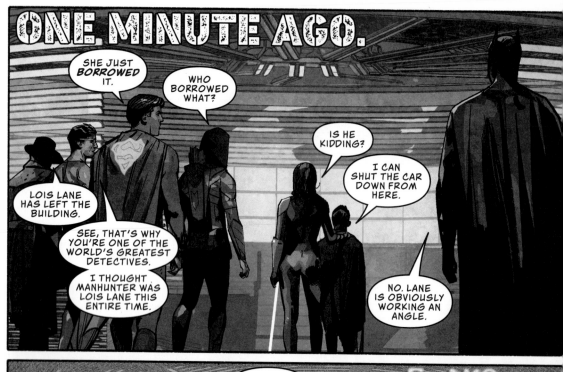

SHE JUST *BORROWED* IT.

WHO BORROWED WHAT?

IS HE KIDDING?

I CAN SHUT THE CAR DOWN FROM HERE.

LOIS LANE HAS LEFT THE BUILDING.

SEE, THAT'S WHY YOU'RE ONE OF THE WORLD'S GREATEST DETECTIVES.

I THOUGHT MANHUNTER WAS LOIS LANE THIS ENTIRE TIME.

NO. LANE IS OBVIOUSLY WORKING AN ANGLE.

YOU'RE WORKING ME.

I'LL PAY FOR THE CAR AND--

I HAVE SOME--

OR SHE'S WORKING *YOU.*

YOU DON'T HAVE IT.

ASTON MARTIN VALKYRIE. 3.2 MILL--

ZZAABATMAM?! THIS IS BATGIRL!

COME IN, BATMAN.

OH, THANK *GOD!*

WHERE ARE YOU?

I'M IN *LEVIATHAN!*

I DON'T HAVE MUCH TIME!

IN LEVIATHAN WHERE?

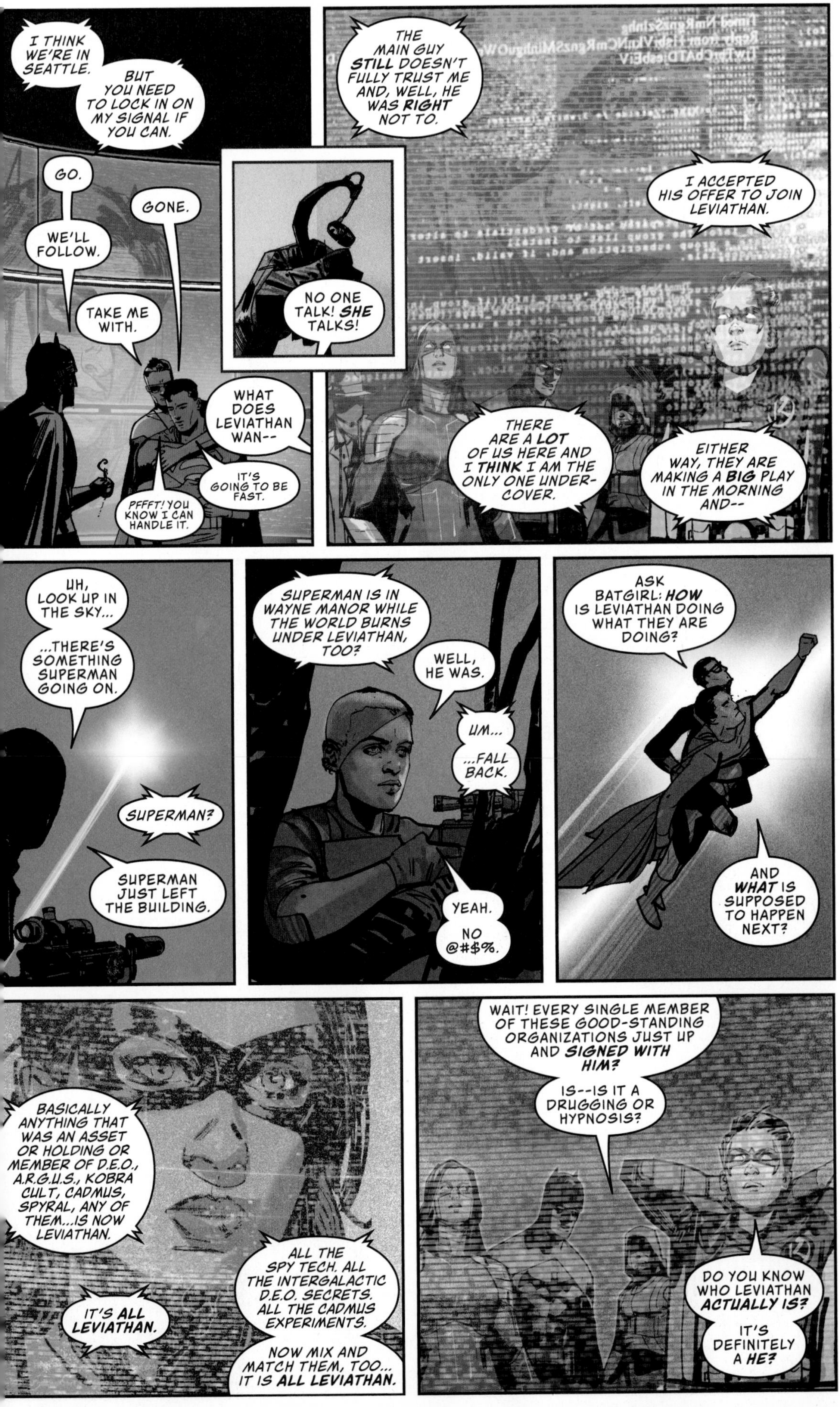
I THINK WE'RE IN SEATTLE.
BUT YOU NEED TO LOCK IN ON MY SIGNAL IF YOU CAN.
GO.
GONE.
WE'LL FOLLOW.
TAKE ME WITH.
WHAT DOES LEVIATHAN WAN--
IT'S GOING TO BE FAST.
PFFFT! YOU KNOW I CAN HANDLE IT.
NO ONE TALK! SHE TALKS!
THE MAIN GUY STILL DOESN'T FULLY TRUST ME AND, WELL, HE WAS RIGHT NOT TO.
I ACCEPTED HIS OFFER TO JOIN LEVIATHAN.
THERE ARE A LOT OF US HERE AND I THINK I AM THE ONLY ONE UNDER-COVER.
EITHER WAY, THEY ARE MAKING A BIG PLAY IN THE MORNING AND--
UH, LOOK UP IN THE SKY...
...THERE'S SOMETHING SUPERMAN GOING ON.
SUPERMAN?
SUPERMAN JUST LEFT THE BUILDING.
SUPERMAN IS IN WAYNE MANOR WHILE THE WORLD BURNS UNDER LEVIATHAN, TOO?
WELL, HE WAS.
UM...
...FALL BACK.
YEAH.
NO @#$%.
ASK BATGIRL: HOW IS LEVIATHAN DOING WHAT THEY ARE DOING?
AND WHAT IS SUPPOSED TO HAPPEN NEXT?
BASICALLY ANYTHING THAT WAS AN ASSET OR HOLDING OR MEMBER OF D.E.O., A.R.G.U.S., KOBRA CULT, CADMUS, SPYRAL, ANY OF THEM...IS NOW LEVIATHAN.
IT'S ALL LEVIATHAN.
ALL THE SPY TECH. ALL THE INTERGALACTIC D.E.O. SECRETS. ALL THE CADMUS EXPERIMENTS.
NOW MIX AND MATCH THEM, TOO... IT IS ALL LEVIATHAN.
WAIT! EVERY SINGLE MEMBER OF THESE GOOD-STANDING ORGANIZATIONS JUST UP AND SIGNED WITH HIM?
IS--IS IT A DRUGGING OR HYPNOSIS?
DO YOU KNOW WHO LEVIATHAN ACTUALLY IS?
IT'S DEFINITELY A HE?

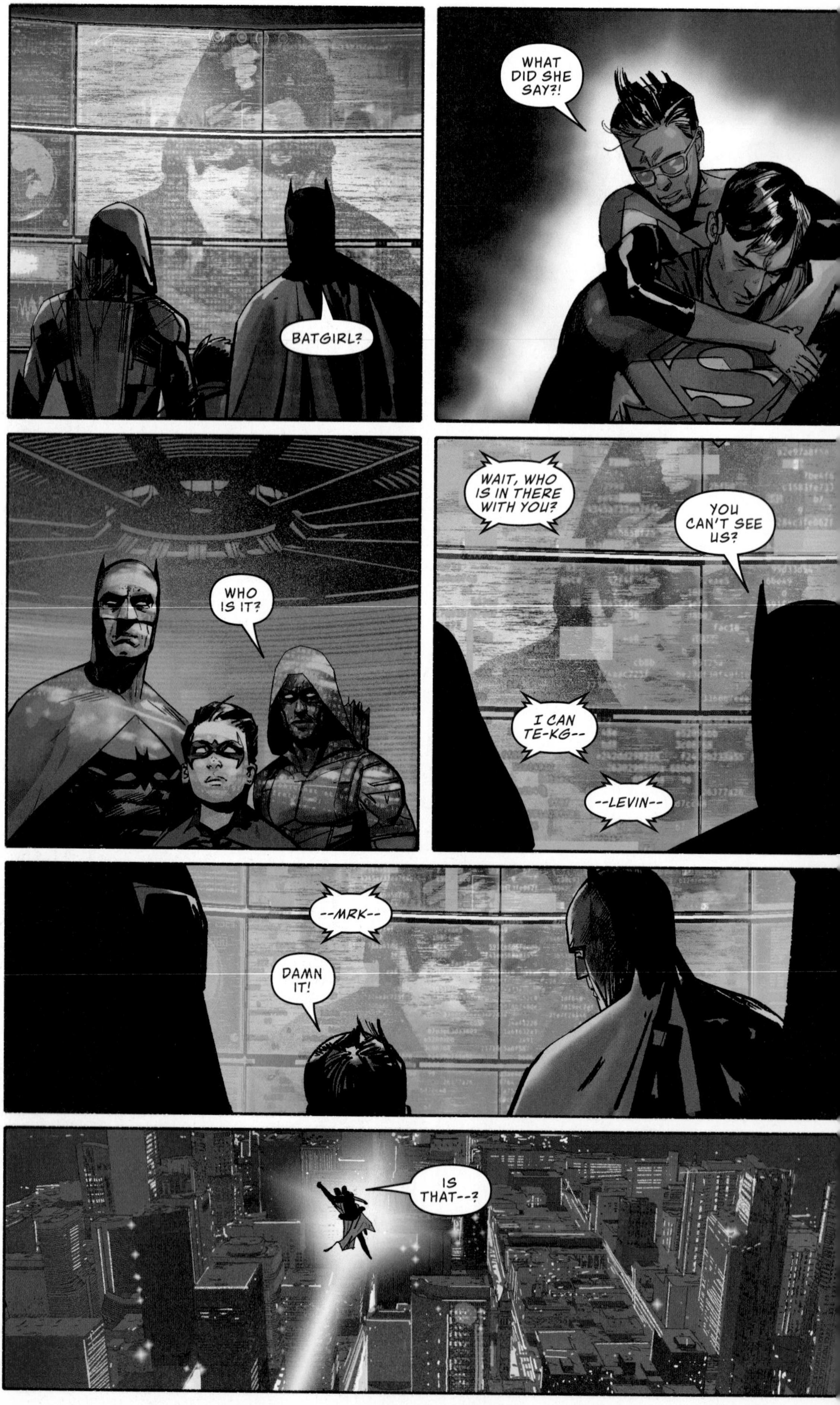
BATGIRL?
WHAT DID SHE SAY?!
WHO IS IT?
WAIT, WHO IS IN THERE WITH YOU?
YOU CAN'T SEE US?
I CAN TE-KG--
--LEVIN--
--MRK--
DAMN IT!
IS THAT--?

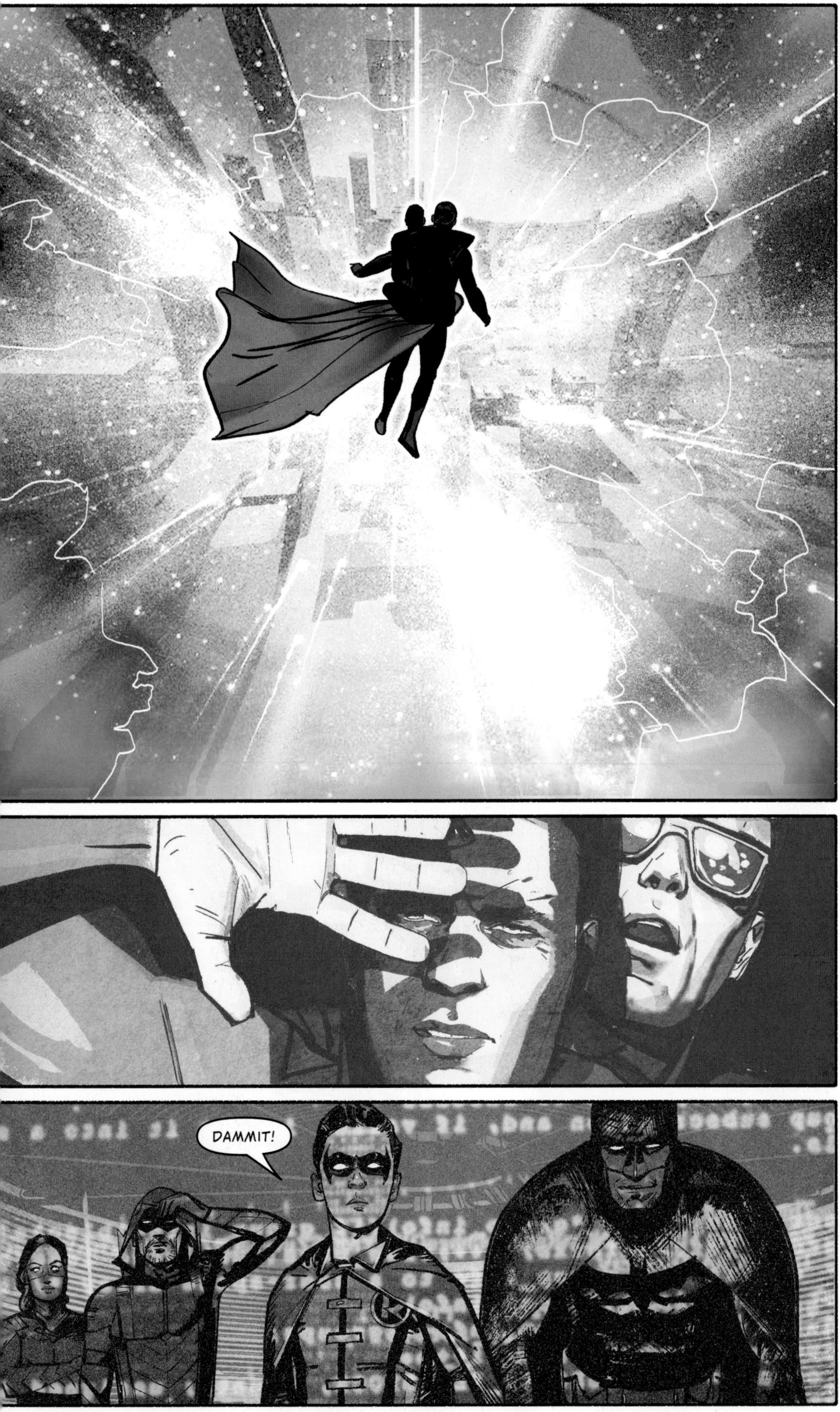
DAMMIT!

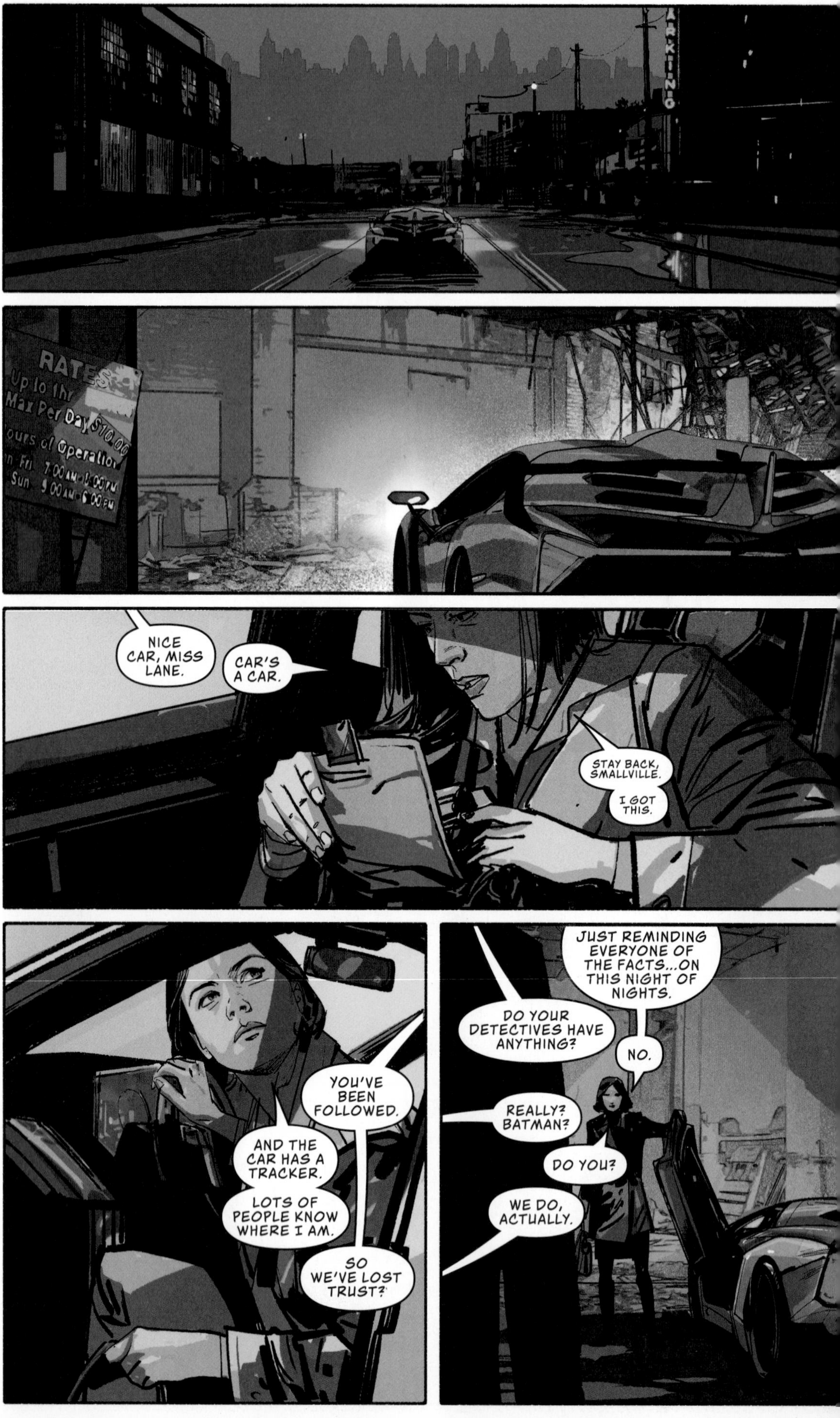
RATES
Up to 1hr
Max Per Day $10.00
Hours of Operation
NICE CAR, MISS LANE.
CAR'S A CAR.
STAY BACK, SMALLVILLE.
I GOT THIS.
YOU'VE BEEN FOLLOWED.
AND THE CAR HAS A TRACKER.
LOTS OF PEOPLE KNOW WHERE I AM.
SO WE'VE LOST TRUST?
JUST REMINDING EVERYONE OF THE FACTS...ON THIS NIGHT OF NIGHTS.
DO YOUR DETECTIVES HAVE ANYTHING?
NO.
REALLY? BATMAN?
DO YOU?
WE DO, ACTUALLY.

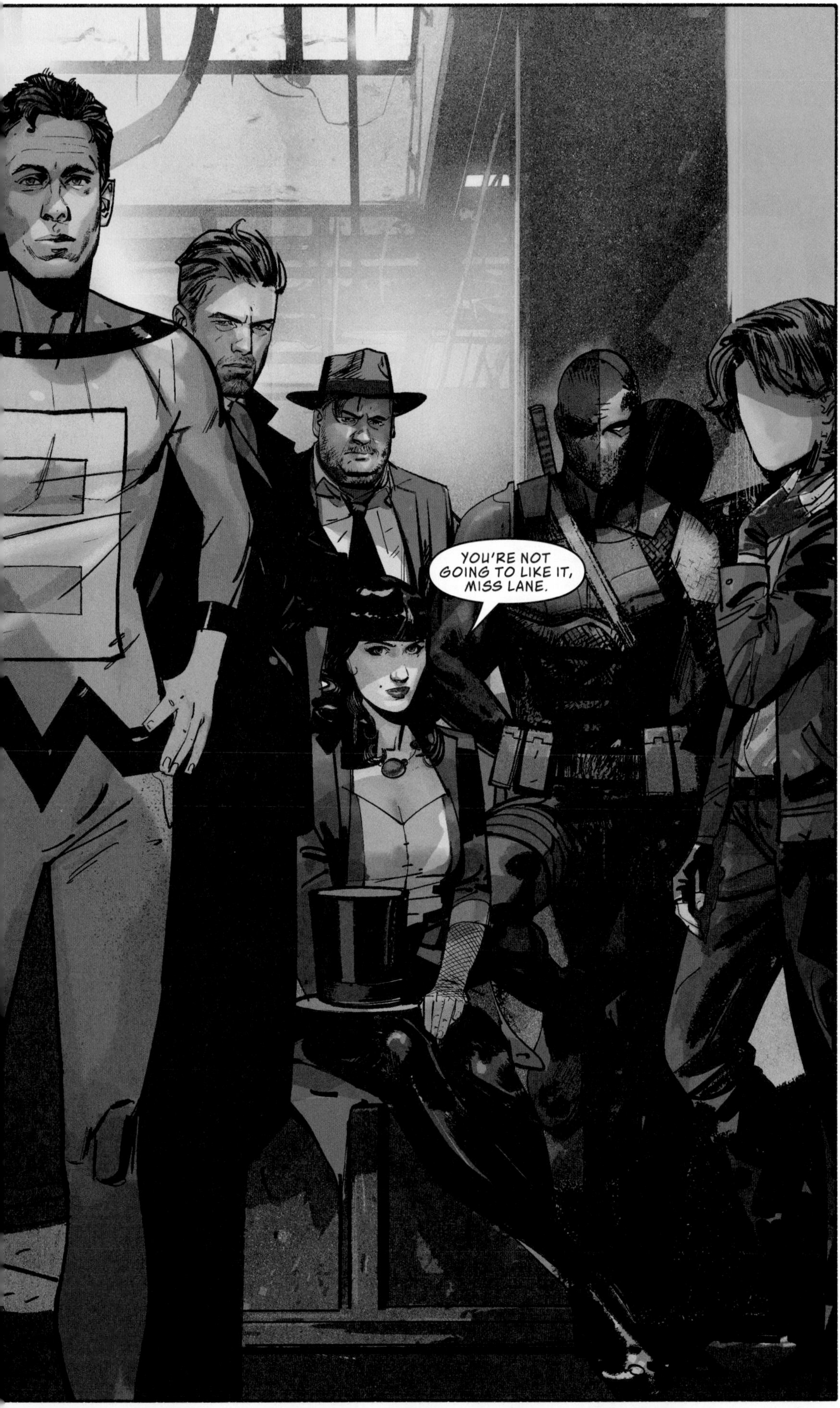
YOU'RE NOT GOING TO LIKE IT, MISS LANE.

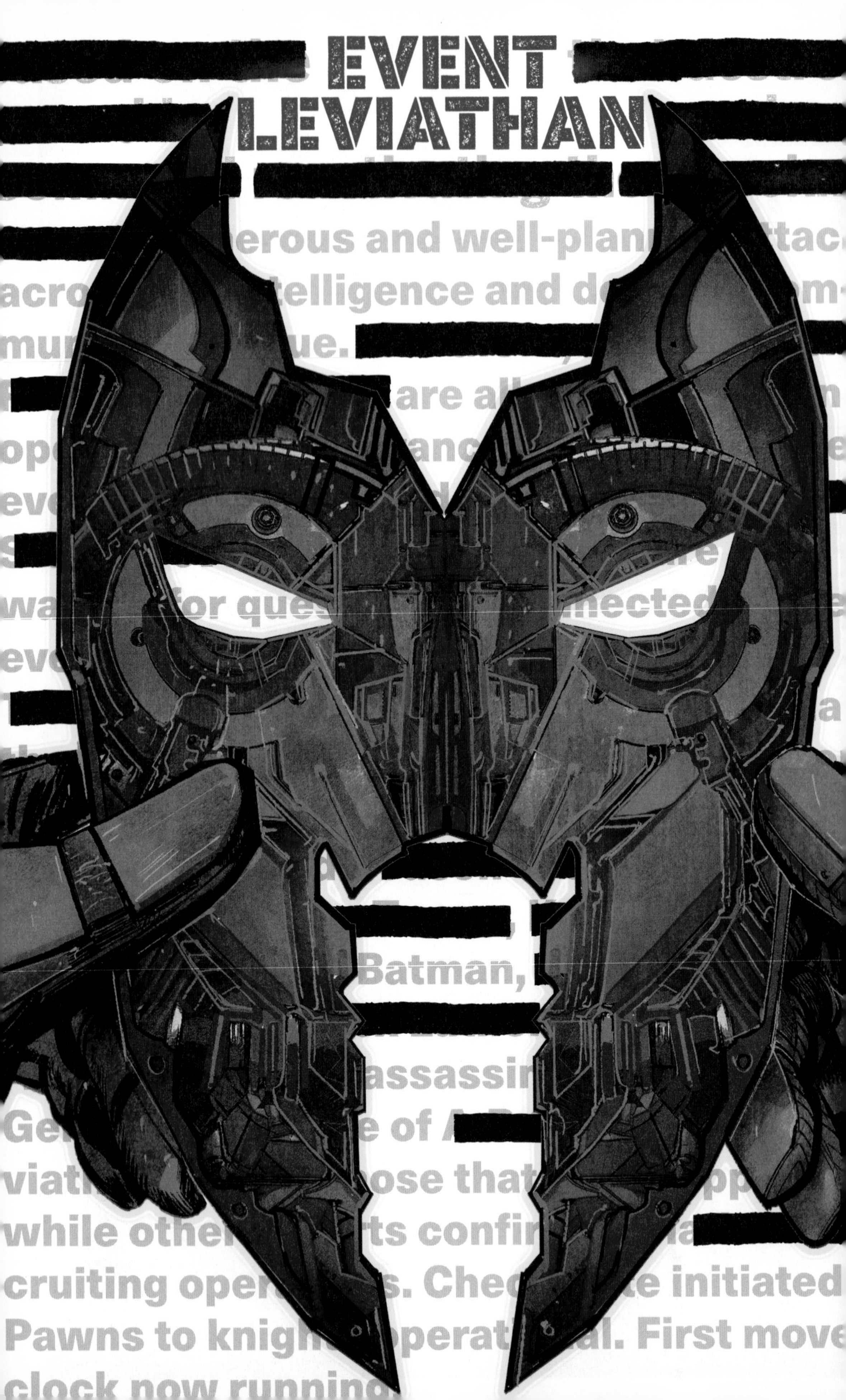
EVENT
LEVIATHAN
Batman,

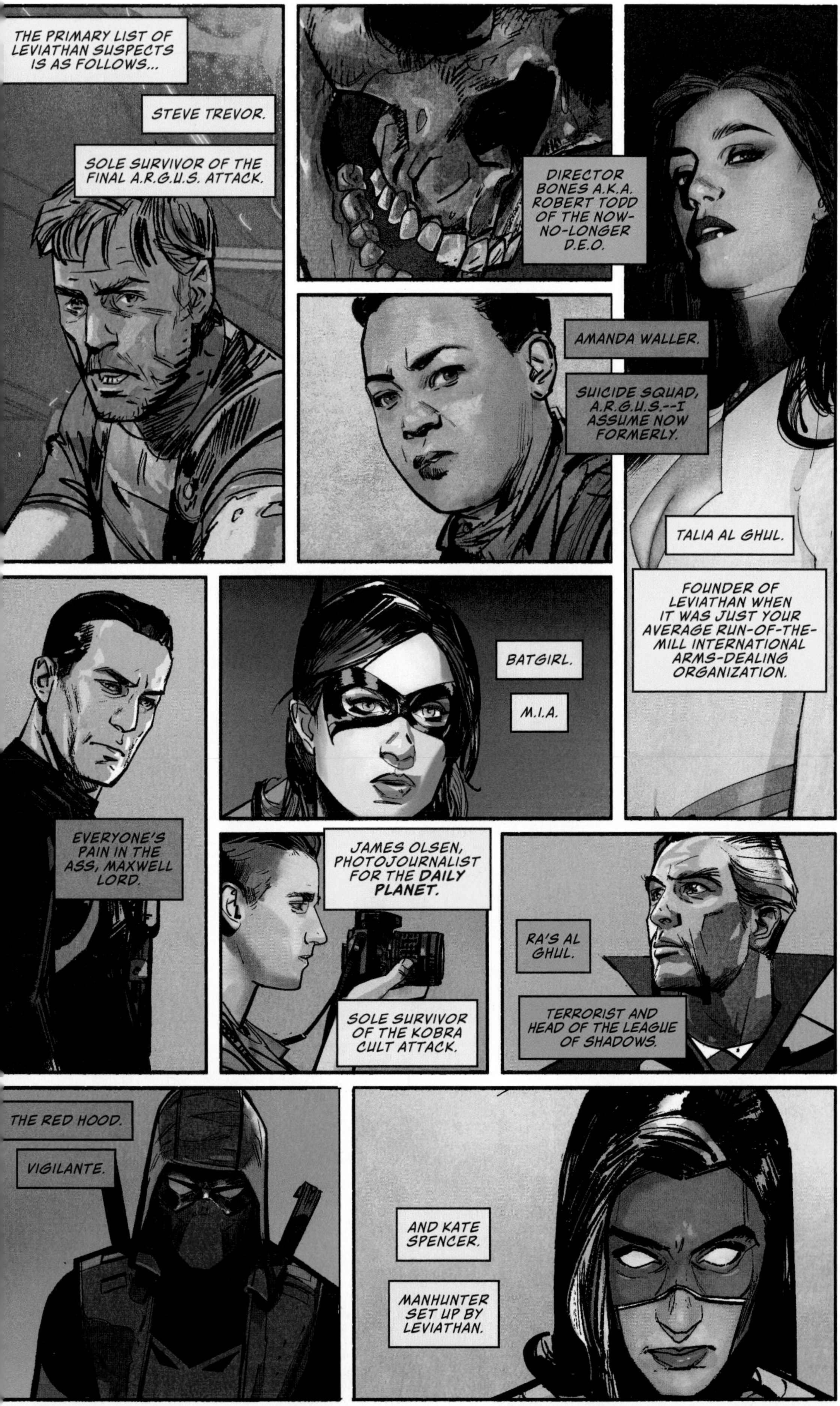
THE PRIMARY LIST OF LEVIATHAN SUSPECTS IS AS FOLLOWS...
STEVE TREVOR.
SOLE SURVIVOR OF THE FINAL A.R.G.U.S. ATTACK.
DIRECTOR BONES A.K.A. ROBERT TODD OF THE NOW-NO-LONGER D.E.O.
AMANDA WALLER.
SUICIDE SQUAD, A.R.G.U.S.--I ASSUME NOW FORMERLY.
TALIA AL GHUL.
FOUNDER OF LEVIATHAN WHEN IT WAS JUST YOUR AVERAGE RUN-OF-THE-MILL INTERNATIONAL ARMS-DEALING ORGANIZATION.
BATGIRL.
M.I.A.
EVERYONE'S PAIN IN THE ASS, MAXWELL LORD.
JAMES OLSEN, PHOTOJOURNALIST FOR THE DAILY PLANET.
SOLE SURVIVOR OF THE KOBRA CULT ATTACK.
RA'S AL GHUL.
TERRORIST AND HEAD OF THE LEAGUE OF SHADOWS.
THE RED HOOD.
VIGILANTE.
AND KATE SPENCER.
MANHUNTER SET UP BY LEVIATHAN.

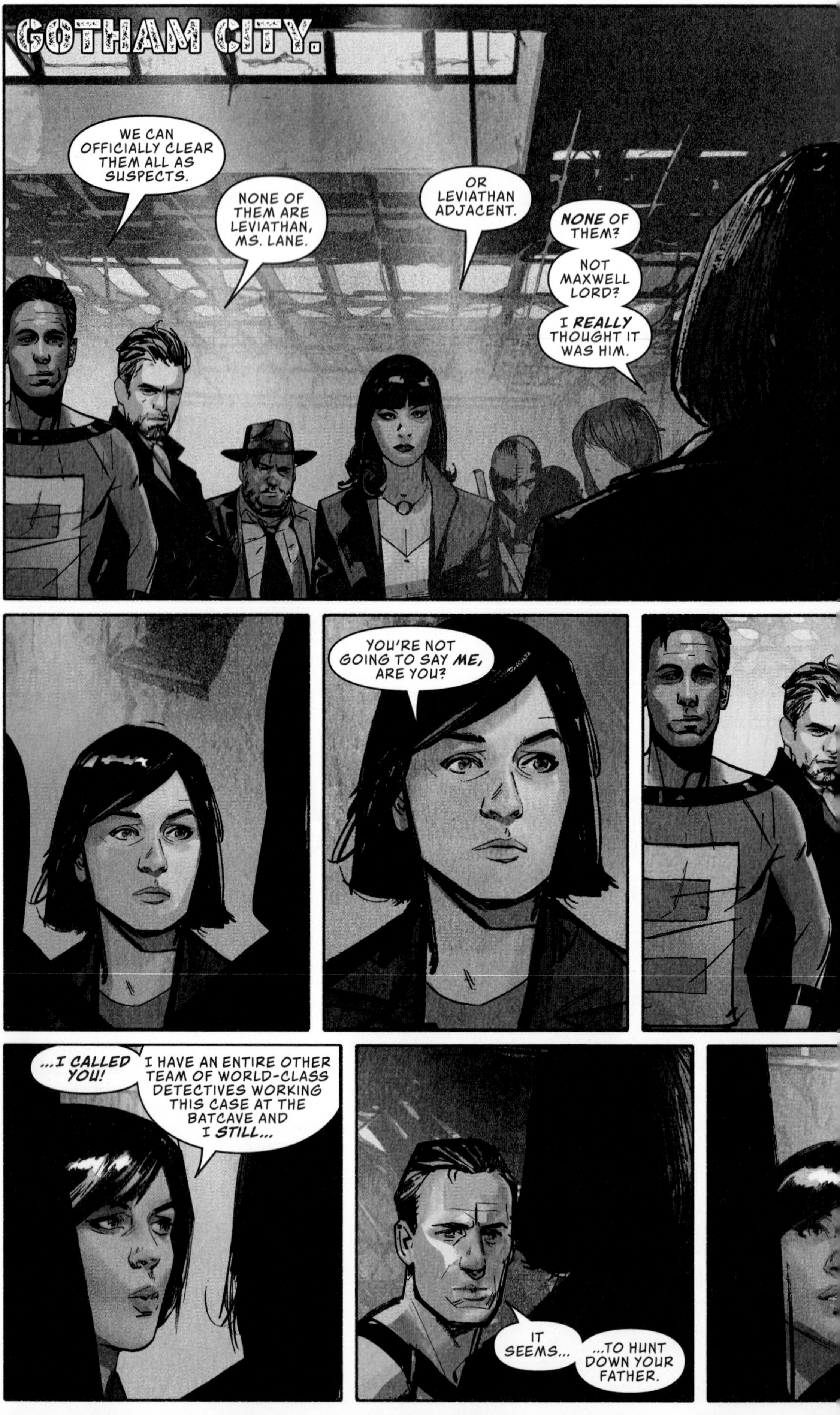
GOTHAM CITY.
WE CAN OFFICIALLY CLEAR THEM ALL AS SUSPECTS.
NONE OF THEM ARE LEVIATHAN, MS. LANE.
OR LEVIATHAN ADJACENT.
NONE OF THEM?
NOT MAXWELL LORD?
I REALLY THOUGHT IT WAS HIM.
YOU'RE NOT GOING TO SAY ME, ARE YOU?
...I CALLED YOU!
I HAVE AN ENTIRE OTHER TEAM OF WORLD-CLASS DETECTIVES WORKING THIS CASE AT THE BATCAVE AND I STILL...
IT SEEMS...
...TO HUNT DOWN YOUR FATHER.

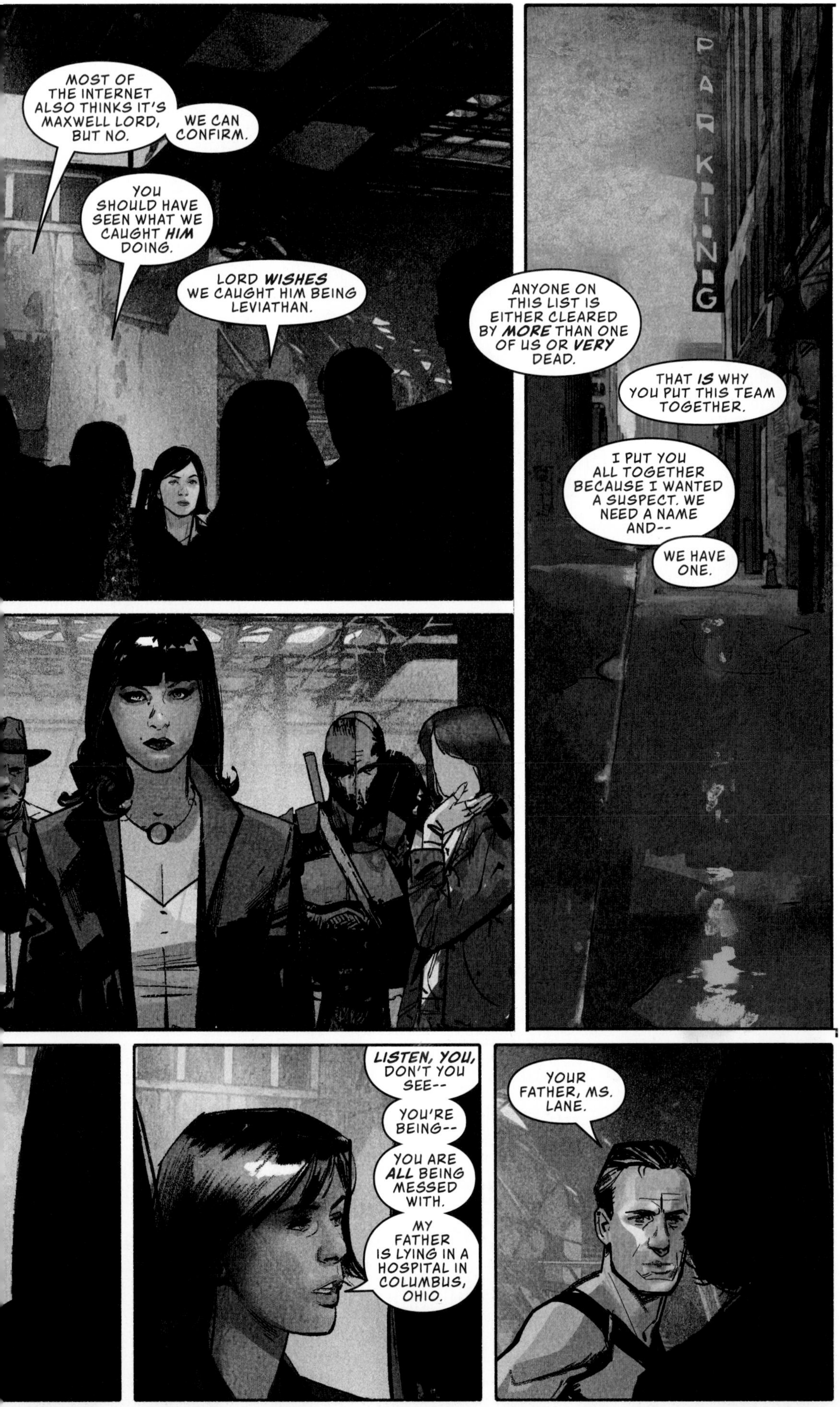
MOST OF THE INTERNET ALSO THINKS IT'S MAXWELL LORD, BUT NO.
WE CAN CONFIRM.
YOU SHOULD HAVE SEEN WHAT WE CAUGHT HIM DOING.
LORD WISHES WE CAUGHT HIM BEING LEVIATHAN.
ANYONE ON THIS LIST IS EITHER CLEARED BY MORE THAN ONE OF US OR VERY DEAD.
PARKING
THAT IS WHY YOU PUT THIS TEAM TOGETHER.
I PUT YOU ALL TOGETHER BECAUSE I WANTED A SUSPECT. WE NEED A NAME AND--
WE HAVE ONE.
LISTEN, YOU, DON'T YOU SEE--
YOU'RE BEING--
YOU ARE ALL BEING MESSED WITH.
MY FATHER IS LYING IN A HOSPITAL IN COLUMBUS, OHIO.
YOUR FATHER, MS. LANE.

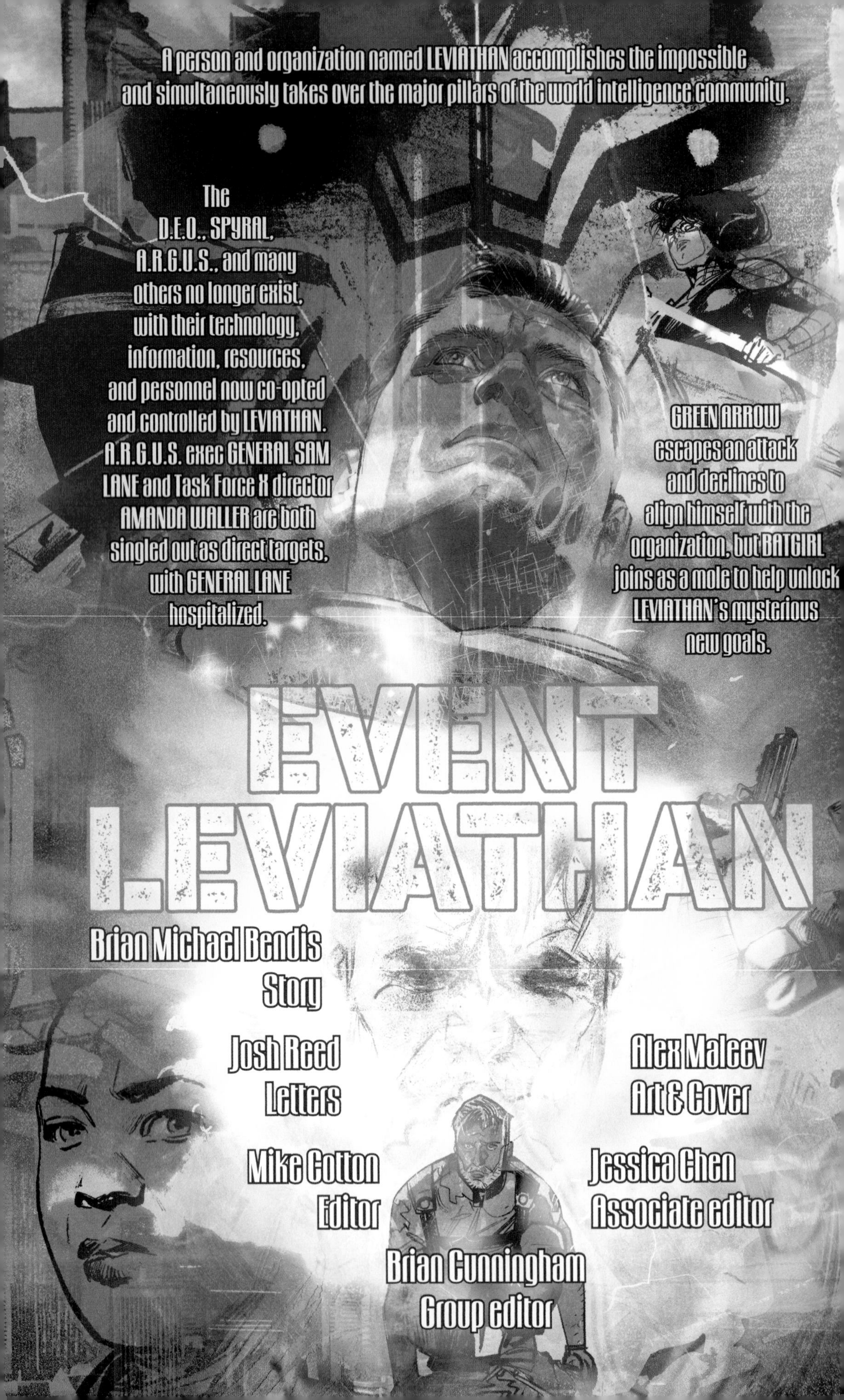

A person and organization named LEVIATHAN accomplishes the impossible and simultaneously takes over the major pillars of the world intelligence community.
The D.E.O., SPYRAL, A.R.G.U.S., and many others no longer exist, with their technology, information, resources, and personnel now co-opted and controlled by LEVIATHAN. A.R.G.U.S. exec GENERAL SAM LANE and Task Force X director AMANDA WALLER are both singled out as direct targets, with GENERAL LANE hospitalized.
GREEN ARROW escapes an attack and declines to align himself with the organization, but BATGIRL joins as a mole to help unlock LEVIATHAN's mysterious new goals.
EVENT LEVIATHAN
Brian Michael Bendis
Story
Josh Reed
Letters
Alex Maleev
Art & Cover
Mike Cotton
Editor
Jessica Chen
Associate editor
Brian Cunningham
Group editor

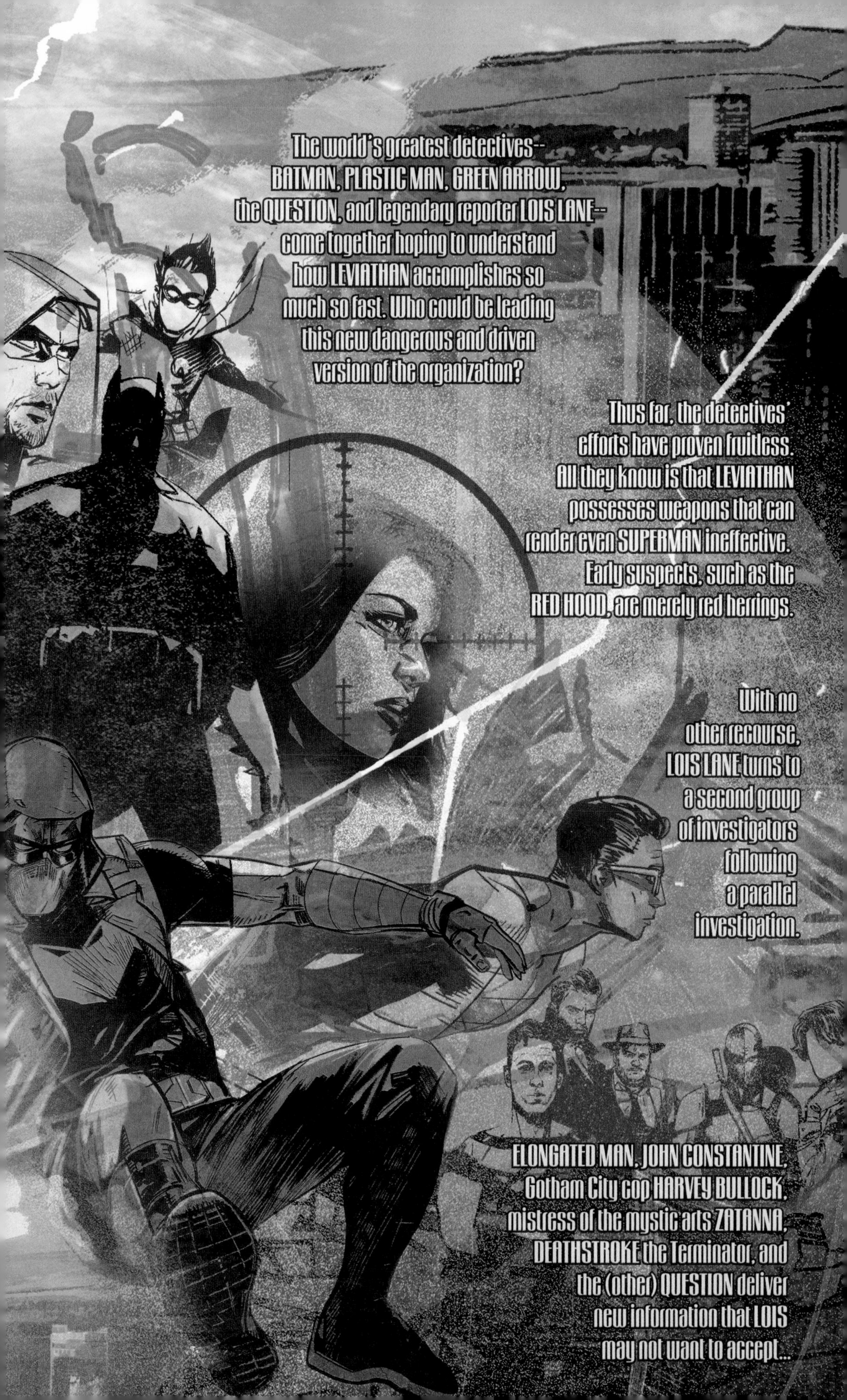
The world's greatest detectives--
BATMAN, PLASTIC MAN, GREEN ARROW,
the QUESTION, and legendary reporter LOIS LANE--
come together hoping to understand
how LEVIATHAN accomplishes so
much so fast. Who could be leading
this new dangerous and driven
version of the organization?
Thus far, the detectives'
efforts have proven fruitless.
All they know is that LEVIATHAN
possesses weapons that can
render even SUPERMAN ineffective.
Early suspects, such as the
RED HOOD, are merely red herrings.
With no
other recourse,
LOIS LANE turns to
a second group
of investigators
following
a parallel
investigation.
ELONGATED MAN, JOHN CONSTANTINE,
Gotham City cop HARVEY BULLOCK,
mistress of the mystic arts ZATANNA,
DEATHSTROKE the Terminator, and
the (other) QUESTION deliver
new information that LOIS
may not want to accept...

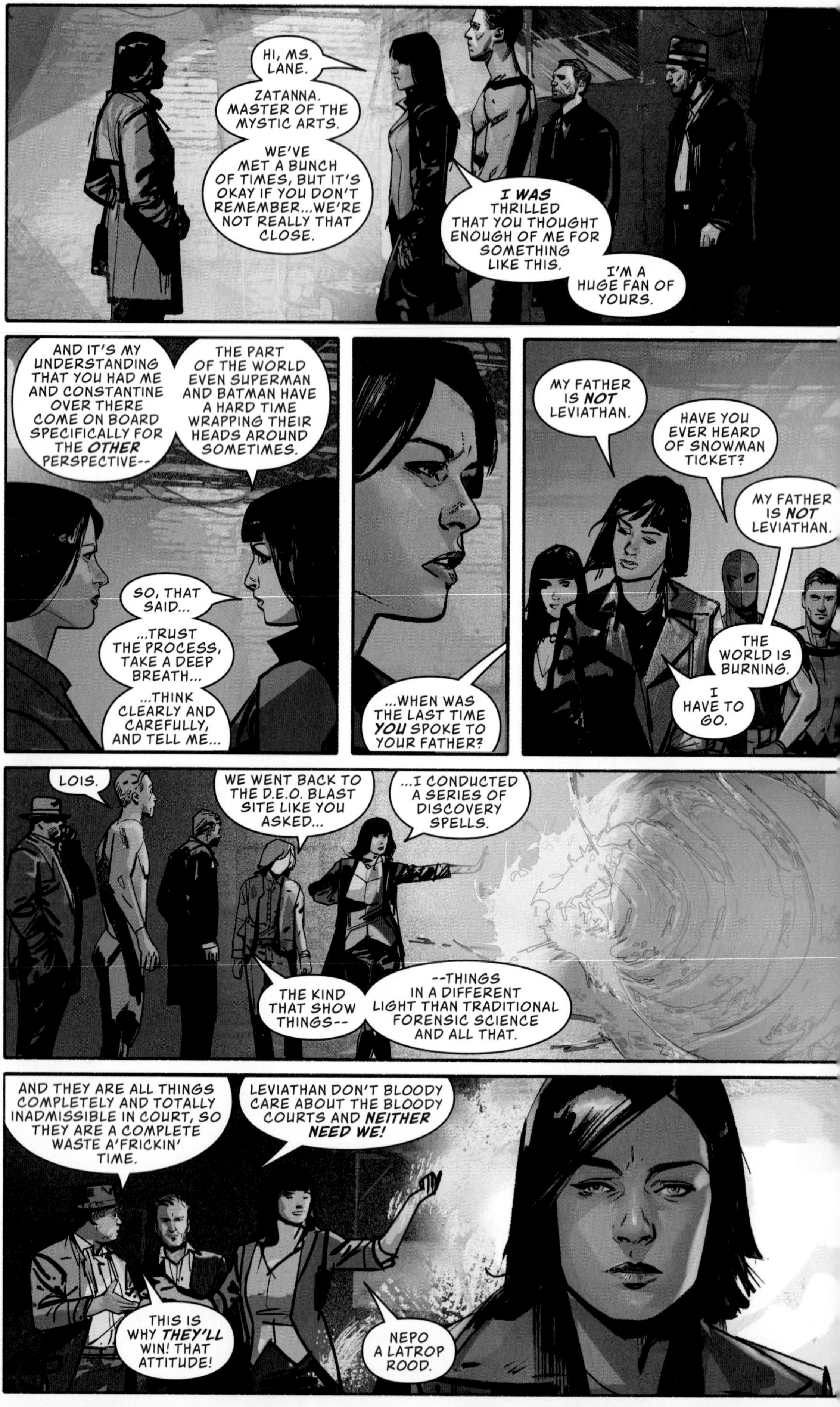
HI, MS. LANE.
ZATANNA. MASTER OF THE MYSTIC ARTS.
WE'VE MET A BUNCH OF TIMES, BUT IT'S OKAY IF YOU DON'T REMEMBER...WE'RE NOT REALLY THAT CLOSE.
I WAS THRILLED THAT YOU THOUGHT ENOUGH OF ME FOR SOMETHING LIKE THIS.
I'M A HUGE FAN OF YOURS.
AND IT'S MY UNDERSTANDING THAT YOU HAD ME AND CONSTANTINE OVER THERE COME ON BOARD SPECIFICALLY FOR THE OTHER PERSPECTIVE--
THE PART OF THE WORLD EVEN SUPERMAN AND BATMAN HAVE A HARD TIME WRAPPING THEIR HEADS AROUND SOMETIMES.
SO, THAT SAID...
...TRUST THE PROCESS, TAKE A DEEP BREATH...
...THINK CLEARLY AND CAREFULLY, AND TELL ME...
...WHEN WAS THE LAST TIME YOU SPOKE TO YOUR FATHER?
MY FATHER IS NOT LEVIATHAN.
HAVE YOU EVER HEARD OF SNOWMAN TICKET?
MY FATHER IS NOT LEVIATHAN.
THE WORLD IS BURNING.
I HAVE TO GO.
LOIS.
WE WENT BACK TO THE D.E.O. BLAST SITE LIKE YOU ASKED...
...I CONDUCTED A SERIES OF DISCOVERY SPELLS.
THE KIND THAT SHOW THINGS--
--THINGS IN A DIFFERENT LIGHT THAN TRADITIONAL FORENSIC SCIENCE AND ALL THAT.
AND THEY ARE ALL THINGS COMPLETELY AND TOTALLY INADMISSIBLE IN COURT, SO THEY ARE A COMPLETE WASTE A'FRICKIN' TIME.
LEVIATHAN DON'T BLOODY CARE ABOUT THE BLOODY COURTS AND NEITHER NEED WE!
THIS IS WHY THEY'LL WIN! THAT ATTITUDE!
NEPO A LATROP ROOD.

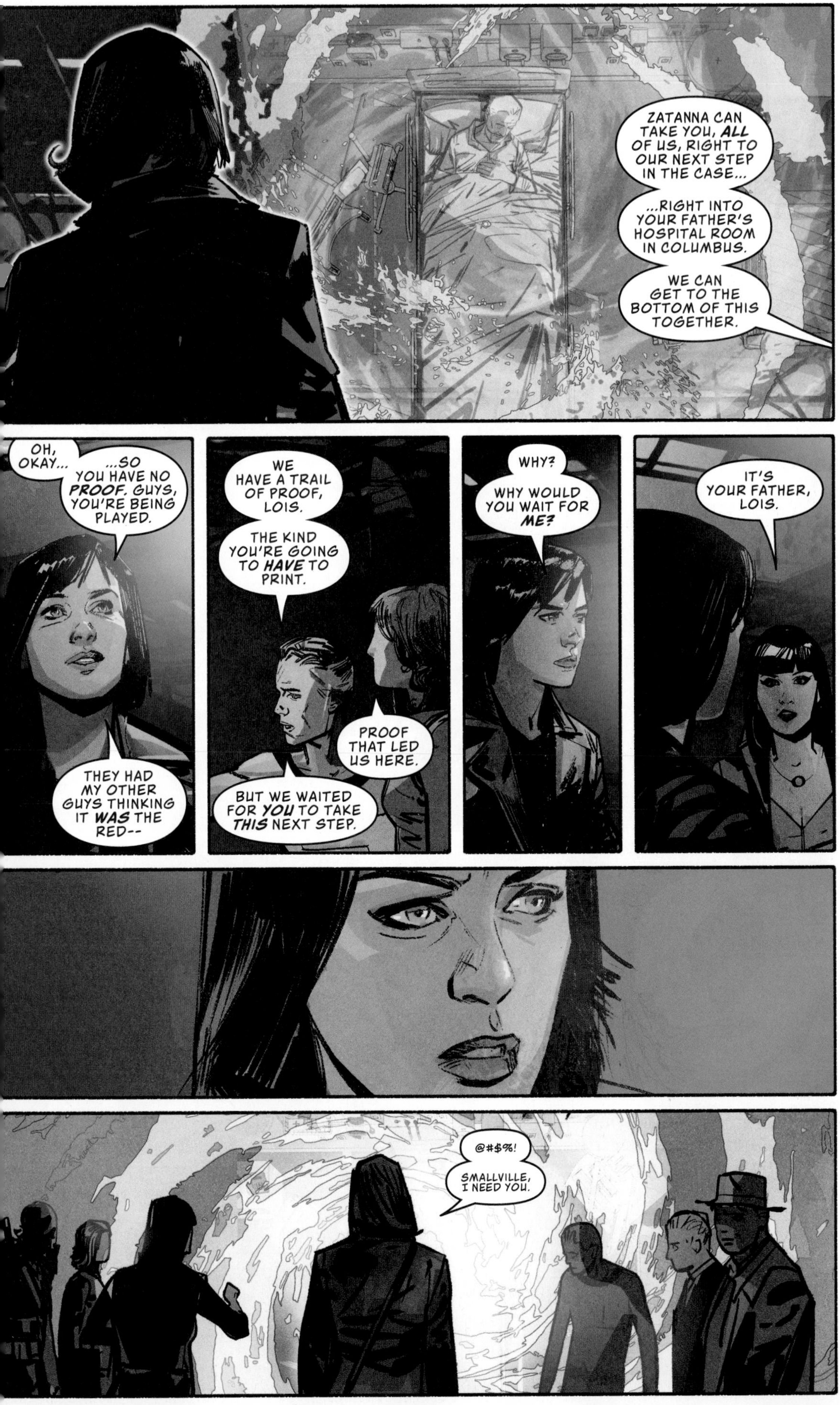
ZATANNA CAN TAKE YOU, ALL OF US, RIGHT TO OUR NEXT STEP IN THE CASE...
...RIGHT INTO YOUR FATHER'S HOSPITAL ROOM IN COLUMBUS.
WE CAN GET TO THE BOTTOM OF THIS TOGETHER.
OH, OKAY...
...SO YOU HAVE NO PROOF. GUYS, YOU'RE BEING PLAYED.
THEY HAD MY OTHER GUYS THINKING IT WAS THE RED--
WE HAVE A TRAIL OF PROOF, LOIS.
THE KIND YOU'RE GOING TO HAVE TO PRINT.
PROOF THAT LED US HERE.
BUT WE WAITED FOR YOU TO TAKE THIS NEXT STEP.
WHY?
WHY WOULD YOU WAIT FOR ME?
IT'S YOUR FATHER, LOIS.
@#$%!
SMALLVILLE, I NEED YOU.

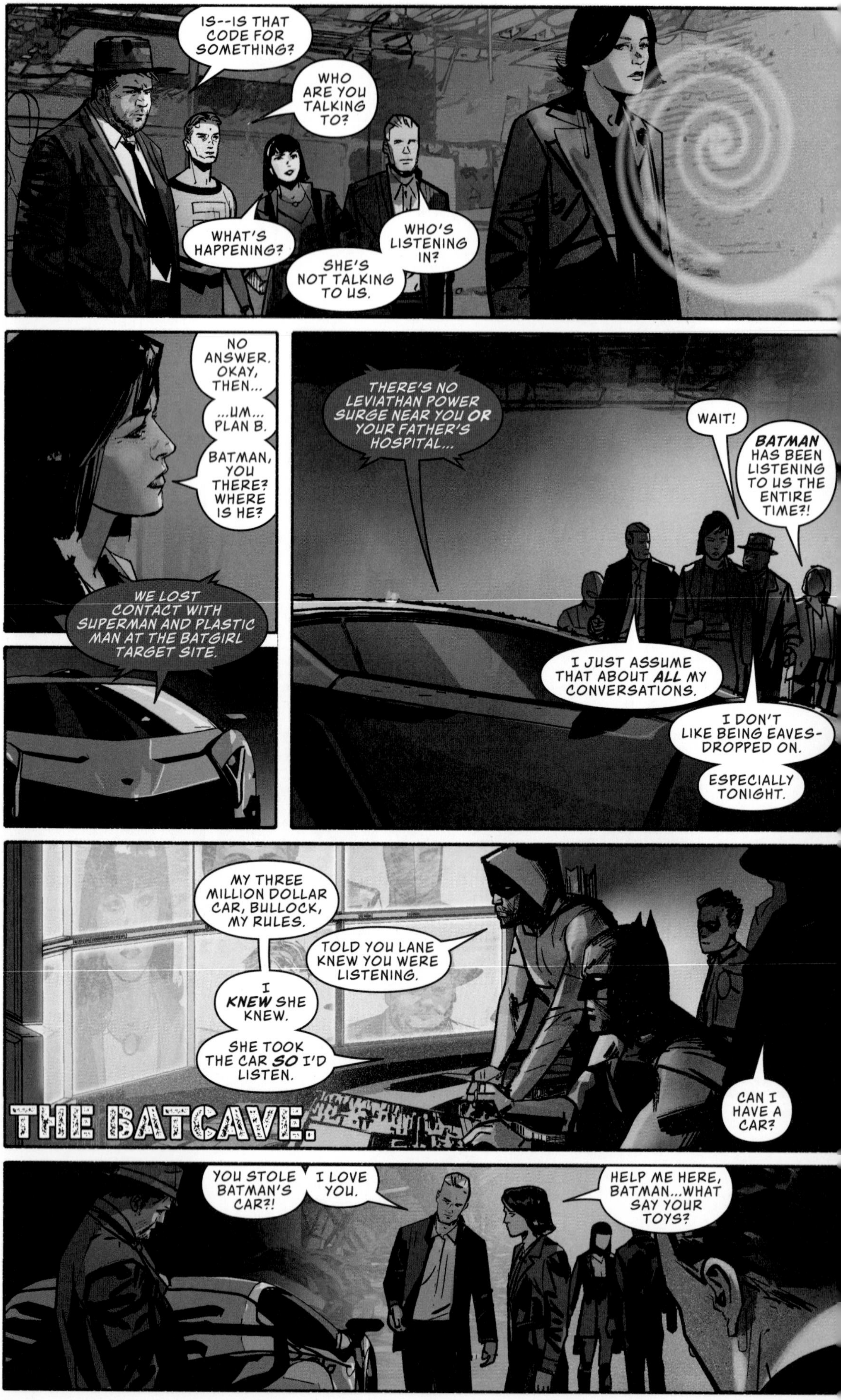
IS--IS THAT CODE FOR SOMETHING?
WHO ARE YOU TALKING TO?
WHAT'S HAPPENING?
WHO'S LISTENING IN?
SHE'S NOT TALKING TO US.
NO ANSWER. OKAY, THEN...
...UM... PLAN B.
BATMAN, YOU THERE? WHERE IS HE?
WE LOST CONTACT WITH SUPERMAN AND PLASTIC MAN AT THE BATGIRL TARGET SITE.
THERE'S NO LEVIATHAN POWER SURGE NEAR YOU OR YOUR FATHER'S HOSPITAL...
WAIT!
BATMAN HAS BEEN LISTENING TO US THE ENTIRE TIME?!
I JUST ASSUME THAT ABOUT ALL MY CONVERSATIONS.
I DON'T LIKE BEING EAVES-DROPPED ON.
ESPECIALLY TONIGHT.
THE BATCAVE.
MY THREE MILLION DOLLAR CAR, BULLOCK, MY RULES.
TOLD YOU LANE KNEW YOU WERE LISTENING.
I KNEW SHE KNEW.
SHE TOOK THE CAR SO I'D LISTEN.
CAN I HAVE A CAR?
YOU STOLE BATMAN'S CAR?!
I LOVE YOU.
HELP ME HERE, BATMAN...WHAT SAY YOUR TOYS?

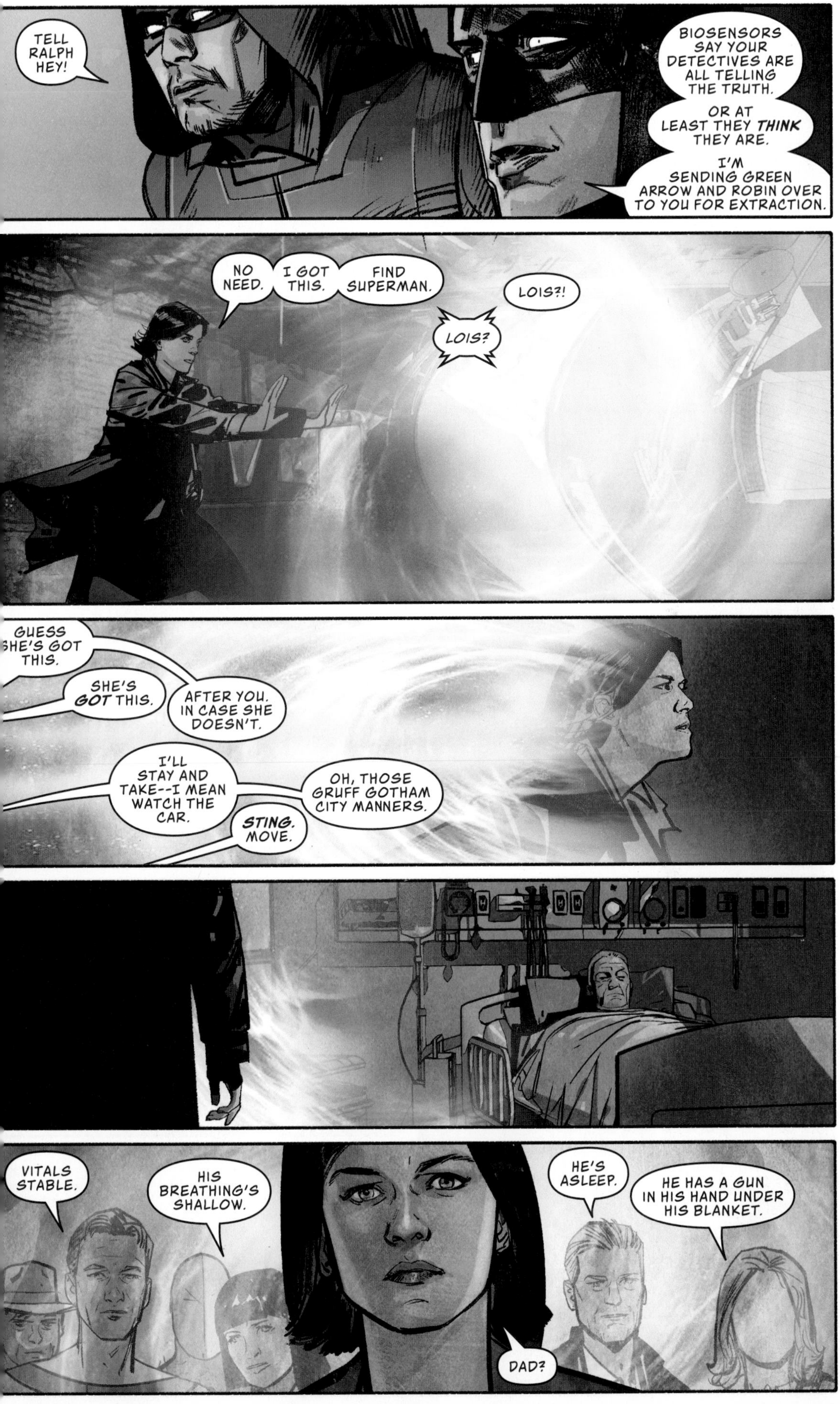
TELL RALPH HEY!
BIOSENSORS SAY YOUR DETECTIVES ARE ALL TELLING THE TRUTH.
OR AT LEAST THEY *THINK* THEY ARE.
I'M SENDING GREEN ARROW AND ROBIN OVER TO YOU FOR EXTRACTION.
NO NEED.
I GOT THIS.
FIND SUPERMAN.
LOIS?!
LOIS?
GUESS SHE'S GOT THIS.
SHE'S *GOT* THIS.
AFTER YOU. IN CASE SHE DOESN'T.
I'LL STAY AND TAKE--I MEAN WATCH THE CAR.
OH, THOSE GRUFF GOTHAM CITY MANNERS.
STING. MOVE.
VITALS STABLE.
HIS BREATHING'S SHALLOW.
HE'S ASLEEP.
HE HAS A GUN IN HIS HAND UNDER HIS BLANKET.
DAD?

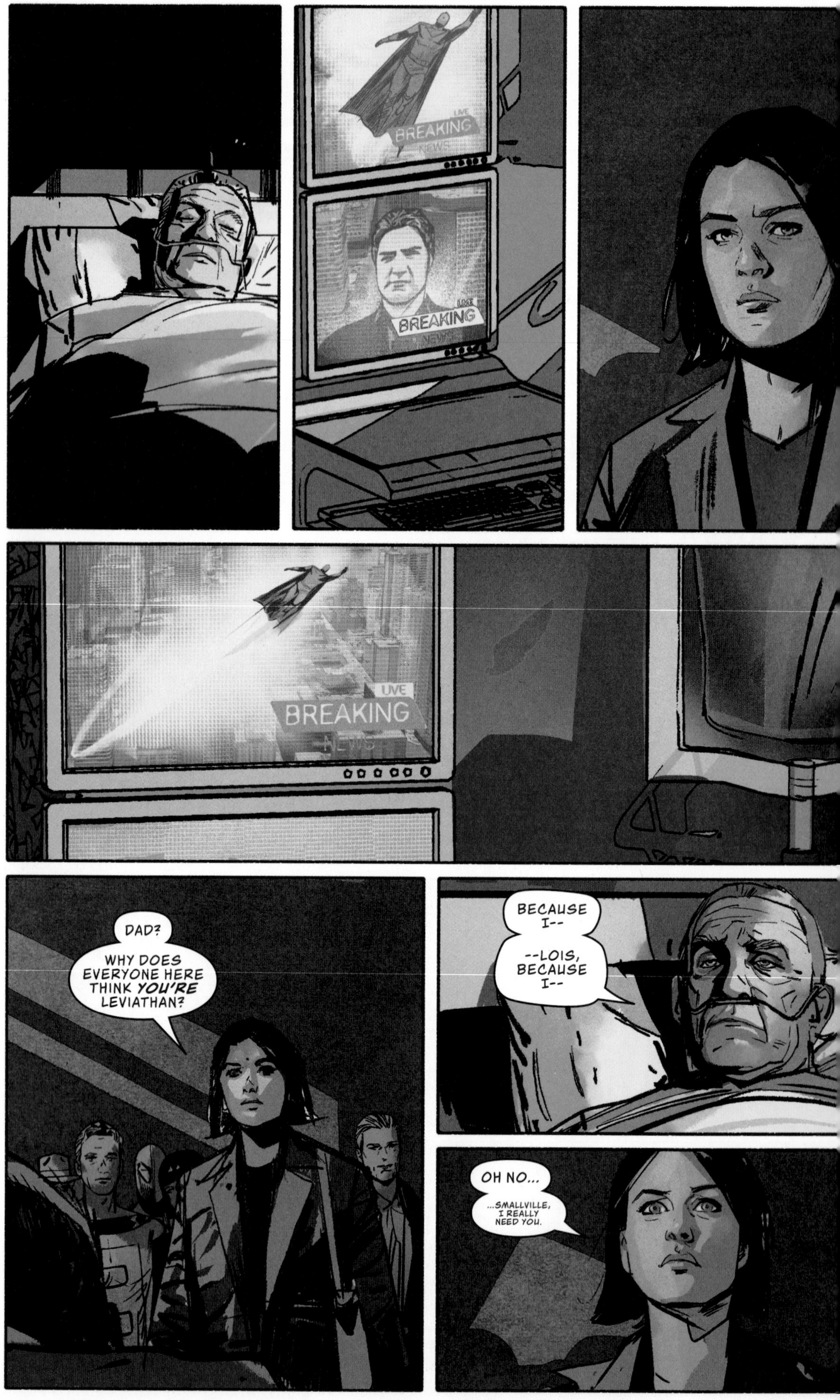
LIVE
BREAKING
NEWS
LIVE
BREAKING
NEWS
LIVE
BREAKING
NEWS
DAD?
WHY DOES EVERYONE HERE THINK *YOU'RE* LEVIATHAN?
BECAUSE I--
--LOIS, BECAUSE I--
OH NO...
...SMALLVILLE, I REALLY NEED YOU.

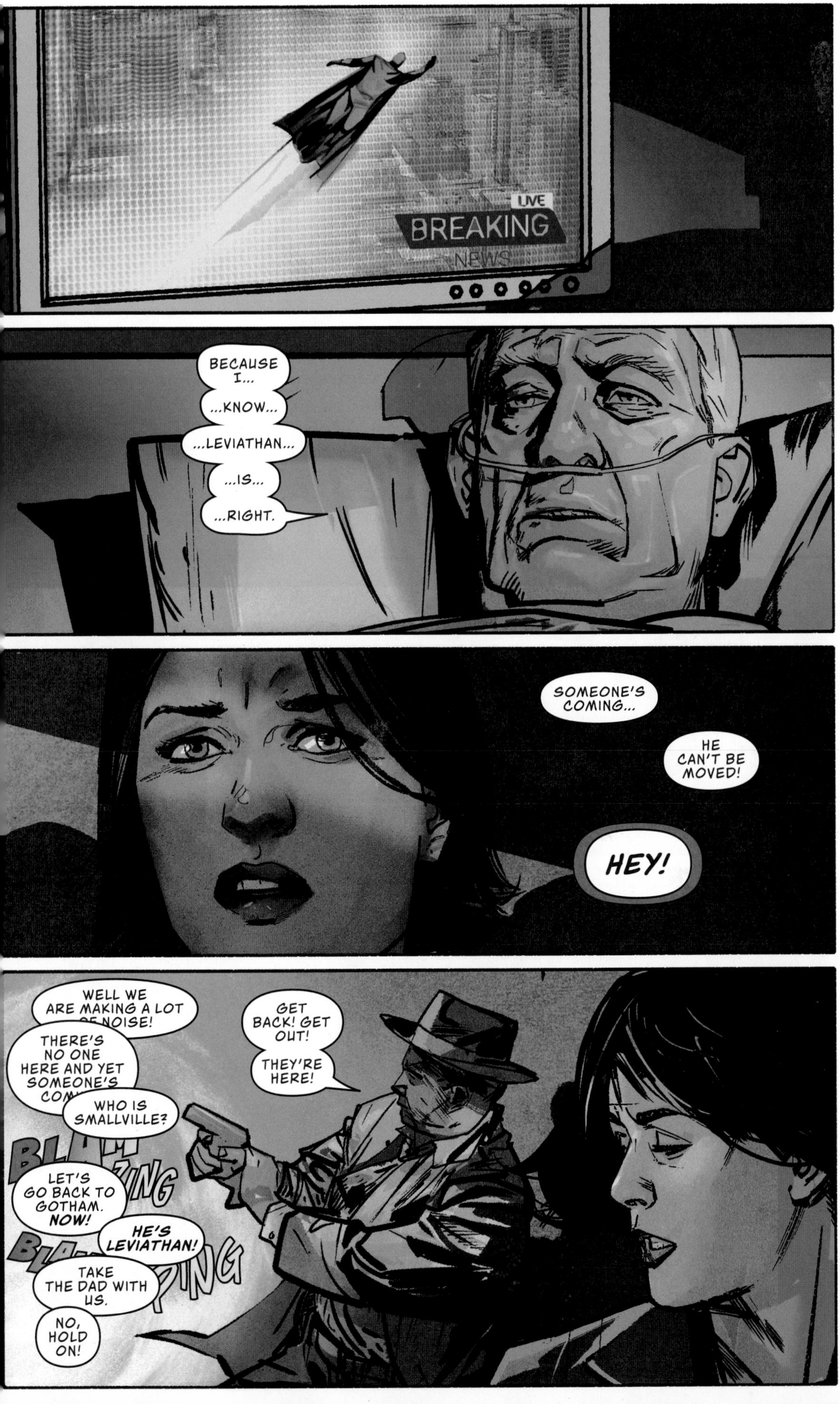
LIVE
BREAKING
NEWS
BECAUSE I...
...KNOW...
...LEVIATHAN...
...IS...
...RIGHT.
SOMEONE'S COMING...
HE CAN'T BE MOVED!
HEY!
WELL WE ARE MAKING A LOT OF NOISE!
GET BACK! GET OUT!
THEY'RE HERE!
THERE'S NO ONE HERE AND YET SOMEONE'S
WHO IS SMALLVILLE?
LET'S GO BACK TO GOTHAM. NOW!
HE'S LEVIATHAN!
TAKE THE DAD WITH US.
NO, HOLD ON!

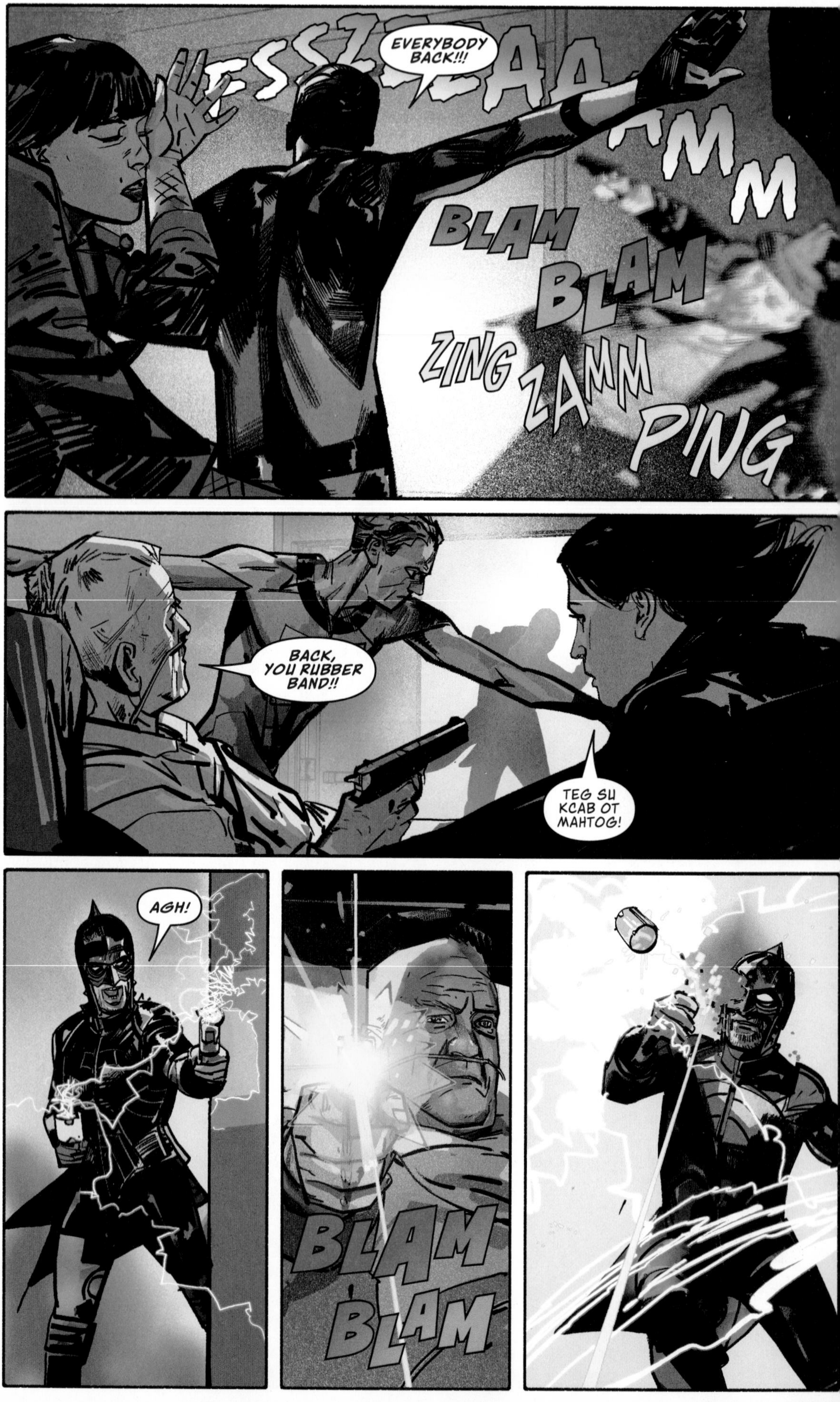
EVERYBODY BACK!!!
ESSZZZAAAAMM
BLAM
BLAM
ZING
ZAMM
PING
BACK, YOU RUBBER BAND!!
TEG SU KCAB OT MAHTOG!
AGH!
BLAM
BLAM

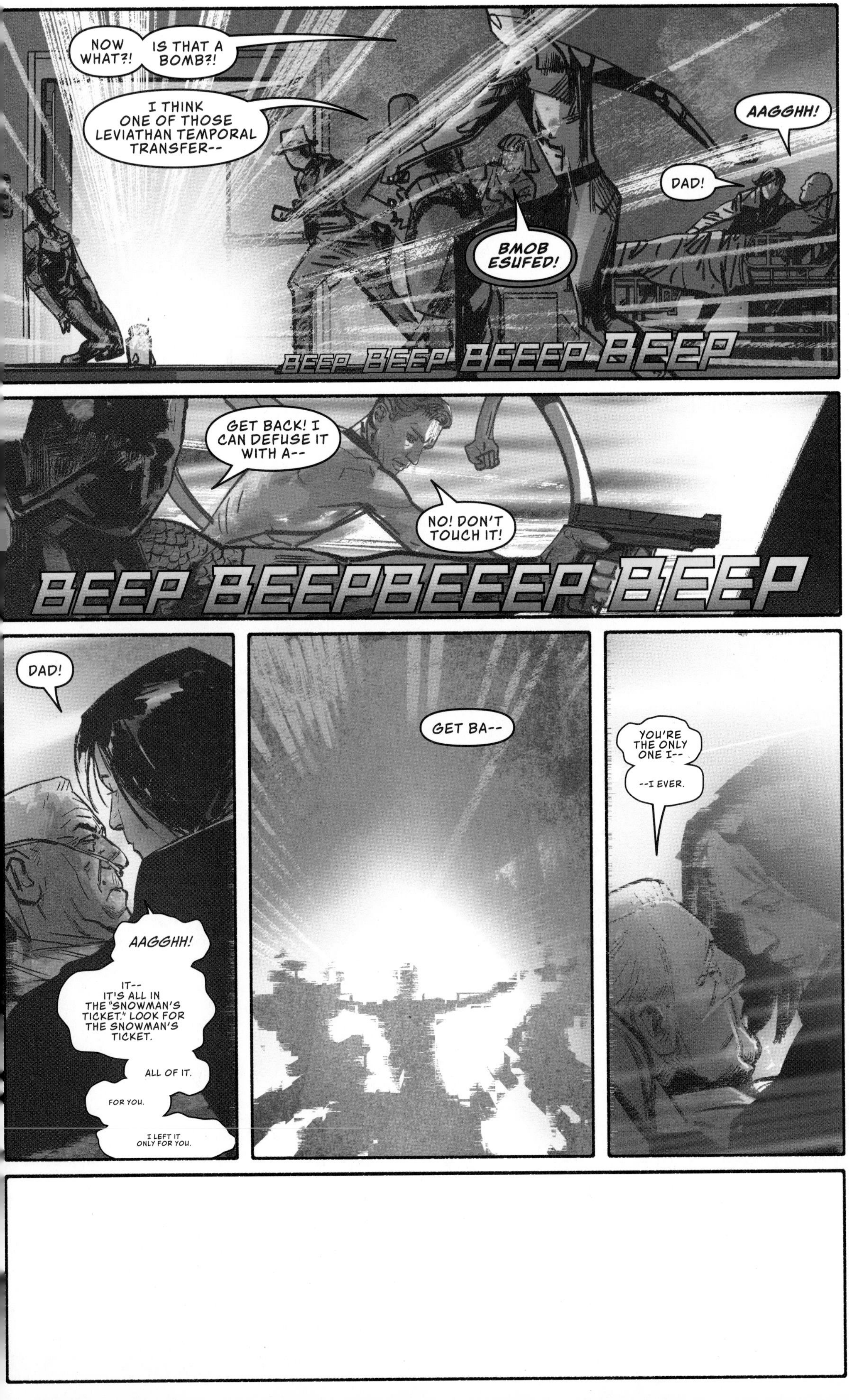
NOW WHAT?!
IS THAT A BOMB?!
I THINK ONE OF THOSE LEVIATHAN TEMPORAL TRANSFER--
AAGGHH!
DAD!
BMOB ESUFED!
BEEP BEEP BEEEP BEEP
GET BACK! I CAN DEFUSE IT WITH A--
NO! DON'T TOUCH IT!
BEEP BEEPBEEEP BEEP
DAD!
AAGGHH!
IT-- IT'S ALL IN THE "SNOWMAN'S TICKET." LOOK FOR THE SNOWMAN'S TICKET.
ALL OF IT.
FOR YOU.
I LEFT IT ONLY FOR YOU.
GET BA--
YOU'RE THE ONLY ONE I--
--I EVER.

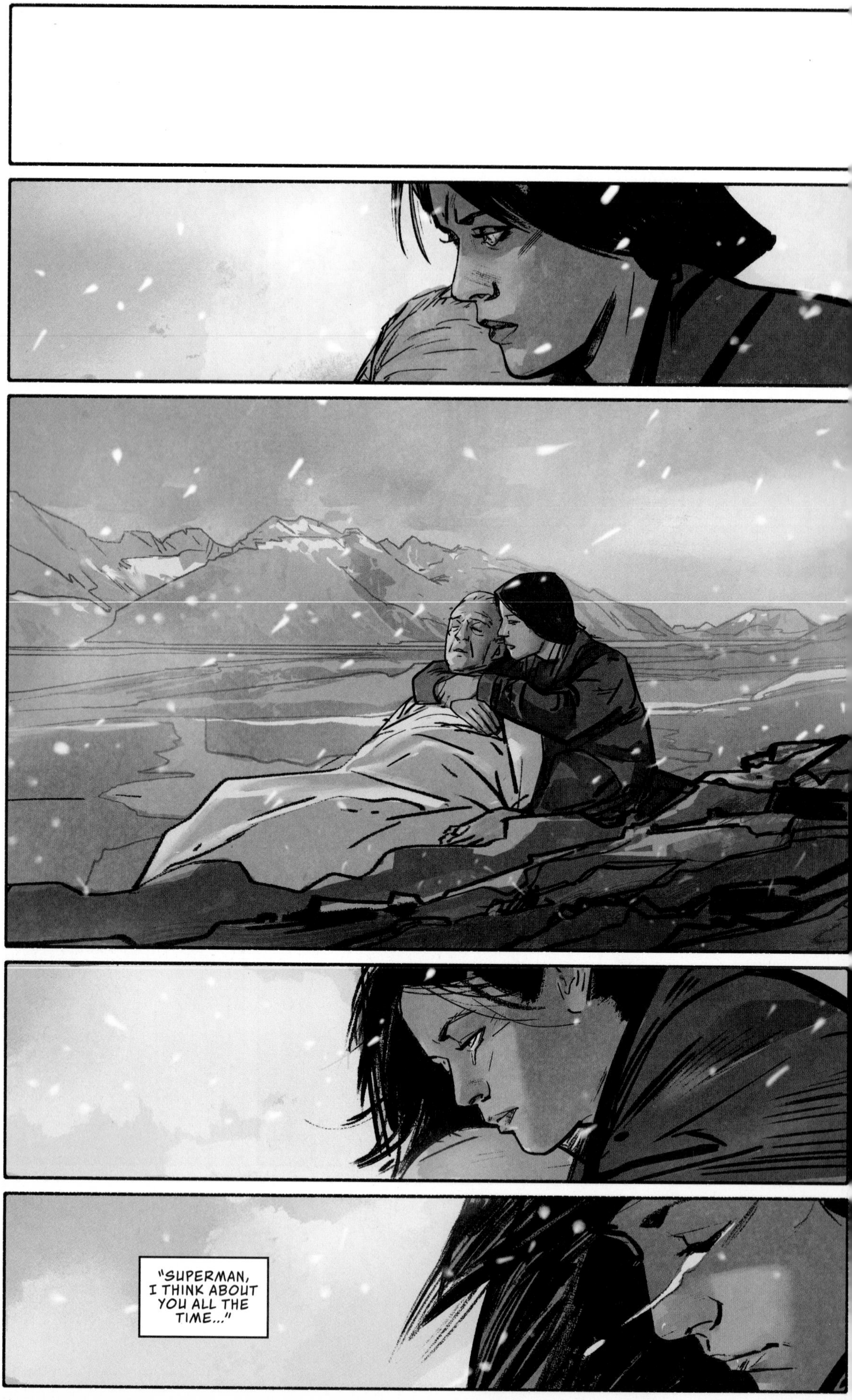
"SUPERMAN, I THINK ABOUT YOU ALL THE TIME..."

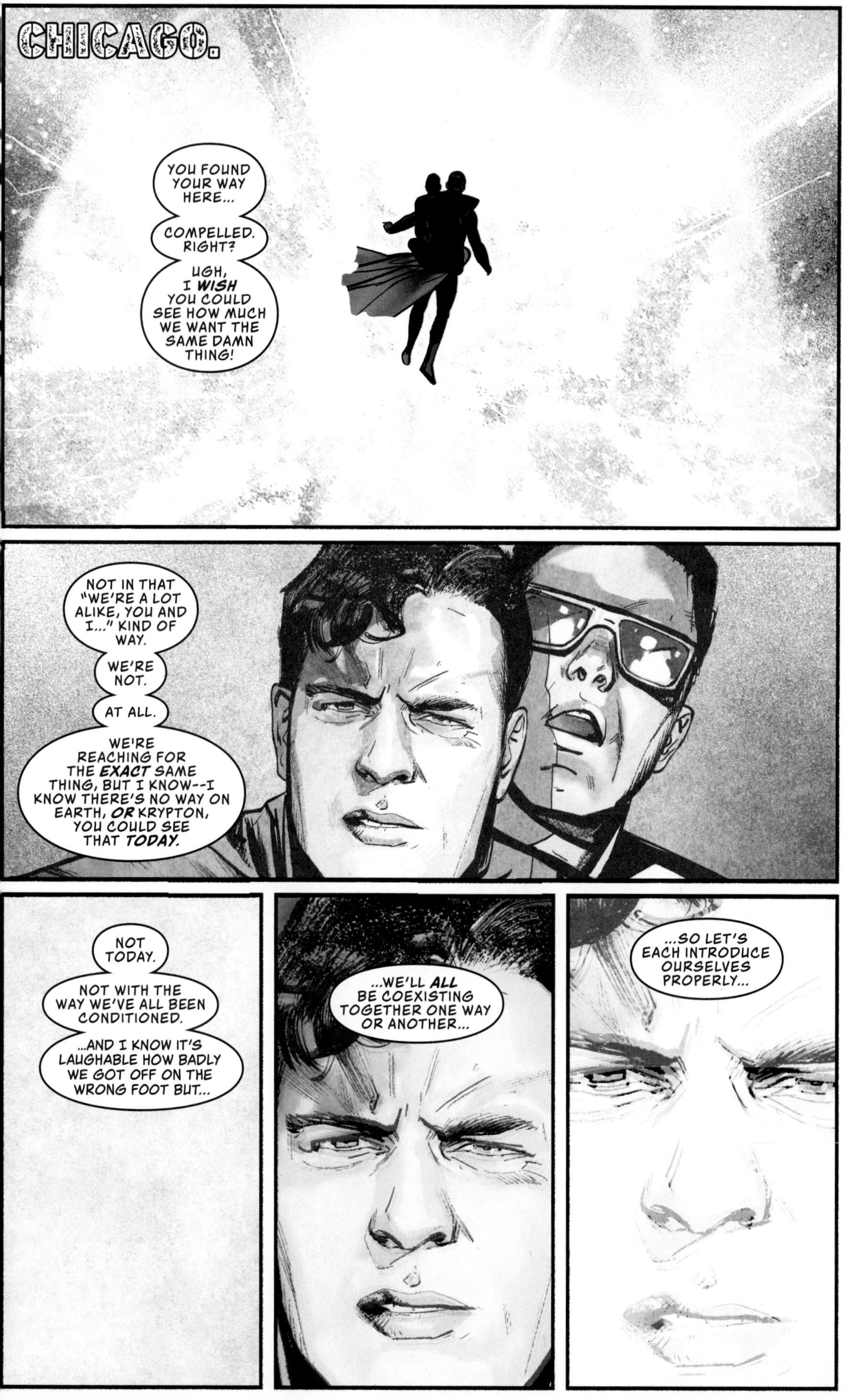
CHICAGO.
YOU FOUND YOUR WAY HERE...
COMPELLED. RIGHT?
UGH, I WISH YOU COULD SEE HOW MUCH WE WANT THE SAME DAMN THING!
NOT IN THAT "WE'RE A LOT ALIKE, YOU AND I..." KIND OF WAY.
WE'RE NOT.
AT ALL.
WE'RE REACHING FOR THE EXACT SAME THING, BUT I KNOW--I KNOW THERE'S NO WAY ON EARTH, OR KRYPTON, YOU COULD SEE THAT TODAY.
NOT TODAY.
NOT WITH THE WAY WE'VE ALL BEEN CONDITIONED.
...AND I KNOW IT'S LAUGHABLE HOW BADLY WE GOT OFF ON THE WRONG FOOT BUT...
...WE'LL ALL BE COEXISTING TOGETHER ONE WAY OR ANOTHER...
...SO LET'S EACH INTRODUCE OURSELVES PROPERLY...

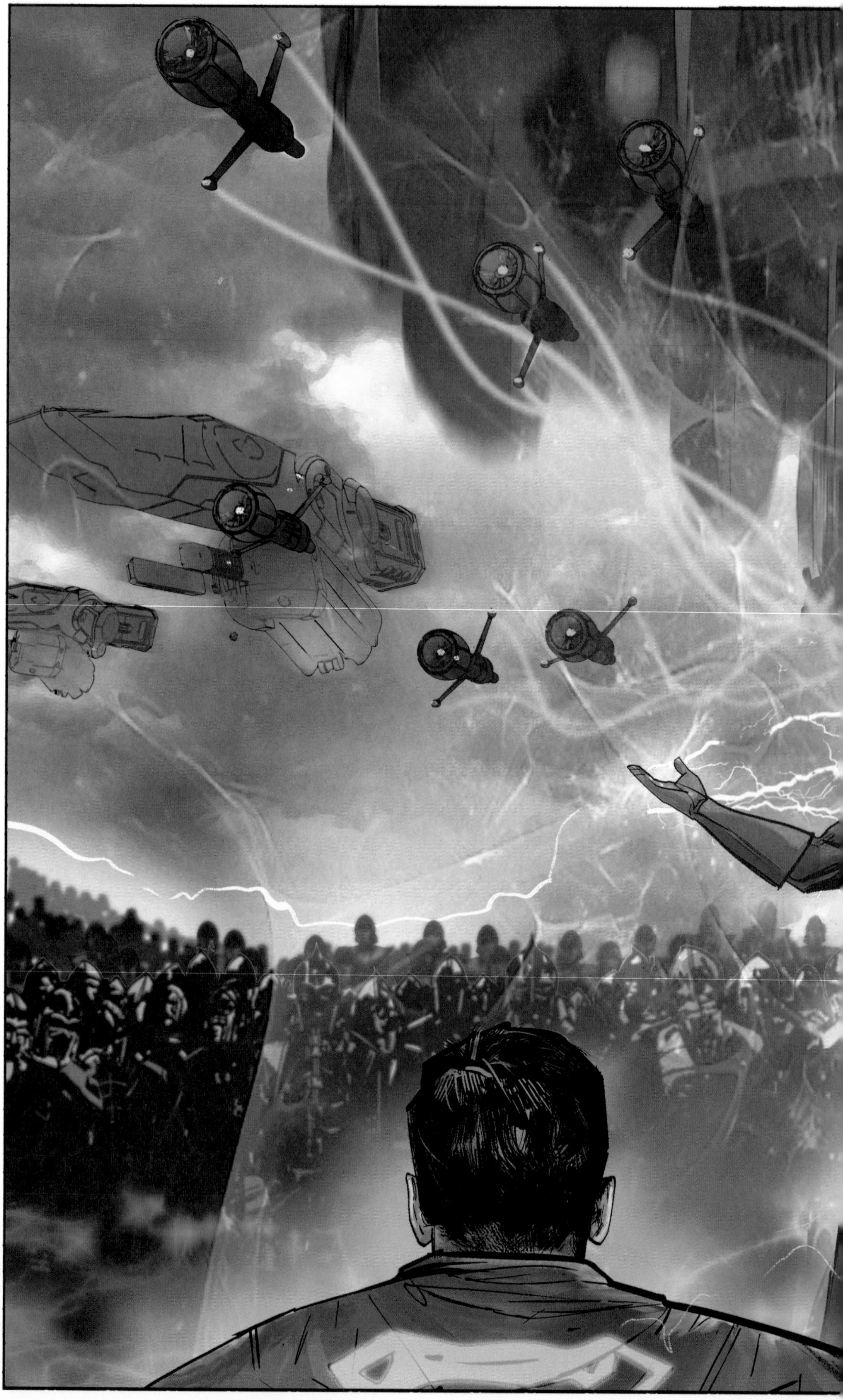

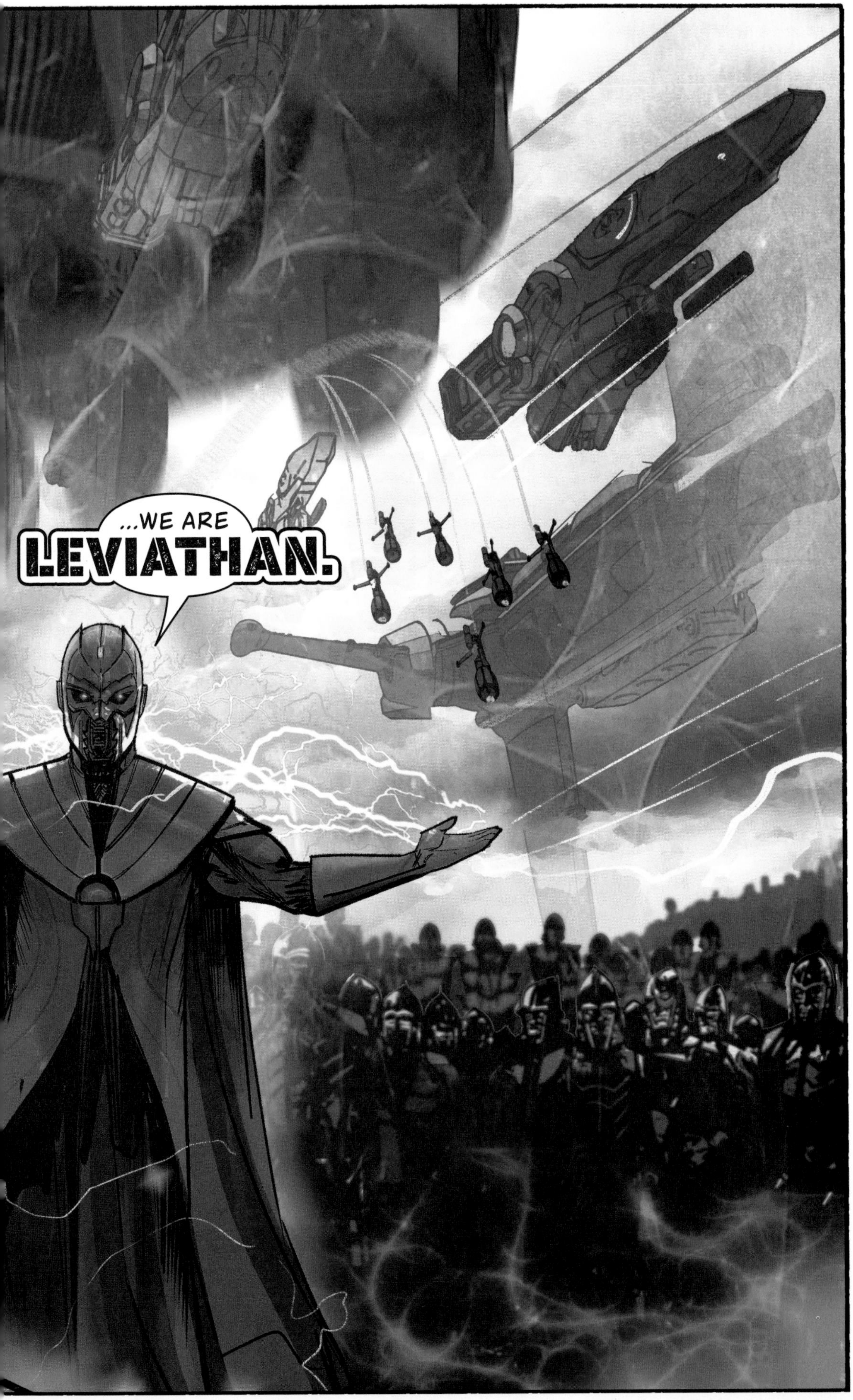
...WE ARE LEVIATHAN.

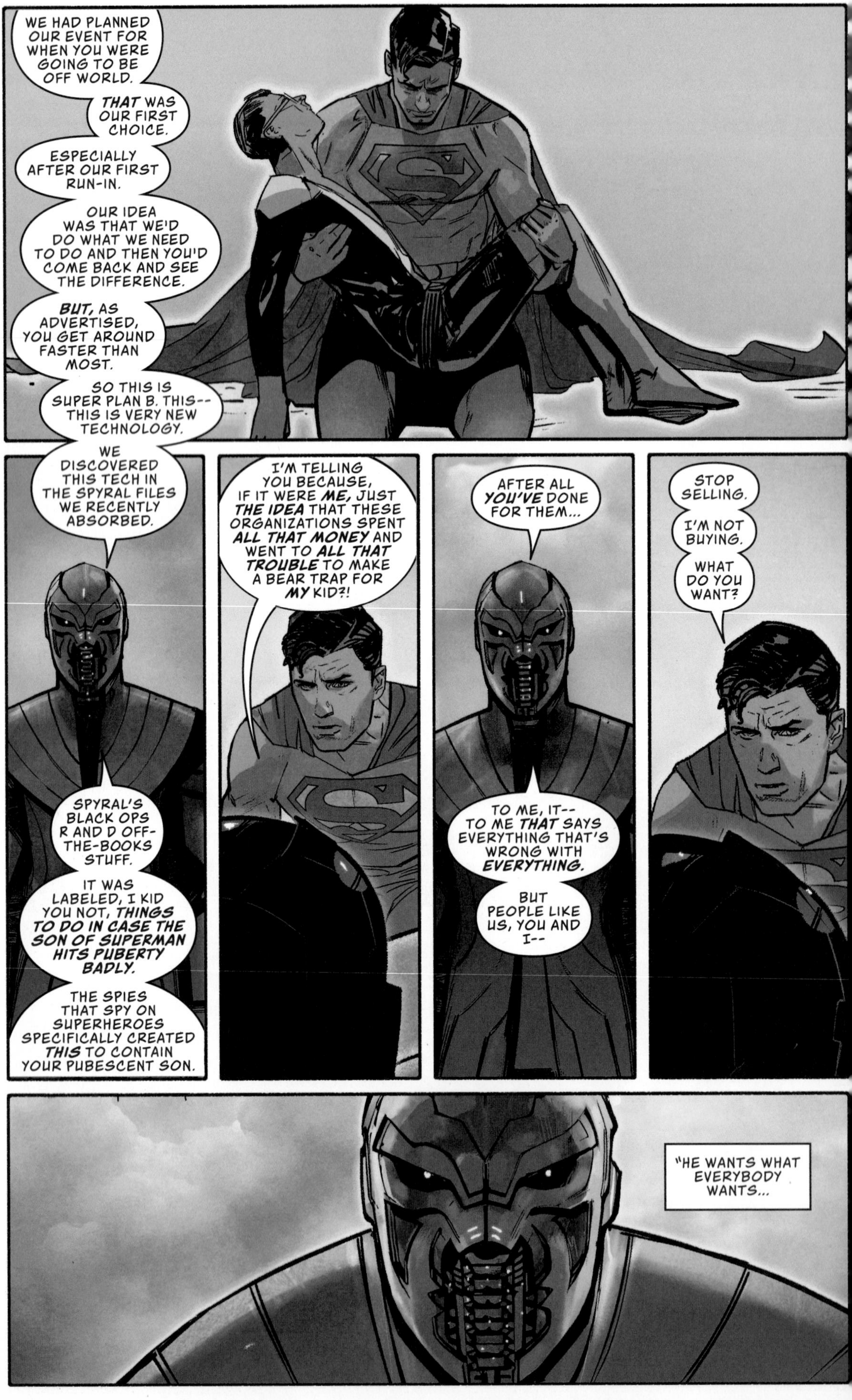
WE HAD PLANNED OUR EVENT FOR WHEN YOU WERE GOING TO BE OFF WORLD.
THAT WAS OUR FIRST CHOICE.
ESPECIALLY AFTER OUR FIRST RUN-IN.
OUR IDEA WAS THAT WE'D DO WHAT WE NEED TO DO AND THEN YOU'D COME BACK AND SEE THE DIFFERENCE.
BUT, AS ADVERTISED, YOU GET AROUND FASTER THAN MOST.
SO THIS IS SUPER PLAN B. THIS-- THIS IS VERY NEW TECHNOLOGY.
WE DISCOVERED THIS TECH IN THE SPYRAL FILES WE RECENTLY ABSORBED.
SPYRAL'S BLACK OPS R AND D OFF-THE-BOOKS STUFF.
IT WAS LABELED, I KID YOU NOT, THINGS TO DO IN CASE THE SON OF SUPERMAN HITS PUBERTY BADLY.
THE SPIES THAT SPY ON SUPERHEROES SPECIFICALLY CREATED THIS TO CONTAIN YOUR PUBESCENT SON.
I'M TELLING YOU BECAUSE, IF IT WERE ME, JUST THE IDEA THAT THESE ORGANIZATIONS SPENT ALL THAT MONEY AND WENT TO ALL THAT TROUBLE TO MAKE A BEAR TRAP FOR MY KID?!
AFTER ALL YOU'VE DONE FOR THEM...
TO ME, IT-- TO ME THAT SAYS EVERYTHING THAT'S WRONG WITH EVERYTHING.
BUT PEOPLE LIKE US, YOU AND I--
STOP SELLING.
I'M NOT BUYING.
WHAT DO YOU WANT?
"HE WANTS WHAT EVERYBODY WANTS...

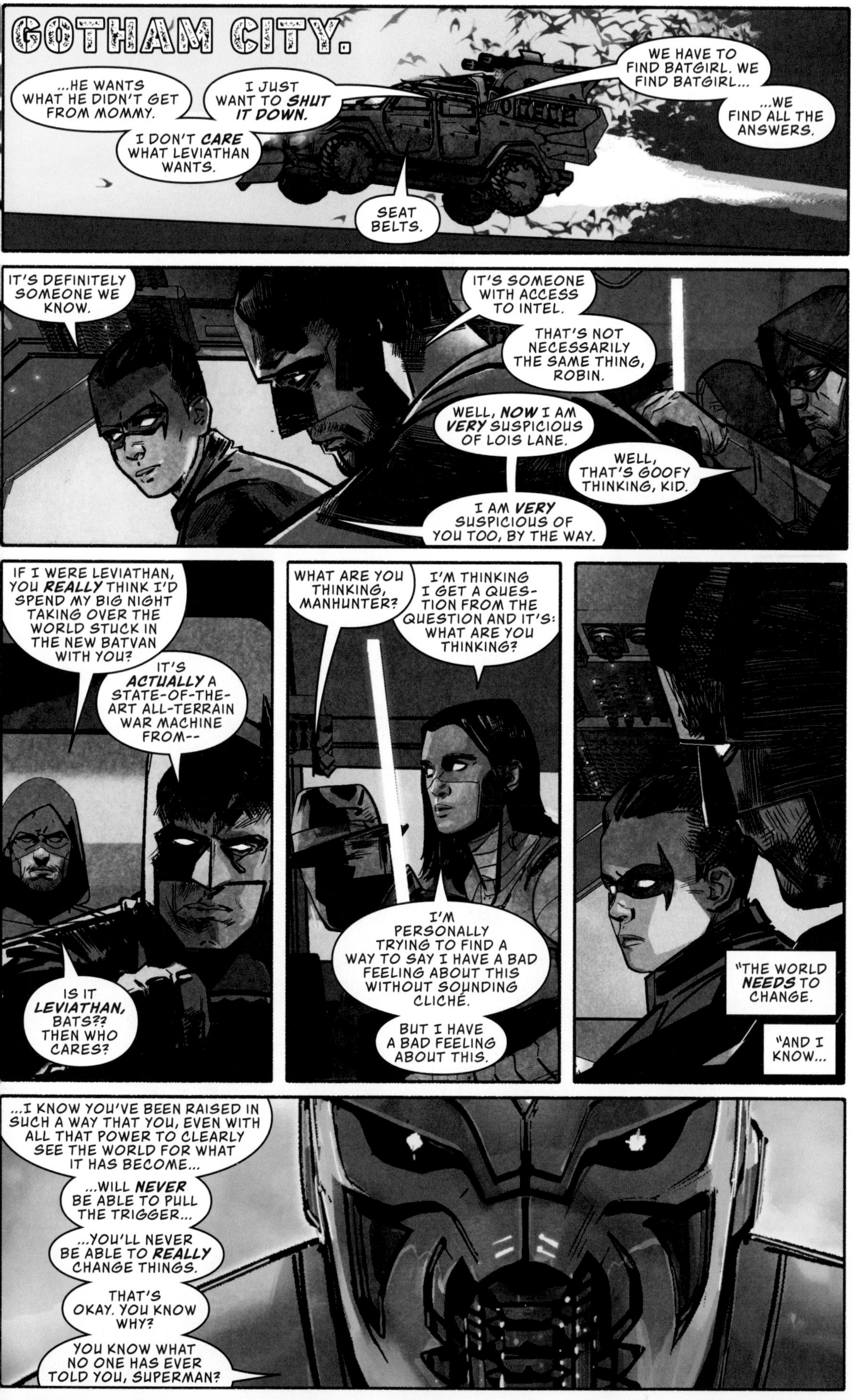
GOTHAM CITY.
...HE WANTS WHAT HE DIDN'T GET FROM MOMMY.
I DON'T CARE WHAT LEVIATHAN WANTS.
I JUST WANT TO SHUT IT DOWN.
SEAT BELTS.
WE HAVE TO FIND BATGIRL. WE FIND BATGIRL...
...WE FIND ALL THE ANSWERS.
IT'S DEFINITELY SOMEONE WE KNOW.
IT'S SOMEONE WITH ACCESS TO INTEL.
THAT'S NOT NECESSARILY THE SAME THING, ROBIN.
WELL, NOW I AM VERY SUSPICIOUS OF LOIS LANE.
I AM VERY SUSPICIOUS OF YOU TOO, BY THE WAY.
WELL, THAT'S GOOFY THINKING, KID.
IF I WERE LEVIATHAN, YOU REALLY THINK I'D SPEND MY BIG NIGHT TAKING OVER THE WORLD STUCK IN THE NEW BATVAN WITH YOU?
IT'S ACTUALLY A STATE-OF-THE-ART ALL-TERRAIN WAR MACHINE FROM--
IS IT LEVIATHAN, BATS?? THEN WHO CARES?
WHAT ARE YOU THINKING, MANHUNTER?
I'M THINKING I GET A QUESTION FROM THE QUESTION AND IT'S: WHAT ARE YOU THINKING?
I'M PERSONALLY TRYING TO FIND A WAY TO SAY I HAVE A BAD FEELING ABOUT THIS WITHOUT SOUNDING CLICHÉ.
BUT I HAVE A BAD FEELING ABOUT THIS.
"THE WORLD NEEDS TO CHANGE.
"AND I KNOW...
...I KNOW YOU'VE BEEN RAISED IN SUCH A WAY THAT YOU, EVEN WITH ALL THAT POWER TO CLEARLY SEE THE WORLD FOR WHAT IT HAS BECOME...
...WILL NEVER BE ABLE TO PULL THE TRIGGER...
...YOU'LL NEVER BE ABLE TO REALLY CHANGE THINGS.
THAT'S OKAY. YOU KNOW WHY?
YOU KNOW WHAT NO ONE HAS EVER TOLD YOU, SUPERMAN?

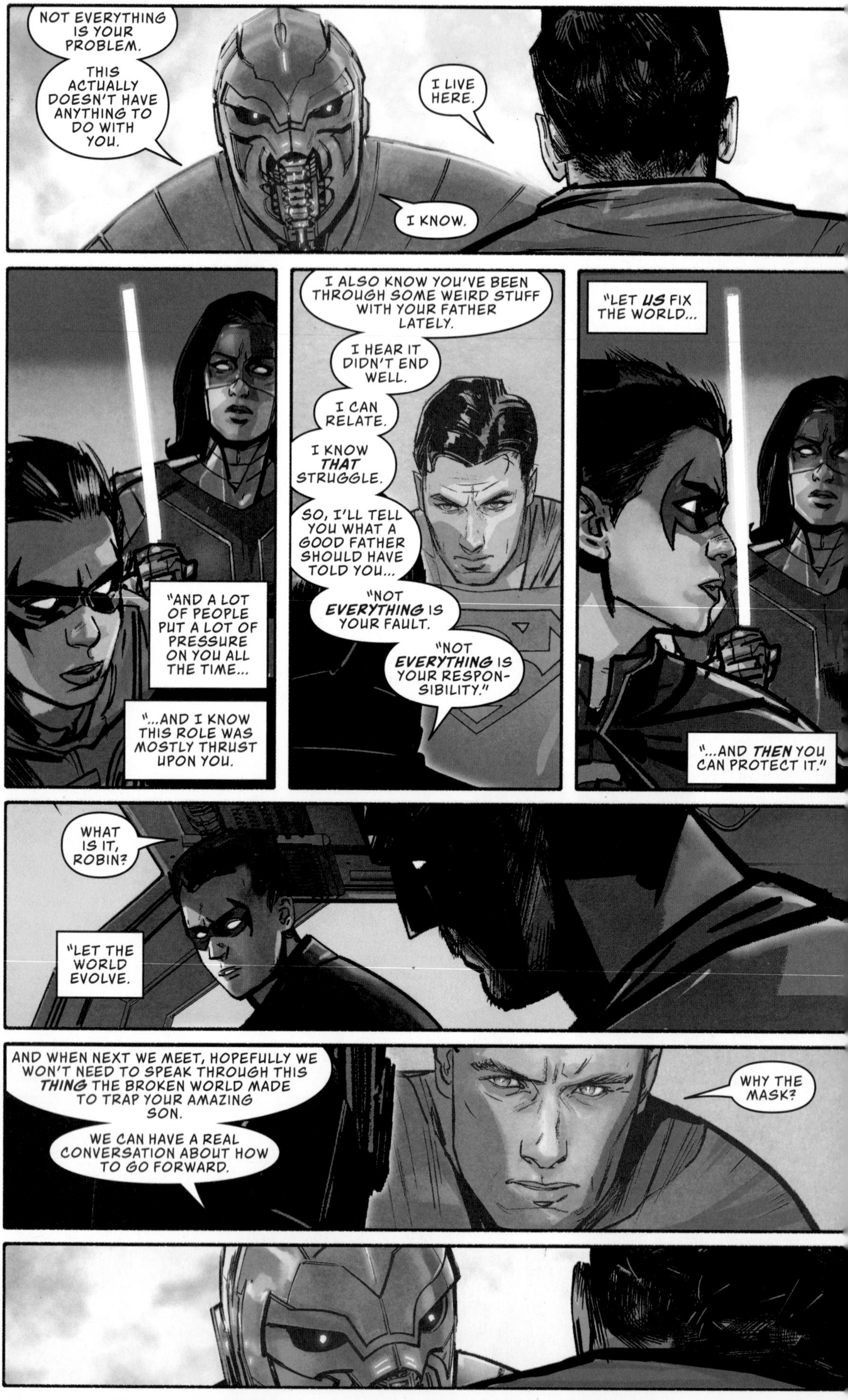
NOT EVERYTHING IS YOUR PROBLEM.
THIS ACTUALLY DOESN'T HAVE ANYTHING TO DO WITH YOU.
I LIVE HERE.
I KNOW.
"AND A LOT OF PEOPLE PUT A LOT OF PRESSURE ON YOU ALL THE TIME...
"...AND I KNOW THIS ROLE WAS MOSTLY THRUST UPON YOU.
I ALSO KNOW YOU'VE BEEN THROUGH SOME WEIRD STUFF WITH YOUR FATHER LATELY.
I HEAR IT DIDN'T END WELL.
I CAN RELATE.
I KNOW THAT STRUGGLE.
SO, I'LL TELL YOU WHAT A GOOD FATHER SHOULD HAVE TOLD YOU...
"NOT EVERYTHING IS YOUR FAULT.
"NOT EVERYTHING IS YOUR RESPONSIBILITY."
"LET US FIX THE WORLD...
"...AND THEN YOU CAN PROTECT IT."
WHAT IS IT, ROBIN?
"LET THE WORLD EVOLVE.
AND WHEN NEXT WE MEET, HOPEFULLY WE WON'T NEED TO SPEAK THROUGH THIS THING THE BROKEN WORLD MADE TO TRAP YOUR AMAZING SON.
WE CAN HAVE A REAL CONVERSATION ABOUT HOW TO GO FORWARD.
WHY THE MASK?

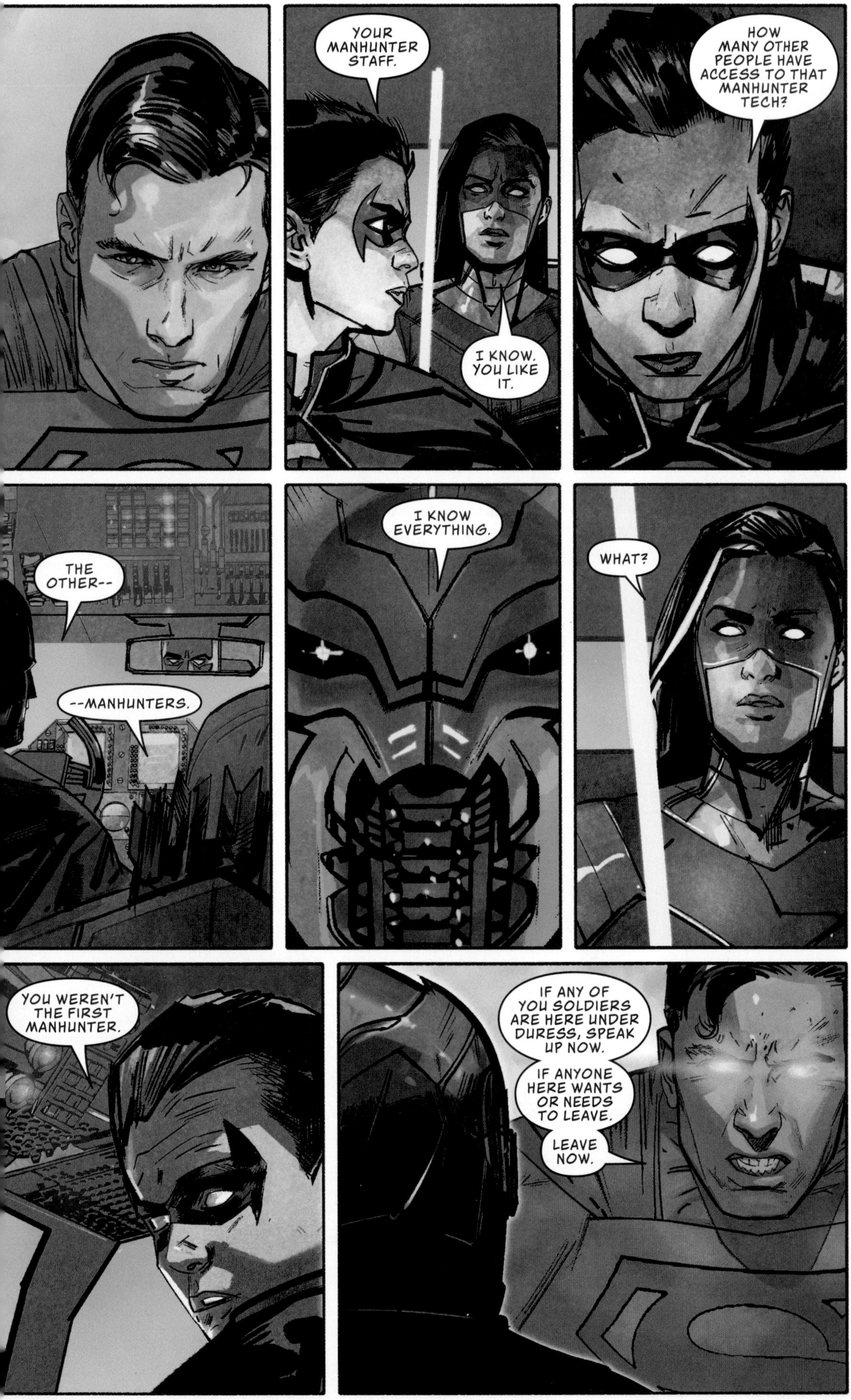
YOUR MANHUNTER STAFF.
I KNOW. YOU LIKE IT.
HOW MANY OTHER PEOPLE HAVE ACCESS TO THAT MANHUNTER TECH?
THE OTHER--
--MANHUNTERS.
I KNOW EVERYTHING.
WHAT?
YOU WEREN'T THE FIRST MANHUNTER.
IF ANY OF YOU SOLDIERS ARE HERE UNDER DURESS, SPEAK UP NOW.
IF ANYONE HERE WANTS OR NEEDS TO LEAVE.
LEAVE NOW.

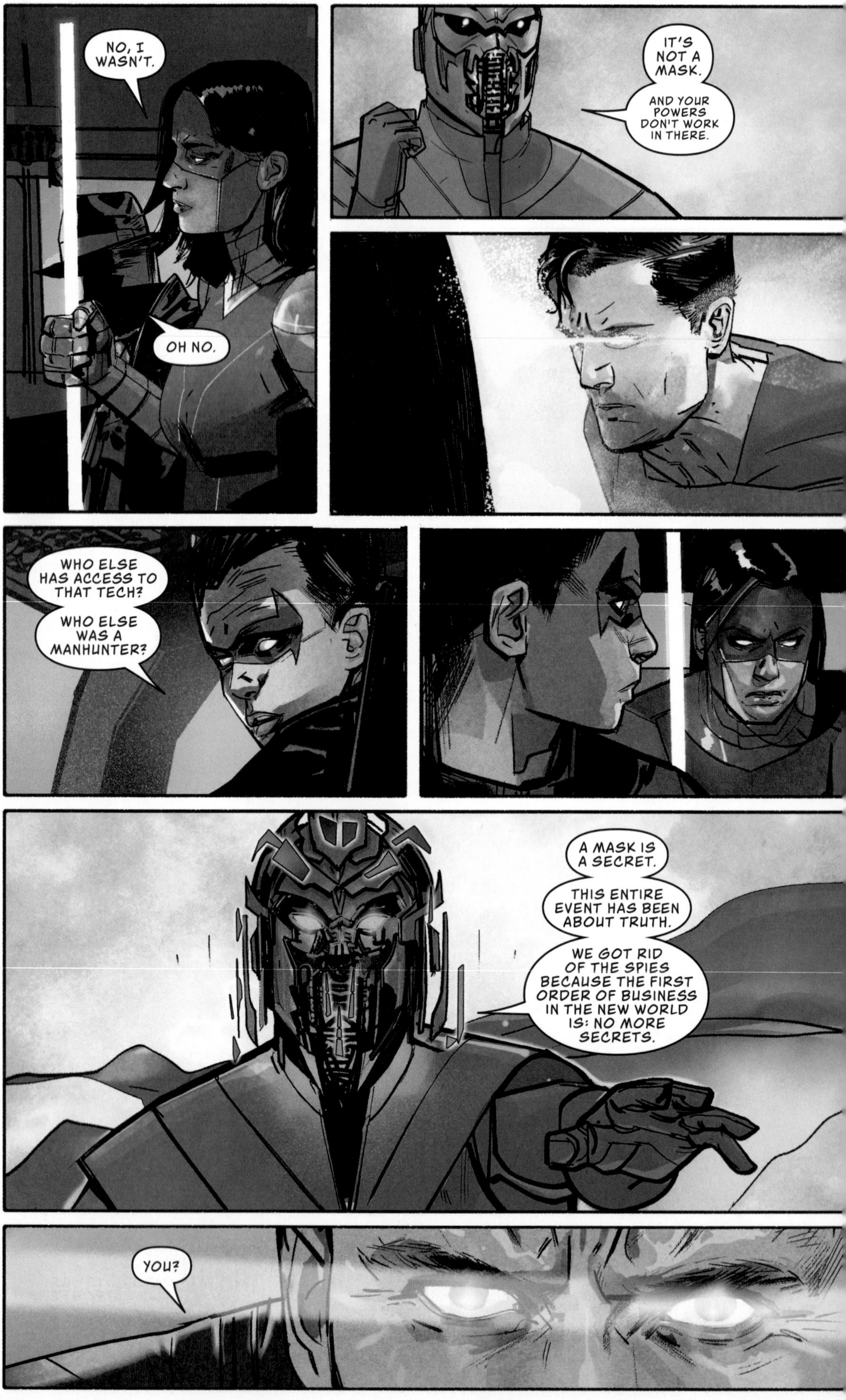

NO, I WASN'T.
OH NO.
IT'S NOT A MASK.
AND YOUR POWERS DON'T WORK IN THERE.
WHO ELSE HAS ACCESS TO THAT TECH?
WHO ELSE WAS A MANHUNTER?
A MASK IS A SECRET.
THIS ENTIRE EVENT HAS BEEN ABOUT TRUTH.
WE GOT RID OF THE SPIES BECAUSE THE FIRST ORDER OF BUSINESS IN THE NEW WORLD IS: NO MORE SECRETS.
YOU?

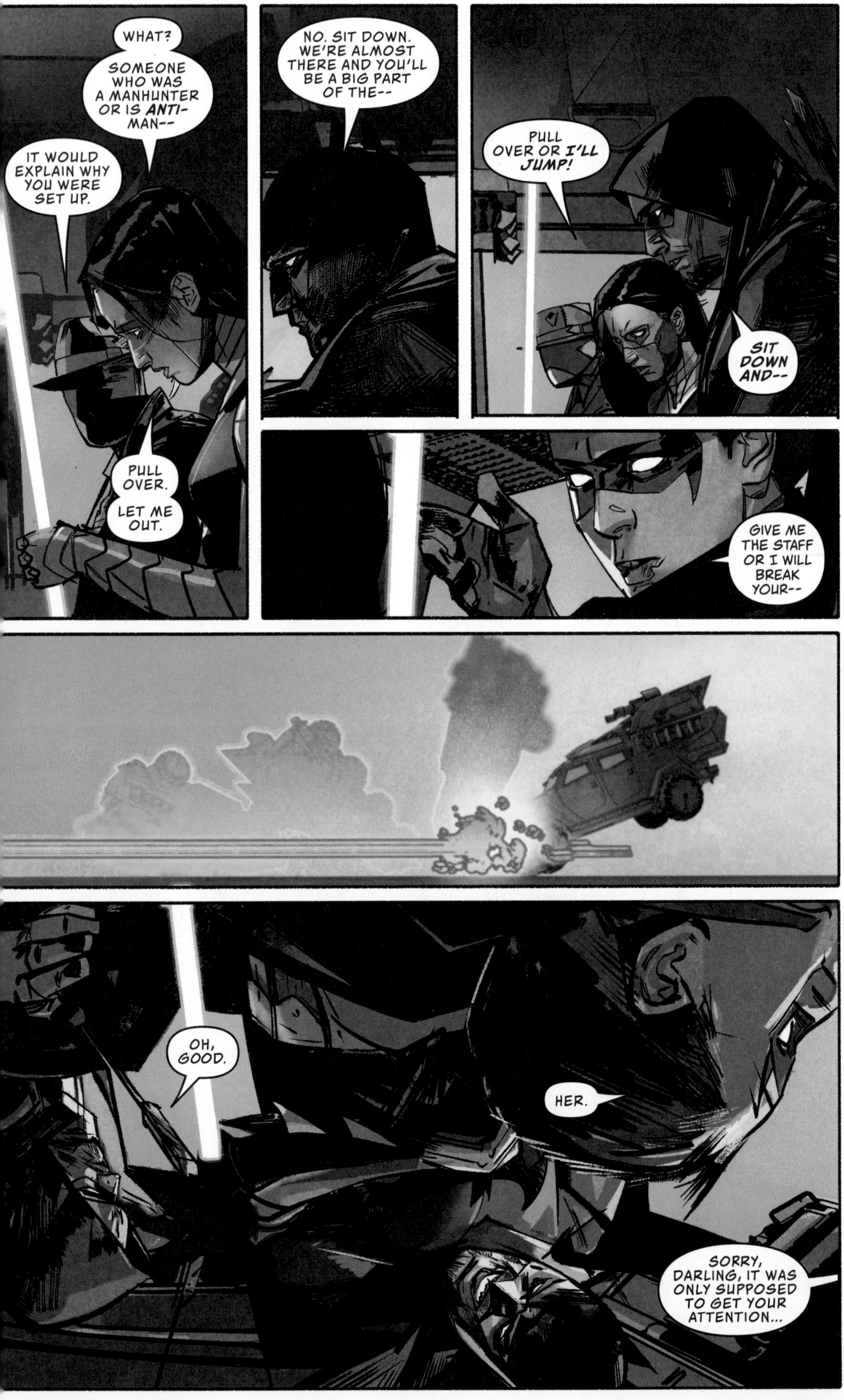
WHAT?
SOMEONE WHO WAS A MANHUNTER OR IS ANTI-MAN--
IT WOULD EXPLAIN WHY YOU WERE SET UP.
PULL OVER.
LET ME OUT.
NO. SIT DOWN. WE'RE ALMOST THERE AND YOU'LL BE A BIG PART OF THE--
PULL OVER OR I'LL JUMP!
SIT DOWN AND--
GIVE ME THE STAFF OR I WILL BREAK YOUR--
OH, GOOD.
HER.
SORRY, DARLING, IT WAS ONLY SUPPOSED TO GET YOUR ATTENTION...

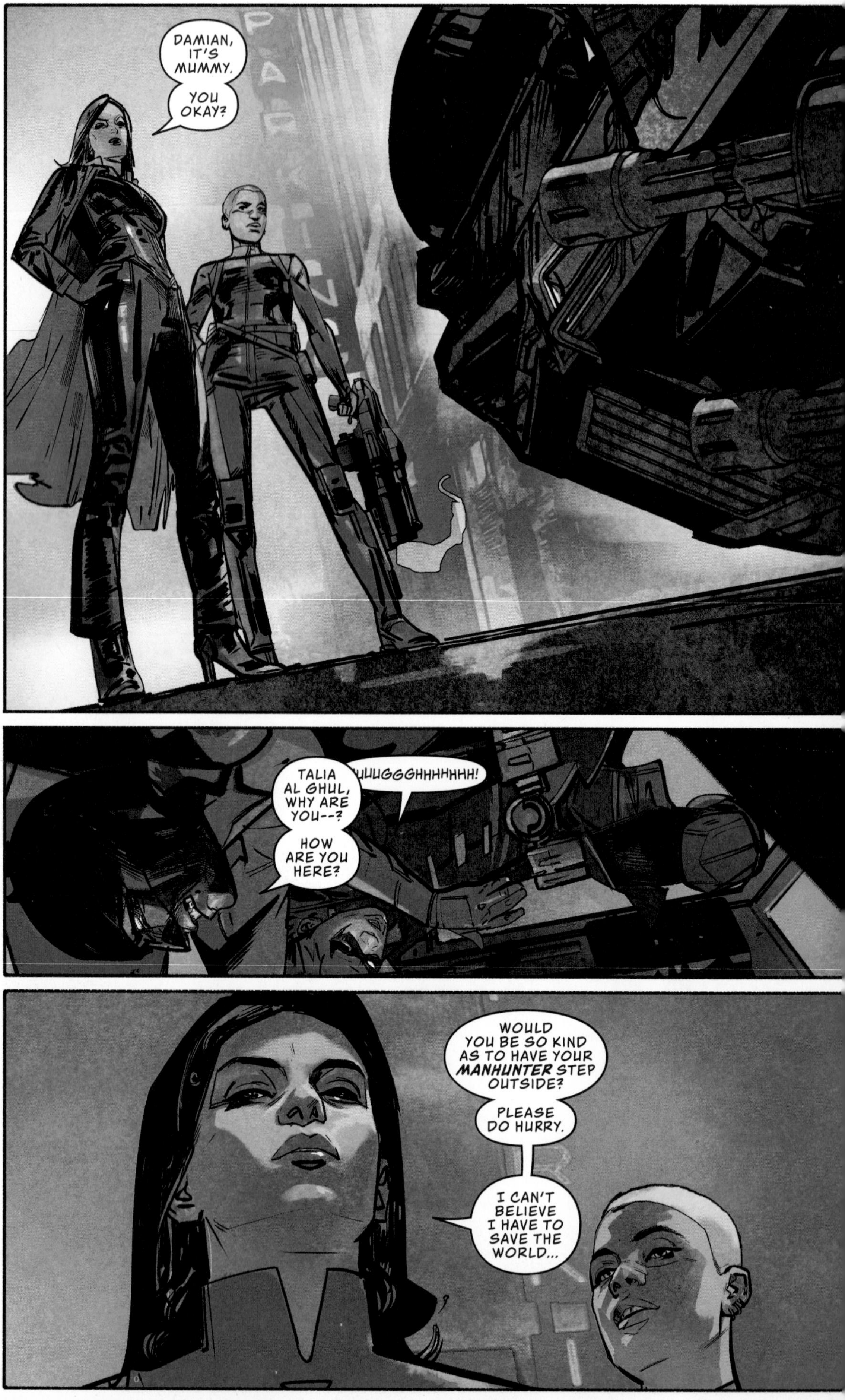
DAMIAN, IT'S MUMMY.
YOU OKAY?
TALIA AL GHUL, WHY ARE YOU--?
HOW ARE YOU HERE?
UUUGGGHHHHHHH!
WOULD YOU BE SO KIND AS TO HAVE YOUR MANHUNTER STEP OUTSIDE?
PLEASE DO HURRY.
I CAN'T BELIEVE I HAVE TO SAVE THE WORLD...

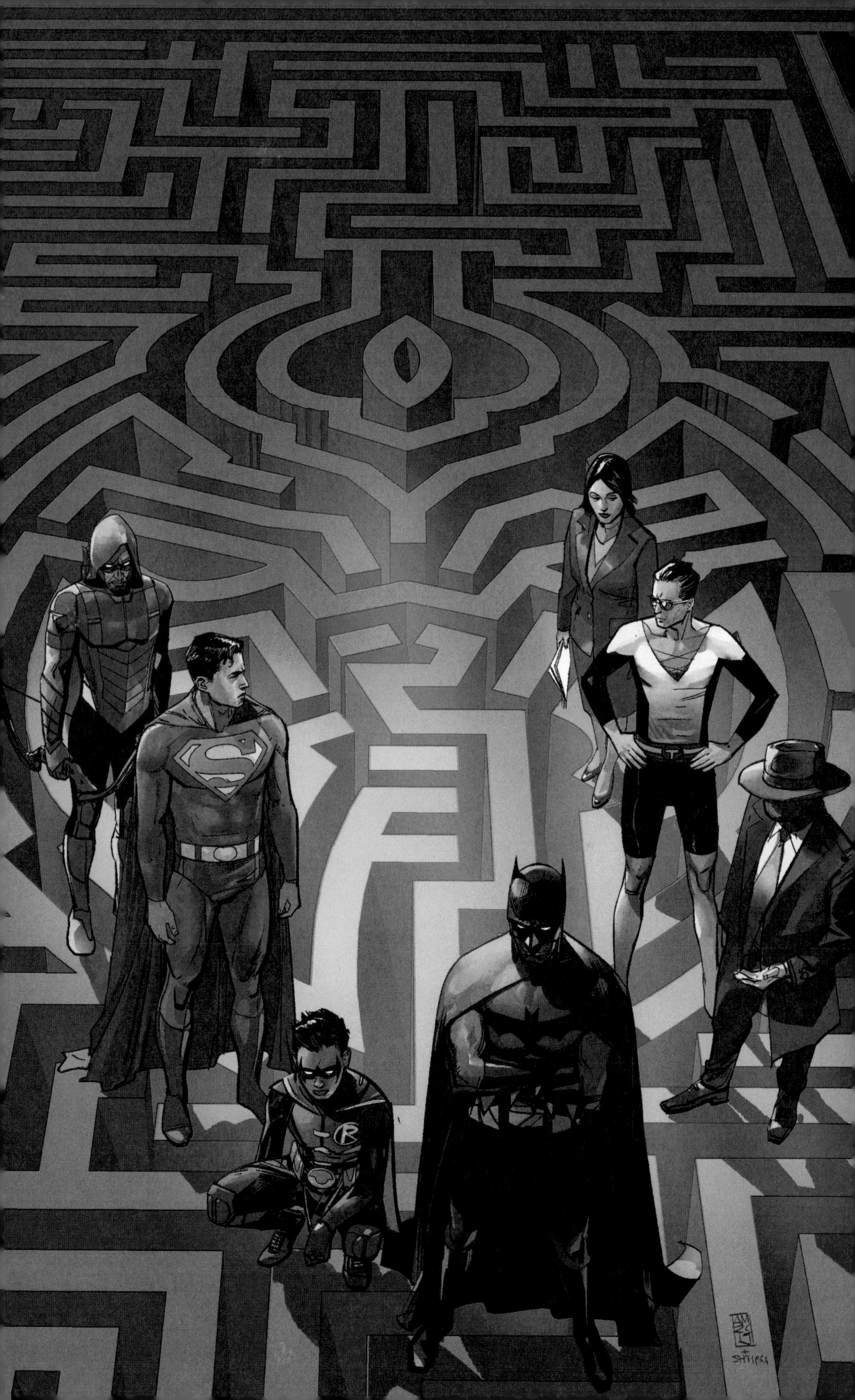

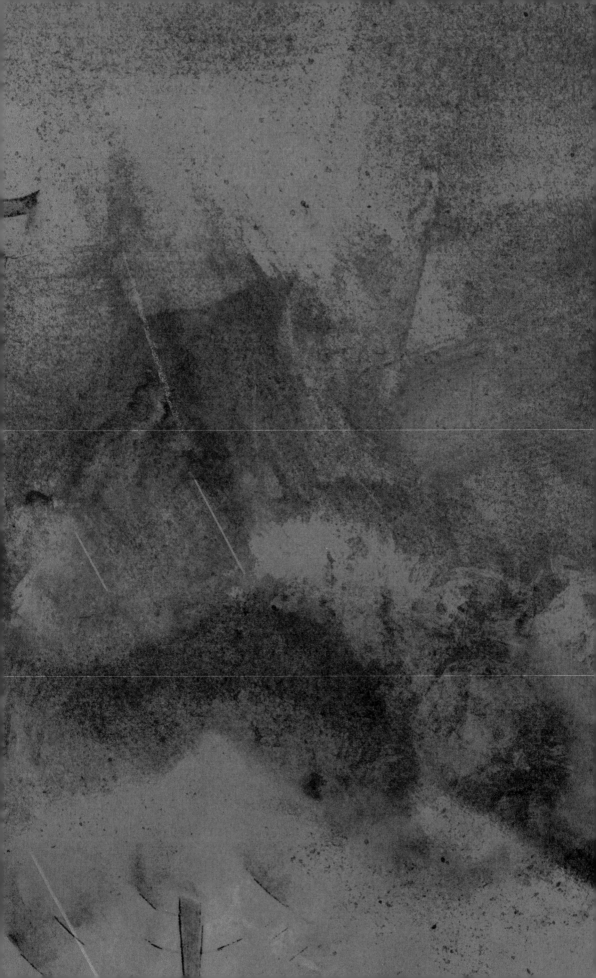

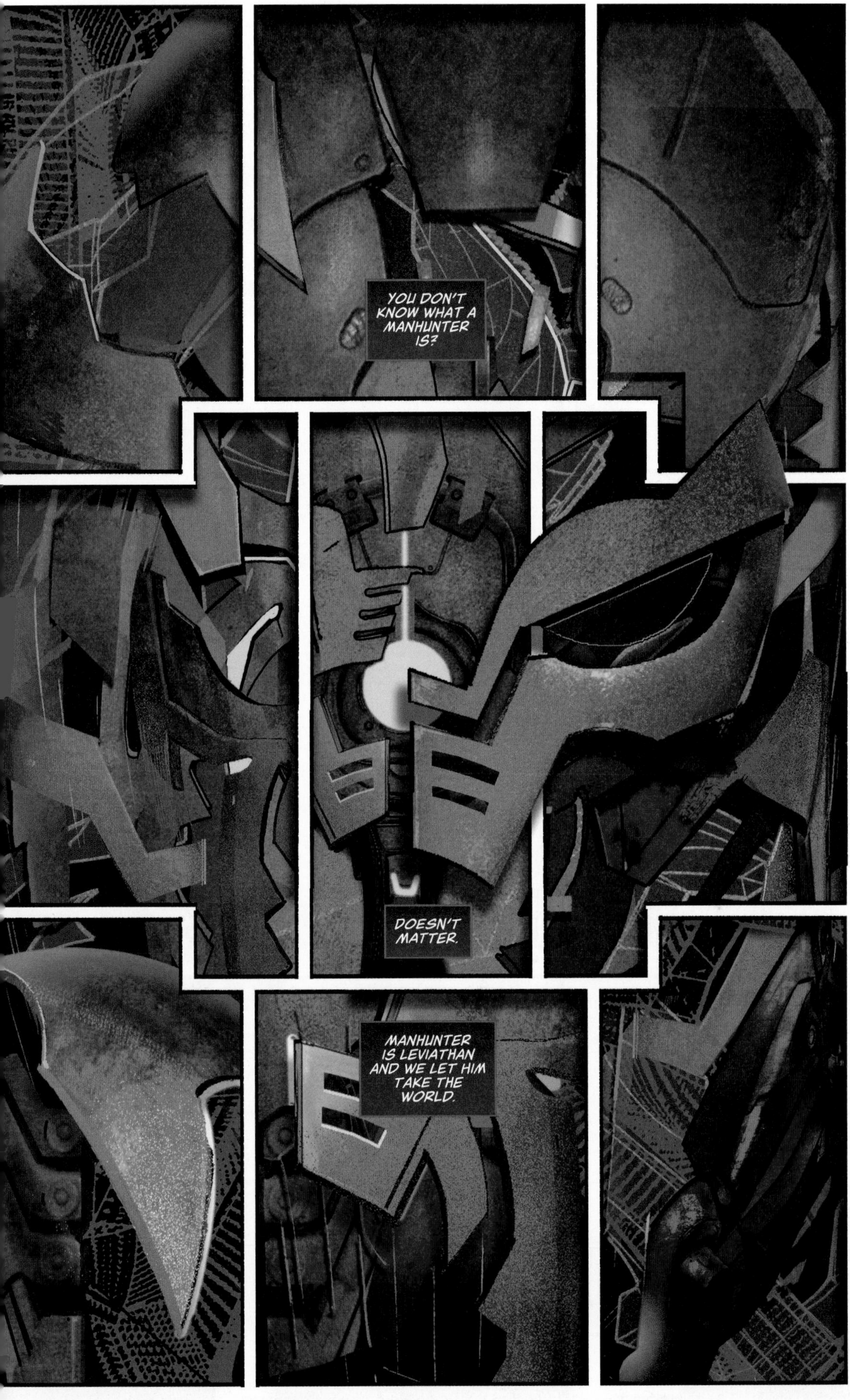
YOU DON'T KNOW WHAT A MANHUNTER IS?
DOESN'T MATTER.
MANHUNTER IS LEVIATHAN AND WE LET HIM TAKE THE WORLD.

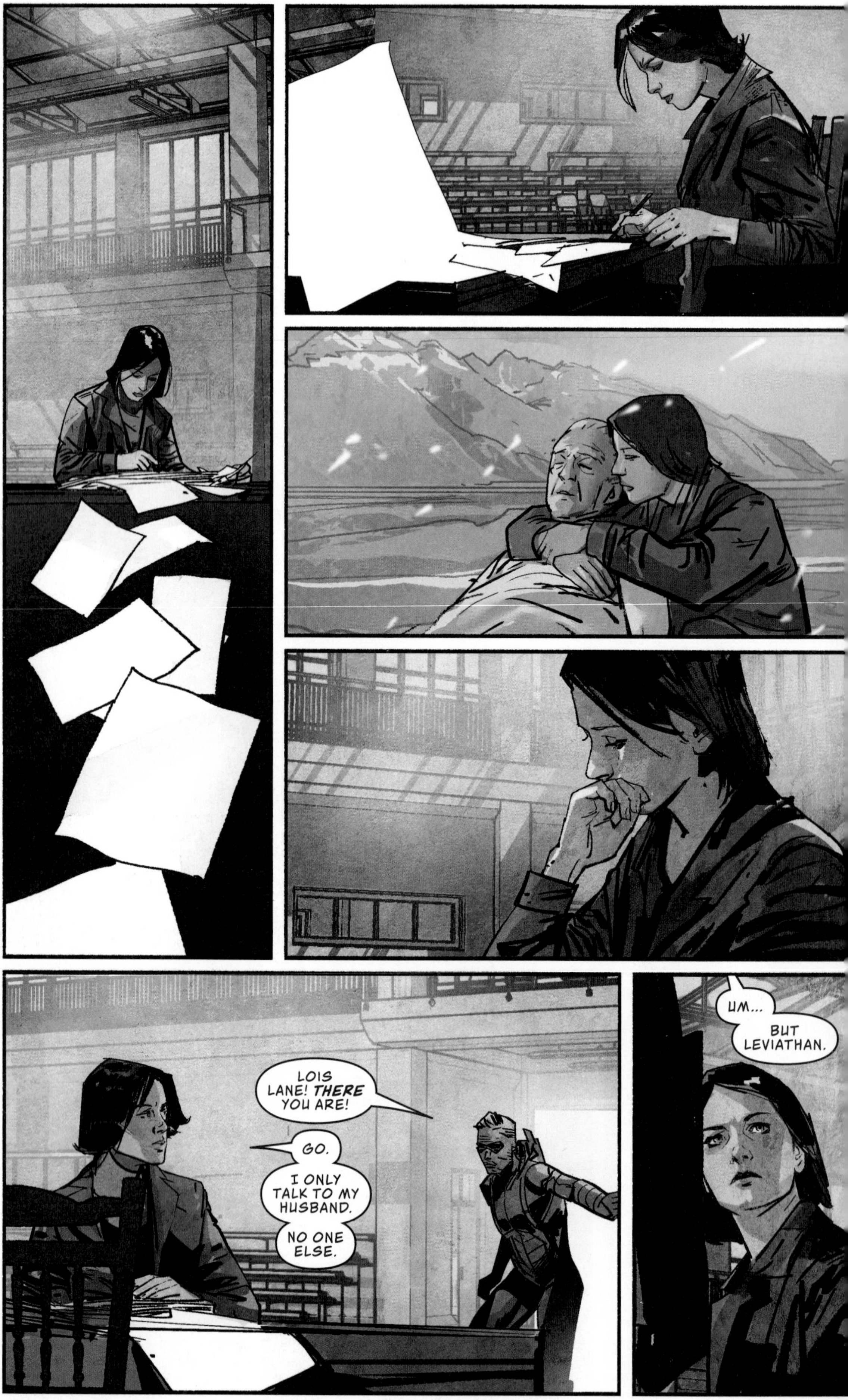
LOIS LANE! THERE YOU ARE!
GO.
I ONLY TALK TO MY HUSBAND.
NO ONE ELSE.
UM...
BUT LEVIATHAN.

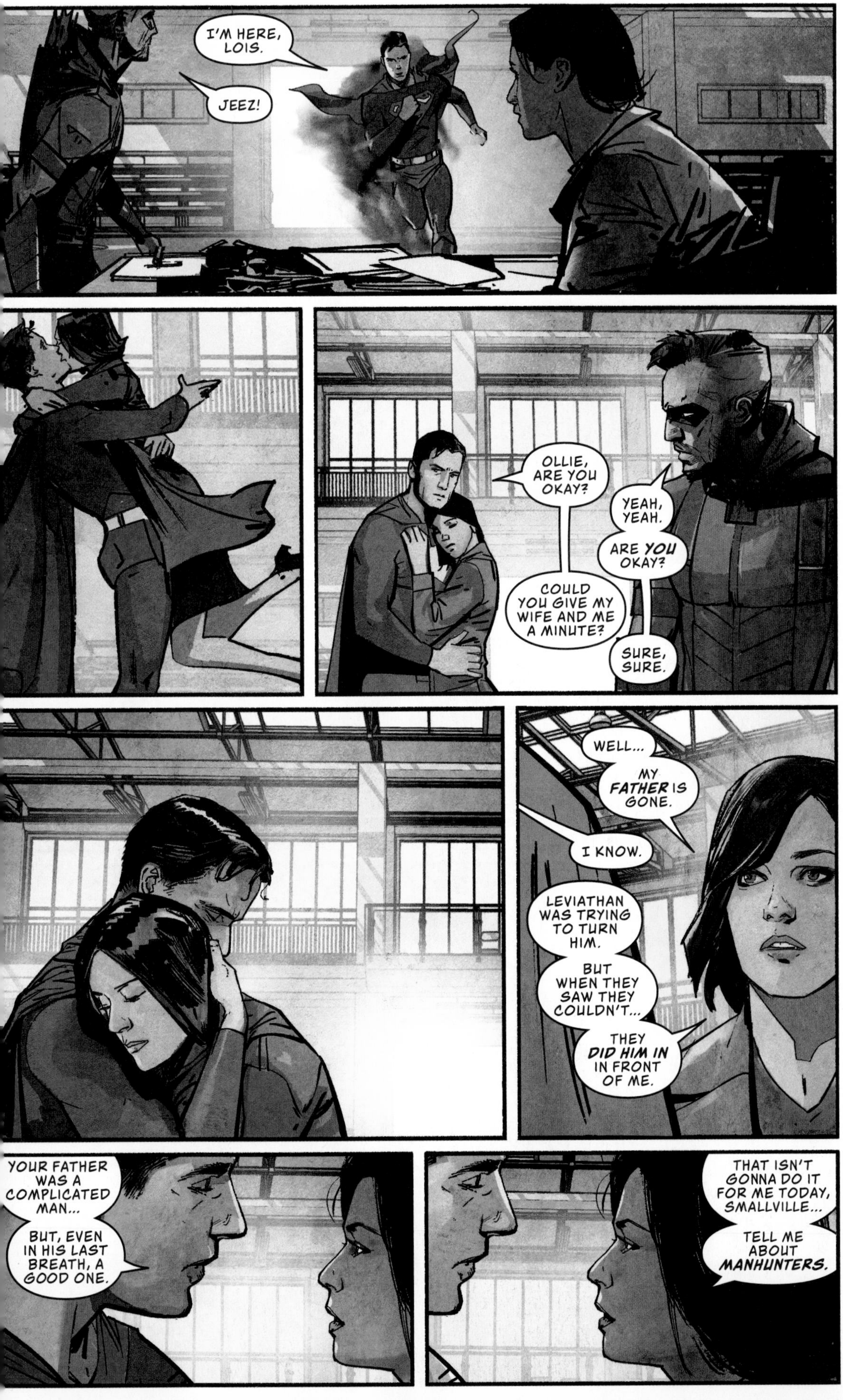
I'M HERE, LOIS.
JEEZ!
OLLIE, ARE YOU OKAY?
YEAH, YEAH.
ARE *YOU* OKAY?
COULD YOU GIVE MY WIFE AND ME A MINUTE?
SURE, SURE.
WELL...
MY *FATHER* IS GONE.
I KNOW.
LEVIATHAN WAS TRYING TO TURN HIM.
BUT WHEN THEY SAW THEY COULDN'T...
THEY *DID HIM IN* IN FRONT OF ME.
YOUR FATHER WAS A COMPLICATED MAN...
BUT, EVEN IN HIS LAST BREATH, A GOOD ONE.
THAT ISN'T GONNA DO IT FOR ME TODAY, SMALLVILLE...
TELL ME ABOUT *MANHUNTERS.*

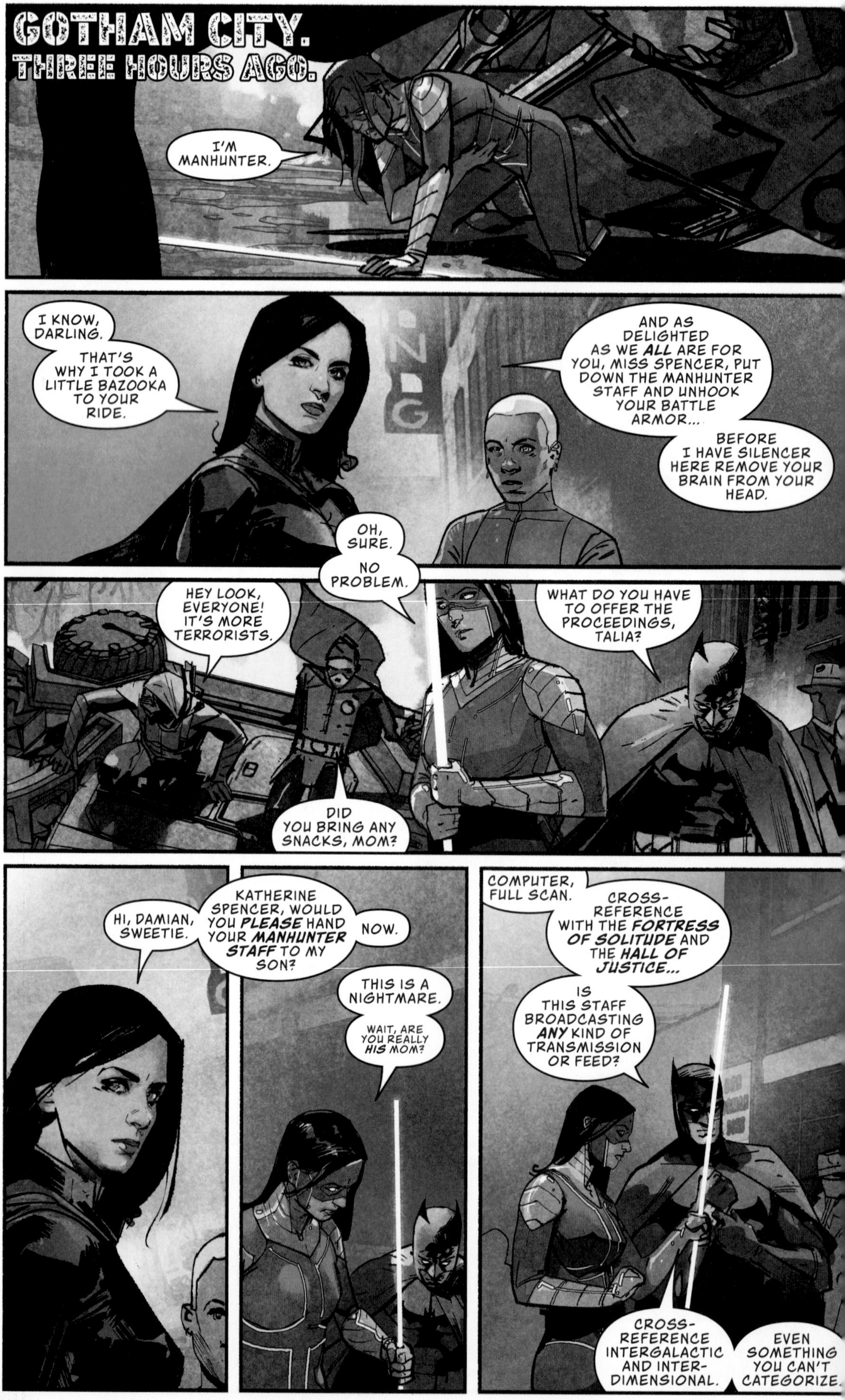
GOTHAM CITY.
THREE HOURS AGO.
I'M MANHUNTER.
I KNOW, DARLING.
THAT'S WHY I TOOK A LITTLE BAZOOKA TO YOUR RIDE.
AND AS DELIGHTED AS WE ALL ARE FOR YOU, MISS SPENCER, PUT DOWN THE MANHUNTER STAFF AND UNHOOK YOUR BATTLE ARMOR...
BEFORE I HAVE SILENCER HERE REMOVE YOUR BRAIN FROM YOUR HEAD.
OH, SURE.
NO PROBLEM.
HEY LOOK, EVERYONE! IT'S MORE TERRORISTS.
WHAT DO YOU HAVE TO OFFER THE PROCEEDINGS, TALIA?
DID YOU BRING ANY SNACKS, MOM?
HI, DAMIAN, SWEETIE.
KATHERINE SPENCER, WOULD YOU PLEASE HAND YOUR MANHUNTER STAFF TO MY SON?
NOW.
THIS IS A NIGHTMARE.
WAIT, ARE YOU REALLY HIS MOM?
COMPUTER, FULL SCAN.
CROSS-REFERENCE WITH THE FORTRESS OF SOLITUDE AND THE HALL OF JUSTICE...
IS THIS STAFF BROADCASTING ANY KIND OF TRANSMISSION OR FEED?
CROSS-REFERENCE INTERGALACTIC AND INTER-DIMENSIONAL.
EVEN SOMETHING YOU CAN'T CATEGORIZE.

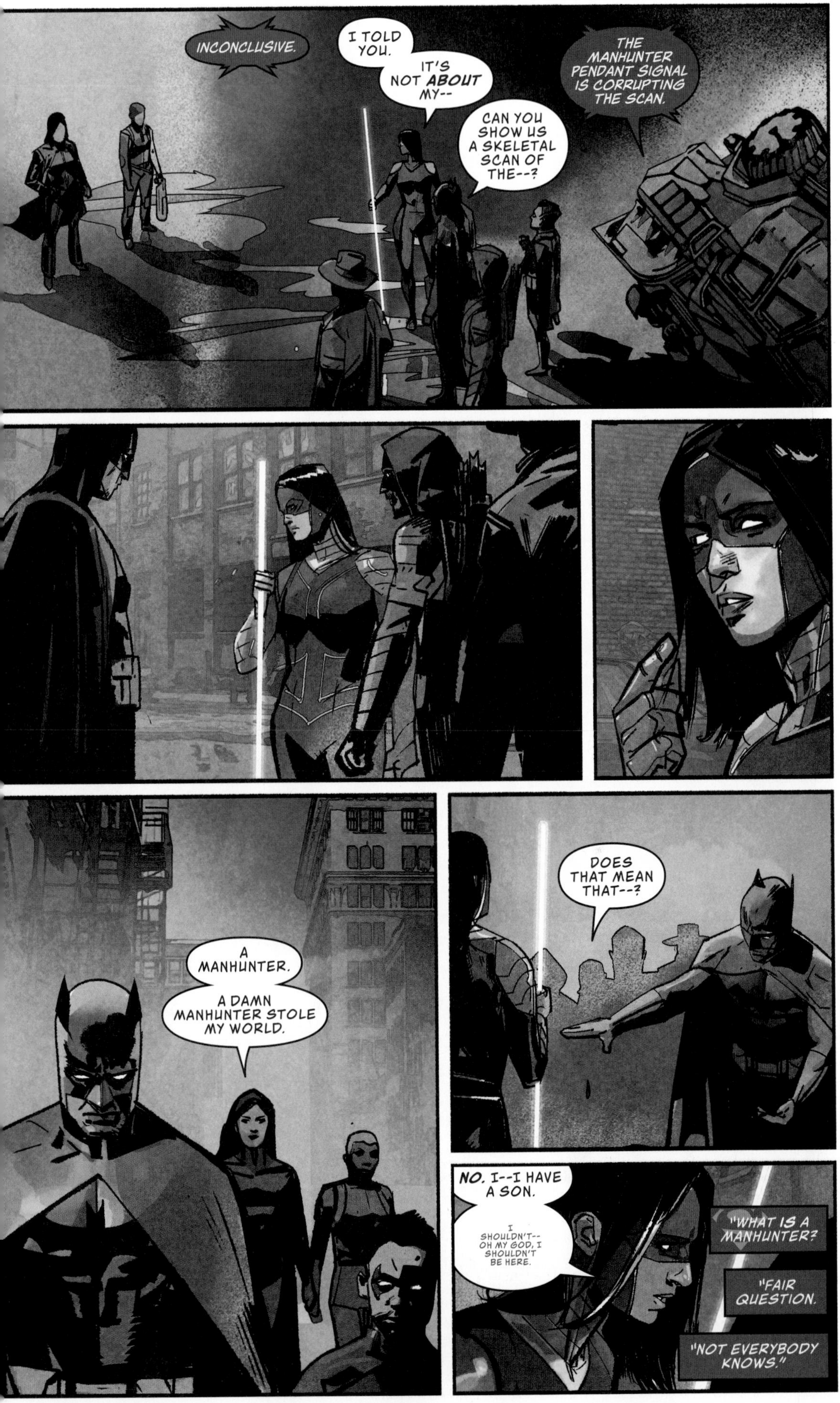
INCONCLUSIVE.
I TOLD YOU.
IT'S NOT ABOUT MY--
THE MANHUNTER PENDANT SIGNAL IS CORRUPTING THE SCAN.
CAN YOU SHOW US A SKELETAL SCAN OF THE--?
A MANHUNTER.
A DAMN MANHUNTER STOLE MY WORLD.
DOES THAT MEAN THAT--?
NO. I--I HAVE A SON.
I SHOULDN'T-- OH MY GOD, I SHOULDN'T BE HERE.
"WHAT IS A MANHUNTER?
"FAIR QUESTION.
"NOT EVERYBODY KNOWS."

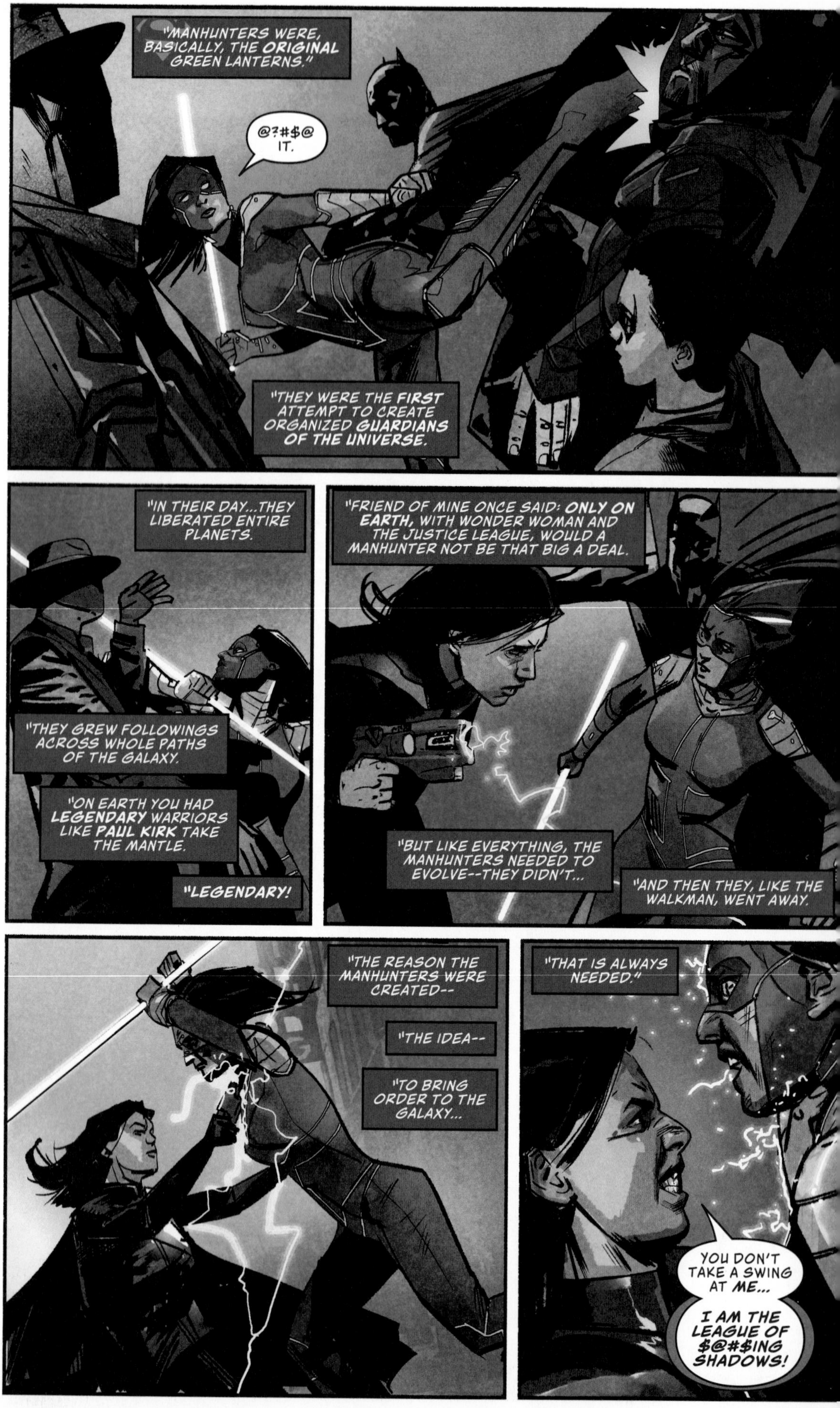
"MANHUNTERS WERE, BASICALLY, THE ORIGINAL GREEN LANTERNS."
@?#$@ IT.
"THEY WERE THE FIRST ATTEMPT TO CREATE ORGANIZED GUARDIANS OF THE UNIVERSE.
"IN THEIR DAY...THEY LIBERATED ENTIRE PLANETS.
"THEY GREW FOLLOWINGS ACROSS WHOLE PATHS OF THE GALAXY.
"ON EARTH YOU HAD LEGENDARY WARRIORS LIKE PAUL KIRK TAKE THE MANTLE.
"LEGENDARY!
"FRIEND OF MINE ONCE SAID: ONLY ON EARTH, WITH WONDER WOMAN AND THE JUSTICE LEAGUE, WOULD A MANHUNTER NOT BE THAT BIG A DEAL.
"BUT LIKE EVERYTHING, THE MANHUNTERS NEEDED TO EVOLVE--THEY DIDN'T...
"AND THEN THEY, LIKE THE WALKMAN, WENT AWAY.
"THE REASON THE MANHUNTERS WERE CREATED--
"THE IDEA--
"TO BRING ORDER TO THE GALAXY...
"THAT IS ALWAYS NEEDED."
YOU DON'T TAKE A SWING AT ME...
I AM THE LEAGUE OF $@#$ING SHADOWS!

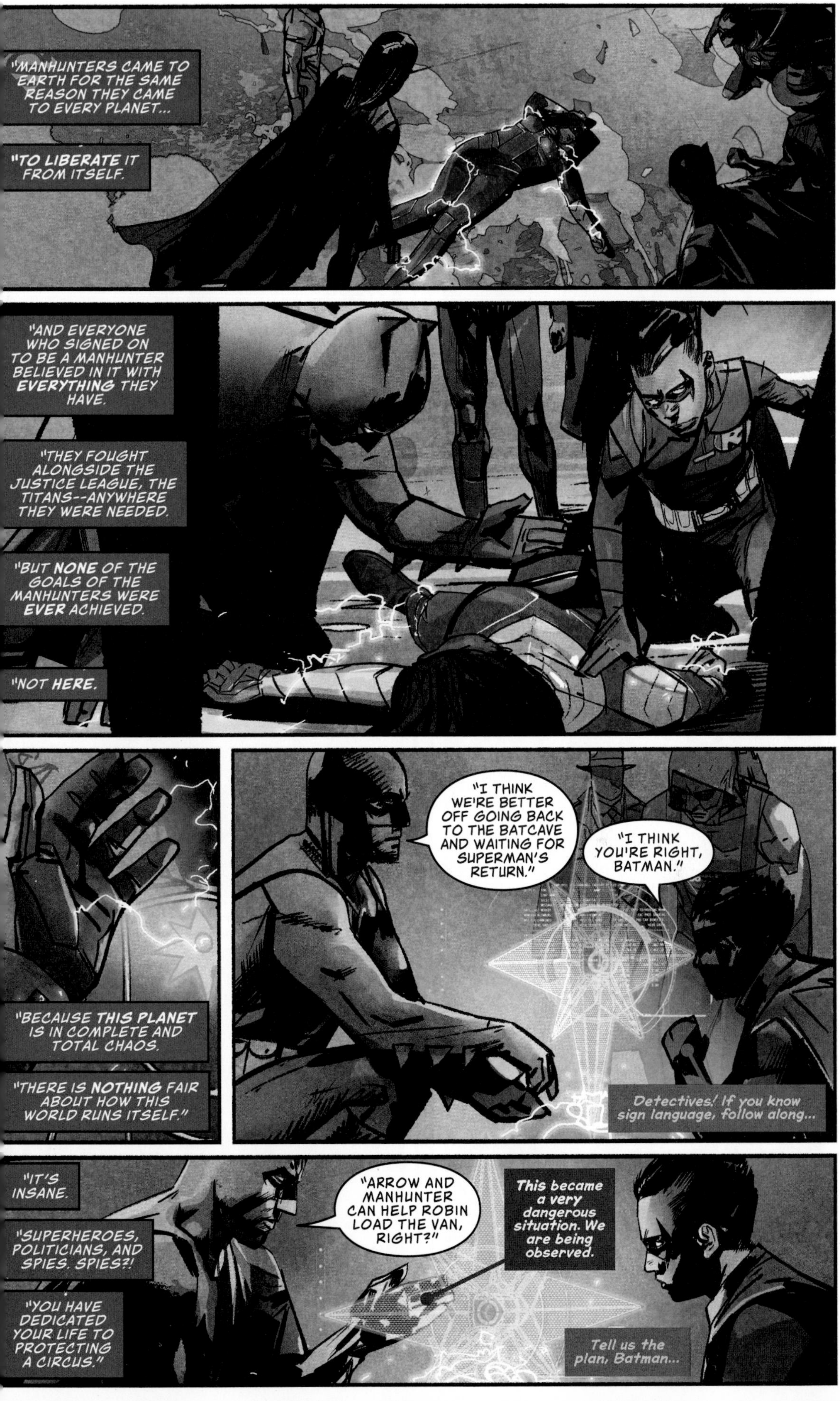
"MANHUNTERS CAME TO EARTH FOR THE SAME REASON THEY CAME TO EVERY PLANET...
"TO LIBERATE IT FROM ITSELF.
"AND EVERYONE WHO SIGNED ON TO BE A MANHUNTER BELIEVED IN IT WITH EVERYTHING THEY HAVE.
"THEY FOUGHT ALONGSIDE THE JUSTICE LEAGUE, THE TITANS--ANYWHERE THEY WERE NEEDED.
"BUT NONE OF THE GOALS OF THE MANHUNTERS WERE EVER ACHIEVED.
"NOT HERE.
"BECAUSE THIS PLANET IS IN COMPLETE AND TOTAL CHAOS.
"THERE IS NOTHING FAIR ABOUT HOW THIS WORLD RUNS ITSELF."
"I THINK WE'RE BETTER OFF GOING BACK TO THE BATCAVE AND WAITING FOR SUPERMAN'S RETURN."
"I THINK YOU'RE RIGHT, BATMAN."
Detectives! If you know sign language, follow along...
"IT'S INSANE.
"SUPERHEROES, POLITICIANS, AND SPIES. SPIES?!
"YOU HAVE DEDICATED YOUR LIFE TO PROTECTING A CIRCUS."
"ARROW AND MANHUNTER CAN HELP ROBIN LOAD THE VAN, RIGHT?"
This became a very dangerous situation. We are being observed.
Tell us the plan, Batman...

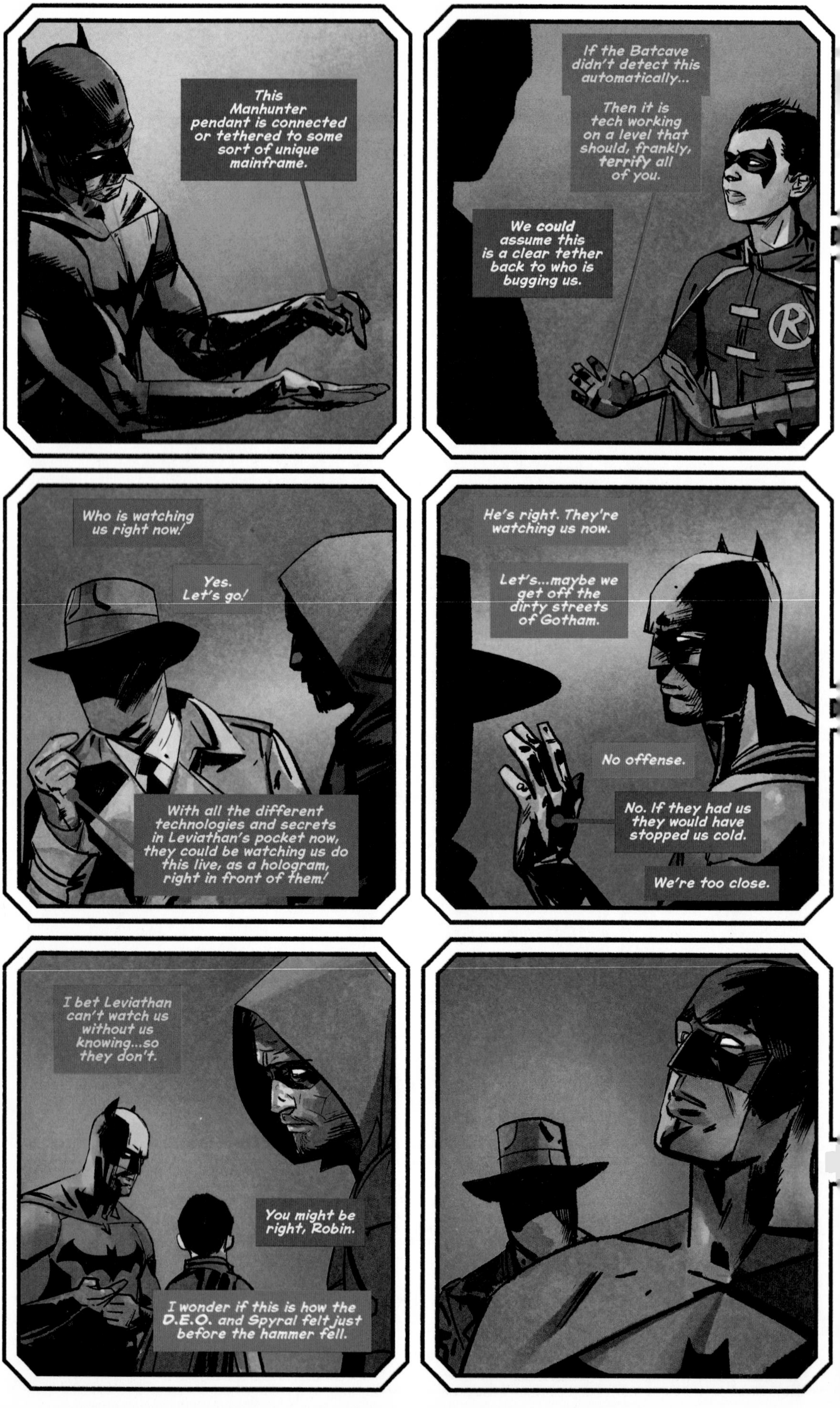
This Manhunter pendant is connected or tethered to some sort of unique mainframe.
If the Batcave didn't detect this automatically...
Then it is tech working on a level that should, frankly, terrify all of you.
We could assume this is a clear tether back to who is bugging us.
Who is watching us right now!
Yes. Let's go!
With all the different technologies and secrets in Leviathan's pocket now, they could be watching us do this live, as a hologram, right in front of them!
He's right. They're watching us now.
Let's...maybe we get off the dirty streets of Gotham.
No offense.
No. If they had us they would have stopped us cold.
We're too close.
I bet Leviathan can't watch us without us knowing...so they don't.
You might be right, Robin.
I wonder if this is how the D.E.O. and Spyral felt just before the hammer fell.

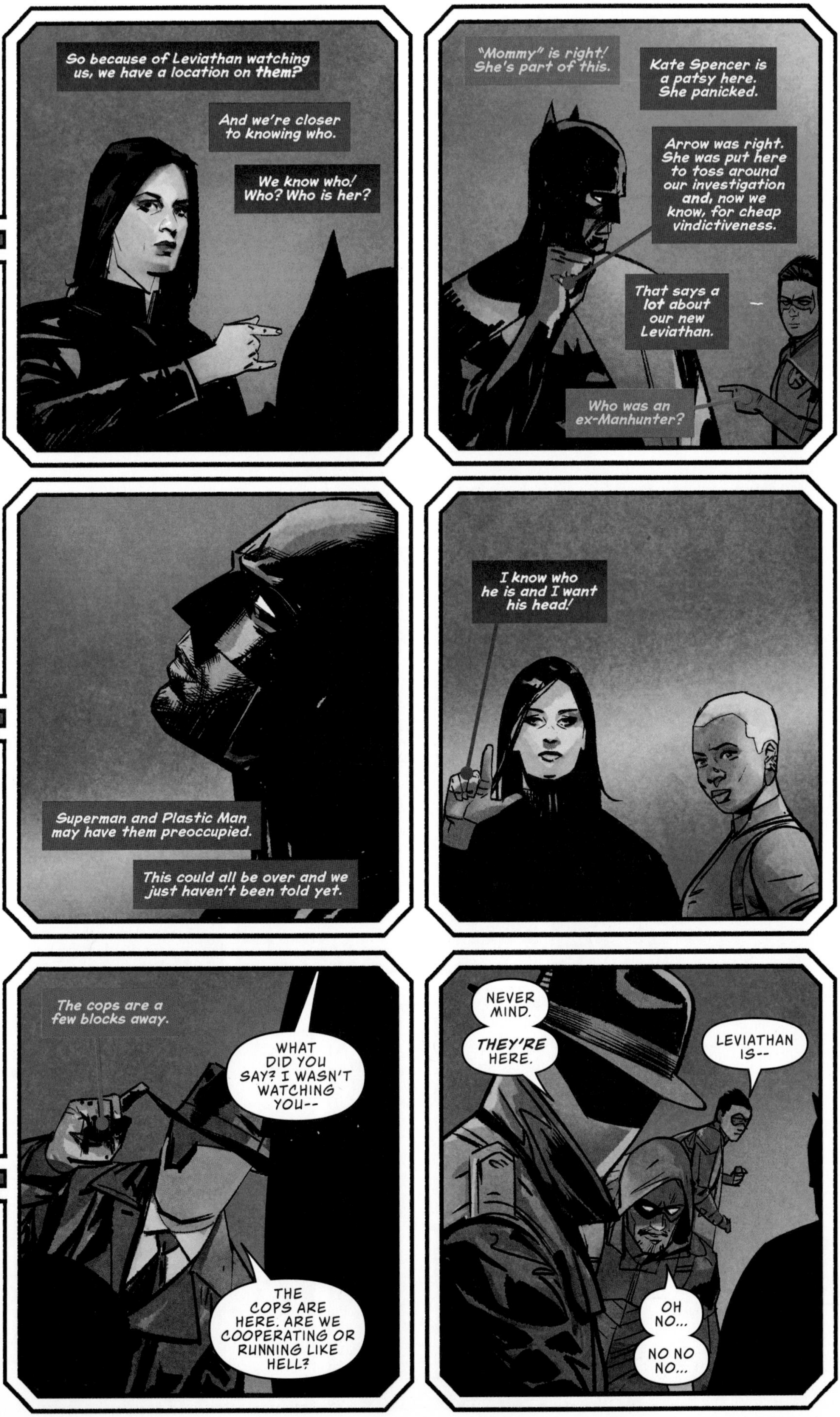
So because of Leviathan watching us, we have a location on them?
And we're closer to knowing who.
We know who! Who? Who is her?
"Mommy" is right! She's part of this.
Kate Spencer is a patsy here. She panicked.
Arrow was right. She was put here to toss around our investigation and, now we know, for cheap vindictiveness.
That says a lot about our new Leviathan.
Who was an ex-Manhunter?
Superman and Plastic Man may have them preoccupied.
This could all be over and we just haven't been told yet.
I know who he is and I want his head!
The cops are a few blocks away.
WHAT DID YOU SAY? I WASN'T WATCHING YOU--
THE COPS ARE HERE. ARE WE COOPERATING OR RUNNING LIKE HELL?
NEVER MIND.
THEY'RE HERE.
LEVIATHAN IS--
OH NO...
NO NO NO...

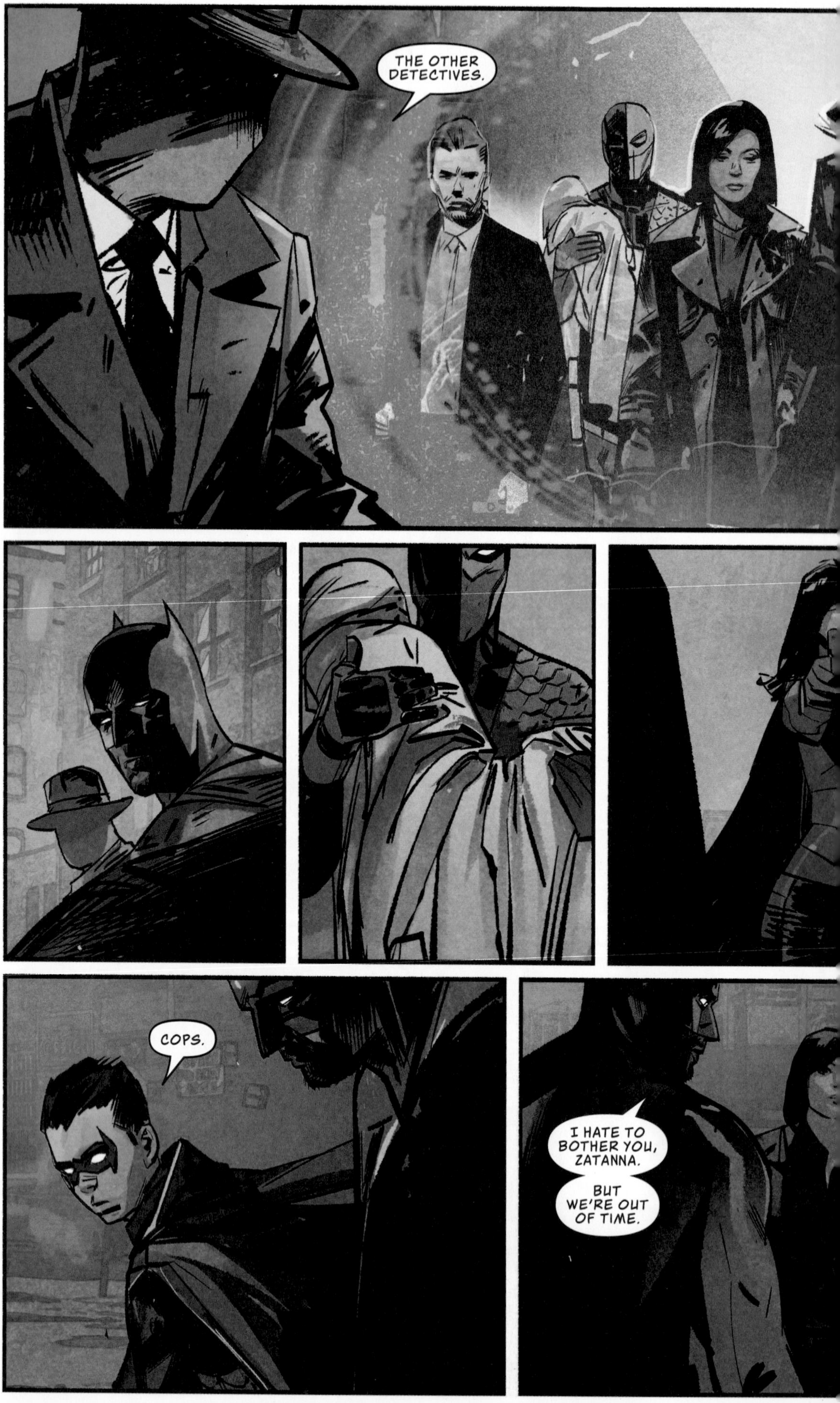
THE OTHER DETECTIVES.
COPS.
I HATE TO BOTHER YOU, ZATANNA.
BUT WE'RE OUT OF TIME.

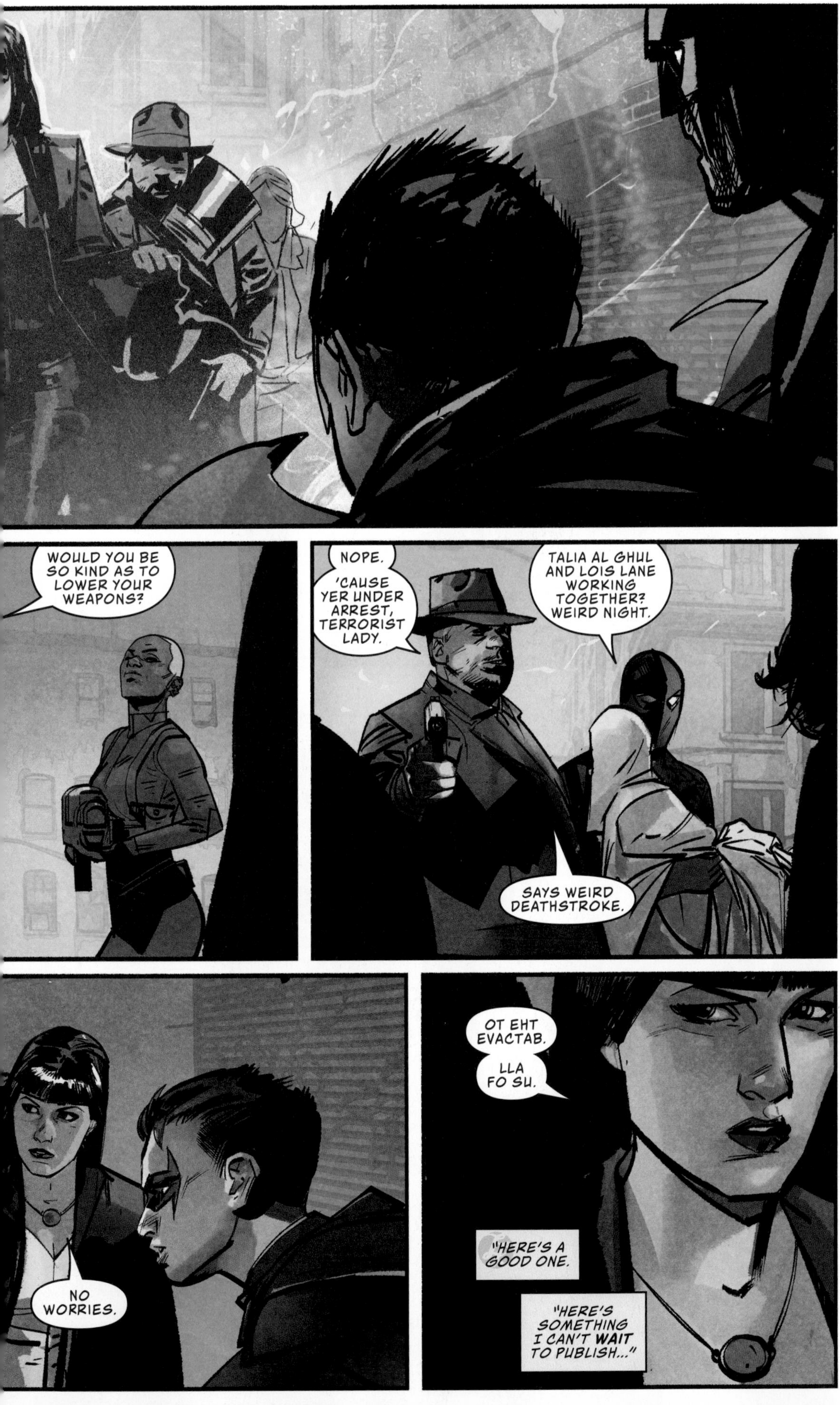
WOULD YOU BE SO KIND AS TO LOWER YOUR WEAPONS?
NOPE.
'CAUSE YER UNDER ARREST, TERRORIST LADY.
TALIA AL GHUL AND LOIS LANE WORKING TOGETHER? WEIRD NIGHT.
SAYS WEIRD DEATHSTROKE.
NO WORRIES.
OT EHT EVACTAB.
LLA FO SU.
"HERE'S A GOOD ONE.
"HERE'S SOMETHING I CAN'T WAIT TO PUBLISH..."

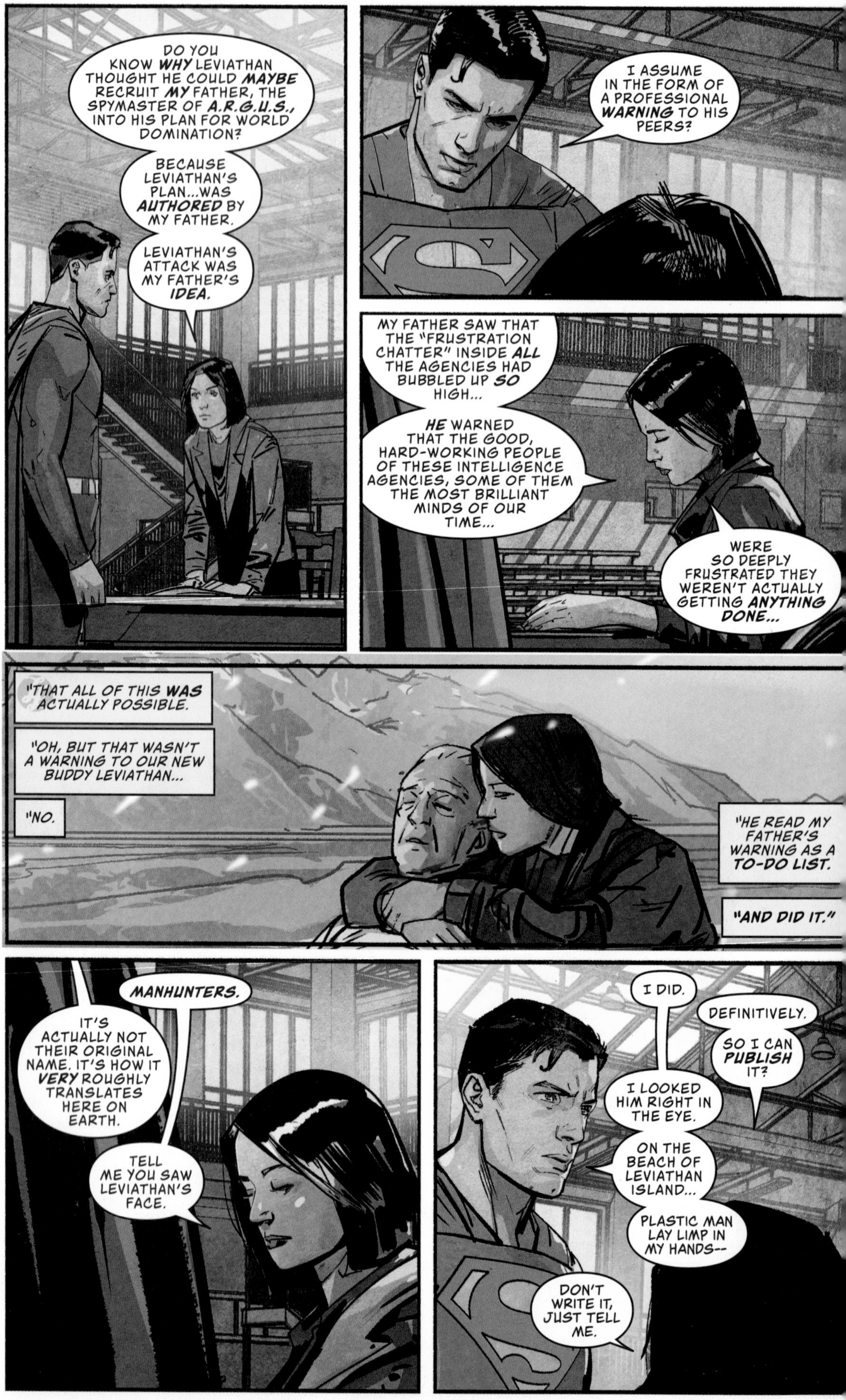
DO YOU KNOW WHY LEVIATHAN THOUGHT HE COULD MAYBE RECRUIT MY FATHER, THE SPYMASTER OF A.R.G.U.S., INTO HIS PLAN FOR WORLD DOMINATION?
BECAUSE LEVIATHAN'S PLAN...WAS AUTHORED BY MY FATHER.
LEVIATHAN'S ATTACK WAS MY FATHER'S IDEA.
I ASSUME IN THE FORM OF A PROFESSIONAL WARNING TO HIS PEERS?
MY FATHER SAW THAT THE "FRUSTRATION CHATTER" INSIDE ALL THE AGENCIES HAD BUBBLED UP SO HIGH...
HE WARNED THAT THE GOOD, HARD-WORKING PEOPLE OF THESE INTELLIGENCE AGENCIES, SOME OF THEM THE MOST BRILLIANT MINDS OF OUR TIME...
WERE SO DEEPLY FRUSTRATED THEY WEREN'T ACTUALLY GETTING ANYTHING DONE...
"THAT ALL OF THIS WAS ACTUALLY POSSIBLE.
"OH, BUT THAT WASN'T A WARNING TO OUR NEW BUDDY LEVIATHAN...
"NO.
"HE READ MY FATHER'S WARNING AS A TO-DO LIST.
"AND DID IT."
MANHUNTERS.
IT'S ACTUALLY NOT THEIR ORIGINAL NAME. IT'S HOW IT VERY ROUGHLY TRANSLATES HERE ON EARTH.
TELL ME YOU SAW LEVIATHAN'S FACE.
I DID.
DEFINITIVELY.
SO I CAN PUBLISH IT?
I LOOKED HIM RIGHT IN THE EYE.
ON THE BEACH OF LEVIATHAN ISLAND...
PLASTIC MAN LAY LIMP IN MY HANDS--
DON'T WRITE IT, JUST TELL ME.

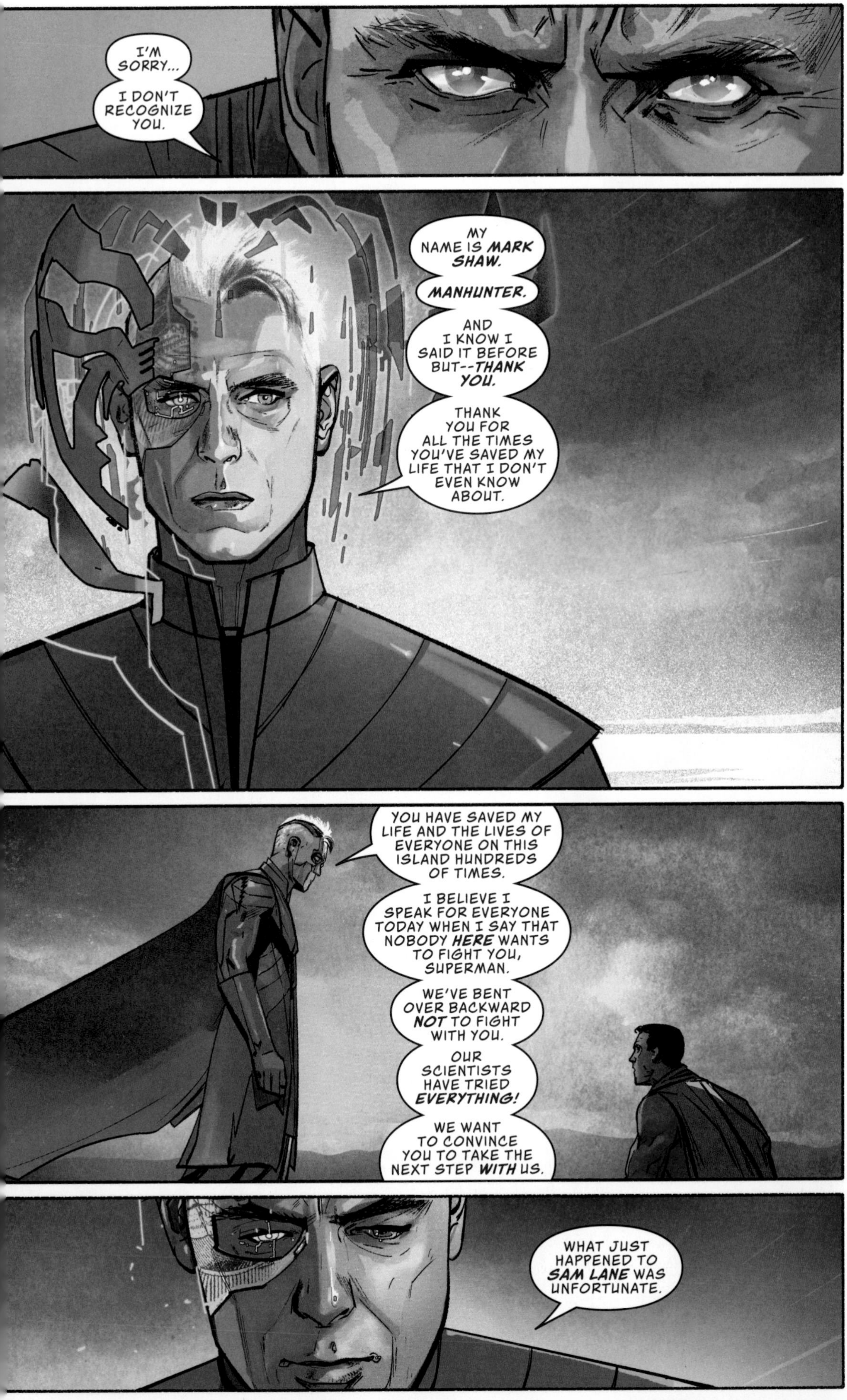
I'M SORRY...
I DON'T RECOGNIZE YOU.
MY NAME IS **MARK SHAW.**
MANHUNTER.
AND I KNOW I SAID IT BEFORE BUT--**THANK YOU.**
THANK YOU FOR ALL THE TIMES YOU'VE SAVED MY LIFE THAT I DON'T EVEN KNOW ABOUT.
YOU HAVE SAVED MY LIFE AND THE LIVES OF EVERYONE ON THIS ISLAND HUNDREDS OF TIMES.
I BELIEVE I SPEAK FOR EVERYONE TODAY WHEN I SAY THAT NOBODY **HERE** WANTS TO FIGHT YOU, SUPERMAN.
WE'VE BENT OVER BACKWARD **NOT** TO FIGHT WITH YOU.
OUR SCIENTISTS HAVE TRIED **EVERYTHING!**
WE WANT TO CONVINCE YOU TO TAKE THE NEXT STEP **WITH** US.
WHAT JUST HAPPENED TO **SAM LANE** WAS UNFORTUNATE.

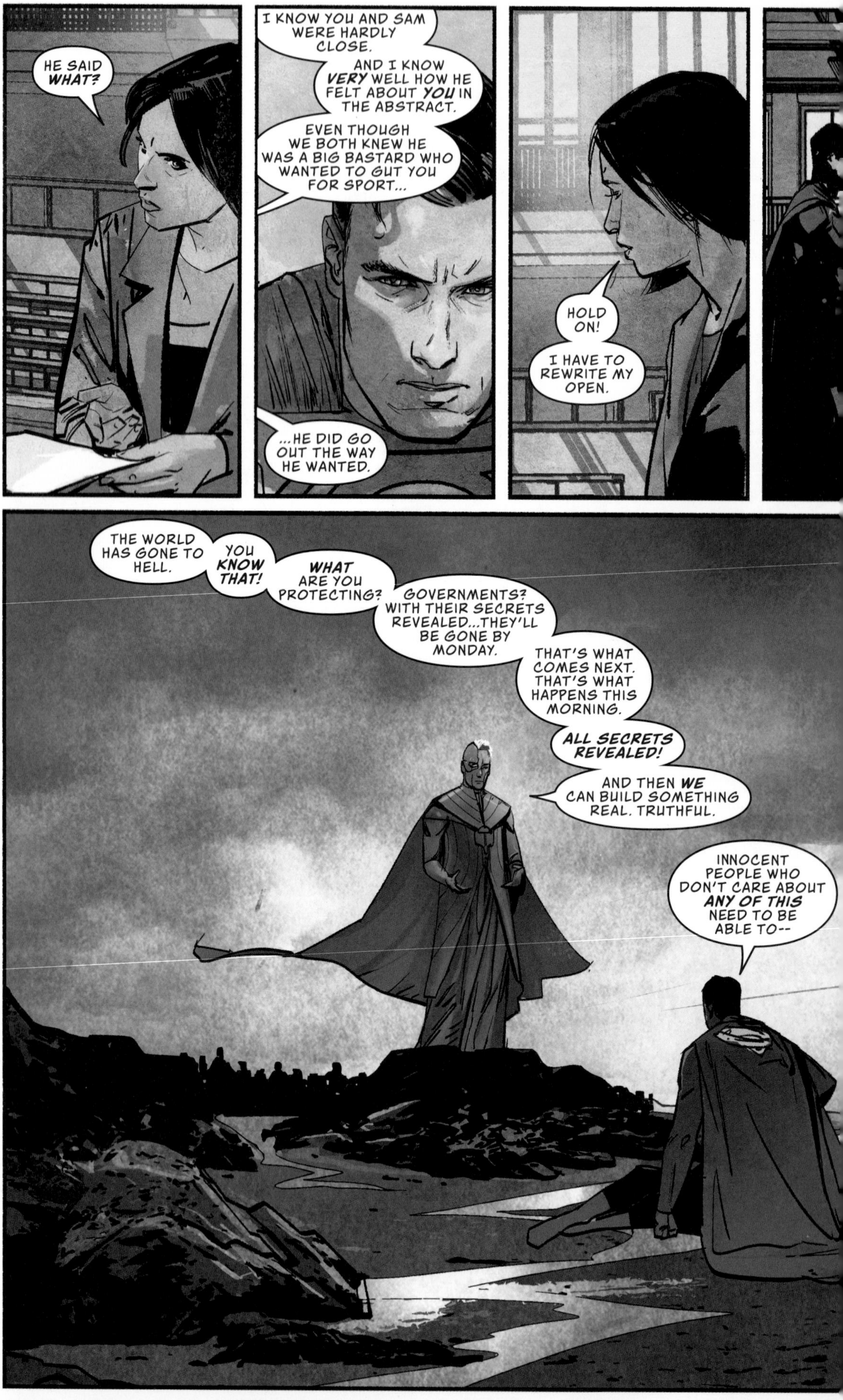
HE SAID *WHAT?*
I KNOW YOU AND SAM WERE HARDLY CLOSE.
AND I KNOW *VERY* WELL HOW HE FELT ABOUT *YOU* IN THE ABSTRACT.
EVEN THOUGH WE BOTH KNEW HE WAS A BIG BASTARD WHO WANTED TO GUT YOU FOR SPORT...
...HE DID GO OUT THE WAY HE WANTED.
HOLD ON!
I HAVE TO REWRITE MY OPEN.
THE WORLD HAS GONE TO HELL.
YOU *KNOW THAT!*
WHAT ARE YOU PROTECTING?
GOVERNMENTS? WITH THEIR SECRETS REVEALED...THEY'LL BE GONE BY MONDAY.
THAT'S WHAT COMES NEXT. THAT'S WHAT HAPPENS THIS MORNING.
ALL SECRETS REVEALED!
AND THEN *WE* CAN BUILD SOMETHING REAL. TRUTHFUL.
INNOCENT PEOPLE WHO DON'T CARE ABOUT *ANY OF THIS* NEED TO BE ABLE TO--

MARK SHAW. EX-SPY.

OF COURSE.

EX-MANHUNTER, EX-SUICIDE SQUAD.

OF COURSE.

HE WAS CHECKMATE WHEN IT COLLAPSED.

TALIA RECRUITED HIM INTO LEVIATHAN NOT KNOWING...

BEFORE THAT HE WAS A TRUSTED PARTNER TO YOUR FATHER.

SO, LEVIATHAN WAS A SPY. SPYCRAFT IS A HOT FIRE GARBAGE WAY FOR A HUMAN TO MAKE A LIVING.

HE *JUST* FIGURED THAT OUT SO *WE* CAN ALL GO TO HELL?

GREAT!

WELL, TO HEAR HIM TELL IT--

YEAH, YEAH...

HOW'D YOU GET OUT OF THERE AND WHERE IS HE NOW?

PLASTIC MAN.

PLASTIC MAN?

PLAS *WASN'T* UNCONSCIOUS.

HE LITERALLY LAID THERE IN MY ARMS USING HIS POWERS TO SQUEEZE PART OF HIMSELF OUT OF OUR *SPYRAL TECH* TRAP.

AND IT WAS *JUST* THEN WHEN *BATMAN* AND ALL THE DETECTIVES TRACED THE LEVIATHAN/MANHUNTER SIGNAL SOURCE TO THIS ISLAND OFF OF ICELAND...

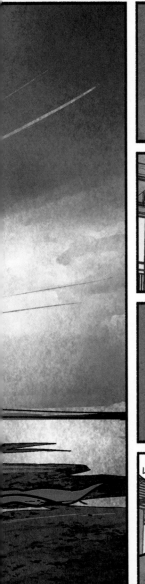

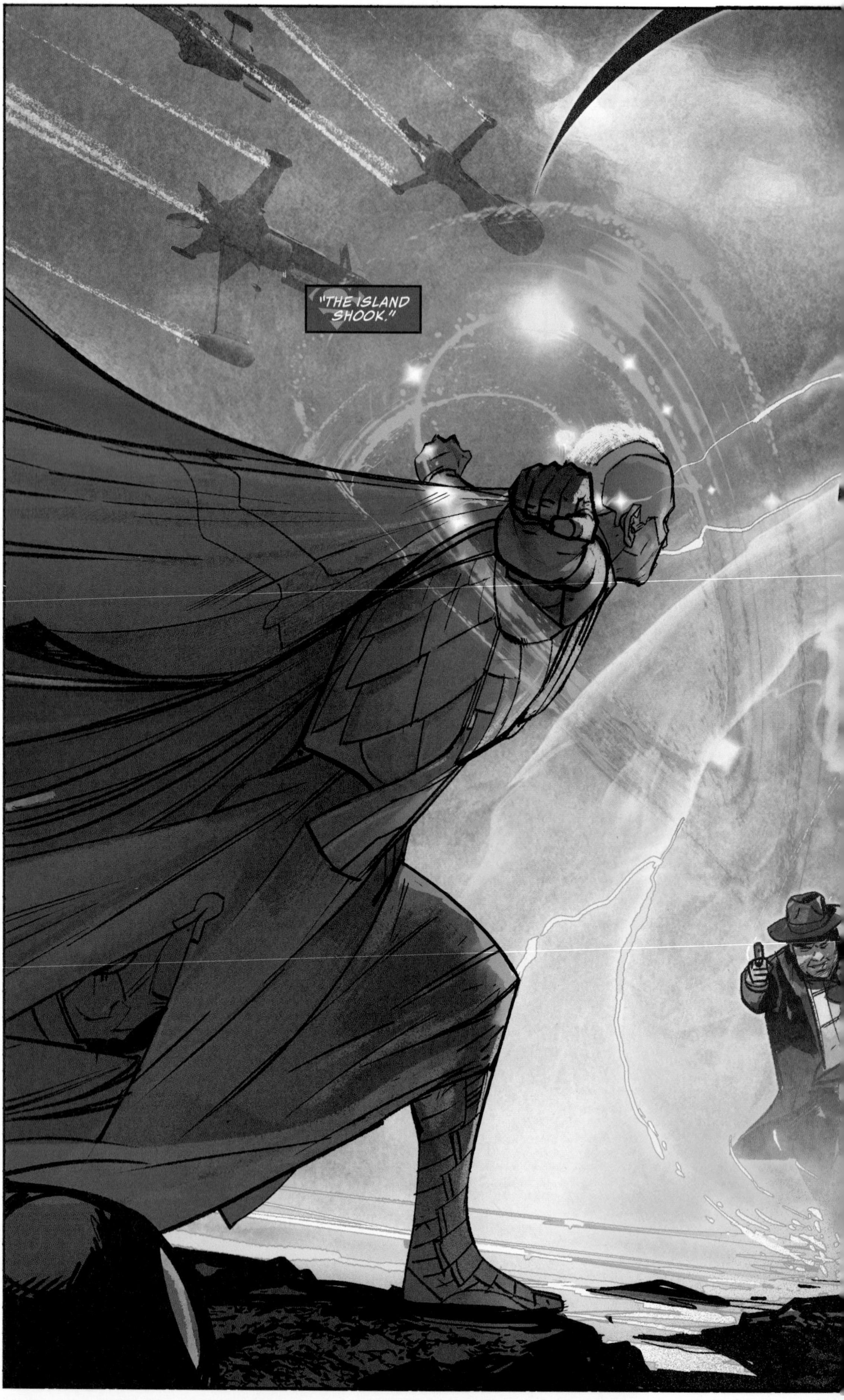
"THE ISLAND SHOOK."

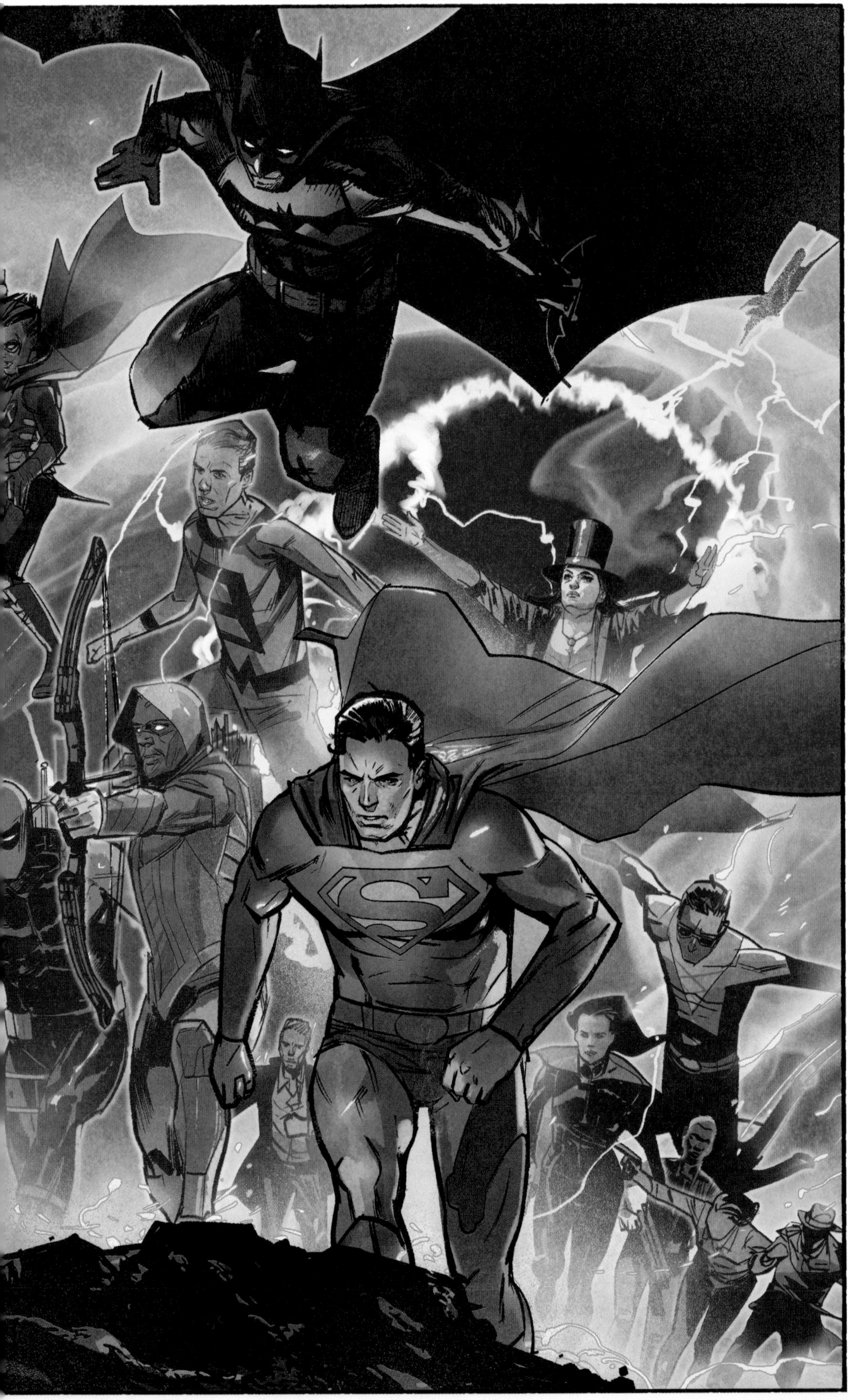

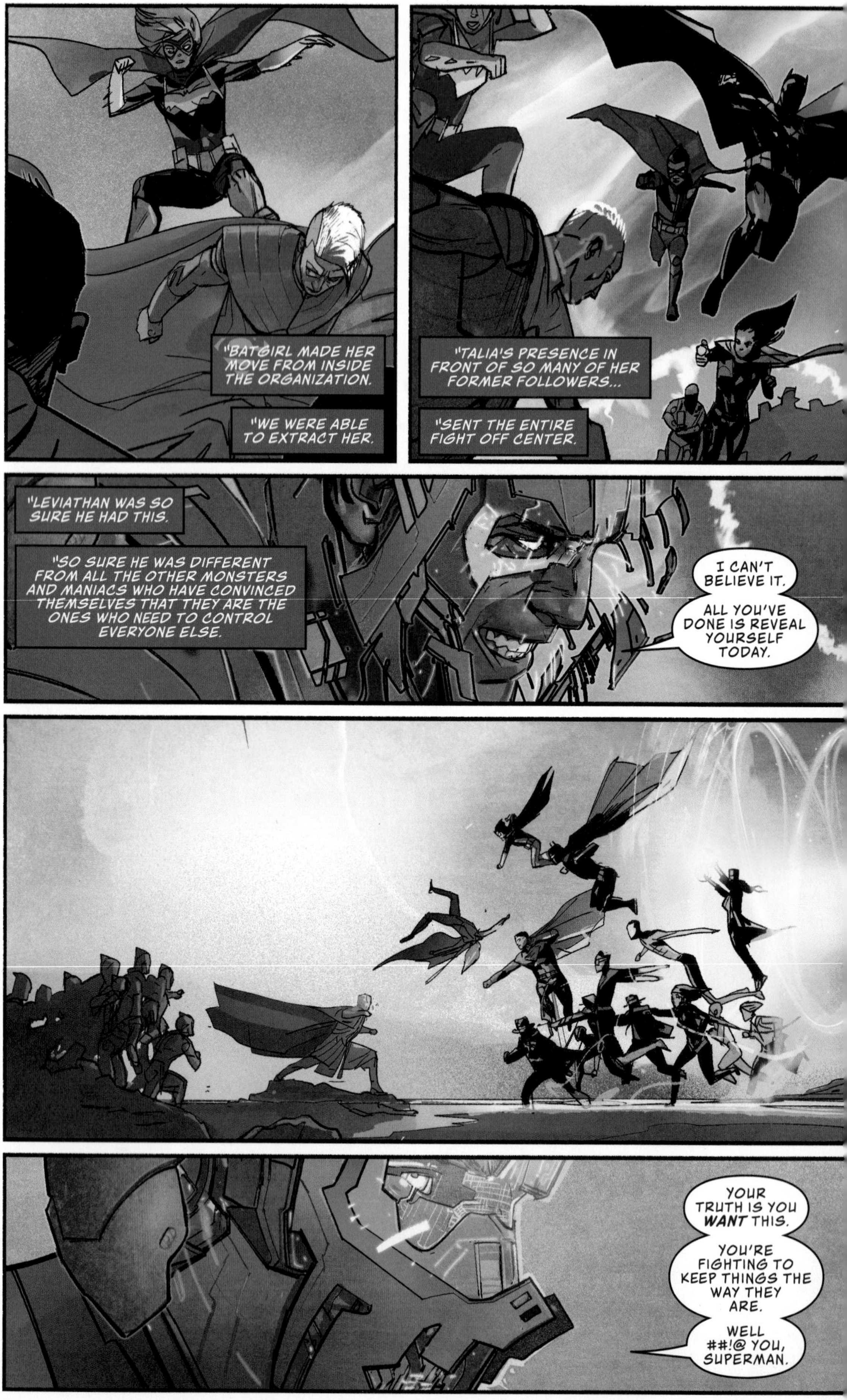
"BATGIRL MADE HER MOVE FROM INSIDE THE ORGANIZATION.
"WE WERE ABLE TO EXTRACT HER.
"TALIA'S PRESENCE IN FRONT OF SO MANY OF HER FORMER FOLLOWERS...
"SENT THE ENTIRE FIGHT OFF CENTER.
"LEVIATHAN WAS SO SURE HE HAD THIS.
"SO SURE HE WAS DIFFERENT FROM ALL THE OTHER MONSTERS AND MANIACS WHO HAVE CONVINCED THEMSELVES THAT THEY ARE THE ONES WHO NEED TO CONTROL EVERYONE ELSE.
I CAN'T BELIEVE IT.
ALL YOU'VE DONE IS REVEAL YOURSELF TODAY.
YOUR TRUTH IS YOU WANT THIS.
YOU'RE FIGHTING TO KEEP THINGS THE WAY THEY ARE.
WELL ##!@ YOU, SUPERMAN.

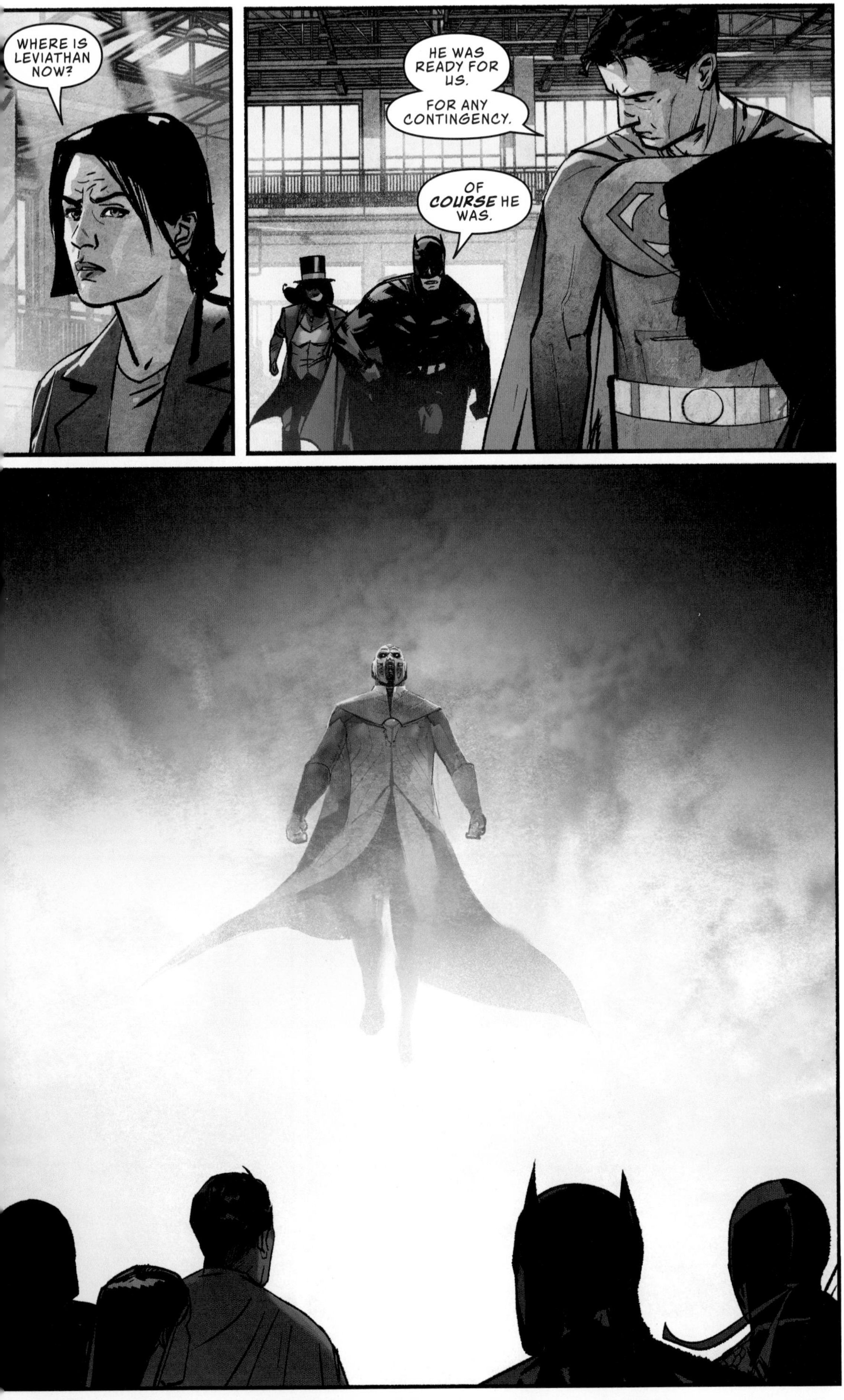
WHERE IS LEVIATHAN NOW?
HE WAS READY FOR US.
FOR ANY CONTINGENCY.
OF *COURSE* HE WAS.

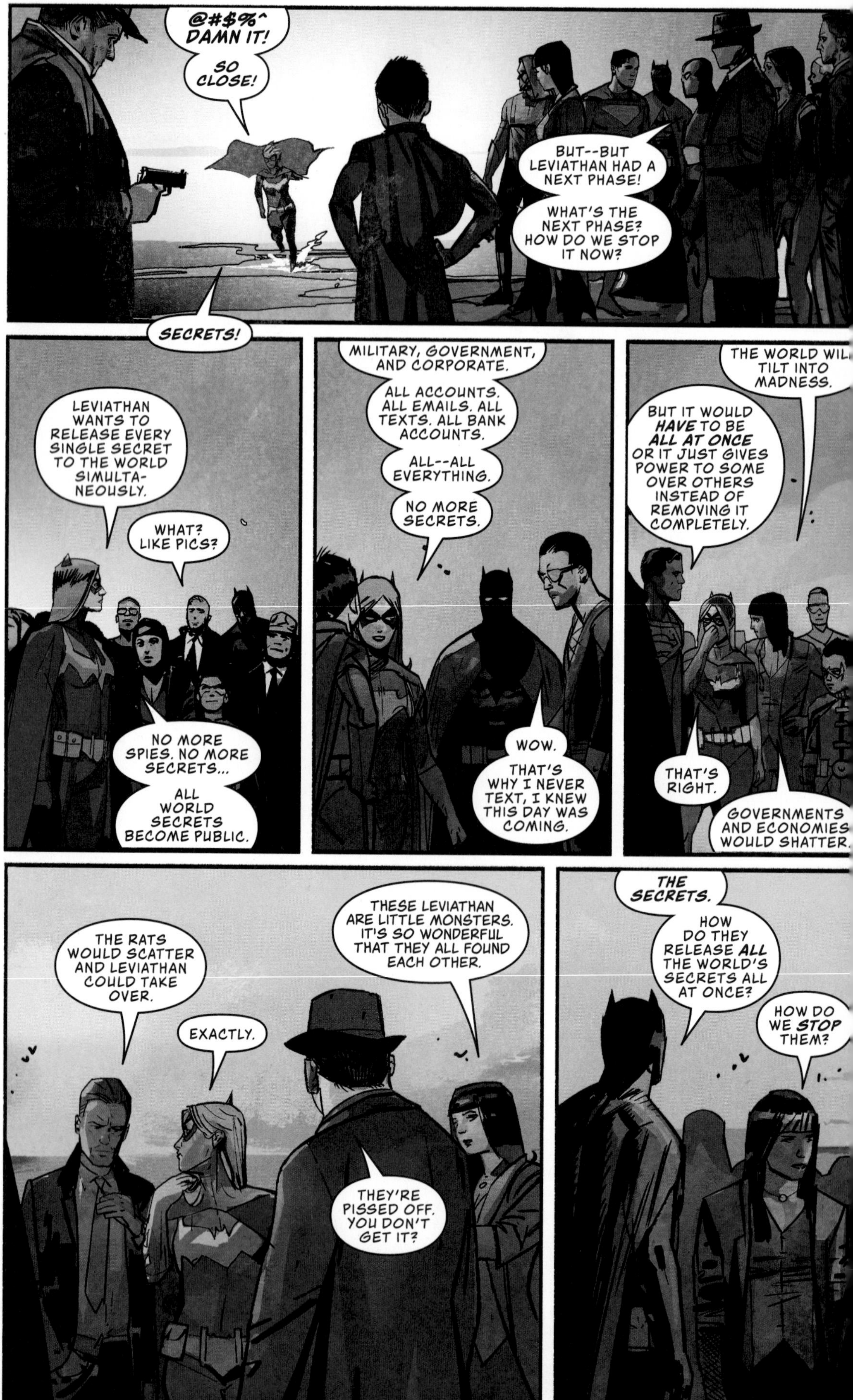
@#$%^ DAMN IT!
SO CLOSE!
BUT--BUT LEVIATHAN HAD A NEXT PHASE!
WHAT'S THE NEXT PHASE? HOW DO WE STOP IT NOW?
SECRETS!
LEVIATHAN WANTS TO RELEASE EVERY SINGLE SECRET TO THE WORLD SIMULTA-NEOUSLY.
WHAT? LIKE PICS?
NO MORE SPIES. NO MORE SECRETS...
ALL WORLD SECRETS BECOME PUBLIC.
MILITARY, GOVERNMENT, AND CORPORATE.
ALL ACCOUNTS. ALL EMAILS. ALL TEXTS. ALL BANK ACCOUNTS.
ALL--ALL EVERYTHING.
NO MORE SECRETS.
WOW.
THAT'S WHY I NEVER TEXT, I KNEW THIS DAY WAS COMING.
THE WORLD WIL TILT INTO MADNESS.
BUT IT WOULD HAVE TO BE ALL AT ONCE OR IT JUST GIVES POWER TO SOME OVER OTHERS INSTEAD OF REMOVING IT COMPLETELY.
THAT'S RIGHT.
GOVERNMENTS AND ECONOMIES WOULD SHATTER.
THE RATS WOULD SCATTER AND LEVIATHAN COULD TAKE OVER.
EXACTLY.
THESE LEVIATHAN ARE LITTLE MONSTERS. IT'S SO WONDERFUL THAT THEY ALL FOUND EACH OTHER.
THEY'RE PISSED OFF. YOU DON'T GET IT?
THE SECRETS.
HOW DO THEY RELEASE ALL THE WORLD'S SECRETS ALL AT ONCE?
HOW DO WE STOP THEM?

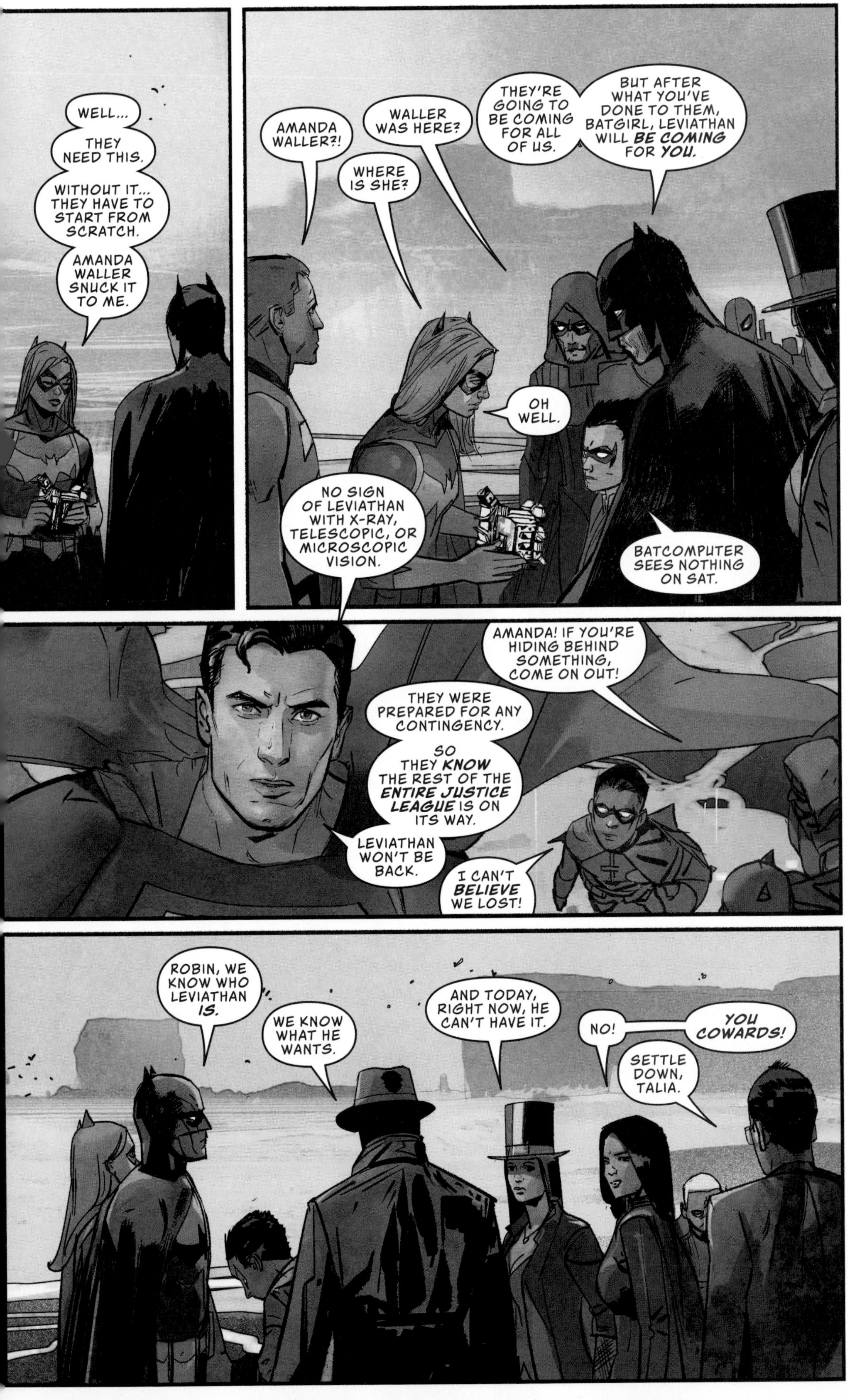
WELL...
THEY NEED THIS.
WITHOUT IT... THEY HAVE TO START FROM SCRATCH.
AMANDA WALLER SNUCK IT TO ME.
AMANDA WALLER?!
WALLER WAS HERE?
WHERE IS SHE?
THEY'RE GOING TO BE COMING FOR ALL OF US.
BUT AFTER WHAT YOU'VE DONE TO THEM, BATGIRL, LEVIATHAN WILL ***BE COMING*** FOR ***YOU.***
OH WELL.
NO SIGN OF LEVIATHAN WITH X-RAY, TELESCOPIC, OR MICROSCOPIC VISION.
BATCOMPUTER SEES NOTHING ON SAT.
AMANDA! IF YOU'RE HIDING BEHIND SOMETHING, COME ON OUT!
THEY WERE PREPARED FOR ANY CONTINGENCY.
SO THEY ***KNOW*** THE REST OF THE ***ENTIRE JUSTICE LEAGUE*** IS ON ITS WAY.
LEVIATHAN WON'T BE BACK.
I CAN'T ***BELIEVE*** WE LOST!
ROBIN, WE KNOW WHO LEVIATHAN ***IS.***
WE KNOW WHAT HE WANTS.
AND TODAY, RIGHT NOW, HE CAN'T HAVE IT.
NO!
YOU COWARDS!
SETTLE DOWN, TALIA.

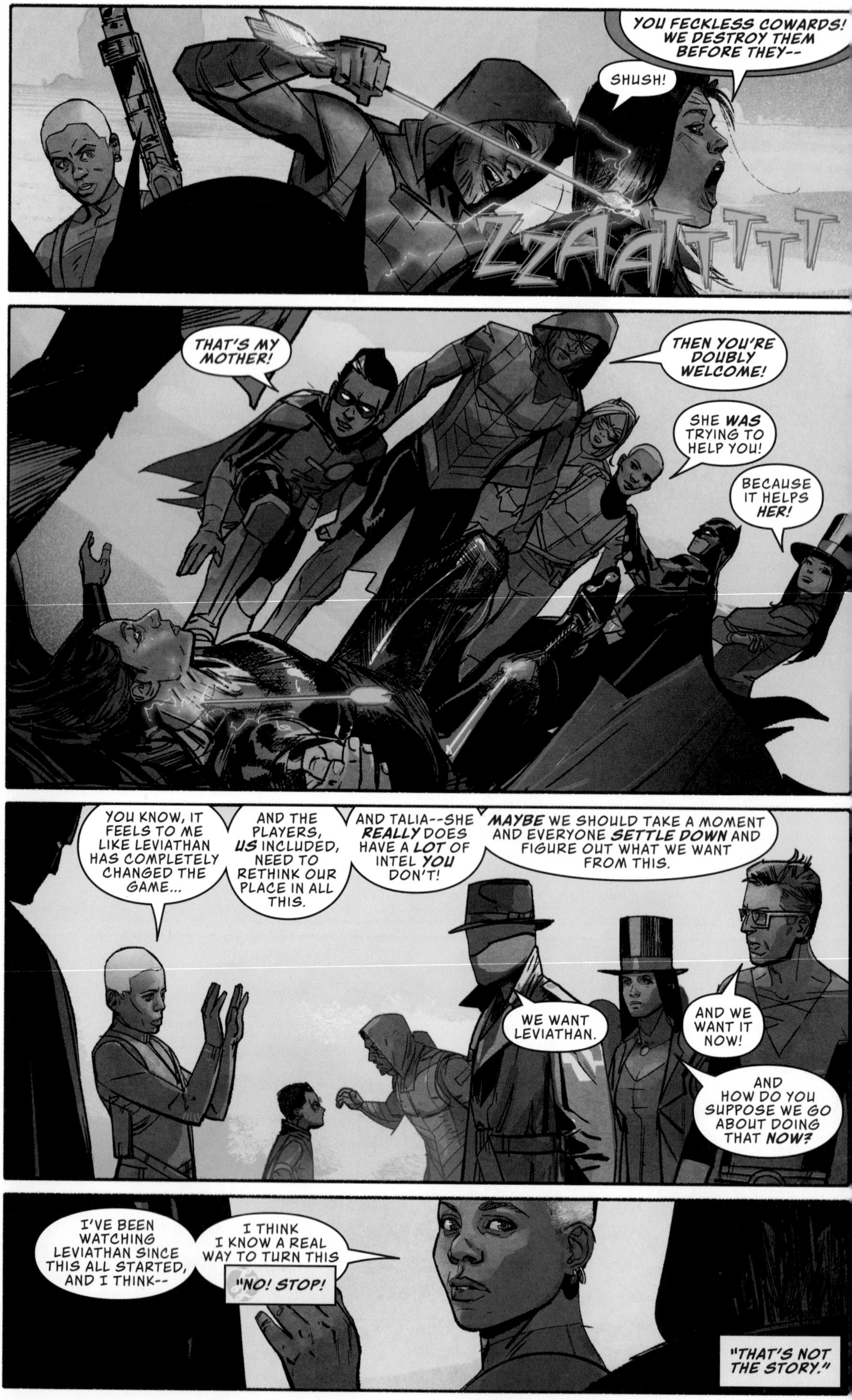
YOU FECKLESS COWARDS! WE DESTROY THEM BEFORE THEY--
SHUSH!
ZZAATTTTT
THAT'S MY MOTHER!
THEN YOU'RE DOUBLY WELCOME!
SHE WAS TRYING TO HELP YOU!
BECAUSE IT HELPS HER!
YOU KNOW, IT FEELS TO ME LIKE LEVIATHAN HAS COMPLETELY CHANGED THE GAME...
AND THE PLAYERS, US INCLUDED, NEED TO RETHINK OUR PLACE IN ALL THIS.
AND TALIA--SHE REALLY DOES HAVE A LOT OF INTEL YOU DON'T!
MAYBE WE SHOULD TAKE A MOMENT AND EVERYONE SETTLE DOWN AND FIGURE OUT WHAT WE WANT FROM THIS.
WE WANT LEVIATHAN.
AND WE WANT IT NOW!
AND HOW DO YOU SUPPOSE WE GO ABOUT DOING THAT NOW?
I'VE BEEN WATCHING LEVIATHAN SINCE THIS ALL STARTED, AND I THINK--
I THINK I KNOW A REAL WAY TO TURN THIS
"NO! STOP!
"THAT'S NOT THE STORY."

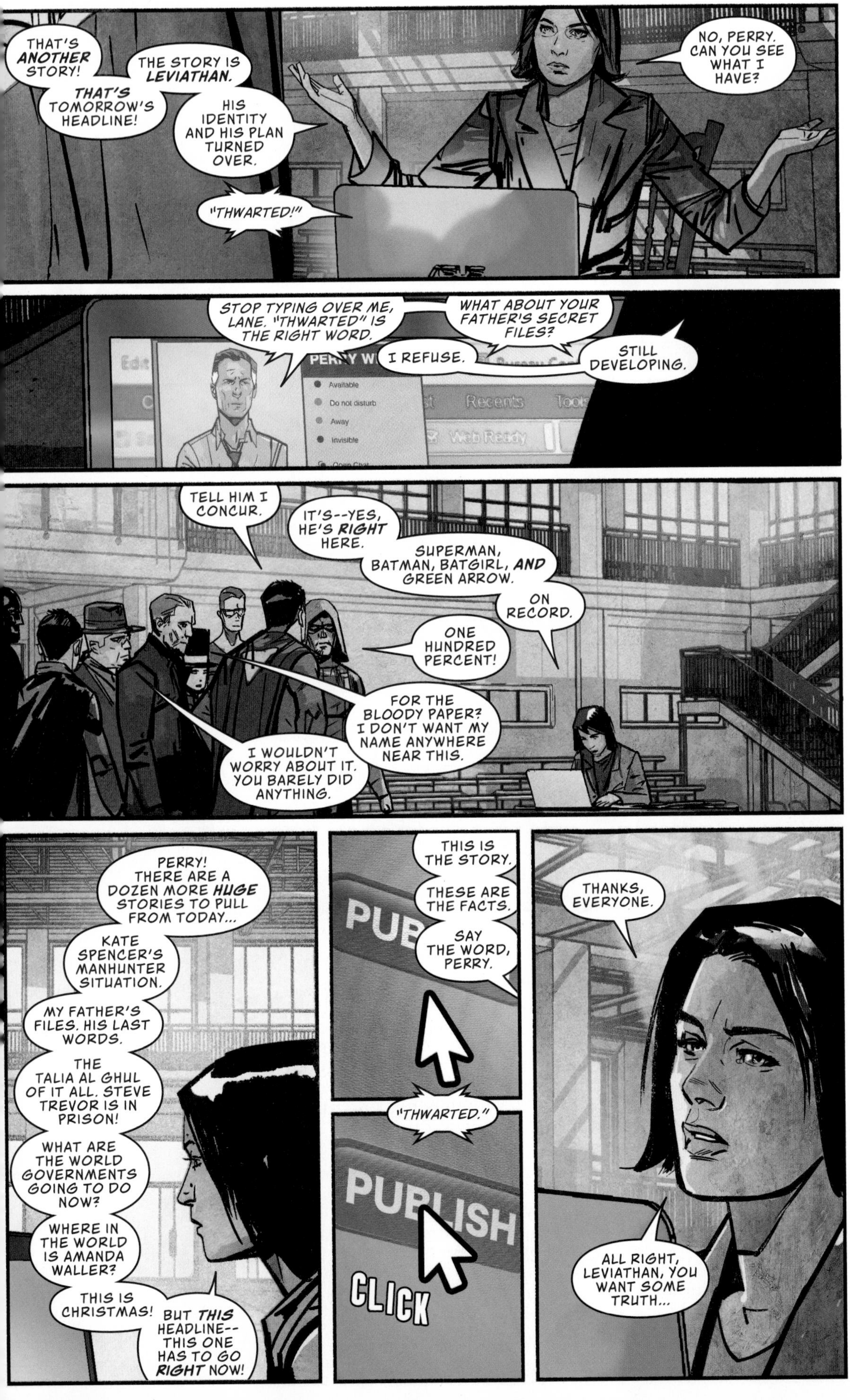
THAT'S ANOTHER STORY!
THAT'S TOMORROW'S HEADLINE!
THE STORY IS LEVIATHAN.
HIS IDENTITY AND HIS PLAN TURNED OVER.
"THWARTED!"
NO, PERRY. CAN YOU SEE WHAT I HAVE?
STOP TYPING OVER ME, LANE. "THWARTED" IS THE RIGHT WORD.
WHAT ABOUT YOUR FATHER'S SECRET FILES?
I REFUSE.
STILL DEVELOPING.
Recents
Tools
Web Ready
Available
Do not disturb
Away
Invisible
TELL HIM I CONCUR.
IT'S--YES, HE'S RIGHT HERE.
SUPERMAN, BATMAN, BATGIRL, AND GREEN ARROW.
ON RECORD.
ONE HUNDRED PERCENT!
FOR THE BLOODY PAPER? I DON'T WANT MY NAME ANYWHERE NEAR THIS.
I WOULDN'T WORRY ABOUT IT. YOU BARELY DID ANYTHING.
PERRY! THERE ARE A DOZEN MORE HUGE STORIES TO PULL FROM TODAY...
KATE SPENCER'S MANHUNTER SITUATION.
MY FATHER'S FILES. HIS LAST WORDS.
THE TALIA AL GHUL OF IT ALL. STEVE TREVOR IS IN PRISON!
WHAT ARE THE WORLD GOVERNMENTS GOING TO DO NOW?
WHERE IN THE WORLD IS AMANDA WALLER?
THIS IS CHRISTMAS!
BUT THIS HEADLINE-- THIS ONE HAS TO GO RIGHT NOW!
THIS IS THE STORY.
THESE ARE THE FACTS.
SAY THE WORD, PERRY.
"THWARTED."
PUBLISH
CLICK
THANKS, EVERYONE.
ALL RIGHT, LEVIATHAN, YOU WANT SOME TRUTH...

ENGLISH ESPAÑOL 中文

DAILY PLANET

NOVEMBER 13, 2019 "A Great Metropolitan Newspaper" Sign In Subscribe

IN THE NEWS WORLD METAHUMANS U.S. POLITICS OPINION SCIENCE HEALTH SPORTS ART STYLE

LEVIATHAN REVEALED

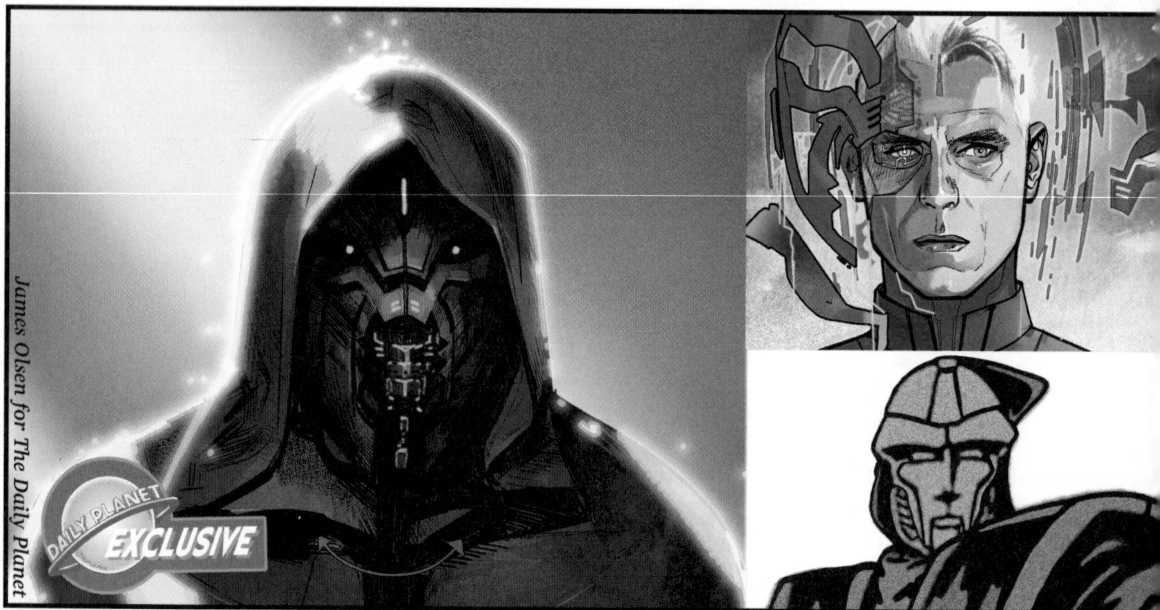
DAILY PLANET
EXCLUSIVE
James Olsen for The Daily Planet

BY **LOIS LANE**

With additional reporting by ***Clark Kent*** *and* ***James Olsen***

The hunt for the person behind the rise of one of the most dangerous organizations in history ended with a Manhunter.

The Daily Planet can exclusively report a onetime costumed adventurer unleashed yesterday's unprecedented, massive attack on the world intelligence organizations. Mark Shaw, once called Manhunter and a former United States intelligence operative, now controls the Leviathan terrorist organization.

While no one was paying attention—not Superman, not Wonder Woman, not any member of the F.B.I. or the Justice League—Shaw took over Leviathan and coerced most of the major intelligence players in the world into joining him in an attempt to overthrow all the world's governments at once.

He was 40 minutes away from making that happen.

1m ago 45 comments

ALSO IN THE NEWS

Brian Michael Bendis
Story

Alex Maleev
Art & cover

Josh Reed
Letters

Jessica Chen
Associate editor

Mike Cotton
Editor

Brian Cunningham
Group editor

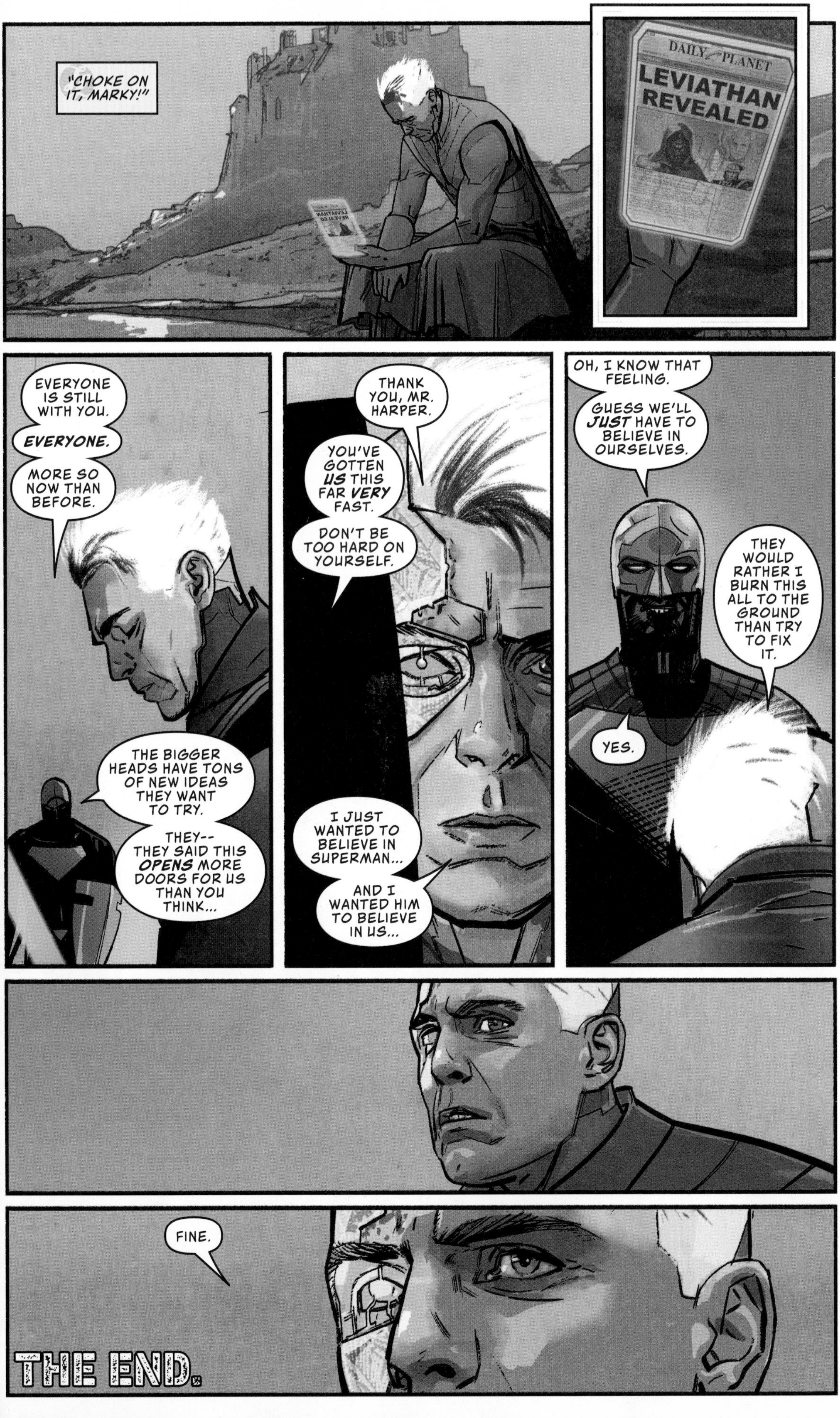
"CHOKE ON IT, MARKY!"
DAILY PLANET
LEVIATHAN REVEALED
EVERYONE IS STILL WITH YOU.
EVERYONE.
MORE SO NOW THAN BEFORE.
THE BIGGER HEADS HAVE TONS OF NEW IDEAS THEY WANT TO TRY.
THEY-- THEY SAID THIS OPENS MORE DOORS FOR US THAN YOU THINK...
THANK YOU, MR. HARPER.
YOU'VE GOTTEN US THIS FAR VERY FAST.
DON'T BE TOO HARD ON YOURSELF.
I JUST WANTED TO BELIEVE IN SUPERMAN...
AND I WANTED HIM TO BELIEVE IN US...
OH, I KNOW THAT FEELING.
GUESS WE'LL JUST HAVE TO BELIEVE IN OURSELVES.
THEY WOULD RATHER I BURN THIS ALL TO THE GROUND THAN TRY TO FIX IT.
YES.
FINE.
THE END.

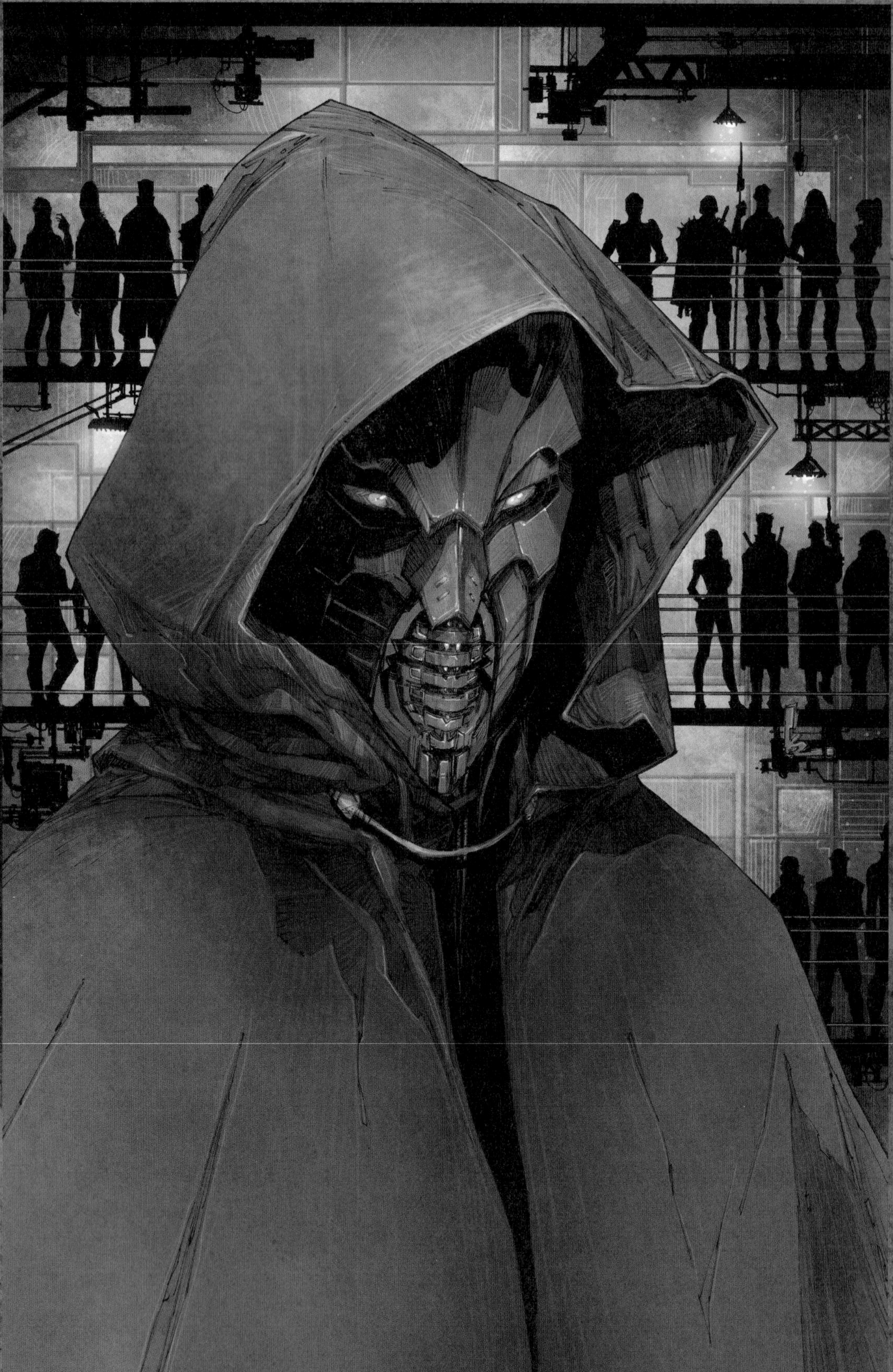

Event Leviathan #1 variant cover by KENNETH ROCAFORT

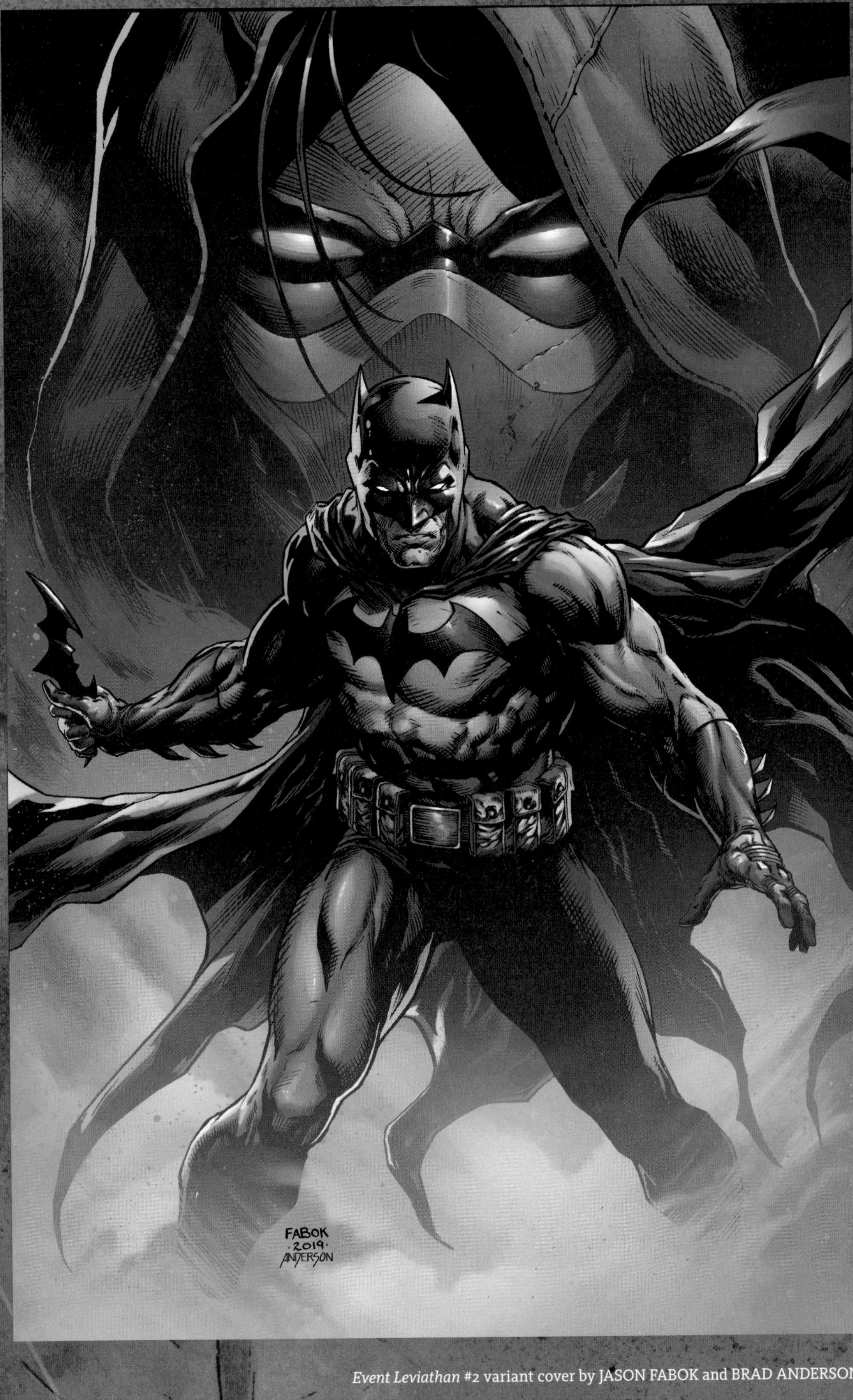
FABOK
·2019·
ANDERSON

Event Leviathan #2 variant cover by JASON FABOK and BRAD ANDERSON

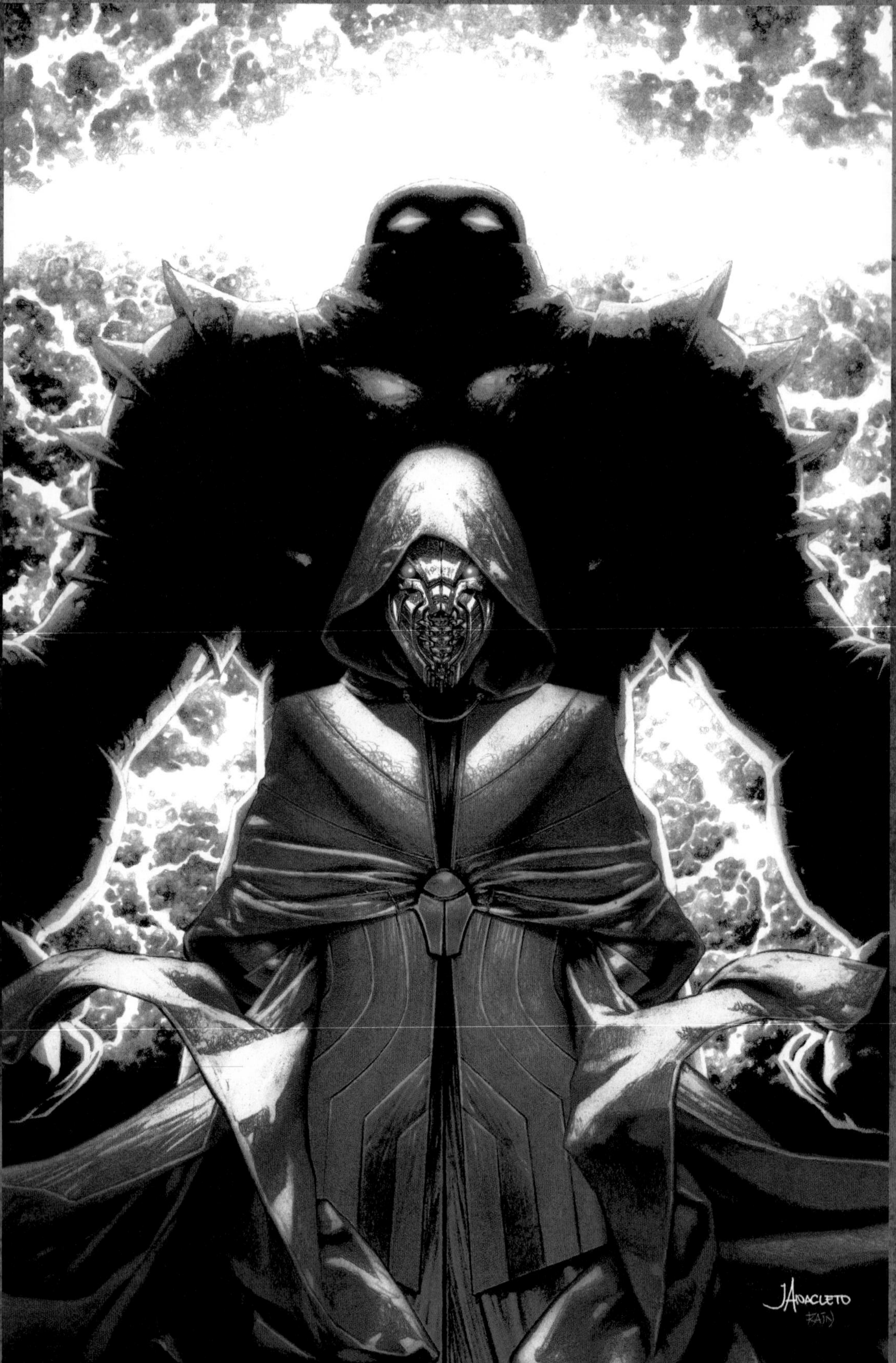
JANACLETO
RAIN

Event Leviathan #3 variant cover by JAY ANACLETO and RAIN BEREDO

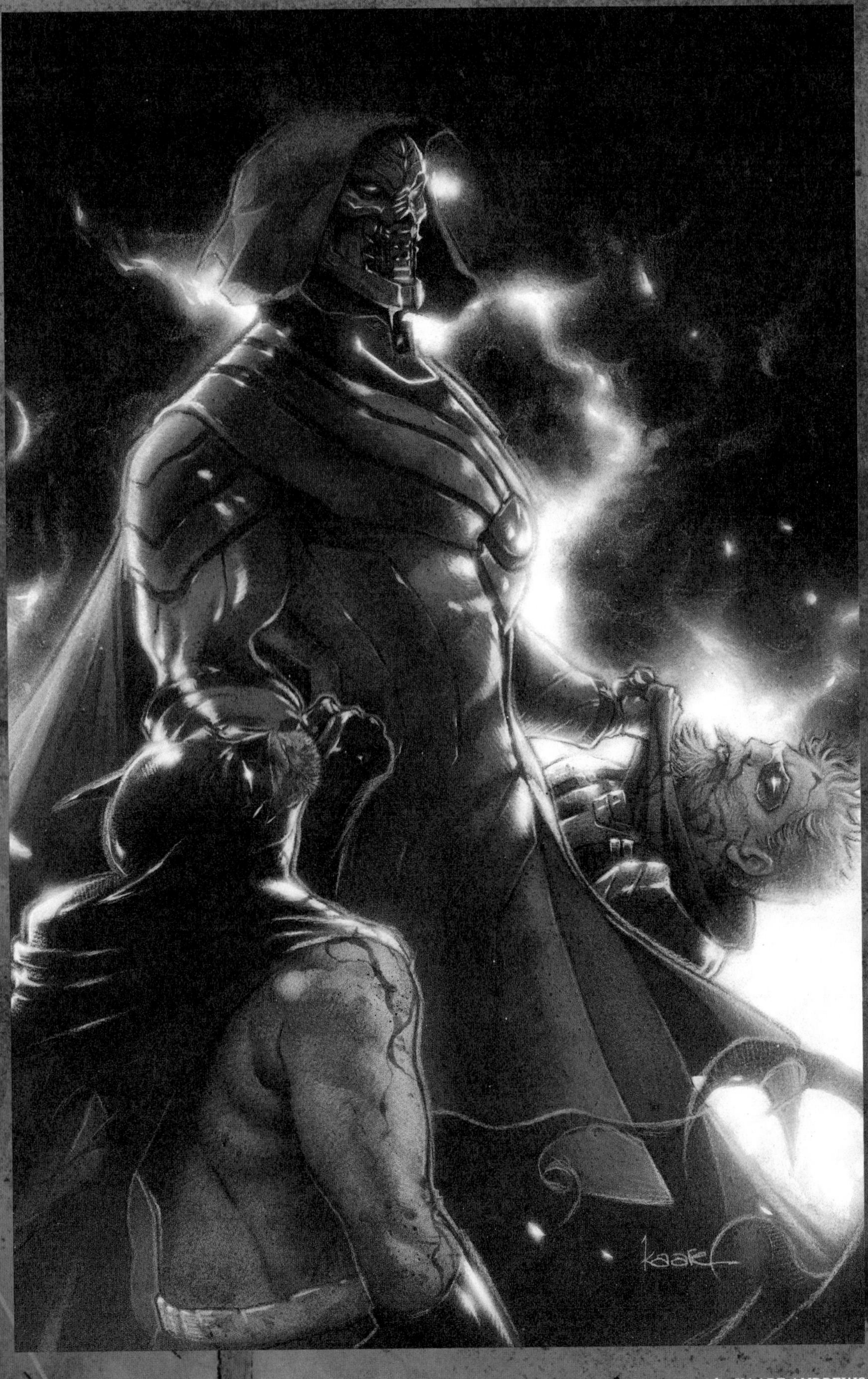
kaare

Event Leviathan #4 variant cover by KAARE ANDREWS

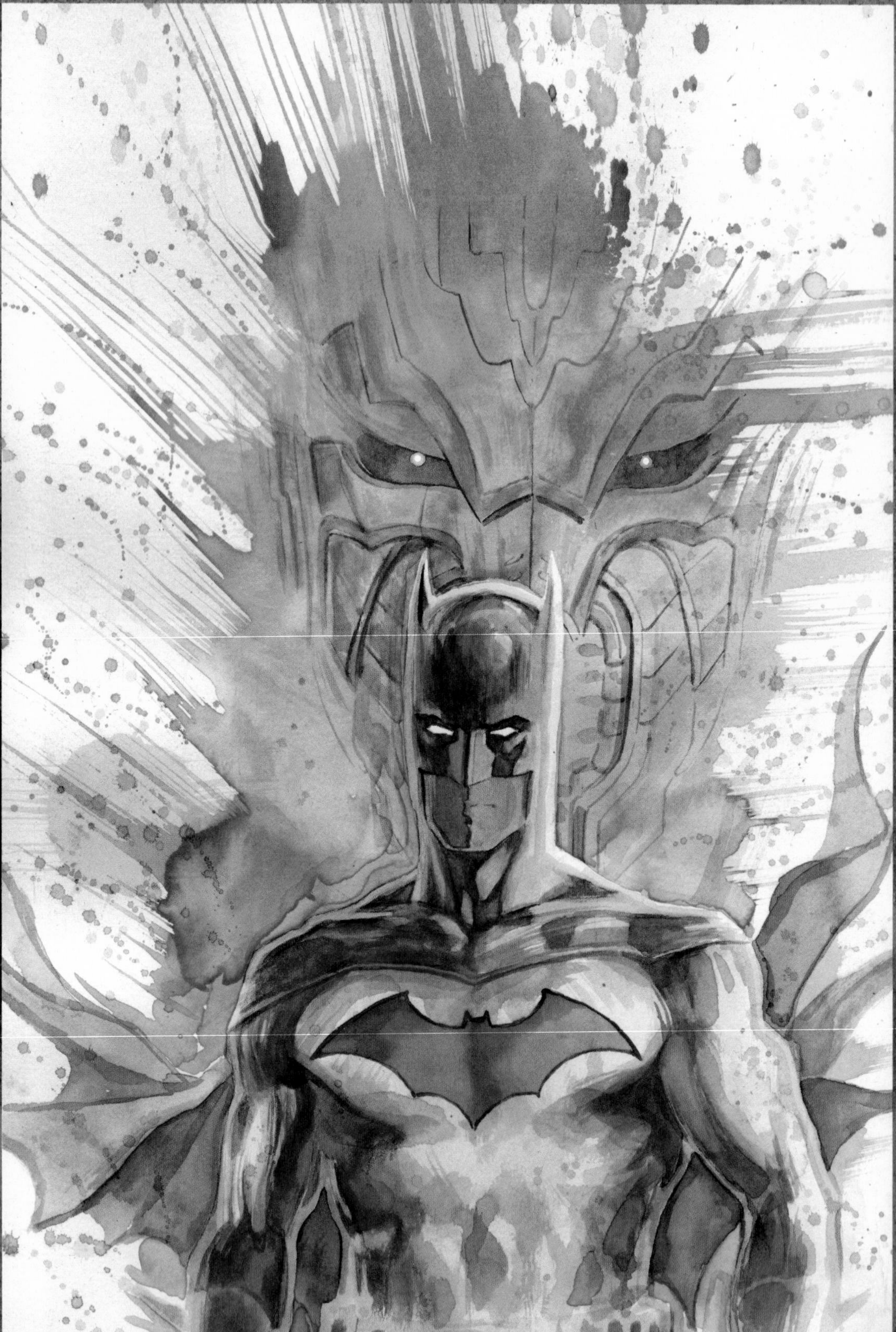
MACK

Event Leviathan #5 variant cover by DAVID MACK

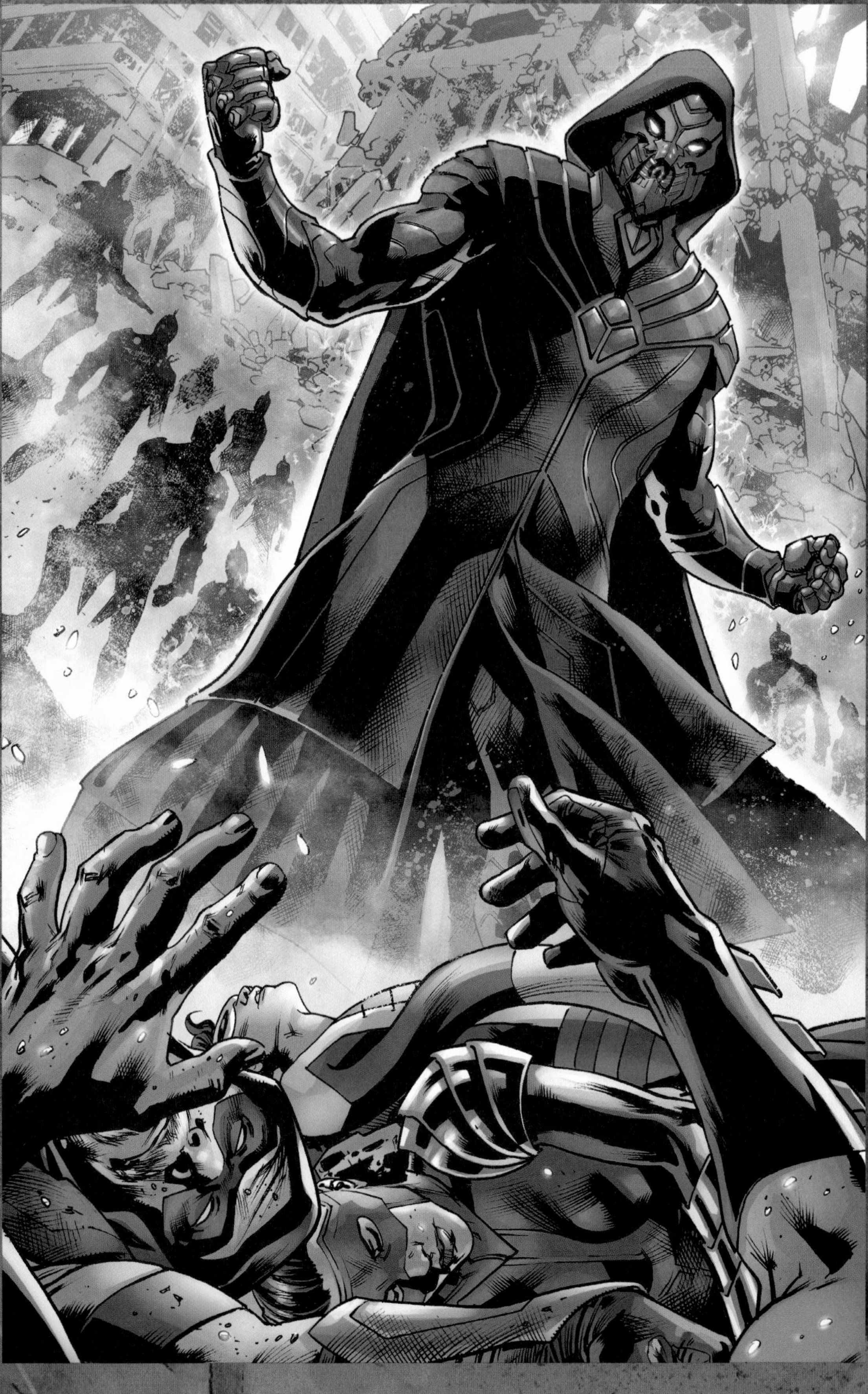

Event Leviathan #6 variant cover by BRYAN HITCH and ALEX SINCLAIR

GROWING LEVIATHAN

Character designs by ALEX MALEEV

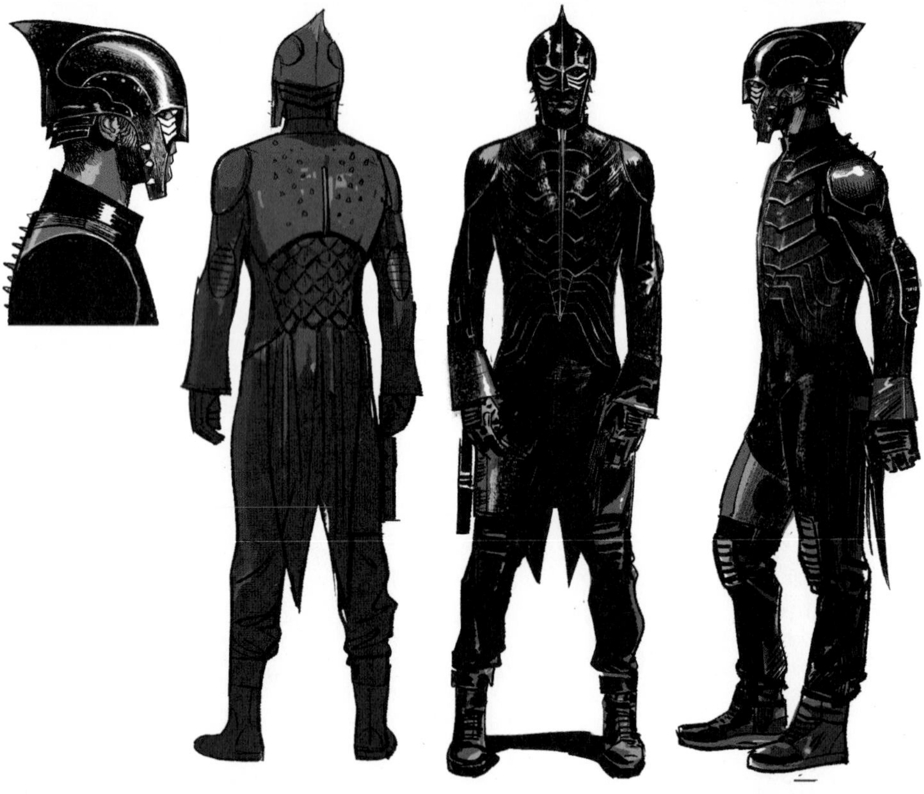

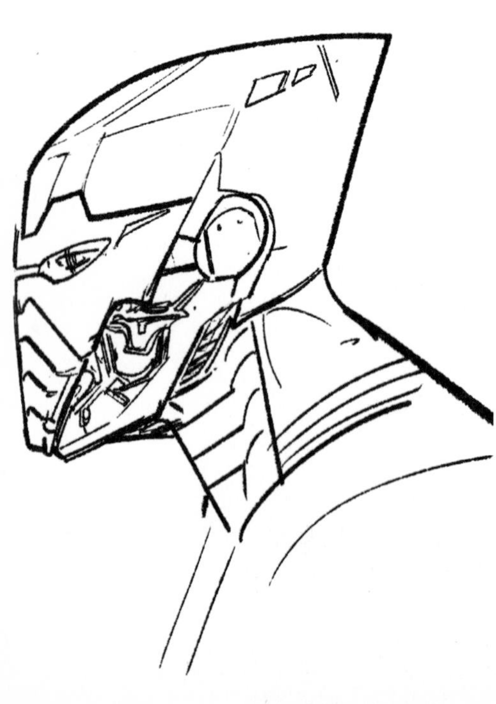

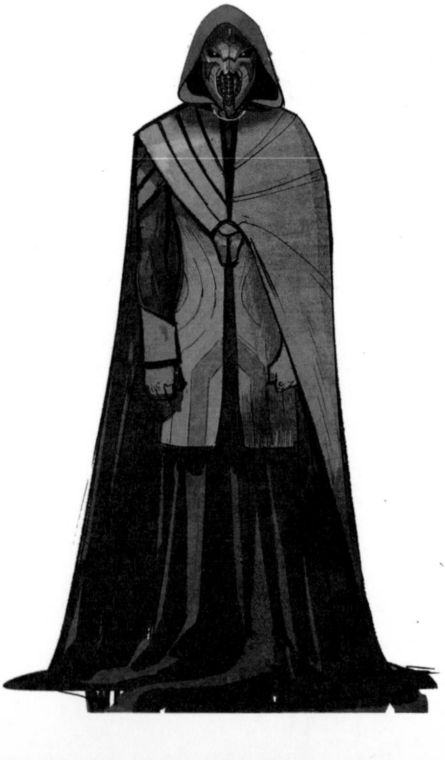

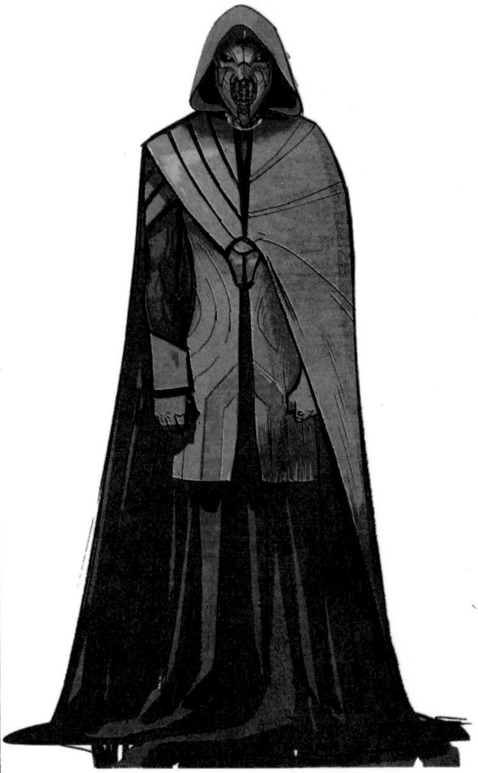

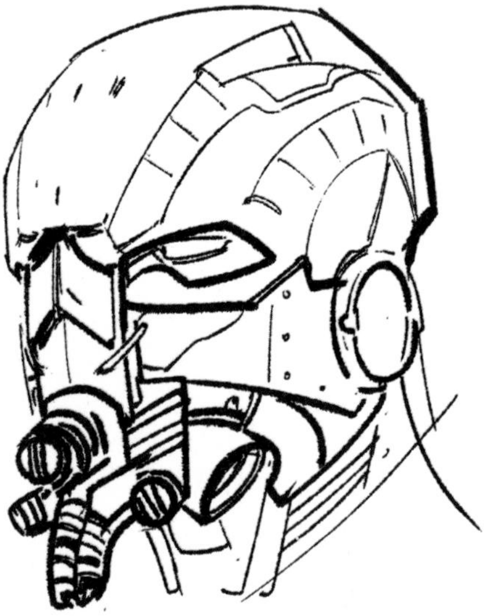

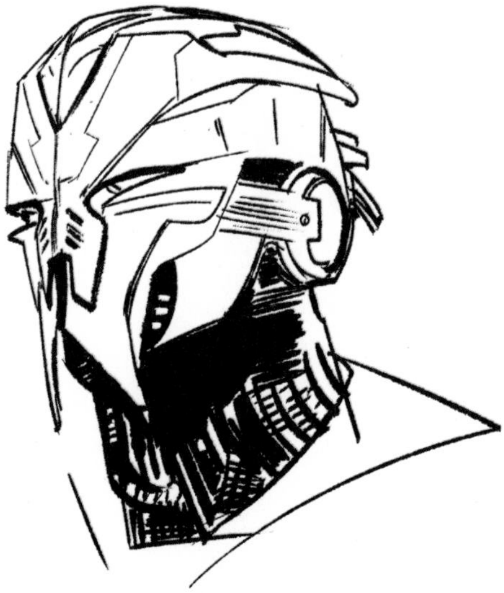

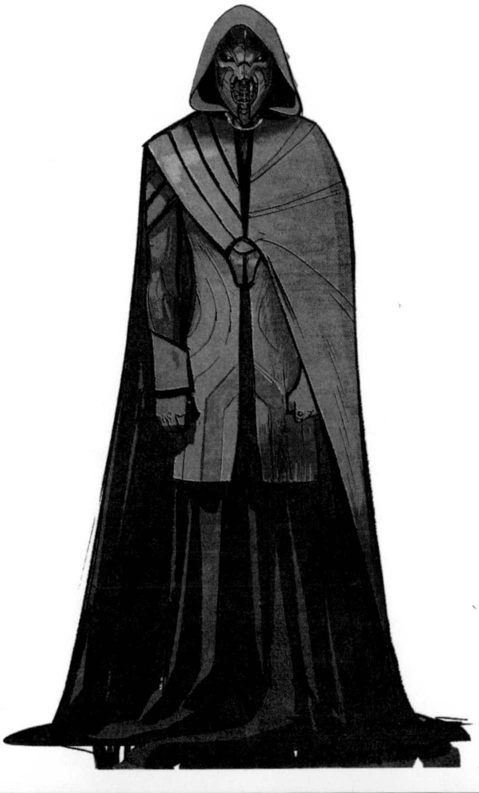

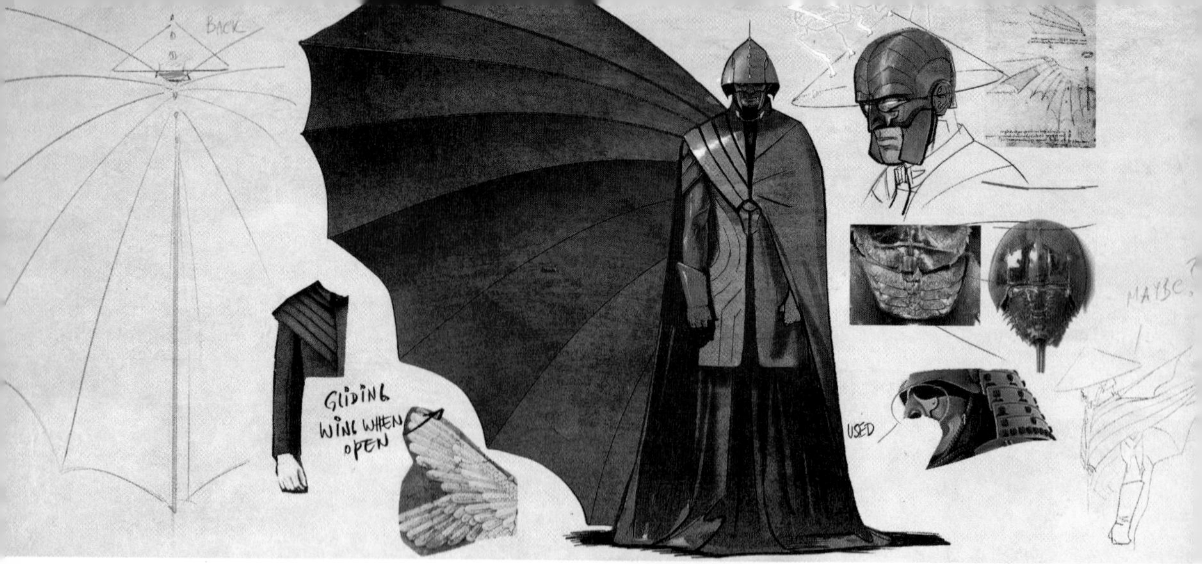
BACK
GLIDING WING WHEN OPEN
USED
MAYBE?

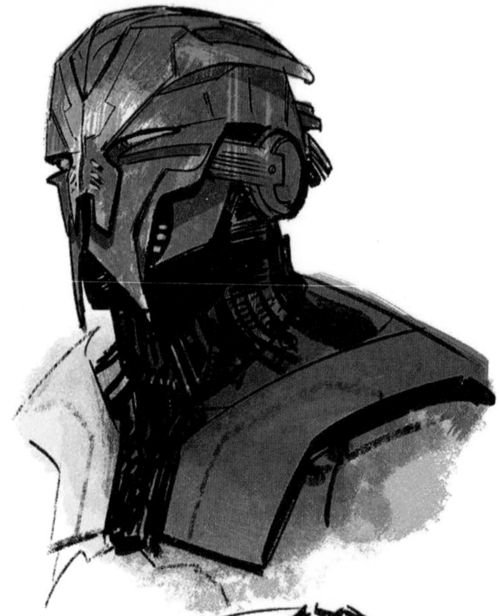

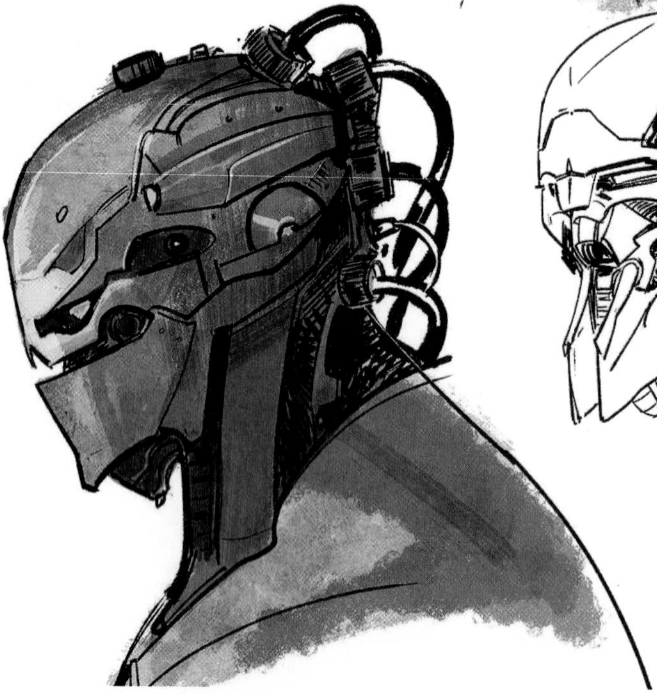

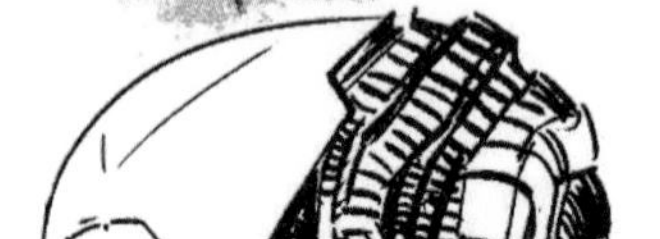

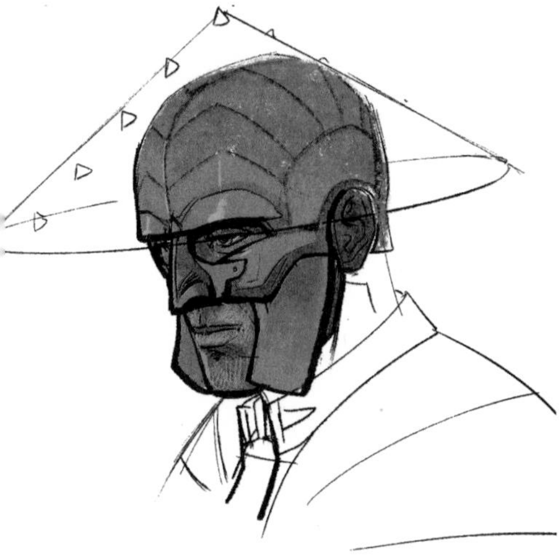
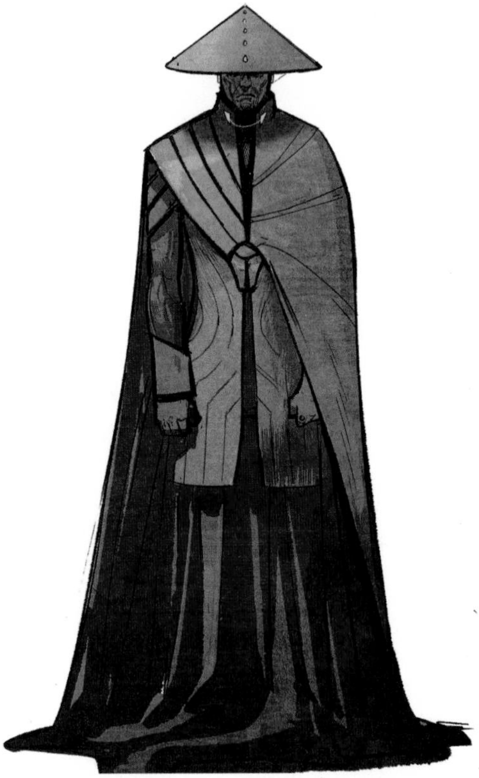
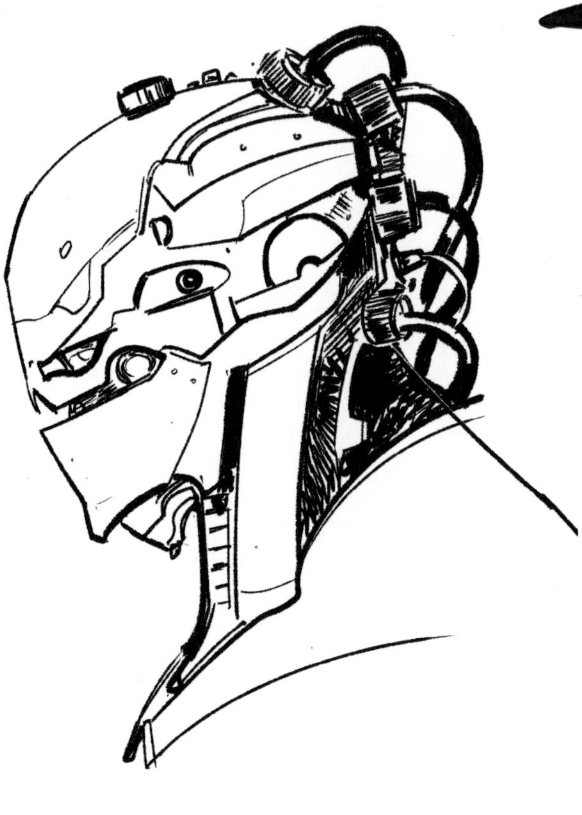
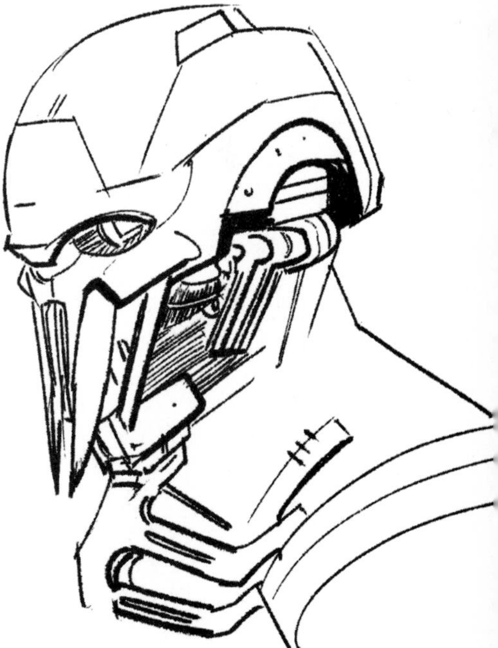

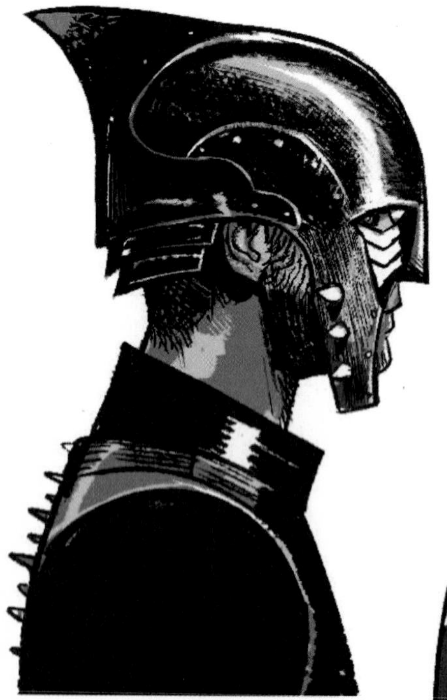

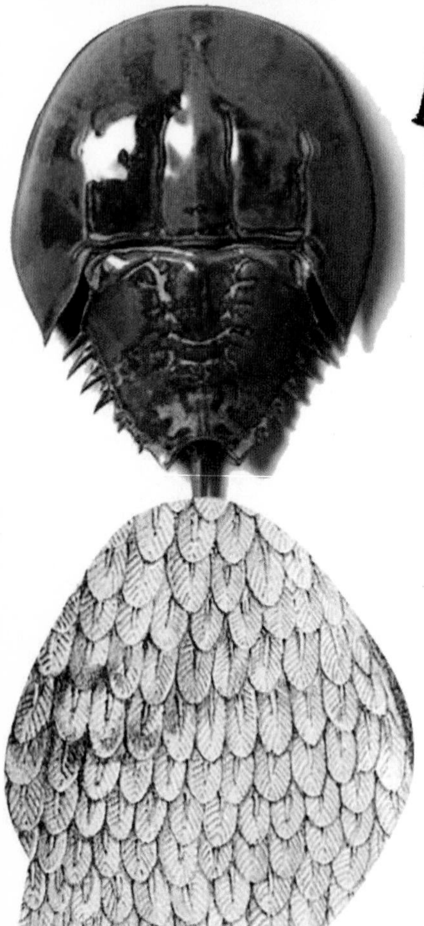

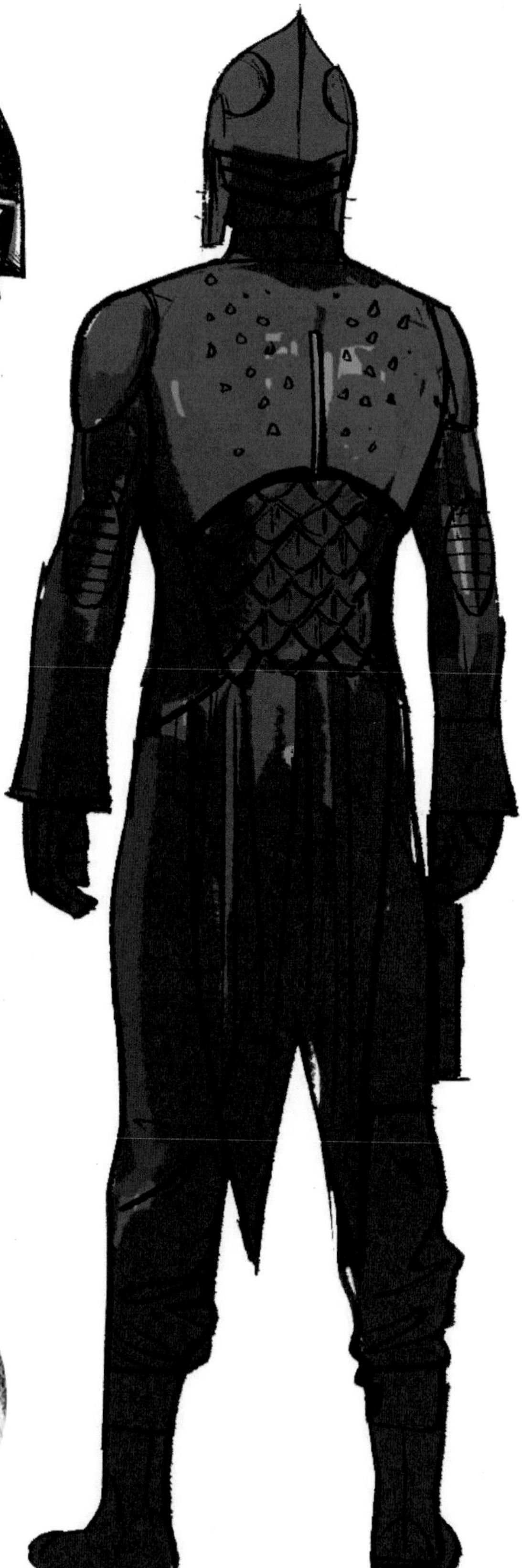

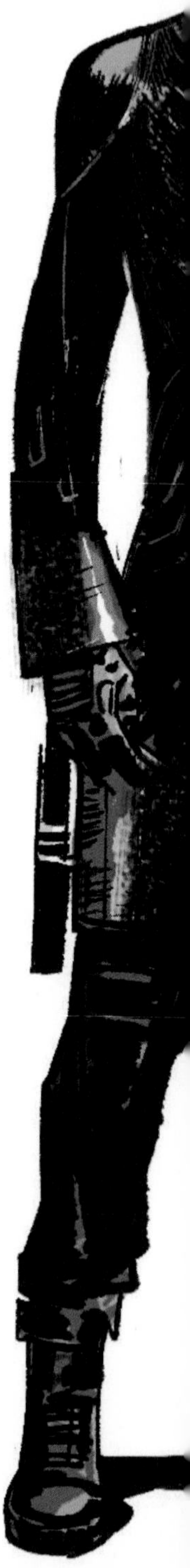

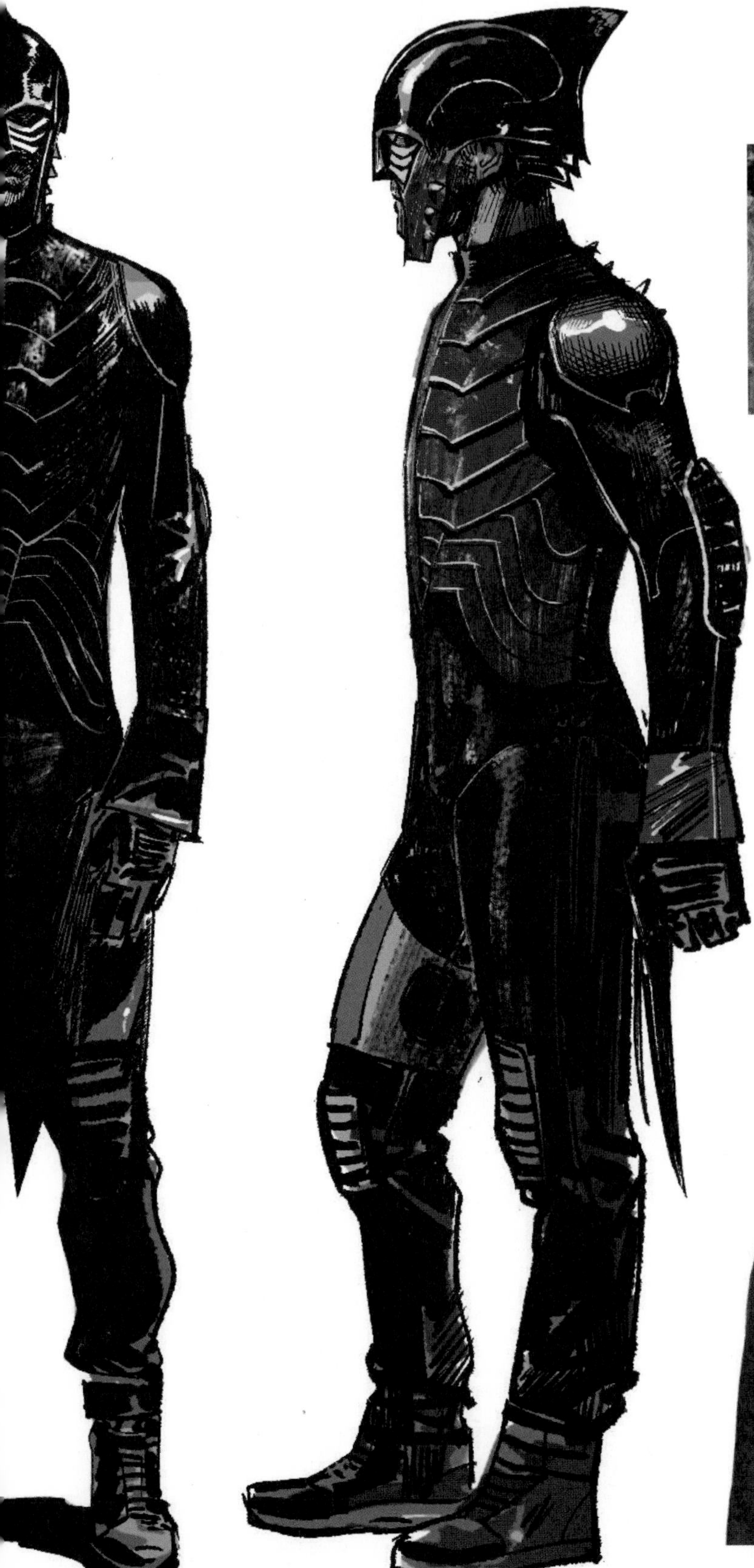

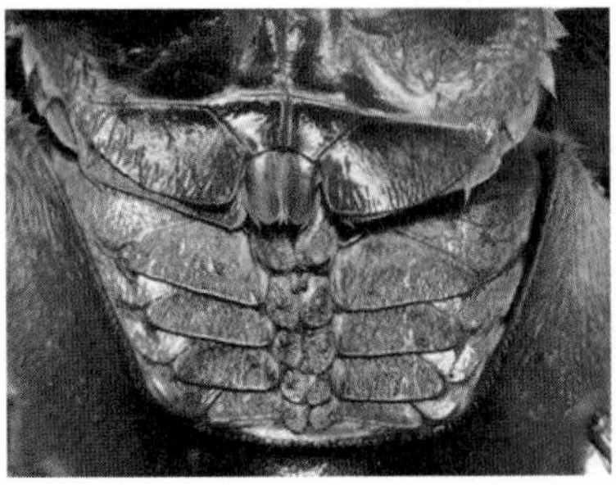

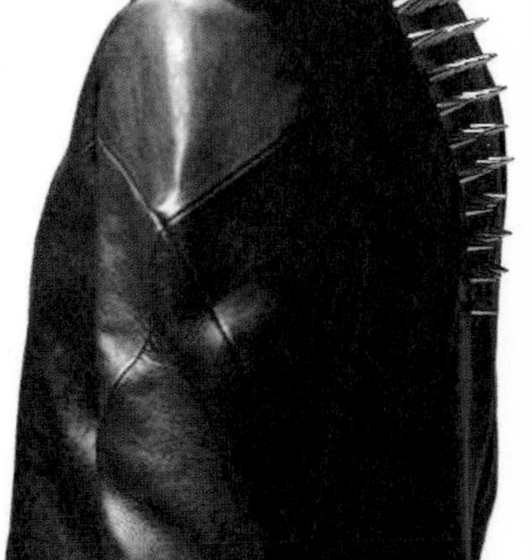

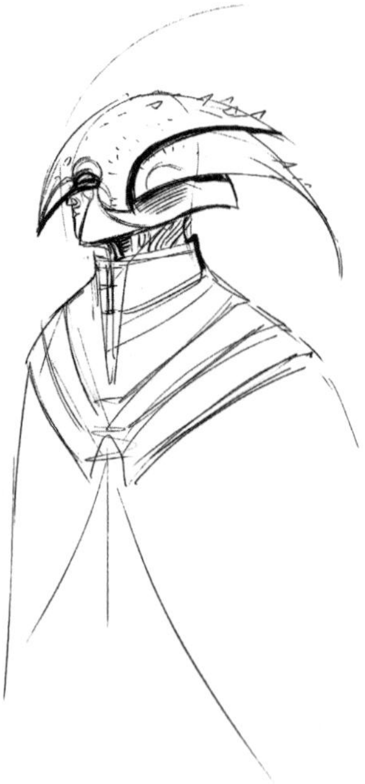
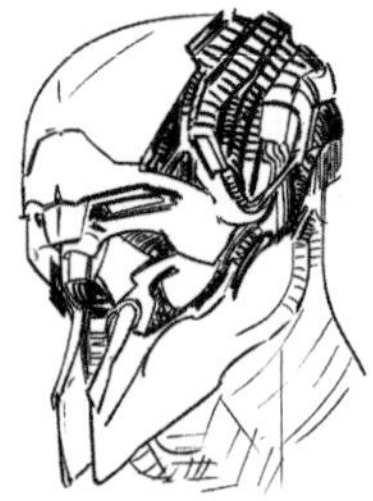
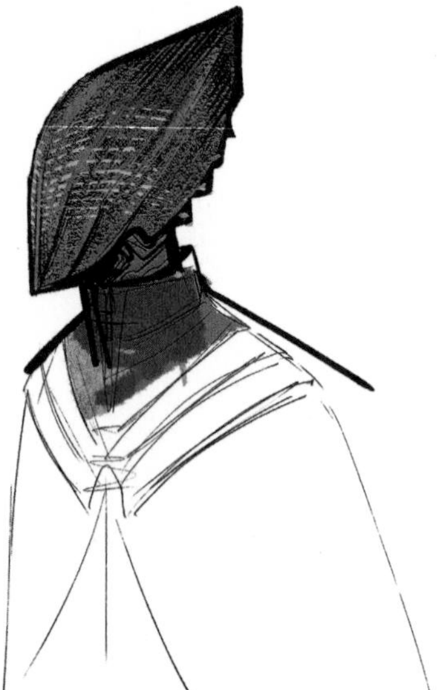
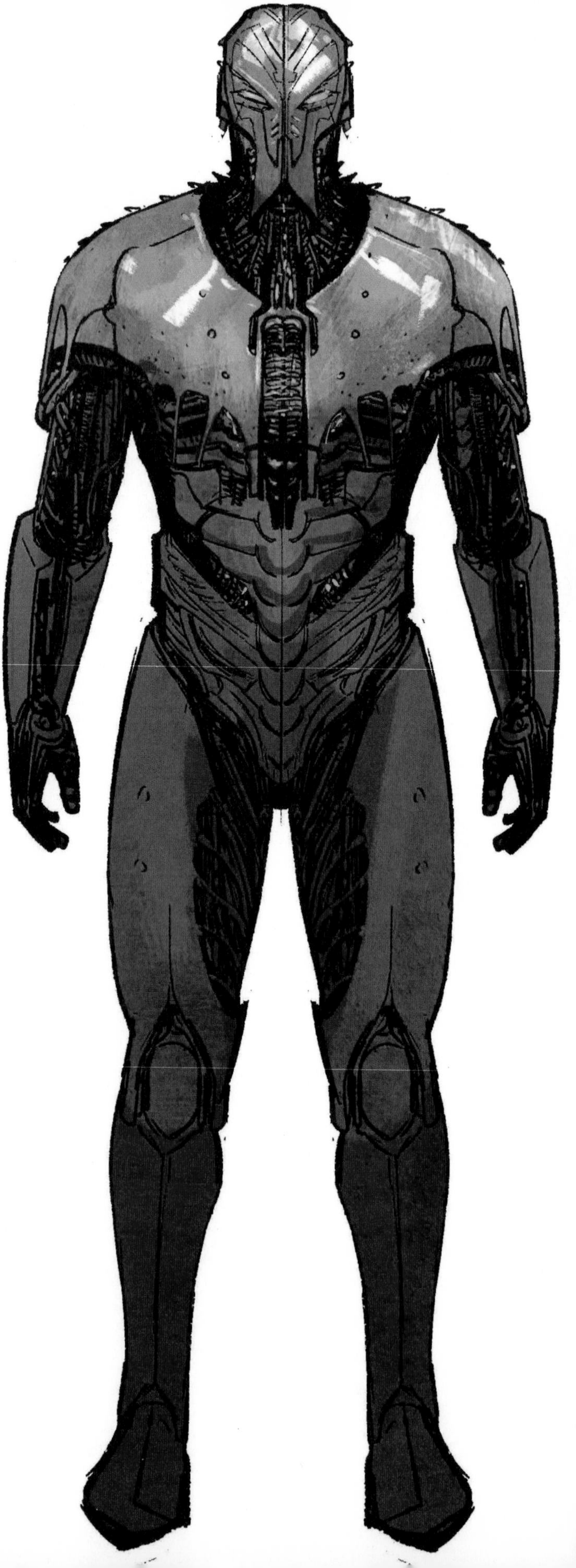

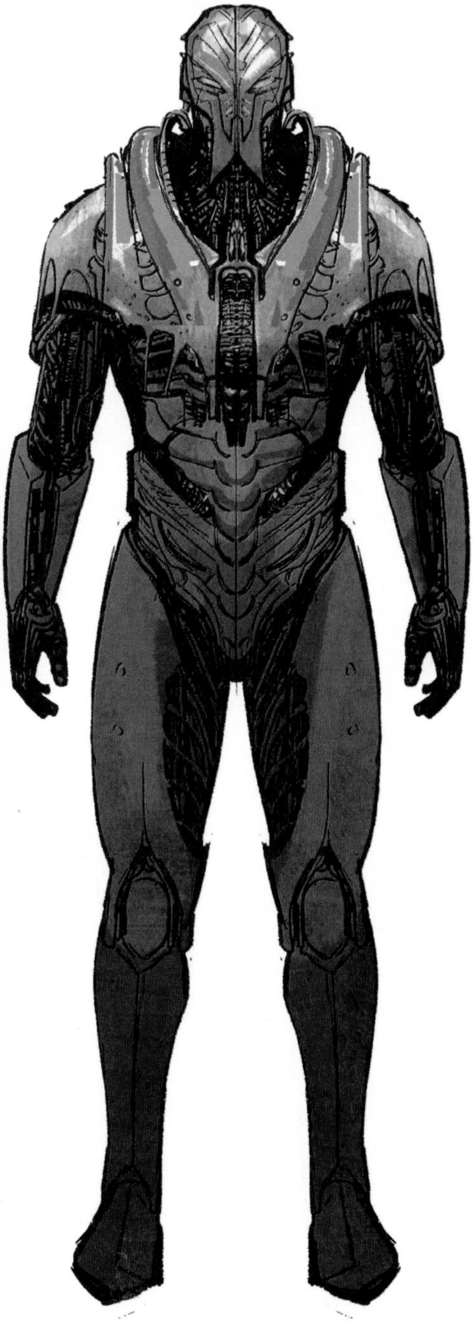

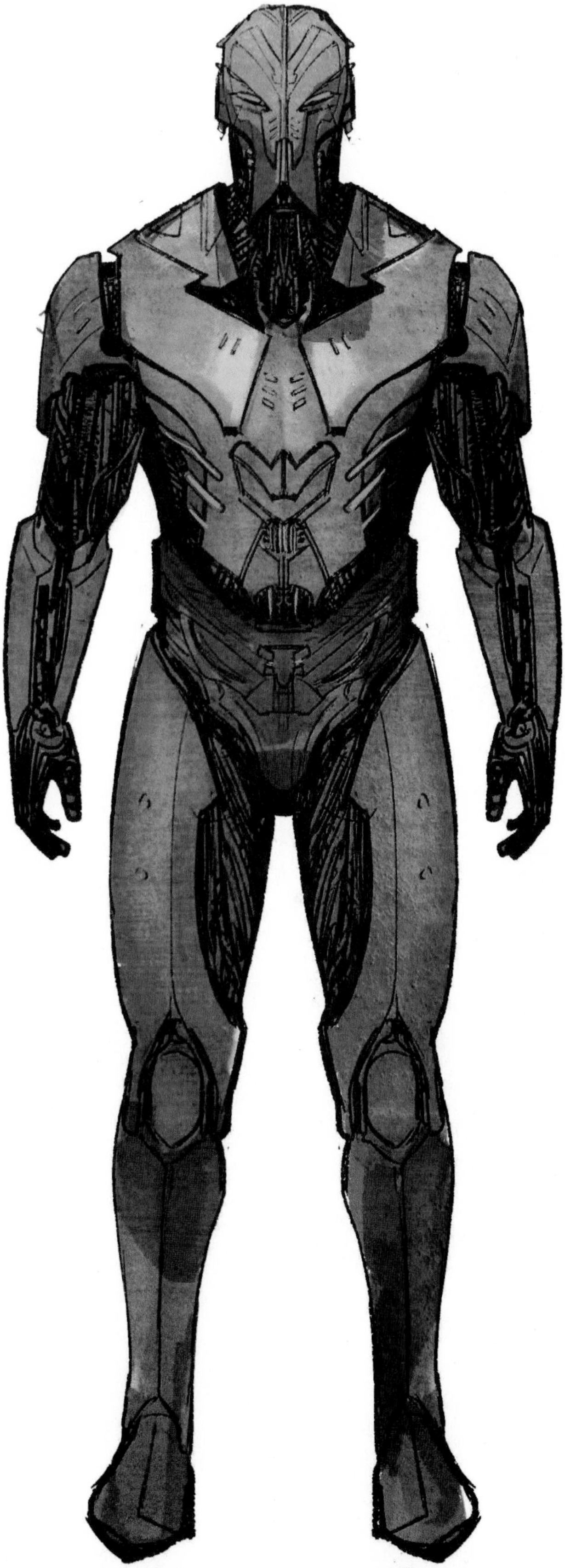

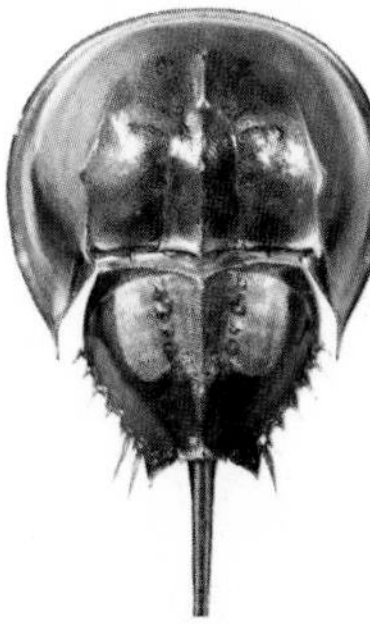

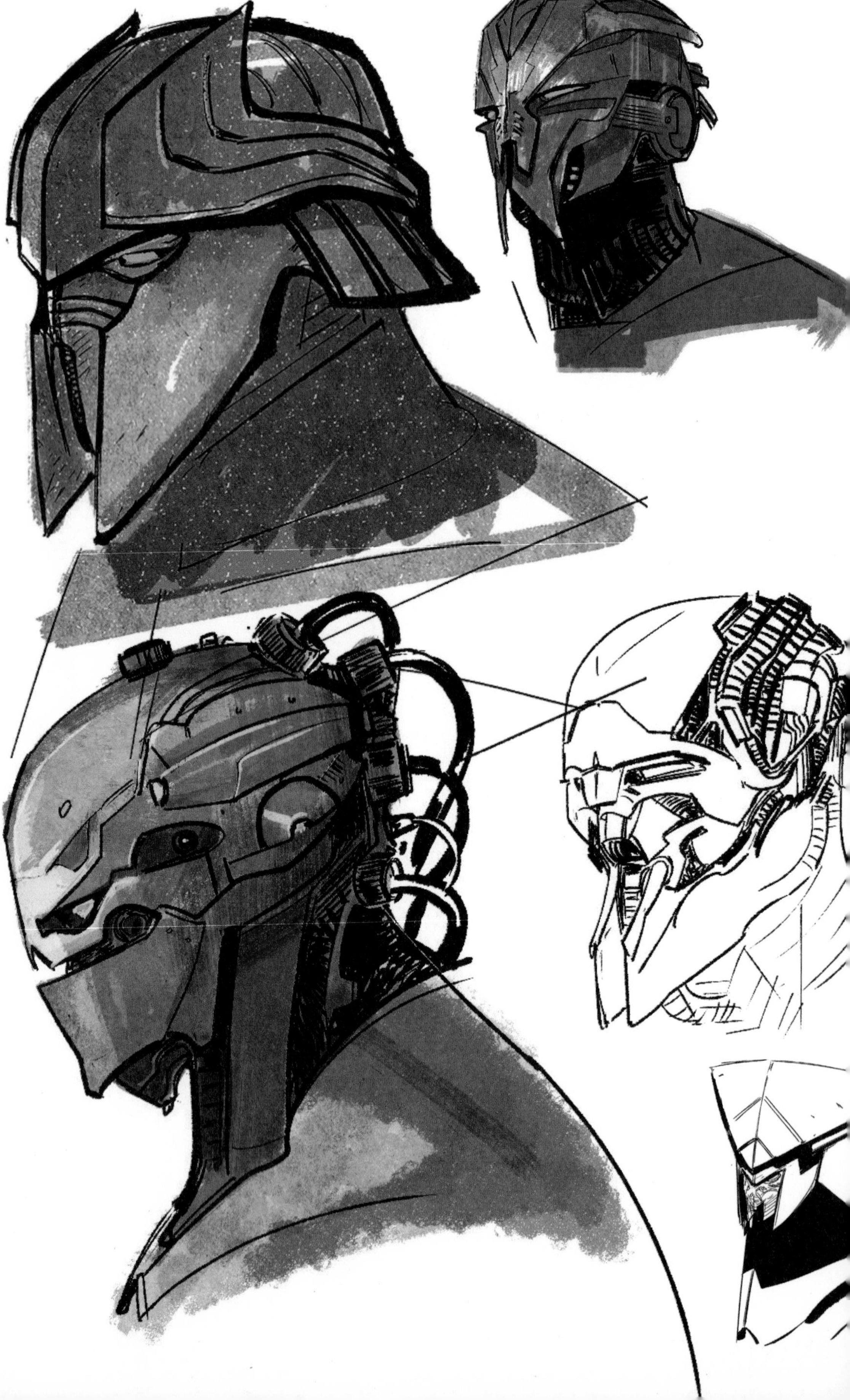

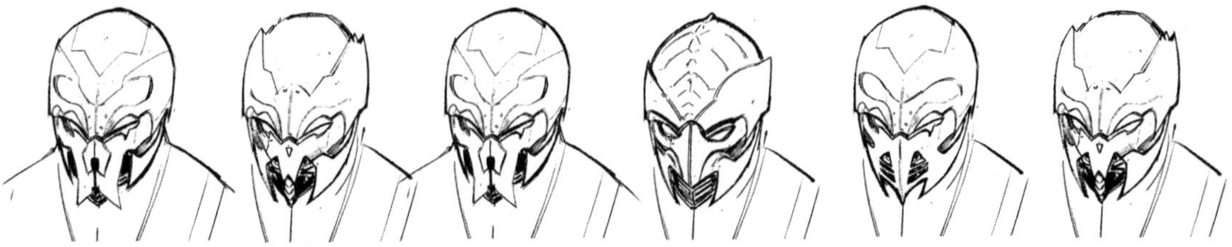

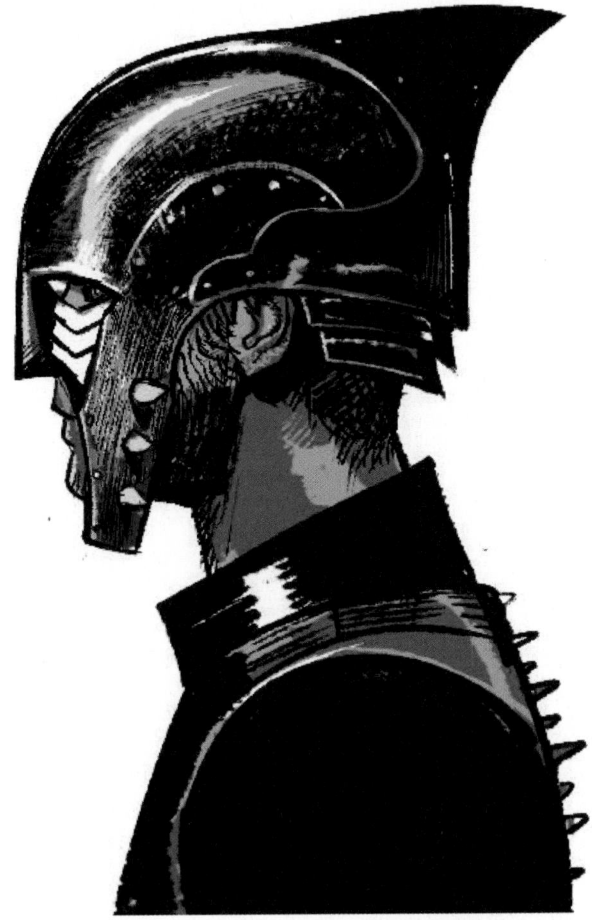

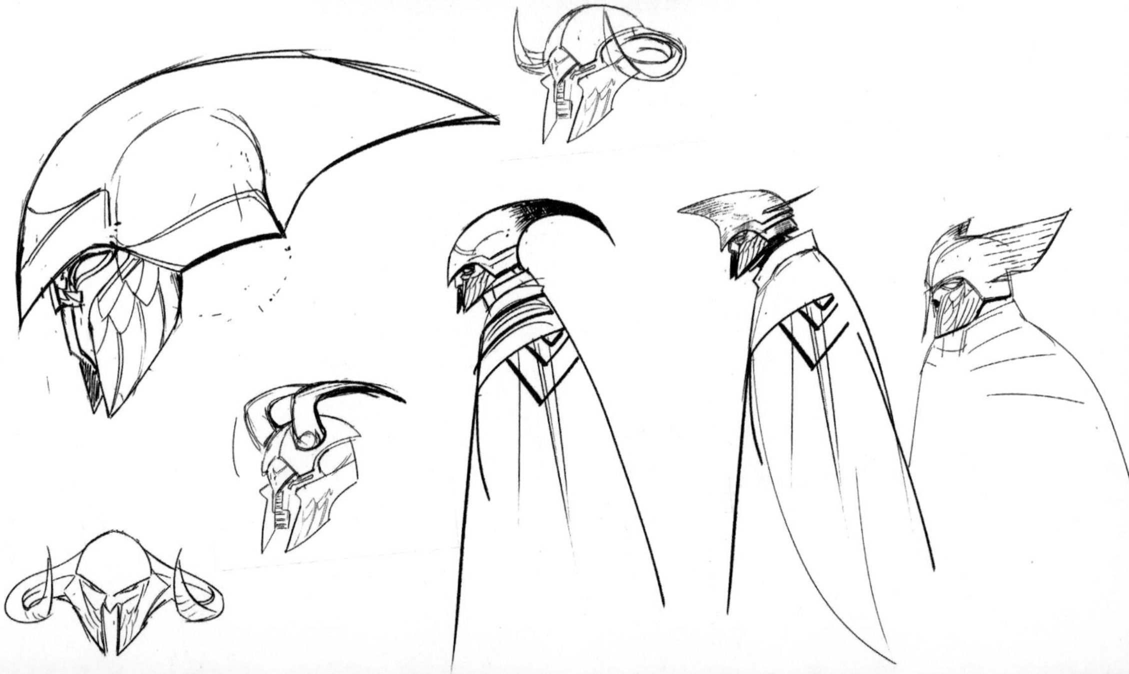

Brian Michael Bendis is a Peabody Award-winning comics creator, an Amazon and *New York Times* bestselling author, and one of the most successful writers working in mainstream comics.

He currently writes *Superman* and *Action Comics* and curates the new Wonder Comics line for DC, which showcases the return of *Young Justice*, *Dial H for Hero*, and *Wonder Twins* and features the debut of *Naomi*, an original new character for the DC Universe.

In addition to his work in print, Bendis was co-creator of *Jessica Jones* on Netflix from Marvel TV, and he was an executive producer and consultant for the Academy Award-winning Sony feature film *Spider-Man: Into the Spider-Verse*, which features the character Miles Morales, the multiracial Spider-Man co-created by Bendis and artist Sara Pichelli.

In his time at Marvel Entertainment, Bendis completed historic runs on *Ultimate Spider-Man* (18 years), *Avengers* (9 years), *Iron Man*, and *Guardians of the Galaxy*, as well as a 100-issue run on the X-Men franchise, and the wildly successful "event" projects *Avengers vs. X-Men*, *House of M*, *Secret War*, *Secret Invasion*, *Age of Ultron*, *Civil War II*, and *Siege*. He was also one of the main architects of Marvel's Ultimate line of comics and part of the company's creative committee that consulted on all of the Marvel movies from the first *Iron Man* through 2018's *Guardians of the Galaxy Vol. 2*.

Bendis has also written the award-winning series *Powers*, the yakuza epic *Pearl* (with Michael Gaydos), the comic book industry spy thriller *Cover* (with David Mack), the youth revolutionary tale *Scarlet* (with Alex Maleev), and the alternate-history mafia saga *United States vs. Murder, Inc.* (with Michael Avon Oeming), all for his own creator-owned comics imprint, Jinxworld.

He has also won five Eisner Awards (including Best Writer two years in a row) and the prestigious Inkpot Award for comics art excellence.

Bendis lives in Portland, Oregon, with his wife and four children.

Alex Maleev was born in Sofia, Bulgaria, in 1971. He received a bachelor's degree in printmaking and later studied at the Kubert School. An award-winning creator, Maleev has worked on a variety of comics, including *Arabian Nights*, *Magic: The Gathering*, *The Crow*, *Alien vs. Predator*, *Sam and Twitch*, *Hellboy: Weird Tales*, and, of course, *Scarlet*. At Marvel he lent his talents to *Daredevil*, *New Avengers: Illuminati*, *Spider-Woman*, *Halo: Uprising*, *Moon Knight*, and *The Dark Tower*. At DC he has worked on *Batman: No Man's Land*, *Batman: The Dark Knight*, and *Superman vs. Predator*. In 1996 Maleev won the Russ Manning Award for Most Promising Newcomer, and in 2003 he (along with Brian Michael Bendis) picked up an Eisner Award for Best Continuing Series for *Daredevil*. Maleev currently lives in Brooklyn, New York.